Collection of ICC Arbitral Awards
1986 – 1990
Recueil des sentences arbitrales de la CCI

COLLECTION OF ICC ARBITRAL AWARDS

1986 – 1990

RECUEIL DES SENTENCES ARBITRALES DE LA CCI

Sigvard Jarvin   *Yves Derains*   *Jean-Jacques Arnaldez*

ICC publishing S.A. Paris – New York
Kluwer Law and Taxation Publishers
Deventer Boston

Kluwer Law and Taxation Publishers
P.O. Box 23   Tel: 31-5700-47261
7400 GA Deventer   Telex: 49295
The Netherlands   Fax: 31-5700-22244

Library of Congress Cataloging-in-Publication Data

Collection of ICC arbitral awards, 1986-1990 = Recueil des sentences arbitrales de la CCI,
    1986-1990 / (compiled by) Sigvard Jarvin, Yves Derains, Jean-Jacques Arnaldez.
        p. cm. -- (ICC publication; 514)
        English and French.
        Includes bibliographical references and indexes.
        ISBN 9284201616 (ICC). -- ISBN 9065446702 (Kluwer)
    1. Arbitration and award, International--Cases. I. Jarvin, Sigvard. II. Derains, Yves. III. Arnaldez, Jean-Jacques.
IV. International Chamber of Commerce. V. Title: Recueil des sentences arbitrales de la CCI,
1986-1990. VI. Series: ICC publication: no. 514.
K2400.A495C65 1993
341.5'22--dc20
                                                                        93-30240
                                                                        CIP

ICC Publication 514

ISBN 92-842-0161-6 (ICC)

ISBN 90 6544 670 2 (Kluwer)

The Collection of the ICC Arbitral Awards 1986-1990 have already been published in the
Yearbook on Commercial Arbitration, the *Journal du Droit International* (Clunet) and *The
International Construction Law Review.*
These extracts are reproduced with permission of the respective editors and publishers.

Table of Contents

Table des matières

The Authors/Les auteurs

Sigvard Jarvin

Membre des Barreaux de Paris et de Suède
Ancien Conseiller Général de la Cour internationale d'arbitrage de la CCI (1982-1987)
Associé de Lagerlöf & Leman

Yves Derains

Avocat au Barreau de Paris,
Ancien Secrétaire Général de la Cour
internationale d'arbitrage de la CCI (1977-1981)

Jean-Jacques Arnaldez

Conseiller, Cour internationale d'arbitrage de la CCI

Foreword To Volume II

1. This second volume of the *Collection of ICC Arbitral Awards* contains the awards that have already been published between 1985 and 1990 in the *"Yearbook Commercial Arbitration,"* the *"Journal du Droit International"* (Clunet) and also in *"The International Construction Law Review."*

2. As in the first volume, the year when the award was rendered may not coincide with the year when it was reported in one of these three publications.

3. Certain awards are reproduced both in English and in French. This is the case with awards that were orignally published simultaneously in the *"Journal du Droit International"* (Clunet) and the *"Yearbook Commercial Arbitration"* or *"The International Construction Law Review."*

4. The Analytical Table of Volume II covers all awards contained in both Volumes I and II of the *Collection of ICC Arbitral Awards.* A page number preceded by "I" refers to Volume I and if preceded by "II," refers to Volume II. Although the extracts of awards that figure in Volume I are not reproduced in Volume II, the reader can therefore limit his search to the Consolidated Analytical Table of Volume II and then look up the case extract in Volume I or II as the case may be.

5. From Volume II onwards, the Consolidated Analytical Table refers to the first page of the award and not necessarily the page where the point in question is to be found, which constitutes a change from Volume I. The reader will thus be directed to start reading the case note from the beginning. In some cases, the reference will already be found in the summary, which will allow the reader to go straight to the part of the commentaries which sometimes follow the award. In other cases, the reference will have to be sought in the text of the award itself or, as may be, in the commentaries that follow.

6. From here on, the Chronological Index is placed before the Consolidated Analytical Table. This index also covers all awards contained in Volumes I and II, the page number being preceded by "I" or "II" to indicate the relevant volume.

The references to the doctrine contained in the Chronological Index have been updated or completed for the awards published in Volume I. It is therefore advisable to consult Volume II only to obtain the most recent references to certain literature where ICC awards have been commented.

7. At the end of Volume II, the reader will find a Table of Cross-Referenced Cases to the *"Journal du Droit International"* (Clunet), the *"Yearbook Commercial Arbitration"* and *"The International Construction Law Review,"* for each of the awards published in Volumes I and II of this Collection. This table will enable the reader, looking at a given award, to rapidly obtain complete references in one or several of these three publications.

8. Finally, Statistics on ICC activities which are regularly supplied by the *"Journal du Droit International"* in its annual Chronicle, has been gathered and now figures in different charts at the end of volume II.

How to use this book?

First situation: the reader knows the case number

The reader who wishes to find the award rendered in case number 5418 will consult the Chronological Index and find that this award figures in English at page 123 of Volume II.

Second situation: the reader is looking for a specific issue

The reader who wishes to know whether a particular question of public policy has been an issue in an ICC arbitration, will consult the Consolidated Analytical Table of Volume II which will send him to the pages of certain awards published in each of the two volumes.

The Consolidated Analytical Table has two versions, one in English which analyses the extracts of awards published in the English language (Volume I : pages 1-176, and Volume II : pages 1-254 and pages 445-549), the other in French which refers to extracts of awards published in the French language (Volume I : pages 177-564, and Volume II : pages 255-444).

The reader as a consequence will consult each of the two versions of the Consolidated Analytical Table, in English under "Public Policy" and in French under "Ordre Public." Each of these key words will eventually indicate a reference to the volume and to the page of a published award, in English or French as the case may be, which deals with the point in question.

The reader who is looking for a particular subject will therefore consult each of the two versions of the Consolidated Analytical Table. Should he not know the exact terminology in one of the two languages, he can consult one of the two Key Word Indexes which will give him the corresponding notion in the other language if the same issue exists in the awards published in that other language.

Third situation: the reader is looking for commentaries on an ICC award which have appeared in another publication

The reader will consult the Chronological Index. When he looks at the case in question, for example award No. 4131, he will find several references to works or publications in which this award has been commented.

Fourth situation: the reader wishes to give the complete references of an award

The reader will consult the Table of Cross-Referenced Cases and will thus obtain for each of the awards:
- on the one hand, its complete references in the *"Journal du Droit International"* (Clunet) or *"The International Construction Law Review"*, in particular with the mention of the initials of the author whose commentaries follow the award, and also in the "Yearbook Commercial Arbitration";
- on the other hand, the indication of the volume and the page where it appears in the *Collection of ICC Arbitral Awards.*

Paris, April 1993

Sigvard Jarvin   Yves Derains   Jean-Jacques Arnaldez

Introduction au second volume

1. Ce second volume du *Recueil des sentences arbitrales de la CCI* regroupe les sentences qui ont déjà été publiées entre 1985 et 1990 au *"Yearbook Commercial Arbitration"*, au *"Journal du Droit International"* (Clunet) et également dans *"The International Construction Law Review"*.

2. Comme dans le premier volume, l'année durant laquelle la sentence à été rendue peut ne pas coïncider avec l'année de sa publication dans l'une de ces trois publications.

3. Certaines sentences sont reproduites tant en anglais qu'en français. C'est le cas de celles qui ont été à l'origine publiées simultanément au *"Journal du Droit International"* (Clunet) et au *"Yearbook Commercial Arbitration"* ou dans *"The International Construction Law Review"*.

4. La Table analytique du second volume couvre l'ensemble des sentences reproduites dans le premier et le second volume du *Recueil des sentences arbitrales de la CCI*. Une page précédée d'un "I" renvoie au volume I et précédée d'un "II", au volume II. Bien que les extraits de sentences qui figurent dans le premier volume, ne soient pas reproduits dans le second, le lecteur limitera donc ses recherches à la Table analytique consolidée du volume II, puis se reportera, selon le cas, au volume I ou II.

5. A compter du second volume, la Table analytique consolidée renvoie à la première page de la sentence et non pas nécessairement à la page où figure la référence recherchée, ce qui constitue un changement par rapport au premier volume. Le lecteur sera ainsi conduit à commencer la lecture de l'affaire à son début. Dans certains cas, la référence se trouvera déjà dans le sommaire, ce qui lui permettra en particulier de se reporter facilement à la partie du commentaire qui suit éventuellement la sentence. Dans les autres cas, la référence devra être recherchée dans le corps même de la sentence ou, suivant le cas, dans les commentaires qui la suivent.

6. Dorénavant, l'Index chronologique est placé avant la Table analytique consolidée. Cet index couvre également toutes les sentences contenues aux volumes I et II, la page mentionnée étant précédée d'un "I" ou d'un "II" pour indiquer le volume.

Les références à la doctrine contenues dans l'Index chronologique ont été mises à jour ou complétées pour les sentences reproduites dans le premier volume. Il est donc recommandé de ne consulter que le volume II pour obtenir les références les plus récentes à certaines sources dans lesquelles des sentences CCI ont été commentées.

7. A la fin du volume II, le lecteur trouvera une Table de correspondance des références au *"Journal du Droit International"* (Clunet), au *"Yearbook Commercial Arbitration"* et à *"The International Construction Law Review"*, de chacune des sentences publiée aux volumes I et II du présent Recueil. Cette table permettra ainsi au lecteur d'obtenir rapidement pour une sentence donnée, ses références complètes dans une ou plusieurs de ces trois publications.

8. Enfin, les Statistiques sur l'activité de la CCI fournies régulièrement par le *"Journal du Droit International"* (Clunet) dans sa Chronique annuelle, ont été réunies et figurent dans différents tableaux à la fin du volume II.

Comment utiliser ce livre ?

Premier cas: le lecteur connaît le numéro de l'affaire

Le lecteur qui souhaite par exemple trouver la sentence rendue dans l'affaire 5418, se reportera à l'Index chronologique et constatera qu'elle est publiée en anglais à la page 123 du volume II.

Deuxième cas: le lecteur cherche une donnée spécifique

Le lecteur qui veut savoir si une question particulière se rapportant à l'ordre public a été abordée dans un arbitrage CCI, consultera la Table analytique consolidée du volume II qui le renverra aux pages de certaines sentences publiées dans chacun des deux volumes.

La Table analytique consolidée comprend deux versions, l'une en anglais qui analyse les extraits de sentences publiés en langue anglaise (volume I: pages 1-176, et volume II: pages 1-254 et pages 445-549), l'autre en français qui se réfère aux extraits de sentences publiés en langue française (volume I: pages 177-564, et volume II: pages 255-444).

Le lecteur devra donc consulter chacune des deux versions de la Table analytique consolidée, en anglais sous "Public Policy" et en français sous "Ordre public". Chacun de ces mots-clés indiquera éventuellement une référence au volume et à la page où une sentence publiée, suivant le cas en anglais ou en français, traiterait de la question posée.

Un lecteur qui cherche un point particulier se référera donc à chacune des deux versions de la Table analytique consolidée. S'il ignore la terminologie exacte dans l'une des deux langues, il s'aidera de l'un des deux Index des mots-clés qui lui fournira la notion correspondante dans l'autre langue dans la mesure où le point en question est traité dans les sentences publiées dans cette langue.

Troisième cas: le lecteur est à la recherche de commentaires sur une sentence CCI publiée dans un autre ouvrage

Le lecteur consultera l'Index chronologique. Au regard de l'affaire en question, par exemple la sentence no. 4131, il trouvera diverses références à des ouvrages ou publications dans lesquels cette sentence a fait l'objet d'un commentaire.

Quatrième cas: le lecteur souhaite donner les références complètes d'une sentence

Le lecteur se reportera à la Table de correspondance des références et obtiendra au regard de
chacune des sentences:
– d'une part, ses références complètes au *"Journal du Droit International"* (Clunet) ou à *"The International Construction Law Review"* avec en particulier la mention des initiales de l'auteur des observations qui la suivent, ou encore au *"Yearbook Commercial Arbitration"*;
– d'autre part, l'indication du volume et de la page de sa publication au *Recueil des sentences arbitrales de la CCI*.

Paris, Avril 1993

Sigvard Jarvin   Yves Derains   Jean-Jacques Arnaldez

Abbreviations / Abreviations

Arb Int	Arbitration International (London)
Boisséson	Matthieu de Boisséson: Le droit français de l'arbitrage interne et international, GLN/Joly, éditions, Paris, 1990
Bulletin ASA	Bulletin de l'Association Suisse de l'Arbitrage (Bâle)
Bulletin ICC	The ICC International Court of Arbitration Bulletin (Paris)
CPP	Craig-Park-Paulsson: International Chamber of Commerce Arbitration (Oceana/ICC) 1983
CPP 2nd ed	Craig-Park-Paulson: International Chamber of Commerce Arbitration, 2nd edition (Oceana/ICC) 1990
DIS	Schriftenreihe des Deutschen Instituts für Schiedsgerichtswesen, Band 6, Band 8, Carl Heymanns Verlag KG, Köln, Berlin, Bonn, München
El-Ahdab	Abdul Hamid El-Ahdab: L'Arbitrage dans les Pays Arabes, Economica, Paris, 1988
Fouchard	Philippe Fouchard: L'Arbitrage Commercial International, Librairie Dalloz, Paris, 1965
ICLR	The International Construction Law Review (London)
JDI	Journal du Droit International (Clunet) (Paris)
JIA	Journal of International Arbitration (Geneva)
Jahrbuch	Jahrbuch für die Praxis der Schiedsgerichtsbarkeit, Band 1, 2, 3, 4, Verlag Recht und Wirtschaft, Heidelberg
Kassis	Antoine Kassis: Théorie Générale des Usages du Commerce, Paris, LGDJ, 1984
Lew	Julian D.M. Lew: Contemporary Problems in International Arbitration, Queen Mary College, London, 1986
Mustill & Boyd	Michael J. Mustill, Stewart C. Boyd: The Law and Practice of Commercial Arbitration in England, London, Butterworths, 1982
RDAI	Revue de Droit des Affaires Internationales / International Business Law Journal (Paris)
Redfern-Hunter	Alan Redfern, Martin Hunter: Law and Practice of International Commercial Arbitration, London, Sweet & Maxwell, 1986
Redfern-Hunter 2nd ed	Alan Redfern, Martin Hunter: Law and Practice of International Commercial Arbitration, 2nd edition, London, 1991, Sweet & Maxwell

Rev Arb	Revue de l'Arbitrage (Paris)
Rubino-Sammartano	Mauro Rubino-Sammartano: International Arbitration Law, Kluwer, 1990
Schlosser	Peter Schlosser: Das recht der internationalen privaten Schiedsgerichtsbarkeit, 2, Auflage, Tübingen, Mohr 1989
Schwebel	Stephen M. Schwebel: International Arbitration - Three Salient Problems, Cambridge, Grotius Publications Ltd, 1987
Wetter	J. Gillis Wetter: The International Arbitral Process, Dobbs Ferry, 1979
YB	ICCA Yearbook Commercial Arbitration (Deventer, The Netherlands)
60ème Anniv.	60 ans après; Regard sur l'Avenir, ICC Publishing S.A., 1984, Paris

Chronological Index

Index Chronologique

Vol I et Vol II

Case/ Affaire N°	Language/Langue (E: English) (F: Français)	Page I = in First Volume/ dans Volume I II = in this Volume/ dans ce Volume	Observations In/Dans:
369	F	I 204	Fouchard: p. 439
519	F	I 193	
536	F	I 203	Fouchard: p. 440
953	E	I 17	CPP II § 5.05; CPP 2nd ed p. 73
1110	F	I 498	4 Arb Int 111; Boisséson n° 593, 667; CPP III § 17.04; CPP 2nd ed p. 83, 307; Kassis p. 489; Lew p. 84, 116; Rev Arb 1984 p. 7, 1986 p. 336; Schlosser p. 235
1250	E	I 30	Boisséson n° 670; CPP II § 8.05; CPP 2nd ed p. 137; Redfern-Hunter p. 96; Redfern-Hunter 2nd ed p. 96; Rev Arb 1983 p. 14
1350	F	I 239	
1397	F	I 179	2 Arb Int 277; CPP III § 17.04; CPP 2nd p. 86, 305; Rev Arb 1982 p. 37; 1984 p. 13, 211; Rubino-Sammartano p. 316
1422	F	I 185	Boisséson n° 670; CPP III §17.02; CPP 2nd ed p. 290; Lew p. 109
1434	F	I 263	2 Arb Int 151; 4 Arb Int 112, 114; Boisséson n° 585, 605, 667, 683, 727; CPP II § 5.09, §7.04, VI § 35.05; CPP 2nd ed p. 99, 128, 627; Kassis p. 339, 468; Lew p. 63, 118; RDAI 1989 p. 986; Rev Arb 1985 p. 504, 583, 642; 1986 p. 350, 392; 1988 p. 161, 483, 485; 1990 p. 91, 92 Rubino-Sammartano p. 49, 218, 277, 367; Schlosser p. 325
1455	E	I 18	4 Arb Int 91; CPP III § 17.02; CPP 2nd ed p. 289; Julian Lew: The Choice of the Applicable Law in International Commercial Arbitration (1977), paras 289, 418
1507	F	I 215	5 Arb Int 26; Boisséson n° 578; Schwebel p. 57;
1512 (Dalmia Dairy Industries v. National Bank of	E F	I 3, 33, 37 I 207	1 Arb Int 64; 4 Arb Int 111, 112; 8 Arb Int 242; Boisséson n° 670, 671, 694, 697, 712, 713, 719; Bulletin ASA 1992 p. 505;

2404	F	I 280	CPP III § 17.02; CPP 2nd ed p. 289; 4 Arb Int 113; Boisséson n° 694; CPP 2nd ed p. 604, 628, 631; Kassis p. 363; Rev Arb 1990 p. 56, 93, 96; Schlosser p. 152
2438	F	I 253	Boisséson n° 670, 671, 694; CPP III § 17.02; CPP 2nd ed p. 291; Kassis p. 363
2443	F	I 276	Boisséson n° 693
2444	F	I 285	CPP IV § 27.02; CPP 2nd ed p. 423, 426; Rubino-Sammartano p. 360, 397
2462	F	I 232	
2476	F	I 289, 323	Boisséson n° 578; CPP III § 11.03; CPP 2nd ed p. 193; Schwebel p. 57
2478	E	I 25	4 Arb Int 105, 111, 113;
	F	I 233	Boisséson n° 683, 697; CPP II § 8.01; VI § 35.03, § 35.04, § 35.05; CPP 2nd ed p. 131, 624, 625, 638, 639; (1989) ICLR 335; Rev Arb 1990 p. 83, 85, 89
2502	F	I 325	
2508	F	I 292	Boisséson n° 697; CPP 2nd ed p. 632; Kassis p. 365, 523; RDAI 1988 p. 171; Rev Arb 1990 p. 97
2520	F	I 278	4 Arb Int 111, 113; CPP VI § 35.04; CPP 2nd ed p. 626; (1989) ICLR 335; Lew p. 125; Rev Arb 1990 p. 90
2521	F	I 282	5 Arb Int 26; Boisséson n° 578; Rev Arb 1984 p. 13; 1985 p. 533; Rubino-Sammartano p. 330; Schlosser p. 247, 540; Schwebel p. 69
2540	F	I 296	4 Arb Int 111; CPP 2nd ed p. 631; Rev Arb 1990 p. 96
2546	F	I 299	CPP 2nd ed p. 634; 1 JIA p. 217; Rev Arb 1990 p. 86
2558	F	I 306	Boisséson n° 587; RDAI 1990 p. 847
2559	F	I 302	
2583	F	I 304	4 Arb Int 91, 101, 113; Boisséson n° 683, 698; CPP 2nd ed p. 629; Kassis p. 523; Lew p. 110, 117; Rev Arb 1990 p. 94; Rubino-Sammartano p. 266
2585	F	I 334	CPP III § 17.02; CPP 2nd ed p. 291;
2602	F	I 303	
2605	F	I 325	

2626	F	I 316	8 Arb Int 133; Boisséson n° 574, 624, 725; Rev Arb 1987 p. 494; 1988 p. 121; 1991 p. 168; Rubino-Sammartano p. 183; Schlosser p. 321
2637	E	I 13	CPP II § 8.04; CPP 2nd ed p. 120, 136; Jahrbuch 3 p. 68
2654	F	I 303	Rubino-Sammartano p. 265
2673	F	I 301	4 Arb Int 91
2680	F	I 334	CPP III § 17.02; CPP 2nd ed p. 291
2689	F	I 335	Rubino-Sammartano p. 265
2694	F	I 320	Boisséson n° 578; CPP III § 17.02, § 18.02; CPP 2nd ed p. 292, 314; Jahrbuch 2 p. 123; Rev Arb 1985 p. 204; Rubino-Sammartano p. 169; Schlosser p. 548; Schwebel p. 57
2699	F	I 299	
2708	F	I 297	CPP IV § 35.03; CPP 2nd ed p. 637; 1 JIA p. 221; Kassis p. 363; Lew p. 118; Rev Arb 1985 p. 204; 1990 p. 88; Rubino-Sammartano p. 399
2730	F	I 490	4 Arb Int 112; Boisséson n° 671, 691, 713; CCP 2nd ed p. 83, 290; 7 JIA 3 p. 57; Lew p. 68, 83; Rev Arb 1986 p. 338; Rubino-Sammartano p. 166, 266, 315, 430; Schlosser p. 540
2734	F	I 333	CPP III § 17.02; CPP 2nd ed p. 292
2735	F	I 301	4 Arb Int 91; Boisséson n° 665, 670; CPP III § 17.02; CPP 2nd ed p. 288; Lew p. 109; Rubino-Sammartano p. 258, 260
2745	F	I 326	Lew p. 118; Rubino-Sammartano p. 447
2762	F	I 326	Lew p. 118; Rubino-Sammartano p. 447
2763	E	I 157	2 Bulletin I p. 15; (1991) ICLR 309
2795	E	I 28	
2801	F	I 303	
2811	F	I 341	2 Arb Int 281; Boisséson n° 589, 730; CPP III § 17.04; CPP 2nd ed p. 86, 305; Rev Arb 1984 p. 211; 1989 p. 3, 19; Rubino-Sammartano p. 316
2879	F	I 346	Boisséson n° 670, 683, 712, 713, 719; CPP III § 17.02, § 18.02; CPP 2nd ed p. 290, 292, 313; Rubino-Sammartano p. 295
2886	F	I 332	4 Arb Int 91; Boisséson n° 672; Lew p. 109; Rubino-Sammartano p. 276

			Rev Arb 1985 p. 651, 657; 1986 p. 33; Rubino-Sammartano p. 271, 277; Schlosser p. 248
3344	F	I 440	4 Arb Int 92, 113, 114; Boisséson n° 690; Bulletin ASA 1992 p. 148; CPP III § 18.02; VI §35.05; CPP 2nd ed p. 314, 626, 627; (1989) ICLR 335; RDAI 1988 p. 66; Rev Arb 1986 p. 349; Rubino-Sammartano p. 48
3380	E F	I 96 I 413	4 Arb Int 91; Boisséson n° 683, 697, 698; CPP 2nd ed p. 125, 604; DIS 8 p. 50; El-Ahdab p. 1053; Rev Arb 1983 p. 14; 1986 pp. 357, 391; 1987 p. 494; 1990 p. 56; Schlosser p. 532
3383	E F	I 100 I 394	Boisséson n° 578; 1 Bulletin ICC 2 p. 16; CPP II § 9.08; III § 11.04, § 15.02; CPP 2nd ed p. 51, 52, 65, 165, 194, 258; 6 JIA 2 p. 69; Redfern-Hunter p. 39; Redfern-Hunter 2nd ed p. 55; Rev Arb 1983 p. 13
3460	F	I 425	Boisséson n° 574; 1 Bulletin ICC 2 p. 18; CPP 2nd ed p. 627; El-Ahdab p. 1055; 6 JIA 2 p. 73; Rev Arb 1988 p. 121; 1990 p. 92
3472	F	I 461	
3493 (the Pyramids case; SPP v. Arab Republic of Egypt L'affaire du plateau des Pyramides)	E	I 124	2 Arb Int 228; 3 Arb Int 214 4 Arb Int 99, 194; 5 Arb Int 24, 265; 7 Arb Int 50; Boisséson n° 607; CPP: Appendix IV; CPP VI § 35.06, § 37.05; CPP 2nd ed p. 200, 339, 604, 653, 670; DIS 6 p. 48; DIS 8 p. 71; (1985) ICLR p. 180; (1990) ICLR 417; Jahrbuch 3 p. 68; 2 JIA I p. 10; 3 JIA I p. 30; 4 JIA I p. 52; 6 JIA I p. 184; RDAI 1990 p. 71; Rev Arb 1986 pp. 3, 105,; 1987 p. 469, 487; 1989 p. 417; 1990 p. 56; 1991 p. 85; Rubino-Sammartano p. 169, 170, 333, 344; Schlosser p. 250, 428, 535; Schwebel p. 113, 123
3515	F	I 424	
3540	E F	I 105 I 399	4 Arb Int 105, 113; Boisséson n° 693, 694, 727; CPP II § 7.04, § 8.05; IV § 26.05, § 35.05; CPP 2nd ed p. 124, 137, 296, 419, 627, 628, 629;

Case	Lang.	Ref.	Citations
3572 (Deutsche Schachtbau und Tiefbohrgesellschaft v. RAKOIL)	E	II 154	(1984) ICLR p. 148; (1991) ICLR 311, 312; Rev Arb 1990 p. 92, 94; Rubino-Sammartano p. 276 5 Arb Int 244; 6 Arb Int 107, 357; 8 Arb Int 7, 254; Boisséson n° 725; (1989) ICLR 336; Jahrbuch 3 p. 69; 7 JIA I p. 11, 119, 123; Rev Arb 1991 p. 241
3742	F	I 486	Boisséson n° 627, 629; CPP 2nd ed p. 98; Rev Arb 1985 pp. 576, 582; Rubino-Sammartano p. 333
3779	E	I 138	
3790	F	I 476	2 Bulletin ICC I p. 15;
	E	II 2	El-Ahdab p. 931;
	E	II 445	(1984) ICLR p. 372; (1985) ICLR p. 339; (1986) ICLR p. 332; (1988) ICLR p. 48, 50; Jahrbuch p. I 71; Rev Arb 1984 p. 451; 1989 p. 626; Rubino-Sammartano p. 160; Schlosser p. 543
3820	E	I 115	CPP II § 7.04; CPP 2nd ed p. 297
3879 (Westland Helicopters v. A.O.I. et al.; L'affaire Westland)	E	II 11	5 Arb Int 25; 7 Arb Int 35, 360; Boisséson n° 607, 618; Bulletin ASA 1992 p. 196, 307; CPP 2nd ed p. 201, 547; 6 JIA I p. 184; 7 JIA 3 p. 25; Rev Arb 1988 p. 490; 1989 p. 427, 514, 547; Rubino-Sammartano p. 239, 329, 510; Schlosser p. 324, 428, 439; Schwebel p. 123
3880	E	I 159	Boisséson n° 670, 697;
	F	I 432	CPP 2nd ed p. 292; Lew p. 108
3881	F	II 257	Rubino-Sammartano p. 315, 424
3894	F	I 449	Boisséson n° 666, 698; El-Ahdab p. 1056
3896 (Framatome c. AEOI)	E	I 161	2 Arb Int 1 p. 152;
	F	I 481	Boisséson n° 626, 683, 715, 728, 757, 762, 763; CPP 2nd ed p. 61, 101, 418; Lew p. 63; RDAI 1988 p. 171; 1990 p. 412; Rev Arb 1985 p. 653; 1986 p. 345; 1990 p. 349; 1991 I p. 44
3902	E	II 450	2 Bulletin ICC I p. 15
3913	F	I 497	4 Arb Int 112; Lew p. 68; Rev Arb 1986 p. 339
3916	F	I 507	4 Arb Int. 112; Boisséon n° 593; CPP 2nd ed 9, 83, 84, 308; DIS 6 p. 30; 5 JIA 4 p. 124; 7 JIA 3 p. 57; Lew p. 68, 84; Redfern-Hunter 2nd ed p. 145; Rev Arb 1984 p. 9; 1986 p. 339;

3938	F	I 503	Schlosser p. 235 CPP 2nd ed p. 143; DIS 6 p. 33; Jahrbuch 2 p. 123; Lew p. 72; Rev Arb 1985 p. 203; Schlosser p. 543, 548
3987	F	I 521	Boisséson n° 578, 727; CPP 2nd ed p. 116, 622; RDAI 1988 p. 170; Rev Arb 1990 p. 81; Rubino-Sammartano p. 137
4023	F	I 528	Boisséson n° 574; CPP 2nd ed p. 204; DIS 6 p. 37; Rev Arb 1988 p. 120
4126	F	I 511	Boisséson n° 757, 762; RDAI 1990 p. 414; Rev Arb 1990 p. 349, 1991 p. 41
4131 (the Dow case; Isover St. Gobain v. Dow Chemical France)	E F	I 146 I 465	1 Arb Int 1 p. 65; 2 Arb Int 142; 2 Arb Int 227; 7 Arb Int 35; Boisséson n° 579, 585, 605, 683; Bulletin ASA 1992 p. 214; CPP II §5.05; CPP 2nd ed p. 72, 74, 96, 97, 135, 200, 604, 619; DIS 6 p. 46; RDAI 1989 p. 796; Rev Arb 1984 p. 137; 1985 pp. 504, 584, 656; 1987 p. 490, 494; 1988 p. 158, 481 1990 p. 56, 77; 1991 p. 167; 1992 p. 102; Rubino-Sammartano p. 143, 179; Schlosser p. 325
4132	E F	I 164 I 456	2 Arb Int 286; Boisséson n° 579, 594, 670; CPP 2nd ed p. 86, 292; 7 JIA 3 p. 57; Rev Arb 1986 pp. 397, 402, 407; 1989 p. 3, 23, 28; Schlosser p. 530, 538
4145	F E	I 559 II 53	Boisséson n° 762; CPP 2nd ed p. 56, 69, 84, 123, 158, 290, 308, 614, 631; El-Ahdab p. 1057; Rev Arb 1988 p. 121; 1990 p. 96; Rubino-Sammartano p. 149, 474; Schlosser p. 321
4156	F	I 515	Boisséson n° 762; CPP 2nd ed p. 417, 426; DIS 6 p. 40; Rubino-Sammartano p. 360
4187	F	I 460	DIS 6 p. 24
4237	E	I 167	4 Arb Int 116; Boisséson n° 670; CPP 2nd ed p. 100, 604, 622, 634, 639; Jahrbuch 3 p. 68; Rev Arb 1990 p. 56, 81; 1992 p. 105; Schlosser p. 611
4265	F	I 499	2 Arb Int 144; CPP 2nd ed p. 310, 313; El-Ahdab p. 1059; 7 JIA 3 p. 57;

			Lew p. 55; Rubino-Sammartano p. 161
4338	F	I 555	Boisséson n° 683; CPP 2nd ed p. 297, 617; Rev Arb 1990 p. 75
4367	E	II 18	Boisséson n° 666; CPP 2nd ed p. 622; Rev Arb 1990 p. 81
4381	F	II 264	Boisséson n° 579, 670, 683; CPP 2nd ed p. 61, 62, 69, 72, 74, 161, 192, 604; (1990) ICLR 424; RDAI 1989 p. 795; Rev Arb 1990 p. 56, 603; Rubino-Sammartano p. 48, 153, 169
4392	F	I 473	2 Arb Int 142; Boisséson n° 579, 585, 607, 627; CPP 2nd ed p. 58, 101; DIS 6 p. 27; Lew p. 53; Rev Arb 1987 p. 494; 1991 p. 168; 1992 p. 103; Rubino-Sammartano p. 141, 142
4402	E	I 153	2 Arb Int 141; CPP 2nd ed p. 98, 100, 198, 199; Lew p. 52
4415	F	I 530	Boisséson n° 588; CPP 2nd ed p. 88, 423; Rubino-Sammartamo p. 360; Schlosser p. 328
4416	F E	I 542 II 460	2 Bulletin I p. 15; (1985) ICLR p. 67; (1988); ICLR 48; Rev Arb 1989 p.619
4434	F	I 458	Boisséson n° 665; CPP 2nd ed p. 290; Lew p. 108; Rubino-Sammartano p. 264
4467	F	I 501	CPP 2nd ed p. 310
4472	F	I 525	Boisséson n° 574, 579; CPP 2nd ed p. 74, 158, 163; DIS 6 p. 37; Rev Arb 1987 p. 492, 495; 1988 p. 120; 1991 p. 168; 1992 p. 103
4491	F	I 539	2 Arb Int 143; Boisséson n° 590; 1 Bulletin ICC 2 p. 18; CPP 2nd ed p. 116; 6 JIA 2 p. 72; Lew p. 54; Schlosser p. 541
4504	F	II 279	Boisséson n° 579, 606, 725, 766; Bulletin ASA 1992 p. 215; CPP 2nd ed p. 98, 100, 200, 254; (1990) ICLR 422; Rev Arb 1987 p. 492; 1988 p. 158, 161, 480, 483; 1991 p. 167; 1992 p. 102; Rubino-Sammartano p. 115, 179, 403
4555	F E	I 536 II 24	CPP 2nd ed p. 69
4567	E	II 27	CPP 2nd ed p. 625;

			Rev Arb 1990 p. 84
4589	E	II 32, 454	CPP 2nd ed p. 91
4604	F	I 546	2 Arb Int 290;
			Boisséson n° 586, 589, 590;
			CPP 2nd ed p. 72, 86;
			Rev Arb 1989 p. 3, 18; 1991 p. 168;
			Schlosser p. 224
4650	E	II 67	CPP 2nd ed p. 292, 300, 611;
			Rev Arb 1990 p. 67
4667	F	II 297	
		II 338	
4695	E	II 33	Boisséson n° 666;
			CPP 2nd ed p. 72, 91, 192, 604, 622;
			Rev Arb 1990 p. 56, 81;
			Rubino-Sammartano p. 158
4707	E	II 477	2 Bulletin ICC 1 p. 15;
			Rev Arb 1989 p. 622;
			Rubino-Sammartano p. 161
4761	E	II 519	Boisséson n° 698;
	F	II 298	CPP 2nd ed p. 143, 275, 299,
	F	II 302	627, 628, 631;
			Rev Arb 1990 p. 92, 93, 96;
			Rubino-Sammartano p. 272, 295, 367
4840	E	II 465	2 Bulletin ICC 1 p. 15;
			Rev Arb 1989 p. 618
4862	E	II 508	2 Bulletin ICC 1 p. 15;
	F	II 309	(1989) ICLR p. 181;
			Rev Arb 1989 p. 622;
			Rubino-Sammartano p. 160, 224
4972	F	II 380	Rev Arb 1990 p. 83
4975	E	II 165	(1991) ICLR 309
4996	F	II 293	Boisséson n° 671;
			CPP 2nd ed p. 290;
			Rubino-Sammartano p. 149, 268
4998	F	II 300	Boisséson n° 715, 727, 757;
			CPP 2nd ed p. 417;
			Rev Arb 1990 p. 349;
			Rubino-Sammartano p. 359
5029	E	II 69	2 Bulletin ICC 1 p. 15;
	E	II 480	3 Bulletin ICC 2 p. 46;
			CPP 2nd ed p. 108, 270;
			Rev Arb 1989 p. 622;
			Schlosser p. 180
5065	F	II 330	Boisséson n° 578, 683;
			CPP 2nd ed p. 64, 192, 199, 297, 622, 625;
			(1990) ICLR 423;
			RDAI 1989 p. 796;
			Rev Arb 1990 p. 81, 84;
			Rubino-Sammartano p. 142, 147, 171
5073	E	II 85	CPP 2nd ed p. 604, 625;
			Rev Arb 1990 p. 56, 85
5080	E	II 80	
5103	F	II 361	8 Arb Int 244;
			Boisséson n° 574, 605, 712;
			Bulletin ASA 1992 p. 213;
			1 Bulletin ICC 2 p. 25;
			2 Bulletin ICC 2 p. 20;
			CPP 2nd ed p. 62, 85, 99, 108, 122, 158,
			284, 604, 622;
			Rev Arb 1990 p. 81

Consolidated Analytical Table

of Awards published in English Language

1974 – 1990

and/et

Table analytique consolidée

des sentences publiées en langue française

1974 – 1990

Consolidated analytical table of arbitral awards

published in English language

1974 – 1990

volume I (pages 1-176)

volume II (pages 1-254 and 445-549)

xlii

xliv

xlvi

1

Table analytique consolidée

des sentences publiées en langue française

1974 - 1990

volume I (pages 177 - 564)

volume II (pages 255 - 444)

A compter du volume II, la Table analytique consolidée renvoie à la première page de la sentence et non pas nécessairement à la page où figure la référence recherchée. L'indication d'une page suivie de la mention (c), indique que la référence recherchée est principalement abordée dans les commentaires qui suivent la sentence.

c

ICC Arbitral Awards

reprinted from *Yearbook Commercial Arbitration*

1986 - 1990

Partial award of 20 January 1983 in case no. 3790

Arbitrators: Sir Charles Fletcher-Cooke, Q.C. (U.K.) chairman, Mr. Abdul Hamid
Ahdab (Lebanon), Mr. Mustapha El Alem (Libya)

Parties: Claimant: French Contractor
Defendant: Libyan Employer

Published in: Summary in *International Construction Law Review* (1984) pp. 372–
375, with comment by S. Jarvin, *id.* pp. 375–376 and G. Westring,
id. pp. 376–377

Subject matters: – arbitrators' power to render partial award
– clause 67 FIDIC (2nd edition)
– powers of the Engineer under FIDIC
– time limit for requesting arbitration
– procedure for requesting arbitration
– release of bank guarantee
– payment of taxes
– currency of payment

FACTS

By a series of contracts a Libyan employer entrusted a French contractor with the
execution of a housing project in Libya. These contracts included a contract called
"Factory Contract", a contract called "Housing Contract" and a contract called
"Public Utilities Contract". Libyan law was declared to be applicable to the
contract. The contracts incorporated to a large extent the FIDIC Conditions for
Works of Civil Engineering Construction (2nd edition). Clause 67 of the FIDIC
Conditions provides:

"Settlement of disputes – Arbitration
If any dispute or difference of any kind whatsoever shall arise between the
Employer or the Engineer and the Contractor in connection with or arising out
of the Contract or the carrying out of the Works (whether during the progress
of the works or after their completion and whether before or after the
termination, abandonment or breach of the Contract) it shall in the first place
be referred to and settled by the Engineer who within a period of 90 days after
being requested by either party to do so shall give written notice of his
decision to the Employer and the Contractor. Save as hereinafter provided
such decision in respect of every matter so referred shall be final and binding
upon the Employer and the Contractor until the completion of the work and
shall forthwith be given effect to by the Contractor who shall proceed with the
Works with all due diligence whether he or the Employer requires arbitration
as hereinafter provided or not. If the Engineer has given written notice of his
decision to the Employer and the Contractor and no claim to arbitration has
been communicated to him by either the Employer or the Contractor within a

period of 90 days from receipt of such notice the said decision shall remain final and binding upon the Employer and the Contractor. If the Engineer shall fail to give notice of his decision as aforesaid within a period of 90 days after being requested as aforesaid or if either the Employer or the Contractor be dissatisfied with any such decision, then and in any such case either the Employer or the Contractor may within 90 days after the expiration of the first named period of 90 days (as the case may be) require that the matter or matters in dispute be referred to arbitration as hereinafter provided. All disputes or differences in respect of which the decision (if any) of the Engineer has not become final and binding shall be finally settled under the Rules of Conciliation and Arbitration of the International Chamber of Commerce in Paris by one or more arbitrators appointed in accordance with the said Rules. The said arbitrator/s shall have full power to open up, review and revise any decision, opinion, direction, certificate or valuation of the Engineer and neither party shall be limited in the proceedings before such arbitrator/s to the evidence or arguments put before the Engineer for the purpose of obtaining his said decision. No decision given by the Engineer in accordance with the foregoing provisions shall disqualify him from being called as a witness and giving evidence before the arbitrator/s on any matter whatsoever relevant to the dispute or difference referred to the arbitrator/s as aforesaid. The arbitrator/s shall not enter on the reference until after the completion or alleged completion of the works unless with the written consent of the Employer and the Contractor provided always

(i) that such reference may be opened before such completion or alleged completion in respect of the withholding by the Engineer of any certificate or the withholding of any portion of the retention money to which the Contractor claims in accordance with the conditions set out in clause numbered 60 to be entitled or in respect of the exercise of the Engineer's power to give a certificate under Clause 63 hereof

(ii) that the giving of the Certificate of Completion under clause 48 he ι shall not be a condition precedent to the opening of any such reference."

During the execution of the project, several disputes arose which were submitted to the Engineer for his decision. Both the Contractor and the Employer filed requests for arbitration with ICC in respect of a number of the Engineer's decision.

The Contractor asked the arbitrators to render a partial award on a number of preliminary issues, *viz.* (a) whether amounts certified by the Engineer were binding on the Employer, (b) whether the Employer's claims were filed with arbitration within the period of time stated in and in conformity with the formalities required under clause 67, (c) whether an amendment to the Housing Contract consisting of an extension of time for the Engineer to render a number of decisions was binding on the Libyan Employer who alleged that the amendment was signed on its behalf by someone who was not authorised to do so, was binding on the Libyan Employer (not reported in the extract as it merely concerns a determination of facts, *held* the person signing the amendment had the power to sign), (d) whether the Contractor's bank guarantee for retension money is to be released on completion of the works or on payment of the final accounts, and (e) the manner in which the sums awarded by the arbitral tribunal in the partial award were to be paid (Libyan taxation and currency).

4

EXTRACT
1. *Power to issue partial award*
At the outset, the arbitral tribunal dealt with the Libyan Employer's objection to
the arbitral tribunal's power to render a partial award:

"The Tribunal applies the rules mentioned in the 'Rules for the ICC Court of
Arbitration'.

"The ICC Rules clearly distinguish in several articles between a final award and
a partial award, particularly in article 21.[1]

"As Libyan law is applied to the contract, the Tribunal finds an explanation for
such convergence between final and partial awards in the wording of article 118
of the Code of Civil and Commercial Procedure as well as in the law relating
to the regulation of the Libyan judiciary. Paragraph 2 of article 118 of the
Code of Procedure provides indeed that:

'. . . if a part of the lawsuit is admissible, the Court is to issue a judgment
as to such part if it deems that a quick judgment may be in the interest of
one of the parties. Moreover, the Court shall take any decision or step
which it may judge necessary as far as the other parts of the suit are
concerned'.

"Both parties agree to such interpretation in chapter VIII of the 'Terms of
Reference':

'Terms of Reference:

B – *Form of the Awards*
The Arbitrators shall seek to ensure that the final arbitral award and
each partial award shall be in a form valid under French and Libyan
law'

as well as in chapter VII of such Terms of Reference which provides:

'F – *Partial Awards*
The Arbitrators shall have such power to make partial awards as is
provided for under the ICC Rules'.

"Therefore the Tribunal finds that it is empowered to issue partial awards.

"After consideration of the four claims by the Contractor, which are entitled as
follows:

---

1. Art. 21 of the ICC Rules provides:
   "Scrutiny of award by the Court
   Before signing an award, whether partial or definitive, the arbitrator shall submit it in
   draft form to the Court. The Court may lay down modifications as to the form of the
   award and, without affecting the arbitrator's liberty of decision, may also drawn his
   attention to points of substance. No award shall be signed until it has been approved by
   the Court as to its form."

> – A – Certified Amounts
> – B – Five Engineer's Decisions
> – C – Eight Engineer's Decisions
> – D – Retention Money Guarantee

the Tribunal deems that they are a part which may be the subject of an award as to their substance.

"Therefore the Tribunal holds to issue an award as to the four preliminary issues."

2. *Certified amounts: position of the Engineer*

The provisions of the Housing and Public Utilities Contracts required that progressive payments were to be made by the Employer within 45 days of the communication of monthly certificates to the Engineer, who was to approve them within 15 days of receipt thereof. Furthermore, each contract provided that on substantial completion of the works, the Contractor's final account is to be paid within 45 days of its communication to the Engineer who was to approve it within 45 days of receipt thereof. The Employer refused to pay a number of these monthly certificates and the final account. The arbitral tribunal considered:

"The Tribunal's mission is restricted to the interpretation of clause 60(f) and (c) in order to determine to what extent the Contract binds the Employer as far as the certificates issued by the Engineer under clause 60 are concerned.

"(. . . .)

"The Tribunal notes that by virtue of those two paragraphs (c) and (f), payment is linked to the Engineer's approval, who is to present a decision within 15 days period as to approval:

(a) of documents relating to works executed monthly;
(b) of the final account.

"This brings up the issue of the nature of the legal bond between the Employer and the Engineer.

"The Tribunal considers that the two contracts entered into by both parties give to the bond uniting the Engineer to the Employer two different legal characters depending on the clause applied. The Engineer is considered to be the Employer's agent:

(*a*) when he pays under clause 60;
(*b*) when, during the course of execution, he orders the renewal of all materials which he deems not to be in accordance with the Contract, by implementation of clause 39;
(*c*) when he orders to execute tests under clause 36(4);
(*d*) when he requires a return in detail of the supervision staff, under clause 53;
(*e*) when he orders the Contractor to stop works, under clause 40;
(*f*) when he gives the order to commence work;
(*g*) when he delivers a certificate after having satisfied himself that the works are provisionally executed;
(*h*) when he proceeds to variations under clauses 51 and 52;

6

(*i*) when he authorises payment for daywork under clause 52(4);
(*j*) when he checks and determines under clause 56 whether the value of the works complies with the Contract;
(*k*) when he issues the final completion certificate under clause 62.

"There is an important difference however between the work executed by the Engineer in his capacity of the Employer's agent and his function when acting as an independent arbitrator under clause 67.

"The Tribunal has noted the effect of article 699 of the Libyan Civil Code.

"The Tribunal considers that the Engineer, with respect to the work which he carries out as the agent of the Employer binds the latter and involves its financial responsibility with respect to such works.

"When acting under clause 67, however, he:

(*a*) does not represent the Employer; and
(*b*) is independent and not bound by the Employer's orders.

"Thus, the Engineer's decision under clause 67 can only bind the Employer if it does not object thereto, whereas the Engineer's orders and decisions as agent of the Employer do immediately bind the latter.

"Clause 67 gives the Employer the possibility to object to the Engineer's certificate by presenting a claim to the Engineer, about which the latter is to render a decision within 90 days. Within 90 days, the Employer may object, before the Court of arbitration, to the Engineer's decisions relating to such certificates. In default of such objection, the Employer is finally bound by the decision.

"The Tribunal notes that the Contractor adjusted the form of the final accounts by deducting the amounts relating to the Engineer's decisions on claims in order to meet the Employer's objections. Accordingly, there is no defence that remains.

(. . . .)

"Therefore the Tribunal holds that the Engineer's approval as to monthly certificates and final accounts binds the Employer and the amount claimed by the Contractor for L.D. 4,259,526.152 should be paid."

3. *Time limit and procedure of clause 67*
The Contractor contended that the Employer (*a*) did not respect the periods of time and (*b*) did not comply with the procedure provided for in clause 67, from which it resulted that its claims to arbitration did not meet the required conditions of its admissibility.

(*a*) The Arbitral Tribunal determined that the Employer received on 1 May 1980 notice of the Engineer's decision. The period of time of 90 days to present its claims to arbitration therefore expired on 1 August 1980. As the Employer filed its claims to arbitration with the ICC on 7 August 1980, the Tribunal held that these claims were time-barred.

(*b*) As to the procedure for making a claim to arbitration, the Arbitral Tribunal observed that:

"[C]lause 67 distinguishes two cases:

"*First Case:*
The Engineer gives written notice of its decision to the Employer and the Contractor within 90 days after being requested to decide. In this case, should one of the parties be dissatisfied with the decision, or wish to object thereto, then a request for arbitration is to be made to the ICC Court of Arbitration and such request should be communicated to the Engineer.

"*Second Case:*
The Engineer does not give written notice of its decision or does not take a decision within 90 days after being requested to decide. In such case, the contract considers that the Engineer's negative behaviour constitutes a neglect of the claim presented by the Contractor or the Employer, which neglect entitled them to resort to arbitration within a restricted period of time.

"Only in the first case is the request for arbitration to be communicated to the Engineer, such communication is not a procedure of mere form but it is a fundamental procedure related to the Engineer's mission to establish monthly payment certificates and particularly the final account.

"Indeed, it is the Engineer, who, under clause 60, adopts the final account which binds the Employer. Such final account varies, depending on whether the amounts fixed by the Engineer's decision are considered to be definitively due or not due subsequently to an objection thereto.

"Unknowingly, the Engineer might order the payment to the Contractor of amounts of the final account, which amounts might be due or not due. It is to prevent such a serious risk that the Contract required that both parties communicate the request for arbitration to the Engineer.

"In the case of the Engineer's not respecting the time limits, the Engineer is considered by the contract as negligent and, in such case, the contract leaves the parties the choice to present a claim to arbitration either to the Court of Arbitration or to the Engineer as there is no need to help the latter to adopt the final account, which he is supposed to examine carefully, when he turns out to have failed to respect the proceedings by not taking the required decisions.

"Moreover, a claim to arbitration without need for particular formalities is to be explicit and clear and clearly show the plaintiff's intention to submit the dispute to arbitration. On the contrary, the expression of a simple dissatisfaction is not enough to show clearly such intention and subsequently, the claim to arbitration expresses a dissatisfaction whereas a dissatisfaction does not express a claim to arbitration.

"On the other hand, after considering the circumstances in which the Employer objected to the Engineer's decision, it appears that:

1. The decisions of the Engineer were notified to both the Contractor on 30 April 1980 and the Employer on 1 May 1980.

8

2. The Contractor filed on 5 June and 25 July 1980 a claim to arbitration with the ICC after asking the Engineer for arbitration, within the 90 days period.
3. On 7 August 1980, the Employer filed a claim to arbitration with the ICC without communicating a request for arbitration to the Engineer within the 90 days period.

"The Engineer took its decision and communicated it to the Contractor on 30 April 1980 and the Employer on 1 May 1980. Thus, it is the first case mentioned in clause 67 which is to be applied here, which is the one with respect to an expressed decision of the Engineer's and not the case with respect to the Engineer's neglect.

"The expression of the dissatisfaction as to the decision is not enough in itself and it is to be accompanied by a claim to arbitration which is to be communicated to the Engineer himself as an objection to his explicit decision, as the mere dissatisfaction has no legal effect on the Engnieer's decisions, only an explicit request for arbitration communicated to the Engineer within the 90 days period suspends the effect thereof.

"The Tribunal rejects the Employer's contentions on both grounds and finds that the Employer has not taken the necessary action under clause 67 of the relevant contract to prevent the eight decisions of the Engineer from being final and binding under that clause.

"Therefore, the eight decisions of the Engineer are final and binding and the Tribunal awards the Contractor L.D. 2,112,274.903."

4. *Release of bank guarantee for retention money*
The Arbitral Tribunal stated the facts for this issue as follows:

"Clause 60(c) and (g) of the General Conditions of the Housing Contract as amended provides:

(c) Monthly payments shall be made to the Contractor for the executed works on the basis of the provisional certificates submitted by him. Such payments shall not be less than the amount fixed in the Appendix to this Contract. They must be made within 45 (forty five) days of presentation of the complete documents to the Engineer, which must approve them within fifteen days of receipt of such documents. The Contractor or his Representative shall, under the Engineer's supervision, prepare the provisional certificates covering the executed works and shall estimate the value thereof according to the rates specified in the Schedule of Rates and Prices.

"After approval of such certificates, 95% of the amount shown thereon shall be paid to the Contractor after deduction of all sums deductible under paragraphs (a) and (b) above and of any other sums to be deducted according to the terms of this contract.

"The Employer shall pay to the Contractor the equivalent of 5% deducted from the payments actually made if the Contractor provides irrevocable letters of guarantee from a Libyan bank representing such percentage, provided that such letters remain valid and renewable until the date of provisional completion of the works.

(g) The 5% retention or else the equivalent letters of guarantee at the same rate, mentioned in paragraph (c) above, and which are deducted from each payment certificate, shall be refunded or returned to the Contractor, on payment of the final statement provided that the Contractor has fulfilled all of its obligations relative to construction of the Contract.

"Under the Housing Contract, the guarantees for retention money to be supplied by the Contractor were in form of an 'on demand' guarantee and reached a value of L.D. 1,200,000 for the Housing Contract.

"The last maintenance certificate for the Housing Contract was issued in March 1978.

"The Contractor contends that the Employer has continued nevertheless to force it to maintain and renew the guarantees for retention money.

"On 6 November 1977, 31 January and 6 December 1978, the Contractor wrote to the Engineer:

'Until now, the financial department of the Employer never took into consideration clause 60(c) of the Contract. We beg you to clear this problem with the Employer . . .'.

"The Contractor contends that, whether clause 60 be construed as meaning that the release or the guarantee is to take place at provisional completion or as meaning to release upon 'payment of the final account', provisional completion took place two years ago and payment of the 'final accounts' was approved by the Engineer on 16 April 1980 (no. 56) and 6 October 1980 (no. 57) (Housing)."

The Arbitral Tribunal held that the Contractor was entitled to an immediate release of the retention money guarantee because provisional completion had taken place two years ago and the employer had failed to make the final payment on the due date, which payment had been approved by the Engineer.

5. *Taxes and currency of payment*
The Housing and Factory Contracts were entered into respectively on 22 November 1973 and 14 March 1973. In September 1973, the Libyan Government promulgated Finance Law no. 64 which provided for a maximum rate of company income tax of 64% which Law repealed Finance Law no. 21 in force until then, which provided for a maximum rate of company income tax of 29%. Clause 70 of the Conditions of the Contracts provided:

"The Contractor shall neither gain a profit nor suffer any loss as a result of changes caused by laws and regulations which cause decreases or increases in due fees and taxes of whatsoever nature and promulgated after the approbation of the Council of Ministers on the project of industrial housing on 17 Ragab 1393 H., corresponding to 16 August 1973 or during its execution."

On the basis of this clause the Contractor claimed a reimbursement of approximately 35/64th of the company income taxes it was obliged to pay on revenues under both Contracts. The Employer contended that neither itself nor the Arbitral Tribunal has the authority to decide upon the amount of taxes the Contractor may have to pay in Libya. It stated also that it would reimburse to the Contractor all the taxes increase which occurred as to the concerned contracts as a result of the Income Tax Law of 1973, but only once the Contractor had actually paid the taxes involved.

10

As regards the currency of payment, the Contractor contended that it had transferred outside Libya less of the contract price than it is entitled under the two Contracts. As clause 60 of the Contract Conditions provided for a percentage of the contract price or value to be paid in foreign currency, the Contractor requested that the Terms of Reference be supplemented by a section providing for the payment of awards in French Francs or U.S. Dollars. The Employer did not object to the Contractor transferring award payments into foreign currencies as provided in the Contracts. It contended that under the relevant provisions of the Contracts and the Libyan exchange control regulations, it could only make payments in Libyan Dinars and not in foreign currency, and that hence the Terms of Reference did not need to be supplemented.

The Arbitral Tribunal declined to decide on the Contractor's requests:

"The Tribunal has been asked to make certain pronouncements about the manner in which the sums which the Tribunal has awarded in this partial award should be paid and also upon the consequences of such award upon the liability of the Contractor as regards Libyan taxation. On neither of these points does the Tribunal feel that it is competent to make such announcements and accordingly it restricts itself to the award in its simple form.

"As far as Libyan taxation is concerned, it is entirely a matter for the relevant authorities in this matter and applicable laws in Libya.

"As far as the currency of payment is concerned, this must be governed by the exact terms of the Contracts and the applicable exchange control regulations."

Interim award of 5 March 1984 in case no. 3879

Arbitrators: Prof. Dr. Eugène Bucher (Switz.), chairman; Mr. Pierre Bellet (France); Mr. Nils Mangård (Sweden)

Parties: Claimant: Westland Helicopters Ltd. (U.K.)
               Respondents: (1) Arab Organization for Industrialization, (2) United Arab Emirates, (3) Kingdom of Saudi Arabia, (4) State of Qatar, (5) Arab Republic of Egypt, and (6) Arab British Helicopter Company (Egypt)

Published in: 23 International Legal Materials (1984) pp. 1071–1089

Subject matters: – multi-party arbitration
                  – competence of arbitrator
                  – supranational organization
                  – arbitration clause binding on founding States
                  – liability of founding States
                  – stay of arbitral proceedings
                  – appointment of arbitrators

FACTS

On 29 April 1975, the States of the United Arab Emirates, Saudi Arabia, Qatar and Egypt concluded an agreement by which they established the Arab Organization for Industrialization (AOI). The object of the AOI was the development of an arms industry for the benefit of the four States. The AOI was directed by a "Higher Committee" composed of ministers delegated by the four States. This Committee established the internal rules of the AOI, which were approved by the four States on 17 August 1975. The head office of the AOI was established in Cairo, and another office was opened in Riyadh.

On 4 January 1978, the Higher Committee signed with the British Government a Memorandum of Understanding, whereby the four States guaranteed the performance of the commitments that the AOI might undertake towards British companies.

On 27 February 1978, the AOI and Westland signed a "Shareholders Agreement" by which they created a "joint stock company" (The Arab British Helicopters Company – ABH). The ABH, of which AOI owned 70% of the shares and Westland 30%, was to be the legal base for manufacturing and selling "Lynx" helicopters developed by Westland. The Agreement contained an arbitration clause referring all disputes to ICC arbitration in Geneva. The Agreement provided for the applicability of Swiss law. On the same day Westland signed with ABH a series of contracts, which also provided for ICC arbitration.

On 14 May 1979, after the Camp David Agreement between Egypt and Israel, Prince Sultan bin Abdul Aziz of Saudi Arabia published in the "Saudi Arabian News Agency" a statement announcing his nomination as Chairman of the AOI; at the same time he gave notice that the United Arab Emirates, Saudi Arabia and Qatar were putting an end to the existence of the AOI as of 1 July 1979, taking into consideration the recognition of Israel by Egypt. The Prince declared that a Liquidation Committee would be established. On 18 May 1979, Egypt promulgated a Decree Law according to which the AOI, having its place of business in Cairo, was still in existence as a legal person.

In June 1980, Westland filed a request for arbitration with the ICC against AOI, United Arab Emirates, Saudi Arabia, Qatar, Egypt and ABH. The AOI, the United Arab Emirates, the Kingdom of Saudi Arabia and the State of Qatar did not appear. The Arab Republic of Egypt and ABH objected to the competence of the Arbitral Tribunal on various grounds.

Before the first arbitration hearing, Egypt commenced proceedings before the Court of Cairo South to have the arbitral proceedings declared null, on the ground of the absence of an arbitration clause validly binding the Arab Republic of Egypt. Notice of the proceedings was given to the arbitral panel in November 1980.

On 18 December 1980, Egypt also filed a petition with the Registry of the Court of Justice of the Canton of Geneva, for the annulment of the arbitral proceedings. Both the Court of Justice and, on appeal, the *Tribunal Fédéral* (Swiss Federal Supreme Court) rejected Egypt's submissions, holding that there existed *prima facie* an agreement to arbitrate.

In an interim award regarding jurisdiction, the Arbitral Tribunal declared itself competent in regard to all the respondents, rejected all other objections of the respondents and refused a stay of the arbitral proceedings.

EXTRACT
1. Egypt contended that (1) the AOI was a legal entity separate from its founding members; (2) the founding members could not be held liable for the AOI's activities; (3) the existence of the AOI could not be terminated unilaterally without one of the founding member's consent; (4) in any case, the Egyptian decree law had had the effect of continuing the existence of the AOI. Further: (5) the liability of Egypt was excluded since, according to its domestic legislation, the Arab Republic of Egypt cannot enter into an arbitration agreement without passing a special law to this purpose; (6) Egypt enjoys the immunity of a sovereign State. ABH presented similar arguments recognizing, however, the validity of the arbitration clauses with Westland.

Identity of AOI
2. By a memorial dated 3 February 1982, Westland specified that the AOI in Riyadh was the sole AOI against which it had intended to press its claims and that the "AOI in Cairo" was therefore to be excluded from the proceedings.

3. Both Egypt and ABH objected and asked for re-introduction of AOI-Cairo. The arbitrators replied:

"The entity 'AOI in Cairo' is wrongly asking 'to be re-introduced' into the present proceedings. Since an award on the merits which may arise from the proceedings will not in any way bind the 'AOI in Cairo', this body has no legitimate interest in being made a party to the proceedings. It goes without saying that neither the Arab Republic of Egypt nor the ABH has any right to request the 'AOI in Cairo' to be re-introduced."

Arbitration clause binding the AOI
4. The arbitrators first considered that the arbitration clause contained in the Agreement between the AOI and Westland constituted an arbitration agreement in written form according to Art. 6(1) of the Swiss Intercantonal Arbitration Convention (Concordat).

Arbitration clause binding the four States
5. The four States did not themselves sign any contract with Westland. However, the arbitrators held:

"In certain circumstances, those who have not signed an arbitration clause are nevertheless bound by it (and can avail themselves of it as a means of objection, if proceedings are instituted against them before the ordinary courts). This is true for the successor in title or any other successor, for example whomsoever may acquire rights over property or a concern with assets and liabilities of the nature referred to in Art. 181 *et seq.* of the Swiss Federal Code of Obligations ('COS') or for an assignee. It is thus that two awards given under the aegis of the ICC held that in cases of subrogation and of universal succession, the subrogated party and the successor were bound by an arbitral clause (Clunet (1978) p. 976 at 980). A partner is bound by the arbitration clause entered into by a general partnership ('*Société en nom collectif*') of which he is a partner, and the co-contracting party may rely upon the arbitration clause if he brings his action against the partner instead of bringing it against the partnership (see, A. Hueck, *Das Recht der offenen Handelsgesellschaft*, 4th ed. (1971) pp. 319–20).

6. "The Concordat, which states that the arbitration clause must be in written form, is not an exception. It does not follow from the requirement of the written form that the clause must be concluded in the name of the party to the proceedings.

(. . . .)[1]

7. "The question whether the four States are bound by the arbitration clause concluded by the AOI in its own name (Shareholders Agreement contracted with Westland, clause 12.1) is exactly the same as the substantive law question whether the four States are bound in general by the obligations contracted by the AOI. If the obligations under substantive law flowing from the Shareholders Agreement are obligations not only of the AOI, but also of the four States, if the *locus standi* to conduct the defence in relation to those obligations can be attributed not only to the AOI, but also to the four States, then the latter are therefore bound by the arbitration clause, just as they might, had they been summoned before an ordinary Court, have availed themselves of this clause as a ground in their defence. The mandatory force of the arbitration clause cannot be dissociated from that of the substantive contractual commitments; the reply to the question as to whether the four States are bound by the acts of the AOI must always be the same, whether the procedural aspect of the arbitration clause is involved or that of the substantive law concerning the financial obligations of the four States."

The supranational status of the AOI
8. The Arbitral Tribunal further examined the legal nature of the AOI, in respect to the intention of the four States in creating it. The arbitrators concluded that the founding States had clearly wanted "to define in an exhaustive and exclusive manner all legal aspects pertaining to the AOI, and above all to exclude the application of any national law". Hence, the AOI had, in the intention of its founding members, a supranational character:

9. "In the opinions submitted by the Arab Republic of Egypt it is maintained that no legal person may exist without a legal foundation within a national legal order. This confuses the legal position of legal persons created by individuals within the framework of private law with the position of the AOI, created by States. Whereas it is true that an individual cannot set up a legal entity without the authorization of a State or a State law, sovereign States may themselves dispense with such a basis. Their acts have the force of law, and if a State alone can create by its acts (even without recourse to its legislation previously in force) a legal person, several States clearly have the same power when they act together and with common intent, as the four States did in the present circumstances.

10. "Having regard to the supranational character of the AOI it is, from the outset, impossible to attribute to it, *a posteriori*, an 'applicable law' according to the

---

1. The arbitral tribunal referred to Swiss Supreme Court [Tribunal Fédéral]: 5 May 1976, *Société des Grands Travaux de Marseille* v. *P. R. of Bangladesh et al.*, ATF 102 I a 574–583, reported in *Yearbook* Vol. V (1980) pp. 217–220; 14 November 1979, *Arab Republic of Libya* v. *Wetco Ltd.*, unpublished.

rules of private international law, that is to say to submit this entity to the law of either the place of its incorporation (which, *in casu*, does not exist), or the place where the centre of its business activities lies, or the place of its management, or any other place. This private law manner of approach is excluded if the legal entity in question is created by States which have wished to give it a supranational character, that is to say to exempt it from being subject to any national law. Fixing the administrative seat in Cairo has no effect on the legal status of this entity.

11. "The later unilateral acts by Egypt, the aim of which was to 'nationalize' the AOI (see Decree Law) cannot in any way change the situation set out. The sovereignty of the Arab Republic of Egypt carries the possibility to exert its *imperium* over its own territory, but that sovereignty does not include a power to change the legal status of the AOI as set up by these treaties with the other States without the agreement of those States themselves, even if the 'seat' (in whatever sense of the word) was situated within Egyptian territory."

Personality of the AOI and liability of the four States
12. The arbitrators held that the attribution of legal personality to the AOI would not affect the liability of the four founding States. The arbitrators considered instances in the Swiss and French legal systems confirming the cumulative liability of a legal person and of the individuals who constitute it (*société coopérative*, Art. 868 cos; *société en commandite par actions*, Art. 764 ff. cos; in France, *société en nom collectif*).

Liability of the four States
13. The liability of the founding States was neither stipulated nor excluded in the Treaty or Basic Statute of AOI. The arbitrators reasoned:

"In the absence of any rule of applicable law [*règle de droit positif*], what is to be deduced from the silence of the founding documents of the AOI as to the liability of the four States? In the absence of any provision expressly or impliedly excluding the liability of the four States, this liability subsists since, as a general rule, those who engage in transactions of an economic nature are deemed liable for the obligations which flow therefrom. In default by the four States of formal exclusion of their liability, third parties which have contracted with the AOI could legitimately count on their liability.

14. "This rule flows from general principles of law and from good faith. It can be supported if one likens the given situation to that which existed during the last century, where commercial organizations were formed without a clear legal basis (whether or not they could be considered as possessing personality). As a general rule, the founding members or the members of such bodies were held liable unless they had excluded their liability in a manner which could not escape third parties' notice which, for example, was the case with the establishment of a joint stock company, the generally known structure of which excluded the liability of shareholders. In the present case, the Basic Statute, despite the fixing of capital, does not classify the AOI as a '*société de capitaux*' such as a limited liability company. The AOI is rather more akin to a general partnership ('*société en nom collectif*') under French, Swiss or German law or a 'partnership' under English or United States law."

15. The arbitrators observed that:

"The foregoing is all the more true given that the personality conferred upon the AOI by the founding States was expressly limited . . . solely to operational needs, as is provided in the articles of many international organizations. The AOI was designated by its founders as an 'organization' and as a 'body', as opposed to the 'joint-stock company' ABH, and the legal status of such a joint inter-state enterprise ['*entreprise commune interétatique*'] – to the extent that it can exist at all – cannot be relied upon in order to eliminate the liability of the States which are partners therein.

16. "Finally, one must admit that in reality, in the circumstances of this case, the AOI is one with the States. At the same time as establishing the AOI, the Treaty set up the Higher Committee composed of the competent Ministers of the four States. . . . This Committee thus played a double role, both as organ of the AOI and as a grouping of States. In fact, in its role as organ of the AOI, it had under its control the operations of the AOI and, as a grouping of States, it signed the Memorandum of Understanding. It was in this way that Westland made arrangements to protect itself against the risks involved, through the signature of a series of documents intended to obtain the effective guarantee of the States themselves.

(. . . .)

17. "All these precautions testify fully to Westland's desire to be protected by the States' guarantees and the latter could not help but be aware of the implications of their actions. Westland would not have entered into the transaction without them."

Equity; abuse of law
18. "Finally, mention must be made of the practical reasons and considerations of equity which have motivated the arbitrators in this matter, quite apart from the legal grounds. It would be wrong if the disagreement which arose between the four States, in May 1979, were to be prejudicial to Westland, rendering all the guarantees worthless. It matters little whether the AOI had disappeared or not. Whether faced with either an Egyptian company which makes itself out as the successor of an international organization ('*société internationale*') – contrary to what had been stipulated – or a liquidation committee, which remains mute, Westland is justified in bringing the four States themselves before the arbitrators. Were this not the case, there would be a real denial of justice.

19. "Equity, in common with the principles of international law, allows the corporate veil to be lifted, in order to protect third parties against an abuse which would be to their detriment."[2]

"Consorité" of the respondents
20. Egypt maintained that Westland improperly instituted a single arbitration against six respondents with conflicting interests. The arbitrators held that:

"Neither the law of the Canton of Geneva nor the Intercantonal Concordat gives any guidance. However, applying Art. 24 of the said Concordat, the Tribunal has referred to the Federal Law of Procedure, where it has found (at

---

2. The arbitral tribunal referred to International Court of Justice, *re* Barcelona Traction, 5 February 1970, in [1970] I.C.J. Rep. 3, 40.

Art. 24) justification for the procedure followed by Westland. Para. 2, of this Article expressly permits a claimant to proceed against multiple defendants jointly if there is among them 'a community at law' (indent a) or if 'claims of the same character, founded upon an essentially common cause of substance and law constitute the subject matter of the dispute' (indent b). In the present case, the request satisfies each of these conditions and, for this twofold reason, it must be declared admissible.

21. "It is true that Art. 24 of the Federal Law concerns court proceedings. As regards arbitral proceedings, one may admit, as was stated by the Court of Geneva, that the position may be slightly different. Everything depends in this case on the intention expressed by the parties in the arbitration clause. It is necessary and therefore sufficient, in principle, that they wished to bind themselves for the arbitrators to have jurisdiction at the same time in respect of them all and for one of them to be able to initiate proceedings against all the other parties within one set of arbitration proceedings. It thus matters little that there are several arbitration clauses when their content shows that they make up a whole in the minds of the parties. Such are the circumstances of the present case.

22. "As has been stated, the series of documents concluded constitutes an indivisible whole and the four States thus truly demonstrated their desire to act together, by joining together under one name. The similarity of the clauses used in the various contracts can only serve to bear out this interpretation. It follows that the Tribunal is not merely competent as regards each of these States, AOI and ABH, but is justified in adjudicating upon their cases in one and the same award.

23. "This reasoning is supported, as once again stated by the Geneva Court, by considerations of a practical nature. It is indeed in the interest of good administration of justice to deliver a single decision applicable to all, so as to avoid either contradictions or conflict between decisions."[3]

Proper appointment of the arbitrators
24. "The parties accepted, in the arbitration clause, an arbitration procedure subject to the Rules of Arbitration of the ICC. The Claimant submitted its Request for Arbitration dated 12 May 1980, in accordance with the said Rules and, also in conformity with them, the Court of Arbitration appointed the arbitrators. That the Court was not able to appoint an arbitrator proposed by the respondents – following the example of the claimant which had made a proposal which was accepted – is the inevitable result of their 'consority' on the one hand and on the other hand of the lack of agreement on the nomination of a joint arbitrator. The appointment of the present Tribunal by the Court of Arbitration of the ICC was in conformity with the Rules of the Court of Arbitration. The arguments raised in this context by the Arab Republic of Egypt have been rejected by the Court of Justice of the Canton of Geneva (judgment of 26 November 1982, pp. 41 *et seq.*); there is no need to repeat them here."

Stay of arbitral proceedings
25. "Now that it has recognized its own jurisdiction, and in the absence of any Swiss legal judgment binding on it on this point, the Tribunal is unable to

---

3. The chairman of the arbitral tribunal filed a dissenting opinion on this issue.

uphold the request for a stay which was placed before it, in a letter dated 25 November 1980, by the representative of the Arab Republic of Egypt, on the pretext that, on the one hand, an appeal was pending before the Court of the Canton of Geneva, and that, on the other hand, other proceedings were before the Egyptian Courts."

Immunity of the four States

26. "The representative of the Arab Republic of Egypt has raised the objection of Egypt's immunity, a ground which must be examined on the Tribunal's own motion for the three non-appearing States as well. The legal principles to apply are those of the place of arbitration. It is necessary to distinguish between immunity from jurisdiction and immunity from execution; only the former enters into consideration here.

"According to a view accepted in Switzerland, as elsewhere, the signing of an arbitration clause implies the waiver of this ground. The four States, in creating the AOI, whose obligations were binding on themselves, could not have overlooked the possibility of being proceeded against at law in respect of these obligations. The creation of the AOI therefore implies a waiver of immunity in respect of obligations entered into by the AOI."

Interim award of 16 November 1984 in case no. 4367

Arbitrators: The Rt. Hon. Peter Thomas, Q.C., M.P. (U.K.), chairman; Prof. Boris I. Bittker (U.S.) and Dr. R. K. Dixit (India)

Parties: Claimant: U.S. supplier
              Respondent: Indian buyer

Published in: Unpublished

Subject matters: – competence–competence
                   – ICC Rules, Art. 8(3) and (4)
                   – waiver of right to arbitrate
                   – estoppel
                   – guarantee agreement
                   – promissory notes
                   – scope of the arbitration clause
                   – claims in tort
                   – amendment of claim (ICC Rules, Art. 16)
                   – additional claim
                   – law applicable to substance

FACTS

Claimant is a New York corporation engaged in the business of manufacturing, selling and servicing of certain equipment and in various ancillary activities. Respondent is an Indian company engaged in the sale of products processed by means of claimant's equipment in India.

By a contract made in August 1964, claimant agreed to sell and supply to respondent equipment and services for a new plant in a location in India. The contract provided that the law of the State of New York would govern the rights and obligations of the parties. The arbitration clause read in relevant part:

18

"Any disagreement arising out of or related to this contract which the parties are unable to resolve by sincere negotiation shall be finally settled in accordance with the Arbitration Rules of the International Chamber of Commerce. As provided in the said Rules, each party shall appoint one Arbitrator, and the Court of Arbitration of the International Chamber of Commerce shall appoint the third Arbitrator . . . . Arbitration proceedings shall be conducted at such time and place as the Court of Arbitration shall decide. Judgment upon an award may be entered in any court of competent jurisdiction."

Disputes arose between the parties and in March 1982 the claimant filed a Request for Arbitration with the ICC, claiming various sums from respondent, *inter alia*, on account of unpaid interest over sums owed by respondent which were overdue.

Respondent filed suit in the Bombay High Court against claimant, seeking, *inter alia*, a declaration that the claims referred to arbitration before the ICC were beyond the scope of the arbitration clause. Claimant, in turn, filed an arbitration petition under Sect. 3 of the Indian Foreign Awards (Recognition and Enforcement) Act 1961, which provision corresponds with Art. II(3) of the New York Convention of 1958. The Bombay High Court, the Court of Appeal, and the Indian Supreme Court (by a decision made in August 1984) held that claimant's claims were to be submitted to arbitration and consequently stayed respondent's suit.

Before the arbitrators, respondent also contended that they lacked competence. The Terms of Reference defined the preliminary issues ensuing from respondent's contentions as follows:

"(a) Whether the arbitrators herein have jurisdiction to determine the ambit or the effect of the arbitration agreement or to entertain and adjudicate upon the claims of the claimant.

"(b) Has the claimant waived its right, if any, to the arbitration proceedings?

"(c) Whether the claimant is estopped from proceeding with the arbitration.

"(d) If the answer to (a) above is 'yes', and the answers to (b) and (c) are 'no', does the claimant's reference to arbitration in respect of its claims herein fall within the purview of [the arbitration clause in] the 1964 agreement? If so, which claims? If not, which claims are not? If all claims are not, no further proceedings are required. If the claims are arbitrable, the following issues remain to be determined.

"(e) Whether the claimant is entitled to enlarge the scope of reference to arbitration or add to the claims already made.

"(f) What is the applicable law?"

The arbitrators rejected respondent's contentions for the following reasons.

EXTRACT
(a) *Competence–competence*

"The respondent submits that we, as arbitrators, have no jurisdiction to determine the extent or the effect of [the arbitration clause in] the 1964 Contract or to entertain or adjudicate upon the claims of the claimant.

"It is not in issue that the 1964 Contract is a valid contract or that it contained an arbitration clause that disputes arising out of or related to the Contract should be settled within the Arbitration Rules of the ICC. The contention of the respondent is, however, that the issue as to whether or not the arbitration agreement covers the claims in dispute cannot be decided by the arbitrators, for by so doing we would be determining the validity of the arbitration agreement in respect of the disputed claims and, in consequence, determining our own jurisdiction, which it is submitted we cannot do.

"We cannot accept these submissions. We are not asked to determine our jurisdiction by adjudicating as to whether the 1964 Contract was void or illegal. It is agreed that a binding Contract containing an arbitration clause was made. It is clear that whether or not a particular claim falls within that arbitration clause is a matter for us to decide as arbitrators.

"In any event, we are bound to act within the ICC Rules. Art. 8(3) and (4) of those Rules specifically state that 'any decision as to the arbitrator's jurisdiction shall be taken by the arbitrator himself'."[1]

(b) *Waiver of right to arbitrate*

"The respondent's submission that the claimant has 'waived its right, if any, to this arbitration and is estopped from proceeding' is based on the accepted facts that in August 1982 the claimant filed a suit in the Calcutta High Court against the respondent's guarantor Bank [in India] for 2.13 million dollars, being the amount of regular interest claimed in this arbitration, and in June 1972 filed a suit in the Calcutta High Court against the same Bank for the rupee equivalent of US$ 740,184 in respect of the 5th promissory note under the 1964 Contract.

"The respondent's contention is that:
(1) There cannot be two tribunals with concurrent jurisdiction to decide the rights of the parties relating to the same subject matter.
(2) The Indian Court's jurisdiction cannot be ousted. Therefore the arbitration tribunal becomes *functus officio*.
(3) The claimant's conduct in litigating on the same subject matter in the Indian Courts is inconsistent with the claim that the parties were obligated to settle their differences by arbitration and the claimant has therefore waived its right to arbitration and in the premises is estopped from proceeding with the arbitration claims.

"The claimant contends that the suits referred to above are separate and independent remedies brought against another party to preserve the security of

---

1. Art. 8(3) and (4) of the ICC Rules provide:
"3. Should one of the parties raise one or more pleas concerning the existence or validity of the agreement to arbitrate, and should the Court be satisfied of the prima facie existence of such an agreement, the Court may, without prejudice to the admissibility or merits of the plea or pleas, decide that the arbitration shall proceed. In such a case any decision as to the arbitrator's jurisdiction shall be taken by the arbitrator himself.
"4. Unless otherwise provided, the arbitrator shall not cease to have jurisdiction by reason of any claim that the contract is null and void or allegation that it is inexistent provided that he upholds the validity of the agreement to arbitrate. He shall continue to have jurisdiction, even though the contract itself may be inexistent or null and void, to determine the respective rights of the parties and to adjudicate upon their claims and pleas."

a guarantee agreement. This we accept. The defendant to the suits is the [Indian] Bank, which is not a party to the 1964 Contract or to the arbitration clause therein, and the claims are brought in respect of a guarantee agreement between the claimant and the Bank dated . . . 1965, which is the basis of the dispute to which the Indian Courts have seisin.

"The fact that the respondent unilaterally has made application to be added as defendant to the suits in no way affects our view that the suits before the Indian Courts are independent remedies separate from those before this Tribunal which do not affect our jurisdiction."

(c) *Estoppel*

"The respondent also submitted for our consideration that it had filed a suit in [an Indian Court] in November 1982 for 'settlement and adjustments of its claims and release from the guarantees given by the [Indian] Bank' and that the suit was 'being contested by the claimant'. In our opinion this suit filed by the respondent has no relevance to the issues of waiver or estoppel on the part of the claimant.

"In our opinion no question of waiver by the claimant of its rights under the arbitration agreement applies, nor is the claimant estopped from proceeding with this arbitration."

(d) *Scope of the arbitration clause*

"As to the question of whether the claimant's claims in this arbitration fall within the purview of [the arbitration clause in] the 1964 Contract, the respondent's primary submission is that the principal claims for regular and delinquent interest arise out of, or are related to, promissory notes, which it contends are contracts separate and independent from the 1964 Contract, and which contain no arbitration clause.

"The respondent's argument was briefly to this effect:
(1) There was no obligation or liability in the 1964 Contract to pay interest after . . . 1967.
(2) The 1964 Contract only provided for execution of promissory notes bearing interest and having due dates of maturity which would enable the claimant to claim interest from the date of the promissory note until the due date and from the due date until date of payment.
(3) The 1964 Contract only prescribed the form of the promissory notes but the promissory notes did not become part of the Contract.
(4) The execution of the promissory notes resulted in the discharge of obligations by the respondent to pay the amounts contemplated by the 1964 Contract and the claim for interest (regular or delinquent) was solely founded on the promissory notes because the right to receive interest is found only in the body of the notes.
(5) Each promissory note is an independent contract containing no arbitration clause.

"The question here for our consideration is whether the notes when executed operated as an absolute discharge of the relevant debts, or only as conditional payment. It is a question of fact and depends on the intention of the parties. The intention must be clear for, as a general rule, a bill or note does not discharge a debt unless it is part of the Contract that it shall do so, for a mere promise to pay cannot be regarded as an effective payment.

"From our consideration of the 1964 Contract we are satisfied that the parties never intended that the promissory notes on execution should operate as payments by way of absolute discharge of the obligation under the Contract. The Contract expressly states that the promissory notes were to be *evidence* of the obligations to make the payments under the Contract. The notes were not handed over to the claimant but were required to be kept in escrow. They would be wholly ineffective if the Reserve Bank of India did not grant permission for the foreign exchange to be remitted abroad. They were liable to be replaced or readjusted in certain circumstances.

"In our view the terms of the 1964 Contract, far from showing that the promissory notes were payments in discharge of obligations under the Contract, clearly indicate that the parties intended that they were to operate as conditional payments. They have to be read as an intrinsic part of the 1964 Contract and cannot stand by themselves.

"In any event, even if, which we dispute, the promissory notes were separate contracts, we would find that the arbitration clause was sufficiently wide to embrace disputes between the parties arising from them.

"The respondent made a further submission that the claim for US$ 2,130,758 was outside the purview of the arbitration clause in the 1964 Contract.

"After setting out the history of the events between the parties from 1964 to the claimant's Request for Arbitration in March 1982, the respondent contended that the claimant's claim for the above sum arose directly out of and related to the Judgment and Order of the Delhi High Court on . . . 1980 (which quashed and set aside the Order of the Government of India of . . . 1969, that payments of interest were subject to tax) as well as certain provisions of the Indian Income Tax Act.

"They submitted that the claim does not in any way arise out of, nor is it related to the 1964 Contract.

"We cannot accept this submission. Any adjudication by a court on the question of exemption by the Government of India from payment of income tax on interest payments arises out of and is directly related to Art. . . . of the 1964 Contract and the Claimant's claim for regular interest could not possibly be formulated except in relation to the Contract.

"The respondent submits that the claimant's claims for US$ 4.4 million and US$ 1.53 million by way of compensatory damages are claims in tort for the wrongful retention of money and therefore do not arise out of the 1964 Contract so as to be within the purview of the arbitration agreement.

"We have already stated our view that the claims for regular and delinquent interest arise from the 1964 Contract and are arbitrable. Accepting *arguendo* the proposition that the compensatory claims are actions in tort, the question for our decision is whether they are directly and inextricably connected with the terms and conditions of the 1964 Contract and, if so, whether the arbitration clause in the Contract is of sufficient width to cover their dispute.

"The claims for compensatory damages depend on the basic question of whether the amounts of regular and delinquent interest were wrongfully retained. The compensatory claims are therefore intimately connected with those claims arising out of the 1964 Contract, and the wide terms of [the arbitration clause in] the 1964 Contract clearly render them arbitrable.

"The respondent has set out in its submissions various other objections to arbitrability. We have considered all of these objections and find them without merit."

(e) *Amendment of claims/Additional claims*

"The respondent further contends that the claimant is not entitled to enlarge the scope of its reference to arbitration by amendment or by the addition of further claims.

"Since the reference to arbitration, and before signature of the Terms of Reference, the claimant has amended its original claims by adding two further (relatively minor) claims plus interest, and by changing the rate of interest claimed on the main claim.

"In our view, these changes are permissible since they were made before the Terms of Reference were signed, thus giving the respondent notice in ample time to respond to the claims on the merits. Moreover, since Art. 16 of the ICC Rules[2] permits changes even after the Terms of Reference are signed, changes before that event are in our view 'a fortiori' permitted.

"We are not satisfied as to whether or not the two additional claims, and consequential claims for damages thereon, are outside the scope of the arbitration agreement as being the subject matters of agreement distinct from the 1964 Contract. Our determination in this respect is set out in [the determination] hereafter."

(f) *Applicable law*

"The respondent contends that in the event of the arbitration proceeding the applicable law should be the law of India. The submission was that the system of law with which the 1964 Contract and its performance have their closest and most real connection was Indian law.

"In the absence of any expressed or clearly inferred intention or agreement by the parties, we agree that respondent's contention would have some force. However, [the applicable law clause in] the 1964 Contract specifically provides that 'the rights and obligations of the parties under this Contract shall be governed in all respects by the laws of the State of New York USA'.

"We are satisfied that this clearly expressed agreement in the 1964 Contract is valid and overrides any other consideration of what the proper law might be."

---

2. Art. 16 of the ICC Rules provides:
   "The parties may make new claims or counter-claims before the arbitrator on condition that these remain within the limits fixed by the Terms of Reference provided for in Article 13 or that they are specified in a rider to that document, signed by the parties and communicated to the Court."

Determination

The arbitrators formulated their decision on the preliminary issues as follows:

"Our answers therefore to the questions in (*a*) to (*f*) . . . are as follows: (*a*) Yes. (*b*) No. (*c*) No. (*d*) Yes as to the claims set out in . . . of the Terms of Reference. We do not feel we have sufficient information about [the two additional claims, and consequential claims for damages thereon] and reserve our determination on whether they fall within the purview of [the arbitration clause in] the 1964 Contract until a subsequent hearing of the arbitration. (*e*) Yes. (*f*) The laws of the State of New York, USA."

Award of February 1985 in case no. 4555

Arbitrator: Samuel A. Stern (U.S.)

Parties: Claimant: U.S. supplier
Defendant: U.S. purchaser

Published in: Journal du Droit International (1985) pp. 964–966 with note by S. Jarvin

Subject matters: – arbitrability of dispute
– unconditional performance guarantee
– material breach of contract
– continued performance regardless of dispute

FACTS

By a Purchase Agreement dated 12 July 1982, claimant was to supply cabinets and wardrobes to defendant. Defendant was in turn to supply these to a Saudi Arabian company ("the Client"). The contract provided for ICC arbitration in Washington, D.C.

According to the contract, claimant was required to provide within 15 days of signing the contract

"[A]n unconditional, irrevocable performance guarantee acceptable to [defendant] opened or confirmed by a US bank in favour of [defendant] in the amount of 10% of the purchase price . . . as a guarantee of this Purchase Agreement." (hereinafter referred to as the "performance letter of credit")

An example of the format of the guarantee was attached to the contract. Defendant was, according to the contract, required to pay by

"[A]n irrevocable, transferable, revolving Letter of Credit in increments of twenty-five (25) per cent of the total price, payable 67 days from date of delivery of documents evidencing receipt. Letter of Credit to be opened in the name of [the claimant] within 15 days after receipt of Client approval." (hereinafter referred to as the "payment letter of credit").

Due to various difficulties not material to the arbitration, the performance letter of credit was not issued in defendant's favour until 20 September 1982. The performance guarantee as issued included a clause stating that the letter would become operative only when defendant opened the payment letter of credit. On 27 September 1982, defendant sent a telex to the claimant stating that the performance letter of credit was unacceptable because it was not "unconditional". It stated that

24

claimant was in breach of contract, and that "if you provide an acceptable guarantee, we will discuss the possibility of going forward." The claimant responded on 29 September 1982 that "[s]ince the only condition on our performance guarantee is in your control, i.e., the opening of your [payment letter of credit], the guarantee is in fact unconditional as to you and for all intents and purposes meets the terms of the contract." Defendant replied, by telex dated 4 October 1982, that the operative clause rendered the performance letter conditional. It concluded, "[d]espite the fact that we gave you more than 60 days to produce an acceptable guarantee, you have failed to do so. Under these circumstances, we have no choice but to hereby cancel your contract for default. We will obtain the goods from a third party."

Claimant commenced arbitration on 22 November 1982, asserting, amongst others, that defendant breached its contractual obligations by (a) asserting that the Purchase Agreement is cancelled, null and void, (b) refusing to cause a payment letter of credit to be issued in favour of claimant, and (c) failing to perform its contractual obligations pending arbitration, and claiming damages resulting from these breaches.

The arbitrator had to decide on the following issues: (1) whether the dispute was arbitrable, (2) whether defendant breached the contract by terminating it, and (3) if so, what damages claimant should receive. The arbitrator decided that the dispute was arbitrable and that defendant's termination of the contract was not in violation of its contractual obligations, and that therefore claimant was not entitled to relief for any injury suffered as a consequence of this termination.

EXTRACT
1. Arbitrability

"I conclude that this dispute is arbitrable. The arbitration clause, by its terms, broadly reaches '[a]ll controversies arising under or in connection with, or relating to any breach of this Agreement . . .'. This is such a controversy.

"Defendant argues that the clause is inapplicable because the contract provides elsewhere that '[t]his Agreement is contingent upon approval of the equipment/material by the Purchaser's client.' No such approval was received, and thus defendant claims the arbitration clause never became effective.

"I do not find this argument persuasive. I conclude that the arbitration clause, like certain other provisions of the contract (e.g., the requirements that claimant must assist defendant in obtaining approval, that a detailed breakdown of the price was to be provided by claimant within 30 days of signing the contract, and the obligation of claimant to open a performance letter of credit), was intended to take effect at the signing of the contract and prior to the approval of the equipment, even though many of the other obligations would not come into play until approval. There is no rational basis for concluding that the parties intended to litigate in court disputes arising before the equipment was approved and to arbitrate only disputes arising thereafter. Indeed, if defendant were correct in arguing that the contractual obligations of the parties never took effect, it would have disproven its own case on the merits, because claimant's obligation to open its performance letter of credit would not have arisen and defendant would thus have had no basis for terminating the contract."

2. Unconditional performance guarantee

"I conclude that claimant did not carry out its contractual obligation to provide an 'unconditional, irrevocable performance guarantee acceptable to [defendant].' I am guided in this decision by the principle that, particularly in international commercial transactions, the terms of an agreement will frequently have an impact on entities beyond the contracting parties; clients, financial institutions, subcontractors and others may rely on their understanding of and be affected by agreements to which they are not parties. International commerce is served by encouraging contracting parties to state the terms of their agreement clearly and fully. It is therefore appropriate, in interpreting such a contract, to place substantial weight on the objective, commonly understood meaning of the contract language actually employed, and to give less weight to unarticulated and undocumented understandings. Consistent with this principle, the reasons for my holdings are:

"(a) The term 'unconditional' is defined generally to mean '[n]ot limited or affected by any condition.' Black's Law Dictionary 1367 (5th ed. 1979). Under this definition, claimant's performance letter of credit was not unconditional, for it was subject to the limitation that it would not be operative until defendant opened a payment letter of credit. This meaning of the term could be overridden by persuasive evidence of standard commercial usage or the clear intent of the parties. See 5 Williston on Contracts § 648 (1961). However, claimant has not provided such evidence. It concedes that the term 'unconditional' has no 'recognized and undisputed meaning when used to describe a letter of credit'. Indeed, the term 'unconditional' is not recognized in the principal publications defining terms used in documentary credits. E.g., 'Uniform Customs and Practices for Documentary Credits' (ICC publ. no. 400); 'Uniform Rules for Contract Guarantees' (ICC publ. no. 325); 'Standard Forms for Issuing Documentary Credits' (ICC publ. no. 323).

"And while the testimony tends to support the view that claimant believed its operative clause was permissible, I conclude that there was no agreement of the parties to this effect. The possibility of an operative clause was discussed by representatives of defendant and claimant prior to the signing of the contract, but this conversation did not contractually commit either party and, even if considered to be an agreement, was nullified by the integration clause incorporated in the subsequently signed contract. The contract on its face, including the annexed sample performance guarantee, does not support claimant's position. And the post-contractual conversation between [representatives of the parties] did not constitute a meeting of the minds amending the contract to authorize the use of an operative clause. Defendant is not estopped from relying on claimant's non-compliance with the contract, nor is reformation of the agreement warranted to authorize claimant's position retroactively.

"(b) The contract expressly stated that claimant must provide an unconditional performance guarantee 'acceptable to defendant'. When the performance letter of credit was issued, defendant informed claimant that, because of the operative clause, the letter was not acceptable to it. Defendant was not unreasonable in taking this position. Defendant gave claimant an opportunity to cure this defect and make the letter acceptable, but claimant declined to do so. Claimant

26

thus failed to provide a performance guarantee meeting the contractual requirement."

3. Material breach and continued performance

"I conclude that this breach entitled defendant to terminate the contract. Claimant argues that termination was not permissible, because (a) any breach that may have occurred was not material, and (b) the arbitration clause required defendant to continue its performance regardless of the dispute. I am not persuaded by these arguments, for the following reasons:

"(*a*) I find that the breach was material, in light of the evidence presented as to the importance to defendant of having an operative performance letter of credit, *Restatement (Second) of the Law of Contracts* § 241(a) (1981), and the fact that claimant was unwilling to remove the operative clause when asked to do so, *id.* § 241(d).

"(*b*) The arbitration clause requires arbitration of all controversies 'arising under or in connection with, or relating to any alleged breach of this agreement' but requires continued performance, pending arbitration, only of disputes 'aris[ing] under' the agreement. These different formulations have distinct legal implications, *see Rochdale Village, Inc.* v. *Public Service Employees Union*, 605 F.2d 1290, 1295 (2d Cir. 1979), and the exclusion of breach claims from the latter portion of the contract provision must be recognized. As this dispute was a claim of breach, which is one of the categories of controversy clearly omitted from the requirement of continued performance, defendant was not obligated by that provision to carry on with the contract. In light of claimant's unwillingness to provide a performance letter acceptable to defendant, and of the materiality of the breach, it was not unreasonable for defendant to seek a substitute supplier that could enable it to meet its own contractual obligations to its customers."

Awards of June 1984 and May 1985 in case no. 4567

Arbitrators: Dr. Jacques Werner (Switz.), chairman; Mr. Bernard White (U.S.) and Mr. Dan Muhlfelder (U.S.)

Parties: Claimant: purchaser from a West-African country
Defendant: U.S. supplier

Published in: Unpublished

Subject matters: – revocation of acceptance in case of non-conforming goods
– contractual limitation of remedy
– amiable compositeur

FACTS

Claimant provides telecommunication services in a West African country. Defendant is a corporation incorporated in Delaware and engaged in the manufacture of telecommunications equipment.

For operational purposes of claimant's earth station in the West African country, the parties signed in April 1978 a contract for the sale, delivery and installation by defendant of a High Power Microwave Amplifier ("HPA"). The contract provided for the applicability of the laws of the State of California. Disputes were to be settled through ICC arbitration to take place in Geneva.

In June 1979, claimant granted factory acceptance of the HPA at defendant's plant in the U.S.A. and in October 1974 on the site in the West African country. Technical problems encountered by defendant resulted in the contractual deadline of 1 July 1979, for the installation of the HPA at the site not being met.

In January 1980, the HPA failed. From that time on, and despite several attempts by both parties to repair it locally, the HPA did not operate normally at site. The HPA's repeated failures were caused by the neutral mismatch, namely, the fact that the HPA had been designed for a grounded neutral power supply system, whereas the power supply system at the site utilized an isolated neutral power system.

In April 1981, the parties finally decided that the HPA would be shipped back to claimant's factory in the U.S.A. Defendant submitted to claimant in May 1981 an offer for the repair of the HPA, which claimant did not accept. Subsequent discussions between the parties on this offer were unsuccessful. On 25 November 1981, claimant revoked its acceptance of the HPA. Claimant made a "cover" by purchasing another HPA from another manufacturer in substitution for the HPA of defendant.

After unsuccessful negotiations to settle the dispute amicably, claimant resorted to ICC arbitration in December 1982, claiming, amongst others, repayment of the contract price, the costs of the cover (i.e., difference between contract price for the original HPA and the substitute HPA), incidental and consequential damages. Defendant requested to reject claimant's claims, and counterclaimed, amongst others, the costs of the repairs.

The arbitral tribunal rendered a partial award and, on the incidental damages, a final award. In these awards, amongst others, the arbitral tribunal declared that claimant was entitled to revoke its acceptance of the HPA, granted claimant's claim for repayment of the contract price, granted in part claimant's claim for cost of cover, rejected claimant's claim for consequential damages (Mr. White dissenting), and granted claimant's claim for incidental damages (Mr. Muhlfelder dissenting). Defendant's counterclaims were rejected by the arbitral tribunal.

The reasoning of the arbitral tribunal on a number of these issues is reproduced below.

EXTRACT
Revocation of acceptance

1. According to Sect. 2608 of the California Commercial Code ("CCC"), a buyer may revoke his acceptance of "a lot or commercial unit whose non-conformity substantially impairs its value to him if he has accepted it" in the following cases:

"(a) On the reasonable assumption that its non-conformity would be cured and it has not been reasonably cured, or

"(b) without discovery of such non-conformity if his acceptance was reasonably induced either by the difficulty of discovery before acceptance or by the seller's assurances."

2. The main point of contention between the parties relates to the realization of the non-conformity condition as laid out by the above provisions of the ccc. The issue was whether the failure of the HPA to operate under the conditions prevailing at the site constituted a non-conformity of the HPA with the contractual specifications. The arbitral tribunal reasoned:

"The arbitral tribunal considers that defendant's contractual obligations concerning the characteristics of the HPA were not only to be derived from the Exhibit B to the contract headed 'Specifications', but also from the provisions of the Contract itself. In this respect of particular relevance are the provisions of the Contract which provide that defendant will not only sell and deliver but also install the HPA at the site (Art. 2a: 'The Contractor shall deliver, install and sell to the Customer the HPA system at the site.', and top of Exhibit A: 'The Contractor shall deliver, install and test at [site] an . . . amplifier and shall manage, control and direct the work to be carried out.').

"Obligation to install at the site did imply the obligation for defendant to ensure that the HPA would be built with all specifications necessary for complying with the conditions prevailing at the site, even if not expressly mentioned in the Exhibit B headed 'Specifications'. By failing to design an HPA having the necessary specifications for operating at the . . . site, defendant did not conform with this obligation.

3. "Should responsibility of defendant for its failure to comply with the above obligation be shared with claimant, as such company knew at the time of the negotiations that the HPA was to comply with the isolated neutral utilized at the site and might have easily completed in this respect the specifications contained in Exhibit B to the Contract? The arbitral tribunal does not consider necessary to examine this question as evidence of the case is that in December 1978, namely during the period of design and construction of the HPA and well before its delivery, Mr. B, defendant's executive in charge of the construction of the HPA, had received notice from one of his engineers on the site that the neutral was isolated. Consequently, defendant knew at material time that the neutral at the site was isolated.

4. "The arbitral tribunal considers consequently that the failure of the HPA to operate under the conditions prevailing at the . . . site did constitute a non-conformity of the HPA with defendant's contractual obligations, and that the requirement of Sect. 2608 of the ccc was met in this respect. The arbitral tribunal considers also that the other legal conditions as laid out by above Sect. 2608 of the ccc for revocation of acceptance were met.

"In view of its above determination, the arbitral tribunal holds that claimant was entitled to revoke its acceptance of the HPA."

Overthrow of limitation of remedy
5. The warranty in the Contract provided:

"[Defendant's] total liability under this warranty shall be limited to the repair or replacement of items delivered under this order which are found to be defective in material and/or workmanship and design. [Defendant] retains the option to make such repair or replacement at the site or at its own plant.

"NO RESPONSIBILITY IS ASSUMED FOR ANY SPECIAL, INCIDENTAL OR CONSEQUENTIAL DAMAGES.

"THIS WARRANTY IS IN LIEU OF ALL OTHER WARRANTIES EXPRESSED OR IMPLIED INCLUDING THE WARRANTIES OF MERCHANTABILITY AND FITNESS FOR A PARTICULAR PURPOSE."

6. Sect. 2719 ccc, however, provides for the overthrow of the limitation of remedy:

"Contractual Modification or Limitation of Remedy
"(1) Subject to the provisions or subdivisions (2) and (3) of this Section and of the preceding Section on liquidation and limitation of damages,

"(a) The agreement may provide for remedies in addition to or in substitution for those provided in this division and may limit or alter the measure of damages recoverable under this division, as by limiting the buyer's remedies to return of the goods and repayment of the price or to repair and replacement of non-conforming goods or parts; and

"(b) resort to a remedy as provided is optional unless the remedy is expressly agreed to be exclusive, in which case it is the sole remedy.

"(2) Where circumstances cause an exclusive or limited remedy to fail of its essential purpose, remedy may be had as provided in this code.

"(3) Consequential damages may be limited or excluded unless the limitation or exclusion is unconscionable. Limitation of consequential damages for injury to the person in the case of consumer goods is prima facie unconscionable but limitation of damages where the loss is commercial is not. (Stats. 1963, c.819, para. 2719)."

7. Regarding the claim for *consequential* damages, the arbitral tribunal rejected this claim in the partial award:

"In order to be entitled to consequential damages claimant had to prove that the exclusion of consequential damages contained in the contract was unconscionable within the meaning of California law. The arbitral tribunal considers that claimant has failed to prove this. California case law, in particular the most recent decision mentioned by claimant, *A. & M. Produce Co.* v. *F.M.C. Corp.*, 135 Cal. App. 3rd 473 (1982), requires for unconscionability procedural and substantive elements which the arbitral tribunal considers as not existing in the present case.

"In view of the contractual exclusion of consequential damages and failure of claimant to prove that such exclusion was unconscionable, the arbitral tribunal does reject claimant's claim for consequential damages. It will order accordingly under point 5 of its orders.

"The arbitrator Mr. White dissents from the opinion of the majority as to consequential damages on the ground that the limitation of remedy fails of its essential purpose."

8. Regarding the claim for *incidental* damages, the arbitral tribunal (Mr. Muhlfelder dissenting) overthrew the contractual limitations:

"As stated in [the partial award], in January 1980 the HPA failed; since that time, and despite several attempts by both claimant and defendant to repair it locally, the HPA did not operate normally on the site. The arbitral tribunal holds consequently that the limited remedy as provided for by the contractual warranty has failed of its essential purpose.

9. "Remaining question to be resolved is whether the condition of unconscionability must be also fulfilled to overthrow the contractual exclusion or limitation of remedy.

"The text of Sect. 2719(3) requires in a clear and unambiguous way the condition of unconscionability for overthrow of limitation/exclusion of consequential damages only, not of incidental damages. It was consequently up to defendant to prove that, in derogation to its clear text, Sect. 2719(3) also applies to incidental damages. The arbitral tribunal considers that defendant has failed to prove this; in particular the case quoted by defendant in support of their contention, *Office Supply Company Inc.* v. *Basic/Four Corp.*, 538 F.Supp. 776, 1982, cannot be considered as decisive in this respect as it was rendered by a first level court, and consequently the interpretation of Sect. 2719(3) it contains may well not be adhered to by the superior competent courts.

10. "The arbitral tribunal considers consequently that the only condition set by Sect. 2719 ccc for the overthrow of the exclusion/limitation of remedy is the failure of its essential purpose. In view of its above determination that the limited remedy provided for by the contractual warranty had failed of its essential purpose, the arbitral tribunal holds that such above condition is met and that claimant is entitled to the incidental damages provided for in Sect. 2715(1) ccc."

Amiable compositeur
11. In the Terms of Reference, the parties agreed that "The arbitral tribunal may act as amiable compositeur". On one occasion, the arbitral tribunal used this power. It concerned the amount of incidental damages claimed on account of technical assistance rendered by a French company for assistance in negotiating the purchase of a substitute HPA:

"For the determination of such amount reasonably incurred, the Arbitral Tribunal has decided to make use of the amiable composition powers granted to it as per point 8. of the Terms of Reference.

"Under the ICC Rules of Arbitration the arbitrators who have been authorized to act as 'amiable compositeurs' may decide a case according to the principles of fairness or equity (cf. in this respect, Craig, Park, Paulsson, "International Chamber of Commerce Arbitration", 1984, chap. 18).

"In use of its power to act as 'amiable compositeur', the arbitral tribunal decides consequently that, out of the US$ 45,070 claimed, US$ 30,000 must be considered as having been reasonably incurred and consequently be awarded to claimant."

12. Mr. White dissented from this finding of the arbitral tribunal stating that:

"The conclusions . . . are not supported by evidence, are speculative, and would appear arbitrary. Claimant incurred the expenses claimed and, in view of defendant's behaviour during performance of the contract and during arbitration, the arbitrators as 'amiable compositeurs' should award the claim for [the French company's] assistance to the claimant."

Interim award of 13 April 1984 in case no. 4589

Arbitrator: Mr. Soumrani (Lebanon)

Parties: Claimant: French contractor
                Defendant: Egyptian employer

Published in: Ahmed S. El-Kosheri, "Some Particular Aspects of Egyptian
                Official Attitudes Towards International Commercial Arbitration", 76
                L'Egypte Contemporaine (1985, no. 400) p. 110 at pp. 120–123

Subject matters: – public policy
                   – place of arbitration
                   – Arts. II and III of the New York Convention of 1958

FACTS

In a dispute concerning a construction contract for a building in Egypt, the Egyptian defendant objected to arbitration in Paris, which place was fixed by the ICC Court of Arbitration under Art. 12 of the ICC Rules.[1]

The Egyptian defendant relied on an opinion of Professor Abou El Wafa in his book *Voluntary and Obligatory Arbitration*, 3d ed. (Alexandria 1978) pp. 83–84. Professor El Wafa takes the view that when an agreement is concluded to arbitrate abroad, it should be ensured that the dispute originally was not within the jurisdiction of the Egyptian courts, or at least that the competence with regard to that dispute is cumulative, i.e., that it can be exercised either by Egyptian or foreign courts. Professor El Wafa opines that, if the subject matter of the arbitration agreement is an issue within the exclusive jurisdiction of the Egyptian Courts, the agreement has to be considered null and void with respect only to the location of the arbitration abroad since this aspect violates Egyptian public policy. In his view, permitting the contrary would lead to fraud against the rules governing the international jurisdiction of Egyptian courts, consolidating the fundamental principles of the judiciary organization. Professor El Wafa considers a judgment of 12 April 1956, of the Egyptian Supreme Court a bad precedent. In that judgment, the Supreme Court held that "the Egyptian legislator does not consider as a matter touching public policy the agreement to submit to arbitrators residing abroad and rendering their awards there".[2]

The arbitrator rejected defendant's objection for the following reasons.

EXTRACT

1. "Whereas the defendant is contending the choice of Paris as the place for arbitration on the ground that Egyptian law considers as a matter of public order, to have all disputes over which Egyptian courts are exclusively competent to be settled either by those courts or by arbitration located in Egypt.

2. "Whereas the validity of an arbitration clause is recognized by the Egyptian Civil and Commercial Procedure Code (Art. 501) if it does not relate to matters that cannot be subject to an out of court settlement.

---

1. Art. 12 of the ICC Rules provides:
    "The place of arbitration shall be fixed by the Court, unless agreed upon by the parties."
2. *Editor's note* – The Egyptian Supreme Court has not (yet) had an opportunity to decide on this question again after the judgment of 1956.

3.   "Whereas such matters are defined by Art. 551 of the Egyptian Civil Code as those in connection with personal status or public order.

4.   "Whereas the present dispute has arisen from the performance of a contracting agreement between two commercial companies and therefore it has no connection of any kind with either the personal status or the public policy's matters.

5.   "Whereas Egypt and France are parties to the New York Convention of 10 June 1958, on the recognition and execution of foreign arbitral awards.

6.   "Whereas Art. II of said Convention recognizes the validity of an arbitration clause giving jurisdiction to an arbitral tribunal located in the territory of a State other than the one on which the execution of the award is to be requested.

7.   "Whereas Art. III of the New York Convention states that each Contracting State will recognize the authority and grant the execution of any arbitral award rendered in the territory of another State.

8.   "Whereas Art. 301 of the Egyptian Civil and Commercial Procedure Code states that the rules governing the execution of foreign judgments and arbitral awards may not affect the provisions of International Treaties between Egypt and the other countries.

9.   "Whereas the parties by agreeing to have their dispute settled under the Rules of the ICC Court of Arbitration are to be considered as having adhered to Art. 12 of said Rules which gives the Court of Arbitration the power to fix the place of arbitration when it is not agreed upon by the parties."

Interim award of November 1984 in case no. 4695

Arbitrators: Prof. Eduardo Jiménez de Aréchaga (Uruguay), Prof. Dr. Karl-Heinz Böckstiegel (F.R.Germ.) and John H. Pickering (U.S.)

Parties: Claimants: parties from Brazil, Panama and U.S.A.
                  Defendant: party from Brazil

Published in: Unpublished

Subject matters: – validity arbitration clause
                  – law applicable to substance and to procedure
                  – international contract
                  – arbitration clause: effects
                  – public policy (of Brazil)
                  – Geneva Protocol of 1923, Art. 1(1)
                  – enforceability of award
                  – Art. 26 of the ICC Rules

FACTS

By a series of contracts, defendant formed with claimants a joint venture for the supply of certain Brazilian raw materials to customers in the United States. The contracts contained the same arbitration clause, reading:

"Whenever any question or dispute shall arise or occur under this [Agreement–Contract], such question or dispute shall (if it is not amicably settled by the parties) be finally settled by arbitration in Paris, France, by one or more arbitrators appointed in accordance with the Rules of Conciliation and Arbitration of the International Chamber of Commerce."

The contracts also provided that the applicable law was:

"This Agreement shall be governed by the law of Brazil in all respects, including matters of validity, construction, performance and enforcement."

A number of disputes having arisen between the joint venture partners, claimants submitted their claims to ICC arbitration on the basis of the above-quoted clause. The defendant objected to the jurisdiction of the arbitral tribunal on various grounds. One of defendant's objections was that, under Brazilian law, there is not a binding arbitration agreement between the parties. The arbitral tribunal rejected this objection for the following reasons.

EXTRACT

1. In support of its objection, the defendant contended that Brazilian law has a unique, constitutionally founded restriction on arbitration; that arbitral clauses are not enforceable and the only form of arbitration agreement which is effective is a full, formal "submission agreement", entered into in accordance with Brazilian statutory requirements, which are not satisfied in this case. Accordingly, it contended that the arbitral clauses relied upon by the claimants are not effective to confer arbitral jurisdiction to the arbitral tribunal.

Distinction between law applicable to substance and law applicable to arbitration; international contract
2. According to the expert opinion submitted by defendant, the procedures provided for in Arts. 1073–1074 of the Brazilian CCP for the constitution of an arbitral tribunal had not been followed in the present case. The arbitral tribunal first inquired whether and to what extent Brazilian law applied to the arbitration clause:

3. "A basic consideration to take into account when examining this premise is that the present case involves a truly international business transaction, whatever test is applied to define international commercial contracts. From the objective point of view the [project] required the investment of substantial foreign capital in Brazil. This investment took the form of a joint venture [to produce the raw material], to transport and to process it, in order to export and market such [material] throughout the world.

"From a subjective point of view the parties to the joint venture and to the relevant Agreements are companies constituted in Brazil, Panama and the United States. It has been further asserted, and not contradicted, that some of these companies are, in turn, controlled or financed, totally or partially, by corporations established in Belgium, Luxembourg, the United States and now Australia.

34

"The agreements were executed in New York and in Washington, D.C., they call for arbitration of disputes in Paris, France, in accordance with the ICC Rules and the substantive law governing them is the law of Brazil.

4. "There is no doubt, and it is admitted by both parties, that in international commercial agreements of this nature the parties are entitled, under the principle of autonomy of the will, to choose the law applicable both to the substance and to the procedure of an eventual arbitration.

"It is also common ground that the parties have chosen Brazilian law as the substantive law governing their agreements.

"But such a choice of substantive law may be put aside by the parties, in certain respects, by a different choice of law, if they elect to do so by means of a specific stipulation in the contract.

5. "And in this case, the arbitration clause itself in all the agreements provides that the arbitrators shall be 'appointed in accordance with the Rules of Conciliation and Arbitration of the International Chamber of Commerce', and that 'each arbitration shall be initiated and conducted in accordance with said Rules'.

"If the principles of the autonomy of the will of the parties, and that of good faith in complying with the engagements undertaken, have the effect attributed to them with respect to the choice of Brazilian law as the substantive law of the contract, those principles must have the same effect with respect to the ICC Rules concerning the appointment of arbitrators and the initiation of proceedings.

6. "The fact that the ICC Rules are not officially issued by a public authority is irrelevant, since their source of validity lies in both cases in the choice of the parties.

(. . . .)[1]

"This specific and explicit choice of the ICC Rules in respect of those procedural matters which concern the constitution of the arbitral tribunal and the initiation of proceedings, necessarily excludes, in respect of an international commercial contract, the application of certain procedural requirements contained in Arts. 1073 and 1074 of the Brazilian Code of Civil Procedure, which are incompatible with the ICC Rules and were obviously designed to apply only to purely Brazilian or domestic arbitrations.

7. "Finally, it might be pointed out that such an interpretation would be in conformity with international contract and arbitration practice, where it is a normal feature to have both an arbitration clause and a choice of law clause. Since the intention of the parties as expressed in the contract is to be regarded as the primary source also for a possible mandate of the arbitrators, a harmonizing interpretation of both clauses together seems to be the right approach. For it cannot be expected that parties, if they include both such

---

1. The arbitral tribunal referred to F. A. Mann, "Lex Facit Arbitrum", in *Liber Amicorum Martin Domke* (The Hague 1967) p. 157 at p. 165; F. E. Klein, *Considérations sur l'arbitrage en droit international privé* (Basle 1955) p. 210.

clauses in the contract, intend one clause to make the other clause ineffective to a great extent. If, therefore, there is a possible interpretation giving the fullest effect to both clauses, that interpretation can be accepted as coming closest to the intention of the parties as expressed in the contract. Such a consolidated interpretation of both clauses is normally employed in international arbitration to the effect that both the arbitration clause and the choice of law clause have to be respected and that this means that it is the arbitrators who have to apply the substantive law chosen. The tribunal does not see any reason why this harmonized interpretation should not be employed in the present case as well."

8. The arbitral tribunal referred to a number of doctrinal authorities who expressly admit the possibility of a disassociation in the choice of substantive and procedural law of an arbitration.[2]

9. The arbitral tribunal then stated:

"In accordance with this conception, it would have been Art. 1009 of the former French Code of Civil Procedure and is now Art. 1455 as introduced by Decree no. 81.500 of 12 May 1981, which would provide the legal foundation for the choice made by the parties in favour of the ICC Rules.[3] These articles grant discretion to the parties to agree on the procedure to be followed in the arbitration."

10. The arbitral tribunal also made reference to published arbitral awards "of great authority" which "carefully distinguish the substantive law applicable to a contract and the procedural law applicable to the procedure of the arbitration itself".[4] Reference was also made to decisions by the English House of Lords.[5]

---

2. Ph. Fouchard, *L'Arbitrage Commercial International* (Paris 1965) para. 114; F. E. Klein, *supra* n. 2, p. 246; G. Wetter, *The International Arbitral Process* (Dobbs Ferry 1979) Vol. II, p. 369; F. A. Mann, *supra* n. 2, p. 164.
3. Art. 1455 of the New French CCP provides:
    "Whenever a natural person or a legal entity is charged with organizing an arbitration, the arbitral mission shall be entrusted to one or several arbitrators accepted by all of the parties.
    "In the absence of such acceptance, the person or entity responsible for organizing the arbitration shall invite each party to appoint an arbitrator and shall, when appropriate, proceed to appoint the arbitrator required to complete the arbitral tribunal.
    "If the parties do not appoint an arbitrator, this is to be done by the person or entity responsible for organizing the arbitration.
    "The arbitral tribunal may also be directly constituted according to the mechanisms set forth in the preceding paragraph.
    "The person or entity responsible for organizing the arbitration may provide that the arbitral tribunal render only a draft award and that if said draft is contested by one of the parties, the case shall be submitted to a second arbitral tribunal. In such a case the members of the second arbitral tribunal shall be appointed by the person or entity responsible for organizing the arbitration, each of the parties having the possibility of having one of the thus appointed arbitrators replaced."
4. *Aramco*, quoted in Wetter, *supra* n. 3, Vol. I, p. 414; *BP* v. *Libya*, Wetter, *supra* n. 2, Vol. I, p. 434; *Kuwait* v. *Aminoil*, 21 International Legal Materials (1982), p. 976 at p. 999 and comment by G. Burdieu, Annuaire Français de Droit International (1982), p. 454 at p. 460 n. 16.
5. *James Miller & Partners Ltd.* v. *Whitworth Street Estates Ltd.*, Wetter, *supra* n. 3, Vol. II, p. 374 and 377; *Compagnie d'Armement Maritime S.A.* v. *Compagnie Tunisienne de Navigation S.A.*, Wetter, *supra* n. 3, Vol. II, p. 389.

Arts. 1073–1074 of Brazilian CCP
11. Returning to Arts. 1073–1074 of the Brazilian CCP, the arbitral tribunal reasoned:

> "[I]t must be observed that the 'terms of reference' which have been adopted in accordance with the ICC Rules comprise all the essential requirements contained in Art. 1039 of the Civil Code of Brazil to wit, the object of the litigation and the names, surnames and domicile of the arbitrators. Referring to the Civil Code and the Code of Civil Procedure, Professor Marotta Rangel has stated that 'the distinction between the two statutory texts is that the CC intends to regulate the substantive legal aspects of arbitration and the CCP the procedural ones'.

12. "Art. 1039 of the Civil Code of Brazil does not contain certain additional procedural requirements made in Arts. 1073 and 1074 of the Code of Civil Procedure: the signature of both parties and two witnesses; the amount at stake in the case (in order to determine the competence of domestic courts) and the provision for judicial costs. But the parties, by agreeing to follow the Rules of the ICC in respect of the constitution of the tribunal and the initiation of its proceedings, have expressly, and by common consent, dispensed with these requirements, which relate exclusively to the form of the instrument (which must always be governed by the rule '*locus regit actum*') and to two other purely procedural matters which only concern domestic courts. It would be against the contractual will and good faith, to deny now the jurisdiction of the agreed arbitration tribunal, by demanding the literal observance of two minor procedural requirements (the amount at stake and the provision for costs) obviously intended for domestic arbitration. In this case, the parties have agreed to execute a 'submission agreement' in accordance with the ICC Rules and not in accordance with the rules established in the Brazilian Code of Civil Procedure."

13. As to Art. 1074, defendant's expert opined that the arbitration clauses did not comply with the requirements of Art. 1074(2) and (3) of the Brazilian CCP as they did not mention the name, profession and domicile of the arbitrators and the object of the litigation. The arbitral tribunal answered this opinion as follows:

> "The answer to this observation is an obvious one. Art. 1074 clearly applies to a 'submission agreement', entered after the dispute has arisen, and not to the 'arbitration clause', agreed at the time the contract is signed, which only contemplates the possibility of eventual disputes which may arise in the future. It would be, not only absurd, but impossible to require an arbitration clause to contain those requirements of Art. 1074(2) and (3), that is to say, to define the object of a dispute which does not exist yet and to indicate the names of the arbitrators, when there is no need for the appointment of an arbitral tribunal."

Arbitration clause and Brazilian courts
14. Defendant's expert also advanced that under Brazilian doctrine and case law the arbitration clause is "absolutely ineffective for purposes of opposing the course of court litigation, which will proceed quite apart from said clause". The arbitral tribunal considered:

> "It is true that under the still prevailing Brazilian doctrine and jurisprudence, an arbitration clause, at least in domestic arbitration, does not 'entail direct,

specific compliance by the Court'; it does not ensure 'satisfaction in kind' when one of the parties, instead of appointing his arbitrator, goes before an ordinary tribunal and asks it to take up the litigation.

"But in the present case such a situation does not exist. The defendant not only has participated in the selection of the arbitral tribunal by choosing one arbitrator, but also he has not gone before a Brazilian court asking it to decide the present dispute. It has gone instead to New York Tribunals,[6] so there is no conflict between Brazilian courts and the arbitral tribunal. This situation is to be distinguished from that decided by Judgment of the Federal Supreme Court. There the Supreme Court stated that the arbitration clause 'does not make the natural judge of the parties incompetent *if recourse is had to him*' (emphasis added).

15. "A second observation, of a more general nature, is that the issue before this arbitral tribunal is whether the arbitration clauses in the agreements, are valid under Brazilian substantive law and, consequently, whether they have the necessary legal effect of conferring jurisdiction to this tribunal.

"The arbitration clauses in question, even if they may not receive specific compliance or satisfaction in kind in Brazilian courts, constitute valid stipulations under Brazilian substantive law.

"It is recognized in [defendant's expert] opinion, that Brazilian courts grant the other party the right to obtain an indemnity for damages in case of non-compliance with the contract. This clearly demonstrates that under Brazilian law, the stipulation of an arbitral clause, even if not subject to specific enforcement, is a valid stipulation and creates a binding obligation. It is considered as an '*obligatio faciendi*', and thus subject to the same legal regime applicable to that type ·of obligations. Its non-fulfilment, says the famous Brazilian jurist Bevilaqua, is 'a breach of the contract which will give rise to civil liability', that is to say, it receives a legal sanction. This valid obligation is based upon two fundamental principles fully admitted in Brazil: the duty to fulfil in good faith the engagements which have been undertaken and the recognition of the autonomy of the will of the parties to a contract.

(. . . .)

16. "The question before this tribunal is not that of enforcing an arbitration clause, among other reasons because this tribunal has no power to enforce arbitration to a reluctant party. It only concerns its power and obligation to exercise its arbitral jurisdiction, if it finds itself in the presence of a contractual stipulation which is a valid one under substantive Brazilian law. This being the case, it must be concluded that it confers jurisdiction to this tribunal to entertain the disputes which have arisen."

17. Defendant's expert further distinguished between the negative (i.e., depriving ordinary courts of jurisdiction) and positive (i.e., granting jurisdiction to the arbitral tribunal) effects of an arbitration clause in Brazilian law. He contended

---

6. *Editor's note* – Before the courts in New York, the defendant had brought an action against claimants to obtain, *inter alia*, a declaratory judgment that it had lawfully rescinded the contracts. At the request of claimants (who were defendants in the New York court action), the New York court referred the parties to the present arbitration.

that since the arbitration clause in Brazilian law has no negative effect, it should also not have the positive effect. The arbitral tribunal reasoned:

"Thus, it seems to be contended that in Brazil once the jurisdiction of an ordinary tribunal is invoked, the jurisdiction of an already established arbitral tribunal would disappear, by virtue of the principles of incompetence or of *lis pendens*.

"We have not found in the record judicial authority for this proposition. On the contrary, it would appear from a *dictum* of the Sao Paulo Court of Appeals that there would be concurring jurisdiction of that Court and an arbitral tribunal.

"But it is not necessary to go into this question, because the above described situation is not the one existing in the present case. The simple answer to the argument is that the jurisdiction of Brazilian courts has not been invoked or recurred to by any of the parties in this case. Consequently, there is not the possibility of conflicting decisions or of *lis pendens* between Brazilian ordinary courts and this arbitral tribunal.

"The defendant has commenced proceedings in New York Tribunals, but this cannot have the effect of depriving this tribunal of its jurisdiction.

"On the contrary, N.Y. federal courts have directed the parties to appear before this tribunal. But in any case, it should be made clear, that this arbitral tribunal is not under any orders of either United States or Brazilian courts. Since the parties have chosen Paris as the seat of the arbitration, only French courts could directly interfere with this arbitration in the very exceptional cases where French law provides for such an interference in international commercial arbitrations.

18. "In a more general way, the suggested equivalence of negative and positive effects of an arbitration clause involves again a 'non-sequitur'. It may be true that in Brazil, if one of the parties to a domestic contract goes before the ordinary judges, despite the existence of an arbitration clause, the ordinary judge is competent to entertain the dispute. But from this it does not follow that the arbitral tribunal, if and when it is established by the parties, would be incompetent. From the absence of a negative effect one cannot infer the absence of a positive grant of jurisdiction to the arbitral tribunal, when it succeeds in being established on the basis of the consent of the parties.

"When the normal situation occurs, that is to say, when the arbitration clause is not infringed, but it is complied with and implemented by the parties by appointing arbitrators, so that the tribunal is constituted, and when no one goes before the Brazilian ordinary court, the natural effect of the clause of conferring jurisdiction to the arbitral tribunal must take place.

"This is, in fact, what currently occurs in Brazil, where [according to defendant's expert] 'the arbitration clause is widely used' and arbitration tribunals, at least in respect of international contracts, function normally and exercise their jurisdiction without difficulties.

19. "The Supreme Court of Brazil has admitted in several cases that arbitration clauses in international commercial contracts which provided for arbitration

outside Brazil were valid and conferred jurisdiction to arbitral tribunals constituted in England or in Hamburg. In one of these cases homologation was denied but for a reason different from that of lack of jurisdiction of the arbitral tribunal constituted in accordance with the arbitral clause."

Brazilian public policy
20. The next objection of defendant, as stated by its expert, was based on Art. 153(4) of the Brazilian Constitution which provides that "the law cannot exclude from consideration by Judicial Authorities any infringement of individual right". According to defendant's expert, "this constitutional guarantee of access to judicial resolution of disputes is a fundamental public policy of Brazil . . . as an integral part of the Brazilian Public Order". The arbitral tribunal observed:

21. "A possible interpretation of this argument would be that all arbitration clauses in Brazil are invalid as contrary to Brazilian public policy, because they might deprive individuals of their right of unimpeded access to judiciary authorities and encroach upon the alleged monopoly of domestic courts to settle disputes, as 'the natural dispensers of justice in Brazil'.

"That would be an extreme and unacceptable proposition, particularly when applied to international commercial contracts, and contrary to current practice in Brazil.

"A more plausible interpretation, and one fully corresponding to Brazilian doctrine and jurisprudence, is that in Brazil the party who has agreed to an arbitration clause in a domestic contract may nevertheless validly resort to the competent judicial authorities and the domestic courts would have jurisdiction to entertain the dispute, when the arbitral tribunal has not been established. But, as already indicated, this is not the situation in the present case, where there is an international commercial contract, no party has attempted to resort to Brazilian judiciary authorities and the arbitral tribunal has been already constituted.

22. "The contention that international commercial arbitration clauses would be contrary to Brazilian public policy or public order is not reconcilable with the fact that Brazil signed and ratified the Geneva Protocol of 1923, which provides [in Art. 1(1)] that:

'Each of the Contracting States recognizes the validity of an agreement whether relating to existing or future differences between parties subject respectively to the jurisdiction of different Contracting States by which the parties to a contract agree to submit to arbitration all or any differences that may arise in connection with such contract relating to commercial matters or to any other matter capable of settlement by arbitration, whether or not the arbitration is to take place in a country to whose jurisdiction none of the parties is subject.'

23. "The competent Brazilian authorities not only ratified the 1923 Protocol but decreed that 'it must be executed and complied with as fully as it itself provides'. (Decree no. 21.187 of 22 March 1932).

"It has been contended [i.e., claimants' expert] that the principles of this Protocol, and the similar ones of the 1958 New York Convention may be controlling in this case, either as customary rules of international law or as

40

rules incorporated in Brazil's municipal law. Without pronouncing on this question, the tribunal finds that the 1923 Protocol whether applicable or not as a treaty, furnishes complete evidence that arbitration clauses in international commercial contracts are not contrary to Brazil's public policy or public order.

24. "It could hardly be otherwise, since arbitration clauses have become an essential guarantee to ensure the flow of international trade and serve the needs of transnational businessmen. They are more indispensable than in domestic contracts, because in international undertakings it is absolutely necessary to ensure in the event of disputes a neutral jurisdiction, whose perceived impartiality cannot be put in doubt. Arbitral clauses therefore, in the terms of the U.S. Supreme Court have become 'an almost indispensable precondition to achievement of the orderliness and predictability essential to any international business transaction'. (U.S. Supreme Court, *Scherk* v. *Alberto-Culver*, 417 U.S. 506, 517 (1974)).

25. "A country like Brazil, more and more involved in the fabric of international trade, both as an importer and an exporter, not just of raw materials, but of manufactured products as well, cannot place itself in a position of 'splendid isolation', which would imperil the ability of its businessmen to enter into international commercial agreements and the expansion of overseas commercial activities by business enterprises based in Brazil.

(. . . .)

26. "A further confirmation of the fact that the recognition and enforcement of arbitration clauses in international commercial contracts is not against Brazil public policy but, on the contrary, in full conformity with it, results from various laws, decrees and contracts issued or agreed by the Government of Brazil and from at least one judgment of its Supreme Tribunal."[7]

27. With respect to the Brazilian DM 150 million bonds 1979/1989, which provide for ICC arbitration in Paris,[8] the arbitral tribunal observed:

"It is not conceivable that the Government of Brazil or Brazilian courts would deny the binding force of this agreement by invoking the procedures in Arts. 1073 and 1074 of the Code of Civil Procedure, the invalidity of arbitration clauses, or even Art. 153(4) of the Constitution of Brazil.

"The acceptance in this important instrument subscribed by the Government of the Federative Republic of Brazil of the ICC Rules for the appointment of arbitrators, as well as the selection of Paris as the seat of arbitration demonstrate, beyond all possible doubt, that such stipulations, identical to those adopted in this case, are in no way contrary to Brazilian public policy or public order."

28. Regarding the Brazilian Supreme Court, the arbitral tribunal noted:

---

7. The arbitral tribunal referred to Brazilian Law no. 1628 of 29 June 1952, which allows in Art. 23 the National Treasury to agree to arbitration; Decree Law no. 1312 of 15 February 1974, which also allows in Art. 11 the National Treasury to agree to arbitration; Euroborrowings made by Brazilian public entities with the guarantee of Brazil, which provide for international arbitration under ICSID Rules (News from ICSID, Vol. 1, no. 2, p. 2).
8. Cited by G. Delaume, "State Contracts and Transnational Arbitration", 75 American Journal of International Law (1981), p. 784 at p. 795 n. 54.

"The Brazilian Supreme Tribunal Federal in the case *La Pastina* v. *Centrofin* confirmed a judgment where it was stated that:

'In the instant case, the arbitration which took place in Hamburg was expressly agreed upon, the dispute is not a state dispute but a commercial one, neither is it exclusively under the Brazilian jurisdiction, not any abuse of process or offence to the public order can be foreseen in it.'

"The President of the Supreme Federal Tribunal in confirming the judgment expressed that 'I can see no offence matter to public order' this being 'a question of commercial bargain and sale'."

Enforceability of award

29. Defendant finally relied on Art. 26 of the ICC Rules which obliges the arbitral tribunal "to make every effort to make sure that the award is enforceable at law". Defendant contended that because of the public order nature of Brazil's limitations on arbitration, any award made by the arbitral tribunal in the absence of (i) a full submission agreement or (ii) a formal submission by defendant to the tribunal's jurisdiction, will not be enforceable in Brazil.

30. The claimants asserted that the jurisdiction of the arbitral tribunal does not depend on whether its award would be enforced in Brazil. They called attention to a publication "International Chamber of Commerce Arbitration" where it is stated that "the question of execution after the award is in no way tied to that of jurisdiction of the arbitral tribunal. The two questions are in effect independent, and the jurisdiction of the tribunal is not conditioned by the fact that the award may not be subject to execution in another country".

31. The arbitral tribunal reasoned:

"Art. 26 of the ICC Rules must be understood as requiring every arbitral tribunal to try to avoid any grounds of nullity, since if the award is unenforceable the whole arbitration proceeding will have been a waste of time and energy.

"But this requirement of Art. 26 is not relevant to the question of jurisdiction. It is obvious that if a tribunal would decline to exercise jurisdiction on the basis of the possible difficulties of a future enforcement in a given country, then there would be no award at all, susceptible of being enforced in other jurisdictions.

"In this case there may be difficulties, perhaps not insuperable, in the enforcement of this tribunal awards, in some national jurisdictions.

"But if the tribunal finds, as it does, that it has jurisdiction, it cannot fail to exercise it. Otherwise, it would be concurring in a failure to exercise jurisdiction and could even be accused of a denial of justice.

"Finally, it must be observed that in the present case the tribunal has been asked by the defendant to take into account considerations relating to enforcement, but it has not been formally requested to decline jurisdiction on this ground."

Final Award of 28 March 1984 in case no. 3267 (ORIGINAL IN ENGLISH)

Arbitrators: C. Reymond (Switz.), F. Duhot (nationality not indicated), P. Chanenet (nationality not indicated)

Parties: Claimant: Mexican Construction Company
             Defendant: Belgian Company (member of a Consortium)

Published in: Unpublished

Subject matters: – *res judicata* effect of partial award
                    – powers of *amiable compositeur*
                    – scope of Terms of Reference
                    – Advance Payment Guarantee and Risk Exposure Guarantee
                    – damages
                    – costs

FACTS

This arbitration was the subject of a partial award rendered 14 June 1979, and reported in *Yearbook*, Vol. VII (1982), pp. 96–106. A related dispute between the claimant and the bank which issued a "risk exposure guarantee" in its favor was decided by an award made 23 October 1979, Case No. 3316 (published in *Yearbook*, Vol. VII (1982) pp. 106–116).

The dispute related to a construction contract entered into in June 1976 between a Saudi Arabian government entity and a Belgian consortium of which the defendant was a member. In January 1977, the defendant subcontracted part of the project to claimant.

The subcontract required claimant to post the standard performance bonds, and also an Advance Payment Guarantee in an amount equal to the entire amount of the advance payment made by defendant to claimant. Claimant pledged to the issuing bank the advance payment as collateral for the Advance Payment Guarantee.

In consideration, defendant caused a "Risk Exposure Guarantee" to be issued in favor of claimant. This guarantee provided for payments to claimant in the event of termination by defendant, in graduated amounts at different phases of completion of the contract.

Difficulties arose in the first few months of performance under the contract. Claimant was unable to meet various milestones, and the defendant made deductions from the sixth and seventh installment payments. On 17 November, claimant gave notice terminating the contract, and on 18 November defendant gave claimant notice.

Claimant thereupon initiated the arbitration. The partial award made 14 June 1979 found in favor of claimant on a certain number of points. It held that claimant's termination of the contract was legitimate, on account of defendant's withholding of certain sums due under the contract. Defendant objected that the amount payable to claimant under the Risk Exposure Guarantee (in excess of $18 million) was excessive, in the nature of a penalty, and should be reviewed by the arbitral tribunal. The arbitral tribunal ruled, however, that such amount was a legitimate liquidated damage amount, which, pursuant to the contract, could be claimed as an alternative to actual damages. Such a contractual term is acceptable under various legal systems and is also a general practice in the construction industry.

As regards the Advance Payment Guarantee and Performance Bonds, the arbitral tribunal held that they should remain in force pending the final award on the merits.

Subsequent to this partial award, there were a number of significant procedural developments. Defendant entered bankruptcy, and its case was thereafter conducted by its trustees in bankruptcy. Defendant initiated criminal proceedings in Belgium against claimant, and sought a review of the partial award pursuant to Art. 41 of the Swiss Concordat. This request, as well as a request for a stay of execution of the partial award, was rejected by the Supreme Court of Justice of Geneva. Furthermore, the claimant proved unable, as a practical matter, to obtain payment of amounts due under the Risk Exposure Guarantee, on account of court actions in Switzerland and Belgium initiated by defendant. After extensive negotiations, amounts due to claimant under the Risk Exposure Guarantee, and to defendant under the various performance guarantees, were deposited into various escrow accounts, and held subject to the final disposition of the case by the arbitral tribunal.

EXTRACT
1. *Effect of Prior Partial Award*
The arbitrators first considered the effect of the partial award on issues remaining to be decided:

> "The fundamental issue in this arbitration was to decide which of the two notices of termination of the contract was effective, claimant's or defendant's. This issue was decided in favour of claimant in the first award. Such award, which was not challenged at the time by defendant as open to it under Swiss law (Art. 36 of the Swiss Concordat sur l'Arbitrage),[1] is now *res judicata*

---

1. Swiss Intercantonal Arbitration Convention, Art. 36 provides:
  "An action for annulment of the arbitral award may be brought before the judicial authority provided for in Article 3, where it is alleged that:
  a. the arbitral tribunal was not properly constituted;
  b. that the arbitral tribunal erroneously declared itself to have or not to have jurisdiction;
  c. that it pronounced on points not submitted to it or, subject to Article 32, failed to make a determination on one of the items in the claim;
  d. that there was a breach of one of the mandatory procedural rules referred to in Article 25;
  e. that the arbitral tribunal awarded to one of the parties something more or other than claimed, without being authorised to do so by a provision of the law;
  f. that the award is arbitrary in that it was based on findings which were manifestly contrary to the facts appearing on the file, or in that it constitutes a clear violation of law or equity;   →

between the parties and binding upon this arbitral tribunal, all the more so that defendant's later petition for review was dismissed by the Geneva Court of Justice.

"This arbitral tribunal is further of the opinion that the binding effect of its first award is not limited to the contents of the order thereof adjudicating or dismissing certain claims, but that it extends to the legal reasons that were necessary for such order, i.e., to the *ratio decidendi* of such award. Irrespective from the academic views that may be entertained on the extent of the principle of *res judicata* on the reasons of a decision, it would be unfair to both parties to depart in a final award from the views held in the previous award, to the extent they were necessary for the disposition of certain issues. By contrast, the arbitral tribunal made clear in other parts of its first award that the views expressed therein on certain other aspects of the case were of a preliminary nature only and without prejudice to its final decision. On such aspects, the arbitral tribunal holds itself entirely free to adopt other views with the benefit of further evidence and investigations."

(. . . .)

As regards the issue of applicable law in the prior award, the arbitrators held:

"In the first award, the arbitral tribunal decided to determine the issues under generally accepted legal principles governing international commercial relations, without specific reference to a particular system of law, which was qualified by a learned commentator as a reference to *lex mercatoria* (Yves Derains, 'Chronique des sentences arbitrales', Journal du droit international, 1980, p. 961, 966–969). In the second phase of this arbitration none of the parties did require the application of any particular system of law, nor did they rely on any specific provision of any municipal system. The arbitral tribunal sees no reason therefore to depart from the view expressed in its first award on this aspect of the cases. Indeed, as it will appear later, all legal issues in this arbitration depend on the construction and system of the contractual documents.

"On the other hand, it was forcibly argued by defendant that, irrespective of the legal principles governing the Contract, the power to act as *amiable compositeur* entitled the arbitral tribunal to modify or disregard the provisions of the Contract, when its application would lead to results contrary to natural justice, or to the principles of equity within the meaning of this word in Civil Law countries.

"This contention raises the question of the nature and extent of the powers of arbitrators acting as *amiables compositeurs*, in addition to the powers deriving from the application of the general principles of international commercial law or of *lex mercatoria* (see Y. Derains, loc. cit.). As a matter of principle, the arbitral tribunal does not reject the view that an *amiable compositeur* may go beyond certain solutions deriving from the normally applicable legal rules, be they those of a municipal legal system or those of *lex mercatoria*. The question

---

g. that the arbitral tribunal made its award after the expiration of the time limit imposed on it in which to accomplish its mission;

h. that the conditions of Article 33 were not complied with or that the order is intelligible or contradictory;

i. that the fees of the arbitrators fixed by the arbitral tribunal are manifestly excessive."

however is how far he can go, especially when faced with specific provisions of a contract. A further question is whether the individual situation and circumstances justify his making use of such power. These two questions shall be dealt with when examining the specific claims in connection therewith."

2. *Claims of Claimant (a–c)*
(a) *Claimant sought payment of the balance of the Advance Payment Guarantee in escrow and reimbursement to it of amounts already drawn down thereunder by defendant.*

The arbitrators described the mechanism of the Advance Payment Guarantee in the context of the particular contract provisions.

"The legal basis on which claimant's claims rest is that the contract required that defendant justify its right to recovery under the Advance Bank Guarantee. The Contract form of bank guarantee required that the notice to be sent by the bank indicate that according to the absolute judgment of defendant, there was a failure by claimant in meeting its obligations. Claimant contends that based upon the first award, the conditions of exercise of the Advance Bank Guarantee were not met and that the amount paid by the bank to defendant and accordingly debited from claimant's cash collateral account should therefore be returned to claimant.

"The determination of this issue requires the resolution of two closely linked but nevertheless distinct questions. Was defendant entitled to call the Advance Bank Guarantee and in the affirmative, is defendant entitled in the final analysis to retain the amount so collected? Claimant argues that defendant was not legally entitled to call such guarantee and that it should therefore return the amount it collected to claimant.

"The arbitral tribunal does not agree with this reasoning: in its first award, the arbitral tribunal has not exonerated claimant from any liability and on the contrary, claimant is now found to have failed to meet certain of its contractual obligations vis-à-vis defendant under the Contract. This in itself justifies the call by defendant of the Advance Bank Guarantee. Thus the arbitral tribunal may now turn to the second question, i.e., whether defendant should reimburse all or part of the amounts so collected by it."

The arbitral tribunal held that claimant was not entitled to reimbursement of sums already drawn down by defendant. As to the balance of the Advance Payment Guarantee, it was to be held pending final accounting and settlement of all amounts due.

(b) *Claimant further sought payment of the entire amount of the Risk Exposure Guarantee, the jurisdiction of the arbitrators continuing until such time as such full payment would be made.*

"The first part of this claim appears to be justified under the terms of the Addendum to the Arbitrators' Terms of Reference if and to the extent that the deposit made under the Escrow Agreement is sufficient to satisfy the payment of any amount which claimant may owe to defendant. As it will be shown later, this is indeed the case and therefore defendant should not be entitled to make a call [on such deposit].

46

"As to the continuance of the jurisdiction of the arbitral tribunal, the present award is a final award by its very terms pursuant to Art. 24(1) of the ICC Rules of Arbitration.[2] Thus, in rendering this present final award, this arbitral tribunal will have discharged its functions. The subclaim contained in the second limb of that claim is to be dismissed. If there was a dispute as to the implementation of the Escrow Agreement, it would lead to a new and distinct arbitration under Art. 9 thereof."

(*c*) *Payment of various claims of claimant, including claims for variation orders, confiscated equipment, insurance premiums, running costs, payment deductions effected by defendant on the 10 November 1977 installment payment, and transportation costs.*

The arbitral tribunal held that claims relating to variation orders, confiscation, insurance and running costs were outside the purview of the terms of reference:

"The arbitral tribunal is a conventional court and its jurisdiction is *per se* not defined by law but by contract. In that respect the basic document which defines the parties' respective claims which are subject to the arbitral tribunal's jurisdiction is the Terms of Reference which is referred to by Art. 13 of the ICC Rules of Arbitration, whether this document is agreed upon by the parties or whether, failing such agreement, it is approved by the Court of Arbitration (Art. 13(2) of the ICC Rules of Arbitration).[3]

"Art. 16 of said Rules[4] provides further that the parties may make any claims or counterclaims before the arbitral tribunal provided that these claims are within the limit fixed by the Terms of Reference provided for in Art. 13 or are specified in a rider to that document signed by the parties and communicated to the Court. The question before the arbitral tribunal is therefore to decide whether the claims made by claimant meet the condition provided for in Art. 16.

"The claims mentioned . . . above and regarding variation orders as well as the claims mentioned . . . above were not included, either expressly or implicitly, in the initial Terms of Reference nor the Addendum thereto. They were filed by claimant during the course of this arbitration proceedings and for most of

---

2. ICC Arbitration Rules, Art. 24(1) provides:
   "The arbitral award shall be final."
3. ICC Arbitration Rules, Art. 13(2) provides:
   "The document mentioned in paragraph 1 of this Article shall be signed by the parties and the arbitrator. Within two months of the date when the file has been transmitted to him, the arbitrator shall transmit to the Court the said document signed by himself and by the parties. Upon the arbitrator's request, the Court may, in exceptional circumstances, extend this time limit.
   Should one of the parties refuse to take part in the drawing up of the said document or to sign the same, the Court, if it is satisfied that the case is one of those mentioned in paragraphs 2 and 3 of Article 8, shall take such action as is necessary for its approval. Thereafter the Court shall set a time limit for the signature of the statement by the defaulting party and on expiry of that time limit the arbitration shall proceed and the award shall be made."
4. ICC Arbitration Rules, Art. 16 provides:
   "The parties may make new claims or counterclaims before the arbitrator on condition that these remain within the limits fixed by the Terms of Reference provided for in Article 13 or that they are specified in a rider to that document, signed by the parties and communicated to the Court."

them, for the first time in claimant's final submission of 28 September 1978. Defendant has argued that such claims were not part of the arbitration proceedings and the arbitration tribunal in its first award has reserved its position.

"It is beyond the authority of the arbitral tribunal, even acting as *amiable compositeur*, to extend the boundaries of its jurisdiction. The above cited claims being not expressly or implicitly covered by the Terms of Reference as amended, the arbitral tribunal cannot pass upon them as it does not have jurisdiction to do so."

The claims relating to payment deductions were held to be waived by claimant, in that it elected to call the Risk Exposure Guarantee, a liquidated damage remedy which precluded claims on actual damages.

The arbitral tribunal granted claimant's claim for transportation payments, on the grounds that such claims were "unsettled claims" according to the terms of the contract, were outside the scope of liquidated damages contemplated by the Risk Exposure Guarantee, and, finally, were within the Terms of Reference.

3. *Claims of Defendant (a–c)*
(*a*) *Liquidation of accounts:*

Defendant sought a liquidation of accounts based on the actual value of the Works at the time of claimant's suspension of activity on site.

"Can it be argued that the contract provides in case of early termination for an estimation of the actual value of the Works made and that in such case, all payments made so far to claimant should be treated solely as advances pending final determination of the amounts really owed to claimant based upon the value of the Works actually delivered? In its first award, this arbitral tribunal already analysed this contract and found that it provides for two parallel but distinct types of obligations, the ones regarding the performance of the Contractor to which are attached associated remedies including financial ones and the others concerning the payment of the contract price by the Owner.

"Nowhere in this contract is there an express or implied provision calling for a valuation of the Works in case of early termination based upon defendant's default. The parties provided at length for their respective rights and obligations in such case of termination.

(. . . .)

"A thorough review of the contract demonstrates that there is no room for a valuation of the Works, irrespective of the type of termination.

"This construction of the contract is in conformity with its general philosophy. As already pointed out in the first award, the contract provides for two independent series of obligations. In particular, there is no necessary correspondence, during the term of the contract, between the quantity of the Works completed by claimant and the amounts paid by defendant. Delays and deficiencies in the performance of the Works are taken care of, in the mechanism of the Contract, by other means than by the reduction of the contract payments, i.e., the delays by the liquidated damages of Clause 13, and any defects under the Guarantee of Good Execution of Clause 22. It would be therefore contrary to the system of the Contract to organize a valuation of the Works performed by claimant. . . ."

Defendant argued that the arbitral tribunal should intervene in its capacity as *amiable compositeur* to cause an accounting of the actual value of the Works:

"Defendant strongly argued that in a case where there was such an imbalance between the amount received by claimant and the work or services delivered by it, an arbitral tribunal, even without the powers to act as *amiable compositeur*, had the authority to reject an abuse of right and that furthermore, an *amiable compositeur* could also depart from the general principles of the *lex mercatoria* or from the contract itself when such departure was justified by fairness or equity.

"In its first award, this arbitral tribunal already expressed its views on the scope of its authority as *amiable compositeur* and intends to strictly adhere to the principles so expressed. It is the duty of ICC arbitrators to apply the provisions of a contract even when empowered to act as *amiables compositeurs* but they may indeed disregard a party's legal or contractual rights only when the enforcement of such rights amounts to an abuse thereof.

"The arbitral tribunal is of the opinion that in the instant case there is not such an abuse which would justify to grant defendant's request. This finding is based on the following elements:

"First, although repeatedly invited to do so by claimant, defendant never communicated its contract with the National Guard, nor any information as to the final amount which it received from the National Guard for the Works subject to the Contract with Claimant or as to any losses (or profits?) it may have incurred (or made) on such Works. Defendant, which has the burden of proof in that matter, did not supply this arbitral tribunal with the factual information which it wanted to be considered in this connection.

"Second, defendant claims that it received from claimant Works and services which it values at SR 35,482,000, while it paid to claimant an amount of SR 135,605,174. These figures are disputed by claimant . . . .

"This arbitral tribunal does not have to decide which of the two parties' valuation is correct. It is sufficient, at this point, for this arbitral tribunal, acting as *amiable compositeur*, to retain as valid some of the objections made by claimant. . . .

"Third and most important, this arbitral tribunal must view its decision from an overall standpoint. In recognizing claimant's right to exercise the REG and to obtain the full monetary benefit thereof it has, as a consequence, denied [claimant] the right to demand payment or obtain credits for a number of claims which would have otherwise been justified. As discussed hereunder, the fairness of this arbitral tribunal's decision must be appreciated within the overall context of its awards in a case where [defendant] has been found in default.

"Based on the foregoing, this arbitral tribunal is of the opinion that it is bound to apply the terms of the Contract, that such contract does not call for a valuation to be made of the Works performed at the time of its terminations and that if the accounts have to be liquidated as between the parties, such liquidation is to be made by applying the terms of the Contract, which provides for a satisfactory method of solution, both at law and from the point of view of fairness and equity."

(. . . .)

(*b*) *Damage claims of defendant:*

The arbitral tribunal sustained certain claims of the defendant, in finding that claimant's performance was deficient in various areas. It rejected, however, defendant's claim for completion costs:

"This arbitral tribunal already rejected defendant's claim 1 seeking to take into account the difference between the so-called 'value' of the Works at the termination date and the amount paid to claimant. It does further reject, as ill founded and contrary to its first award, the claim for reimbursement of the extra cost incurred in having the Works completed by another contractor. . . . This arbitral tribunal found in its first award that the Contract had been legitimately terminated by claimant and that the notice of termination issued subsequently by defendant was of no legal effect. The additional expenses of replacing claimant by another contractor is a direct consequence of the termination and should in no way be borne by claimant. The remedies to claimant's defaults or deficiencies as to Work and materials are defined in the Contract (. . . particularly clauses 19 and 22) which calls for either repairs or replacement of the defective Works or materials at the cost of the Contractor.

"By contrast, this arbitral tribunal finds that defendant is entitled to be credited for all expenses which should normally have been borne by claimant during the course of the Contract or which are already covered by the REG."

(. . . .)

(c) *Interest*

"In the final analysis, either in its first award or in the present final award, this arbitral tribunal has not granted any interest to any of the two parties. This overall solution which entails that the claims for interest from both parties are disposed of in the same manner, complies with the principle of fairness which this Tribunal must take into account as *amiable compositeur.*"

(. . . .)

4. *Role of Tribunal as Amiable Compositeur*

"This arbitral tribunal has been entrusted to act with the powers of *amiable compositeur.* It already made clear in its first award its view as to the extent and limit of such powers and throughout these proceedings it consistently acted according to such views.

"As these proceedings come to an end, it feels bound vis-à-vis both parties and especially vis-à-vis defendant, which argued at length in favor of a much broader view of the authority of *amiable compositeur,* to assess the end result of these proceedings from an overall standpoint and to verify that it is consistent with principles of fairness.

"This case started in December 1977, that is more than six years ago, and involved a valid termination by claimant of its Contract with defendant based upon recognized violations by defendant of its contractual obligations.

"In order, probably, to obtain a speedy remedy, claimant elected to exercise the REG, a first demand guarantee issued by a first class Belgian bank for an amount in excess of US$18,000,000. In making such election, claimant in effect waived its rights to obtain payment from defendant of outstanding amounts contractually owed to it, as well as damages for its expenses and losses (including loss of expected profits). To achieve the same objective of a speedy resolution of the dispute, claimant chose to initially limit these arbitration proceedings to specific issues relating to the termination of the Contract, leaving outside of the scope of said proceedings a number of unsettled claims which appeared at least partially justified.

"From all the documents and briefs filed by claimant, it appears that [claimant] estimates the total aggregate amount so waived or left outside of these proceedings in exchange for a prompt remedy through the exercise of the REG to be far in excess of the amount of the REG.

"This arbitral tribunal is of the opinion that such aggregate amount could indeed be not out of line with the amount of the REG.

"The arbitral tribunal has given the REG and claimant's option to exercise the REG their respective full effects both beneficial and detrimental to claimant.

"More than six years after the initiation of these proceedings, claimant has not yet received the principal amount of the REG and seems to receive the interest thereon only since about three years, i.e., since the end of 1980 when the corresponding amounts were transmitted to the [escrow bank] which used them as collateral to issue its Bank Guarantee . . . . Using a present discounted value basis and expressed in the currency of the Contract, the funds representing the REG as of the end of 1980 represent substantially less than they would have at the end of 1977 when claimant should have normally cashed them.

"Defendant attempted to persuade this arbitral tribunal that its bankruptcy was due to claimant's failure to meet its contractual obligations which resulted in huge losses in its contract with the National Guard but at the same time, it chose not to give the arbitral tribunal any real information on its main contract with the National Guard and the financial impact of such contract on defendant. Without expressing any opinion on the defendant's bankruptcy proceedings where the members of the defendant Consortium are also the main creditors, this tribunal is satisfied that such bankruptcy was not caused solely by the dispute with claimant and the ensuing termination by claimant of its Contract with defendant.

"This arbitral tribunal believes that as a result of claimant's attempt to obtain a speedy solution – an attempt which ultimately failed – claimant is now obtaining remedies which, at today's present value, do not exceed and are probably less than those which it would have obtained without exercising the

REG, in the ordinary course of an arbitration proceedings, not burdened by unusual – and sometimes unnecessary – delays.

"Defendant also attempted to persuade this arbitral tribunal that at the time of termination, the 'value' of the Works was far less than the amounts then paid to claimant. But at the same time, it elected to withhold for reasons of its own any information as to the 'value' recognized to such Works by its client, the National Guard. For the arbitral tribunal, the real value of the Works aside from any independent valuation is really measured by the price which the ultimate customer is willing to pay for such Works. Without such basic information, the arbitral tribunal was not in a position to even consider defendant's argument had it wished to do so.

"The arbitral tribunal has granted defendant all remedies which it was entitled to in order to cure claimant's deficiencies in fulfilling its contractual obligations and gave defendant credit for expenses which should have been claimant's or for advances which were to be repaid by claimant. In other words, through a decision on the merits, these arbitration proceedings shall enable defendant to retain SR24,340,779 representing deductions it withheld from Contract Payments, US$3,291,851 which it already received from the exercise of the Advance Bank Guarantee and to receive in addition as will be seen later amounts of 19,822,667 Belgian Francs and 3,840,397 US Dollars.

"This arbitral tribunal is therefore satisfied that in the conduct of these proceedings and in the decisions resulting therefrom its strict adherence to the terms of the Contract and to widely accepted general principles governing international commercial law was also totally consistent with the principles of fairness, *équité*, and that it is thereby properly discharging its functions of *amiable compositeur*."

5. *Decision*

The arbitral tribunal thus credited each party with amounts awarded to them, finding a net balance of US Dollars 4,850,000 in favor of defendant, a net balance of Saudi Riyals 3,563,900 in favor of Claimant, and a net balance of Belgian Francs 19,822,667 in favor of defendant. After satisfaction of such amounts, the balance of amounts in escrow was ordered released to claimant.

As regards the costs of the arbitration, the arbitral tribunal held:

"In this matter, the arbitral tribunal enjoys a wide amount of discretion, both under ICC Rules and as *amiable compositeur*.

(. . . .)

"In view of the final result of this arbitration for each party, it is an equitable solution to decide that the costs of the arbitration proper are to be borne by the parties in the same proportion as their advances therefor, which were made approximately one third by claimant and two thirds by defendant, and this arbitral tribunal shall so order.

"As for legal costs between party and party, for the same reasons, the equitable solution is to decide that each party is to bear its own legal costs, and this arbitral tribunal shall order accordingly."

Interim awards and final award of 1983, 1984 and 1986 in case no. 4145

Arbitrators: DDr. Franz Matscher, (Austria) chairman; Me Jean-Claude Fivaz (Switz.); Prof. Dr. Sang Hyun Song (South Korea), who resigned after the interim awards and was replaced by Prof. W. Michael Reisman (USA)

Parties: Claimant: Establishment of Middle East country X
Defendant: South Asian construction company

Published in: 112 Journal du droit international (Clunet) 1985, p. 985, with commentary Y. Derains

Subject matters: *First interim award:*
– law applicable to arbitration agreement
– deficient arbitration agreement (rejected)
– separability arbitration clause
– icc Rules, Art. 8(4)
Second interim award:
– law applicable to substance (choice for two laws; no cumulative applicability; *favor negotii*)
– bribery (rejected)
– extortion (rejected)
– consultancy agreement (qualification)
– brokerage agreement (qualification)
Final award:
– waiver of claim
– changed circumstances (*rebus sic stantibus*)
– trade usages
– icc Rules, Art. 13(5)

FACTS

In the seventies, a Ministry of Middle East country X was calling for tenders for a project involving the construction of certain buildings for social purposes (hereinafter: the "Project").

During that period, defendant was trying to enter the construction market in country X. Its efforts were relatively unsuccessful. When the tender for the Project came out in 1978, defendant was eager to be the successful bidder, as were its competitors.

Defendant then entered in 1978 into an agreement with claimant, an establishment of country X, by the terms of which defendant appointed claimant as representative for the promotion and contracting of the Project (hereinafter: the "Agreement"). The services to be rendered by claimant were described in the Agreement as follows:

"Consultant shall, in consideration of the compensation hereinafter agreed to be paid to it by Company, provide Company with such counsel, guidance liaison assistance, facilities, value engineering, complete tender studies, inspections of site, or any additional service as shall be reasonably necessary and required from a Consultant and shall, in general use its best efforts to promote and further the sale of the Projects. Further, the increased price sale of the Project through his services or through the services of other Consultants that he may hire out of his own funds."

Upon the conclusion of the Agreement, defendant signed similar agreements with companies related to claimant providing for a cooperation on other projects in the country concerned.

After negotiations lasting some eight months, defendant was awarded in early 1979 the Project for a final price equivalent to approximately US$374 million.

Thereupon, in a letter from defendant to claimant's bank in Geneva, defendant undertook the irrevocable and unconditional commitment to pay immediately upon receipt of its down payment from the Ministry "for services which were received in full in connection with the above mentioned Agreement" the sum of US$50 million. That sum was subsequently remitted by defendant to claimant's bank.

At the same time, the chairman of defendant expressed in a telex to the principal representative of claimant his "sincere thanks on your excellent efforts."

When negotiating an extension with the Ministry in 1979, claimant and defendant signed an amendment to the Agreement relating to the extension (hereinafter: the "Amendment").

In 1980 defendant obtained the extension of its original contract by the award of additional works for a total amount equivalent to approx. US$54.5 million, consisting of two parts: (1) works according to the Bill of Quantities ("BOQ") in the original contract (US$40 million) and (2) works which have no BOQ (US$14.5 million).

Having received the amount of US$50 million in 1979, claimant complained that this was not the full amount it was entitled to, which according to it, was US$57 million, the result being that it should receive US$7 million more.

Subsequently, claimant asked for compensation relating to the extension of the original contract, that is US$7 million (relating to the US$40 million) and US$2.5 million (relating to the US$14.5 million).

Defendant refused to pay anything more and, as the parties could not reach a settlement, in 1981 claimant submitted the case to the ICC for arbitration pursuant to the arbitration clause in the Agreement (which clause is quoted below), asking for the payment of US$ (7 + 7 + 2.5 =) 16.5 million plus interests and costs.

In absence of an agreement of the parties on the place of arbitration, the ICC Court of Arbitration fixed Vienna as place of arbitration.

In a first interim award, rendered in 1983, the arbitral tribunal held that it had jurisdiction to decide the case for the reasons partly reproduced below.

In a second interim award, rendered in 1984, the arbitral tribunal held that the Agreement was valid under Swiss law and rejected defendant's motion to

54

dismiss the arbitration on the ground of forgery, with prejudice for the reasons partly reproduced below.

In the final award, rendered in 1986, the arbitral tribunal ordered defendant to pay an equivalent of US$1.5 million with 5% interest, for the reasons partly reproduced below.

EXTRACT
First Interim Award
1. Sect. 11 of the Agreement reads as follows:

"Validity, Construction and Arbitration
The validity and construction of this Agreement shall be governed by the laws of the Canton of Geneva, Switzerland or country X, or both. Any controversy or claim between the Parties hereto arising out of or in connection with the Agreement which might be subject of any action at law or suit in equity under the Rules of Conciliation and Arbitration of the International Chamber of Commerce [*sic*]. The award of a majority of the arbitrators, including the apportionment of the expenses of the arbitration, shall be final and binding upon the parties, and judgment upon the award rendered may be entered in any court having jurisdiction."

2. The arbitral tribunal reasoned with respect to this clause:

"The claimant considers that Sect. 11 of the Agreement includes a valid agreement to arbitrate. Notwithstanding its linguistic deficiencies, it would express without any doubt the parties' intention to submit any controversy between them to ICC-arbitration.

3. "As far as applicable law (to govern the validity of the agreement to arbitrate) is concerned, the claimant firstly relies on the 'validity rule', namely that the agreement would be valid, if it could be based upon at least one of the legal systems referred to by the parties in Art. 11 of the said Agreement ('the laws of the Canton of Geneva, Switzerland or country X, or both'). Now, following the relevant provisions of Swiss Law, there would be a valid clause to arbitrate. Under these circumstances, any further investigation concerning the position of the law of country X would be irrelevant. Should, however, the arbitral tribunal be of the opinion that there is no precise applicable law clause in the Agreement, then Austrian Law would have to be advanced as the law of the seat of arbitration. Also following the relevant provisions of that law there would be no doubt about the validity of the agreement to arbitrate.

4. "In the opinion of the defendant, the Agreement really does seem to contemplate some kind of arbitration, but the crucial element of an agreement to arbitrate would be lacking, namely submission to the adjudicatory jurisdiction of an arbitral tribunal. The arbitral forum being an exceptional one, arbitration agreements are to be interpreted restrictively. Therefore, the arbitrators are not called upon to cure contractual deficiencies by means of interpretation.

5. "Moreover, following the 'center of gravity-test', the whole agreement (including the arbitral clause) would be governed by the law of country X, Swiss Law playing a suppletive role only. Then, the Agreement would be unenforceable under the law of country X as well as under Swiss Law or under the applicable principles of international public order, mainly because of the illicitness of its object. Indeed, following the submissions of the defendant – contested by claimant – the main purpose of the Agreement was to influence the price of the Project, to which the defendant competed, by illegal means. Therefore, the Agreement was immoral per se and its object was illicit. Accordingly, the arbitral tribunal should dismiss the claim on jurisdictional grounds so as not to support a contract which is contrary to public policy and moral standards.

6. "For these reasons, defendant concludes that the arbitral tribunal dismiss the claim by a preliminary award.

7. "The arbitrators do not share the views underlying defendant's conclusion. They admit that the arbitration clause included in Sect. 11 of the Agreement, is deficient in the linguistic sense. Nevertheless, they are satisfied that Sect. 11 shows in a sufficiently clear manner the parties' intention to submit their disputes resulting from the Agreement to icc-arbitration. Indeed, no other reasonable meaning can be deduced from the wording of sentences 2 and 3 of Sect. 11. This conclusion would be reached by applying Swiss Law as well as the law of country X (as the possible leges contractus) or Austrian Law (as the lex fori). In accordance with these laws, for the interpretation of contractual clauses (including agreements to arbitrate) the clear intention of the parties has to prevail over an incorrect or unprecise wording. Contrary to defendant's submission, this interpretation, based on the investigation of the real intention of the parties, has nothing to do with extensive or restrictive interpretation.

8. "On the other hand, the question of validity or nullity of the main contract, for reasons of public policy, illegality or otherwise, is one of merits and not of jurisdiction, the validity of the arbitration clause having to be considered separately from the validity of the main contract (see Art. 8(4) icc Rules).[1]

9. "Notwithstanding the fact that § II of the Terms of Reference indicated that a decision on the applicable law must precede any preliminary decision on jurisdiction, having concluded that the agreement to arbitrate would stand under any one of the possibly applicable laws or any combination thereof, the arbitral tribunal reserves judgment as to the applicable law or laws to a later date. This preliminary award respecting jurisdiction is consistent with such deferral and should not be considered to have any bearing on the issue of governing law."

Second Interim Award
10. In the second interim award, the arbitrators first dealt with the law applicable to the substance. The claimant contended it to be Swiss Law, whilst defendant asserted it to be the law of country X.

---

1. Art. 8(4) of the icc Rules provides:
   "Unless otherwise provided, the arbitrator shall not cease to have jurisdiction by reason of any claim that the contract is null and void or allegation that it is inexistent provided that he upholds the validity of the agreement to arbitrate. He shall continue to have jurisdiction, even though the contract itself may be inexistent or null and void, to determine the respective rights of the parties and to adjudicate upon their claims and pleas."

11. The arbitrators observed:

> "The principle of autonomy – widely recognized – allows the parties to choose any law to rule their contract, even if not obviously related with. (See: Vischer – von Planta, *Internationales Privatrecht* 2 (1982) pp. 174 and 175; footnote 30, p. 174).

12. "This is what the parties have done in mentioning Swiss Law, although at first sight less related with the Agreement than the law of country X. Such mention of Swiss Law in first place (before the law of country X) is in this respect an important indication.

13. "Moreover, Swiss Law constitutes a highly sophisticated system of law, which answers all the questions that may arise from the interpretation or fulfilment of an agreement of the kind of the one entered into.

14. "On the other hand, the law of country X, might partially or totally affect the validity of the Agreement.

15. "It is then reasonable to assume that from two possible laws, the parties would choose the law which would uphold the validity of the Agreement.

16. "It is also a general and widely recognized principle that from two legal solutions, the judge will choose the one which favours the validity of an agreement (*favor negotii*).

17. "In these circumstances, the arbitrators definitely decided to choose Swiss Law as the applicable law, assuming that this choice corresponds to what the parties had in mind by inserting the above mentioned provision in Art. 11 of the Agreement.

18. "(There is no reason to envisage the cumulative application of both Swiss Law and the law of country X to the Agreement, such solution being rejected by most of the authors; Vischer – von Planta, op. cit. p. 174)."

19. The arbitral tribunal then considered the issue of the validity and enforceability of the Agreement. Defendant contended that the Agreement was null and void because of bribery and extortion.

20. With respect to the issue of bribery, the arbitrators reasoned:

> "The defendant has insisted that the Agreement was an agreement for bribery or was abused by the claimant for bribery. The claimant denied such allegation, stating that the Agreement was a consultancy agreement.

21. "This question has to be solved by trying to interpret the real intention of the parties, according to Art. 18 of the Swiss Code des Obligations (CO) which says:

> '(1) As regards both the form and content of a contract, the real intent which is mutually agreed upon shall be considered, and not an incorrect statement or method of expression used by the parties, whether due to error, or with the intention of concealing the true nature of the contract.

'(2). . . .'

22. "According to this provision, interpretation means trying to find the real intention of the parties, beyond the words used in their agreement.

23. "Circumstances prior and contemporary to the agreement as well as posterior to the agreement – especially the way parties have fulfilled their obligations – have to be taken into consideration (Becker, *Berner Kommentar VI, Obligationenrecht. Allgemeine Bestimmungen* (Art. 1–183 OR) 2 (1941/45), ad Art. 18 CO, p. 70 et seq.; Engel, *Traité des obligations en droit suisse. Dispositions générales du CO* (1973), p. 165 et seq., especially p. 169; Jäggy-Gauch, *Zürcher Kommentar. Obligationenrecht* (1980), ad Art. 18 CO, no. 308, p. 79; ATF 95, 1969 II p. 320, 326).

24. "It is obvious that if the said Agreement were an agreement for bribery, it would be null and void, according to Art. 20 CO, which states:

'(1) A contract providing for an impossibility, having illegal contents, or violating bonos mores, is null and void.

'(2) . . .'

25. "Bribery is considered as immoral (*contra bonos mores*) in Swiss law (Heritier, '*Les pots de vin*', p. 104 et seq., especially p. 106 and 111; Engel, op. cit., p. 202 ad c).

26. "It must be stressed that nullity implies that *both parties* agree on the immoral purpose to be achieved or on the immoral means to be used in order to achieve a certain result (Von Tuhr, *Partie générale du Code Fédéral des Obligations*, 2 (1933/34), pp. 224–225; Engel, op. cit., p. 205; various decisions of the Federal Court quoted ad Art. 20 – footnote c, p. 12 of the Swiss Code des Obligations annoté par Scyboz et Gilliéron, 1983).

27. "The defendant's accusation is not supported by direct evidence or even circumstantial evidence to be retained as convincing.

28. "In this respect, it must be stressed that, following general principles of interpretation (also recognized in Swiss Law; see ad Art. 8 Code Civil Suisse; ATF 105 III 43; ATF 74, p.202; 90 p. 227; 104 p. 68, 216) a fact can be considered as proven even by the way of circumstantial evidence. However, such circumstantial evidence must lead to a very high probability.

29. "This is not the case in the present litigation:
 – The Agreement obviously does not mention any bribery;
 – Mr. A – the own defendant's principal witness – who was the man who signed the Agreement on behalf of defendant and with whom it was essentially discussed, categorically denied that any bribery was ever intended (three times: 'No').

His declaration is of the utmost importance if one considers that Mr. A's declarations had been carefully prepared in advance (see his Affidavit drafted in defendant's counsel office in Paris) and that it was decisive for the defendant's thesis that the answer to such a question would be: 'Yes'.

– The way the relations between defendant and the Ministry developed does not really support the idea of a bribery.

30. "The final price of the contract was certainly higher than the original price of defendant's bid, but it has been shown (both parties' declarations match on this point) that there has been a constant upgrading of the initial project, so that the final price for which the contract was awarded to defendant, was not at all due to a sheer increase in the price, without counterpart – which would certainly have been suspect – but to a considerable increase in quantity and quality of the work offered by defendant in its first bid.

31. "Moreover, the file shows that the final price mentioned by defendant after constant upgrading of the Project, was [equivalent to US$415 million] and that the Ministry cut it down to [equivalent of US$374 million], which is a considerable reduction, hardly understandable under the assumption that the Ministry would be bribed on money obtained by the claimants from the difference between the basic price and the 'increased price'.

32. "The Project was from the beginning (and the claimant knew it: see confidential correspondence from Mr. B's correspondence file) under the constant supervision of the World Bank team and of the committee of the Ministry. It would have been a very hazardous enterprise to start bribing all these people or to bribe only part of them. The granting of the Agreement on abnormal conditions would certainly have raised the suspicion of the unbribed.

(. . . .)

33. "The fact that the claimant has obviously not rendered the considerable amount of work it claims to have performed is also not a sufficient ground to conclude that the Agreement was in reality an agreement for bribery.

34. "The implication of this fact will be examined underneath, as well as the implication of Art. 10(3) of the Agreement which is certainly not quite compatible with a consultancy agreement but which certainly does not reflect any idea of bribery.

35. "The arbitrators are convinced that various circumstances lead to the conclusion that the Agreement, is not only a consultancy agreement – as they will explain underneath – but do not find sufficient reasons to arrive at the conclusion it was an agreement for bribery.

36. "In this respect, it must be once more pointed out that, according to Swiss Law, an agreement is null and void only if both parties agree on bribery, which has been clearly denied by defendant's own principal witness, Mr. A."

37. With respect to the issue of extortion, the arbitrators reasoned:

"As already mentioned above (with regard to the letters attributed to Mr. C, claimant's principal representative), there is no material evidence that defendant would have been the victim of an extortion.

38. "Moreover, the accusation of extortion is absolutely incompatible with the acknowledgement that ' . . . full services' had been rendered and with the telex of congratulation sent by defendant [see Facts, above].

39. "One does not imagine someone being threatened into paying US$50,000,000 and thanking heartily the author of the threat for the result achieved.

40. "On the other hand, one knows that defendant was ready to enter into new agreements with the claimant and with other companies related with it, long after having paid US$50,000,000. An attitude which is also not understandable from a company which would have been the victim of an extortion.

41. "Eventually, it must be pointed out that, according to Swiss law (Arts. 29 and 31 CO), such threat would not directly affect the validity of an agreement but would give to the victim the possibility of invalidating the agreement within one year, which defendant never did.

42. "Art. 29 states that:

'(1) Where a contracting party has been unlawfully forced to conclude a contract while under duress, whether originating from the other party or a third person, the party acting under duress is not bound by the contract.

'(2) . . . .

43. "Art. 31 CO states:

'(1) If the party influenced by error, deception or threat fails, within one year, to declare to the other party that he is not bound by the contract, or fails to demand restitution, then the contract is deemed to be ratified.

'(2) Such period runs, in the event of error or deception, from the time of its discovery, and in the event of threat, from the time of its removal.

'(3) . . . .' "

44. Thereafter, the arbitral tribunal determined the object of the Agreement as follows:

45. "As the parties disagree on the real object of the Agreement, the arbitral tribunal is compelled to determine the true intention of the parties, according to the principles stated in Art. 18 CO already quoted.

46. "The arbitral tribunal will do so by analysing the very nature of the Agreement and then by examining the various circumstances, among which the way the Agreement was fulfilled by both parties.

47. "(A) *The Agreement.* If one carefully reads the Agreement, one finds various elements which imply that the said Agreement is not a sheer consultancy agreement as it appears to be at first sight.

- *Article 2*
  The Company defendant hereby appoints . . . for the promoting and *contracting* of the Projects to the Customers (the Ministry). . . .
- *Same Article, paragraph 2*
  . . . any increase in the (base price) because of the Consultant's efforts
  . . . .
- *Article 5*
  According to which the Consultant is paid on a contingency basis, which means his compensation depends on a result: the granting of the Project to defendant.
- *Article 10(3)*
  Such waiving of the normal defendant's rights is incompatible with an agreement the sole object of which would be consultancy services.
- Claimant's affirmation in its first Memorandum (30 April 1981) according to which they succeeded in getting a better price.

48. "These elements convey by themselves the strong impression that the Agreement was not intended to be a sheer consultancy agreement, but also an intermediary or brokerage agreement, which, as such, would not be invalid under Swiss Law as it will be set out later.

49. "(B) *Other elements confirming the existence of an intermediary or brokerage agreement, among which the way the Agreement was fulfilled by both parties.* Certain services were undoubtedly performed by the claimant, of a nature which fits with the notion of consultancy services and with the notion of mandate, as stated in Art. 394 CO. The said article has the following content:
    '(1) By accepting a mandate, the agent is obligated to carry out the contractually agreed business transactions or services with which he has been entrusted.
    '(2) . . . .
    '(3) . . . .'

50. "These services have been already described and are the following:
    - Day to day services
    - Financial assistance
    - Assistance in preparing the negotiations with the Ministry
    - Site surveys."

51. At an earlier stage in the interim award the arbitral tribunal has determined that these services consisted of the following:

52. *Day to day services*: Several of claimant's witnesses asserted that claimant's companies or their employees had rendered numerous small services such as typing, translations, messengers' services, and general administrative services. Defendant had not denied these services, but qualified them as insignificant. However, one of defendant's principal witnesses had admitted that defendant needed assistance, its own official agent having done nothing on the day to day work. The arbitral tribunal stated to be "satisfied that certain services of the alleged kind having been rendered."

53. *Financial assistance*: Claimant had provided defendant with a US$1 million loan in order to help it overcome a transitory liquidity problem in 1979. Furthermore, claimant had assisted in obtaining an advance payment guarantee of US$20 million.

54. Assistance in preparing negotiations with the Ministry: Although defendant contested having obtained any assistance, the arbitral tribunal found that Mr. A, at the relevant time defendant's chief executive in country X, had admitted in his testimony having made copies of tape recordings of the meetings with the Ministry and having them handed over to claimant in order to get their help. He had also admitted that during the tender period he had frequent contacts with Mr. C, claimant's principal representative (once or twice monthly, generally after the meetings with the Ministry). The arbitral tribunal concluded that it was "satisfied that claimant assisted defendant in preparing the meetings with the Ministry".

55. Site surveys: Defendant contested that any services of that kind had been rendered by claimant. From the tape recordings with the Ministry it resulted that defendant's representatives were not aware of the soil conditions. The arbitral tribunal considered: "Under these circumstances, the arbitral tribunal believes it to be probable that claimant's companies performed at least some superficial soil inspections for the defendant".

56. The arbitral tribunal continued its considerations regarding the determination of the object of the Agreement as follows:

57. "It has been already explained that claimant had failed to bring evidence of the other important services it pretended to have rendered, especially the technical services.

58. "It is then hardly understandable that defendant would have been ready to pay US$50,000,000 for 'full services' rendered, that is for the limited services enumerated above.

59. "In the same line, it is hardly conceivable that defendant would have taken the trouble to send Mr. C. [claimant's principle representative] a telegram (that is three days after the Agreement was signed with the Ministry) expressing defendant's . . . sincere thanks on your excellent effort'.

60. "Under the circumstances, this could only mean that the effort exerted by claimant had permitted the award of the contract to defendant.

61. "Taking into consideration that the sole consultancy services rendered by claimant were not of a nature to achieve alone such a result, arbitrators are led to the conclusion that defendant was referring to some other activity – that is convincing the Ministry and/or the World Bank team to deal with defendant, better than with other competitors. Consequently, the Agreement concluded by the parties, was intended to be more than a consultancy agreement. It obviously was also an intermediary agreement.

62. "Claimant did certainly enjoy excellent connections with the Ministry and/or the World Bank's experts that enabled it to provide the defendant with important informations and to exert a certain influence on the decision to be taken.

(. . . .)

63. "It is also significant that before Mr. A. met Mr. C., claimants were not at all sure to get the contract from the Ministry as they recognized it

themselves. After Mr. A. had met Mr. C. and the Agreement was signed things changed very quickly and defendant remained as the only candidate, the Ministry having rejected the other competitors, among which the Korean firm Z. (as mentioned by Mr. A. himself).

64. "It is interesting to consider that the defendant admits the idea of an intermediary agreement (adding that bribery was intended, which was not evidenced) and that the claimant itself indirectly acknowledge its existence in producing (with its last Memorandum) a legal opinion on commission in intermediary agreements and in having tried to convince by any means, the arbitral tribunal that the intended Agreement was only a consultancy agreement, for the obvious reason it feared that the Court might apply the law of country X to an intermediary agreement, with the consequence that it might be invalid. In the same line, one has to consider the claimant's insistence to have Swiss Law applicable, which does not contain the same restrictive provisions concerning intermediary agreements as the law of country X does.

65. "According to Swiss Law, an intermediary agreement is perfectly valid, even if the foreseen contract is to be concluded with a public corporation (see, for instance, decision of the Federal Court, JT 1951, p. 491 et seq., which concerns an intermediary agreement involving the Town of Zurich).

66. "The intermediary agreement is ruled, in Swiss Law, by Art. 412 et seq. CO. It is a kind of agreement which is generally submitted to the rules of mandate.

"Art. 412 states:

'(1) A brokerage contract is an agreement whereby the broker is granted a mandate to provide against compensation an opportunity to conclude a contract or to act as an intermediary thereto.

'(2) In general, the brokerage contract is subject to the provisions governing the ordinary mandate.'"

Final award
  (a) *Causal nexus*
67. Having qualified the Agreement in the words of the arbitrators "as being mainly an intermediary agreement on a contingency basis", defendant contended that, even assuming that the Agreement is to be considered as such, claimant was not instrumental to the awarding of the Project and in particular of the extension.

68. The arbitral tribunal rejected this contention:

"The first premise of that contention is contradicted by defendant's chairman's congratulatory telex and by defendant's letter to the Bank (see the Facts above). While these relate only to the awarding of the Project, the award of the extension was a consequence of the award of the Project. Generally speaking, the extension, negotiated between defendant and the Ministry and awarded to the former in 1980, was considered by both parties to be an extension of the Project (see the language of the Amendment).

69. "Moreover, some ancillary services were rendered by claimant to defendant even after the award of the initial Project, e.g. securing the US$1 million loan (see the Second Interim Award, nrs. 52–55 above).

70. "Therefore, the arbitral tribunal has satisfied itself of the existence of a causal link between the activities of the intermediary and the award of the projects to the extent required by Art. 413 CO.[2] According to that provision, the causal nexus exists as soon as some influence has been exerted on the decision, even though such influence might be indirect and/or accessory (see ATF 76, 378)."

(b) Compensation for initial contract

71. Defendant contended that the US$50 million was in full settlement of any compensation due on the initial contract, claimant being therefore barred from any further claim in this regard. Claimant asserted that the payment of US$50 million was provisional or only on account.

72. One of claimant's arguments was that the accounting document made in 1979 contained no waiver language evidencing claimant's intention to waive any further claim. The arbitral tribunal stated that "it is true that in case of doubt, the waiver of a claim is not to be presumed". It found, however, that the accounting document made in 1979 was sufficiently clear to demonstrate both sides' intentions: it was headed "final offer" (of US$50 million) which was "confirmed" and "accepted and acknowledged" by claimant.

73. Another argument of claimant was that defendant's letter to the bank in Geneva written the same day as the accounting document read: "If the contract awarded to us is increased or decreased, the attached calculations will be revised accordingly". The arbitral tribunal found that this language merely related to a possible extension of the contract.

74. For the foregoing and some other reasons, the arbitral tribunal rejected claimant's claim for further compensation regarding the initial contract (i.e., US$7 million).

(c) Compensation for extension

75. The arbitral tribunal then turned to the claim for compensation for the extension which as mentioned under Facts above was divided into "new items" and "BOQ Works". It noted that notwithstanding the considerable amount of – partly contested, partly contradictory – documents and the divergent explanations given by both sides' expert witnesses, made it impossible to establish true or even reliable figures to be used in the computation of compensation.

76. With respect to the "new items", the arbitral tribunal concluded for various reasons (mainly because of a failure of proof by both parties) that they must be

---

2. Art. 413 of the Swiss Code of Obligations provides:
   "1. The broker is entitled to compensation from the moment when the indication which he had provided or the negotiations which he has conducted result in the conclusion of a contract.
   "2. When the contract has been concluded under a suspensive condition the compensation is not to be paid until the condition has been fulfilled.
   "3. If it has been agreed that the expenses incurred by the broker shall be reimbursed to him, he shall be entitled to them, even when the contract has not been concluded."

deemed to have generated no profit and no losses with which the agreed compensation was linked. Hence, no compensation was held to be due for the "new items".

77. As for the "BOQ Works", the arbitral tribunal found that there had been a profit. However, the tribunal would not accept the profit as calculated by claimant (i.e., 50%) on the basis of which the compensation was to be calculated. The arbitral tribunal reasoned:

78. "[If] the original formula would produce a disproportionately high remuneration for claimant, and a disproportionately severe deprivation for the defendant, the arbitral tribunal must address two possibilities: either the parties did not contemplate this development or they did contemplate it. In both cases, Swiss Law provides an explicit remedy.

79. "As to the first possibility, *clausula rebus sic stantibus,* originally based on Art. 373 CO,[3] implies the following conditions: a very important change of circumstances; unforeseen by the parties; such as to destroy the economy of the contract, that is to render the execution of the contract excessively hard for one of the parties (ATF 104, 314). These conditions are fulfilled in the present matter and the judge is entitled to proceed to correct the contract.

80. "As to the second possibility, the same result is required even when the change was arguably foreseen by the parties. According to Swiss Law, the party whose interests are jeopardized by the change of circumstances can rely on Art. 2(2) CCS,[4] even if it has expressly or implicitly renounced the right to an adaptation of the contract. The judge will refuse a compensation that would appear as abusive in the light of the change of circumstances. The judge is authorized to proceed to a correction of the contract to take into account such change of circumstances. This is certainly the case here for the above mentioned reasons. It would be abusive for claimant to insist on getting an extremely high compensation disproportionate to the real profit accrued from BOQ Works.

81. "These problems have been thoroughly studied by recent authors, among others Schönle, in *Le Centenaire du Code des obligations,* édition universitaire, Fribourg, 1982 p. 436 et seq. See also Deschenaux: *Traité de droit civil suisse; le titre préliminaire du Code civil,* p. 190 et seq. with references to court decisions: *Le dépassement du risque objectivement imputable.*

---

3. Art. 373 of the Swiss Code of Obligations provides:
   "1. In case a contract price has been fixed, the contractor must perform the work for the fixed amount; he will not be permitted to claim a higher amount even if more work or costs were involved then were anticipated.
   "2. Nevertheless, if the execution of the contract has been rendered impossible or excessively difficult due to extraordinary unforeseeable circumstances or circumstances excluded by agreement of the parties, the court can, on the basis of its own evaluation, allow either an increase in the fixed price or the cancellation of the contract.
   "3. The principal shall pay the full price even if less work was involved than was anticipated."
4. Art. 2(2) of the Swiss Civil Code provides:
   "A manifest abuse of rights is not protected by the law."

82. "In view of these observations, the arbitral tribunal will correct the Agreement of the parties by applying trade usages that are relevant (see also Art. 13(5) of the Rules of the ICC).[5] For most contracts for which a tariff has been issued, the rates applicable in Switzerland are generally in the range of 2 to 5%. This is the case for instance for the rates of commission applicable in Geneva and Vaud for brokerage concerning the sale of real property. The Federal Court has recognized that commission rates for brokerage concerning the sale of real properties fluctuate between 2 and 5% (see ATF 90 II 107, ad 417 CO). The agent commission is also limited by statute to 5% in country X.

83. "The same result is achieved by using a completely different approach based on Art. 417 CO.[6] That provision requires the judge, in certain contracts, to reduce the agreed compensation when it appears to be excessive. As already explained, the Federal Court has recognized a rate of 2 to 5% as usual. It has judged that a rate of 11% was absolutely excessive (ATF 83 II 153).

84. "Art. 417 CO is normally applicable to sales of real property and labour contracts, but an analogical application to other kinds of contracts is possible. The ratio legis of Art. 417 CO is a public policy seeking to prevent the prices of real property from being increased excessively by disproportionate brokerage commissions and to prevent workers from having to face excessive claims from brokers after getting the jobs they sought. Swiss courts have, on certain occasions, analogized 417 CO to other kinds of contracts: e.g. an architect who got a job through a broker as well as an emphyteotic lease.

85. "The arbitral tribunal is convinced that analogical application of Art. 417 CO would be justified in the present case. It is clear that an excessive commission would cause the prices of buildings and real properties to be artificially increased, which is undesirable from a social point of view, whether one considers future transactions between private persons or even the impact of an excessive commission of the costs of buildings erected by the State for social purposes. . . .

86. "Although the compensation is, in a brokerage agreement, based on the result achieved and not on the efforts of the broker, this aspect of the problem is not completely put aside by Swiss courts' decisions (see ATF 90 II 107).

87. "Taking into account these various elements, including the fact that the awarding of the extension required less efforts than the awarding of the main contract, the arbitral tribunal fixes claimant's remuneration at a rate of 4% on [the equivalent of US$40 million] which equals [the equivalent of US$1.5 million)."

---

5. Art. 13(5) of the ICC Rules provides:
   "In all cases the arbitrator shall take account of the provisions of the contract and the relevant trade usages."
6. Art. 417 of the Swiss Code of Obligations provides:
   "When an excessive compensation has been agreed to, either for providing the opportunity to conclude an individual labour contract or the sale of real property, or for having negotiated such a contract, this compensation may, upon request by the debtor, be reduced by the court according to equity."

Interim Award of 1985 in case no. 4650

Arbitrators: Dr. Robert Briner (Switz.) chairman; René Merkt (Switz.); Thomas
R. A. Morison, QC (UK)

Parties: Claimant: American architect
                    Respondent: Saudi Arabian company

Published in: Unpublished

Subject matters: – law applicable to substance
                   – direct choice of law
                   – *lex mercatoria*
                   – trade usages

FACTS
In 1976 the parties concluded two agreements (Service Phase I and Service
Phase II) which basically involved the preparation by claimant of drawings and
other related construction documents as well as an involvement in connection
with negotiations with potential contractors regarding a building project in
Jeddah, Saudi Arabia. The parties agreed on ICC arbitration to take place in
Geneva. No choice of law was expressed in the agreements.

When a dispute arose about the amount of the fee, claimant commenced
arbitration. Defendant made a counterclaim for alleged overpayment. By a final
award rendered in 1986, the arbitrators dismissed both the claim and the
counterclaim.

The interim award was rendered in 1985. It dealt with the question of which law
was applicable to the substance.

The claimant contended that this law should be the law of the State of Georgia,
USA, as all significant work provided under the agreements was carried out
there. Claimant submitted in the alternative that Swiss substantive law, being
the *lex fori,* or, possibly, the *lex mercatoria* should apply. Finally, claimant
relied on "analogous international rules regarding the provision of engineering
services which suggest that the law of the place of domicile of the engineer
rather than of the employer will govern the legal relations between the parties,
in the absence of any express agreement to the contrary".

Defendant submitted that Saudi Arabian law should be applied because
claimant's obligations were partly performed in Georgia and partly in Saudi
Arabia, whilst defendant's obligations were to be wholly performed in Saudi
Arabia. Moreover, under the Service Phase II Agreement, claimant's obligations
were all to be performed in Saudi Arabia. With regard to trade usages,
defendant contended that there exist no such usages which have any direct
bearing on the provision of architectural services by an American architect for a
project in Saudi Arabia. Finally, defendant submitted that neither Swiss
substantive law nor the *lex mercatoria* should be applied.

The arbitrators held that the law of the State of Georgia applied for the reasons reproduced below.

EXTRACT

1. "It is not disputed that the parties did not make an express choice of law in their agreement.

2. "Based on the evidence presented to the arbitral tribunal the question of the governing law did not appear to have been discussed between the parties and it would seem obvious that no tacit agreement or understanding had been reached. In the absence of any evidence regarding an actual agreement or concurrent intentions of the parties, the arbitral tribunal is of the opinion that one cannot consider that the parties had chosen Swiss substantive law or the *lex mercatoria*. It would seem to the arbitral tribunal that the choice of such a law would require an agreement between the parties which in the present case was not reached.

3. "Based on the evidence produced by the parties regarding the services which claimant was to render under the agreement there can be no doubt that the work needed to render such services was predominantly performed in Georgia. Occasional visits for fact finding and liaison purposes by representatives of the claimant to Saudi Arabia do not shift the centre of the characteristic work from Georgia to Saudi Arabia. The bulk and characteristic part of the work of the claimant, for which an amount of 5,135,997 Saudi Rials was paid, was, the tribunal finds, carried out and performed in Georgia, USA.

4. "The arbitral tribunal does not deem it necessary in this case to decide on a specific rule of conflict to designate the proper law of the contract in view of the fact that most major rules in some form or other point to the place of the characteristic or dominant work and that in the opinion of the arbitral tribunal there can be no doubt that the dominant or characteristic work performed under the agreement was performed in Georgia, USA.

5. "The arbitral tribunal notes that a decision in favour of the laws of the State of Georgia would be consistent with international rules regarding the provision of engineering services.

6. "The arbitral tribunal holds that it does not have to examine the hypothetical case of what would have been the applicable law if Service Phase II had been carried out. It is not disputed that the parties deliberately chose to provide for two separate agreements regarding the involvement of the claimant in the project and it is furthermore not disputed that Phase II was never commenced and that the parties have, at least in this arbitration, not alleged that there exist any obligations or liabilities arising from the Service Phase II Agreement. In view of these facts, the arbitral tribunal is not persuaded that the same governing law would necessarily apply to the two Service Phase Agreements. Accordingly, what might have been the governing law of the Service Phase II Agreement cannot constitute a sound basis for determining the issue which the tribunal is called upon to decide. There is no doubt that the various conflict of law rules take into consideration to a

68

considerable extent the actual facts and the characteristic work actually carried out under the contracts. In view of the fact that no Service Phase II work was performed, the arbitral tribunal only needs to take into consideration the actual facts of the case and not potential future activities governed by a separate agreement which were never carried out."

Interim Award of 16 July 1986 in case no. 5029

Arbitrators: Loek J. Malmberg (Neth.) chairman; Sir Charles Fletcher-Cooke, QC (UK); Dr. Mohammed Zaazoue (Egypt)

Parties: Claimant: French contractor
Defendant: Egyptian employer

Published in: 3 International Construction Law Review (1986) Pp. 473–476 (portions regarding time-bar under Clause 67)

Subject matters: – law applicable to arbitration
– international contract
– reference to the ICC in arbitration clause
– legal nature of joint venture
– power of attorney of lawyer
– capacity of party to commence arbitration
– Clause 67 FIDIC and time-bar

FACTS

In 1981 a joint venture called X consisting of the French company A, its 100% French subsidiary B, and two Egyptian companies, C and D, entered into a contract with an Egyptian entity for the construction of certain civil works in Egypt. The contract incorporated the FIDIC conditions (3d edition 1977). Clause 67 of these conditions provides for a two-tier system for resolving disputes: disputes have first to be referred to the Engineer and, if a party is dissatisfied with the Engineer's decision, he can submit the dispute to ICC arbitration.

Following the rejection of a number of claims by the Engineer, the French company A and its subsidiary B filed a request for arbitration against the Egyptian employer in 1984. The place of arbitration was determined by the ICC Court of Arbitration to be The Hague.

The Egyptian defendant objected to the jurisdiction of the Arbitral Tribunal on a number of grounds. By an interim award of 16 July 1986 the Arbitral Tribunal rejected the jurisdictional defences (the Egyptian arbitrator dissenting).

EXTRACT

A. *Law governing the arbitration*

1. Art. 5(1)(*b*) of the Contract provided:

> "The Contract shall be deemed to be an Egyptian Contract and shall be governed by and construed according to the laws in force in Egypt."

2. "Defendant claimed that the law governing the arbitration proceedings is Egyptian civil procedural law. He argued that the choice of law clause, quoted above, covered not only substantive law aspects but also procedural ones, including arbitration. According to defendant in a letter received by the Secretariat of the Court of Arbitration, the text of Clause 67 of the Contract 'clearly expressed the intention of the parties that arbitration is a local arbitration and not international' and 'that it is internal and not external'. Defendant further asserted that the foregoing is not altered by Art. 11 of the ICC Rules.[1]

3. "Whilst claimant agreed with defendant that Egyptian law rules of interpretation should be applied, claimant asserted that the parties intended to agree and in fact did agree to an international, external arbitration under the auspices of the International Chamber of Commerce in view of various foreign elements connected with the contract. Claimant further contended that a distinction, made in all systems of law, must be made between substantive law and procedural law. The former is governed by the law chosen by the parties (i.e., Egyptian law), whilst the latter is governed by the mandatory provisions of the arbitration law of the place of arbitration, i.e., Dutch arbitration law."

4. The arbitral tribunal reasoned:

> "The choice of law clause contained in Art. 5(1)(*b*) of the Contract means that the Contract must be interpreted in accordance with the rules of contract interpretation of Egyptian law, in particular Arts. 150 et seq. of the Egyptian Civil Code.[2] The Arbitral Tribunal will follow these rules of interpretation in respect of all the jurisdictional issues.

5. "The Arbitral Tribunal holds that the law governing the arbitration is the arbitration law of the Netherlands. The Arbitral Tribunal notes at the outset that the Contract is a truly international contract involving parties of different

---

1. Art. 11 of the ICC Rules provides:
"The rules governing the proceedings before the arbitrator shall be those resulting from these Rules and, where these Rules are silent, any rules which the parties (or, failing them, the arbitrator) may settle, and whether or not reference is thereby made to a municipal procedural law to be applied to the arbitration."
2. Art. 150 of the Egyptian Civil Code provides:
"When the wording of a contract is clear, it cannot be deviated from in order to ascertain by means of interpretation the intention of the parties.

"When a contract has to be construed, it is necessary to ascertain the common intention of the parties and to go beyond the literal meaning of the words, taking into account the nature of the transaction as well as that loyalty and confidence which should exist between the parties in accordance with commercial usage."

nationalities (i.e., French and Egyptian), the movement of equipment and services across national frontiers, and the payment in different currencies (i.e., Egyptian Pounds and US Dollars). The international character of the Contract is inconsistent with the defendant's allegation that the parties intended to provide for domestic, internal (i.e., Egyptian) arbitration. Such intent cannot be derived from the choice of law clause contained in Art. 5(1)(*b*) of the Contract, providing for the applicability of Egyptian law, whilst Clause 67, providing for arbitration under the Rules of the ICC, clearly expresses the contrary. As it is recognized in virtually all legal systems around the world, a basic distinction must be made between the law governing the substance and the law governing the procedure. That distinction is also recognized in Egyptian conflict of laws: whereas Art. 19 of the Egyptian Civil Code provides for the law governing the substance of the dispute, Art. 22 is concerned with the law governing the procedure. Accordingly, if the parties had wished that the arbitration be governed by Egyptian procedural law, they should have made a specific agreement thereon. Art. 5(1)(*b*) of the Contract is not such a provision as it does not mention specifically that arbitration is governed by Egyptian law. Failing such agreement, the arbitration law of the place governs the arbitration. This principle is in accordance with Art. V(1)(*a*), (*d*) and (*e*) of the New York Convention of 1958 to which Egypt and the Netherlands have adhered. See also Prof. Moshen Chafik, 'National Report Egypt', in IV *Yearbook Commercial Arbitration*, 1979, p. 44 at p. 50 and pp. 53–54.

6. "The agreement of the parties to arbitration under the Rules of the International Chamber of Commerce in Clause 67 meant that, failing their agreement on the place of arbitration, they gave, under Art. 12 of the Rules, a mandate to the Court of Arbitration to fix the place of arbitration on their behalf. It is to be noted that defendant itself proposed in the alternative The Hague as the place of arbitration (see letter received by the Secretariat of the Court of Arbitration on 10 August 1984, p. 3 sub no. 8). The prevailing interpretation of the Rules of the ICC nowadays is also that the mandatory provisions of the arbitration law of the place of arbitration govern the arbitration, irrespective of the law governing the substance. Whereas Art. 13(3) of the Rules contains the contractual conflict of laws rules for determining the law governing the substance of the dispute, Art. 11 is concerned with the rules governing the proceedings. In respect of the latter provision, it is stated in *Guide to Arbitration* (ICC Publication no. 382) p. 39:

> 'To make sure that the award will be enforceable at law, the mandatory rules of national law applicable to international arbitrations in the country where the arbitration takes place must anyway be observed, even if other rules of procedure are chosen by the parties or by the arbitrator.'

7. "The Arbitral Tribunal emphasizes that the applicability of Dutch arbitration law in the present case by no means implies that the Dutch rules concerning proceeding before Dutch State Courts are applicable. According to Dutch arbitration law, parties are free to agree on the rules of procedure and, failing such agreement, the arbitrator determines the conduct of the proceedings, subject to a few necessary mandatory provisions. See generally P. Sanders, 'National Report Netherlands', VI *Yearbook Commercial Arbitration*, 1981, p. 60 et seq.; *Arbitration Law in Europe* (Paris 1981) p. 277 et seq. By referring to the Rules of the International Chamber of Commerce, the parties have 'internationalized' the arbitration within this legal framework."

B. *Inadequate Reference to the ICC*

8. "The defendant contended that Clause 67 does not clearly refer to the Rules of the Paris International Chamber of Commerce as it only mentions the Rules of Conciliation and Arbitration of the International Chamber of Commerce. This text, according to defendant, is 'abstruse and unintelligible' because 'it does not tell which international Chamber of Commerce has the competence to settle the dispute, since there are, as it is well known, a large number of international chambers of commerce in the world'.

9. "Claimant took the view that the words of Clause 67 are 'absolutely unambiguous and clear'. To claimant's knowledge, there is only one International Chamber of Commerce, there exists only one set of 'Rules of Conciliation and Arbitration of the International Chamber of Commerce', and defendant has failed to submit proof of the contrary. Claimant also relied on the decision rendered in the ICC case no. 3460. Claimant further submitted that the omission of the word 'Paris' is entirely irrelevant. Finally, claimant argued, the drafting history of Clause 67 clearly demonstrates the parties' common intent that disputes would be referred to the International Chamber of Commerce with which it filed its Request for Arbitration. Claimant also questioned defendant's good faith in advancing these contentions."

10. The Arbitral Tribunal considered:

    "The Arbitral Tribunal does not have the slightest doubt that Clause 67 refers to the Rules of Conciliation and Arbitration of the International Chamber of Commerce having its registered offices in Paris. Arbitration under the Rules of the International Chamber of Commerce, being the leading institution in international arbitration as of its inception in 1923, is so well-known around the world, that a party cannot in all sincerity contend that a reference to it is 'abstruse and unintelligible', certainly not in a case where the reference is contained in a standard clause (i.e., Clause 67 of FIDIC) which clause is commonly used in international construction contracts and is in relevant part modelled after the standard clause recommended by the ICC itself. Defendant has failed to submit proof of its contention that 'there are, as it is well known, a large number of international chambers of commerce in the world'. The Arbitral Tribunal is not aware of any International Chamber of Commerce other than the one whose Court of Arbitration has appointed it under its 'Rules of Conciliation and Arbitration'.

11. "Claimant relies on the decision in ICC case no. 3460, reported in *Journal du Droit International,* 1981, p. 939. In that case the arbitration clause referred to the 'International Chamber of Commerce in Geneva'. The Arbitral Tribunal subscribes to the reasoning of the arbitrators in that case, who reached the conclusion that the words 'International Chamber of Commerce in Geneva' meant arbitration under the auspices of the International Chamber of Commerce having its registered offices in Paris. A fortiori, the reference in Clause 67 to the International Chamber of Commerce and its Rules of Conciliation and Arbitration means arbitration under the auspices of said International Chamber of Commerce.

12. "Defendant's contention that the arbitration clause in the present case should have specified 'in Paris' is misplaced. To the contrary, if Clause 67 had read

'International Chamber of Commerce in Paris' an ambiguity could have arisen as to whether the words 'in Paris' referred to the registered offices of the ICC or to an agreement of the parties as to the place of arbitration. Furthermore, the history of Clause 67's inclusion in the Contract clearly shows that defendant was fully aware of the meaning of arbitration under the auspices of the ICC and its Rules of Conciliation and Arbitration. In addition, ICC arbitration is well known in Egypt."

(. . . .)

C. *Claimant's Locus Standi*

13. As mentioned under *Facts* above, the Contractor was a joint venture called X consisting of the French company A, its 100% French subsidiary B, and two Egyptian companies C and D. The joint venture was based on a number of successive joint venture agreements which provided that the parties to the joint venture would be jointly and severally liable to the Employer. They further also contained provisions regarding the administration of the joint venture (supervisory board, the project manager, the site manager), financing, distribution of profit and losses, and termination. The French company A was appointed as leader of the joint venture and the project manager. In the Contract with the Employer, the Contractor was identified as "X joint venture of companies A, B, C and D". All four companies affixed their signature to the Contract.

14. Shortly after the request for arbitration was filed by the French company A and its subsidiary B in 1984, the latter terminated the joint venture agreement with respect to the Egyptian companies C and D for lack of financial contributions by these companies. The defendant contended that the Arbitral Tribunal had no jurisdiction because the French companies A and B lacked the capacity to commence the arbitration, both companies not having been specifically authorized to do so by the other partners of the joint venture.

15. Defendant argued more specifically:

"– The joint venture X is a mere contractual relationship between the companies A, B, C and D which does not constitute a separate entity enjoying legal personality nor a *Sharikat Al Mohassa* because the latter's existence was disclosed to defendant.[3]

"– In the relationship with defendant, the parties to the joint venture X are joint and several debtors of defendant under the Contract. To the extent that they are creditors of defendant under the Contract, they can only exercise their rights jointly, including the right to arbitrate claims against defendant. Consequently, in order for companies A and B to initiate arbitration proceedings against defendant under the Contract, they need a power of attorney from companies C and D, which must conform to the requirements of

---

3. *Editor's note.* A *Sharikat Al Mohassa* is a legal entity which may be compared with the Swiss *société simple* and the French *société en participation*.

Art. 702 of the Egyptian Civil Code.[4] Companies A and B do not possess such special mandate. If such special mandate was given at all, it was revoked or nullified by companies A and B terminating companies C and D as parties to the joint venture X."

16. Claimant denied defendant's contentions as follows:

"– The joint venture X is a contractual relationship between companies A, B, C and D, constituting a *Sharikat Al Mohassa* under Arts. 59–64 of the Egyptian Commercial Code.

"– A *Sharikat Al Mohassa* is not a legal person; however, vis-à-vis a third party to whom its existence is disclosed, the *Sharikat Al Mohassa* operates like a legal entity in terms of its management and representation.

"– In the case of joint venture X, whose existence was disclosed to defendant, company A was appointed as manager of joint venture X with full powers to represent joint venture X in any and all matters pertaining to the project, including arbitration of claims against defendant. Company A did not need a special mandate from companies C and D as mentioned in Art. 702 of the Egyptian Civil Code in order to commence the present arbitration.

"– Joint venture X was not dissolved as a *Sharikat Al Mohassa,* by company A expelling companies C and D from further participation. This was a mere internal matter, changing the internal relationship between the parties. Vis-à-vis defendant, joint venture X continued to exist as the Contractor under the Contract with company A remaining the only person authorized to represent joint venture X, also in the present arbitration.

"– The provisions of Art. 702 of the Egyptian Civil Code do not apply to international arbitration."

17. The Arbitral Tribunal rejected defendant's contentions for the following reasons:

"[A] preliminary remark concerns the distinction between a power of attorney for a lawyer to act on behalf of his client in an arbitration and the authorization of one party to act on behalf of another party in an arbitration.

18. "A power of attorney for a lawyer to act on behalf of his client in an arbitration is a matter pertaining to the procedural law of the forum, which, as observed before, is Dutch arbitration law. Dutch arbitration law does not require a power of attorney in a special form for a lawyer to act in an

---

4. Art. 702 of the Egyptian Civil Code provides:
"A special mandate, in respect of any act which is not an act of management, is required, and in particular for a sale, a mortgage, a gift, a compromise, an admission, an arbitration, the tendering of an oath and representation before the Courts.

"A special mandate to carry out a certain category of juridical acts is valid, save as regards gratuitous acts, even though the object of such acts is not specified.

"A special mandate only confers on the mandatary a power to act in matters specified therein and in matters necessarily incidental thereto in accordance with the nature of each matter and prevailing custom."

arbitration. In any case, company A did submit a power of attorney dated 10 December 1984, authorizing its lawyers to act on its behalf in the present arbitration. The power of attorney for a lawyer to act in an arbitration, therefore, is not at issue in the present arbitration.

19. "The authorization of one party to act on behalf of another party in an arbitration is a different matter. Here the question is whether one party can commence arbitration on behalf of another party in a case where the other party is also linked to the contract which forms the subject matter of the arbitration. That question must, in principle, be decided under the law governing the contract at issue. It is this question which constitutes claimant's *locus standi* issue.

(. . . .)

20. "Defendant's main argument for denying company A's capacity to initiate the present arbitration is that the four parties to joint venture X can exercise their rights only jointly, including the right to arbitrate claims, against defendant and that, consequently, company A needs a special mandate from companies C and D in accordance with the provisions of Art. 702 of the Egyptian Civil Code in order to represent these parties in the present arbitration.

21. "The Arbitral Tribunal cannot accept the point of view that the four parties to joint venture X are joint creditors of defendant under the Contract so that defendant can be sued upon its obligations under the Contract only by these four parties together. Such a joint creditorship of the four parties to joint venture X does not follow from any of the joint venture agreements entered into by them, nor from the Contract. To the contrary, Clause 9(2) of Part II of the conditions of Contract, which deals specifically with the case of two or more parties acting as the Contractor, provides that 'the receipt, signature or any other act whatsoever of each member in relation to the Contract shall bind every member', thus recognizing that any of the parties forming the Contractor may act individually.[5] In the respective joint venture agreements of 25 April 1980, 12 May 1980 and 31 December 1980, companies C and D agreed, *inter alia,* that they were to be represented by company A in matters pertaining to the Contract. Such an agreement creates an agency relationship and not an undertaking to exercise any rights arising under the Contract against defendant only jointly.

22. "The four parties to joint venture X not being joint creditors of defendant under the Contract, their creditorship must fall within one of the following categories of creditorship recognized by Egyptian law:

"(*a*) the four parties to joint venture X are joint and several creditors of defendant in accordance with the provisions of Art. 279 et seq. of the Egyptian Civil Code; or

---

5. The complete text of Clause 9(2) reads:
"In the case of two or more companies or persons acting as the Contractor under the Contract their liability shall be joint and several. No such member shall retire nor shall any new member be admitted without the prior written consent of the Employer. The Employer or the Engineer may validly deal with any of the said members as representing all of them, and the receipt, signature or any other act whatsoever of each member in relation to the Contract shall bind every member."

"(*b*) each of the four parties to joint venture X is an individual creditor of defendant and entitled to enforce the rights under the Contract for its share independently of the other parties; or

"(*c*) the four parties to joint venture X are co-creditors of defendant, whose obligations under the Contract are indivisible in accordance with the provisions of Art. 300 et seq. of the Egyptian Civil Code.

23. "Art. 279 of the Egyptian Civil Code provides under the heading 'Joint and Several Obligations':

'Solidarity between creditors or between debtors is not presumed. It is created by agreement or by law.'

"Since it is not possible to point to any law or agreement between the parties making them joint and several creditors in respect of defendant's obligations under the Contract, the possibility of joint and several creditorship (see sub (*a*), above) must be ruled out by the Arbitral Tribunal.

24. "As to the remaining possibilities mentioned sub (*b*) and (*c*), above, the Arbitral Tribunal holds that the four parties to joint venture X are co-creditors of defendant whose obligations under the Contract are indivisible for the following reasons.

25. "Art. 300 of the Egyptian Civil Code provides with respect to indivisible obligations:

'An obligation cannot be divided:
(. . . .)
(b) if it is the intention of the parties or it follows from the purpose pursued by the parties that the performance of the obligation should not be divided.'

"In the Arbitral Tribunal's view, it was the intention of defendant as the Employer and the four parties to joint venture X as the Contractor that the performance of the obligations of both the Contractor and the Employer under the Contract should not be divided.

26. "As to the Contractor's obligations, it was not intended by the parties that each of the four parties to joint venture X is to be responsible for the completion of a certain portion of the works under the Contract. To the contrary, the Contract stipulates that the four parties to joint venture X are – jointly and severally – responsible for the completion of the whole of the works to be carried out thereunder. Similarly, the obligations of the Employer under the Contract were intended to be indivisible. The Contract looks at the four parties to joint venture X as being *one* Contractor for the obligations to be fulfilled by the Employer under the Contract. It provides, for example, for delivery by the Employer of the whole of the site to the Contractor and not for delivery of a certain part of the site to each of the four parties to joint venture X (Clause 42(1) of Part I of the Conditions of Contract). Another example is that under the payment terms, the contract price is to be paid to the Contractor in its entirety in instalments and not in certain portions of each instalment to each of the four parties to joint venture X (Clause 60 of Part II of the Conditions of Contract).

27. "The intended indivisibility of the Employer's obligations under the Contract is further evidenced by Clause 9(2).[6] That clause lays down in the first sentence a joint and several liability of the parties forming the Contractor vis-à-vis Employer. Clause 9(2) stipulates in the third sentence that 'The Employer may validly deal with any of the said members *as representing all of them,* and the receipt, signature or *any other act whatsoever* of each member in relation to the Contract shall bind every member' (emphasis added). The very broad wording of this sentence – especially the words 'any other act whatsoever' – includes not only the Employer's rights, corresponding with joint and several obligations of the parties forming the Contractor, but also the Employer's obligations, corresponding with the rights of the parties forming the Contractor. When the Employer can validly deal with one of the members 'as representing all of them' in respect of the former's obligations, it means that the parties intended the Employer's obligations to be indivisible."

28. "Having established that the parties intended defendant's obligations to be indivisible under the Contract, the next question is whether claimant company A is entitled to demand performance thereof. Defendant argues that an indivisibility of an obligation does not mean that one of the co-creditors of such obligation can demand performance thereof. His expert gives in his opinion at page 3 the example of the sale of a car by (A) to (B) and (C). He states that there is an indivisible obligation on the part of (A) to deliver the car, whilst (B) and (C) may be committed by agreement jointly and severally to pay the price in instalments. Defendant's expert then states:

'While the obligation of the seller is indivisible in view of the nature of its object, the obligation of the purchasers is divisible but in the same time joint and several and coupled with a term. In the event of suing the seller to carry out his commitments following a divergence of views relating to the validity of the sale, the purchasers are to institute the proceedings together. None of them could represent the other neither under the rules of indivisibility of the obligation nor under the rules of their joint and several liability. In point of fact, such joint and several liability may give each of them a limited power to represent the other, only when he is sued as a co-debtor and only if and when his defense as debtor may procure a benefit for the two debtors.'

29. "Defendant's expert also maintains at pages 9–10 of his opinion that Art. 302 of the Egyptian Civil Code concerning the case of a plurality of creditors of an indivisible obligation is limited to liquidated and undisputed debts. Furthermore, according to defendant's expert, Art. 302 cannot be extended to damages (pages 10–11 of the opinion).

30. "Claimant argues that, considering the indivisibility of defendant's obligations under the Contract, claimant is entitled to submit to arbitration the Contractor's claims under the Contract by virtue of Arts. 300–302 of the Egyptian Civil Code. As regards the question whether Art. 302 is limited to liquidated and uncontested debts, claimant's expert states in his opinion at page 2:

'Not a single judicial decision or doctrinal opinion expressed by the authorities under Egyptian Law suggests that the applicability of Arts. 300–302 of the Egyptian Civil Code has to be restricted to uncontested

---

6. See *supra* n. 5.

liquidated debts. The scope of the said articles is wide enough to cover all obligations which may be deemed to emerge from the contract or which may be assumed to be existing thereunder.'

31. "Art. 302 of the Egyptian Civil Code provides:

'When there are several creditors in respect of an indivisible obligation or several heirs of a creditor in respect of such an obligation, each of the creditors or heirs may demand the performance in its entirety of the indivisible obligation. If one of the creditors or the heirs contests such a demand, the debtor shall effect payment to all the creditors together or deposit the object of the obligation in Court.

'Co-creditors will have remedies against a creditor who has received payment, each one for his share.'

32. "The Arbitral Tribunal finds the opinion of claimant's expert convincing. The text of Art. 302 is broadly worded and employs in particular the words '*demand* the performance *in its entirety*' as opposed to 'receive payment of his share'. Defendant has been unable to submit any judicial decision or doctrinal writing which supports a narrow reading of these clear words. The reliance of defendant's expert on the *travaux préparatoires* cannot lead to a different interpretation. The legislative history as quoted by defendant's expert reads:

'Art. 302 is coping with the case of plurality of creditors. In such case each creditor may receive the debt in full.'

"This observation, however, does not say anything as to why the words 'demand the performance' should be read as 'receive payment'.

33. "The interpretation of defendant's expert that Art. 302 cannot be extended to damages, is not supported by the broad wording of Art. 302. In any case, claimant is in fact asking performance by defendant of its obligations under the Contract on the basis of an alleged non-payment of a part of the contract-price and non-payment for extras. The claims have, in principle, not the character of damages.

34. "The Arbitral Tribunal finds the opinion of defendant's expert that an indivisibility of an obligation does not mean that one of the co-creditors of that obligation can demand performance, far from convincing (see paragraph *28*, above). Indeed, a distinction must be made between an indivisible obligation of one debtor vis-à-vis several creditors and a joint and several obligation of several debtors vis-à-vis one creditor. In the example of defendant's expert, the obligation of the seller to deliver the car is indivisible, whilst the obligation of the buyers to pay the purchase price is joint and several. When it comes to enforcing the obligation to deliver the car, each of the purchasers may, by virtue of Art. 302 of the Egyptian Civil Code, demand the performance of this obligation of the seller. The Arbitral Tribunal fails to see why the joint and several obligation of the purchasers to pay the purchase price would imply that delivery of the car can only be demanded by all the purchasers together. The text of Art. 302 simply says the contrary.

35. "Having established that company A could validly submit the Contractor's claims against defendant in this arbitration in its own behalf and on behalf of the parties forming joint venture X, it should be noted no other party to joint venture X has contested company A's demands in this arbitration. On the contrary, notwithstanding the fact that company A did not need an authorization from the other parties to joint venture X to commence the arbitration against defendant, the other parties did give company A such authorization. In the successive joint venture agreements company A was appointed 'sponsor of the joint venture' and granted a power of attorney 'in all matters relating to . . . the Contract' (Agreement of 25 April 1980). According to the joint venture Agreements of 12 May 1980 and 31 December 1980, company A, being appointed as Project Manager, is to represent 'the joint venture towards the Employer and the Engineer'. More in particular, in the minutes of meeting of 24 November 1982, the Supervisory Board of the joint venture decided to pursue claims 'including a recourse to arbitration', in which connection it is stated: 'It empowers the Project Manager accordingly.' The minutes of meeting of 24 February 1983 and 8 May 1984 also indicate that company A is to conduct the arbitration against defendant. It may be added that defendant itself wished to deal mainly with company A in relation to the Contract. It insisted that company A was the 'leader' and 'sponsor' of the joint venture. It would make no sense to regard company A as no longer the 'leader' or 'sponsor' when it comes to arbitration.

36. "The foregoing is not altered by the purported termination of the joint venture agreement by company A as far as companies C and D are concerned. Notwithstanding the purported termination, all parties to joint venture X wished to pursue the arbitration against defendant. See minutes of meeting of 8 May 1984. Moreover, as noted before, the termination had legally not taken effect but was only requested by companies C and D to be declared in an arbitration amongst these parties. Company A's request for an order ratifying their decisions terminating joint venture X with respect to companies C and D does not mean that the joint venture agreement must be deemed legally terminated. In any case, it has never come that far since, as also noted before, the parties to joint venture X have settled their differences and withdrawn the arbitration, without an arbitral award having been rendered.

37. "It should be pointed out that if one creditor demands performance of an indivisible obligation, he does legally so on behalf of all creditors, although he does not need the authorization of his co-creditors for making the demand. If the creditor has received payment, his co-creditors have recourse against that creditor (Art. 302(2) of the Egyptian Civil Code, quoted in paragraph 36, above). But that is an internal affair amongst the creditors (i.e., the parties to joint venture X) which is of no concern to the debtor (i.e., defendant). In the present case, the other parties to the joint venture X have, in addition to the foregoing, expressly entrusted company A with the task of demanding performance. Consequently, in all circumstances company A could validly commence arbitration on behalf of the other parties to the joint venture X.

38. "In view of the above considerations, it is not necessary to decide on the other arguments advanced by the parties in relation to the issue of claimant's *locus standi* and in particular on the question whether the joint venture constitutes a *Sharikat Al Mohassa*."

D. *Time-bar under Clause 67*
39. "Clause 67 of the Contract, which is identical to Clause 67 of the FIDIC Conditions (3d edition, 1977), provides for a two-tier system for the settlement

of disputes between the parties. All disputes between the Employer (defendant) and the Contractor (claimant) or between the Engineer and the Contractor shall in the first place be referred to and settled by the Engineer. The Engineer must give a decision within 90 days after having been requested to do so. A party who is dissatisfied with the Engineer's decision can 'require that the matter or matters in dispute be referred to arbitration' within 90 days after the Engineer has given a decision. The same applies if the Engineer has failed to give a decision. In that case a party can 'require that the matter or matters in dispute be referred to arbitration' within 90 days upon the lapse of the 90 days after the Engineer has been requested to render a decision. In the event that a party does not require arbitration within the second 90 days' period, the Engineer's 'decision shall remain final and binding upon the Employer and the Contractor'."

40. For each of the claims filed in the arbitration, the Engineer had issued a decision. For each Engineer's decision so given, the claimant had communicated to the Engineer, within 90 days following the latter's decision, that the claimant required that the claim be referred to arbitration. However, the claims had actually been filed in the arbitration after the expiration of the 90 days' period.

41. Defendant contended that the Engineer's decisions regarding the claims had become final and binding because claimant had failed to file a request for arbitration with the ICC within 90 days after the relevant decisions had been given.

42. The Arbitral Tribunal interpreted Clause 67 as requiring a party who is dissatisfied with a decision of the Engineer, in order not to lose his right to have the matter resolved by arbitration, solely to notify the Engineer, within 90 days after the Engineer has rendered his decision, that he requires the dispute be referred to arbitration. The reasoning of the arbitral tribunal regarding this issue is reproduced in full in the International Construction Law Review (1986) pp. 473–476 with a comment by S. Jarvin.[7]

Final Award of 1985 in case nr. 5080

Arbitrator: Roger Ph. Budin (Switz.)

Parties: Claimant: US company
Defendant: Spanish company

Published in: Unpublished

Subject matters: – apparent power of attorney
– amendment of contract
– written form for agreement under Swiss law
– ratification of legal transaction by subsequent behaviour

---

7. *Editor's note.* In another case the arbitral tribunal rendered the opposite conclusion as to the time-bar in Clause 67 of FIDIC, holding that a request for arbitration must be filed with the ICC within the second 90 days. ICC award no. 4707 published in 3 International Construction Law Review (1986) pp. 470–473 with comment by S. Jarvin. See also Christopher R. Seppala, "The Pre-Arbitral Procedure for the Settlement of Disputes in the FIDIC (Civil Engineering) Conditions of Contract", 4 International Construction Law Review (1986) pp. 315–337.

FACTS

A Sales Representation Agreement, concluded in 1982, gave rise to the question whether the US company was entitled to commissions on sales to a country (Lebanon) which was outside the territories described in the Agreement. The Agreement provided for ICC arbitration in Geneva. Swiss law was declared in the Agreement to be the applicable law.

One of the issues between the parties was whether they had subsequently agreed to an inclusion of the other countries in the territories described in the Agreement. The Spanish company contended in respect of this issue that the Agreement required that amendments be in writing and no such amendment was carried out. Moreover, the only telexes and letters exchanged in this respect had not been signed by a person authorised to represent the Spanish company.

The sole arbitrator rejected both contentions for the following reasons.

EXTRACT

1. "Respondent has . . . admitted as a matter of law that Mr. X represented it as export manager and was authorized to sign on behalf of respondent. . . .

2. "Even if Mr. X had only an apparent power of attorney, rather than an actual one, this appearance was largely sufficient under the principle of good faith as far as a co-contracting party was concerned, such as claimant. If respondent did not intend to be bound by Mr. X's signature or co-signature, then it should have expressly emphasized it, before entering into the representation agreement. Therefore, respondent cannot invoke against claimant a situation which it has created itself.

3. "Moreover, this is also the case under Art. 37 of the Swiss Code of Obligations, which deals with the cancellation of a power of attorney by the represented party.[1] According to this provision, unless the other party was duly notified of such cancellation, it may believe in good faith that the power of attorney remains valid. This legal provision applies to the case at hand, even though respondent claims that Mr. X's name was never entered in the commercial registry as an executive of the company. The relevant fact is that Mr. X has co-signed a contract in the name of respondent with the latter's express agreement.

   (. . . .)

4. "Art. 2 of the Agreement provides, as stated above, that amendments to the Agreement would have to be made 'in writing by one of the executives'. It must therefore be determined what an 'agreement in writing' is, under Swiss law.

5. "Art. 11 of the Code of Obligations provides that 'the validity of agreements is only subject to the observation of any particular form, in case such form

---

1. Art. 37 of the Swiss Code of Obligations provides:
   "1. As long as an agent is not aware of the termination of his powers, the principal or his legal successors automatically become a creditor or debtor as if these powers were still in force.
   "2. This does not apply to a third party who knew that these powers had terminated."

is required by a special provision of the law'. No such form is required with respect to representation agreements.

6. "Art. 12 of the Code specifies that 'if the law requires that an agreement be made in writing, this rule also applies to modifications of the agreement, *except for complementary and accessory stipulations which do not contradict the agreement.*'

7. "This legal provision would apply to the extent that one admitted that the three Lebanese contracts entered into by respondent had been the subject of 'complementary and accessory' provisions, and had not 'contradicted the Agreement'.

8. "Art. 16 of the Swiss Code of Obligations provides that:

    'the parties who have agreed to give a specific form to an agreement for which the law does not require any form, are deemed to have intended to be bound only upon the accomplishment of such form.

    'If this be the written form, without further specifications, one must refer to the legal prescriptions provided for such form where it is required by law.'

9. "Art. 12 of the Code of Obligations applies here, including its terms regarding 'complementary stipulations', in accordance with the parties' intent.

10. "In the case at hand, the parties have given sufficiently precise indications regarding the form which must be observed in case of amendments. Therefore, the agreement of the parties prevails on this issue, i.e., the amendment must be entered into 'in writing by one of the executives referred to in para. 12 hereof'.

11. "As already stated, the identity of the 'executives' concerned is known. The question arises, however, of what the parties exactly meant by the terms 'in writing', and whether these terms made the actual setting of signatures necessary.

12. "The answer is to be found at Art. 14(1) and (2) of the Code of Obligations: In order to bind oneself in writing, one must either sign by hand, or else 'proceed with any mechanical device', but only in transactions where this is admitted by custom. The Code gives as an example (which is in no way limitative) the signature of negotiable instruments issued in very large numbers.

13. "It must, however, be recognized that, since the implementation of the Code of Obligations, 'mechanical devices' of communication, including most of all the telex, have been considerably developed in the field of business transactions. The telex, which is such a 'mechanical device', is generally deemed sufficient for such transactions. The speed of modern transactions and the distance between the persons taking part in them requires a quick communication of offers and answers, which can only be achieved by way of telex or telecopier. It is therefore not, *a priori,* out of the ordinary that, in a particular case, parties who had to make special provisions for certain transactions have done so by way of telex.

82

4. "They could, however, have confirmed their agreement subsequently by exchanging signed documents, in accordance with Art. 2 of the Agreement, and such documents could of course have been signed, on the basis of that same article, by Mr. Y on the part of claimant, and by Mr. X on the part of respondent.

(. . . .)

5. "In the light of the foregoing observations of the tribunal, it arises that respondent has expressly accepted this transaction, which was brought to it by its sales representative, but that the formalities required by Art. 2 of the Agreement have not been strictly adhered to, as explained hereabove, and this is in fact the essential ground raised by the respondent to refuse the payment of the commissions claimed by claimant on the three shipments made to Lebanon.

6. "It must therefore be examined whether in spite of these formal flaws, respondent nevertheless bound itself to pay the said commissions.

(. . . .)

7. "Art. 2 of the Agreement requires the written form with respect to *both parties* and not to claimant alone, but for each of them respectively, the signature of one 'executive' is sufficient and we know that the executives were Mr. X for respondent and Mr. Y for claimant.

8. "On the other hand, it is also obvious that the requirement of a written and signed agreement is only meant to protect the party which denies being bound. In this regard, one notes that although it is claimant's signature which is missing, claimant itself is the plaintiff and it bases its claim, in particular, on Mr. X's letter . . . 1983, duly signed by him. Even though such letter did not constitute in itself an express agreement to pay the commissions, it remains that the invoices relating to the shipments concerned were enclosed with it, and one fails to see the reason why these invoices were sent by Mr. X to claimant unless they were to serve as a basis of calculation, i.e., in view of the payment of a commission.

(. . . .)

9. "The issue is, therefore, whether in this particular context, respondent validly and specially agreed to pay a commission on these three sales, even though the final consignee had its registered offices outside the 'Served Territory'.

20. "Swiss law recognizes the principle of the ratification of legal transactions by conclusive behaviour, even where such transactions were originally not valid in terms of form, and even if they had a major defect. Art. 31 of the Code of Obligations states in this respect that:

'The agreement which is vitiated by an error or by fraud, or which was entered into by reason of a justified fear is deemed ratified in case that the party who is not bound by the agreement fails to notify to the other party its decision not to maintain the agreement, or does not claim back the monies which it has paid.'

21. "According to Swiss federal case law (e.g., Journal des Tribunaux 1959, 486), it is sufficient for a party who does not intend to be bound by an agreement, to so declare within a period of one year. Consequently, under Swiss law, a major vice, such as those referred to in Arts. 23 et seq. of the Code of Obligations, may be cured by a simple lack of reaction. The Code therefore favours the ratification of acts which are null and void, or even illegal, simply by a tacit behaviour amounting, in this case, to a ratification.

(. . . .)

22. "However, it does not appear from the wording of the telexes exchanged between the parties that they ever intended to extend the Representation Agreement as such to Lebanon. In other words, respondent never agreed to pay commissions to claimant on all the transactions which it would enter into with any Lebanese customer.

(. . . .)

23. "In the present case, the parties have agreed on certain complementary provisions in the framework of the Agreement, *which are, however, strictly limited to the three shipments considered*. As already explained hereabove, these exceptions constituted complementary and accessory stipulations which extended the Agreement and did not contradict it.

24. "As for these three transactions, not only have the parties extended the Agreement, in that they have exchanged telexes referring to the reduced amount of the commission concerning the shipments, etc., but mainly and conclusively, respondent acknowledged the customer without any reservation towards claimant, delivered the goods to it and received payment. This is clearly and beyond doubt a case of ratification by conclusive behaviour and, in this sense, even though from a strictly formal point of view, the telexes and other documents exchanged between the parties were perhaps not sufficient to modify in a general manner the served territory covered by the Agreement, this Agreement has in fact been amended as far as those three transactions are concerned, through the positive attitude of respondent towards the customer, on the one hand, and towards claimant, on the other.

25. "This is even more so the case since a representation agreement is not a simple contract whereby each party may pursue its own interests exclusively, such interests being usually opposed to those of the other contracting party, but is on the contrary a contract of cooperation whereby both parties concur in pursuing the same object: to obtain sales contracts from customers introduced by the representative to the represented party. There exists a duty of loyalty between the representative and the represented party, somewhat similar to that which binds partners, or principal and agent. This duty of loyalty at the very least obliged respondent to make reservations vis-à-vis claimant to the effect that the latter was not authorized to deal with that case."

Partial award in case no. 5073 of 1986

Arbitrators:	Lic. José Luis Siqueiros (Mexico), Chairman; Prof. George A. Bermann (US); Dr. Antonio Boggiano (Argentina)
Parties:	Claimant: US exporter Defendant: Argentine distributor
Place of arbitration:	Port of Spain, Trinidad and Tobago (agreed by the parties)
Published in:	Unpublished (original in English)
Subject matters:	- distributorship agreement - partial award - choice of substantive law and adhesion contract - termination of agreement - retraction of termination of agreement - precontractual relationships - mitigation of damages

Facts

By an International Distributor Agreement (the Agreement) made 8 August 1979, claimant appointed defendant as its distributor for the sale of certain equipment (the Products) in Argentina.

Article 15 of the Agreement provided that in case of any dispute or difference between the parties which could not be settled by amicable negotiation, the parties would submit to arbitration under the rules for the International Chamber of Commerce (''ICC''). The place of arbitration (as amended on 31 August 1979) was fixed at Trinidad and Tobago, West Indies.

The Agreement provided for a duration of two years at which time it would terminate automatically, but could be extended beyond the two-year period upon mutual written agreement. The Agreement expired on 8 August 1981.

However, claimant and defendant entered into several short-term extensions and each party thus continued to perform under the Agreement.

On 9 March 1983, claimant informed defendant that claimant was in the process of updating its new International Distributor Agreement and that it would be a few months before the new instrument was completed. Therefore, claimant extended the existing Agreement until two months after claimant should present defendant the new one, thus allowing time for the latter to consider it. In fact, the new Agreement was never submitted to defendant.

The matter of possible mandatory integration by the new Argentine government continued to be discussed by the parties and gradually became an important issue for claimant. In the month of November of 1983, claimant decided that commercial requirements with respect to its Argentine operations had changed so as to require actual manufacture in Argentina. Claimant thus wished to appoint another company, better qualified in its judgment, to act as a partner and distributor.

On 2 December 1983, claimant sent a telex to defendant in which it formally notified its decision to terminate the successively renewed agreement, effective 1 February 1984. In the same telex claimant informed defendant that another Argentine company would be assuming the distribution role.

Defendant objected to claimant's telex, informing claimant that in view of the unilateral termination of the Agreement it might commence legal proceedings in the Argentine courts. Claimant responded by suggesting that the parties attempt to negotiate and resolve amicably the change in the commercial relationship, requesting that defendant travel to California for that purpose. Claimant then sent a telex to defendant on 11 January 1984, rescinding the termination announced in the 2 December 1983 telex in order to "allow both companies to negotiate in good faith an agreement concerning a continued presence of [claimant] in Argentina". Claimant and defendant met in California during February 1984, but were unable to resolve their differences.

A series of communications, by letters and telexes ensued. Different alternatives were presented to arrange for a gradual phase out of the existing Argentine operations, but defendant rejected claimant's proposals to that effect, claiming that the unilateral breach of the Agreement by claimant entitled the distributor to be legally indemnified.

Claimant, in a telex dated 29 March 1984 formally offered to extend the Agreement on the same original terms and conditions for a period of two years from the date of defendant's acceptance. By telex dated 4 April 1984, defendant rejected claimant's offer, maintaining that claimant had improperly terminated the parties' relationship as of 2 December 1983.

On 16 May 1984, defendant executed an exclusive distributor agreement with a French concern, a competitor of claimant. Claimant in turn executed an exclusive distributor agreement with another Argentine company during the month of April 1985.

In August 1984, claimant filed a request for arbitration with the ICC, seeking an arbitral award "declaring that the Agreement has been properly and effectively terminated" and "prohibiting defendant from commencing legal proceedings in Argentina".

Defendant counterclaimed an approximate total of US$ 19 million in damages relating, inter alia, to (a) stock of spares, (b) equipment owned by defendant and leased to others, (c) leasing contracts, (d) maintenance contract, (e) loss of sales of upgrades of installed equipment, (f) loss of contracts in course of materialization, (g) lost profit for loss of future market, and (h) travel allowance.

The Terms of Reference were signed by the parties and the arbitrators on 26 November 1985. The issues to be decided by the arbitrators were defined therein as follows:

"*Claim by claimant*

"(1) Whether or not the telex sent by claimant to defendant on 2 December 1983, whereby the former notified the latter its intention (or decision) to terminate, effective 1 February 1984, the Agreement between the parties, implies or not a wrongful termination (material breach) of the Agreement and its agreed extensions.

"(2) Whether or not, even assuming the 2 December 1983 telex constituted a material breach of the Agreement, claimant's telex of 11 January 1984 which was responded to by defendant's telex of 19 January 1984, constituted a valid retraction of such breach.

"(3) Whether or not claimant's offer of 29 March 1984, to extend the Agreement on the same terms and conditions contained in the original instrument (for an additional period of two years), coupled with defendant's telex of 4 April 1984, rejecting that offer on the grounds among others of its not having been made in good faith, terminated their business relationship and released claimant from any further liability or obligation to defendant.

"(4) Whether or not claimant's dealing with the [other Argentine company] or defendant's dealings with [the French concern], or their acts or dealings with still other parties, constituted at any time a material breach of any obligation of good faith or otherwise owed to the other contracting party.

"*Counterclaim by defendant*

"(5) Whether or not defendant is entitled to be compensated by claimant for the various damages and losses set forth in the former's counterclaim and which were rebutted by the claimant in its reply.

"(6) If assuming that defendant were to be indemnified, whether it is entitled to receive the amounts it has claimed or if such amounts must be adjusted pursuant to claimant's defences.

"*Arbitration Costs*

"(7) Which party or parties shall bear the arbitration costs and legal fees originating from this arbitration and, in the latter case, in what proportion those costs and fees will be allocated as between the parties."

By a submission of 16 January 1986, defendant readjusted the amount of the counterclaim, increasing it to an approximate total of US$ 27.5 million.

In the partial award rendered in the course of 1986, the arbitrators decided with respect to the above issues:

(1)   claimant's notice of termination was unreasonably abrupt, and to this extent implied a wrongful termination;

(2)   claimant's telex of 11 January 1982 did not constitute a valid retraction of the breach;

(3)   claimant's offer of 24 March 1984 to extend the Agreement on the same terms and conditions coupled with defendant's telex of 4 April 1984, rejecting the offer terminated their business relationship, without relieving claimant of its liability to compensate defendant for the resulting losses and damages;

(4)   the parties' dealings with (potential) competitors were not sufficiently established by evidence;

(5)-(7) will be decided at the time of issuance of the final award.

Excerpt

A.   Arbitrators' power to render partial award

[1]   "Art. 21 of the ICC Rules of Procedure distinguishes between partial and definitive awards. There is no doubt that arbitrators may issue preliminary determinations with respect to clear obligations prior to

resolving other issues which may require more lengthy proceedings. The rendering of a partial award may under appropriate circumstances advance the conduct of the proceedings by narrowing the issues, without depriving the parties of the right in due course to present evidence and argument on all matters that are relevant.

[2]   "In the instance case claimant's original claim is that it properly and effectively terminated the Agreement and did not thereby incur liability to defendant. On the other hand, defendant's claim for damages is based precisely on the existence of such liability. The arbitrators believe that the issue of liability or non-liability can most conveniently be decided before entering into an analysis of the amount of damages claimed in the counterclaim.

[3]   "This means in effect that the first four issues to be determined under the Terms of Reference should be resolved prior to examination of the three remaining issues dealing with defendant's counterclaim and the arbitration costs.

[4]   "Although defendant opposes the rendering of this partial award, the arbitrators do not find that its objections are properly supported. The tribunal also notes that the Arbitration Act of Trinidad and Tobago, place of the arbitration, provides that the arbitrators or umpire may, in their discretion, make an interim award. (First Schedule, Art. 10)."

B.   *Law applicable to substance of dispute*

[5]   "The Agreement provides (clause 16) that it shall be construed under and governed by the laws of California. For purposes of determining the law applicable to this dispute, however, defendant claims that the contract must be characterized as a contract of adhesion, while claimant submits it is not. Defendant more specifically argues that the contractual choice of law clause should be disregarded by this arbitral tribunal at least to the extent that the provisions of California law 'were more unfavorable for defendant than those included in the Argentina Law, which is the one that should naturally have governed the circumstances occurred between the parties, since it is the law of the place where the object of the contract was to be performed'.

[6]   "Claimant, on the other hand, insists that California substantive law applies to all aspects of the performance or breach of the Agreement, that law having been chosen by the parties themselves in an International Distributor Agreement that cannot plausibly be construed as a contract of adhesion.

[7]   "In the unanimous view of the arbitrators the law applicable to
         determining whether the International Distributor Agreement before
         us is an adhesion contract and whether the choice of law clause it
         contains is valid and effective is the law that would govern the contract
         if the choice were valid, i.e., in the present case, California law. The
         clause in question covers not only the interpretation of the contract,
         but impliedly also its characterization.

[8]   "This general principle of private international law applies to this case
         with particular clarity since both parties have addressed the adhesion
         contract question on the basis of California case law. Defendant, it is
         true, has carefully included arguments based on Argentina law.
         However, invoking both laws in order to secure the law more favorable
         to one's own claim is, with the utmost respect, a form of law shopping,
         and law shopping like forum shopping is not to be encouraged, least of
         all in arbitration procedures.

[9]   "In fact, under both California and Argentina law claimant and
         defendant are to be regarded as commercial parties. Both acted as such
         in the course of entering into the International Distributor Agreement
         and in their difficulties with one another under that agreement.
         Evidence shows that both parties were capable of conducting their
         business relationships.

[10]   "Certainly, defendant cannot claim to be or have been a consumer.
         That term would not properly characterize 'the most prominent
         company in the market' in Argentina .... Moreover, the agreement
         before us cannot be considered an inflexible printed form dictated by
         claimant and presented to defendant on a 'take it or leave it' basis.
         This simply does not appear to be the case. Defendant does not claim
         that claimant had a monopoly, or that all manufacturers in this special
         trade used the same standard forms. Defendant does not even argue
         that it was compelled to accept the standard form provided by
         claimant. We do not, of course, imply that there was exact equality of
         bargaining power on both sides or that it is always easy to draw a sharp
         line between consent reluctantly given and an absence of consent.
         Here, however, lack of consent was not alleged at all when the contract
         was entered into, either with respect to the choice of law clause
         incorporated into the contract or with respect to the International
         Distributor Agreement as a whole.

[11]   "Moreover, it appears from the evidence that the defendant indeed
         had opportunities to discuss and negotiate the terms of the agreement.
         That the place of arbitration was changed from London to Trinidad

and Tobago at defendant's request is sufficient evidence that the conditions of the deal were to some degree effectively bargained for between the parties.

[12] "Finally, defendant has failed to show that the choice of California law will work fundamentally unfair or unreasonable legal results. Proof of this is defendant's continual reliance on California precedents when considered favorable to its cause. Thus, the arbitrators cannot accept the view that defendant agreed to an unconscionable choice of law clause. We conclude that under California law, to which both parties advert on this particular issue, the International Distributor Agreement is an international standard contract but not a contract of adhesion.

[13] "Putting aside the adhesion contract issue, we submit that the choice of California law clause is valid not only under California law but also under the Restatement (Second) of Conflict of Laws, under Argentine Private International Law, and under Trinidad and Tobago law.

"Section 16 of the Agreement provides:

'16. *Choice of law*

'This Agreement shall be construed under and shall be governed in accordance with the laws of the State of California, USA.'

[14] "In *S.A. Empresa de Viacao Aerea Rio Grandense (Varig Airlines) v. The Boeing Company*, 641 F.2d 746, 749 (9th Cir. 1981), it was held that California will apply as substantive law the one designated by the contract unless the transaction falls within either of two exceptions: (1) when the chosen state has no substantial relationship to the parties or the transaction, or (2) when application of the law of the chosen state would be contrary to a fundamental policy of the state.

[15] "In this case, the Agreement obviously has substantial relationship to at least one of the parties to the transaction and neither party claims that California substantive law offends against any fundamental policy or principle of any law otherwise applicable to the contract, even assuming *ex hypothesis* that Argentina law would be that otherwise applicable law. At least we have not heard defendant make arguments to that effect. In fact, the chosen law appears to provide reasonable protection for the distributor.

[16] "Finally, any argument that the choice of California law includes California rules of conflict of laws, thus allowing a possible *renvoi* to

domestic Argentina law, is not in conformity with California law (see *Varig Airlines*, supra). To the same effect, Sect. 187 of the Restatement (Second) of Conflict of Laws states that: '... (3) In the absence of contrary indication, the reference is to the local law of the State of the chosen law'.

[17]   "The legal principles which guide an Argentine court on the question of proper law of a contract are now well settled. Argentine private international law allows the parties to choose a law to govern their contract. See In re *Banco de Rio Negro y Neuquen v. Independencia Transportes Internacionales*, 97 "El Derecho" 604 (Nat'l Comm. Ch. App. 20 October 1981) (note by Malbran, 98 "El Derecho" 865); In re *Cicerone v. Banco de Entre Rios*, 101 "El Derecho" 179 (19 February 1982) (note by Malbran); In re *Deutsches Reisburo GM v. Speter*, Armando, 108 "El Derecho" 233 (27 February 1984) (note by Perugini de Paz y Geuse, "La Ley", 19 November 1984); In re *Arrebillaga, Arturo Ernesto y otra v. Banco de la Providencia de Santa Cruz*, 109 "El Derecho" 715 (note by Goldschimidt); In re *Expreso Mercurio S.A. v. Maupe*, (7 May 1984), in "Doctrina Judicial", 2 January 1985 (note by Najurieta). The authorities are cited in Boggiano, Sociedades y Grupos Multinacionales 311-36 (Buenos Aires 1985). See also 2 Boggiano, Derecho Internacional Privado 699 et seq. (2d. ed. Buenos Aires); Boggiano, 'International Contracts in Argentina', 47 Rabels Zeitschrift 431-77 (1983).

[18]   "Argentina law therefore is in accord with the well-known statement by Professor Pierre Lalive on the validity of a choice of law clause:

'There are few principles more universally admitted in private international law than those referred to by the standard terms of the "proper law of the contract" according to which the law governing the contract is that which has been chosen by the parties, whether expressly or (with certain differences or variations according to the various systems) tacitly (ICC Award no. 1512, Doc. No.410/1935, 24 February 1987).'

[19]   "Finally, Trinidad and Tobago law also allows the parties to international contracts to agree on the governing law through a contractual choice of law clause. In matters of contract law, Trinidad and Tobago follows English common law, under which the interpretation and effects of contracts, as well as the rights and obligations of the parties, are governed by the law which the parties agree or intend shall govern it, or which they are presumed to have

intended to govern it. This law is known as the proper law of the contract. Thus, the law expressly stipulated by the parties, as the proper law of contract, should govern their disputes.''

C. *Wrongful termination (point no. 1 of the issues)*

[20]   "In order to decide whether claimant committed a material breach of its contract with defendant when it gave notice of termination of the existing distributorship by its telex of 2 December 1983, this tribunal must analyze the legal status of the relationship between the parties as of that date, especially in light of claimant's previous letter to defendant of 9 March 1983. We analyze that status as follows. The original distributorship agreement between the parties, dated 8 August 1979, expired by its terms two years later, on 8 August 1981. It was subsequently renewed on five occasions for shorter fixed periods, the last in that sequence covering the two-month period ending 30 April 1983. We assume in all these instances that, apart from the contract term, all provisions of the original contract carried over. Among those carried-over terms are (1) the provision that the agreement should terminate automatically at the end of the stated contract period, subject to further extension upon mutual written agreement by the parties (agreement, para. 2a), and (2) the provisions that either party in addition might, upon thirty days' notice, terminate the agreement for any of four categories of breach by the other party set out in the contract (agreement, para. 2b). We note that since claimant does not claim to have terminated the distributorship on account of any breach by defendant, the latter provision does not furnish an adequate basis for the termination.

[21]   ''Periodically over the course of 1982 and 1983, defendant expressed dissatisfaction over these short renewal terms and sought assurances from claimant of a more durable relationship. Eventually, on the occasion of a visit by defendant's personnel to claimant's offices in [California] and at defendant's request, claimant submitted to defendant a document, dated 9 March 1983, that is of critical importance to this case. In that document, claimant extended the contract then in force 'until two months after we present to you the new one', the latter term referring to a new form International Distributor Agreement which claimant claimed to be in the process of preparing for purposes of putting its international distributorships on an improved legal basis.

[22]   "Thus, midstream in the final two-month renewal period ending 30
          April 1983, claimant extended the agreement for an indefinite period
          of time – indefinite in that it would expire two months after the
          unspecified moment of presentation to defendant of a new
          International Distributor Agreement. Despite semantic differences,
          the parties essentially agree that the letter of 9 March 1983 represented
          a prolongation of the agreement. However, they disagree on the legal
          effect of the indication in that letter that a new agreement would be
          forthcoming from claimant and that defendant would have two
          months in which to decide whether to accept it.

[23]   "This tribunal finds that, as in many cases of factual and legal
          ambiguity, the correct answer lies somewhere between the positions
          adamantly asserted by the opposing parties. We shall be as precise as
          possible in setting forth our analysis.

[24]   "On the other hand, this tribunal cannot find, despite claimant's
          periodic references to the parties' future relationship, that claimant
          was categorically barred by its 9 March 1983 letter from terminating
          the existing agreement without first submitting to defendant a revised
          International Distributor Agreement for its acceptance or rejection. To
          begin with, the legal relationship between the parties as of 9 March
          1983 was basically a contract of indefinite duration which, under
          California law, must be regarded (unless the contract otherwise
          provides) as terminable by either party, provided a reasonable length
          of time has elapsed and sufficient notice is given to the other party.
          Alpha Distributing Co. of California, Inc. v. Jack Daniel Distillery,
          454 F.2d 442 (1972), reh'g denied, 493 F.2d 1355 (9th Cir.), cert.
          denied, 419 U.S. 842 (1974); *Hunt Foods v. Phillips*, 248 F.2d 23 (9th
          Cir. 1957); *J.C. Millet Co. v. Park & Tilford Distillers*, 123 F.Supp.
          484 (N.D.Cal. 1954); *Aronowicz v. Nalley's, Inc.*, 30 Cal. App. 3d 27,
          106 Cal.Rptr. 424 (1972). Moreover, unless the parties have agreed
          otherwise, the right of a party to terminate a contract of indefinite
          duration is not under California law subject to a requirement of good
          cause. *Alpha Distributing Co. of California, Inc.*, supra; *Gianelli
          Distributing Co. v. Beck & Co.*, 171 Cal.App.3d 1132, 215 Cal.Rptr.
          667 (1985); *Kolling v. Dow Jones & Co., Inc.* 137 Cal.App.3d 709,
          187 Cal.Rptr. 797 (1982). See also *Triangle Mining Co., Inc. v.
          Stauffer Chemical Co.*, 753 F.2d 734 (9th Cir. 1985) (Idaho). On the
          basis of a history of several short-term extensions of the original
          agreement and in light of the California cases cited above, this tribunal
          is inclined to assume that claimant extended the Agreement on 9 March

1983 for a period of indefinite duration. Under such assumption claimant normally would have been privileged to terminate this contract of indefinite duration as it did, some eleven months later upon two months' prior notice.

[25]   "However, in this case, the contract was not simply extended for an indefinite period, but ostensibly so extended in order to allow for the preparation of a new and improved distributorship contract between the same parties. As pointed out later in this award, this is a factor of no small importance. Nevertheless, we think the parties should be aware of the fact that conditions over the course of a contract of indefinite duration are basically subject to change. In this case, defendant knew of the importance that a requirement of integration in Argentina would hold for claimant; by the latter half of 1983, it also knew the reservations claimant was expressing about relying upon defendant as an integration partner. Moreover, we are influenced by the fact that the new provisions of the contemplated distributorship agreement – the performance criteria, the duration, among others – had not been defined. It does not appear that the parties had reached agreement on any of those particulars, or indeed had substantially discussed them, either by 9 March 1983 or at any time prior to the notice of termination the following December.

[26]   "This uncertainty, reflected in the vague notion of a 'second phase' in the development of the Argentinian market, cannot be ignored in determining the weight and legal effect of claimant's references to a new international distributor agreement. Under established California law agreements to agree are not enforceable contracts. 'Where an agreement is not sufficiently definite to enable a court to give it an exact meaning or where an essential element is reserved for future agreement of both parties, a legal obligation cannot result'. *Transamerica Equipment Leasing Corp. v. Union Bank*, 426 F.2d 273 (9th Cir. 1970). See also *White Point Company v. Herrington*, 268 Cal.App. 2d 458, 73 Cal.Rptr. 885 (1968); *Carter v. Milestone*, 170 Cal.App.2d 189, 338 P.2d 569 (1959); 14 Cal.Jur.3d Contracts Sect. 40 (1974). The cases cited by defendant on this issue are not to the contrary. *Pacific Mills Corporation v. Duggan*, 199 Cal.App.2d 806, 19 Cal.Rptr. 291 (1962); *Mann v. Mueller*, 140 Cal.App.2d 481, 295 P.2d 421 (1956).

[27]   "For these reasons, we conclude that claimant was not legally barred from terminating the contract without submitting a revised contract to defendant. To rule otherwise would leave claimant no choice in

responding to legitimate concern over changed circumstances in the course of a contract of indefinite duration but to offer to defendant a new contract containing provisions that defendant could not possibly accept.

[28]   "That does not, however, conclude our analysis of this first issue. Notwithstanding what has been said, this tribunal finds that the express statement by claimant on 9 March 1983 about a forthcoming revised agreement that defendant might accept or reject, coupled with a series of other express or implied indications on its part in the course of 1982 and 1983 on the subject of claimant's and defendant's future relationship, reasonably raised defendant's expectations about the prospects of a long term relationship. Under such circumstances, claimant cannot plausibly maintain that it enjoyed the same degree of freedom in terminating the relationship established in March 1983 as if those statements and indications had not been given. On the contrary, we find that claimant's termination of the contract was unreasonably abrupt. Relevant to this finding is the fact that the Argentinian political party committed to integration had been defeated in the national elections held on 30 October 1983. While the tribunal is prepared to accept that integration concerns were the primary factor in claimant's decision to terminate, it does not appear that the predicted mandatory integration had by November or December 1983 yet become a reality.

[29]   "In effect, claimant argues that defendant showed sufficient evidence in 1983 and earlier of insecurity over the status and future of its relationship with claimant to bar it from asserting a claim based on reliance. The record does reflect insecurity on its part, as indeed does much of the testimony of witnesses presented by both sides in this case. Defendant's overtures during this period to [the French concern], a competitor of claimant, are further evidence of that. But the record also shows both oral and written encouragement by claimant to defendant during the same time. In short, the signals to defendant must be described as at least mixed. They were positive enough on 9 March 1983 and thereafter to refute claimant's claim that defendant deserved no greater notice of termination that would have been appropriate in a contract of indefinite duration had no assurances ever been given at all.

[30]   "This part of our ruling is likewise firmly grounded in California law. Although, as noted above, California law does not in principle enforce

mere agreements to agree or broadly embrace precontractual liability, it does impose upon each of the parties to a contract an underlying duty of good faith and fair dealing toward the other party in its performance. *Seaman's Direct Buying Service, Inc. v. Standard Oil Co.*, 36 Cal.3d 752, 206 Cal.Rptr. 354, 686 P.2d 1158 (1984); *Egan v. Mutual of Omaha Ins. Co.*, 24 Cal.3d 809, 169 Cal.Rptr. 691, 620 P.2d 141 (1979), app. dism., 445 US 912 (1980); *Flying Tiger Line, Inc. v. United States Aircoach*, 51 Cal.2d 199, 331 P.2d 37 (1958); *Brown v. Superior Court*, 34 Cal.2d 559, 212 P.2d 878 (1949); *Cleary v. American Airlines, Inc.*, 111 Cal.App.3d 443, 168 Cal.Rptr. 722 (1980); Restatement (Second) of Contracts Sect. 205 ('Every contract imposes upon each party a duty of good faith and fair dealing in its performance and its enforcement'). See also U.C.C. Sect. 1-203. In this case, the good faith that claimant owed to defendant in the performance of the contract as extended on 9 March 1983, obligated it to provide more ample notice of termination than it in fact did. The same result follows from the related notion of promissory estoppel according to which 'a promise which the promisor should reasonably expect to induce action or forbearance on the part of the promisee ... and which does induce such action or forbearance is binding if injustice can be avoided only by enforcement of the promise. The remedy granted for breach may be limited as justice requires.' Restatement (Second) of Contracts Sect. 90(1). California law expressly recognizes this equitable principle. See *Drennan v. Star Paving Co.*, 51 Cal.2d 409, 333 P.2d 757 (1958); *Aronowicz v. Nalley's Inc.*, supra.

[31] "None of the cases specifically brought by claimant to the tribunal's attention suggests a contrary result. In both *Tozuku Shida v. Japan Food Corp.*, 251 Cal.App.2d 864, 60 Cal.Rptr. 43 (1967), and *A.B.C. Distributing Co. v. Distillers Distributing Co.*, 154 Cal.App.2d 175, 316 P.2d 71 (1957), the manufacturer terminated the distributorship as of the exact termination date specified in the contract or, more precisely, declined to renew it. In neither case was the contract, like the agreement as extended in the case at hand on 9 March 1983, a contract of indefinite duration. Nor was the contract accompanied by statements contemplating a new arrangement.

[32] "In sum, for the reasons already stated, we find under the circumstances that two months was an insufficient notice period prior to termination and that the termination was therefore unreasonably abrupt. To this extent, we find a wrongful termination (material breach) of the agreement and its extensions."

D. Retraction of termination (point no. 2 of the issues)

[33]   "The California Commercial Code Sect. 2-611(1) provides that until the repudiating party's next performance is due, he can retract his repudiation, provided the aggrieved party has not yet materially changed his position or otherwise indicated that he considers the repudiation final. The California courts have in some cases held that a retraction by the repudiating party nullifies the breach. *Taylor v. Johnston*, 15 Cal.3d 130, 123 Cal.Rptr. 641, 539 P.2d 425 (1975); *Guerrieri v. Severini*, 51 Cal.2d 12, 330 P.2d 635 (1958); *Sacket v. Spindler*, 248 Cal.App.2d 220, 56 Cal.Rptr. 435 (1967). Claimant thus argues that its telex dated 11 January 1984 effectively retracted the breach, if any, that occurred when it sent the 2 December 1983 telex to defendant.

[34]   "However, the same line of cases cited above underscores that to constitute an express retraction, the repudiating party's conduct must be unequivocal in its intention and refrain from imposing new conditions. *Pichignau v. City of Paris*, 264 Cal.App.2d 138, 70 Cal. Rptr. 147 (1968). It must propose to reinstate the parties' legal relationship as it existed at the time of breach. Claimant's telex dated 11 January 1984 did not in fact mention reinstatement of the distribution contract; on the contrary, it was captioned: 'Negotiation to resolve existing claimant-defendant relationship'. We believe that the telex is better characterized as an invitation to negotiate a phasing-out of defendant than as a restoration of the prevailing status quo. As stated by the Supreme court of California in *Taylor*, the injured party faces an election of remedies: 'he can treat the repudiation as an anticipatory breach and immediately seek damages for breach of contract, ... or he can treat the repudiation as an empty threat ...'. Nor do we find that defendant's reply dated 19 January 1984 constituted a waiver. It only expressed its willingness to travel to [California] 'to try to arrive at a solution satisfactory to our rights, which would spare us to have to resort to the courts'.

[35]   "For the stated reasons, but without implying that the parties are foreclosed from invoking the communications exchanged in January and February 1984 in making their arguments on possible mitigation of damages owed for the abrupt termination of the Agreement, the arbitrators rule that claimant's telex of 11 January 1984 did not constitute a valid retraction of such breach.''

E. *Termination of the business relationship (point no. 3 of the issues)*

[36] "Under California statutory law, specifically in accordance with its Civil Code, Sect. 1485, an obligation is extinguished by an offer of performance. The offer must be made with intent to extinguish the obligation and in good faith. When properly made, it has the effect of putting the other party in default if it refuses to accept. *Still v. Plaza Marina Commercial Corp.*, 21 Cal.App.3d 378, 98 Cal.Rptr. 414 (1971). See also *Bidegaray v. Ormaca*, 48 Cal.App. 655, 192 P.176 (1920).

[37] "The tribunal believes that the offer contained in the telex dated 29 March 1984, sent by Mr. Y on behalf of claimant to Mr. X, President of defendant, formally offering 'to extend the existing agreement upon the same terms and conditions as in the past', that is, for a period of two (2) years from the date of defendant's acceptance, constituted a good faith and reasonable proposal to continue performing under the original contract.

[38] "Defendant may have found the terms of the original agreement, notably its duration of two rather than five or ten years, not entirely satisfactory, particularly in light of the strains which had impaired the parties' relationship over the preceding year and a half. However, upon receipt of the offer, defendant could have expressed any specific objections to its terms, including its duration term, thus allowing the offeror to consider modifications of its offer. California Civil Code, Sect. 1501. See *Noyes v. Habitation Resources Inc.*, 49 Cal.App.3d 910, 123 Cal.Rptr. 261 (1975). Instead defendant's management chose to regard the offer as absolutely unacceptable and malicious, and for this reason expressly rejected it by telex 2379, dated 4 April 1984. In the arbitrators' view such rejection had the effect of putting that party in default.

[39] "Our ruling on point no. 3 of the issues does not relieve claimant of its liability in damages. We have already ruled that claimant abruptly notified defendant of the termination of the contractual relationship on 2 December 1983. The distributor is therefore entitled to compensation for the resulting loss it can prove, though presumably only for the loss or damages suffered as of that period of time ending when the distributor improperly rejected the offer of delayed performance.

[40] "In other words, under the whole of chapter 2 of the California Civil Code (Sects. 1485 through 1505 and particularly Sect. 1492), when a

party has delayed performance of its obligations or committed a breach through the abrupt termination of the existing agreement, that party is obligated to compensate the aggrieved party for its legal injury in the meantime.

[41]   "The tribunal finds in accordance with Sect. 1492 of the California Civil Code that the delay in performance is capable of exact and entire compensation to the aggrieved party. Time had not been declared to be of the essence to the obligation; in fact, a contract that had been in force for more than four years and had become one of an indefinite duration when terminated cannot be characterized as one in which time is of the essence. *Katemis v. Westerlind*, 142 Cal.App.2d 799, 299 P.2d 383 (1956).

[42]   "This result is entirely consistent with, and meant to be understood in light of, the rule of California law on mitigation of damages. *Valencia v. Shell Oil Co.*, 23 Cal.2d 840, 147 P.2d 558 (1944); *Sackett v. Spindler*, 248 Cal.App.2d 392, 220, 56 Cal.Rptr. 435 (1967) cf. *Green v. Smith*, 261 Cal.App.2d 67 Cal.Rptr. 796 (1968) (tort action). That rule required defendant to mitigate the damages flowing from claimant's abrupt termination of the contract. At a minimum, it appears that claimant's offer of 29 March 1984 to renew the contract for two years presented defendant with an appropriate opportunity to mitigate its damages. The tribunal believes that it would be unfair for one of the parties to deny the other the opportunity to correct a situation created by its improper conduct.

[43]   "The arbitrators do not decide at this point how the damages that allegedly ensued from the wrongful termination should be measures or mitigated. That will be dealt with in the final award when the tribunal, upon all the evidence, makes a ruling on points five and six of the issues to be determined."

F. Dealing with (potential) competitors

[44]   "The arbitral tribunal has already stated that California law recognizes an implied covenant of good faith and fair dealing which requires that neither party do anything to injure the right of the other to receive the benefits of the agreement.

[45]   "From the extensive documentary and testimonial evidence submitted by both parties, the arbitrators take note of the various dealings and informal negotiations that claimant and defendant conducted with ..., and still other potential competitors. In all fairness,

neither party seems to have conducted itself at all times in strict good faith when effecting such overtures and dealings.

[46]   "To this extent, any material breach of the obligation of good faith owed to the other party would appear to be reciprocal. More important, we do not propose to weigh the equities between the parties in such dealings because, whatever that balance, neither party has effectively satisfied its burden of persuasion that the other's alleged misconduct in this respect was sufficiently serious to warrant redress."

Partial award in case no. 5195 of 1986

Arbitrators:	Robert A. MacCrindle, QC (UK), Chairman; Prof. Henry Lesguillons (France); Prof. Berthold Goldman (France)
Parties:	Claimant: French contractor Defendant: Ministry of Finance of African country X
Place of arbitration:	Paris, France (agreed by the parties)
Published in:	Unpublished (original in English)
Subject matters:	- construction contract - attack by People's Liberation Army - frustration of contract

Facts

By a contract dated 15 December 1981, the French contractor undertook the construction, completion and maintenance of certain civil, building, mechanical and electrical works for the Ministry of African country X at the airport of that country (the "Airport Project"). The Contract contained an arbitration clause referring to the ICC. The substantive law was, according to the Contract, the law of country X, which originates from English law.

At the time, the contractor was already carrying out another contract for the Ministry of Irrigation of country X, namely an excavation of a canal (the "Canal Project"), which was situated some 300 km. from the airport site. The

Canal Project also gave rise to ICC arbitration (case no. 5277). The first and second interim award in that case are reported in this Yearbook as well.

The Contractor commenced work on the airport in January 1982. The works were to be completed on 15 June 1984. During 1982 and 1983 the Contractor carried out a substantial part of the work under the contract at the airport site. At the same time, it continued to carry out work on the Canal Project.

The subsequent facts were established by the arbitrators[1]:

[1]   "During the night of 15 and 16 November 1983, the Contractor was the subject of an attack on its advance camp, which was one of the camps used on the Canal Project and which was 290 kilometres (as the crow flies) from the airport. The attack was made without any prior warning by an organization hostile to the established Government of country X, calling itself the X People's Liberation Army ('PLA') identified with the X People's Liberation Movement (the "PLM"). The attackers kidnapped 9 hostages (7 Frenchmen and 2 Pakistanis), 8 of whom were employees of the Contractor and one of whom was an employee of a supplier of plant and equipment. The attackers removed the radio equipment which connected the camp to the base camp. Before they left with the hostages the attackers left a message written in Arabic and English, which set out both the conditions which they required to be fulfilled if the hostages were to be released and their threats as to the fate of the hostages if those conditions were not complied with. The document required, inter alia, that work should cease forthwith on the digging of the Canal.

[2]   "As a result of the situation which had arisen, the Contractor stopped all excavation work on the Canal Project on 16 November 1983, thus fulfilling the main condition required for the release of the hostages. The 9 hostages were released by the captors, and returned on 18 November 1983 to the camp, which was then evacuated. Thereafter the activities of the Contractor on the Canal Project were limited to minor maintenance work at the base camp and the Contractor's staff there was reduced to the minimum.

[3]   "The Engineer under the Canal Project subsequently claimed (in a letter to the Contractor dated 7 December 1983) that, as a result from 18 November 1983 'a situation of back to normal conditions ... prevailed ... at the camp as well as throughout all sites of work along

---

1. *Note General Editor.* The names are modified in order not to reveal the identity of the parties.

the canal', that 'more reinforcement of effective security measures have been undertaken by the Employer [i.e., the Ministry of Irrigation of the Government] all along the canal' and that since 'the Employer has provided the adequate security measures and created conditions to facilitate the normal execution of the works and the Employer is prepared to provide any further security measures', the Contractor should resume work on the Canal Project. The Contractor, however, expressed its disagreement, and requested the Ministry of Irrigation to acknowledge formally that the situation fell under the 'Special Risks' provisions in the Canal Project Contract. The discussions which followed concerned only the Canal Project (i.e., did not concern the Contract or the work thereunder at the airport) but we were told that they concluded by the Ministry of Irrigation agreeing in a letter to the Contractor dated 4 January 1984 that the aforesaid attack did indeed give rise to the application of the 'Special Risks' provisions under the Canal Project Contract. The Contractor did not resume excavation work on the Canal Project. It did, however, agree to commence the transfer of the base camp, which had been planned for 1984.

[4]   "Although in November 1983 it stopped excavation work on the Canal Project the Contractor did not then cease activity at the airport. It had no particular reason to think that the organization behind the attackers was concerned with anything more than preventing work continuing on the Canal Project, since the message which had been left at the camp mentioned only the Canal Project. No threats had been received in relation to the works at airport. Work therefore continued uninterrupted at airport in and after November 1983. By early February 1984, the Contract work was roughly 90% complete, and had reached a stage which would have permitted it to be completed in the ordinary course within a further three months or so.

[5]   "Because all excavation work on the Canal had stopped there was, after November 1983, very little traffic on the road built alongside the Canal. On 6 February 1984, however, a truck belonging to the Contractor was transporting a maintenance crew and some local civilians along that road. At about 50 kilometres south of Y it detonated a mine which had been laid in the road. The truck was destroyed, twelve people were killed, and some twelve men were wounded. The Contractor had received no prior warning that the road had been mined. The PLM later claimed responsibility for having laid the mine.

"Four days later, at 5 am on 10 February 1984, the Contractor's base camp was attacked by a force of armed men dressed in military fashion. The attack lasted until 10 am. During the five hours of the attack there were exchanges of fire between the attackers and the modest contingent of the Government's army stationed close to the base camp. The camp was itself subject to prolonged fire and overrun by the attackers, who took with them when they withdrew 7 hostages (5 men, one women who was pregnant, and her young son aged 2). One of those men was found dead later in the day by Government forces. Responsibility for the attack was claimed by PLM/PLA.

[6]   "As soon as the attackers withdrew, the base camp was evacuated by the Contractor, using a barge which had arrived that morning under machine-gun fire from the banks of the river. The Contractor decided that it should immediately also evacuate the camp which was being used for the Canal Project, and that no further presence at all should be maintained in relation to that Project, so that the whole area of the site should be abandoned and all plant, equipment and supplies of the Contractor should be left in the care of the Government. This accordingly took place. The last of the hostages was not in fact released until January 1985. The Canal Project was never resumed by the Contractor, and remains unfinished to this day.

[7]   "In the light of the above-mentioned attacks, the Contractor concluded that there was a real risk that the Airport Project might well imminently be a target of the PLM. It was mindful that the two attacks on the Canal camps had been made without any prior warning. In evidence submitted to us, representatives of the Contractor testified that it decided that it could not continue at that time to put at risk the lives and safety of its employees, that it accordingly on or about 12 February 1984 decided to evacuate most expatriate women and children from the airport site and that at or about the same time it decided to reduce the number of male expatriates to the minimum required merely to ensure custody of plant, equipment and tools at the airport. All productive work on the Airport Project in fact ceased on 12 February 1984, though the Contractor did not at that stage exclude the possibility of returning at an uncertain future date when conditions might be safer.

[8]   "On 13 February 1984, the French Embassy in London received three communications. These communications were copies of letters addressed to the Contractor but which in fact the Contractor had not then received. They were respectively (i) a letter dated 30 November 1983, purporting to emanate from 'People's Liberation Movement';

(ii) an undated letter (probably written on 7 December 1983) also purporting to emanate from the said PLM; and (iii) a copy of a letter dated 8 February 1984, purporting to emanate from 'PLM UK and Europe Branche'.

[9]   "We think it clear that the PLM had considerable military strength, that (as appears from these communications) one of its objects was the stopping of work on the Canal Project, and that it was prepared to use armed violence to achieve that object.

[10]   "On the evening of 13 February 1984 the French Embassy in London caused the text of communication (iii) above to be transmitted to the Contractor in France. The next morning at 10:15 am the Contractor transmitted it to its representatives in country X. The same day (14 February 1984) the Contractor in France received via the French Foreign Ministry the text of communications (i) and (ii), and telexed them at once to those representatives in country X.

[11]   "The Contractor further adduced evidence to the effect that on or about 15 February 1984 it received both by telephone and in the form of a tape-recording the essence of the text of a fourth communication which subsequently was received by it in the form of a letter dated 16 February 1983 purporting to emanate from the said PLM UK and European Branch. This included the passage:

'Further the [Contractor] is hereby notified that they must immediately stop the construction of ... Airport. If the work continues as from the date of this letter, the [PLA] forces will take drastic action as they have already shown themselves capable of at the Canal zone. Should we be forced to take such action the [PLA] and [PLM] will not be responsible for any loss of life and]or property that may ensue.'

[12]   "It is not clear to us whether the text of this fourth communication was ever transmitted to the Contractor's representatives in country X. What is clear is that the Contractor had substantially evacuated the site at the airport before it knew of that communication. In a letter to the Ministry dated 15 February 1984 (which had been drafted by the Contractor in Paris on 14 February 1984) the Contractor's local area manager suggested that the parties should discuss how far the work not yet completed might be carried out in part by the Contractor and in part by local (i.e., X) contractors, and asserted that the Ministry should recognize that the 'Special Risks' provisions of the Contract applied to the situation which had arisen. At 17:57 Paris time on the same day he

received a telex from the Contractor in Paris ordering al work to be stopped immediately, and all expatriates to be sent home. Forthwith the Contractor evacuated completely its camp at the airport. It did not expect to return. It has not returned.''

In January 1985, the Contractor filed a request for arbitration with the ICC against the Ministry of Finance. The Contractor alleged that by reason of the matters referred to above that took place in country X in 1983 and early 1984, the completion by the Contractor of the works required by the Contract became effectively impossible. It further alleged that by virtue of the terms of the Contract, the Contractor was entitled to suspend work thereunder, was entitled not to resume such work at any time prior to the request for arbitration, and to recover from the Ministry various sums representing the Contractor's increased costs or losses. Alternatively, the Contractor alleged that the Contract had become frustrated under the law of country X.

The Ministry of Finance disputed the entitlement of the Contractor to the relief claimed and counterclaimed damages for breach of contract.

In December 1986, the arbitrators rendered a partial award in which they declared, inter alia, that the Contractor was entitled to suspend work under the Contract in February 1984 and never became obligated to resume such work, that the Contractor became frustrated by mid 1984, that the relief (if any) as the Contractor may be entitled to obtain against the Ministry falls to be determined in a subsequent award, and that the Ministry is not entitled to recover damages or to obtain other relief against the Contractor.

Excerpt

With respect to the Contractor's claims, the arbitrators considered the *following:*

A. *Frustration of Contract*

[13]   ''We do not think that when the Contract was concluded in December 1981 a reasonable business man in the position of the Contractor was entitled to assume, in the light of the known internal political, ethnic and economic problems of country X, that this job would be free from risk to those engaged upon it. Nor, in the situation prevailing in mid-February 1984 do we think that it would have been literally and absolutely impossible for the Contractor to have carried out thereafter (doubtless with some additional delay) the 10-15% of the Contract work which remained to be done at the Airport. It is not literally or

absolutely impossible that one who sets out to cross an uncharted mine-field will safely reach the other side.

[14]   "But in a commercial bargain one is concerned with pragmatic rather than abstract considerations – with commercial practicability rather than theoretical possibility. Where events beyond the control of either side supervene which merely render performance financially more onerous for a contracting party he will not, under most systems of law, be excused from further performance or (in the absence of some special contractual or statutory provision – nowadays not infrequently to be found) entitled to insist upon extra compensation. It appears to us that X law is no exception.

[15]   "But events which go beyond merely increasing the financial burden on the party performing, and which reach a point where they render performance unacceptably hazardous to the lives and safety of those performing, are in a different category altogether. If such events supervene, and if the risk which they create is unlikely to be removed within a reasonable time, under many legal systems further performance will be excused. Whether it is will usually depend upon such matters as the foreseeability, character, and expected duration of the risk, as they would have appeared to an objective, informed observer.

[16]   "We have concluded, on the basis of the expert evidence which we heard of X law (the proper law of the Contract), that these are equally the criteria to be applied to the assessment of the impact on the Contract of the events which we have described. In making that assessment in retrospect one must be on one's guard not to be too critical of decisions taken by those who were under the pressure of disquieting contemporary events.

[17]   "We see no reason to suppose that the Contractor was anxious in February 1984 to snatch at any pretext for not completing the modest proportion of the Contract work remaining. There was evidence to suggest that the Contractor had until that time been anxious to obtain further work in country X. In our view in February 1984 the Contractor was effectively prevented, by a real and substantial risk to the safety of its personnel and plant, from continuing with the work at the airport. That risk was of an appreciably greater order than anything that could have been reasonably contemplated in 1981. The Contractor could not humanly ignore the risk to those of its workmen who were already being held as hostages.

[18]   "Moreover, the Contractor is in our view not to be blamed for

declining to expose its workmen and their families at the airport to the significantly increased risk to their safety – we believe that many a responsible employer would have found it equally impossible to do so. So long as there was a fair possibility that the situation might improve within a reasonable time the Contract would in law remain alive, and the Contractor might well have been entitled to a corresponding extension of time.

[19]   "Once it became clear (as in our view it did by not later than mid-1984) that there was to be no material change for an unacceptably long time – perhaps years – the Contract was in law discharged by frustration, whether under [a section of an Act of country X], or under General Condition 136(2), or under the provisions of Special Condition 136 dealing with frustration.

[20]   "In our judgment this conclusion is not affected in law by the fact that had the Contractor completed the work by the original program date (which we find to be not later than 15 January 1984) none of these problems would have arisen. It appears to us that the Contractor was in January 1984 entitled to contractual extensions of time at least sufficient to take the Completion Date well beyond mid-February 1984. This conclusion is supported by the fact that both the Engineer and the Works Supervisor later recommended in this connection an extension of 51 days. But in any event, the Contract was certainly still alive in mid-February even if (contrary to our finding) the Contractor would already by then have been liable to pay liquidated damages for delay. The real question is simply whether the circumstances then and thereafter were such as to bring about its frustration.

[21]   "No conduct of the Contractor's caused the circumstances referred to – they were beyond the control of all. No question of 'self-induced frustration' arises here. It is not sufficient to show that but antecedent delay those circumstances might never have had any impact. *Post hoc* is not *propter hoc*. The frustration would not be 'self- induced' in law unless both (a) there was antecedent delay which was a breach of contract, and (b) that delay itself *caused* the occurrence of the new events creating frustration. We are not satisfied that either (a) or (b) is satisfied here.

[22]   "We would add two comments. First, after-events have now demonstrated that anyone who judged in mid-1984 that the situation would not speedily improve was not being unduly pessimistic. Secondly we prefer not to base our decision on any alleged illegality involved in continuing the work in the conditions indicated. The

bargain embodied in the Contract was not illegal, even if to have continued to attempt to perform it might have exposed one party to it (the Contractor) to penalties or damages at the suit of third parties in respect of physical risks to workmen employed by it (rather than by its subcontractor(s)) to carry out the work."

B. Consequences of Frustration

[23] "The consequences of our conclusion that the Contract was frustrated are as follows:

[24] "(a) During the period between mid-February 1984 and the moment (which we have held to be not later than mid-1984) when the Contract became discharged by frustration, the Contract remained alive. The Contractor incurred no expense in the execution of any work during that period. Any demobilization expenses which it incurred would have had to be incurred in due course in any event. Its plant and equipment grew a little older, but we can see nothing during this period in the nature of 'any increased cost of or incidental to the execution of the Works' (cf. Special Condition 136(4)). No work whatever was executed during the period or at any time thereafter. The fact that plant was retained on site may have meant that it was not put to good use elsewhere, but that is not an increased cost of or incidental to the execution of work. Nevertheless, during this period the Contractor was effectively prevented from working, and it is possible that it might be able to prove that the effluxion of time during that prevention but prior to the moment when the Contract became frustrated caused it financial loss of some sort.

[25] "The Contractor claimed alternatively to be indemnified in respect of any such loss under General Condition 136(2)(4) which purports to afford to the Contractor 'an indemnity based on the injury suffered'. In our view, however, General Condition 136(2)(4) does not apply unless it is established positively that the circumstances did 'not make it impossible to complete the Contract'. That is not this case. On the contrary, during the period under discussion (mid-February to June/July 1984) it was, on the Contractor's own case, effectively impossible to do any work at all – this was a period during which no notional objective observer would have asserted flatly that the circumstances did *not* make it impossible to complete the Contract. Such an observer would have said (as the Contractor indeed submits) that the circumstances certainly *did* make it impossible for the

Contractor to work for the time being, and *might* well continue to make it thus impossible for an intolerably long time. He could not have excluded the latter, and hence could not have said that completion was *not* impossible. It *was* impossible unless and until circumstances changed for the better, which they might never do (and in the event never did). Thus, the impartial observer could only have counselled patience to see if the current impossibility was temporary only.

[26]　　　"In fact it was not. In retrospect it can be seen that there was no time after mid-February 1984 when the circumstances did not make it impossible to complete the Contract, because the circumstances never again became such as to make it practicable to work. Something which makes it impossible to work today, and which (as it turns out) continues to make it impossible to work at all material times thereafter, cannot properly be described as something which does *not* make it impossible to work.

[27]　　　"But General Condition 136(2)(4) requires it to be established that the circumstances *do not* make it impossible to complete, or that existing circumstances make it *impossible to say* whether or not it will ever again become not impossible to complete. We consider that General Condition 136(2)(4) applies only to a case where it can be affirmatively established that the circumstances did not in fact make it impossible to complete the Contract without delay of a radical nature. It does not apply so long as no one can yet say whether it will be possible or impossible to complete without such a delay, still less to a case where it never again in fact becomes possible. General Condition 136(2)(4) deals with a case where the Contractor's obligation to complete the Contract never disappears, i.e., where the circumstances have never truly made it impossible to complete it without delay of the radical nature mentioned. In such a case, that provision will go far to protect the Contractor against many of the additional financial burdens (including those arising from unavoidable delays) which circumstances beyond its control may have imposed upon it in carrying out the task of completing the work. But the provision is not designed to deal with a case where the Contractor ceases to be under any obligation to complete and does not attempt to do so.

[28]　　　"We accordingly reject claims by the Contractor for financial losses attributable to cessation of work during this period and not otherwise recoverable under (b) below.

[29]　　　"(b) Once the Contract became frustrated it was *ipso facto* from that

moment discharged or rescinded without fault on either side. Neither side can claim damages resulting from such discharge. Under X law (as under the statutory law of the United Kingdom relating to frustration) the Contractor is prima facie entitled to be paid whatever (if anything) was owing to it for what it had done and for expenses that it had incurred under the Contract when it was discharged up to a ceiling figure equal to the value of the benefit conferred on the Ministry – see [a section of an Act of country X]. Subject to that ceiling, anything contractually payable for work done or expenses incurred, which had not been paid when frustration occurred, remained payable thereafter.

[30] ''The Contractor is therefore to be paid for the work which it has done. It is also entitled to recover (under Special Condition 136 and probably also on general principles of X law) in respect of any contractual claims for damages for breach of contract which may have accrued at the time when frustration occurred, and in respect of which the Ministry has no other good defence in law. It is entitled to no more.

[31] ''By parity of reasoning, however, it has a good defence against any counterclaims by the Ministry for failure to do further work. The Ministry has no valid claim against the Contractor for failing to complete such work, for the Contract has gone.

[32] ''On the evidence of the distinguished lawyers of country X who testified before us we judge that this conclusion is in accord with X law.

[33] ''But we are fortified in reaching it by what appears to us to be the justice of the result on the facts of the present case. We see no basis in law or equity for saying that the Ministry, rather than the Contractor, must under the Contract bear all the risks arising from the exceptional circumstances discussed, which were beyond the practical control of either of them. When frustration occurs the rights and obligations of the parties are those which have accrued at the time of such occurrence. As to the future, the loss lies where it falls. To grant the Contractor an extension of time to a point *after* frustration of the Contract has occurred would not only be devoid of logic but of no practical value to the Contractor. To grant the Contractor an extension of time to any *earlier* point would not afford the Contractor any cause of action against the Ministry. To order that the Ministry should pay the Contractor for work done or expenditure incurred a sum in excess of that calculated in accordance with the Contract mechanisms (and *a fortiori* to order that it should pay for work not done at all) would be as unjust as to order that the Contractor should compensate the Ministry for the Contractor's failure to complete the Contract work after events

beyond the Contractor's control rendered it effectively impossible to do so.

[34] "Thus as regards work done under the Contract, the Contract rates *prima facie* apply. To the extent that these have been paid to the Contractor, no further sums are due from the Ministry for that work. As regards the 'Supplemental Claims' of the Contractor, all or most of these appear to relate to matters arising from mid- February 1984. *Prima facie* therefore certain of these may be recoverable to the extent that they may meet the criteria of being claims which had accrued by mid-1984 either under the Contract or by way of damages for breach of it, and in respect of which the Ministry has no good defence in law. We are not, however, asked to rule upon the Supplemental Claims at the present stage. ....''

As regards the Ministry's counterclaims, the arbitrators considered:

[35] "As regards the Ministry's counterclaims, those relating to the cost of completion of the work, and to damage or injury to the Ministry's property are dismissed. The former is unsustainable in law, and the latter was insufficiently particularized or proved. The counterclaim for liquidated damages for delay is also dismissed. We judge that the Contractor was not, by mid-February 1984, in breach of its obligation to complete the Contract work within the contractual period plus such extensions thereof as it could already then justify. To any allegation of delay between mid-February 1984 and the time when the Contract became frustrated the Contractor could compellingly have answered by a claim under [a section of an Act of country X] for an extension of time arising from exceptional and unpredictable events causing delays beyond its control. To any allegations of culpable delay after the time when the Contract was frustrated the frustration itself would be a complete answer. No other counterclaims have been established before us.''

Second interim award in case no. 5277 of 1987

Arbitrators: Mark Littman, QC (UK), Chairman; Prof. Giorgio Bernini (Italy); Prof. Berthold Goldman (France)

Parties: Claimant: French contractor
                            Defendant: Ministry of Irrigation of African country X

Place of arbitration: Paris, France (agreed by the parties)

Published in: Unpublished (original in English)

Subject matters: - construction contract
                            - attack by People's Liberation Army
                            - frustration of contract
                            - damages, measure of -
                            - clause 67 FIDIC and time-bar
                            - economic dislocation and inflation
                            - prohibition of interest

Facts

By a contract dated 28 July 1976, as amended by a Supplemental Agreement dated 13 March 1980, the Ministry of Irrigation of African country X employed the French contractor to construct a canal of approximately 280 km. in that country. The conditions of contract included FIDIC 2nd edition (July 1969). The contract provided for the law of country X, which originates from English law as applicable law.

The facts of the case are similar to case no. 5195 also reported in this Yearbook. Case no. 5195 involved the same French contractor with respect to the Airport Project in the same African country X.

The Canal Project in the present case (no. 5277) required the employment of a giant bucket wheel excavator with which the French contractor had constructed a canal in an Asian country where the excavator had excavated at the rate of 3,000 m. per hour. Two years were required to bring the bucket wheel excavator weighing 2,300 tons and dismantled into 750 units for carriage to the site and for erection in country X. The excavation works commenced in June 1978.

By 15 November 1983 some 260 km. of the Canal had been excavated by the French contractor and paid by the Ministry. Since that date all work on the Canal had stopped due to attacks by the People's Liberation Army of country X (see the facts in case no. 5195 in this Yearbook).

In the ICC arbitration, which commenced on 12 April 1985, the French contractor sought (a) the decision of the arbitrators as to the date upon which the contract was frustrated; (b) damages and/or an award for payment of monies in respect of the period of "special risks," of frustration (clauses 65 and 66, respectively), of "major economic dislocation" (clause 67), of delays in the execution of the works allegedly due to a lack of fuel, and of the US$ amounts contained in six certificates issued by the Engineer, as well as interest thereon together with costs. The Ministry filed various counterclaims.

In a first interim award, the arbitrators refused a request for interim relief by the French contractor which request was prompted by the demand for payment by the Ministry under the advanced payment guarantee issued by a French Bank for account of the French contractor in favor of the Ministry.

In the second interim award, reported below, the arbitrators declared that: (1) the contract was frustrated on 1 August 1984; (2) the French contractor was entitled to recover the fair market value of the equipment in country X on 1 August 1984; (3) that the claims were not time-barred; (4) that the claim for "major economic dislocation" cannot comprise internal inflation; (5) the claim for fuel shortage is not barred by any permission of what has been granted by the Ministry to the French contractor to operate its own transportation of fuel; (6) that the French contractor is entitled to recover the unpaid certificates less a deduction for any element of interest contained therein and arising otherwise than under Clause 60 of the Conditions of Particular Application of the Contract; and that the Ministry's counterclaim for remeasurement is dismissed.

Portions of the arbitrators' reasoning in respect of a number of the above declarations are reproduced below.

Excerpt

A. *Claims under clauses 65 ("special risks") and 66 (frustration)*

1. The arbitrators summarized clauses 65 and 66 as follows:

> "By clause 65(1) the employer agreed to compensate the contractor for 'any loss of ... property of the contractor used or intended to be used for the purposes of the works and occasioned either directly or indirectly by' (inter alia) 'civil war'. By clause 65(4) the employer agreed to repay to the contractor any increased cost of or incidental to the execution of the works attributable to such a special risk. By clause 66, it was agreed that 'in the event of the contract being frustrated ... the sum payable by the employer to the contractor in respect of the

work executed shall be the same as that which would have been payable under clause 65 hereof if the contract had been terminated under the provisions of clause 65 hereof'. Clause 65(5) provided for a right of termination upon an outbreak of war. Clause 65(7) provided that 'if the contract is so terminated the contractor shall be paid by the employer for all work executed prior to the date of termination at the rates and prices provided in the contract' and in addition certain other sums which included at clause 65(7)(*d*) 'any additional sum payable under the provisions of sub-clause 1 ... and 4'.

2. With respect to the date of frustration, the arbitrators considered:

"Notwithstanding the position taken up by the Government and the engineer prior to the arbitration, it was conceded at the hearing that frustration had in fact occurred. The concept of 'frustration' is a familiar one in English law. It is not a term which is used in [an Act of country X] in connection with the law of contract, but [a section in the Act] provides 'The contract is the law of the parties.'. Sect. ... (which relates to the effect of change of circumstances) and Sect. ... (which relates to impossibility of performance) permit us and indeed require us to adopt the English concept in accordance with the will of the parties, especially in the absence of any suggestion by either party to the contrary.

"However, in relation to both of these claims there was an issue before us as to the date at which frustration had occurred. We were informed by a witness called on behalf of the Government that the position previously adopted by the Government in denying frustration previously had a political motivation. The Government did not wish to concede that the rebels had achieved their objective of preventing the completion of the Canal. Indeed, at the hearing it was contended for the defendant that frustration had occurred as early as 10 February 1984. The claimant on the other hand contended that notwithstanding the terms of its own letter dated 15 November 1984 (which suggested the 15 November 1984 as the date when frustration had occurred) the correct date which should be taken for frustration was 1 March 1985.

[3] "We find on the evidence that the date of frustration was 1 August 1984. This date was during the rainy season which would normally come to an end in about October. The evidence was that it would have required about three months to remobilize the labor force. If,

therefore, any real prospect had been perceived of recommencing work in time for the dry season 1984/85, this remobilization would have to have commenced not later than 1 August 1984. In fact, of course, no such remobilization was even considered at that date, much less undertaken. We consider, therefore, that 1 August 1984 is a fair date to take. Accordingly, any payments by the defendant under clause 65 (Special Risks) in respect of a period after 1 August 1984 are repayable to the defendant.''

4. As regards the claim for the value of the lost equipment, in particular the bucket wheel excavator, the arbitrators considered:

"A considerable part of the claim under clauses 65 and 66 is for the value of this equipment. The equipment may still be there and is still the property of the claimant. However, since at least February 1984 and to a considerable extent since 15 November 1983, the claimant has been deprived of all use of this equipment and has indeed had no access to it. We have had evidence that the bucket wheel excavator has been attacked from time to time and this and all the other equipment has no doubt deteriorated very considerably for want of maintenance and repair. However, the important point is we have found that from 1 August 1984 there was no likelihood of the claimant being able to recover access to and use of this equipment for the foreseeable future. On this basis we find, therefore, that the claimant has suffered a loss of all this equipment.

(....)

[5] "In our view the claimant is entitled to recover for this loss either under clause 65(1) or alternatively under clause 66. There can be no doubt that the claimant has lost the equipment as the result of the civil war and that this loss crystallized at the date of frustration. Accordingly, one or other or both of these clauses apply.

[6] "As to the basis of valuation, we hold that the correct measure is market value of the equipment existing in country X on 1 August 1984 and not written down book value. Clause 65(1) provides that the employer 'shall compensate the contractor for any loss of ... property of the contractor ...'. We hold that upon the true construction of clause 65 this is the compensation which is appropriate.''

B. Time-bar

7. The Ministry had raised the objection that certain claims were out of time inasmuch as the request for arbitration was not made within the second period of 90 days contemplated by clause 67 of FIDIC (2nd edition). Clause 67 provides for a two-tier system for resolving disputes: disputes first have to be referred to the engineer and, if a party is dissatisfied with the engineer's decision, he can submit the dispute to ICC arbitration. The part of clause 67 in FIDIC (2nd edition) reading:

> "The arbitrator(s) shall not enter on the reference until after the completion or alleged completion of the Works unless with the written consent of the employer and the contractor."

was replaced in the Conditions of Particular Application by the words:

> "The arbitrator(s) may enter on the reference at any time before or after the completion or alleged completion of the works."[1]

8. The arbitrators observed:

> "This question raises a point on which there has been considerable difference of opinion. The defendant's case is that upon the true construction of clause 67 and in particular the words 'require that the matter ... in dispute to be referred to arbitration as hereinafter provided' there must be an actual reference to arbitration within the second period of 90 days if the claim is not to become time-barred and any engineer's certificate given is not to become final and binding. The reference has to be by the submission of a formal request for arbitration under the ICC Rules. It is common ground that no such request was made within the specified time. The claimant's case, on the other hand, ... is that it was sufficient that they gave notice stating that they required that the matter or matters in dispute be referred to arbitration without actually filing the request within the specified period.
>
> [9] "Upon this point we were referred to a number of decisions of arbitrators and text-book articles in which both points of view received support. Thus, the contention of the claimant is supported by an article by Mr. I.N. Duncan Wallace, QC in the International

---

1. *Note General Editor.* These words correspond with the text of clause 67 in FIDIC (3d edition).

Construction Law Review: 'The Time Bar in FIDIC Clause 67'; and the award in ICC cases no. 1896 and 5029,[2] while the contention of the defendant is supported by the award in ICC cases no. 3790[3] and 4707[4]. We were also referred to certain English decisions but we did not find them to be directly in point. We were not referred to any decisions by the courts of country X, but our attention was called to [three Articles in an Act of country X, one of which provides]:

'*Construction in Case of Doubt*

'In cases of doubt the construction shall be in favor of the party who is aggrieved by the condition ...'.

[10]   "But for this article [in the Act], we would have preferred the strict interpretation, i.e., the one for which the defendant contends, for the following reasons:

[11]   "(1) It would give a more definite and commercial effect to the stipulation in question. Clause 67 provides that in certain circumstances the engineer's decision (if any) shall be final and conclusive. It then goes on to say that it shall not be final and conclusive in a certain event. One would, therefore, expect that event to be a definitive and binding event such as an actual submission to arbitration. If all that is called for is a notice that at some unspecified time thereafter the matter will or may be referred to arbitration it is difficult to see what real purpose is served by the notice since it would be no more than a statement of intention which could be abandoned at any time thereafter. On the strict construction, however, a real purpose is evident, i.e., to cut down quite drastically the ordinary legal period of limitation. We note that in some of the writing supporting the defendant's construction stress is laid upon the necessity for the warning being a *serious* warning because of the use of the word 'require'. It is conceded that a mere vague warning of a possible future challenge by arbitration is not sufficient. However, we are unable to see what difference this would make since a statement, being merely a

---

2. Reported in Yearbook XII (1987) p. 113, 123-123, and in 3 International Construction Law Review (1986) p. 472.

3. Reported in Yearbook XI (1986) p. 119, 123-125, and 1 International Construction Law Review (1984) p. 372 with comment by S. Jarvin, id. p. 375 and G. Westring, id p. 376.

4. Reported in 3 International Construction Law Review (1986) p. 470 with comment by S. Jarvin.

statement of intent, would not be binding in any event and could be abandoned at any time.

[12] "(2) The wording employed is not ideal on either approach. Thus, if the intention is to make a warning sufficient one would have expected some such words as 'serve notice that at any time thereafter the matter may be referred to arbitration'. On the other hand, it can also be said that much clearer words could have been used to achieve the 'strict' effect, e.g., 'submit the matter ... to arbitration as hereinafter provided', or 'must ... submit a request for arbitration to the ICC in respect of the matter or matters in dispute'. However, on balance we think that words used are more favorable to the defendant's contention than the claimant's. Thus, the word 'require' bears a flavor of something that is compelling or imperative rather than a mere non-binding statement of intention. This point gains force by its close conjunction with the words 'to arbitration as hereinafter provided'.

[13] "(3) The word 'require' in the context of ordinary English arbitration (such as was envisaged by earlier editions of this form of contract) has sometimes been used to refer to a subject which actually commenced in arbitration, e.g., Sect. 27 of the Arbitration Act (1950); Sect. 27(3) of the Limitation Act (1939), which provides that:

'... an arbitration shall be deemed to be commenced when one party to the arbitration serves on the other party or parties a notice requiring him or them to appoint an arbitrator or to agree to the appointment of arbitrator or, where the arbitration agreement provides that the reference shall be to a person named or designated in the agreement requiring him or them to submit the dispute to the person so named or designated.'

[14] "See also, *The Agios Lazaros* (1976) 2 Lloyd's Rep. 47 per Lord Denning M.R. at p. 51, where the learned Judge pointed out that an arbitration in England is commenced by the service of a notice containing:

'... a requirement. It must require the other party to do one or other of two things: (1) Either "to appoint an arbitrator" or (2) "to agree to the appointment of an arbitrator".'
(....)
'It seems to me that a notice which says: "I require the difference between us to be submitted to arbitration" is sufficient to commence

the arbitration: because it is by implication a request to agree to the appointment of an arbitrator.'

[15]   "(4) However, we must also take account of [the above quoted article in the Act of country X] and ask ourselves whether this is a 'case of doubt'. If so, we must give the benefit of the doubt to the claimant since the effect of the strict interpretation would be to make, as we have said, a drastic reduction in the period of limitation. We have come to the conclusion that this is a case of doubt. We accept, of course, that the doubt must be reasonable one and not merely fanciful. Nevertheless, it has to be borne in mind that this is a form of contract used throughout the world and used by parties who would not necessarily be familiar with the background of English law and practice in relation to arbitration. What has happened is that the former provision for ordinary English arbitration has been replaced by ICC arbitration but the introductory wording has not been changed. This has led, we think, to a certain lack of clarity in the wording which lays the words open to a possible construction which, although not the one we prefer, cannot be rejected as wholly unreasonable or fanciful. In these circumstances, we hold that the letters served by the claimant were a sufficient notice.

[16]   "The defendant has also contended in the alternative that the prior correspondence indicates that these matters were referred to the engineer before 30 August 1984 and 17 October 1983, respectively. However, we find that this contention is not made out by this earlier correspondence which we find was only of a preliminary nature.''

C.   *Economic dislocation*

[17]   "One of the matters discussed before us was the application of clause 71 (Special Conditions). This reads as follows:

'In the event of there being subsequent to the date of tender such a major economic dislocation within the country in which the works are being or are to be constructed as to result in the imposition by the Government of that country of currency restrictions or in devaluation of the currency of that country the employer shall pay to the contractor any increased costs of or incidental to the execution of the works which is howsoever attributable to or consequent on or the result of or in any way whatever connected with such economic dislocation provided always that nothing in this clause contained shall prejudice the right of the contractor to exercise any other rights or remedies to which the contractor may be entitled in such event.'

[18]   "There is no dispute that there was subsequent to the date of tender a 'major economic dislocation' in country X which resulted in devaluation of the X currency. The claimant accordingly contends that it is entitled to be paid certain increased costs of or incidental to the execution of the work resulting from such economic dislocation, i.e., increased costs incurred in country X as the result of internal inflation which mirrored and which was approximately of the same magnitude as the devaluation (i.e., the fall in the external value of the currency). Part of this claim does not relate to any foreign currency losses, nor to items payable in X currency which were subject to an escalation clause, e.g., labor costs and petroleum product costs. It is essentially for increased costs of other items purchased or incurred in country X which were compensated in the contract at fixed unit rates and for which the claimant had to pay far larger sums due to internal inflation in country X.

[19]   "In our view such costs related exclusively to internal inflation are not recoverable under this clause. The employer is liable under this clause to pay increased costs resulting, etc. from 'such economic dislocation'. We consider that the latter words refer to major economic dislocation resulting in the imposition of currency restrictions or devaluation of the currency. We think that the word devaluation means a change in the external value of the currency and that this clause is not intended to give compensation for internal inflation as such. Under this form of contract if a contractor wishes to be protected from internal inflation he must do so by appropriate escalation clauses. Accordingly on this ground we declare that such part of the claim under ... as relates exclusively to internal inflation fails as not being within the scope of clause 71."

D.   Interest

20.   As regards the claim for interest on the unpaid certificates, the Ministry objected to this part of the claim on the ground that interest is not recoverable under the law of country X. The arbitrators considered this objection in the following terms:

[21]   "Upon this question we were assisted by experts in X law called on behalf of both parties. Prior to 19-- the law was governed by [a Section in an Act of country X]. This placed no bar on the recovery of contractual interest and in addition gave a court power to award what is sometimes called 'legal interest' upon a principal sum from the date of such until the date of settlement or until such other date as the court should think suitable. The maximum rate was 9% for commercial debts and 6% for other debts.

[22]   "... [T]he position was radically changed by [the introduction of a new Act in country X], which prohibited any order by a court for the payment of interest. This law was designed to give effect to Islamic principles. Several years later this law was relaxed as regards contracts made (as was this contract) prior to 19--. There was some difference of view between the legal experts as to the effect of this law but we find that its effect was as follows.

[23]   "(1) Since 19-- there has been no bar on a court giving effect to any contractual agreement for the payment of interest provided the contract was entered into prior to 18 August 19--.
"(2) That as regards any contract made thereafter the court cannot award contractual interest.
"(3) That since 19-- the court has had no power to award non-contractual or 'legal' interest in any circumstances.

[24]   "Applying these principles to the claims in this case we find that the only power we have to award interest is under clause 60 of the Conditions of Particular Application of the Contract, i.e., on unpaid certificates at the rate of 12% per annum but as regards clause [no number indicated in the award] that power exists in respect of any period whether before or after 19--. The prohibition does not extend to damages simply upon the ground that they contain an item for the payment by either party of bank charges.

[25]   "It is not, however, possible in our view for the prohibition on interest to be circumvented by describing it as a claim for damages for loss of the use of the money. We accept the evidence of Dr. A that a court in country X would not uphold a claim for interest even though it was dressed up in such a way."

Final award in case no. 5418 of 1987

Arbitrators:	Dr. Kurt Heller (Austria), Chairman; Anthony Colman (UK); Dr. Gyula Gal (Hungary)
Parties:	Claimant: Importer in the UK Defendant: Exporter in Hungary
Place of arbitration:	Paris, France (as agreed by the parties)
Published in:	Unpublished (original in English)
Subject matters:	- exclusive distributorship agreement - commission contract under Hungarian law - contract of sale and of delivery under Hungarian law - effect of Government order authorizing parallel exports - waiver of right - loss of profits - standard of proof - mitigation of damages by party - mitigation of damages by arbitrators

Facts

By an agreement of 14 June 1977, the Hungarian foreign trade company ("Exporter") granted the English company ("Importer") the sole and exclusive rights for the import and sale in the territory of the United Kingdom of certain Hungarian wines, including in particular a wine called X. As far as wine X was concerned, the agreement provided that it would continue until 31 December 1987 with a further ten year extension unless either party gave a written notice of termination prior to 31 December 1986. Furthermore, the agreement provided also for ICC arbitration in Paris and designated Hungarian law as the applicable law.

Until 1984 there were no major disputes or misunderstandings between the parties. During that period, Exporter had a monopoly position in the export of wine X.

In February 1984, the Hungarian producer of wine X (the "Combinate") filed an application with the Foreign Trade Ministry to obtain the right to parallel export of its wines. Exporter raised objections to said application. The Ministry, however, by order of 30 March 1984, granted the application:

"From 1 April 1984 the Combinate has authority:

- to realize export subject to convertible accounts of wines, resp. all kinds of viticultural goods deriving from own and/or contractual production, or procured in the denomination of which the place name of ... figures;
- in the course of export subject to convertible accounts of these wines and viticultural products the Combinate is to be regarded a base-company. Furthermore:
- to realize parallel export subject to convertible accounts of wines and viticultural products, as well as viticultural by-products deriving from the wine species cultivated, or which can be planted on the croplands of the traditional wine districts ... and of other adequate vineyard determined by ....''

It stipulated in the order

"that in the course of prosecution of foreign trade activity licensed in the present decision the Combinate is obliged to act with observance of stipulations of the attached letter.''

The letter, which was made part of the order, advised inter alia:

"Therefore, it is necessary that when exercising the independent right to export, you should reckon with the home and foreign market situation that has developed up to the present, ensure – jointly with [Exporter] – the continuity and enlargement of export and contribute to the increase of returns in foreign exchange resulting from the export of Hungarian wines.''

Exporter, Importer and the Combinate engaged in discussions in order to solve the situation created by the Order. Attempts to replace the agreement between Exporter and Importer by an agreement between the Combinate and Importer failed.

On 9 January 1985, the Combinate informed Importer that it had decided to enter into an agreement with another English importer. On 10 January

1985, Exporter terminated the agreement with Importer as of 1 January 1985 referring to the "force majeure situation".

Importer resorted to ICC arbitration against Exporter, claiming damages for wrongful repudiation of the agreement, consisting, in essence, of loss of profits (UK£ 797,000), together with interest and costs.

The arbitrators decided that Exporter was liable to pay Importer UK£ 500,000 with interest and costs for the reasons reproduced in part below.

Excerpt

A. *The legal background*

[1]   "(a) Foreign trade in Hungary is a state monopoly (Sect. 3 Act III of 1974 on Foreign Trade). The right to engage in foreign trade activity is granted by the Minister of Foreign Trade. In the course of economic reform developments after 1968 the number of firms of foreign trade has been increased by extending this right to certain producing enterprises.

[2]   "(b) A further step of liberalization was the discontinuation of the monopolistic position of traditional foreign trade firms. Upholding the state monopoly of foreign trade the Directive No. 10/1981/Kk.E.10. of the Foreign Trade Minister made it possible that under conditions stipulated in the said norm a parallel foreign trade activity could be granted.

[3]   "The decision M-325-5/1984 of 30 March 1984 of the Minister of Foreign Trade was a measure the effect of which was that the Combinate was authorized 'to realize parallel export subjected to convertible accounts of wines' produced in a specific region and to export as base company subjected to convertible accounts of wines in the denomination of which the place of origin ... figures.

[4]   "(c) The Combinate before having received foreign trade rights, exported various wines, among them X, through the intermediary of Exporter. Their legal relation was based on a commission contract. This kind of contract between producer enterprises and foreign trade enterprises is subject to the Governmental Order No. 32/67/IX.23/ amended by G.O. No.54/1978/XII.7/ and G.O. No. 21/1981/ VII.17/, respectively in its background rules in the Civil Code of the Hungarian People's Republic (the "CC").

[5]   "Under the commission contract the commission-agent enters into a

contract of sale in his own name, for the benefit of the principal, against remuneration. Sect. 507 CC.

(....)

[6]   "In terms of G.O. 32/1967, the inland principal authorizes the foreign trade company to conclude foreign trade contracts in its own name.

[7]   "Under a contract concluded on the basis of commission it is the commission agent who acquires rights and accepts obligations in relation to the party having entered into the contract with him. Sect. 509 CC.

(....)

[8]   "Therefore, no legal relationship will be established between the foreign party who contracts with the Hungarian foreign trade company and the principal of the latter (producer).

[9]   "On the other hand, the commission agent of foreign trade has no more right to enforce the fulfilment of the foreign trade contract against the principal than agents do in general (Sect. 21-33 G.O. No. 32/1967 regulating the rights and obligations of the parties to the commission contract contains no stipulation concerning this issue).

[10]   "Between the foreign trade company and the producer there is no contract of delivery or sales contract the performance of which could be enforced by suit. The principal is only liable for damages caused to the commission-agent by non-performance.

[11]   "(d) The law of contracts, breach of contracts, responsibility for damages caused otherwise than by breach of contract are regulated in the CC Chapters XVII-L.[Act IV of 1977 on the amendment and Consolidated Text of Act. IV of 1959]. Concerning foreign trade contracts the rules of the CC are applicable with the modifications contained in the Law-Decree No. 8 of 1978 (the "Decree").

[12]   "(e) Hungarian civil law differentiates between contract of sale and contract of delivery. The latter can be entered into only by economic organizations (i.e., Hungarian state enterprises, co-operatives, etc.) according to special provisions contained in Governmental Decree No. 7/1978. These provisions are not applicable to this case. Foreign trade contracts under Hungarian law are governed by the general principles of contract law quoted above.

[13]   "(f) The basic rule of legal consequences of non-performance is contained in Sect. 312 CC.

(....)

[14]   "Where performance has become impossible for a reason the obligor is responsible for, the obligee may claim damages for non-performance. (al.2).

[15]   "Where the impossibility is the consequence of a fact the obligee is responsible for, the obligor shall be relieved of his obligation and may claim damages. (al.3). If none of the parties is responsible for impossibility of performance, the contract ceases to be in existence. (al.1).

[16]   "The performance may become impossible due to legal and physical reasons, but judicial custom in certain cases accepts also economic impossibility. At any rate the third alternative (al.1) presupposes an objective fact, being independent from the will, influence or activity of the parties to the agreement.

[17]   "(g) For non-performance for which one of the parties is responsible, Sect. 315 CC stipulates that any person who employs some other person for the discharging of an obligation, will be responsible for the conduct of the person so employed. (....)

[18]   "(h) To the liability for breach of contract and to the extent of damages the rules of liability for damages caused otherwise than by breach of contract apply with the difference that, unless exception is made by a provision of law, the damages cannot be reduced. Sect. 318 al.1. (....)

[19]   "(i) Under Hungarian law rules of responsibility for damages caused by breach of contract or otherwise than by breach of contract are identical and are set forth in Chapter XXIX 'General Rules of Compensation of Damages' of the CC. This identity applies also to measure of compensation which is regulated in Chapter XXXI for both categories.

[20]   "Sect. 339 CC sets forth that whoever unlawfully causes damage to another person shall be bound to compensate it. He shall be relieved of responsibility if he proves having acted in such a way as might reasonably be expected in the given situation.

[21]   "Concerning statement of damage Subsect. 2 of this Section makes possible that for circumstances deserving special appreciation the court may partly relieve the person responsible for the damage of his responsibility.

[22]   "The exclusion of this possibility for damages caused by breach of contract stipulated in Sect. 318(1) CC is not valid for damages caused

by breach of foreign trade contracts. Decree law No. 8 of 1978 ('KPTK') Sect. 15 amending Sect. 318 CC renders possible that the parties to the contract exclude or restrict the liability for breach of contract; the compensation of damage can also be mitigated by the court (arbitral tribunal).

[23]   "(j) From Sect. 339 CC quoted above, the following elements of liability may be abstracted: (a) damage; (b) unlawfulness; (c) causation; and (d) imputability.

[24]   "*Ad (a):* Without damage there is no compensation even if the act or omission was unlawful.

[25]   "*Ad (b):* Causing damage itself is illegal (general civil law violation). Statements of facts are not specified as in old laws or in criminal law. Apparently unlawful is the causing of damage by breach of contract. A special problem in theory and practice is the effect of prohibitions or permissions contained in other branches of the legal system such as, e.g., administrative law. It seems to be an accepted principle of court practice, that a behavior corresponding to rules of administrative law does not exclude civil law liability.

[26]   "*Ad (c):* The causal relation is a link between unlawful and imputable behavior and damage. The link should be relevant.

[27]   "*Ad (d):* Imputability in the general form of culpability may be expressed by terms of Sect. 339, al. 1: '... did not act in such a way as might reasonably be expected in the given situation'. 'Expectation' is a subjective element of legal qualification depending on reasonable demands towards the obligee in the given situation. Burden of proof: Claimant should prove (a) occurrence of damage, (b) unlawfulness of behaviour, and (c) causal link between them. Defendant has to prove (d) that he acted in such a way as might reasonably be expected in the given situation.

[28]   "Main rules for measure of compensation as stipulated in Sect. 355, al. 1 and al.4 are the following:

[29]   "The person responsible for the damage should restore the original situation (*in integrum restitutio*).

[30]   "Should this be impossible, he shall be given compensation for the loss suffered.

[31]   "By way of compensation the loss of value in the property of the injured person and the loss of profit sustained as a consequence of the damaging act, as well as the indemnification of expenses needed for the reduction or elimination of the financial and non-financial losses shall be given."

B.   Effect of the order of 30 March 1984 (issue no. 1)

32.   The arbitrators answered in the negative the first issue whether Exporter had lost its right to export wine X because of the Order of 30 March 1984 issued by the Hungarian Ministry of Foreign Trade:

> "There was nothing in the Order of 13 March 1984 which prohibited Exporter from selling wine X to Importer. If the Combinate had been willing to supply the wine, it would have been lawful for Exporter to sell it to Importer. The consequences of the Order will be explained in detail in the answer to issue 2."

C.   Exporter's wrongful refusal to perform the agreement (issue no. 2)

33.   The arbitrators answered affirmatively the second issue whether Exporter had wrongfully refused to perform the Agreement with respect to wine X:

> "It has not been established that Exporter at any time had a sale and purchase contract with the Combinate or any other organization under which the Combinate or such other organization was under a duty to deliver such wine X as Importer would require in order to perform the Agreement which Exporter had with Importer. Exporter had a commission contract with the Combinate.

[34]
> "A contract of sale between Exporter and the Combinate would have been inconsistent with their commission contract. The commission contract is a common type of contract between Hungarian foreign trade companies and producing economic organizations not having foreign trade rights.

> 'Under a contract of sale made on the basis of commission it is the commission agent who acquires rights and obligations in relation to the party having entered into the contract with him (Sect. 509(1) of the Hungarian CC).'

[35]
> "The Hungarian Supreme Court has explained the legal consequences of this provision as follows (p.toerv.v. 21.186/1976/2 ZR.- Collegium):

> 'There is no legal relation between the principal and the third person with whom the commission agent has signed the contract: In relation to this third party the rights are those of the commission agent and he

has to fulfill obligations even in case when the third party knew of the commission contract and the principal. The third party can only raise claims against the commission agent.'

[36]   "The Supreme Court ruled in another decision (GF.ii. 30.881/1973/4):

'The commission agent concludes the foreign trade contract in his own name but for the account of the principal. The principal has therefore to fulfill the obligations. Consequently, the foreign party can raise its claims under the foreign trade contract only against the foreign trade organization, the latter can take recourse against the principal for payments made by him.'

[37]   "The tribunal concluded that
"- performance had not become impossible for a reason that none of the parties is responsible for (Sect. 312(1) of the CC)
"- even if the Tribunal accepts that the defendant as commission agent acted in such a way as might reasonably be expected in the given situation (Sect. 339(1)) by reason of Sect. 509(1) as applied in Hungarian court practice the defendant should be held responsible for the impossibility of delivering the wine to the claimant for reasons under the control of the principal.

[38]   "Foreign trade partners of Hungarian export organizations may claim damages from the latter and not from their principals with whom they have no legal relationship. Whether under issue 2 the defendant acted wrongfully must be decided in accordance with the principles stated above. It is apparent that it is against the commission agent that claims under the contract can be made. On the other hand, the commission agent has the opportunity of taking recourse against the principal if the principal's conduct caused the breach of contract and wrongful act.

[39]   "Exporter has also relied on the fact that the trademark in wine X had to be transferred to the Combinate at the beginning of 1985 and that Exporter therefore could not continue to permit the claimants to market the wine. The tribunal considers that, just as Exporter, in accordance with the principles stated above, is to be held responsible for its failure to supply wine where its principal has caused the impossibility of continuing to supply wine, so also Exporter must be

held responsible if its principal no longer allows the use of its trademark by the claimant.''

D.   Waiver of right by importer (issue no. 3)

40.   The arbitrators answered in the negative the third issue whether Importer had expressly or impliedly waived its right to claim that Exporter had wrongfully refused to perform the agreement. Reviewing the circumstances of the case, the arbitrators concluded that there was ''no proof or even indication, that Importer waived its rights unconditionally and whether or not a new contract with the Combinate was ultimately entered into''.

E.   Loss of profits (issue no. 4)

41.   Turning to Importer's claim for damages, which essentially concerned loss of profits, the arbitrators considered this claim at length and made the following pertinent observations:

> ''As described ... above (the law), the compensation of damages under Hungarian law includes loss of profit (Sect. 355(4) of the Hungarian CC).
> ''When estimating the damages the tribunal has to try to arrive at an amount of damage which is plausible under the given circumstances. The plausibility has, however, to be proven by the claimant, who has – in general – the burden of proof for damages.
>
> [42]   ''The estimation of a loss of profit is mainly based on expectations of the future. In this context the tribunal has to start by taking into account the history of developments in the past. It was, therefore, an appropriate method of the claimant to present the calculation of their profit during the years 1980 through 1984 and for the first three months of 1985 .... The tribunal has no reason to doubt the correctness of these figures. They have been confirmed by Price Waterhouse, a very reputable international firm of certified public accountants. They were the official auditors of the group of companies to which the claimant belongs.
> (....)
>
> [43]   ''A claimant who seeks to recover damages for loss of profit upon wrongful termination of a long-term sales contract and who seeks to persuade a tribunal that the lost profit would be more substantial than had been earned in the period immediately preceding termination of

the contract has to adduce strong and compelling evidence that marketing circumstances would have significantly improved had the contract continued. Forward predictions are necessarily to some extent speculative and it is therefore particularly important that a tribunal which is asked to award damages for loss of increased future sales should require a high standard of proof that such increases were probable. The evidence adduced by the claimants in this case falls well short of convincing this tribunal that such an increase would probably have occurred. Mere commercial optimism is not enough. It has to be supported by evidence of actual market developments and characteristics strongly indicating increased sales. In the present case the kind of evidence which would have carried weight would have established a substantial and sustained increase in actual demand for wine X or substantially similar wines after 1984. No such evidence has been adduced.

[44]   "Indeed, the evidence presented by the claimant did not convince the tribunal that the figures for 1985 through 1987 for wine X would be substantially different from those in previous years. Therefore, the tribunal concluded that the sales volumes for 1985, 1986 and 1987 would probably be about the same overall as the average of the three previous years.

(....)

[45]   "It follows that the tribunal has reached the conclusion that the claimant has established that had the agreement been performed until the end of its term in 1987 the net profit which the claimant would have derived from it would have been most likely UK£ 692,000."

F.   Mitigation of loss by importer (issue no. 5)

46.   The arbitrators answered in the negative the fifth issue whether Importer had failed to mitigate its loss without justification:

    "(....)

[47]   "The tribunal is of the view that the claimants were not acting unreasonably in declining to attempt to expand their sales of Hungarian generic wines. If they had thought that it was reasonably possible to sell larger volumes profitably they could easily have obtained supplies from the defendants and would no doubt have done so. The tribunal accepts the evidence of Mr. S. that they could not substantially increase sales of generic wines and the evidence both of

Mr. S. and Mr. G. that to have any chance of increasing such sales would have required the launching of a new brand. This in turn would have involved a very substantial capital investment presented by promotion costs, with great uncertainty as to the likely degree of success.

[48]   "Sect. 340(1) of the CC provides as follows:

'The injured person shall make such effort in order to prevent or to mitigate the damage as might reasonably be expected generally in the given situation. Such part of the damages as has been caused by the injured person having omitted to comply with the said duty does not entitle him to compensation.'

[49]   "The tribunal considers that the prospects of increased sales of generic wines were so uncertain and the capital expenditure in launching them was so great that the claimants were quite justified in refusing to take the risk of losing their capital. There was therefore no breach of the duty to mitigate."

G. *Compensation to be paid by exporter (issue no. 6)*

50. Exporter argued that even if Importer had suffered losses as a result of Exporter's breach of the agreement, Exporter was not liable for the whole of the claim for damages as a matter of Hungarian law, in particular on the basis of Sect. 318(1) of the Hungarian CC as amended by Sects. 10, 15, and 18 of Decree no. 8 of 1978:

"Sect. 318(1): To responsibility for the breach of contract and to the extent of damages the rules governing liability for damage caused otherwise than by breach of contract shall apply with the difference that unless exception is made by a provision of law, the damages cannot be reduced.

[51]   "Sect. 10 of Decree no. 8 of 1978 (to Sect. 246(2) of the CC): Damages to be paid for breach of foreign trade contract cannot exceed penalty.

[52]   "Sect. 15 of Decree no. 8 of 1978 (to Sects. 314 and 318 CC): The parties may exclude or limit their liability for breach of contract. Damages may be mitigated by the court (arbitration tribunal) as well.

[53]   "Sect. 18 of Decree No. 8 of 1978 (to Sect. 318(1) and 335(1) of the CC): The party who caused the damage shall redress the damage which is the direct consequence of his conduct and which he could take into

consideration as a possible consequence of breach of contract at the
time the contract was made.

[54]   ''Sect. 339(2): For circumstances deserving special appreciation the
court may partly relieve the person responsible for the damage of his
responsibility.''

55.   Exporter's request that the arbitrators "should ask for independent
information about Hungarian law,'' was rejected by the arbitrators:

''Dr. F. stated on behalf of the defendant, that the tribunal should ask
for independent information about Hungarian law.

[56]   ''In international arbitration cases the tribunal is not bound by specific
rules for the taking of evidence provided that both parties were allowed
to present their case (Art. $V(1)(b)$ of the Convention on the
Recognition and Enforcement of Foreign Arbitral Awards and other
international documents).

[57]   ''When determining the law the tribunal may either make its own
research or appoint an expert under Art. 14(2) of the [ICC] Rules or
may hear experts presented by the parties. It is a matter of the
circumstances of the given case whether the tribunal assumes that one
or the other way is more appropriate.

[58]   ''In the present case the tribunal decided to do its own research and to
hear the experts of the parties. In particular the discussion of legal
issues with the experts of the parties was very helpful together with the
tribunal's own research. The specific circumstances in which the
tribunal did not – in addition – appoint an expert were the
following:

''- one of the arbitrators, Dr. Gal, is a Hungarian lawyer and expert in
Hungarian law who contributed the correct interpretation of
relevant rules by studying Hungarian court practices and works of
leading Hungarian authorities on civil law;
''- all relevant provisions of Hungarian law were made available to the
tribunal in an English translation, which Dr. Gal checked against
the Hungarian text;
''- the tribunal was given a number of additional supporting texts like
the pronouncement of the Decree No. 8/1978 by the Ministry of
Justice and commentaries to Hungarian Civil Law;
''- there are no settled court rules by the Hungarian Supreme Court
relating to Decree No.8/1978. Even Dr. X., a judge of this Supreme

Court, was unable to name any decision. Therefore, the tribunal had to make its own interpretation of the Decree No.8/1978 without being able to rely on court decisions as the prime authority to interpret Hungarian law.''

59.   After a number of general considerations, the arbitrators applied Sects. 10, 15 and 18 of Decree No. 8 of 1978:

[60]
''Sect. 10: As explained above this provision is irrelevant for this case.
''Sect. 18: The tribunal takes the view that the loss of profit for which the claimant claims compensation in damages is a direct consequence of the breach of the agreement by the defendants in failing to make continued deliveries under the agreement. The tribunal is further of the view that this is just the kind of loss which at the time when the agreement was entered into was the reasonably foreseeable consequence of refusal to continue supplies of wine X to the claimant as exclusive British distributor and which would result from the consequent marketing of that wine by another British distributor.

[61]
''Therefore the tribunal is justified in awarding the claimant damages based on the claimant's loss of profit and lost resales.

[62]
''Sect. 15: No decision of the Hungarian courts concerning this provision were presented to the tribunal. The lack of legal practice was confirmed by the Hungarian Ministry of Foreign Trade.

[63]
''When answering issue 2 the tribunal explained the reasons why Exporter is legally responsible for the breach of its contract with Importer. The tribunal took, however, notice that this breach of contract was partly the indirect consequence of the way how the parallel export rights were granted to the Combinate, whereby no proper considerations were made to harmonize it with existing foreign trade contracts. Exporter was, therefore, to some extent the victim of the uncoordinated introduction of parallel export rights. This does not – as explained under issue 2 above – relieve Exporter from its responsibility, but the way in which the damage was caused amounts to circumstances deserving special appreciation in the same sense as provided by Sect. 339(2) CC and therefore some mitigation under Sect. 15 would be justified.

[64]
''When deciding on the amount of reduction due to Sect. 339(2) CC and Sect. 15 of the Decree No. 8/1978 the main weight has to be given to the fact that the claimant suffered from a breach of contract and was

in no way connected with the reorganization of the Hungarian foreign trade.

[65] "Taking into account the specific facts of this case the tribunal regards a moderate diminuation of the losses justified. The amount of recoverable losses of profit shall therefore be reduced to UK£ 500,000 (instead of UK£ 692,000).

[66] "One member of the tribunal has felt considerable hesitation about applying Sect. 15 on the facts of this case, particularly in view of the complete lack of Hungarian judicial decisions on this section and because in his view the damage suffered by the claimants and by Exporter (due to this award) has been substantially caused by the failure of the Combinate, the principals of Exporter, to act in good faith and because it appears likely that the Combinate is liable to indemnify Exporter. However, in his opinion it was appropriate in view of the continuing trading relationship between the claimants and Exporter that there should be a unanimous award.''

Final award in case no. 5460 of 1987

Arbitrator: Paul Sieghart (UK)

Parties: Claimant: Austrian franchisor
                       Defendant: South African franchisee

Place of
arbitration: London, United Kingdom (fixed by the ICC Court of
                       Arbitration)

Published in: Unpublished (original in English)

Subject matters: - applicable conflict rules
                       - proof of foreign law
                       - law applicable to the substance
                       - period of limitation and applicable law

Facts

By a contract concluded in August/September 1979, an Austrian Mr. X concluded a franchise contract with a South African company relating to the manufacture by the South African company of certain equipment of Mr. X's design and the payment by the South African company to Mr. X of certain royalties thereon (the "Contract"). By clause 10.4 of the contract, the parties submitted "to the jurisdiction of the International Chamber of Commerce, as the arbitration court."

When the South African company failed to pay the minimum royalties under the Contract, Mr. X started court proceedings on 25 January 1983 in the Supreme Court of South Africa, claiming from the South African company SA Rand 288,000 together with interest thereon at 11%.

In a Special Plea entered in the said action on 11 October 1983, the South African company stated that the contract contained the arbitration clause referred to above, that the said action was in respect of disputes which were covered by the arbitration clause, and that the South African company was and remained ready and willing to do all things necessary to the proper conduct of an arbitration in terms of the said arbitration clause; accordingly, it prayed that the action be stayed pending the arbitration proceedings, and that the claimant be ordered to pay the costs of the action.

By a request for arbitration dated 12 November 1985, Mr. X thereupon instituted ICC proceedings, claiming from the South African company the sum of AS 4,896,000 (being the equivalent, under the Contract, of the sum of SA Rand 288,000 referred to above), together with interest thereon at the rate of 11% per annum, and the costs of the arbitration.

By its reply to the said request dated 13 December 1985, the defendant contended that:
(a) because proceedings in respect of the same claim were pending in the Supreme Court of South Africa, "it was not competent for the claimant to institute the arbitration proceedings";
(b) the claimant's claim "might have become prescribed";
(c) the claimant had failed to perform his obligations under the Contract;
(d) accordingly, the claimant was not entitled to the payment of the sum claimed, or of any sum, from the defendant.

Despite repeated reminders and extensions of time by the ICC Court of Arbitration, the South African company refused to sign the Terms of Reference. It also refused to participate in the arbitral proceedings, although it was duly invited.

In the course of 1987, the sole arbitrator (appointed by the ICC Court of Arbitration) rendered an award, ordering the South African company to pay Mr. X AS 4,896,000 together with interest from 25 January 1983 at the rate of 11% per annum and costs.

Excerpt

A. *Applicable law*

[1]   "The place of this arbitration is London, and on any question of choice
             of law I must therefore apply the relevant rules of the private
             international law of England. Under those rules, questions of
             performance or breach of a contract fall to be determined in accordance
             with what we call the 'proper law' of the contract. Unlike the laws of
             some other countries, the principal consideration here is not the *lex
             loci contractus*, but rather the law of the place with which the contract
             has its closest connection – which, in practice, means the place on
             which the principal obligations under the contract are to be
             performed.

[2]   "In the present case, virtually all the obligations of both parties fell to
             be performed in South Africa. It was there that the claimant's
             drawings and other documents were to be delivered; it was there that
             the defendants had to obtain the appropriate exchange control consent
             before dispatching the royalties to claimant; above all, it was there that
             the equipment was to be made and sold. On any commercial view, the
             principal place of performance of this Contract, and the place with
             which it had its closest connection, was South Africa. Insofar as it may
             be necessary for the purposes of this award, I therefore hold that the
             proper law of the Contract was South African law.

[3]   "Under the rules of English private international law, foreign law is a
             question of fact, to be established by expert evidence; failing evidence
             to the contrary, English private international law compels me to
             assume that any foreign law is the same as English domestic law.
             Neither party has furnished me with any evidence about the South
             African substantive law of contract. Accordingly, I am bound to
             assume that it does not differ from the law of England."

B. *Period of limitation*

[4]   "Under the rules of English private international law, questions of
             prescription (or, as it is called here, limitation) are to be determined by
             the *lex fori* – that is, in the present case, by the domestic law of
             England. By that law, the period of prescription or limitation for a
             claim arising under a contract is six years. The present Contract was
             concluded in September 1979. The present arbitration commenced in

November 1985. No part of the claimant's claim is founded on any alleged breach of the Contract more than six years before the commencement of the arbitration – that is, within the first two months of its currency.

5]   "That is enough to dispose of this question. However, even if I were to apply to it the provisions of South African or Austrian law – both of which, according to the pleadings in this arbitration, provide a prescription period of three years from the time when the cause of action arose – I would still come to the same conclusion. The defendant's obligations under clause 11 of the Contract were to manufacture certain minimal annual numbers of an equipment during the contractual period, and to pay the agreed royalties thereon to the claimant. It is not disputed that the defendant did neither. Under clause 9.1 of the Contract, this gave the claimant the right at any time, after not less than 30 days' notice, to bring the Contract to an end, whereupon he would become entitled to payment of the minimum royalties which he now claims.

6]   "By a letter dated 28 October 1982, the claimant's South African attorneys demanded from the defendant that it should confirm, by 15 November 1982, that it would abide by the Contract and pay the royalties stipulated under it. That letter was not an exercise by the claimant of any right vested in him to bring the Contract to an end: on the contrary, it was an affirmation of the Contract. Not until 25 January 1983, when he issued his summons in the Supreme Court of South Africa, did the claimant, by para. 9 of the Particulars of its claim annexed to that summons, exercise its right to terminate the Contract under the terms of clause 9.1 thereof. This was therefore the date on which the claimant's cause of action for payment of the minimum royalties arose, and it was less than three years after this that the present arbitration was commenced.

7]   "In support of their plea of prescription, the defendant relies on a copy of a letter dated 13 June 1980, written by their then attorneys, saying that the defendant 'has cancelled the contract', 'does not consider itself bound by it', and 'deems the whole Contract nul [sic] and void'. That letter was in fact addressed, not to the claimant, but to a quite different Austrian entity apparently called … . At the hearing, the claimant told me that he has never seen the original of this letter, and that he did not hear of its alleged existence, or of the fact that the defendant's attorneys claimed to have written it, until some time in the following year. I have no reason to disbelieve him, but even if it h   had come to his notice earlier it could not have started any prescription period running. It was addressed to a third party, and at its highest it evinced an intention by the defendants not to be bound by the Contract – that is, a unilateral repudiation of it, which it would have been open to the claimant either to accept or to reject. Acceptance of a repudiation must be within a reasonable time; without it, the contract continues in force and no cause for action arises for such an 'anticipatory breach'. In fact, the claimant's attorneys' letter of 28 October 1986, referred to above, expressly refers to this letter and says that the claimant does *not* accept the repudiation.

[8]   "Accordingly, I conclude that the claimant's claim in this arbitration has not become prescribed."

C.   *Competence to institute arbitration proceedings*

[9]   "This issue can be disposed of briefly. When the claimant instituted his action in the Supreme Court of South Africa on 25 January 1983, he had a choice of two remedies: that action, or the institution of arbitration proceedings under the Rules of the ICC. He chose the first. Thereupon, the defendant too had a choice: to let the dispute be decided in the action, or to rely on the arbitration clause in the Contract and apply for a stay of the action pending the institution of arbitration proceedings. Having considered the matter for several months, it chose the second course by entering their Special Plea on 11 October 1983. On the claimant's motion, the Supreme Court on 23 October 1984 ordered that this Special Plea should be decided separately, and prior to the trial of the matter, and that the action should meanwhile be stayed. Thereupon, the claimant instituted the present arbitration proceedings.

[10]   "Having submitted a voluminous reply to the request for arbitration and conducted a good deal of correspondence with me – in the course of which it sought more than once, and received, an assurance from me that its clients would be entitled to be heard in the arbitration even if they failed to pay their share of the advance for costs to the ICC – the defendant's representatives in this arbitration, under cover of a brief letter dated 18 August 1986, sent me a copy of a document purporting to be a Notice of Withdrawal of the Special Plea, prepared by the attorneys acting for the defendant in the action before the Supreme Court of South Africa (who are not the same as the defendant's representatives in this arbitration), and dated '-- day of August 1986'.

[11]   "Even on the assumption that a dated original of this copy has been duly submitted to the Supreme Court, it cannot retrospectively affect the competence of the present arbitration. Were it otherwise, a defendant in similar circumstances could send a claimant from pillar to post in perpetuity, by calling for arbitration if the claimant chooses litigation and thereupon, reversing his position, calling for litigation if the claimant accepts that invitation and chooses arbitration. In my judgment, once the defendant has elected to claim arbitration (as it was perfectly entitled to do), and once the claimant, in response to that election, has instituted arbitration proceedings, it is no longer open to the defendant to resile from it.

"Accordingly, I conclude that it was competent for the claimant to institute the present arbitration proceedings, and that it is competent for me to determine them."

D.   Claimant's failure to perform

12.   The arbitrator found that Mr X. had not committed any of the breaches of the obligations under the Contract which the South African company alleged.

E.   Currency, interest and costs

[13]   "It follows that the claimant's claim in this arbitration must succeed. Under clause 9.1, he became in the events which have happened entitled to payment of the minimum royalties calculated in accordance with clause 11, which sets them out in both SA Rand and AS. They amount to SA Rand 288,000 claimed in the action in the Supreme Court of South Africa, or AS 4,896,000 claimed in this arbitration, the rate of exchange being fixed by the Contract itself.

[14]   "In addition, the claimant claims interest on this sum at the rate of 11% per annum, being the rate awarded now, and over recent years, by the Austrian courts. That appears to me to be a perfectly proper rate. The claimant further asks for compound interest, but I am not disposed to award this. The date from which the interest should run is 25 January 1983, being the date on which, in the Particulars of his claim annexed to his summons in the Supreme Court of South Africa, the claimant first exercised his right to terminate the Contract under clause 9.1, whereupon the whole of the sum now claimed became immediately due and payable to him.

[15]   "The claimant is clearly entitled to an order for his costs. Apart from

the costs of the arbitration, the claimant also claims the 'normal legal costs' incurred by him, in accordance with Art. 20.2 of the Rules. Mr. Y's bill – drawn up in accordance with the principles, and at the normal rates, applicable to Austrian patent agents - amounts (after deduction of the deposits for costs paid to the Court of Arbitration of the ICC, which are included in it) to AS 274,900.''

Preliminary award in case no. 5505 of 1987

Arbitrator:	Georges Muller (Switz.)
Parties:	Claimant: buyer from Mozambique
	Defendant: seller from the Netherlands
Place of arbitration:	Lausanne, Switzerland (fixed by the ICC Court of Arbitration)
Published in:	Unpublished (original in English)
Subject matters:	- law applicable to substance
	- law applicable to procedure
	- applicable conflict of laws rules
	- law applicable to arbitration clause
	- validity of choice of law

Facts

The contract for the sale of seed potatoes between the Dutch seller and the Mozambique buyer contained the following clause contained in an Annex II:

"*Arbitration*:

"Both parties undertake to fulfill this contract in good faith. Any dispute arising in consequence thereof, or in connection therewith, should be settled through an amicable negotiation. Should no agreement be arrived at, they must finally undertake to submit the matter according to the regulation for agreement and arbitration of the International Chamber of Commerce to one or more arbitrators as per the said laws. The arbitration will take place in Switzerland, the law applicable is that known in England.''

The parties disputed the meaning and effect of the words ''the law applicable is that known in England'' as appearing in the last sentence of the above quoted clause. The arbitrator held that the words meant a valid choice in favor of English substantive law for the following reasons.[1]

Excerpt

A. *Introduction*

[1]   ''The claimants assert that English substantive law applies to the dispute. Their position is based on the clause 'Arbitration' of Annex II to the contract executed by the parties. They consider this provision as embodying a valid choice in favor of English substantive law.

''The defendants hold that the arbitrator should apply Dutch substantive law to resolve the dispute. Their contention is based on several arguments regarding the interpretation, the validity, and the effects of the provisions contained in Annex II.

[2]   ''There is no dispute that the arbitration clause contained in Annex II has been agreed upon by the parties and that it should govern these arbitration proceedings.

''(....)

''Further, it is not disputed that the parties have agreed to have any dispute among them settled in accordance with the rules of conciliation and arbitration of the ICC Court of Arbitration.

''Finally, the parties have chosen Switzerland as the place of arbitration.

''The sole issue to be determined by the arbitrator at this stage relates to the substantive law which he should apply to resolve the dispute.

[3]   ''In this respect, the arbitrator must first consider the ICC Rules which the parties have adopted.

''Under Art. 13(3) of the ICC Rules,

'The parties shall be free to determine the law to be applied by the

---

1. *Note General Editor.* After issuance of the preliminary award, the parties reached a settlement.

arbitrator to the merits of the dispute. In the absence of any indication by the parties as to the applicable law, the arbitrator shall apply the law designated as the proper law by the rule of conflict which he deems appropriate.'

"The parties to an agreement are free, under the ICC Rules, to adopt the substantive law which should govern their agreement and an arbitral tribunal has to apply the law so adopted. It is only if there is no designation by the parties of the applicable law that the arbitral tribunal shall resort to a rule of conflict of laws. An arbitral tribunal should probably also deviate from the law chosen by the parties if it would appear that such a choice, if applied by the arbitral tribunal, could prevent that the award be implemented (Art. 26 of the ICC Rules;[2] L. Craig, W. Park, J. Paulsson, *International Chamber of Commerce Arbitration*, Part III, p. 88, Paris 1984).

[4]   "In the present instance, the parties are in conflict as to whether or not they have made an election in the contract for a substantive law to apply.
            "Therefore, the arbitrator shall first make a decision upon the meaning of the words 'the law applicable is that known in England'. Does it or does it not represent a choice of substantive law?
            "If the decision is that it does not represent such a choice, then the arbitrator will have to select a proper rule of conflict of laws.
            "If the decision is that it represents such a choice, then the arbitrator will have to consider whether it is a valid choice of laws and whether there are clear indications that the application of English law to resolve the dispute could obstruct the implementation of the award either in the Mozambique or in the Netherlands.''

B.   Rules of construction

[5]   "In making that decision, one has first to select which system or principles of law one has to apply.
            "One could construe the disputed sentence by applying English law

---

2. Art. 26 of the ICC Rules provides:
       "In all matters not expressly provided for in these Rules, the Court of Arbitration and the arbitrator shall act in the spirit of these Rules and shall make every effort to make sure that the award is enforceable at law.''

as being the law presumably chosen by the parties, or by applying Swiss law as the *'lex fori'*, or by resorting to principles of law generally admitted (among others: L. Craig, W. Park, J. Paulsson, *International Chamber of Commerce Arbitration*, Part II, p. 17, Part III, p. 67 et seq., Paris 1984; P. Fouchard, *L'arbitrage commercial international*, p. 62 et seq., 319 et seq., 362 et seq., Paris 1965; E. Bucher, "Arbitration under the ICC Rules in Switzerland and the 'Concordat'", *Recueil de Travaux suisses sur l'arbitrage international*, p. 134-135, Zurich 1984; J. Robert, *L'arbitrage*, 5th ed., p. 231 et seq., 269 et seq., 279 et seq., Paris 1983; P. Lalive, "Les règles de conflict de lois appliquées au fond du litige par l'arbitre international siégeant en Suisse", in *L'arbitrage international privé et la Suisse*, p. 67 et seq., Geneva 1977; O. Lando, "The law applicable to the merits of the dispute, Contemporary problems" in *International Arbitration*, p. 104 et seq., London 1986).

"It does not seem adequate to apply English law to determine the issue as it could lead to preempting the solution. Therefore, the arbitrator will be guided by Swiss law and general principles of law (P. Jolidon, *Commentaire du Concordat suisse sur l'arbitrage*, p. 455, Bern 1984).

"It has to be noted that in the present instance there is no absolute need to resort to a specific system of law to construe the said sentence.

6] "Under Swiss law, the wording of contracts forms the basis of their construction, but Swiss judges also look at all the circumstances which seem appropriate to establish the common intention of the parties (ATF 99 II 285).

"The statements of a party must be construed as the other party had to understand them *bona fide*, i.e., as an honest and reasonable person would have understood them under the same circumstances (ATF 101 I a 43). If the real intention of the parties cannot be proven, the judge will look at the objective meaning of the contract, defined in accordance with the general experience of life and the principle of good faith (ATF 95 II 437).

"Generally, the judge may assume that the words of the agreement have been used in their common meaning (ATF 82 II 452) or, in contracts between specialists, in their technical meaning (ATF 100 II 145). If the text of a contract is clear, it should not be altered on an interpretation based on extrinsic evidence (ATF 99 II 285). Swiss law further accepts the principle according to which the terms of a contract are to be construed more strongly against the maker of the contract (ATF 100 II 153). However, this principle applies only in cases of ambiguity, and not if both parties have taken part in the making of the contract.

"In the present case, there are no facts known to the arbitrator which could help establishing the common intention of the parties as regards the disputed sentence. Nor did the parties bring any extrinsic evidence in their memorials.

"(....)

"The construction of the disputed sentence shall therefore rest on its terms."

C. *Possible meanings*

[7]   "The arbitrator is of the opinion that the parties to the contract did not include inadvertently the said sentence into Annex II, but that they were rather willing to give to that sentence a definite meaning in the context of the arbitration clause.

"In the said context, one may elaborate four possible meanings, that is,

- a choice of substantive law
- a choice of procedural law
- a choice of a rule of conflict of laws
- a choice of a law to determine the validity and effect of the arbitration clause.

"The arbitrator will review whether the disputed sentence may be regarded as a choice of procedural law, or a choice of a rule of conflict of laws, or a choice of a law to determine the validity and effect of the arbitration clause, or a choice of substantive law. In this connection, the arbitrator will address the argument made by the defendants that clauses which embody a choice of substantive law have to be clear, specific and unambiguous.

"In reviewing the possible meanings of the disputed sentence, the arbitrator will apply the following test: How could that sentence be understood in good faith by a reasonable man active in the international trade."

D.   *The word "law"*

8]   "Beforehand, the arbitrator notes that the word 'law' appears twice in
              the arbitration clause of Annex II.
                 "The first reference is to 'as per said laws'. The 'said laws' obviously
              refer to the Rules of Conciliation and Arbitration of the ICC. Another
              construction is not reasonable and the parties do not pretend to the
              contrary.
                 "The second reference to the word 'law' appears in the disputed
              sentence, in connection with the word 'applicable'. The defendants
              allege that 'the law applicable' could refer to 'as per said laws'. This
              does not seem, however, to be a valid construction of these words.
                 "The word 'law' has several meanings and there is no reason why it
              should not have been used under two imports. As far as the form is
              concerned, it is difficult if not impossible to connect the 'law' and the
              'said laws'. As regards the substance, it makes no sense to do that kind
              of reference.
                 "Therefore, one shall admit that the 'law applicable' does not refer
              to the 'said laws'.''

E.   *Does the "law applicable" indicate a choice of procedural law?*

9]   "It is quite uncommon to find in an arbitration clause an indication of
              the law which shall govern the procedure under which the arbitration
              shall take place (among others, see P. Fouchard, *L'arbitrage
              commercial international*, p. 304, Paris 1965).
                 "Parties adopting an arbitration clause expect mostly to escape
              procedural particularities of local courts; the designation of a
              municipal law is most often contrary to the advantages sought in an
              arbitration clause (L. Craig, W. Park, J. Paulsson, *International
              Chamber of Commerce Arbitration*, Part III, p. 68, Paris 1984).
                 "In this case, the choice of the ICC Rules was well sufficient to settle
              the problems of procedure (Art. 11 of the Rules for the ICC Court of
              Arbitration[3]). The choice of Switzerland as the place of arbitration

---

3. Art. 11 of the ICC Rules provides:
        "The Rules governing the proceedings before the arbitrator shall be those resulting from
        these Rules and where these Rules are silent, any rules which the parties (or, failing
        them, the arbitrator) may settle, and whether or not reference is thereby made to a
        municipal procedural law to be applied to the arbitration."

implied in any case the application of the Swiss mandatory provisions Nothing indicates that the parties could have reasons to avoid the application of Swiss procedural law and to choose specifically English procedural law. Moreover, such a choice could bring with it numerou difficulties.

"Therefore, quite clearly, if the parties intended a reference to procedural law, they would have made it plain and would not have used the words 'the law applicable' which designate ordinarily the substantive law (see hereafter).

"Further, one cannot understand why the parties would have chosen such an extraordinary law of procedure under the circumstances but not a substantive law.

"The arbitrator is therefore of the opinion that a reasonable man active in the international trade could not have understood the disputed sentence as a reference to a choice of procedural law."

F.   Does the "law applicable" indicate a choice of a rule of conflict of laws?

[10]   "It seems unlikely that parties to an international contract choose a rule of conflict of laws, but not the substantive law: it is hard to understand how the parties cannot agree to a proper law, but can agree to the rules of conflict that determine the proper law. This may sometimes happen, but for certain reasons (L. Craig, W. Park, J Paulsson, *International Chamber of Commerce Arbitration*, Part II, p. 67, Paris 1984).

"In this case, there is no evidence of any reason of that kind.

"Further, one may assume that, if the parties had in mind to refer to a rule of conflict of laws, as opposed to a substantive law, they would have made it clear.

"Finally, it would have been contradictory and therefore unreasonable to choose at the same time a rule of conflict of laws and a substantive law, as this is assumed by the defendants.

"The arbitrator is therefore of the opinion that a reasonable man active in the international trade could not have understood the disputed sentence as a reference to a rule of conflict of laws."

G.   Does the "law applicable" indicate a choice of a law to determine the validity and effect of the arbitration clause?

[11]   "Parties may submit an arbitration agreement to a law which is not the

148

substantive law of the main contract. But in that case, they almost always designate the law governing the arbitration agreement *and* the law applying to the contract. If not, they indicate that the selected law applies specifically to the arbitration agreement. Obviously, the parties to an international contract are likely to have in mind the problems of jurisdiction or arbitration, possibly of substantive law, but not of the law governing the arbitration clause itself, which is mostly thought to be governed either by the selected law or by the 'lex fori' (the law of the place of arbitration).

"In this case, there is no evidence that the parties might have intended or at least had reasons to submit the arbitration clause to a specific law.

"The arbitrator is therefore of the opinion that a reasonable man active in the international trade could not have understood the disputed sentence as a reference to a law that would have determined the validity and effect of the arbitration clause."

H. Does the *"law applicable"* indicate a choice of substantive law ?

[12]   "Universally, the words 'the law applicable' or 'the law which applies' are used in the context of the determination of the substantive law governing private international relationships (example: Art. 13(3) of the Rules of the ICC Court of Arbitration [quoted above under [3]; G. Delaume, *Transnational Contracts, Applicable Law and Settlement of Disputes, Law and Practice*, Part II, Conflict issues, chapter VII, Party autonomy and express stipulations of applicable law; P. Sanders, "The Netherlands", in *Yearbook Commercial Arbitration* VI (1981), p. 75).

"In contracts containing no arbitration clause, the choice of the 'applicable law' unambiguously refers to the substantive law, the procedure being in any case governed by the 'lex fori'. The word 'substantive' therefore never or very rarely appears in connection with the expression 'the law applicable', although always implied. This usage certainly extends to contracts containing an arbitration clause.

"Whereas the reference to the law known in England cannot be construed as a designation of the procedural law, or of the rule of conflict of laws, or of the law governing the arbitration clause, there are clear indications which speak in favor of the designation of a substantive law.

"The parties had valid reasons to refer to the substantive law known in England. English law is neutral; its provisions are adapted to the needs of international commerce; it is fairly well accessible and known to lawyers of other countries, such as Switzerland, Mozambique and the Netherlands; English is far more common than Dutch, Portugese or even French.

"The parties could thus consider the application of English law as perfectly acceptable and the presence of a choice of substantive law clause under the title 'Arbitration' was in nothing peculiar.

"The arbitrator is therefore of the opinion that a reasonable man active in the international trade should have understood the disputed sentence as a reference to a substantive law.

[13]   "Although somewhat unusual, the expression 'the law known in England' is not ambiguous. It is wide enough to include, as appropriate, international rules and usages recognized in England. However, this expression cannot reasonably imply a reference to a national law other than the English. The parties cannot have intended to designate all the laws of the world. Considering the plain meaning of the words, the arbitrator finds that the use of the expression 'the laws known in England' does not affect the validity of the clause.

[14]   "The argument has been made by the defendants that a clause of choice of substantive law should be clear and unambiguous.

"Under Swiss law, the choice of the applicable law is considered as the result of a contract between the parties, which is separate from the main contract (F. Fischer, *Internationales Vertragsrecht*, p. 66 et seq., Bern 1962; ATF 91 II 248; ATF 102 II 143). This 'choice of law' is not subject to any formality and can be express or implied (TC VD, 8 February 1980, Marks).

"Whereas implied choice of law has to result clearly and unambiguously from the terms of the contract or the circumstances, express choice of law clauses do not have to be drafted with such a degree of clarity that they should not be construed. It does not seem that any decision of a Swiss Court has ever set particular requirements as to the form, wording or precision of clauses mentioning expressly the 'law applicable'. The draft of the Swiss Statute on International Private Law does not either require any form for express choice of law clauses, as it states that 'the choice of law must be express *or* result with certainty from the provisions of the contract or from the circumstances of the case' (Art. 113(2)).[4]

"Finally, the Hague Treaty on the law applicable to international sales of goods (1955), which applies in Switzerland, does not provide for any form requirement regarding choice of law clauses. The draft of Protocol of the Treaty discussed at the 14th Session of the Hague Conference (1980) certainly states that the choice of law must be express and in writing, therefore unambiguous, but the Protocol only deals with a matter unrelated with this case, the purchase by consumers (M. Pélichet, ''Mémoire sur les ventes aux consommateurs'', *Actes et documents de la 14ème Session de la Conférence de La Haye de droit international privé*, Vol. II, p. 7 et seq.; Von Mehren, *Report of the Special Commission*, ibidem, p. 38).

"In this case, the arbitrator finds that the express election in favor of English law is sufficiently clear to be regarded.

"As a preliminary conclusion, the arbitrator decides that the contract between the parties contains an express choice of substantive law in favor of the English law.''

I.   The validity of the choice of English law

[15]   "The defendants allege that the parties were not free to choose English law as the law applicable to their contract, for there being no connection between the matter and English law.

"Whether English law is a valid choice of law has to be scrutinized both under Swiss law and English law (B. Dutoit, F. Knoepfler, P. Lalive, P. Mercier, *Répertoire de droit international privé suisse*, Vol. 1, p. 31, Bern 1982; M. Keller, K. Siehr, *Allgemeine Lehren des internationalen Privatrechts*, p. 376, Zurich 1986; also Art. 113(3) of the draft of the Swiss Statute on International Private Law).[4]

---

4.   Art. 113(3) of the draft Swiss Statute on International Private Law (the equivalent of Art. 116 in the final version) provides:

"1.   The agreement is governed by the law chosen by the parties.

"2.   The choice of law must be express or result in a clear fashion from the provisions of the agreement or from the circumstances surrounding the case; furthermore, the choice of law is governed by the substantive law chosen by the parties.

"3.   The choice of law may be made or modified at any time. If it is subsequent to the conclusion of the agreement, it has retroactive effects as from the conclusion of the agreement, subject to the right of third parties.''

[16]   "Under Swiss law, the freedom of the parties as to their choice of the applicable law has not been finally settled. Swiss courts do not require the existence of a 'natural connection between the matter and the chosen law' and recognize the validity of a choice of law in each case where the parties have a reasonable interest in the application of the chosen law (ATF 91 II 44, 51; ATF 102 II 143). Such an interest exists for example when the chosen law contains a regulation of the matter which seems appropriate, when the parties are willing to submit their relationship to certain usages assuming the application of the chosen law or when the contract is in connection with another business submitted to the chosen law. It does not seem that any decision of a Swiss court has ever denied the existence of a reasonable interest of the parties in the application of a chosen law (B. Dutoit, F. Knoepfler, P. Lalive, P. Mercier, *Répertoire de droit international privé suisse*, Vol. 1, p. 30, Bern 1982). The draft of the Swiss Statute on Private International Law of 10 November 1982 does not limit the choice of the parties with any requirement regarding the connection with a chosen law. The Federal Council regards the criterion of the 'reasonable interest of the parties' as inappropriate and useless. It has limited the choice of the applicable law only for the types of contracts in which a party needs special protection (*Message du Conseil Fédéral concernant une loi fédérale sur le droit international privé*, 10 November 1982, p. 141-142).

[17]   "Under English law, the question of the connection between the matter and the chosen law seems to be somewhat controversial. There seems to be no reported case in which an English court refused to give effect to an express choice of law because of the deficient connection between the contract and the chosen law (Dicey and Morris, *The Conflict of Laws*, 10th ed., vol. 2, p. 755, London 1980). In *Vita Food Products Inc. v. Unus Shipping Co. Ltd.* (1939, AC 277 (PC)), it was stated that 'a connection with English law is not, as a matter of principle, essential'. In this decision, the judge mentioned in particular the importance of English law in international commercial relationships, even unconnected with England. He considered reasonable for the parties to commercial contracts to submit their transaction to English law, although that law might have nothing to do with the facts of the particular case.

"Swiss and English laws largely reflect the international practice. 'In most countries, the parties to transnational contracts enjoy a large degree of autonomy in selecting the proper law of their contract.

Except in those situations in which compliance with mandatory rules is required, the parties are generally free to choose by way of express stipulation the law applicable to their relationship. In the overwhelming majority of cases, the law stipulated applicable is the domestic law of a specific country to which the contract bears some connection or the law of a "third" country selected for reason of expertise (such as English law in regard to maritime matters) or of "neutrality" (such as Swedish, Swiss or French law) …' (G. Delaume, *Transnational Contracts, Applicable Law and Settlements of Disputes, Law and Practice*, Part II, Conflict issues, Chapter VII, Party Autonomy and Express Stipulations of Applicable Laws, p. 2; also, M. Keller, K. Siehr, *Allgemeine Lehren des internationalen Privatrechts*, p. 384, Zurich 1986).

[18]   "In this case, the arbitrator finds that the parties have a reasonable interest in the application of English law. The choice of English substantive law cannot be held for invalid for there being no connection between the matter and English law.

"There is further no indication that the choice of English substantive law was made to escape some mandatory provisions of the laws of the Netherlands or Mozambique.

"Nor is there any indication that an award which would be based in English substantive law would not be enforceable in the Netherlands (see also *New York Convention of 10 June 1958*) or in the Mozambique.

[19]   "Therefore, the arbitrator considers that the parties have made a valid choice in favor of English substantive law. In accordance with Art. 13(3) of the Rules for the ICC Court of Arbitration, the arbitrator shall apply English substantive law."

Final award in case no. 3572 of 1982

Arbitrators: Pierre Folliet (Switz., chairman); Bjørn Haug (Norway);
                          Cedric Barclay (UK)

Parties*:   Claimants: Deutsche Schachtbau- und Tiefbohrgesellschaft
                          mbH (DST) (FR Germ.) et al.
                          Defendants: The Government of the State of R'as Al
                          Khaimah (UAE) and The R'as Al Khaimah Oil Company
                          (Rakoil) (UAE)

Place of
arbitration: Geneva, Switzerland

Published in: Unpublished

Subject matters: - evidence of "commercial quantities" of oil
                          - misrepresentation
                          - competence-competence
                          - Arts. 8(3), 8(4), 13(3) and 20 ICC Rules (1975)
                          - Swiss Arbitration Concordat, Art. 8
                          - separability of arbitration clause
                          - concurrent court proceedings
                          - international principles of law governing contractual
                            relations
                          - Government party to contract signed by agency
                          - simple and compound interest

Facts

In 1973, a concession agreement was concluded between the Government of R'as
Al Khaimah and an exploration company to explore for oil and gas in the territorial
waters of R'as Al Khaimah. The parties subsequently signed an Operating

---

* For the policy of publishing the parties' names, see note General Editor at p. 45.

Agreement on 24 February 1974 (the Original Operating Agreement) in which the exploration company was designated as Operator.

The exploration work was carried out by the "Consortium", a group of companies, to which contractual rights had been assigned by the Operator. The Consortium was to carry out certain seismic work and the drilling of two exploratory wells, "Well B-1" and "Well A-1". The Government was not to participate in the costs of these operations until and unless "commercial quantities" of oil or gas had been discovered.

Well B-1 was drilled and proven "dry". The Government and Rakoil and the Consortium – after an agreement dated 23 July 1976 failed to enter into force because one of the Consortium members did not sign it – on 1 September 1976 entered into an "Assignment Agreement" which contained as an annex the 1976 "Operating Agreement". By these agreements, Rakoil, inter alia, acquired a 48.78 percent participating interest and also undertook to cover a corresponding part of the future exploration costs, the percentage later to increase to 50 percent.

The Government through Rakoil also exercised its acquired right under the Assignment Agreement to decide upon drilling two additional exploratory wells as so called "sole risk" operations. DST, which on 1 January 1979 had succeeded the exploration company as Operator, and another member of the Consortium exercised their rights to participate in these ventures. In this connection, the Government entered into an agreement with Sea and Land Drilling Contractors Inc. (hereinafter referred to as "Sea and Land") to perform certain services.

In 1978, the Government stopped all payments of its share of the exploration costs.

A request for arbitration was filed on 7 March 1979 with the ICC by DST as agent for the group of companies against the Government and Rakoil, based on the arbitration clauses contained in the Concession Agreement and the 1976 (Joint) Operating Agreement asking to be awarded damages of US$ 3,220,070 plus costs and expenses and interest.

At the beginning of April 1979, Defendants filed suit with the R'as Al Kaimah court against DST and the original Operator requesting that the Agreements be set aside and that DST and the original Operator be restrained from continuing with the reference to arbitration thereunder; an order to that effect dated 3 December 1979 was issued.

Defendants, by letters 5 April and 14 May 1979 from their legal advisors to the Secretary General of the ICC, challenged the jurisdiction of the arbitral tribunal and denied liability, and did not participate further in the arbitration.

Defendants claimed they entered into the Assignment Agreement and the 1976 Operating Agreement as a result of the representations of the Consortium that substantial quantities of oil had been discovered but that such representation were actually contrary to fact.

Claimants alleged that daily reports were sent to the Government in the same form as they were communicated to all Consortium members and that the Government also had the benefit of the analysis of the test results that "hydrocarbons were present in Structure B, but that pending further exploration, it was impossible to say in just what quantities" and that "test results were not promising".

According to Claimants' account of events, the Government, wishing to conduct drilling operations in the Concession area, and had been prepared to assume a 50 percent participation in Concession area operations provided the Consortium would commit itself to the drilling (and assuming of 50 percent of the cost) of two additional wells instead of 100 percent of the cost of the single additional well required under the Concession Agreement.

The arbitrators first settled the disputed factual issues, deciding that neither the Assignment Agreement nor the Agreement of 23 July 1976 contained an affirmation or representation that commercial quantities had been discovered, nor were there misrepresentations. The arbitral tribunal held that it was competent to rule on its own jurisdiction and further held "internationally accepted principles of law governing contractual relations to be the proper law applicable to the case". It concluded that the agreements were valid and that the Government was also a party to these agreements, awarding claimant US$ 4,635.664, which included accrued interest, and arbitration and legal costs.

The ensuing UK judgment of the Court of Appeal, 24 March 1987, rejecting the appeal made by Rakoil against the leave to enforce the award granted to DST, as well as refusing to lift an injunction, restraining Rakoil from removing assets which consisted of payments by Shell to Rakoil from the jurisdiction, is published in Yearbook XIII, (1988) pp. 522-536 (UK no. 22). The judgment of the House of Lords, 23 June 1988, reversing the court of Appeal's decision, is published in this Yearbook, pp. 737-750 (UK no. 27).

Excerpt

A. Evidence

[1]   The arbitrators reasoned as follows regarding the factual issues:

"No documentary evidence as to information on Well B-1 issued to the Government has been produced. The Arbitration Tribunal can only express regret that Claimants merely produced copies of telexes from [the first Operator] to DST, instead of copies of telexes from [the first Operator] to the Government. On this point, evidence produced by Claimants consists of the witness statements...."

[2]   The witness statements gave an account of the reporting procedures and information reported which supported Claimant's allegation on this matter and the arbitral tribunal saw no reason to reject these statements. They held them to be confirmed by other evidence as follows:

[3]   "While the Draft Agreement of 23 July 1976 (reference to which is made by Claimants as well as by Defendants, states in its preamble that operations by the Consortium have resulted in the discovery 'of hydrocarbons', it expressly provides that 'notwithstanding any other provision (of the Concession Agreement) or any test results of the Consortium's RAK No. 1 well, to the contrary, the parties agree that (A) Commercial Quantities have been established in the Concession area...'. Claimants say that this draft was signed by the Ruler but did not come into effect due to the refusal of [one of the Consortium members] to ratify it.

[4]   "Defendants state that it never became binding (which is undisputed) and say that it is the consequence of the refusal of [the Consortium member]. They do not directly confirm that it was agreed upon by the Government, but they admit it implicitly by that statement. Anyhow, it is obvious that the Government had knowledge of it. The Arbitration Tribunal cannot give to its para. 1 (inception and subpara. A) any other meaning but that the parties were informed that no commercial quantities had been effectively discovered. The fact that the Agreement did not become binding does not alter this conclusion.

[5]   "The Arbitration Tribunal deems it unlikely that the Government would have entered into an Agreement which would lead to heavy immediate disbursements (US$ 2,514,315.46), and to even greater expenditure at a later date, without first requesting information about the outcome of the tests which it obviously knew had been made.

[6]   "It would have been easy for Defendants to substantiate their assertion as to misrepresentations by the Consortium, in particular by specifying what information they had received in what form and when. In fact, Defendants, in their statement, seem to rely on the wording of the Assignment Agreement. It says that 'operations conducted by the Assignors and their associates ... have resulted in the discovery of hydrocarbons and the Government therefore wishes to take a working interest...', the Arbitration Tribunal noted that this wording does not contain any reference to 'commercial quantities' within the meaning of the Concession Agreement, but only relates to the discovery of hydrocarbons without reference to quantities (as had already been the case for the (non-binding) Agreement of 23 July, 1976); the Assignment Agreement replaced the provision of para. 1

(inception and subpara. A) by the wording 'The provisions of paragraph 6.A. of the Concession Agreement shall have no application whatsoever as among the parties to this Agreement'. This seems to have a similar meaning. In any event, the Arbitration Tribunal does not read in the Assignment Agreement (nor in the Agreement of 23 July 1976) an affirmation or representation that commercial quantities had been discovered.

[7]   "The Arbitration Tribunal cannot therefore admit that Defendants entered into the Assignment Agreement (incorporating the 1976 Operating Agreement) because of misrepresentations by the Consortium concerning quantities discovered. There were no misrepresentations.''

B. Jurisdiction

[8]   "The direct basis of Claimants' claim is the 1976 Operating Agreement. The said Agreement supplements the Concession Agreement and the Assignment Agreement. The Concession Agreement and the 1976 Operating Agreement include identical arbitration clauses, reading as follows:

'A (resp. 1): All disputes arising in connection with the interpretation or application of this Agreement shall be finally settled under the Rules of Conciliation and Arbitration of the International Chamber of Commerce by three arbitrators appointed in accordance with the Rules.

B (resp. 2): The arbitration shall be held in Geneva, Switzerland and shall be conducted in the English language.' ''

[9]   The arbitral tribunal held:

"By virtue of the above arbitration clauses, the parties have made the Rules of Conciliation and Arbitration of the ICC an integral part of their Agreement.
  "Art. 8(3) and (4) of the Rules read as follows:

'Should one of the parties raise one or more pleas concerning the existence or validity of the agreement to arbitrate, and should the Court be satisfied of the prima facie existence of such an agreement, the Court may, without prejudice to the admissibility or merits of the plea or pleas, decide that the arbitration shall proceed. In such a case any decision as to the arbitrator's jurisdiction shall be taken by the arbitrator himself.

'Unless otherwise provided, the arbitrator shall not cease to have jurisdiction by reason of any claim that the contract is null and void or allegation that it is inexistent provided that he upholds the validity of the agreement to arbitrate. He shall continue to have jurisdiction, even though the contract itself may be inexistent or null and void, to determine the respective rights of the parties and to adjudicate upon their claims and pleas'.

[10] "Art. 8 of the Swiss Intercantonal Arbitration Convention, which is the procedure law on arbitration applicable in Geneva, the place of arbitration according to the arbitration clauses, reads as follows (translation from Comité Suisse de l'Arbitrage, *Concordat Suisse sur l'Arbitrage* (Ed. Payot 1974)):

'If the validity of the arbitration agreement or its content or scope are disputed before the arbitral tribunal, that tribunal shall in an interlocutory order or final award determine its own jurisdiction'

[11] "Defendants in the letters of Peter T. James and Co. of 5 April 1979 and 14 May 1979, challenge the validity of the arbitration clause of the 1976 Operating Agreement substantially on the ground that said Agreement and the Assignment Agreement incorporating it are null and void because Defendants were induced to enter into them by representations of the Consortium not in accordance with the facts.

"Defendants, however, admit the validity of the arbitration clause of the Concession Agreement (see first letter mentioned).

"Cf Sanders, "l'Autonomie de la clause compromissoire", in *Hommage à Frédéric Eisemann*, p. 31. Cf also Swiss Federal Supreme Court in BGE 59 I 177, 88 I 100 (as to plea based on the alleged invalidity of the entire contract and not on grounds for the invalidity of the arbitration clause specifically).

"On the basis of the above, the arbitration tribunal finds and holds that it has competence and jurisdiction to determine its own jurisdiction with regard to the validity of the arbitration clause.

[12] "To determine the validity of the arbitration clause of the 1976 Operating Agreement, it will in principle be necessary to determine what body of law shall apply to this Agreement. As will be discussed below, the arbitration tribunal considers internationally accepted principles of law governing contractual relations to be the proper law applicable to this matter. As follows from the arbitration tribunal's findings in regard to the facts, it will be clear that invalidity of the arbitration clause cannot be upheld.

[13] "The arbitration tribunal will add that the action instituted in the courts of R'as Al Khaimah at the beginning of April 1979, or the order by the R'as Al Khaimah court of 3 December 1979, cannot stay the competence and jurisdiction

of this arbitration tribunal to proceed with the arbitration and to award on the merits of the case.''

C. Law applicable to substance

[14] ''The 1976 Operating Agreement which is the direct basis of Claimant's claim does not include a clause of choice of law, neither do the Assignment Agreement and the Concession Agreement.

[15] ''However, Art. 13(3) of the Rules of Conciliation and Arbitration provide that:

> 'The parties shall be free to determine the law to be applied by the arbitrator to the merits of the dispute. In the absence of any indication by the parties as to the applicable law, the arbitrator shall apply the law designated as the proper law by the rule of conflict which he deems appropriate'.

[16] ''The Arbitration Tribunal holds that: the Concession Agreement, the Assignment Agreement and the 1976 Operating Agreement are contracts between, on one hand, a number of companies organised under various laws, and, on the other hand, a State respectively a company which is actually an agency of such State.

[17] ''Reference either to law of any one of the companies, or of such State of the State on whose territory one or several of these contracts were entered into, may seem inappropriate, for several reasons.

[18] ''The Arbitration Tribunal will refer to what has become common practice in international arbitrations particularly in the field of oil drilling concessions and especially to arbitrations located in Switzerland. Indeed, this practice, which must have been known to the parties, should be regarded as representing their implicit will. Reference is made in particular to the leading cases *Sapphire International Petroleums Ltd. v. National Iranian Oil Company* (International Law Reports 1967, 136 ff), *Texaco Overseas Petroleum Company v. The Government of Libyan Arab Republic* (International Law Reports 1979, 389 ff).[1] See also Lalive, 'Les Règles de conflit de lois appliqueés au fond du litige par l'arbitre international siégeant en Suisse', *L'arbitrage international privé et la Suisse*, 1977; see also Derains, 'L'application cumulative par l'arbitre des systèmes de conflit de lois intéressés au litige', in Revue de l'arbitrage 1972, p. 100.

[19] ''The Arbitration Tribunal therefore holds internationally accepted principles of law governing contractual relations to be the proper law applicable to the merits of this case.''

---

1. Reported in Yearbook IV (1979) pp. 177-187.

D. Validity of Agreements

[20] "As explained above [see supra, A. *Evidence*], the Arbitration Tribunal does not find, as a fact, that Defendants were induced [to] enter into the said Agreements as a result of representations by the Consortium which representations were contrary to the true facts related to the quantities of oil effectively discovered. The allegation of Defendants that such Agreements are void on the ground of misrepresentations must be rejected.

[21] "Neither has there been presented to the Arbitration Tribunal any facts or circumstances that can give rise to questions of invalidity of the agreements on the grounds of mistake on the part of Defendants or for any other reason.

[22] "For these reasons, the choice of the law to be applied to the agreements is of little significance, if any, under the prevailing circumstances."

E. Government party to agreement

[23] "It has been alleged that since the 1976 Operating Agreement designated Rakoil but not the Government as party to the Agreement, the said Agreement is not binding upon the Government, and claims thereunder cannot be awarded against the Government.

[24] "The Arbitration Tribunal holds as follows:

"The Concession Agreement in para. 1.G contains the following clause:

'Government shall include any duly authorized representative or agency of the State of R'as Al Khaimah and any body, corporate or other, which may be designated by the State to enjoy any rights or discharge any obligations under this Agreement'.

"The Concession Agreement was signed by the Government only, as was the Original Operating Agreement which supplemented it.

"The Assignment Agreement was signed both on behalf of the Government and Rakoil. Although the agreement assigned to Rakoil 50% of the Consortium members's working interests and made Rakoil the only governmental party to the annexed 1976 Operating Agreement, there is no clause in the agreements or any other indication to the effect that the Government should be substituted by Rakoil and excluded as a party to the rights and obligations under the Concession Agreement and the Supplemental Operating Agreements.

[25] "In the negotiations leading up to the signing of the Assignment Agreement, as well as in the relationship between the parties in the following period, the Government acted and was regarded as a direct participant. Thus, the

cash calls in the subsequent period were met directly by the Government and during the period after the payments were stopped, the Government acted directly and actively in the attempts to find a solution acceptable to all interests. Also, both the Government and Rakoil appear as Claimants in the application filed with the R'as Al Khaimah Court in April 1979.

[26] "The Arbitration Tribunal holds that Rakoil must be seen as an instrument chosen by the Government to enjoy certain rights and discharge certain obligations on behalf of the Government, but not to the exclusion of the Government's own rights or obligations. This holding is supported by the information submitted by the Claimants, and it has not been refuted as information by the Defendants that no indication of the formation of a separate legal body corporate has appeared in the R'as Al Khaimah official gazette or has been evidenced to the Arbitration Tribunal.

[27] "Therefore, the Arbitration Tribunal holds that the claims as mentioned below, may be directed against the Government and Rakoil who must be held jointly and severally liable if an Award is made against them."

F. Liabilities and damages

[28] Claimant's claim regarding the principal amount was US$ 2,963,218 of which US$ 726,149 related to the Sea and Land contract. Defendants, in the letter of their legal representative of 5 April 1979, contested the accuracy of the figures in Claimant's request for arbitration and requested an audit of Claimant's accounts and records and of their predecessor. The arbitrators noted that the matter in litigation concerned the accounts starting with the fiscal year 1979 only and continued as follows:

[29] "Para. 4 sub. a and b of the 'Accounting Procedure' ... provide as follows:

'a. Operator's accounts and records shall be subject to an audit in respect of each calendar year which shall be carried out by Operator's auditors whose certificate shall be conclusive evidence of such audit.

'b. A non-Operator, upon notice to Operator and all other Non-Operators, shall have the right to call for an audit of Operator's accounts and records relating to the accounting hereunder for any calendar year within the twenty-four (24) month period following the end of such calendar year; provided, however, that Non-Operators must take exception to and make claim upon Operator for all discrepancies disclosed by said audit within said twenty-four (24) month period. As far as is reasonably possible audits will be performed by a Joint Audit Group of all Non-Operators and not on an individual company basis. Non-Operators shall make every reasonable effort to ensure that audits are conducted in a manner which will result in a minimum of inconvenience to Operator and Operator will make every reasonable effort to assist such audits'.

[30]   "In connection with the declaration of Defendants (letter of [Defendant's legal counsel] of 5 April 1979) that they sought an audit of the Operator's accounts, the Arbitration Tribunal has noted that there is no indication that Defendant took any step to arrange such an audit. Accordingly, they omitted to substantiate their own accounts and thus challenge those accounts presented by the Operator.''

[31]   Claimants produced witness statements and audited financial statements and reports regarding the amounts claimed, as well as information that the Commerzbank's prime rate fell from 11.875% (as at 4 June 1980) to 11% (as at date of hearing). The arbitral tribunal found the items regarding the principal amount to be proven to its satisfaction.

[32]   Regarding the Sea and Land contract the arbitral tribunal held:

"The existence of a debt towards Sea and Land under the contract previously mentioned is proven satisfactorily by the statements of Mr. Kluge as a witness and by the attachments submitted in evidence.

[33]   ''Claimants have themselves affirmed that the said contract was between Sea and Land and the Government. Prima facie therefore, the said indebtedness is exclusively that of the Defendants. However, the Government entered into the Sea and Land contract in connection with 'sole risk' operations in which DST also participated and was Operator under the 1976 Operation Agreement.

"Accordingly the contract entered into by the Government was brought into said venture, and was in fact performed by the Operator under conditions similar to those of any other operation.

[34]   ''The Arbitration Tribunal holds therefore that the Operator is entitled to claim payment from the other party in the venture, just as it would do for any other operation.

"One cannot fail to note that the Operator, in his capacity as partner in this venture, has a strong legitimate interest in bringing this matter to a prompt and orderly settlement.''

G.   Interest up to date of award

[35]   ''The Arbitration Tribunal considers that the absence of the word 'simple' in para. XIII.1 – which would otherwise define interest in the same way as in para.

V.6, is not sufficient to imply that the parties intended to compound interest under para. XIII.1. The Tribunal holds therefore that interest should be calculated as simple interest.''

(. . . .)

H. Collection expenses and costs

[36] ''The Arbitration Tribunal holds that, besides the provision of Art. 20 of the Rules of Conciliation and Arbitration,[2] para. XIII.1 of the 1976 Operating Agreement provides for payment by a party in default of 'all costs paid or incurred by non-defaulting parties including, but not limited to collection expenses, solicitor's fees, and court costs'.

''It will later be seen (Issue J) that the Arbitration Tribunal feels it should allow the said expenses and costs in full.''

(. . . .)

I. Interest until payment

[37] ''The Tribunal is unanimous in awarding interest up to the date of this Award. This interest is included in the sum finally awarded.

[38] ''In regard to interest for the period after the date of the award, a majority of the Tribunal holds that the right to interest according to the contract does not lapse by virtue of the arbitration dispute or the Award sought by the Claimants.

''Thus, a majority holds that the Claimants are entitled to simple interest on the US\$ 4,635,664.- or the unpaid portions thereof until fully paid, at the rate per annum of 3% above the prime rate of Commerzbank.

[39] ''Since this interest rate in all probability might fluctuate, the Claimants at the hearing altered their claim in regard to interest after the date of the Award to 11% + 3% = 14% per annum. However, since the contractual stipulated interest may fall below this figure, our award is made for interest after the date of the award

---

2. ICC Rules 1975 provide in Art. 20:

''1. The arbitrator's award shall, in addition to dealing with the merits of the case, fix the costs of the arbitration and decide which of the parties shall bear the costs or in what proportions the costs shall be borne by the parties.

''2. The costs of the arbitration shall include the arbitrator's fees and the administrative costs fixed by the Court in accordance with the scale annexed to the present Rules, the expenses, if any, of the arbitrator, the fees and expenses of any experts, and the normal legal costs incurred by the parties.

''3. The Court may fix the arbitrator's fees at a figure higher or lower than that which would result from the application of the annexed scale if in the exceptional circumstances of the case this appears to be necessary.''

t an annual rate according to the contract, however limited to 14% per annum. This interest is to be payable on the total sum of the award, or the unpaid portions thereof, until the debt discharged.

40] "The Arbitration Tribunal is unanimous in holding that the Claimants are entitled to such interest rate as may be due on the award according to applicable law."

I. Costs

[41] "The Arbitration Tribunal has tested the evidence and is satisfied that these costs [collection costs, legal costs and arbitration costs, i.e. US$ 395,837] have been properly and reasonably incurred, and it holds and finds that these costs shall be borne by the Defendants in full."

Final award in case no. 4975 of 1988

Arbitrators:	Mr. Mark Littman, QC (UK, chairman); Mr. D. Gardam, QC (UK); Mr. R.A. MacCrindle, QC (UK)
Parties:	Claimants: Main contractor (Jersey, Channel Islands) Respondents: Sub-contractors (FR Germ.)
Place of arbitration:	London, UK and Geneva, Switzerland
Published in:	Unpublished
Subject matters:	- hearing - Arts. 11 and 14 ICC Rules - pre-contractual negotiations - interpretation of contract - delay and suspension of performance - repudiation of contract - exchange losses

Facts

By a contract dated 31 October 1977, which contained an arbitration clause, the Main Contractor agreed to design, supply, construct and commission a plant in

Saudi Arabia. According to Tender Specification no. S.1234/X ("1234/X"), the Main Contractor was also to provide a specified product for the functioning of the plant. The value of the Main Contract exceeded 2.5 billion Saudi Riyals.

On 8 May 1978, the Main Contractor and respondent no. 1 signed a Supply Contract under which respondent no. 1 agreed to design, manufacture and supply the said product at the price of SR 99,145,555. On 29 June 1979, the Main Contractor entered into an Erection Contract with respondent no. 2; the latter was to erect, commission and maintain the product supplied by respondent no. 1. Both contracts contained an ICC arbitration clause and elected Geneva as the seat of the arbitration proceedings. The contracts were amended on several occasions. On 10 November 1979, it was agreed that the Supply Contract and the Erection Contract should be regarded as a single contract. On 23 September 1980, a "P. Agreement" was signed which was supplemental to the Supply Contract; by this agreement the contract value was *inter alia* fixed at DM 91,316,433, and it was agreed that the conversion of the DM value into SR would be the subject of a later agreement.

In the meantime, shipments of equipment to the site had commenced in November 1979, and by January 1980, when the P. Agreement was signed, about 80% of the value of the total supply had been delivered. By June 1981, nearly 60% of the erection work had been completed.

Towards the end of 1981, respondent no. 1 pressed the Main Contractor for arrears of payment alleged to be due under the contracts. The Main Contractor replied that "due to unexpected delays in [the Employer's] payments ... we may not be able to process any of your outstanding payments".

In January 1982, these sums still being outstanding, the Main Contractor issued four promissory notes. The first two promissory notes were duly paid, but the last two were dishonoured on 22 April and 24 May 1982, respectively.

Meanwhile, respondent no. 1's economic difficulties came to a critical point in the first half of 1982 and, on 23 August 1982, the Main Contractor informed the bank that issued the promissory notes that they were not paying the promissory notes because they were concerned about the financial problems of respondent no. 1, which they said might lead to respondent no. 1 being unable to complete their work on the project.

Further negotiations resulted, on 18 October 1982, in the "J. Agreement", by which the Main Contractor agreed to pay certain sums, and respondent no. 1. to promptly supply certain goods and services.

Respondents resumed work under the contracts and in December 1983, respondent no. 1 delivered and installed its product under the Supply Contract. On 21 December, the respondents gave the Main Contractor formal notice under Art. 73 of the Uniform Law on the International Sale of Goods that they were suspending all further performance on their part until the outstanding monies due to them were paid.[1] Notwithstanding this, respondent no. 1 made certain performances under the contract, allegedly to avoid the risk of further damage to their business relations with [the Employer's Government].

On 10 April 1984, the Main Contractor wrote to the respondents making allegations of default on their part and requiring the defects to be remedied. On 16 April 1984, the Main Contractor wrote again to the respondents giving immediate notice of termination of all contracts between the parties, on grounds of alleged default on the respondents' part.

On 11 April 1984, immediately after the first letter to the respondents, the Main Contractor submitted a Request for Arbitration to the Court of Arbitration of the ICC.

The Respondents continued work until 25 April 1984, when the Main Contractor demanded withdrawal from site of all persons working for the respondents. On 18 May 1984, the respondents gave notice to the Main Contractor that they regarded the Main Contractor as having repudiated the contracts, and they accepted such repudiation, thereby bringing the contracts to an end.

Excerpt

A. *Claimants' application for further hearing*

[1] "At the hearing on 22/26 September 1986 the claimants asked for a further hearing. This was opposed by the respondents who submitted that the arbitrators should proceed to an award on the material before them. The claimants' application was, however, granted and a date for a final hearing was fixed for 16/19 March 1987. At the commencement of this hearing the claimants applied for an adjournment on the grounds that their legal representatives were not fully

---

1. Art. 73 of the Uniform Law on the International Sale of Goods 1964 reads:

"(1) Each party may suspend the performance of his obligations whenever, after the conclusion of the contract, the economic situation of the other party appears to have become so difficult that there is good reason to fear that he will not perform a material part of his obligations.

"(2) If the seller has already despatched the goods before the economic situation of the buyer described in paragraph (1) of this Article becomes evident, he may prevent the handing over of the goods to the buyer if the latter holds a document which entitles him to obtain them.

"(3) Nevertheless, the seller shall not be entitled to prevent the handing over of the goods if they are claimed by a third person who is a lawful holder of a document which entitles him to obtain the goods, unless the document contains a reservation concerning the effects of its transfer or unless the seller can prove that the holder of the document, when he acquired it, knowingly acted to the detriment of the seller."

prepared. This application was opposed by the respondents and refused by the tribunal who nevertheless granted the claimants permission to file a further written memorandum on any aspect of the case within six weeks from 19 March 1987. The claimants accordingly filed such a memorandum dated 30 April 1987 containing 67 pages.

[2] "In such memorandum the claimants applied for a further hearing. This application was opposed in a letter from the respondents' solicitors dated 27 May 1987.

[3] "The first reason given for this application was that further oral submissions were necessary. We were, however, of the view that the claimants had had abundant and equal opportunity to make submissions both orally and in writing and that no further hearing for that purpose was necessary or justified.

[4] "The second ground for this application (…) was that such further hearing should be for the purpose of the tribunal hearing or re-hearing the claimants' witnesses. The claimants asked the tribunal to disregard the respondents' witness statements insofar as those witnesses were not examined before the tribunal. In support of this the claimants expressed concern over the procedure adopted for resolving the issues between the parties in this arbitration (…). They contended that the practice adopted was 'not a practice followed by Swiss Courts or Arbitration Tribunals' and was 'wholly alien to Continental practice'. In response, the respondents' solicitors in their letter of 27 May 1987 stated 'we see no need for any further hearing in this arbitration and, having taken advice from Geneva lawyers, are satisfied that it has been conducted in a perfectly proper manner'.

[5] "Having carefully considered this application we decided not to grant it for the following (amongst other) reasons:

"(i) The application is in contradiction to a procedure laid down by an Agreed Order dated 18 September 1985 made after lengthy discussions on two occasions at the commencement of the arbitration. (. . . .)

"(iii) This agreed procedure was followed subsequently throughout the course of the arbitration. The only occasions on which witnesses for the respondents did not give their evidence in person were when the claimants elected not to require their attendance for cross-examination. Thus, on 6 January 1986 the claimants' solicitors wrote: 'In accordance with the tribunal's Order dated 18 September 1985 we enclose in triplicate copies of the following documents … (3) Bundle of witness statements'. In their letter of 18 April 1986 the claimants' said solicitors themselves referred to 'the advantages of the reduction of the case to writing' and referred to the proposal that the parties identify witnesses for cross-examination at the September hearing by a defined dated as 'a very helpful suggestion'.

"(iv) The arbitrators considered that the procedure followed in the arbitration with the full consent of both parties was appropriate in the context of the ICC Arbitration Rules and in particular Arts. 11 and 14.[2] The arbitrators at all times had in mind that the legal seat of the arbitration was Geneva but they were not satisfied that there was anything in the law of Geneva which rendered such a procedure not permissible. The first suggestion that the procedure in some way offended against the law of Geneva was made in the claimants' Supplementary Submissions delivered six weeks after the close of the final hearing.

[6]   "For these reasons and having regard to the general circumstances of the case, including the delay that had already taken place and the greater delay and expense that would be involved in granting the claimants' application, we decided in our discretion to refuse it."

B.   *Analysis of Main Contractor's claims*

[7]   "In their Amended Statement of Claim [Main Contractor] list a number of heads of damages said to result from breaches of contract of a repudiatory nature. Some of these breaches are [product]-related, either in whole or in part, and some not. In the arbitration [Main Contractor] placed great emphasis on alleged breach of contract by the respondents in relation to the [product]. We shall, therefore, deal with this question first and necessarily at some length. It is important to bear in mind, however, that the [product] represented only a comparatively small part in monetary value of the whole of the Supply and Erection Contracts.

---

2.   Arts. 11 and 14 of the 1975 ICC Rules provide, respectively:

Article 11 :
"Rules governing the proceedings
"The rules governing the proceedings before the arbitrator shall be those resulting from these Rules and, where these Rules are silent, any rules which the parties (or, failing them, the arbitrator) may settle, and whether or not reference is thereby made to a municipal procedural law to be applied to the arbitration."

Article 14:
"The arbitral proceedings
"(1)   The arbitrator shall proceed within as short a time as possible to establish the facts of the case by all appropriate means. After study of the written submissions of the parties and of all documents relied upon, the arbitrator shall hear the parties together in person if one of them so requests: and failing such a request he may of his own motion decide to hear them.
"In addition, the arbitrator may decide to hear any other person in the presence of the parties or in their absence provided they have been duly summoned.
"(2)   The arbitrator may appoint one or more experts, define their terms of reference, receive their reports and/or hear them in person.
"(3)   The arbitrator may decide the case on the relevant documents alone if the parties so request or agree."

[8]   ''The essential complaint in respect of the [product] is that what was tendered was not in compliance with the contract and that as a result [Main Contractor] have been required to replace it. We, however, have to confront the fact that on 16 April 1984, when the installation was admittedly incomplete and had not yet been fully tested and commissioned, [Main Contractor] purported to terminate all contractual relationships, and shortly thereafter required [Respondent no. 1] to withdraw completely from the site. Since the question of compliance or non-compliance with contractual requirements can normally only be tested after commissioning, it is, in our view, an essential ingredient of [Main Contractor]'s claim that they were justified in giving the notice of 16 April 1984. In other words, [Main Contractor] must show that by reason of the conduct of the respondents prior to 16 April 1984 [Main Contractor] was on that date entitled to, and did, terminate the contract, either (as they claimed) under clause 19.1 of the Supply Contract and clause 19.1 of the Erection Contract, or because the respondents were at common law in repudiation of those contracts. We propose to deal first with that question for it is plain that unless it is answered favourably to [Main Contractor] its letters of 16 May 1984 (and its direction to the respondents to withdraw) were themselves repudiatory of the contracts. That question is accordingly dealt with ... below. We will then deal ... with claims which may arise independently of repudiation.

[9]   ''There are three main strands of the [Main Contractor's] case that [Respondent no. 1] and [Respondent no. 2] had repudiated the contracts.

   ''[a]   Non-compliance with 1234/X (paras. 10-19 below).

   ''[b]   Non-compliance with Annex 1 (paras. 20-21 below).

   ''[c]   Delay in and suspension of performance (paras. 22-24 below).

   ''We will deal with these three elements seriatim.''

C.   Compliance with contractual requirements

[10]   On the ''1234/X'' question, the arbitral tribunal considered:

[11]   ''From a fairly early stage after the making of the contracts the respondents evinced an intention not to comply with Specification 1234/X – an attitude they maintained throughout the whole history of the contracts. If, therefore, compliance with this Specification was a term of the contracts, [Main Contractor] would be well on their way to proving a case of repudiation. The crucial question is whether it was in fact a term of the contract. The question has been very fully addressed in the Cases and Supplementary Cases filed on behalf of the parties and was the subject of the hearing in Geneva which occupied three days between 2 and 4 June 1986.

[12]   ''[Main Contractor] rely upon:

"[a]   Preliminary negotiations leading up to the making of the contracts.

"[b]   The terms of the Supply Contract.

"[c]   Page 67 of Annex 1 of the Supply Contract referring back to the respondents' proposal of 23 February 1977, Supplement 1 of 28 June 1977 and the Tender of 15 November 1977, referring to 1234/X.

"[d]   The P. Agreement."

a) Previous negotiations

13]   "Having regard to the decisions in *Penn v. Simmonds* (1971) 1 WLR 1381 at 1383 to 1384 and *Reardon Smith Line v. Hansen-Tangen* (1976) 1 WLR 989 at 996 and 997 preliminary negotiations can only be taken into account as part of the surrounding circumstances in which the contracts were made. The wisdom of this rule is exemplified in the present case since the negotiations show the position of the parties changing and each trying to obtain the best bargain from its own point of view.

'. . . .)

14]   "We do not find much assistance from the preliminary negotiations. For the true nature of the legal bargain between the parties we must look primarily to the actual wording of the contract itself. In other words, we must seek in the words the parties themselves have chosen what were their presumed intentions."

b) Supply contract

'. . . .)

15]   "We have no doubt that [Main Contractor] wished to obtain from Respondent no. 1] a contractual obligation to comply with Specification 1234/X which matched their own obligation to [the Employer]. Such a desire is clearly evidenced by the recitals of the Supply Agreement itself. On the other hand, it seems equally clear to us and must, we think, have been clear to [Main Contractor] that what [Respondent no. 1] were tendering was a system which departed in several major respects from that contemplated by 1234/X. No doubt both parties hoped that the Engineer could in the course of time be persuaded to accept the respondents' ideas (embodied in Annex I) in place of 1234/X. In some important respects the Engineer was persuaded but in other respects he was not. It appears to us that the real question of construction arising under the contract is where the parties intended the risk to lie should the Engineer not be completely persuaded and insist on the Main Contract being performed according to 1234/X. It is the claimants' case that risk was borne by [Respondent no. 1] and that [Respondent no. 1] was obliged, if the Engineer insisted, to comply with Specification 1234/X at [Respondent no.1]'s expense. It is the essential case for the respondents that upon a true construction of these agreements [Respondent no. 1]'s obligation was confined to carrying out Annex I and they were only obliged to comply with Specification 1234/X where the latter was not inconsistent with Annex I and then only insofar as it related to Annex I. They contend that the risk of the Engineer not being persuaded was to be borne by [Main Contractor] and that [Main Contractor] was only entitled to secure compliance by [Respondent no. 1] with the Engineer's requirements which went beyond Annex I by issuing a variation order which would have placed the burden of the extra cost upon [Main Contractor].

[16] "As we have said, the answer to this question must be found upon the true construction of the written contract by which the parties had reduced their bargain into writing, surrounding circumstances being duly taken into account.

(. . . .)

[17] "The most that can be said is that because 1234/X formed part of the package of Contract Documents it must by implication be a document to which regard could properly be had for purposes of interpreting Annex I. Its role was subsidiary and interpretative. The basic scope of work and supply was to be that laid down in Annex I. In the event of any ambiguity in the text of Annex I, or any puzzle as to its meaning arising from its silence on something which needed to be ascertained before it could be understood, the gap might be filled by reference to an express provision of 1234/X clarifying the point. Similarly 1234/X might help as to the manner or method of executing the defined work. But 1234/X was not to play a governing part. It was to be an aid to the construction of Annex I, but even in that capacity it was to be available only subject to the qualifications discussed ... above."

(c) *Annex I*
(. . . .)

(d) *The P. Agreement*
(. . . .)

[18] "In short, while the language used certainly leaves room for argument the terms of the P. Agreement are not considered by us to be sufficiently clear to bring about any fundamental change in the role of 1234/X in relation to the contract. It left untouched the essential provisions of the contract as to the work obligations imposed on [Respondent no. 1]. As before, [Respondent no. 1] could not be required at no extra consideration to do work to a standard conflicting with the standards of Annex I, or which would affect the conceptions of the systems and their interconnections which Annex I required to be furnished, or which would simply be wholly outside the scope of Annex I. It could not be so required even if that work would have been necessary to comply with 1234/X. If, however, [Main Contractor] required work to be done *within* that scope (but, for example, by a

method or in a manner upon which Annex I was silent but which 1234/X
specified), the contract price mechanism would be applicable and no question of a
variation would be involved. The above inevitably leaves room for debate on
difficult border-line cases, but this is the consequence of the imprecision of the
language used by the parties."

(e)   *Findings with respect to compliance with contractual requirements*
(. . . .)
[19]   "It follows that all the claimants' claims based upon non-compliance with
Specification 1234/X fail on the ground that compliance with this specification was
not a term of the Supply Contract except to the limited extent set out ... above. We
do not find that the claimants have established any breach of the Supply Contract
or Erection Contract in respect of Specification 1234/X."

D.   *Non-compliance with Annex I*

[20]   "The second strand in contention of [Main Contractor] that the respondents
were in repudiation is founded on alleged non-compliance of the respondents with
Annex I.
(. . . .)
[21]   "We accept the evidence of Mr. X that the [product] did not, as at April
1984, comply in certain respects with Annex I. As we have said, however, the
[product] supply represented only a relatively modest proportion of the very
substantial amounts covered by the Supply and Erection Contracts, and on any
view such defects as may have existed were not irremediable. Furthermore, even if
(contrary to our view) the condition of the [product] on 10 April 1984 were capable
of leading to an inference that the respondents were renouncing these contracts,
[Main Contractor] did not elect to 'accept' any such repudiation. On the contrary,
by its letters of 10 April 1984 with knowledge of all the relevant facts, it elected to
affirm the contracts and called for further work to be done thereunder. Whatever
the defects required to be remedied may have been, [Main Contractor] thereby in
law waived any right to treat them as repudiatory breaches entitling it to terminate
the contracts at common law without further notice. Nor in fact did [Main
Contractor] thereafter ever purport so to do."

E.   *Delay and suspension in performance*

[22]   "A third strand in the argument of [Main Contractor] that the respondents
had repudiated the contracts was its allegation that the respondents delayed

performance; that for a prolonged period commencing in the summer of 1982 they actually suspended performance; that to the extent to which they did resume performance they did so only partially and not for the purpose of honouring the contracts but only for their own ends, i.e., to preserve their own reputation and their standing with the Government of [the Employer]. [Main Contractor] say that this non-performance and delay began early in 1982 ...; that on 4 July 1982, in response to a request from [Main Contractor]'s Contract Manager [for] proper performance, the respondents on 5 July 1982 stated that 'due to the extreme stringent financial condition [Respondents nos. 1 and 2] have been facing we are unable to respond to your letter' (...); that on 19 August 1982 the respondents withdrew from the site (...); and that the respondents had not properly resumed performance at any time before [Main Contractor] gave notice purportedly under clause 11.3 of the Supply Contract and clause 19.1 of the Erection Contract on 16 April 1984.

[23] "We find that [Respondents nos. 1 and 2] did slow down the pace of their work in the first half of 1982; that in August 1982 they suspended performance; that subsequent acts of performance were somewhat intermittent; and that the notice of suspension was never formally removed. Such conduct is capable in some circumstances of amounting to a repudiation, especially in the context of a sub-contract for a large project such as the one under consideration.

[24] "However, we hold that in the present case it did not amount to a repudiation for the following reasons:

"[a] During the whole of the period in question and up to the present time [Main Contractor] has been in heavy arrears of payments due under the contracts. Thus, we find that on 12 October 1982 in the J. Agreement, the claimants admitted arrears of SR 38 million and the indebtedness has remained very substantial since that date. By clause 5.6 of the Supply Contract and Clause 5.3 of the Erection Contract time for payment is made of the essence of the contract. In these circumstances we hold that the respondents were not obliged to perform further while such arrears existed. The claimants seek to respond to this by relying upon the Convention on the International Sale of Goods, which they contend gave them a right to suspend payment inasmuch as [Respondent no. 1]'s financial difficulties gave [Main Contractor] good reason to fear that the respondents would not perform a material part of their obligations. We accept that there may well have been such a legitimate doubt from about 5 July 1982 until 12 October 1982. From the latter date, however, it is clear from the J. Agreement that [Main Contractor] fully expected that the respondents, if they were paid the arrears, would be able to proceed. Furthermore, even if [Main Contractor] were entitled, for a time, to suspend payment that does not mean that the respondents were obliged to proceed without payment. In our view there was in that period a state of mutual justified suspension.

"[b] Even if the delayed or suspended performance had been a repudiation entitling [Main Contractor], by 'accepting' it as such, to end the contracts, [Main Contractor] did not take that course. As we have indicated in dealing with the arguments based upon defects in the [product] [Main Contractor] chose by its notices of 10 April 1984 to affirm the contracts. Such additional culpable delay (if any) as may have occurred in the ensuing six days on no view amounted to a fresh repudiation. [Main Contractor] by its letters of 16 April 1984 did not so assert, nor did those letters profess to be an acceptance at common law of repudiations (if any) of the contracts. They sought to invoke the contracts themselves and to exercise express contractual options. But that is a different story, and is dealt with below."

F. Conclusion on Main Contractor's contentions

[25] "We have examined the various complaints of [Main Contractor] referred to above in considerable detail out of deference to the arguments addressed to us. Although (for reasons which in part have already been indicated) we think that it is not strictly necessary for us to decide the point, we have concluded that none of the alleged breaches (and in particular none of the alleged defects in the equipment supplied) taken alone or cumulatively, were sufficiently grave or irremediable as to have been tantamount to a repudiation of these contracts by the respondents, or to have demonstrated that they were incapable of performing them. We have, on the other hand, found that the [product] did not, in April 1984, comply with Annex I in certain respects some of which were quite serious, e.g., the characteristics referred to in page 8 of Mr. X's report. We accept in this regard the Reports of Mr. X. (whose evidence was not in our view seriously challenged by either side). But in summary:

"(i) In the light of the expert evidence of Mr. X. and of [a scientific institution] in particular, we do not regard such non-compliance at that stage, viewed in context, as evincing a repudiatory refusal by the respondents to perform their obligations in respects going to the root of the entire contracts, of which the [product] formed a relatively small part.

"(ii) Even if it were capable of being so regarded, [Main Contractor] by its letters of 10 April 1984 did not elect to treat it as such. These letters, on the contrary, *affirmed* the contracts and called for their performance. Repudiatory conduct in English law gives the innocent party an election. He may 'accept' it as such within a reasonable time, thereby terminating the contract while preserving his right to damages. Alternatively, he may positively affirm the contract and hold the other party to its bargain. He cannot do both. In doing the latter he waives any prior repudiatory conduct as a ground for terminating, and the contract thereafter remains binding on both sides. This is what [Main Contractor] did on 10 April 1984.

"(iii)   There is no evidence of any repudiatory conduct by the respondents in the few days which elapsed between 10 and 16 April 1984. Nor did the notices of 16 April 1984 even claim to be 'acceptances' at common law by the claimants of repudiatory conduct by the respondents. They claimed to exercise a contractual option.

"(iv)   There is no evidence that the respondents were *incapable* (within a period not so long as to have frustrated the whole venture) of remedying such defects as there may have been – on the contrary, it is plain that they were not irremediable, and that the cost of remedying them would have been but a small proportion of the aggregate contract prices (by then some SR 240 million).

"(v)   Whether *in fact* [Respondent no. 1] would have chosen to remedy them without extra remuneration is at least questionable. But [Main Contractor], by its letters of 16 April 1984 purporting to terminate the contracts with immediate effect, clearly in law waived any further obligation on [Respondent no. 1] to do any further work at all. Indeed, they refused to allow the respondents to remain on the site. If such termination was justified under some express contractual option vested in [Main Contractor], the contracts then ended. If it was not, the contracts remained in existence unless and until [Respondent no. 1] should itself elect to treat such unjustified termination as a repudiation of the contracts by [Main Contractor] and to claim damages from [Main Contractor] on the basis of such repudiation. On either view [Main Contractor] cannot in law complain that [Respondent no. 1] *thereafter* failed to remedy any defects. On either view, the conduct of [Main Contractor] deprived [Respondent no. 1] of its right to choose to do so. [Respondent no. 1] through that repudiation by [Main Contractor] lost the opportunity of earning under the contracts, in exchange for the further expenditure necessary to rectify any defects, the outstanding sums payable thereunder. The value of that loss is the difference between those sums and that expenditure.

"(vi)   The notices of 16 April 1984 were not effective exercises by [Main Contractor] of the contractual provisions conferring rights of termination (clause 11.3 of the Supply Contract and clause 19.1 of the Erection Contract). Those provisions by their express terms could not be invoked unless and until the respondents had been given by [Main Contractor] written notice to rectify specified contractual defects, and had failed to do so after a reasonable time had elapsed from the service of such notice. These requirements were not satisfied.

"(vii) The notices of 16 April 1984 left no doubt that [Main Contractor] was treating the contracts as at an end with immediate effect. Since [Main Contractor] had in any event only a few days before elected to affirm the contracts, and since the notices did not on any view comply with the conditions of the contractual clauses upon which they were expressed to be based, they themselves evinced a refusal to continue with the contracts which was legally unjustified. The respondents were entitled to, and did, 'accept' those notices as repudiatory by their letters of 18 May 1984. The contracts thereupon in law ended.''

G.   *Rights of the parties under the contracts became thus discharged*

[26]   ''(a)   The respondents were relieved from any obligation of further performance.

''(b)   [Main Contractor], having itself repudiated the contracts, could not claim damages for loss of the bargain or for any failure thereafter by the respondents to complete the work.

''(c)   [Main Contractor] was itself liable for all sums due for work done under the contracts up to 18 May 1984, and was also potentially liable to the respondents in damages for wrongful repudiation of the contracts.

''(d)   In calculating the amounts so recoverable by the respondents credit should be given to [Main Contractor] for diminution in the value of the work done arising from the need to repair or replace it so as to correspond to the standards of the contracts. We reject the submission by the respondents that effectively all the sums owing by [Main Contractor] under the contracts as at 18 May 1984 are recoverable by the respondents in this arbitration without giving such credit.

''(e)   [Main Contractor] would no doubt theoretically be entitled to set off against any claim by the respondents in respect of work done or goods supplied such accrued claims (if any) as it might have against the respondents for any breaches of the contracts by them, *which breaches were complete at the time the contracts ended on 18 May 1984.*

''(f)   But the contracts being alive until 18 May 1984, [Main Contractor] is not in fact in a position to point at that date to any final breaches of contract by the respondents in respect of any defects then affecting the [product]. Nor, since it refused to allow *further* work to be done, can it complain of failure thereafter to complete performance. It can at best set up, against the respondents' own claims for sums payable under the contracts, any diminution in value arising from defective work. Such diminution in value would not in our view, on the facts of this case, exceed any additional costs which the respondents would have been obliged to incur had they been permitted to complete, and had they completed, the work to the full contractual standard.

''(g)   On the evidence before us, we consider in order to have put the [product] into a condition complying with Annex I it would in 1984/85 have been necessary to spend an amount of the order of DM 2,65 million. We note that the [product] was later replaced with a superior new model, supplied and installed by other manufacturers, for some US$ 2.9 million.

"(h) We hold that against their claims under the contracts the respondents must give credit under this heading for DM 2,65 million."

(. . . .)

H. Exchange losses

[27] The arbitral tribunal dealt in detail with the subcontractors' counterclaims. One of them concerned exchange losses in respect of which the tribunal considered

[28] "The respondents also advanced a counterclaim ... for DM 26,288,519 in respect of foreign exchange losses. The basis of such counterclaim was as follows. The respondents conduct their affairs largely in Deutsch Marks. Under the contracts many of the payments which [Main Contractor] would thereafter become obliged to make to the respondents were to be in Saudi Riyals. To protect themselves against depreciation in the exchange value of the SR against the DM the respondents entered into forward exchange contracts under which they sold SR forward for DM. These afforded a hedge against the possibility that when the SR were ultimately paid their spot value in terms of DM would have fallen below the rate at which the forward bargain was struck. We find that the existence and purpose of such exchange contracts (though not their details) was at all material times within the knowledge of [Main Contractor], as is indeed admitted by [Main Contractor] in ... of its Points of Reply.

[29] "It is obvious that such forward contracts protect their maker against a diminution in value, prior to payment, of the Saudi Riyals in which payment is made on the due date. It is equally obvious that if payment is not made at all on the due date the maker will still be obliged to deliver Saudi Riyals under those forward contracts, that to do so he may have to acquire those Saudi Riyals in the foreign exchange market, and that if the Saudi Riyal has in the interim risen against the DM he will have to pay more for those Saudi Riyals in DM terms than the amount of DM at which he has committed himself to deliver them. The respondents contend that by reason of the failure of [Main Contractor] to pay on the due dates they suffered the losses complained of. They claimed to recover those losses either as damages for [Main Contractor's] failure to pay DM under the contracts when due, or by virtue of express contractual commitments allegedly undertaken by [Main Contractor] requiring a compensatory adjustment in the contractual prices payable.

[30] "We reject these claims. In the first place the nature, extent and timing of any foreign exchange contracts which may have been made were entirely a matter

for the respondents. They did not have to (and did not promise to) maintain any such contracts. Such contracts were in the nature of an insurance or a speculation. We do not think that [Main Contractor] ever bound itself by any warranty that the contracts would not show a loss, or that [Main Contractor] could have had any legal interest in any profit which they might show. We are not satisfied that any language used by the parties gave rise to an express contractual commitment on the part of [Main Contractor] to shoulder any losses on forward contracts. Nor are we satisfied that the losses complained of on such contracts in fact flowed entirely from breaches of the contracts by [Main Contractor]. The forward currency management of the respondents does not appear to us to have been particularly professional. Moreover, prima facie in English law the damages recoverable for late payment are represented by interest. No doubt there are exceptions. But under these contracts it is expressly stipulated that for delay in payment [Main Contractor] is to pay interest at the Saudi Riyal loan rate charged by [the Bank] for the period of the delay (see clause 5.6 of the Supply contract and clause 5.4 of the Erection Contract). On the face of it the respondents could have borrowed Saudi Riyals, or 'rolledover' their obligation to deliver them under their forward exchange contracts, for sums approximately equal to such interest and the respondents would be adequately compensated by an award of that amount (see below). In our view the damages for late payment in the present case should not extend in addition to so-called exchange losses as claimed by the respondents. In the circumstances we do not proceed to consider whether in any event a claim for such losses would be barred under clause 7 of the contracts which excludes liability for damages on the terms therein set out.''

I.   Decisions

[31]   "We award and adjudge that the claims of the claimants herein do fail and are dismissed.

[32]   "We award and adjudge that the respondents do recover from the claimants in respect of the respondents' counterclaims the sums of SR 87,789,216 and DM 4,001,287, such sums being inclusive of interest allowed by us up to the date of this award, but any balance(s) of such sums from time to time remaining unpaid after that date to bear interest from that date until payment at the loan rate for Saudi Riyals and Deutschmarks respectively charged by [the Bank] as from time to time prevailing.

[33]   "We award and adjudge that the claimants do pay to the respondents a contribution to the respondents' legal costs and expenses and the costs of the expertise which contribution we assess at [UK]£ 500,000.

[34]   "We award and adjudge that the claimants do pay the costs of this

arbitration, including our fees and expenses and the administrative costs fixed by the Court of the International Chamber of Commerce in the total amount of US$ 480,000 and that if in the first instance the whole or any part thereof shall have been paid by the respondents via deposit with the International Chamber of Commerce or otherwise the claimants do refund to the respondents such amount so paid.''

Final award in case no. 5294 of 22 February 1988

Arbitrator: Robert Karrer (Switz.)

Parties: Claimant: Danish firm
                         Defendant: Egyptian firm

Place of
arbitration: Zürich, Switzerland

Published in: Unpublished

Subject matters: - place of arbitration (determination)
                         - public policy
                         - contents arbitration clause
                         - Art. 502(3) Egyptian CCP
                         - concurrent court proceedings
                         - delay in execution of works
                         - termination of contract
                         - damages (calculation)
                         - completion of works by employer himself
                         - amendment of claim
                         - interest (rate)

Facts

On 26 March 1983, the Danish firm entered into a contract with an Egyptian employer for the construction in Egypt of a cattle abattoir. On 9 March 1983, the Danish firm subcontracted the civil works to the defendant, an Egyptian firm. The contract, which was subsequently amended, contained an arbitration clause. The Egyptian firm agreed to erect ten buildings and one water reservoir, and to execute additional site works such as landscaping and the building of roads and fencing.

Pursuant to disputes about delays in the execution of the works by defendant, at the end of January 1985 claimant took over the further execution of the works as provided for in an Amendment Agreement dated 19 September 1984 and finished the unexecuted part of the works itself. On request of the claimant, a quality surveyor's report was made to determine what work had been completed up to 31 January 1985.

On 7 May 1985, the Danish firm filed a request for arbitration in Zürich with the ICC, claiming EGP 555,000 (amended on 30 April 1987 to EGP 230,097) and Dkr 7,262,997. On 10 September 1985, a sole arbitrator was appointed by ICC, which also confirmed Zürich as the place of arbitration. Defendant did not sign the Terms of Reference, contested the arbitrator's jurisdiction and did not formally participate in the proceedings. However, the arbitrator received various communications from Mr. A and Mr. B, who claimed to be counsel for defendant.

The arbitrator examined the issue of his own jurisdiction *ex officio*, finding that he could hear the case before him. As to the merits, he deemed claimant's allegations to be contested by defendant, and held that the Danish firm was allowed compensation for the part of the works which it had rightfully executed itself.

Excerpt

A. *Jurisdiction*

[1] "Since Zurich is the place of the arbitration, the procedure is governed by the ICC Rules and the Zurich Rules of Civil Procedure. The provisions of the Zurich Rules of Civil Procedure referring to arbitration were changed as of 1 July 1985 (replacement of the earlier Zurich Rules by the Swiss Intercantonal Concordat on Arbitration). Since this arbitration was, however, commenced before 1 July 1985, it is still the former Zurich law (more particularly Sects. 238-257 of the Zurich Rules of Civil Procedure as enacted on 13 June 1976) which governs (Law of 8 May 1985 on the accession of the Canton Zurich to the Concordat Art. III(2) – OS 49 p. 370). This is of practical importance mainly because of the necessity of a formally separate award on jurisdiction with a different type of appeal than against the award on the merits."

[2] "The decision on his own – disputed – jurisdiction is to be taken by the arbitrator himself (Sect. 241 Zurich Rules of Civil Procedure and Art. 8(3) ICC Rules).[1]

---

1. Sect. 241 of the Zürich Rules of Civil Procedure of 13 June 1976 reads: →

[3] "The arbitration clause invoked by claimant is contained in Art. 14 of the Agreement between the parties of 9 March 1983 (doc. 2/2 = C2) and reads as follows:

> 'Any disputes and deviations which cannot be solved amicably between the parties shall be resolved and settled by arbitration under the rules of conciliation and arbitration of the International Chamber of Commerce, Zurich, Switzerland, in accordance with Swiss law of the Canton of Zurich.'

"This clause could, in and of itself, give rise to a doubt inasmuch as it refers to the rules of conciliation and arbitration of the 'International Chamber of Commerce, Zurich, Switzerland': the International Chamber of Commerce has its seat in Paris and there is no International Chamber of Commerce in Zurich.

[4] "For a correct construction of the clause, its background must be considered. The Agreement between the parties of 9 March 1983 was intimately connected with the main contract between claimant and the Egyptian [employer] of 26 March 1983 (...); the latter formed an 'integral part' of the former (...) and was, therefore known to both parties. The main contract contains, as Annex F, also an arbitration clause (which runs to one and a half pages). It provides for arbitration in Zurich with application of Swiss laws, but by an ad hoc arbitral tribunal of three members, the election of which is carefully described. Art. 14 of the Agreement between the parties which is relevant differs clearly in providing for 'arbitration under the Rules of Conciliation and Arbitration of the International Chamber of Commerce, Zurich'; i.e., for institutional, rather than ad hoc arbitration, but it also refers to Swiss law 'of the Canton of Zurich'. The term 'Rules of Conciliation and Arbitration' is generally used distinctively for the arbitration rules of the – only – International Chamber of Commerce (with seat in Paris), which is also widely known throughout the world for its arbitration organization. The rules of the local Zurich Chamber of Commerce are, on the other side, known as 'rules of *mediation* and arbitration'. Under these circumstances it must be concluded that the true

---

"The Court of Arbitration may rule on its own jurisdiction pursuant to Art. III even when the validity of the arbitration agreement is contested."

Art. 8(3) of the 1975 ICC Rules reads:

"Should one of the parties raise one or more pleas concerning the existence or validity of the agreement to arbitrate, and should the Court be satisfied of the prima facie existence of such an agreement, the Court may, without prejudice to the admissibility or merits of the plea or pleas, decide that the arbitration shall proceed. In such a case any decision as to the arbitrator's jurisdiction shall be taken by the arbitrator himself."

meaning of the clause applicable here is an arbitration in Zurich under the ICC Rules with Swiss/Zurich law applicable to the substance of the case. This construction is concordant with at least one decision of a Zurich court *(Kassationsgericht des Kantons Zürich* in H.c.P. of 28 August 1985 [not published] and with other ICC-cases (ICC no. 4472, reported in Clunet 1984, 946; ICC no. 4023, reported in Clunet 1984, 950; ICC no. 3460, reported in Clunet 1981, 939), where similar clauses had been construed to refer to arbitrations taking place in Zurich under the Rules of the ICC (in Paris).The organization of the present arbitration (introduction of the action by claimant with the ICC Court of Arbitration and the appointment by the ICC Court of Arbitration of an Arbitrator for an arbitration to be held in Zurich) conforms exactly to the clause.

[5] "Defendant also appears to take the view that the arbitration clause is deficient and violates Egyptian 'ordre public' by not appointing the arbitrator itself. The exact argument does not appear directly from the writings addressed to the arbitrator by defendant, but obliquely in a copy of a request by defendant to the Egyptian Court ...There, defendant claims that the arbitration clause in case is invalid because it does not comply with Art. 502(3) of the Egyptian Code of Civil Procedure, which provides that arbitrators should be appointed and named in the agreement on arbitration or in a separate agreement.[2]

[6] "It is undoubtedly true that, in the present case, the arbitration clause did not nominate the arbitrator directly but only provided for ICC arbitration, and that the arbitrator was – pursuant to the ICC Rules – nominated by the ICC. This does not, however, make the arbitration clause invalid. It is not governed by Egyptian law, but by the *lex fori* of the arbitrator (...). It may be noted that also under Art. 22 of the Egyptian Civil Code (quoted in award 5029) the law applicable to the arbitral procedure will be the law of the place where the arbitration is held.[3] Under the

---

2. Art. 502(3) of the Egyptian Code of Civil Procedure reads:

   "The arbitrator cannot be a minor (not possessing full legal capacity) or subject to curatorship or deprived from his civil rights as a result of criminal penalty or declared bankrupt unless he has his status restored.
      "In case of plurality of arbitrators, their number should be in all cases uneven. Otherwise, the arbitration is null.
      "Without prejudice to what is provided for in special laws, the appointment of the arbitrators has to be contained in the arbitration agreement or in a separate agreement."

   Translation kindly provided by Prof. Ahmed El-Kosheri.

3. Art. 22 of the Egyptian Civil Code reads:

   "Principles of competence of courts and all questions of procedure are governed by the law of the country in which the action is brought, or in which the proceedings are taken."

applicable procedural law (ICC Rules and Zurich Code of Civil Procedure in the 1976 version) it is self-evident that the agreement to arbitrate is binding even without nomination of the arbitrators by the parties in that agreement; this result already from the detail provisions as to the nomination of arbitrators after a controversy has arisen and to the procedure to be followed when one party refuses to nominate an arbitrator and / of if the parties' nominated arbitrators cannot agree on a third arbitrator.

[7] "It should also be noted that on 26 April 1982 the Egyptian Cour de Cassation (in case no. 714 of the judicial year 47) held that Art. 502(3) of the Egyptian Code of Civil Procedure could not be used in the case of an agreement to arbitrate in England and that, furthermore, a foreign law which was different from Art. 502(3) Egyptian Code of Civil Procedure would not violate public policy (and would therefore not be unenforceable in Egypt) under Art. 28 of the Egyptian Civil Code (cited after Prof. Achmed El-Kosheri, 'Arbitration and Domestic Laws: Egyptian Law', Conference Institute of International Business Law and Practice, International Chamber of Commerce, Paris, 17/18 December 1984).

[8] "Defendant's point of view that the arbitration clause is invalid for not confirming to Art. 502(3) of the Egyptian Code of Civil Procedure is, therefore, unfounded.

[9] "Already by telex of 20 November 1985, Mr. [A], on behalf of defendant informed the arbitrator that defendant had introduced an action to declare the arbitration clause void introduced at the [Egyptian court] and requested a suspension of the arbitration until a decision of that litigation in Egypt. By telex of 29 January 1987, Mr. [B], on behalf of defendant, referred to a Court Order by the [Egyptian Court] ordering the holding of all arbitration procedures until a decision in a further procedure in the same court.

[10] "No order of any Egyptian Court was actually ever notified or submitted to the arbitrator either directly or by either of the parties. This is, however, immaterial. As the arbitrator pointed out already in his telex of 21 November 1985 to Mr. [A] (with copy to the claimant), court proceedings in Egypt did and do not have any direct influence on the present arbitration proceedings, since Egyptian Courts would not have jurisdiction of either these proceedings or the arbitrator. They certainly do not have any influence on the arbitrator's jurisdiction in the present case.

[11] "Based on the foregoing considerations, the result is that there is a valid arbitration agreement for ICC arbitration in Zurich and that, therefore, the arbitrator has jurisdiction. This is to be recorded in a formally separate award. (. . . .)"

3. *Merits*

12] "It is therefore proven, and the arbitrator finds so as a fact, that defendant vas in delay in the work on 8 January and 16 January 1985 in the sense of Art. 7 of he contract amendment of 19 September 1984, without it being necessary to xplore further the entire scope of defendant's delays.

13] "The documents submitted do not contain indications that would prove the lelays were attributable to reasons beyond defendant's control. Under the .pplicable Swiss law, such circumstances would, anyway, had to be alleged and roven by defendant since fault is presumed in breaches of contract under Swiss aw. Art. 97 of the Swiss Code of Obligations provides that if an obligation cannot e fulfilled at all or not correctly, the debtor has to pay damages for the damage aused thereby if he does not prove that no fault whatsoever is attributable to him.[4] Vo such allegations were made (at least not in a substantiated form) or proof ffered by defendant.

14] "Art. 107 of the Swiss Code of Obligations provides generally that in a ilateral contract one party may, when the other is in default with performing the ontract, impart a time limit for curing the default and can furthermore, if the lefault is not cured within that time, reject to have the contract performed by the ther side and claim damages instead.[5] These damages can include the cost of naving the defaulting party's obligation performed by a third party or by the reditor himself (see: Von Tuhr/Escher, *Allgemeiner Teil des Obligationen-*

. Art. 97 of the Swiss Code of Obligations reads:

"If the performance of an obligation cannot at all or not duly be effected, the obligor shall compensate for the damage arising therefrom, unless he proves that no fault at all is attributable to him.

"The means of enforcement are governed by the provisions of the Law on Enforcement and Bankruptcy, and by the Federal and cantonal laws concerning execution."

Translation taken from *Swiss Contract Law*, a publication of the Swiss-American Chamber of Commerce.

. Art. 107 of the Swiss Code of Obligations reads:

"If the obligor is in default in the case of a bilateral contract, the obligee shall be entitled to fix an appropriate time limit for subsequent performance, or to have it fixed by the competent authority.

"If, at the expiration of this time limit, there is no performance, the obligee may still sue for performance plus damages due to delay. Alternatively, if he so declares without delay, he may waive future performance and ask for compensation for damages arising out of the non-performance, or he may withdraw from the contract."

Translation taken from *Swiss Contract Law*, a publication of the Swiss-American Chamber of Commerce.

rechtes, II, Zurich 1974, p. 92/93, Bücher, *Schweizerisches Obligationenrecht, Allgemeiner Teil*, Zurich 1979, p. 296/297). For so-called 'contract for works' (which includes construction contracts), Art. 366 of the Swiss Code of Obligations specifically provides that when it can be foreseen in the course of the work that through the fault of the contractor the work will be executed contrary to the terms of the agreement, the employer may fix to the contractor a reasonable time within which the defaults have to be cured, intimating that otherwise the continuation of the work will be entrusted to a third person at the contractor's risk and expense.[6] This provision differs from the general provision of Art. 107 only in that Art. 366 does not presuppose that there is already technically a default but only that the execution contrary to the agreement can be clearly foreseen.

[15] "Art. 7 of the Amendment Agreement of 17 September 1984[7] is perfectly compatible with these legal provisions of Swiss law, which are in no way mandatory.

---

6. Art. 366 of the Swiss Code of Obligations reads:

"If the contractor does not commence the work on time, or delays the carrying out in violation of the contract, or is, without fault of the principal, so behind schedule that the timely completion can no longer be anticipated, the principal may, without waiting for the delivery date, withdraw from the contract.

"If, during the carrying out of the work, performance can definitely be anticipated to be faulty or otherwise in breach of the contract, and by fault of the contractor, then the principal may set an appropriate time limit for a remedy, or have it set, with the warning, that in the event of his failure to perform the correction or continuation of the work will be conferred upon a third party at the contractor's risk and cost."

Translation taken from *Swiss Contract Law*, a publication of the Swiss-American Chamber of Commerce.

7. Art. 7 of the Amendment Agreements reads in pertinent part:

" ....

"Second: provided [defendant] do not keep up their time schedules, manpower or material plans, ref. Art. 5 and 6, then at the end of each month a manager from [defendant] and a manager from [claimant] will visit the site and verify the delays.

"If their are delays, and the delays are caused directly by [defendant] or their sub-suppliers and the delays are not attributed to reasons beyond [defendant's] control, then [defendant] have to remedy the delayed work within 7 days after this meeting, if not, then [claimant] have the right after 7 days written notice to take over the delayed work and withhold the expenses in the first due interim certificate, in accordance with the invoiced amount to [claimant] for the work elaborated to catch up with the delays.

"Third, in case [defendant] fail to keep up their time schedules, manpower or material plans a second time – on the same conditions as stated in Art. 7(2) – then [claimant] have the right to take over the complete work and withhold all expenses from the forthcoming payments from the interim certificates. ..."

The procedure agreed there is, in fact, only an adaptation of principles which would generally obtain under Swiss law, to a particular contractual situation. Under the principle of freedom of contract (which is one of the basic rules of Swiss contract law), the parties were free to make such an agreement. The case can and must therefore be decided under the said Art. 7 of the Amendment Agreement without further inquiries into Swiss law. In particular, the question as to whether the Agreement between the parties was a joint venture/partnership agreement (as it states itself) or a contract for works (which would be more in line with its substance) can remain open.

[16] "Without being very clear, defendant seems to be of the view that its termination of the Agreement by unilateral action of claimant was not possible without prior arbitration or court proceedings. This is erroneous. Contrary to French law (and possibly Egyptian law), Swiss law allows a party to terminate an agreement (or modify it in the sense of converting a debtor's obligation to do something into an obligation for damages by unilateral declaration in case of default of the other party) by its own declaration (if the conditions are met) and does not require a court decision to terminate or rescind the agreement. Art. 7 of the Amendment Agreement which provides for such unilateral action is therefore perfectly compatible with Swiss law. (. . . .)"

[17] "From the above description of the facts it is clear that claimant was entitled to invoke Art. 7.3 of the Amendment Agreement on 16 January 1985 and acted correctly according to Art. 7 of the Amendment Agreement in rejecting defendant's further services as from 31 January 1985 and continuing by a third party or itself a construction work which ought to have been done by the defendant. Claimant is therefore entitled to recover the cost expended in good faith for such completion of the works, less the net amounts received for such work from the [Egyptian employer]. (. . . .)"

[18] "While claimant gave the above details of expenditure as per cost category, its bookkeeping system would not allow it to correlate costs to the individual items of work remaining to be done according to the [quantity surveyor's] report. On the other side, it is readily apparent that the cost expended by claimant to complete the job (on which work had already been performed) substantially exceeded the total sum contractually allotted to the performance of all the civil works. ... In these circumstances it was necessary to check the appropriateness of the expenses incurred. For that purpose, Mr. ... a chartered quantity surveyor, was appointed by the arbitrator as expert to produce an estimate of what the cost of completing the items listed in column 3 of the [first quantity surveyor's] report would have been if done by an Egyptian civil contractor and, alternatively, if done by an international civil contractor. In his written report of 27 March 1987 (doc. 74), the expert explained that he had priced the remaining work as per the [first quantity

surveyor's] report on the basis of prices obtained from four different sources, i.e., an Egyptian general contractor, a Korean contractor operating in Egypt, a large Egyptian civil contractor, and a Japanese civil contractor with a local joint venture partner in Egypt. In each case he had ignored the highest and lowest rate of labour/material basic prices and interpolating the two remaining, used his expertise to convert the prices into unit rates for the items of work described in the [first quantity surveyor's] report. The report comes to the conclusion that reasonable cost for completion of the work in column 3 of the [first quantity surveyor's] report would have been EGP 1,425,500 for execution by an Egyptian civil contractor and EGP 1,275,400 plus DKr. 5,817,700 for execution by an international civil contractor (all non-Egyptian cost converted in DKr at mid1985 rates of exchange for ease of comparison). The arbitrator considers the methodology used by the expert as correct and his results as plausible and trustworthy.(. . . .)''

[19] ''There remains the question if the defendant must absorb the additional expense caused by the claimant assuming the work itself rather than using another Egyptian contractor. The arbitrator is satisfied that claimant's action was, under the circumstances, a reasonable if not the only solution. There had already been considerable delays in the execution of the project which was undertaken as a whole under a tight time schedule vis-à-vis the Egyptian [employer]. It is reasonable to assume that the involvement of another Egyptian contractor would have involved more time for getting started on the job and would have made the necessary intricate scheduling of building and installation work more difficult and would also have involved the risk of not meeting the employer's deadlines. Claimant was acting diligently and in good faith in carrying out itself the work in lieu of the defendant. Claimant is therefore entitled to full recovery of its expenses as detailed above. (. . . .)''

[20] ''It should be mentioned that the original Request for Arbitration (and the Terms of Reference) only mentioned an amount of EGP 555,000, i.e., considerably less than the amount claimed now. It must, however, be noted that the amounts claimed now, were already included in the calculation of loss supplied with the first brief of claimant on 30 July 1986 requested by the arbitrator. In the Request for Arbitration, claimant had reserved the right to increase its claims; this was also noted in the Terms of Reference. The full claims of claimant are therefore admissible. (. . . .)''

[21] ''The interest rate is the Swiss statutory rate for moratory interest of 5% (Art.

104 of the Swiss Code of Obligations[8]). The higher rates (7% for DKr and 6% for
EGP) demanded by claimant have not been sufficiently justified.(. . . .)''

Final award in case no. 5428 of 1988

Arbitrators: Dr. Eugene Cotran (UK, chairman); Dr. Nael G. Bunni
                        (Ireland); Dr. Ahmed S. El Kosheri (Egypt)

Parties: Claimant: European contractor
                        Defendant: Middle East employer

Published in: Unpublished

Place of
arbitration: Paris, France

Subject matters: - time bar and clause 67 FIDIC (2d ed.)
                        - clauses 44(1), 52(5), 56 and 60(1) FIDIC (2d ed.)

Facts

The case concerns the contract between a European contractor (claimant) and the
Ministry of Public Works of a Middle East country for the construction of a
highway. The contract, which declared the law of the Middle East country to be the
governing law, incorporated the FIDIC conditions (2d edition). Clause 67 of the
FIDIC Conditions provides:

---

8. Art. 104 of the Swiss Code of Obligations reads:

    "If an obligor is in default as to the payment of a financial obligation, he shall pay penalty interest
    at five percent per annum, even if the contract provides for a lower rate.

    "If a higher interest rate than five percent has been agreed upon in the contract, whether directly
    or by stipulation of a periodic bank charge, such higher interest may be claimed for the period of the
    default.

    "As between merchants, penalty interest may be calculated at this higher rate when the usual
    bank discount at the place of payment is higher than five percent."

    Translation taken from *Swiss Contract Law*, a publication of the Swiss-American Chamber of
    Commerce.

"If any dispute or difference of any kind whatsoever shall arise between the Employer or the Engineer and the Contractor in connection with or arising out of the contract or the carrying out of the works (whether during the progress of the works or after their completion and whether before or after the termination abandonment or breach of the contract) it shall in the first place be referred to and settled by the Engineer who within a period of 90 days after being requested by either party to do so shall give written notice of his decision to the Employer and the Contractor. Save as hereinafter provided such decision in respect of every matter to referred shall be final and binding upon the Employer and the Contractor until the completion of the work and shall forthwith be given effect to by the Contractor who shall proceed with the works with all due diligence whether he or the Employer requires arbitration as hereinafter provided or not. If the Engineer has given written notice of his decision to the Employer and the Contractor and no claim to arbitration has been communicated to him by either the Employer or the Contractor within a period of 90 days from receipt of such notice the said decision shall remain final and binding upon the Employer and the Contractor. If the Engineer shall fail to give notice of his decision as aforesaid within a period of 90 days after being requested as aforesaid or if either the Employer or the Contractor be dissatisfied with any such decision then and in any such case either the Employer or the Contracter may within 90 days after the expiration of the first named period of 90 days (as the case may be) require that the matter or matters in dispute be referred to arbitration as hereinafter provided. All disputes or differences in respect of which the decision (if any) of the Engineer has not become final and binding as aforesaid shall be finally settled under the Rules of Conciliation and Arbitration of the International Chamber of Commerce by three arbitrators appointed in accordance with the said Rules. The said arbitrators shall have full power to open up review and revise any decision opinion direction certificate or valuation of the Engineer and neither party shall be limited in the proceedings before such arbitrators to the evidence or arguments put before the Engineer for the purpose of obtaining his said decision. No decision given by the Engineer in accordance with the foregoing provisions shall disqualify him from being called as a witness and giving evidence before the arbitrators on any matter whatsoever relevant to the dispute or difference referred to the arbitrators as aforesaid. The arbitrators shall not enter on the reference until after the completion or alleged completion of the works unless with the written consent of the Employer and the Contractor provided always:

"(i) that such reference may be opened before such completion or alleged completion in respect of the withholding by the Engineer of any certificate or the withholding of any portion of the retention money to which the Contractor claims in accordance with the conditions set out in Part II in the clause numbered 60 to be entitled or in respect of the exercise of the Engineer's power to give a certificate under clause 63(1) hereof or in respect of a dispute arising under Clause 71 hereof.

"(ii)   that the giving of a Certificate of Completion under Clause 48 hereof shall not be a condition precedent to the opening of any such reference."

In the arbitration, which took place in Paris, the European contractor submitted claims for extension of time, extra works, additional expense, delay, disruption costs and miscellaneous other cost items. The Ministry objected that certain claims were "inadmissible" and that all other were "produced" in view of Clause 67 and some other Provisions of the FIDIC Conditions.

The arbitral tribunal rejected these objections. A number of the tribunal's considerations are reproduced below.

Excerpt

A.   *"Inflated claims"*

[1]   Defendant argued that any "inflated claim", i.e., a claim submitted to arbitration which is more than that submitted to the Engineer, cannot be arbitrated on. The arbitral tribunal considered:

"We reject this argument which suggests that any amount which is above what was put to the Engineer is barred in the arbitration. This is especially so in the light of the specific 'full power' given to the arbitrators by clause 67 'to open up review and revise any decision opinion direction certificate or valuation of the Engineer'.
[2]   "The tribunal therefore holds that it is not barred either by clause 62(2) or clause 67 from adjudicating on any claim on account of the fact that the claimant has claimed a larger sum than he did for the same claim to the Engineer."

B.   *"Preclusion"*

(a)   *The relevant clauses in FIDIC*

[3]   "Under this heading the defendant submits that all the other claims are precluded by the application of clauses 52(5), 44(1), 67, 60(1)(6) and 56 of the contract. Clause 67 has already been set out. The other clauses relied on read as follows:

'*Clause 52(5)*
'The Contractor shall send to the Engineer once in every month an account

giving particulars as full and detailed as possible of all claims for any additional expense to which the Contractor may consider himself entitled and of all extra or additional work ordered by the Engineer which he has executed during the preceding month and no claim for payment for any such work will be considered which has not been included in such particulars. Provided always that the Engineer shall be entitled to authorize payment to be made for any such work notwithstanding the Contractor's failure to comply with this condition if the Contractor has at the earliest practicable opportunity notified the Engineer that he intends to make a claim for such work.

'*Clause 44(1)*

'Should the amount of extra or additional work of any kind or other special circumstances of any kind whatsoever which may occur be such as fairly to entitle the Contractor to an extension of time for the completion of the work the Engineer shall determine the amount of such extension. Provided that the Engineer is not bound to take into account any extra or additional work or other special circumstances unless the Contractor has within 28 days after such work has been commenced or such circumstances have arisen or as soon thereafter as is practicable delivered to the Engineer full and detailed particulars of any claim to extension of time which he may consider himself entitled in order that such claim may be investigated at the time.

'*Clause 60(1)(6)*

'Signature by the Contractor of payment certificates implies his acceptance of all matters relative to such certificates. In case the Contractor signs with reservations he shall within a period not exceeding fourteen (14) days from the date of his signature make known the reasons therefore [sic] to the Employer. No reservations shall be accepted after that date.

'*Clause 56*

'The Engineer shall except as otherwise stated ascertain and determine by admeasurement the value in accordance with the contract of work done in accordance with the contract. He shall when he requires any part or parts of the works to be measured give notice to the Contractor's authorized agent or representative who shall forthwith attend or send a qualified agent to assist the Engineer in making such measurement and shall furnish all particulars required by either of them. Should the Contractor not attend or neglect or omit to send such agent then the measurement made by the Engineer or approved by him shall be taken to be the correct measurement of the work. For the purpose of measuring such permanent work as is to be measured by records and drawings the Engineer shall prepare records and drawings month by month of such work and the Contractor as and when called upon to do so in writing shall within 14 days attend to examine and agree such records and drawings with the Engineer and shall sign the same when so agreed and if the Contractor does not so attend to examine and agree any such records and drawings they shall be taken to be correct. If after examination of such records and drawings the Contractor does not agree the same or does not sign the same as agreed, they shall nevertheless be taken to be correct unless the Contractor shall within 14 days of such examination lodge with the Engineer for decision by the Engineer notice in writing of the respects in which such records and drawings are claimed by him to be incorrect.' ''

(b) *Clause 52(5) and 44(1)* FIDIC

[4] ''On Clause 52(5) the defendant argues that its effect is that unless the claimant (a) *includes* in his monthly account his claim for (i) additional expense, and (ii) extra or additional work, and (b) *gives* full and detailed particulars of them, then no claim for payment for either heads can be entertained by the Engineer. As to the proviso, the defendant submits that the discretion of the Engineer is limited by the first part of the clause with the effect that notice of intention to claim must relate to work done in the previous month.

[5] ''On Clause 44(1) it is said that in relation to extension of time the requirement of 28 days notice or 'as soon as practicable' for giving full and detailed particulars, are mandatory and must be complied with, failing which the claim is barred.

''For his submissions, the defendant relies on a passage from André Brabant *Le Contrat International de Construction* (Edition Bruyland, Brussels 1981) at p. 325 and also on paras. 106-107 of Duncan Wallace's *First Supplement to the International Civil Engineering Contract* (London, Sweet & Maxwell 1980). Although the comment of André Brabant does support the defendant's argument it is in the most general of terms. Duncan Wallace's comment supports the claimant's argument that the bar to payment relates to *extra work* and not to claims for additional expense, so that the latter can be claimed without notice or particulars being given each month. A work claim, argue the claimants can be considered if notice is given *at the earliest practical opportunity*: this does not have to be the next month. Finally, the claimants say that in any event clause 52(5) only bars the Contractor's entitlement to an interim payment and not to final payment and they cite in support the English cases of *Tersons Ltd. v. Stevenage Development Corporation* (1965) 1 G.B. 37, and *Mommouthshire County Council v. Costello & Kemple* (1965) 63 LGR 429.

[6] ''We do not propose to go into a detailed analysis of these legal submissions. It seems to us that the purpose and intent of the FIDIC scheme is that notice of claims of whatever nature should be made to the Engineer in writing (see clause

62(2) above) at the earliest practicable opportunity and when made should be as detailed as possible having regard to the nature of the claim. In many instances if, for example, they are of a continuing nature, preliminary notice of the claim can be given but the quantum may well increase as the contract goes on and is eventually finalised.

[7] "The purpose of clause 52(5) is to give a wide discretion to the Engineer and to enable him to give fair consideration to any claims. In that clause, as in clause 44(1) notice should be given at the earliest possible opportunity and must be as detailed as possible in the circumstances.

[8] "The position in this case is that every single item that is being claimed in the Request for Arbitration (except for one to which we will refer later – paras. 36 to 38) as is clear from the History of Claims ... *was in fact made to the Engineer*. We accept that in a few cases, the sums claimed herein are more, but we have dealt with this point already. We are of the view that they were all made at the 'earliest practicable opportunity'. But even more important *they were accepted* by the Engineer as valid claims. They were in every case sufficiently detailed. The Engineer did not say that he will not consider them because they were not included in the monthly account, or that they were not received within 28 days, or that they were not sufficiently detailed. In each and every case he considered them and rejected them on the merits. The argument on clauses 52(2) and 44(1) appears *for the first time* in the submission of [counsel for defendant] dated 30 September 1986. We do not accept it.

[9] "The tribunal holds that neither clause 52(5) nor clause 44(1) bars the claimant from pursuing any of his claims in this arbitration."

(c) *Clause 67 FIDIC*

[10] "As we understand it, the defendant's argument here is that the Engineer makes one decision only on a claim. Once he makes it, he has settled the 'dispute' or 'difference' under clause 67 and the time of 90 days begins to run from then.

[11] "With respect, this argument is without merit, taken for the first time in [counsel for defendant]'s submission of 20 September 1986, and runs contrary to the whole well known two-tier system of the FIDIC Contract Conditions.

[12] "There is a world of difference between a 'claim' as opposed to a 'dispute' or 'difference'. The FIDIC scheme is clear. The Engineer is the port of first call if the Contractor has a claim during the performance of the contract. The claim may be for extension of time, extra expense, etc. Of whatever nature, the Contractor must give notice of it to the Engineer as soon as reasonably practical and he must, at the earliest that he can, quantify it and detail it. When that 'claim' – of whatever description – goes to the Engineer, the Engineer may grant it in full, or in part, or

reject it altogether. This is the *first tier* of decision making by the Engineer. The Contractor may be happy with the result. That would be the end of the matter and there is no 'dispute' or 'difference'. If, however, he is unhappy, he goes to the Engineer again. This time there is a 'dispute' or 'difference' and we get to the *second tier* of the FIDIC system where the Engineer acts (or should act) in a quasi-judicial role specifically under clause 67.

[13]   "Under claim 67 that 'dispute' or 'difference' must be settled by the Engineer within 90 days after he had been requested to settle the matter. If the Engineer does not so settle it within 90 days or if he does so, then the aggrieved party has a further 90 days to give notice requiring that the matter be referred to ICC Arbitration, failing which the Engineer's decision becomes final and binding.

[14]   "In this case, as will be seen in the history given for each claim outlined above and in the summary given below, the following steps were taken:

(a)   except for the claim referred to below, the claimant had given notice to the Engineer of each of his claims at the earliest practical opportunity, giving as much detail as he can:

(b)   after its rejection (or in the case of [part of the works] the grant of 181 days) he specifically asked for a clause 67 decision on the 'dispute' or 'difference';

(c)   a decision on the 'dispute' or 'difference' was given by the Engineer specifically under clause 67, and

(d)   notice requiring ICC Arbitration was given by the claimant within 90 days of (c).

[15]   "The tribunal therefore holds that the time of 90 days begins to run not from the Engineer's decision on any 'claim' but from the Engineer's decision on a 'dispute' or 'difference' referred to him under clause 67 and that none of the claims in this arbitration (except for the one referred to in paras. 36 and 38) is barred by virtue of clause 67."

(d)   *Clause 60(1)* FIDIC

[16]   "It is argued by [counsel for defendant] that unless the Contractor gives reasons for his reservations within 14 days, he 'forfeits his right to claim at a later date'.

[17]   "This clause is relied upon in relation to the claims of Bridges [X] and [Y]. It is said that when the claimant made his reservation under Interim Payment Application Form no. 39 of 13 October 1983, he stopped there and did not give his reasons after 14 days. It seems to us that would be perfectly right in a situation where the claim is being raised for the first time under the reservation. But that was not the case. The fact is that long before 13 October 1983, there was long correspondence between the parties about Bridges [X] and [Y], and the problems

which occurred with them, each party attributing fault to the other (...). Furthermore, formal notice to claim for Bridges was given in the letter of 7 March 1983 (...) and specifically for Bridge [Y] on 3 November 1982 (...), and for Bridge [X] on 17 July 1984 (...).

[18] "It would have been pointless in the circumstances for the claimants to give reasons within 14 days of the reservation on 13 October 1983 in Interim Payment Application Form no. 39. The Engineer knew full well what their reasons were.

[19] "We hold therefore that clause 60(1) did not bar the claimants from pursuing their claims for Bridges [X] and [Y] to the Engineer and does not bar them from pursuing the claims to this Tribunal."

(e) *Clause 56 FIDIC*

[20] "It is argued that this clause bars the claim for median filling by reason of its measurement provisions. It is said that [the Engineer]'s Resident Engineer, Mr. Z., by letter dated 7 November 1984 (MPW Doc. 56) asked the claimant to come to a meeting to agree on final measurement and the claimant failed to attend. Therefore, says the defendant, since he did not attend, the records of the Resident Engineer must be taken as correct under clause 56.

[21] "This argument overlooks the fact that there was much argument about this matter some two years earlier in 1982. This culminated in the rejection of the claim by [the Engineer] on 9 February 1982 (MPW Doc. 53). On 17 July 1982, the Engineer made a clause 67 decision on the matter (MPW Doc. 54). The claimants replied on 17 October 1982 (MPW Doc. 55) saying that they received Doc. 54 on 24 July 1982 and requiring that the matter be referred to arbitration.

[22] "The claimants therefore say that there was little point in going to a meeting two years later and in any event, their response to the request to go to the meeting in 1984 was that the dispute or method of measurement had already been referred to arbitration.

[23] "The tribunal holds that clause 56 is inapplicable to the dispute on median filling measurement, the dispute having already been referred to arbitration 2 years before the meeting fixed for November 1984."

(f) *"Preclusion" of the various claims*

[24] "We now finally go to each of the claims and deal briefly with the clauses relied upon in the Conditions of Contract as a justification for the 'preclusion' argument.

[25] "*(1) Parts P and Q of the Works*
       The claims for these were made, as the correspondence in Chapter 8 ... shows

in June 1982. In our view both claims were made promptly. The Engineer chose to sit on the matter for 6 months when on 18 December 1982 he rejected any extension for time for [P] and awarded 119 days for [Q] (...). After further representations made in January 1983, the Engineer again chose to sit on the matter for a further 6 months and wrote on 17 April 1983 maintaining his decision on [P] and giving another 62 days (total 181) for [Q] (...).

[26]   "If blame for delay is to be attributed to anybody, it must surely be attributed to the Engineer, not the claimants.

[27]   "The argument here is that the 18 December 1982 and 17 April 1983 decisions of the Engineer on [P] and [Q] are clause 67 decisions. We have rejected this argument. Those two decisions are the first-tier decisions and the 90 day period referred to in clause 67 does not apply to them.

[28]   "The clause 67 decisions for both [P] and [Q] were requested on 13 September 1983. They were given by the Engineer on 26 November 1983. Notice requiring arbitration was given by the claimant on 12 December 1983, well within the 90 day period. We hold they are not barred.

[29]   *"Earthworks/Asphalt claim*

"As we have said earlier the origin of this problem goes back to the testing procedure for compaction and according to the claimant the delays that this caused to his whole earthworks programme. The matter was firstly raised by the Engineer on an official level on 22 February 1983 (...). An immediate reply by the claimant on 7 March 1983 gave notice to the Engineer of a claim under these two heads (...). Then on 24 October 1983 came the 3rd interim claim for the earthworks operation (...).

[30]   "After 7 months, on 7 May 1984 (...), the Engineer rejected the claim.

[31]   "On 8 July 1984 the claimant made further representations to the Engineer (...), but to no avail (Engineer's letter dated 12 August 1984 ...).

[32]   "It is argued by [counsel for defendant] that the 7 May 1984 and 12 August 1984 decisions by the Engineer are clause 67 decisions. We disagree for reasons given earlier.

[33]   "Accordingly we hold: A clause 67 decision was sought for earthworks and asphalt in the claimant's letter dated 17 July 1984. The claimant gave notice requiring arbitration on 18 November 1984, well within the 90 day period. Consequently, the earthworks/asphalt claim is not barred.

(. . . .)

[34]   "Finally, in relation to some of these claims the defendant makes two additional points:

"(i) That when the claimant gave notice requiring arbitration, his notice or letter arrived to the Engineer long after the 90 days. What the defendant overlooks is that the 90 day period runs from *receipt* of the Engineer's decision until the day

the claimant gives his notice requiring arbitration. If the claimant's notice i
delayed through transmission or for some other reason that is an irrelevan
consideration for purposes of the 90 day rule. It is also alleged that the 1
November 1984 letters giving notice requiring arbitration were fraudulently 'back
dated'.

"The tribunal is not impressed by this suggestion which really ought not to
have been made without an iota of evidence. The claimants produced at the
hearing their mail register which clearly shows the letters were sent on that day, i.e.
18 November 1984.

[35] "(ii) It is also said that the claimant in certain instances gave his notice
through the Resident Engineer of [the Engineer] and that will not do. The tribuna
notes, however, that the claimants were told to do so by letter of the Enginee
himself dated 11 May 1980 (...). But in any event the notices though sent via the
Resident Engineer are all addressed to the Chief Engineer.

[36] "We hold that such notices under clause 67 requiring arbitration which were
sent to the Engineer via or through the Resident Engineer were validly given under
clause 67, and were not back-dated.

[37] "We have dealt in considerable detail with the 'inadmissibility' and
'preclusion' arguments made by the defendant in his numerous volumes of
submissions. We have dismissed all the arguments he made on clauses 62(2), 67,
52(5), 44(1), 60(1) and 56 with one exception. The exception relates to the claim
under the heading of 'Additional Bridge Costs'.

[38] "It is clear to us that this claim, which really has nothing to do directly with
Bridges [P] and [Q] was never made the subject of a proper separate claim to the
Engineer. As pointed out ... it was part of Interim Claim no. 4, as 'additional costs'
to the [X] and [Y] bridge claims. However, it is clearly a separate claim. As pointed
out ... and as particularised in the Request for Arbitration and the submissions of
the claimants, the basis of this claim is for 'demoralization' of the work force and
the resultant loss of production in the building of *all the bridges* and not only
Bridges [X] and [Y]. We shall indicate later in this award that this claim is without
merit.

"As at this stage it is our duty to say that it was not put to the Engineer on that
basis, nor 'settled' by him on that basis, as can be seen from his decision of 13
October 1984 (...) where *he does not* refer to it specifically, nor do the claimants
refer to it specifically when they gave notice requiring arbitration on 18 November
1984 (...).

[39] "In the premises we hold that we have no jurisdiction to deal with the claim
for 'Additional Bridge Costs' in the sum of ... as we are barred from doing so under
the provisions of clause 67 of the contract.''

Final award in case no. 5485 of 18 August 1987

Arbitrators:	M. de Haas (France, chairman); B. Cremades (Spain); D.L. Lopez Sanchez (Spain)
Parties:	Claimant: Bermudian Company Defendant: Spanish Company
Place of arbitration:	Paris, France
Published in:	Unpublished
Subject matters:	- validity arbitration clause under Spanish law - domestic and international public policy - separability of arbitration clause - validity contract - validity of clause for alternative fora - determination of distributable profits of joint venture - voting agreement - filling of contractual gap by application of trade usages

Facts

On 7 October 1972, parties entered into a "Basic Agreement" for the formation of a new Spanish joint venture ("X"), the initial object of which was to construct and operate facilities in Spain for the manufacture and sale of petrochemical products. The corporation was to be owned fifty percent by claimant and fifty percent by defendant.

According to the Basic Agreement, the directors of either shareholder had the right to veto a proposition to expand the business of X beyond the production and sale of its products or to invest in additional facilities for their production beyond the facilities initially approved. The payment of dividends, however, was not subject to unilateral veto of either shareholder. The Basic Agreement, in Art. 4(9), provided that, unless otherwise agreed by the annual meeting of shareholders, the shareholders would be paid each year the maximum dividend consistent with maintaining mandatory legal reserves.

Art. 5(13) of the Basic Agreement contained the clause that shareholders were obliged to "so cast their votes at general meetings of shareholders of [X] and otherwise expend their efforts to assure that [X] will be managed and operated in a manner ... consistent with the provisions of the Basic Agreement".

On 24 June 1985, the annual report, balance sheet and profit-and-loss statement for the fiscal year 1984 were unanimously approved by the shareholders. The report indicated that approximately 359 million pesetas were available for distribution to the shareholders. After approval of the annual report, claimant proposed distribution of this sum as dividend. Defendant opposed this, taking the view that the amount should be assigned to a freely disposable reserve until the financing schedule for a proposed increase in X's production capacity was established. Prior to the shareholders meeting, this proposal to increase the production capacity of X's facilities had been presented to the Board of Directors, but had been voted down by the directors of claimant.

Claimant stated that, consequently, defendant was obliged to vote for the distribution of a dividend in accordance with Art. 4(9), and that defendant, in accordance with Art. 5(13) was obligated to vote to assure that the Basic Agreement was accomplished. Defendant, however, maintained that the amount was necessary for the proposed expansion of X's production.

On 5 September 1985, at another shareholders meeting, claimant again proposed that the dividend would be paid and informed defendant, which once again refused its approval, that it was in violation of the Basic Agreement.

Claimant requested for arbitration at the Court of Arbitration of the ICC on 27 November 1985, claiming that defendant, by refusing to approve the distribution of the dividend, was in breach of the Basic Agreement; that claimant was entitled to receive its share of the dividend; and that it had been damaged in an amount equal to fifty percent of the dividend to be distributed. On 15 August 1986, claimant sent a supplemental request for arbitration to include the problem of the distribution of dividends for the fiscal year 1985 (1055 million pesetas).

Defendant contended that the Arbitral Tribunal lacked jurisdiction, because the arbitral agreement was null and void under Spanish law.

Excerpt

A. Jurisdiction

[1] "Whereas the defendant has alleged that the Tribunal lacks jurisdiction because the arbitration clause in the Basic Agreement (Art. 17(2)) ... is void at law since it is contrary to Art. 57 of the Spanish law for Civil Procedure ('Ley de

Enjuiciamiento Civil', LEC)[1] and, more precisely, that said Art. 17(2) of the Basic Agreement is contrary to the prohibition against submitting to alternative fora, established in Art. 57 LEC, such prohibition being Spanish public policy, which is to say, in short, that the arbitration clause is in conflict with the Spanish law which governs the contract (Art. 17(1) of the Basic Agreement). The Tribunal should, in first instance, resolve the question of its own jurisdiction since whether or not to consider the substance of the dispute between the parties depends on the resolution of this previous question.''

[2]   The arbitrators considered that under Spanish law the parties to a contract may, by expressly submitting to a judge, designate their own judge:

[3]   ''Art. 57 LEC states that 'express submission (to a judge) is that which is made by the interested parties when they clearly and conclusively waive their own forum and designate, with all precision, the judge to whom they submit'.''

[4]   The arbitral clause provided as follows:

[5]   ''''[E]xcept for those disputes to be resolved pursuant to Art. VI of this Basic Agreement, all disputes which may arise under, out of or in connection with this Basic Agreement shall be settled by arbitration conducted in the English language. Should [the Bermudian company] be the Party requesting arbitration, the arbitration shall be conducted at Madrid or Paris, at such Party's option; should [the Spanish company] be the Party requesting arbitration, the arbitration shall be conducted at New York or Paris, at [the Spanish company]'s option. Arbitration in New York shall always be conducted under the rules of the American Arbitration Association in effect at the time hereof, and arbitration in Paris always under the Rules of Arbitration of the International Chamber of Commerce in effect at the time hereof. Arbitration in Madrid shall be conducted in accordance with the Law of Private Arbitration of 22 December 1953, as arbitration of laws; for the purposes of said Law, this paragraph 17(2) shall be considered as a preliminary arbitration agreement. Arbitration hereunder shall always be conducted by three (3) arbitrators, appointed in accordance with the rules applicable as stated above to the arbitration in question; provided, however, that should a Party fail to cooperate in an arbitration requested hereunder, the arbitration may nonetheless proceed, the

---

1. *Note General Editor* Translation of Spanish legal texts provided by Mr. A. Tejada. Art. 57 of the Spanish Code of Civil Procedure (LEC) provides:

    ''Express submission shall be understood as that made by the parties renouncing clearly and definitively their own jurisdiction and precisely designating the judge to whom they may submit.''

three (3) arbitrators being appointed by a third party in accordance with the applicable rules. The Parties hereto agree that service of any notice in the course of such arbitration at their addresses as designated in or pursuant to this Basic Agreement shall be valid and sufficient. The arbitration shall be final and enforceable and judgment upon any award rendered by the arbitrators may be entered as being a final adjudication in any court having requisite jurisdiction thereof.' ''

[6]   The arbitrators classified the arbitration as an "international commercial arbitration":

[7]   "Whereas this arbitration is an international commercial arbitration since interests of international trade are involved. The parties have, in addition, different nationalities and residences. The parties themselves even foresaw the institutional arbitration of the ICC, a body with an international character, as a means of resolving their differences, applying its rules of arbitration in a neutral place of arbitration (Paris).

[8]   "Whereas in international commercial arbitration the arbitrators have the authority to determine their own jurisdiction (see Art. V(3) of the European Convention on international commercial arbitration signed in Geneva on 21 April 1961 – hereinafter, the Geneva Convention – ,[2] Art. 8(3) of the ICC Rules of Arbitration,[3] confirmed by the ICC arbitral awards handed down in case nos. 1507 of 1970, 2138 of 1974 and 3896 of 1982,[4] among others).

Further, the parties have not contested the authority of the Tribunal to determine their own jurisdiction, and indeed so expressly admit such authority

---

2.   Art. V(3) of the Geneva Convention of 1961 provides:

"3. Subject to any subsequent judicial control provided for under the *lex fori*, the arbitrator whose jurisdiction is called in question shall be entitled to proceed with the arbitration, to rule on his own jurisdiction and to decide upon the existence or the validity of the arbitration agreement or of the contract of which the agreement forms part."

3.   Art. 8(3) of the 1975 ICC Rules provides:

"Should one of the parties raise one or more pleas concerning the existence or validity of the agreement to arbitrate, and should the Court be satisfied of the prima facie existence of such an agreement, the Court may, without prejudice to the admissibility or merits of the plea or pleas, decide that the arbitration shall proceed. In such a case any decision as to the arbitrator's jurisdiction shall be taken by the arbitrator himself."

4.   Reported in Yearbook X (1985) p. 47.

when asking the Tribunal to declare its jurisdiction (claimant's position) or its lack of jurisdiction (defendant's position).''

9] The arbitrators then considered the separability of the arbitration clause and concluded that separability is recognized both in international commercial arbitration and under Spanish law:

10] "Whereas the separability (autonomy) of the arbitration clause has long been recognized as a general principle of international commercial arbitration, from the point of view of conflicts (the law applicable to the arbitration clause can be different from the law applicable to the contract, see, for example, Art. V(1)(a) of the Convention for the Recognition and Enforcement of Foreign Arbitral Awards signed in New York on 10 June 1958 – hereinafter, the New York Convention – ,[5] Art. VI(2)(a) of the Geneva Convention,[6] the award handed down in ICC case number 4131 of 1982, or the interim ICC arbitral award handed down on 23 September 1982 in the *Dow Chemical/Isover-Saint Gobain* case),[7] as well as from the point of view of substance (the nullity of the contract does not necessarily imply the nullity of the arbitration clause, see, for example, Art. V(3) of the Geneva Convention[8] and Art. 8(4) of the ICC Rules of Arbitration,[9] as well as the

---

5. Art. V(1)(a) of the New York Convention of 1958 provides:

"1. Recognition and enforcement of the award may be refused, at the request of the party against whom it is invoked, only if that party furnishes to the competent authority where the recognition and enforcement is sought, proof that:
(a)   The parties to the agreement referred to in article II were, under the law applicable to them, under some incapacity, or the said agreement is not valid under the law to which the parties have subjected it or, failing any indication thereon, under the law of the country where the award was made;....''

6. Art. VI(2)(a) of the European Convention of 1961 provides:

"2. In taking a decision concerning the existence or the validity of an arbitration agreement, courts of Contracting States shall examine the validity of such agreement with reference to the capacity of the parties, under the law applicable to them, and with reference to other questions
(a)   under the law to which the parties have subjected their arbitration agreement;....''

7. Reported in Yearbook IX (1984) p. 131.
8. *Supra*, note 2.
9. Art. 8(4) of the 1975 ICC Rules provides:

"Unless otherwise provided, the arbitrator shall not cease to have jurisdiction by reason of any claim that the contract is null and void or allegation that it is inexistent provided that he upholds the validity of the agreement to arbitrate. He shall continue to have jurisdiction, even though the contract itself may be inexistent or null and void, to determine the respective rights of the parties and to adjudicate upon their claims and pleas.''

ICC arbitral awards handed down in cases nos. 1526 of 1968 or 2476 of 1976).

[11]   "(Moreover, the separability of the arbitration clause is also recognized in Spanish law. Gullon – *Curso de Derecho Civil. Contratos en especial. Responsabilidad extracontractual*, Madrid 1968 – indicates that if the clause is included in a contract, 'despite such formal dependence, the arbitration clause is independent "per se"' (p. 411); Gonzalez-Campos – 'Sobre el convenio de arbitraje en el Derecho Internacional Privado Espa[n]ol', Anuario de Derecho Internacional, 1975.II, p. 39 – also holds this position, which is widely accepted today. The parties have not stated anything to the contrary, and the Spanish Supreme Court has even admitted the principle of separability of the arbitration clause in, for example, its Ruling of 17.06.83)''.[10]

[12]   The arbitrators considered that an express reference was made to the ICC Rules of Arbitration and concluded, after having taken these rules into consideration, that the arbitral clause was valid:

[13]   "Whereas for the purposes of this arbitration proceeding the parties have expressly agreed to apply the ICC Rules of Arbitration rather than a specific national procedural law (which could have been applied had the parties so desired), and such specific reference to the rules of an international arbitration institution converts such rules into the source of law governing the arbitration agreement excluding other procedural rules (see, for example, Art. IV(l)(a) of the Geneva Convention);[11] therefore the appraisal of the validity of the arbitration clause must be made in accordance with the ICC Rules of Arbitration. The ICC Rules of Arbitration in no way nullify, nor have the parties sustained any argument to the contrary, the arbitration clause which the parties agreed to and, therefore, the clause is to be understood as perfectly valid and effective.

[14]   "Whereas Art. 13(5) of the ICC Rules of Arbitration[12] obligates the arbitrators to take account of the relevant international trade usages and practices

---

10. *Ludmila C. Shipping Co. Ltd. (Cyprus) v. Maderas G.L. S.A. (Spain)*, reported in Yearbook XI (1986) pp. 525-526 (Spain no. 7).

11. Art. IV(1)(a) of the European Convention of 1961 provides:

"1. The parties to an arbitration agreement shall be free to submit their disputes:
(a) to a permanent arbitral institution; in this case, the arbitration proceedings shall be held in conformity with the rules of the said institution;...."

12. Art. 13(5) of the 1975 ICC Rules provides:

"In all cases the arbitrator shall take account of the provisions of the contract and the relevant trade usages."

The Tribunal has examined such usages and practices and has concluded that nothing thereof opposes the full validity and effectivity of the arbitration clause agreed upon by the parties, nor have the parties sustained any argument to the contrary.

[15] "Whereas Art. 26 of the ICC Rules of Arbitration[13] establishes that the arbitrators shall make every effort to make sure that the award is enforceable at law. As the place of this arbitration is the city of Paris (France), the Tribunal has examined French law (Nouveau Code de Procédure Civile, Arts. 1492 to 1497) and have concluded that said law contains nothing which is in conflict with the full validity and effectiveness of the arbitration clause in dispute. Again, the parties have sustained nothing to the contrary."

[16] The arbitral tribunal continued that also under Spanish international law – bilateral and multilateral treaties and conventions ratified by Spain being part of the Spanish internal legal system – the arbitral clause was considered to be valid.

[17] "Whereas under Spanish law no internal law refers directly to international arbitration. While internal (domestic) arbitration is governed by the Law of Private Arbitration of 22 December 1953 (hereinafter, the Law of 1953), international arbitration is governed in Spanish law, not by the Law of 1953 – only applicable to domestic arbitration – , but by a complete (self-sufficient) and autonomous body of rules whose conventional character underscores the international character of the arbitrations that it regulates and whose direct application by Spanish tribunals is established both at the constitutional level (Art. 96(1) of the Spanish Constitution of 27 December 1978, hereinafter, the Constitution) as well as at the level of ordinary Laws (Art. 1(5) of the Spanish Civil Code, 'Código civil', CC); [a] body of rules which is made up of both bilateral and multilateral treaties and conventions which, ratified by Spain, form part of the Spanish internal legal system (Rulings of the Spanish Supreme Court of 14-01-83,[14] 1-06-83[15] and 22-12-83[16]), even with a ranking superior to that of ordinary Laws (Ruling of 17-06-83) such as the Law of 1953 or the LEC.

---

13. Art. 26 of the 1975 ICC Rules provides:

   "In all matters not expressly provided for in these Rules, the Court of Arbitration and the arbitrator shall act in the spirit of these Rules and shall make every effort to make sure that the award is enforceable at law."

14. *X S.A. (Panama) v. Y (Spain)*, reported in Yearbook XI (1986) pp. 523-525 (Spain no. 6).

15. Reported in this Yearbook pp. --- (Spain no. 16).

16. *Fletamentos Maritimos S.A. (Spain) v. Star Dispatch Shipping (Liberia)*, reported in Yearbook XI (1986) p. 531 (Spain no. 11).

[18] "In this case, neither the New York Convention, ratified by Spain, nor the Spanish-French Treaty for the Recognition and Enforcement of Judicial and Arbitral Decisions and Authentic Records in Civil and Commercial Matters, signed in Paris on 28 May 1969 (hereinafter, the Spanish-French Treaty) and also ratified by Spain, allow the validity of the arbitration clause to be protested."

[19] The arbitrators determined that defendant had not proved that (1) Art. 57 of the Spanish Law for Civil Procedure (LEC) is applicable in matters of international arbitration, nor (2) that it forms part of Spanish public policy affecting this arbitration, nor (3) that it prohibits submission to alternative fora:

[20] "Whereas (1) as stated earlier, international arbitration is governed in Spanish law by a complete (selfsufficient) and autonomous body of rules, directly applicable, made up of bilateral and multilateral treaties and conventions, LEC does not form part of said body of rules, and, given that the parties have not expressly agreed to the principal or subsidiary application of the LEC to this arbitration, LEC does not apply to this arbitration. Actually, the LEC (along with the 'Ley Orgánica' 6/1985) constitutes the basic legislative body in Spanish law regulating the organization and jurisdiction of the Spanish Courts.

[21] "Moreover, Art. 57 LEC in no way refers to arbitration (neither domestic nor international), but rather refers exclusively to the jurisdiction and competence of the (Spanish) courts to which disputes are submitted by the parties, as confirmed, for example, in Art. 70 LEC, included in the same Book I, Title II, LEC, which reads:

'The preceding decrees on jurisdiction will apply to those foreigners who resort to the *Spanish courts* giving rise to acts of voluntary jurisdiction, participating in them, or appearing in court as plaintiffs or defendants, against Spaniards or against other foreigners, when it is proper for the *Spanish courts* to exercise jurisdiction in accordance with the laws of the Kingdom or treaties with other nations.' (emphasis added)."

[22] According to the arbitrators, also the analogous application of Art. 57 LEC was inadmissible, because there was no legal vacuum, the New York Convention and the Spanish-French Treaty governing the case:

[23] "In the case at issue before us, the defendant does not, at any time, claim direct application of Art. 57 LEC in this arbitration, but rather its analogous application, which is also inadmissible since it overlooks (i) that in this case there exists no legal vacuum which must be filled by analogy to Art. 57 LEC, as the New York Convention and the Spanish-French Treaty govern, in Spanish law, expressly

and sufficiently the arbitration clause which has been agreed to; and (ii) that there do not exist common characteristics between the case regulated by Art. 57 LEC and the case presented to us, given the substantive differences existing between internal judicial process and international arbitration, both requirements (i) and (ii) to which the analogous application of the legal norms, by Art. 4(1) CC, is subject: Art. 4(1) CC states that 'analogous application of legal norms will be admitted when these norms (i) do not regulate a given case, but (ii) do regulate other similar cases that share common characteristics'.''

[24]   The arbitrators concluded that the Spanish Law for Civil Procedure (LEC) is not part of Spanish international public policy:

[25]   "Whereas (2) for the purposes of Arts. V(2)*(b)* of the New York Convention[17] and 4(2) of the Spanish-French Treaty and consequently for this arbitration, Spanish public policy includes only (a) those laws whose observance is established as necessary for the safeguarding of the political, social and economic organization of Spain, together with (b) those principles, concepts and values protected as essential to the Spanish legal system.

[26]   "Whereas (a) by no interpretation can LEC be understood to form part of the Spanish international public policy affecting this arbitration, nor has the defendant proved otherwise.

[27]   "Indeed, this conclusion is supported in the Spanish Supreme Court Ruling of 11-02-81,[18] later confirmed in its Ruling of 8-10-81,[19] and consistently reiterated in many others to date (see, for example, more recent Rulings of 22-12-86 and 12-03-86). Since there exists in international commercial arbitration the principle of freedom of will of the parties, the Conventions do not mandate observance of the legislation of the forum and therefore the parties may freely contravene said laws of the forum. To understand said principle in any other way would make the purpose pursued in such international Conventions illusory (Ruling of 8-10-81). Moreover, the Conventions confer on the parties wide authority in arbitration proceedings,

---

17. Art. V(2)*(b)* of the New York Convention of 1958 provides:

"2. Recognition and enforcement of an arbitral award may also be refused if the competent authority in the country where recognition and enforcement is sought finds that:
(. . . .)
(b) The recognition or enforcement of the award would be contrary to the public policy of that country."

18. *Shipowner (Finland) v. Charterer (Spain)*, reported in Yearbook VII (1982) pp. 356-358 (Spain no. 1).

19. *S.A. X (Switzerland) v. Y (Spain)*, reported in Yearbook VIII (1983) pp. 406-407 (Spain no. 2).

allowing them to freely elect an 'ad hoc' or institutional arbitration (Ruling of 23-03-82), choose the arbitrators, indicate their number, determine the place of arbitration and fix the rules of procedure to be observed (Ruling of 8-10-81), both without ties to any national law (which does not offend Spanish international public policy: Ruling of 17-06-83), as well as by reference to the rules of an international arbitration institution (which reference binds the parties and stops either from claiming lack of due process because of a violation of those procedural steps established in the Law of 1953: Ruling of 14-01-83). 'To understand that the Law of 1953 forms part of (Spanish international) public policy or that Art. 954 LEC is applicable, would convert those Conventions into a dead letter' (Rulings of 8-10-81, 14-01-83 and 13-10-83) and would, in addition, violate Art. 96(1) of the Constitution (which requires the intervention of the Parliament to supersede, modify or suspend such Conventions). Further, subscribing to any other legal position would have no more basis 'than that of a unilateral and illegal disposition to refuse to comply with the commitments assumed and to refuse to recognize the jurisdiction which was freely and spontaneously accepted, with an inadmissible disdain for the most elemental principles of international trade' (Ruling of 11-02-81).''

[28]   The arbitrators further observed that the arbitration clause did not violate the principles of international public policy which are contained in Art. 57 LEC and Art. 24 of the Spanish Constitution:

[29]   ''Whereas (b) the only public policy contained in Art. 57 LEC is the prohibition against those clauses of submission which offend the principles, concepts and values of equality of the parties, due process and legal certainty *(seguridad jurídica)*, principles which do form part of Spanish international public policy (Art. 24 of the Constitution). In the case at issue before us, the arbitration clause in no way violates this essential content of Art. 57 LEC: the arbitration clause is clear and precise: it designates two alternative arbitral fora which each party may choose, and it selects the applicable procedural rules; if the choosing party wishes to abandon the neutral forum (Paris, ICC) he may do so only by choosing the forum where his opponent is located. Therefore the arbitration clause is not contrary, but rather conforms to Art. 57 LEC, and its validity and effectiveness must, in consequence, be reiterated.''

[30]   The arbitrators considered clauses of submission to alternative fora not to be illegal ''per se'' in Spanish law:

[31]   ''Whereas (3) precisely because of that stated in (b) above, all clauses of

submission to alternative fora are not illegal 'per se' in Spanish law: for example, the Spanish Supreme Court in Judgments of 04-10-35 and 12-12-40 struck down two clauses of alternative submission (to Spanish courts); but in Judgments of 15-10-31 and 13-01-42, it upheld the validity of other analogous clauses, each case being judged on its merits; on the other hand, LEC itself establishes alternative fora in its Arts. 62 and 63 (and many other legal dispositions: see, for example, the second additional disposition of Spanish law 30/1981 of 7 July; thus it cannot be understood that a general prohibition against all clauses of submission to alternative fora exists in Spanish law, constituting international public policy or, for that matter, domestic public policy, but rather that such prohibition exists only against those clauses which violate (and depending on the extent of that violation) the essential content of the above-mentioned Art. 57 LEC, which is not the case here, as previously stated.''

[32]   The arbitrators concluded that the Tribunal had jurisdiction:

[33]   "The validity and effectiveness of the arbitration clause in the Basic Agreement is recognized, the previous question presented by the defendant is dismissed and the jurisdiction of this Tribunal is declared so that it can proceed to hear the merits of this dispute.''

B.   Merits

[34]   The arbitrators, following Art. 13(5) ICC Rules,[20] considered that, the parties having so designated, Spanish law was applicable to the merits of the case, and that the Basic Agreement and relevant international trade usages would be taken into account. The arbitrators came to the conclusion that the Basic Agreement fulfilled the requirements of Spanish law and that the Basic Agreement, therefore, was a valid contract:

[35]   "Whereas the Basic Agreement is in fact a valid contract under Spanish law inasmuch as Art. 1261 CC states that 'there is no contract unless the following requirements are met: (a) consent of the contracting parties; (b) a determinate object as the matter of the contract; and (c) cause *(causa)* of the obligation to be established,' requirements which are all satisfied by the Basic Agreement:

(a) consent of the contracting parties: exists and is manifested, not only by the signature of the Basic Agreement, but also by the subsequent precise and repeated acts of the parties themselves, performed consistently with their

---

20. *Supra*, note 13.

original consent, given more than 10 years ago;

(b) object of the contract: a determined and specific 'joint venture' between mercantile companies; and

(c) cause *(causa)*: the creation by the parties of a common fund for the purpose of sharing and distributing commercial benefits *(causa asociativa)*.

See, in addition, Art. 1255 CC.

The Tribunal concludes that the Basic Agreement is a valid contract between the parties.''

[36]   The arbitrators did not agree with defendant's view, that Art. 4(9) of the Basic Agreement was contrary to Spanish law:

[37]   ''Whereas the defendant argues that Art. 4(9) of the Basic Agreement which states 'unless otherwise agreed to at the annual general meeting of the shareholders, the dividend policy of [X] will be to pay its shareholders each year the maximum dividend consistent with maintaining mandatory legal reserves, using maximum depreciation rates, repayment of shareholder loans, and providing for future cash requirements of [X]', is in some respect contrary to Spanish law because said Art. 4(9) lacks two of the three requirements imposed by Art. 1261 CC .. (consent, object and cause); more precisely, the defendant claims that Art. 4(9) of the Basic Agreement lacks object (or determined object) and cause.

[38]   ''Nevertheless, the Tribunal observes that: (1) Art. 1261 CC is included in Book IV ('Obligations and contracts'), ...; (2) Art. 1285 CC, Chapter IV of said Book IV, Title II ('Interpretation of contracts') states: 'Each article of a contract should be interpreted in view of the content of the others, attributing the sense extracted from the articles taken as a whole, to those whose meaning is not clear'; and (3) Art. 1255 CC, Chapter I of said Book IV, Title II ('General provisions') states: 'The contracting parties may establish such agreements, articles and conditions as they deem convenient, provided that such are not contrary to the laws, morals or public policy'; and there is no Spanish norm in which consent, object and cause are set out as requirements for each article of a contract (nor has the defendant argued the contrary).

[39]   ''The Tribunal can infer from the above that under Spanish law (1) the three conditions of Art. 1261 CC are required for the existence of any contract as a whole, but not for the existence of each article of that contract; (2) the articles of a contract are not independent of one another, but are always interdependent; and (3) Spanish law recognizes the validity of the articles of a contract insofar as they do not oppose laws, morals and public policy.

[40]   ''It is the judgment of the Tribunal that Art. 4(9) of the Basic Agreement is not contrary to Art. 1256 CC since there is nothing in said Art. 4(9) in conflict with

ie laws, morals or public policy (nor has the defendant proved otherwise). The
efendant's argument is rejected.''

41] According to the arbitrators, Art. 4(9) of the Basic Agreement was clear and
ad to be applied literally:

42] ''Whereas the rule *pacta sunt servanda* implies that the contract is the law of
he parties, agreed to by them for the regulation of their legal relationship, and
enerates not only the obligation of each party to a contract to fulfill its promises,
ut also the obligation to perform them in good faith, to compensate for the
lamage caused to the other party by their non-fulfillment and to not terminate the
ontract unilaterally except as provided for in the contract. These principles are also
art of Spanish law: [See Arts. 1101, 1124, 1257 and 1258 CC].[21]
43] ''Whereas Art. 4(9) of the Basic Agreement is clear and, from the evidence
resented in this arbitration, effectively reflects what the parties wanted to contract
and effectively did contract), and should therefore be literally applied: *in claris*

---

1. Art. 1101 of the Spanish Civil Code provides:

''Those persons who, whilst complying with their obligations commit fraud, are negligent or delay
payment, and those who in any way go against the spirit of their obligations, shall be liable to
indemnify the damages caused.''

Art. 1124 of the Spanish Civil Code provides:

''In bilateral obligations, it is understood that an implied right exists to cancel the obligation should
one of the parties fail to fulfil his obligations.''

Art. 1257 of the Spanish Civil Code provides:

''Contracts are only effective between the contracting parties and their heirs; except, with regard to
the latter, in cases where the rights and obligations deriving from the contract are not transferable,
either by their nature, or by agreement, or according to the provisions of the law.
    Should the contract contain any provision in favour of a third party, the latter may demand its
execution, if he already has communicated his acceptance to the person under the obligation and
prior to its cancellation.''

Art. 1258 of the Spanish Civil Code provides:

''Contracts become enforceable by mere consent and from then on not only oblige compliance with
the express provisions of the contract, but also that all consequences resulting therefrom, according
to their nature, be in keeping with good faith, common practice or the law.''

non fit interpretatio. [See Art. 1281 CC].[22] Art. 4(9) of the Basic Agreemen\
establishes:

(1) that the parties are obligated to determine the amount of distributable profits o\
their 'joint-venture', which, unless the parties agree otherwise in the future\
will be the maximum dividend 'consistent with maintaining mandatory lega\
reserves, using maximum depreciation rates, repayment of shareholders loans\
and providing for future cash requirements of [X]';

2) that the parties are obligated to distribute (to pay) the amount that has beer\
determined according to the foregoing, unless they agree otherwise in th\
future.''

[44]   The arbitrators considered that parties had reached an agreement on the\
total amount available for distribution and judged that the distributable profit\
must be paid:

[45]   ''Whereas on 24 June 1985, at a duly convened ordinary [X] shareholders'\
meeting, the parties unanimously adopted a resolution acknowledging the\
existence of a total of 1,414 million pesetas as profits available for distribution, o\
which 359 million pesetas correspond to the 1984 fiscal year, and 1,055 million\
pesetas correspond to profits distributable for the 1985 fiscal year.

[46]   ''Therefore, the parties have reached an agreement, within the scope of Art.\
4(9) of the Basic Agreement, determining the amount of distributable profits of it\
'joint-venture'; and although the defendant has questioned whether such figure\
are 'consistent with maintaining mandatory legal reserves, using maximum\
depreciation rates, repayment of shareholders loans, and providing for future cash\
requirements of [X],' the Tribunal will not take it upon itself to decide whether o\
not such figures are consistent with said parameters or if the agreement reached by\
the parties has disregarded such parameters, because even this would be expressly\
authorized by Art. 4(9) of the Basic Agreement ('unless otherwise agreed'); and\
even if Art. 4(9) does not contemplate it, the parties can come to anothe\
agreement at any time. Neither has the defendant alleged that there was error on it\
part or any other reason that would invalidate the consent then freely given: the\
defendant is now stopped from arguing against its own acts.

[47]   ''Whereas (2) to the contrary, there does not exist any proof that the partie\

---

22. Art. 1281 of the Spanish Civil Code provides:

''If the terms of a contract are clear and leave no doubt as to the intention of the contracting parties,
the clauses shall be interpreted literally.''

have agreed not to pay the distributable profits, or made any other agreement with respect to the distribution of said profits. Therefore, in the case here in question, the general rule established by the parties for this situation should be strictly applied: the distributable profits previously determined must be paid.''

[48] The arbitrators concluded that defendant, by failing to vote for the distribution of the dividends, was in breach of the Basic Agreement:

[49] ''Whereas the two obligations contained in Art. 4(9) imply the obligation of the parties to do whatever may be necessary in order that the parties' obligation may be carried out; this is confirmed by Art. 5(13) of the Basic Agreement, which states that [the Bermudian company] and [the Spanish company] 'shall so cast their votes at general meeting of shareholders of [X] and shall otherwise expend their efforts to assure that [X] will be managed and operated in a manner which will accomplish and be consistent with the provisions of the Basic Agreement ...'. We note that confirmation by Art. 5(13) is not necessary since these obligations are clearly implicit in Art. 4(9).

''The Tribunal understands that under Arts. 4(9) and 5(13) of the Basic Agreement [defendant], as a party to the Basic Agreement, agreed with [claimant] to vote to assure that the terms of the Basic Agreement were properly executed and that, by failing to vote for the distribution of the dividends previously determined to be distributable profits under Art. 4(9) of the Basic Agreement, [defendant] was in breach of the Basic Agreement.''

C. *Damages*

[50] The arbitrators considered that the divergent positions of the parties made it impossible to approve a resolution regarding the distribution of the profits of the fiscal years 1984 and 1985. In failing the vote Defendant had not performed its obligations under the Basic Agreement:

[51] ''Whereas Art. 5(13) of the Basic Agreement obligates the shareholders to cast their votes in a manner consistent with the provisions of the Basic Agreement and, as it is pertinent here, to cast their votes in such a manner as to permit the distribution of dividends thus giving effect to Art. 4(9) of the Basic Agreement.
[52] ''The obligation assumed by the parties in Art. 5(13) of the Basic Agreement constitutes an obligation to do something, which obligation is to be performed by voting, as a shareholder of [X], in order to adopt the resolutions that shall make it possible to attain the purpose of the Agreement. In accordance with Art. 1098 of

the Spanish Civil Code[23] and Art. 924 of the Spanish Code of Civil Procedure,[24] the parties are obligated to perform any obligations to do something that the parties have assumed. If any of the parties should fail to do so in accordance with the manner instructed in execution of judgment and within the period specified therefor by the Judge, execution shall be ordered at the defaulting party's expense. However, the act of voting at General Meetings of Shareholders being a very personal act in nature, it is not possible to act in substitution or representation of the defaulting party, for which reason it shall be deemed, in such event and in accordance with the second of the aforesaid legal provisions, that the defaulting party has opted for payment of damages.

[53] "The Tribunal understands under Art. 5(13) of the Basic Agreement, [defendant], as a party to the Basic Agreement, was obligated to vote to assure that the terms of the Basic Agreement were properly executed and that, by failing to vote the distribution or the dividends previously determined as declared and payable under Art. 4(9) of the Basic Agreement, [defendant] was in breach of the Basic Agreement."

[54]   According to Spanish law the party refusing to perform shall be regarded as having opted for payment of damages:

[55]   "Whereas, in the light of the legal provisions described above, the Arbitral Tribunal considers that it is adequate to order the two parties in dispute, i.e., [claimant and defendant], to call a Special General Meeting of Shareholders of [X], to be held within 30 calendar days from the date of notification of this award, for the purpose of adopting the resolution that will permit distribution and payment

---

23. Art. 1098 of the Spanish Civil Code provides:

> "If the person who is under an obligation to do something does not comply, compliance will be ordered at his cost.
> The same will apply if he acted aginst the spirit of his obligation. Moreover it may be decreed that he undo the wrong perpetrated."

24. Art. 924 of the Spanish Code of Civil Procedure provides:

> "If the party against whom judgment is made to do something, does not comply with said judgment within the time period laid down by the judge, compliance will be ordered at his cost; and if this is not possible due to the personal nature of the act, it will be understood that he has opted to pay compensation for damages caused.
> If the sum to be paid in case of non-compliance has been laid down in the judgment, the procedure, in accordance with the provisions of Art. 921, with respect to compliance with a judgment handed down which includes a sum fixed for damages, will be followed.
> In any other case the procedure as laid down in Arts. 928 et seq. will be followed."

of a dividend, against the profits of the financial years of [X] ended on 31 December 1984 and 31 December 1985 and in the amount specified in this award. In the event that any of the two parties fails to vote in favor of distribution and payment of such dividend, the refusing party shall suffer the consequences established in Art. 924 of the Spanish Code of Civil Procedure, it being deemed that such refusing party has opted for payment of damages in the amount that for such case is likewise specified in this award.

[56] "Whereas, the Arbitral Tribunal considers, in the light of the allegations submitted by the parties, that the covenant contained in Art. 4(9) of the Basic Agreement is a valid and binding covenant whose legal and practical interpretation and scope must be determined in accordance with the provisions of Arts. 1281 to 1289 of the Spanish Civil Code.

[57] "Such interpretation shall permit deducting what was the evident intent of the contracting parties when they agreed to distribution of a maximum dividend that is consistent, inter alia, with providing for future cash requirements of [X].... Neither from the allegations of the parties nor from the terms of the Agreement or from any other element of proof submitted with the briefs, is it possible to determine, exactly and conclusively, the quantitative scope of the factor which is to define, in respect of the maximum profit distributable by [X], the agreed concept of a maximum dividend."

[58]   The arbitrators applied trade usages to fill the contractual gap:

[59] "Based on the provisions contained in Arts. 1287 and 1289 of the Spanish Civil Code, it is necessary to take into consideration the uses and customs that constitute the business practice, and to resolve any doubts, this being an onerous contract, in favor of a greater reciprocity of interests.

[60] "For this purpose the Arbitral Tribunal has considered the reports of experts in business and financial matters, in order to issue a decision that shall fill the existing gap contained in the express covenant between the parties."

[61]   The maximum distributable dividend was calculated to be 75% of the profit available.

[62] "Whereas, the circumstances and interests to be taken into account in the interpretation of the covenant contained in Art. 4(9) are, on the one hand, those of the shareholders proper ... and ... the interest of [X] proper, as a company independent and different from its own shareholders and living an autonomous business reality within its own market. In the analysis and joint application of all the legal, business, economic, financial and practical factors described above the

Arbitral Tribunal considers that, as relates to the financial years ended on 31 December 1984 and 31 December 1985, the maximum dividend whose distribution is contemplated by the parties in Art. 4(9) of the Basic Agreement must be established at 75% of the profit available for distribution which was submitted to consideration by the shareholders at the General Meetings of Shareholders held on 24 June 1985 and 20 June 1986, respectively. In this manner and in accordance with the will of the parties, the objective of distributing a maximum dividend consistent with providing for future cash requirements of [X] is attained.

[63]   "The value of 75 percent has been retained, because according to the Tribunal, it is the normal ratio which has to be distributed in such circumstances...."

[64]   It was decided by the arbitrators that, if defendant did not vote in favor of the defined dividend, it had to pay damages. Interest was due from the time of default:

[65]   "Whereas, for reasons stated above, if [defendant] in the fixed delay does not vote the defined dividend, it would have to indemnify [claimant] for damages caused. In the judgment of the Tribunal, the damages sustained by [claimant] as a consequence of [defendant]'s breach of the Basic Agreement should be: 75 percent of one-half of the aggregate sums available for distribution to [X]'s shareholders, that is to say 530,363,340 million pesetas.

[65]   "In any case, [defendant] will pay to [claimant] interest from the time of default. [Defendant] has been in default of its obligations of the Basic Agreement, from 24 June 1985, in respect to undistributed dividends corresponding to fiscal year 1984, and from 20 June 1986, in respect of undistributed dividends corresponding to fiscal year 1985. Interest should be computed from these dates (effective dates) at the Spanish statutory rates. (. . . .) The interest accrues from the respective effective dates until the date of final payment by [defendant]."

Final award in case no. 5649 of 1987

Arbitrators:	Pierre Bellet (France, chairman); Jacques Piot (France); Abdelhay Sefrioui (Morocco)
Parties:	Claimant: French bank Defendant and counter-claimant: Moroccan company
Place of arbitration:	Paris, France
Published in:	Journal du Droit International (Clunet) (1987) pp. 1054-1060 (original in French) with note by S. Jarvin, pp. 1060-1061
Subject matters:	- performance bond - *caution* (surety) - guarantee - technical expertise

Facts

By a contract concluded on 20 September 1982 with the Moroccan company, a French construction company agreed to build a turnkey complex in Morocco for the price of FF 211,200,000 and 60,264,000 Dirhams. The contract between the parties contained an ICC arbitration clause.

The construction company further agreed to have a performance bond issued by a French bank for 20 percent of the contract price. By a letter dated 9 November 1984, the French bank, claimant in the present case, established a guarantee for the maximum of FF 54,575,438.16, being 20 percent of the contract price. It declared (original in French):

"Expressly renouncing our right of discussion and division, we shall pay all or part of the above mentioned sum upon written request on your part, accompanied by an expert report made by an expert from the International Centre for Technical Expertise of the International Chamber of Commerce."

It was also agreed that the amount of the guarantee would decrease as the works progressed. According to a letter of 9 November 1984, all disputes concerning the guarantee were to be submitted to ICC arbitration.

In 1984, a dispute arose between the French construction company and the Moroccan company and was submitted to ICC arbitration on 10 September 1985. This procedure is still pending and concerns the issue whether the parties have correctly performed under the contract.

On 10 October 1985, the Moroccan company requested the International Centre for Technical Expertise to appoint an expert, in the sense of the 1984 letter of guarantee. On 12 November 1985, the Centre appointed a Swiss national, who submitted his report in April 1986, after having inspected the works. The expert affirmed in his report that reservations could be made with respect to the execution of the works by the French constructor, and quantified his reservations at FF 16,902,000 and 13,076,000 Dirhams.

On 21 April 1986, the Moroccan company requested the French bank to pay the sum fixed by the expert. On 2 May 1986, the bank refused payment and on 22 May 1986, resorted to ICC arbitration. The present award concerns this procedure.

The French bank asserted that the guarantee given to the Moroccan company was only a *caution* (surety as opposed to a guarantee) and therefore depended on the outcome of the arbitration proceedings between the Moroccan company and the French company. It also contended, in case it were found that the guarantee was a documentary guarantee based on the mere requirement of an expert report, that the report had been obtained fraudulently. It finally asserted that there were difficulties in the interpretation of the report, which meant that the guarantee could not be paid out automatically.

The Moroccan company contended that the report had been obtained regularly, that it met the requirements set forth in the letter of guarantee, and that the letter itself had an independent and autonomous status. It also counterclaimed the payment of the sum determined by the expert (FF 16,902,000 and the equivalent in FF of 13,076,000 Dirhams), interest thereon, the costs of the arbitration proceedings and of the expert report, and FF 1,500,000 to cover the economic and material damages suffered.

Excerpt

A. *On the principal claim*

1. *Caution or autonomous guarantee*

[1]   "The letter of guarantee is very ambiguous in its terminology. In fact, on the one hand the bank uses the words *caution bancaire de bonne fin*, *caution solidaire*,

and 'renouncing the right of discussion and division', which are typical of a *caution*. On the other hand, it promises that it shall pay 'upon written request from your part, accompanied by a report by an expert'. The bank mentions three points which in its opinion would characterize the letter of guarantee as a *caution*. Firstly, the bank alleges that it has promised to pay 'all or part' of the sum indicated in its letter because this payment would be subordinated to the payment of the principal sum which the construction company might be found to owe. Secondly, the bank points out that the guarantee decreased as the works progressed and, thirdly, it alleges that the presence of an arbitration clause concerning difficulties of interpretation or execution of the guarantee shows that the guarantee itself was not to be executed automatically.

[2]   "These three aspects do not characterize a *caution* any more than they characterize an autonomous guarantee. On the first point, the promise to pay all or part of the sum simply derives from the fact that the Moroccan party could request the payment of a sum smaller than the total amount of the guarantee. On the second point, the fact that the guarantee decreased as the works progressed is totally independent from the issue whether the guarantee is autonomous or accessory. On the third point, the insertion of an arbitral clause for all difficulties of interpretation or execution does not imply that the guarantee was not autonomous. On the contrary, if the effects of the guarantee depended on the result of the arbitration between the Moroccan company and the construction company, it would not have been necessary to provide for a second arbitration. The fact that the guarantee decreased as the works progressed was enough in itself to create difficulties which made arbitration necessary.

[3]   "Therefore the contradiction remains between the words *caution de bonne fin* and *caution solidaire* on the one hand and the promise to pay 'upon request' on the other hand. The arbitral tribunal, forced to choose between these contradictory terms, and regretting that a bank has allowed such a discrepancy to exist, finds that in the present case it is a bank guarantee of the documentary type, i.e., independent from the main obligation and subordinated only to the requirement of the submission of a document. In fact, when refusing to pay on 2 May 1986, the bank never alleged that its obligation to pay depended on the result of the dispute between the other two parties: it only affirmed that it was 'impossible' to execute the guarantee.

[4]   "It would be impossible to understand why the requirement of an expert report would have been imposed on the Moroccan company if the bank were merely bound by the guarantee after resolution of the dispute between the other two parties. The requirement of a report was meant to avoid unfounded requests for payment of the guarantee, without being as strict a requirement as the 'justified'

proof of the damage by the Moroccan company, which the bank had originally proposed.

[5] "This compromise solution was, however, more advantageous to the bank and consequently to the French party than the freezing of a certain sum as a 'standby letter of credit'.

[6] "In fact, the ambiguity in the terminology used derives from the fact that this is a compromise solution between:

- the *caution stricto sensu* suggested by the bank in a letter of 10 October 1984; it is not contested that this form has been excluded,
- the guarantee at mere first demand, suggested by the Moroccan company which has also been excluded.

"However, the bank has continued to use the term *caution* in its general meaning which is synonymous of a guarantee *lato sensu*, and not in its specific juridical meaning. Hence, the bank cannot allege that the letter of 9 November 1984 establishes a *caution*.

[7] "The arbitral tribunal, considering that the bank established a documentary guarantee in favor of the Moroccan company, holds consequently that the report by the Swiss expert is the requirement – set by the bank itself – for the guarantee's execution."

2. *Question whether the report has been obtained fraudulently or irregularly*

[8] "The expert report was not at all meant to facilitate or accelerate the solution of the dispute between the Moroccan and the French party; ... it aimed at avoiding unfounded requests for payment of the guarantee by the Moroccan company, by submitting to a competent and neutral expert the quantification of the claim of the Moroccan company against the French construction company, and was to result in the automatic payment of the guarantee. This report has no legal relevance in the arbitration proceedings involving the French construction company, neither for the arbitrators nor the parties. There have been no contradictory proceedings involving the French construction company, since the report cannot be opposed to it. The expert was appointed according to the requirements of the letter of guarantee and according to the rules on technical expertise referred to in the letter. Moreover, not only the bank, but also the French party were informed of the appointment of the expert, who saw and heard them, had meetings with them, visited the site and, upon request of the French party, another similar site as well. There has been no irregularity, let alone fraud, in the sense determined by case law on bank guarantees. Consequently the report cannot be set aside."

3.   *Question whether the difficulties in interpreting the report make execution of the guarantee impossible*

[9]   "This is the main reason for the bank's refusal to pay. Later, the bank contended that the expert's remarks were incorrect, that the expert erroneously interpreted the terms of the contract, and that he drew hypothetical conclusions.
[10]   "On this point too, we must take into consideration what has been said on the nature of the guarantee. The submission of a report by an expert appointed as agreed upon by the parties must, as a general rule, suffice [for the guarantee to be executed], of course only if the findings of the expert do not contradict the allegations by the Moroccan company. Obviously, had the expert concluded that there was no right to reimbursement, the Moroccan party could not have succeeded in its request. On the contrary, after careful research, the expert exactly quantified the amount of the possible claims by the Moroccan party, and it is this sum that the Moroccan party mentioned in its request.
[11]   "In the absence of a manifest or blatant mistake by the expert, it is not possible to control the factual or legal aspects of his work. He has not given himself over to hypotheses; he has classified his remarks and evaluations in three different categories and he has also added for the sake of conscience that his evaluations could be changed if the situation changed. These are not dubious remarks.
[12]   "Also, we cannot ascertain whether the amount of the guarantee decreased with the progress of the works, since the bank filed neither a request to this purpose nor furnished precise facts which can confirm its allegations. There is, therefore, no contradiction, doubt or difficulty which makes it impossible to execute the guarantee, and a suspension cannot be granted in relation to the execution of the main contract between the Moroccan and the French party."

B.   *On the counterclaim*

[13]   "From all the preceding considerations, it follows that the Moroccan company can request execution of the guarantee and that the bank must, furthermore, pay the damage resulting directly from its refusal to pay. The Moroccan company has grounds to claim on this point, apart from the sums fixed by the expert:
(1)   Interests on the above mentioned sums, starting from the formal notification requesting payment by registered mail on 21 April 1986; this interest is to be calculated according to the applicable French law, i.e., at the rate of 9.5 percent per year.
(2)   Compensation for the consequential and material damages suffered for the same reason by the Moroccan company, independently from the delay in the

execution of the guarantee. The arbitral tribunal evaluates all this at FF 1,300,000.
[14]   "The Moroccan party does not have grounds to request payment of the costs
of the expert report, which was anyway at his expense. As to the costs of the
arbitration (administrative fees of the ICC and fees of the arbitrators), the tribunal
deems it equitable that they be paid as follows:
-   three quarters by the bank
-   one quarter by the Moroccan party."

Final award in case no. 5713 of 1989

Parties:	Claimant/counterdefendant: Seller
	Defendant/counterclaimant: Buyer
Place of arbitration:	Paris, France
Published in:	Unpublished
Subject matters:	- applicable law
	- Art. 13(3) and (5) ICC Rules
	- Hague Convention of 1955 on the Law Applicable to the International Sales of Goods
	- Vienna Sales Convention of 1980
	- international trade usages
	- set-off
	- Art. 70 French New Code of Civil Procedure

Facts

In 1979, the parties concluded three contracts for the sale of a product according to certain contract specifications. The buyer paid 90% of the price payable under each of the contracts upon presentation of the shipping documents, as contractually agreed.

The product delivered pursuant to the first and third contracts met the contract specifications. The conformity of the second consignment was disputed prior to its shipment. When the product was again inspected upon arrival, it was found that it did not meet the contract specifications. The product was eventually sold by the buyer to third parties at considerable loss, after having undergone a certain treatment to make it more saleable.

The seller initiated arbitration proceedings to recover the 10% balance remaining due under the contracts. The buyer filed a counterclaim alleging that the seller's claim should be set off against the amounts which the buyer estimates to be payable to the buyer by the seller, i.e., the direct losses, financing costs, lost profits and interest.

Excerpt

I. Applicable Law

[1] "The contract contains no provisions regarding the substantive law. Accordingly that law has to be determined by the Arbitrators in accordance with Art. 13(3) of the ICC rules.[1] Under that article, the Arbitrators will 'apply the law designated as the proper law by the rule of conflicts which they deem appropriate'.
[2] "The contract is between a Seller and a Buyer [of different nationalities] for delivery [in a third country]. The sale was f.o.b. so that the transfer of risks to the Buyer took place in [the country of the Seller]. [The country of the Seller] accordingly appears as being the jurisdiction to which the sale is most closely related.
[3] "The Hague Convention on the law applicable to international sales of goods dated 15 June 1955 (Art. 3) regarding sales contracts, refers as governing law to the law of the Seller's current residence....[2] [The country of the Buyer] has adhered to the Hague Convention, not [the country of the Seller]. However, the general trend in conflicts of law is to apply the domestic law of the current residence of the debtor of the essential undertaking arising under the contract. That debtor in a sales contract is the Seller. Based on those combined findings, [the law of the country of the Seller] appears to be the proper law governing the Contract between the Seller and the Buyer.
[4] "As regards the applicable rules of [the law of the country of the Seller], the

---

1. Art. 13 of the ICC Rules of 1975 (not amended by the 1988 amendments) reads in relevant part:

    "3. The parties shall be free to determine the law to be applied by the arbitrator to the merits of the dispute. In the absence of any indication by the parties as to the applicable law, the arbitrator shall apply the law designated as the proper law by the rule of conflict which he deems appropriate.
    (. . . .)
    5. In all cases the arbitrator shall take account of the provisions of the contract and the relevant trade usages."

2. Art. 3 of the Hague Convention on the Law Applicable to the International Sales of Goods reads in pertinent part:

    "In default of a law declared applicable by the parties under the conditions provided in the preceding article, a sale shall be governed by the domestic law of the country in which the vendor has his habitual residence at the time when he received the order...."

Arbitrators have relied on the Parties' respective statements on the subject and on the information obtained by the Arbitrators from an independent consultant .... The Arbitrators, in accordance with the last paragraph of Art. 13 of the ICC rules, will also take into account the 'relevant trade usages'.''

II. Admissibility of the Counterclaim

(a). Under [the law of the country of the Seller]
(. . . .)

(b). Under the international trade usages prevailing in the international sale of goods
[5]   ''The Tribunal finds that there is no better source to determine the prevailing trade usages than the terms of the United Nations Convention on the International Sale of Goods of 11 April 1980, usually called 'the Vienna Convention'. This is so even though neither [the country of the Buyer] nor [the country of the Seller] are parties to that Convention. If they were, the Convention might be applicable to this case as a matter of law and not only as reflecting the trade usages.
[6]   ''The Vienna Convention, which has been given effect to in 17 countries, may be fairly taken to reflect the generally recognized usages regarding the matter of the non-conformity of goods in international sales. Art. 38(1) of the Convention puts the onus on the Buyer to 'examine the goods or cause them to be examined promptly'. The Buyer should then notify the Seller of the non-conformity of the goods within a reasonable period as of the moment he noticed or should have noticed the defect; otherwise he forfeits his right to raise a claim based on the said non-conformity. Art. 39(1) specifies in this respect that:

'In any event the buyer shall lose the right to rely on a lack of conformity of the goods if he has not given notice thereof to the seller within a period of two years from the date on which the goods were handed over, unless the lack of conformity constituted a breach of a guarantee covering a longer period'.

[7]   ''In the circumstances, the Buyer had the shipment examined within a reasonable time-span since [an expert] was requested to inspect the shipment even before the goods had arrived. The Buyer should also be deemed to have given notice of the defects within a reasonable period, that is eight days after the expert's report had been published.
[8]   ''The Tribunal finds that, in the circumstances of the case, the Buyer has complied with the above-mentioned requirements of the Vienna Convention. These requirements are considerably more flexible than those provided under [the

law of the country of the Seller]. This law, by imposing extremely short and specific time requirements in respect of the giving of the notices of defects by the Buyer to the Seller appears to be an exception on this point to the generally accepted trade usages.

[9] "In any case, the Seller should be regarded as having forfeited its right to invoke any non-compliance with the requirements of Arts. 38 and 39 of the Vienna Convention since Art. 40 states that the Seller cannot rely on Arts. 38 and 39, 'if the lack of conformity relates to facts of which he knew, or of which he could not have been unaware, and which he did not disclose'. Indeed, this appears to be the case, since it clearly transpires from the file and the evidence that the Seller knew and could not be unaware [of the non-conformity of the consignment to] contract specifications."

(c). Art. 70 of the New French Code of Civil Procedure[3]
[10] "This provision, even assuming that it may apply in the circumstances, does not in any way require the tribunal to reject the counterclaim if its examination might delay that of the main claim. It simply states that the counterclaim for setting off is always admissible except only that the tribunal may find it appropriate to sever the counterclaim from the main claim lest a concurrent examination of the counterclaim should excessively delay the judgment on the merits. In the present case, the main Claim and the Counterclaim, in accordance with the Terms of Reference, have been examined together so as to be the subject of a single award, and there is no reason to separate them."

[11] The Tribunal awarded the Seller the full amount of its claim and set it off against part of the counterclaim filed by the Buyer.

---

3. Art. 70 of the New French Code of Civil Procedure reads:

"Counterclaims and additional claims are admissible only if they are sufficiently connected to the main claim.

A set-off claim is admissible in the absence of such a connection; however, the judge may sever it from the main claim if he deems that the set-off could excessively delay the decision on the whole dispute."

Final award in case no. 5989 of 1989

Parties:	Claimant: Contractor
	Defendants: Employers A and B

Place of arbitration:	Geneva, Switzerland

Published in:	Unpublished (original in French)

Subject matters:	- jurisdiction based on arbitration clauses in the connected contracts
	- suspensive condition
	- resolutory condition
	- expiration of contract by mutual consent
	- allocation of payments
	- interest on contested debt

Facts

At the end of the Seventies, employer A, a State organization of country X, wished to reorganize its fuel distribution network and to this aim entered into an agreement with a foreign contractor. Because of the complexity and urgency of the programme, the parties first entered into a "Basic Agreement" which was signed in March 1978 and entered into force on 1 November 1978. The parties agreed by this Basic Agreement to conclude Application Contracts to further specify their contractual obligations in the course of their relationship.

Art. 4.3 of the Basic Agreement provided that in case of termination of the same, employer A would have the right to purchase the materials imported into the country by the contractor. Art. 20 provided for the creation of a Coordination Committee which would "coordinate the activities of each of the parties and solve disputes which may arise in the course of the execution of the contractual obligations". Art. 21 of the Agreement provided that all disputes which could not be amicably settled with the intervention of the Coordination Committee were to be settled by ICC arbitration in Geneva according to law X, as in force at the moment of the signing of the contact.

On the same day as the signing of the Basic Agreement, the parties also signed Application Contract no. 1.

In June 1981, employer A notified by telex the contractor that it terminated Application Contract no. 1. It further expressed its intention to discuss the modalities of the purchase of the materials.

In the meantime, due to a reorganization of state agencies, employer B succeeded to the original employer A. The succession became formally effective as of 1 January 1982.

In July 1981, a Purchase Contract was signed by the contractor and initialled by employer B. This contract contained a clause providing that all disputes were to be referred to a sole arbitrator. In case the parties did not agree on a sole arbitrator, the dispute was to be settled by ICC arbitration in Geneva, according to law X.

In January 1982, a Technical Assistance and Services Contract was signed by the contractor and initialled by employer B. This contract was complementary to the Purchase Contract.

In March 1982, the Purchase Contract as well as the Technical Assistance and Services Contract had not yet been signed by employer B, lacking the previous approval of the competent authorities of country X. Contractor consequently suspended all activities under the contracts. In August 1982, employer B signed the Purchase Contract; however, the execution of the contract was again delayed because of customs difficulties.

Discussions and meetings ensued. In July 1986, contractor formally requested payment of certain amounts due under the Purchase and the Technical Assistance Contract. It further asked for a meeting of the Coordination Committee and proposed that a sole arbitrator be appointed to settle the dispute. It also stated that it would initiate arbitration proceedings in case the Coordination Committee did not meet or reached a solution, or the parties did not agree on a sole arbitrator.

In September 1986, the Coordination Committee held a meeting at which employer B and contractor were present. In the course of this meeting, an agreement was reached concerning the payment of the amounts claimed by contractor. The agreement was laid down in the minutes of the meeting, which were signed by contractor and initialled by employer B. A Termination Agreement was subsequently prepared by employer B and was signed on 1 October 1986 by contractor, which added the following sentence to Art. 6 of the draft:

"In case the amounts mentioned in Arts. 2 and 3 are not paid according to Art. 5 [i.e., before 20 December 1986], the parties reserve all rights under the provisions of the Basic Agreement."

The Termination Agreement was only initialled by employer B.

Part of the amounts agreed upon were paid by employer B before 20

December 1986. In April 1987, employer B invited the contractor to participate in a meeting to discuss the final settlement of the dispute. Contractor replied that the dispute had been definitively settled by the agreement of September 1986 and it refused to be present at a further meeting. In May 1987, employer B, having been authorized to do so by the competent authorities of country X, signed the Termination Agreement and paid a certain amount to contractor. Contractor acknowledged receipt of the amount and stated that it considered it to be an advance payment on the interest due. It also affirmed its intention to proceed to arbitration.

Contractor initiated ICC arbitration proceedings against employers A and B. It requested the arbitral tribunal to declare that the September 1986 agreement was terminated because of breach of contract by employer B, and claimed various amounts due under the Technical Assistance Contract and the Purchase Contract and interest thereon.

Excerpt

I. Request for Arbitration Based on Two Different Arbitration Clauses

[1]   "Contractor founds its request for arbitration on the clauses contained in the Basic Agreement and in the Purchase Contract. Employer B contends that this request is inadmissible because it is based on two different arbitration clauses, and asks the arbitral tribunal to declare that it has no jurisdiction over the request by contractor based on the Purchase Contract. Employer B alleges that the arbitration clauses at issue provide for two different mechanisms for the settlement of disputes: the Purchase Contract does not provide for the intervention of the Coordination Committee as does the Basic Agreement, but provides that a dispute which cannot be amicably settled must be referred to a sole arbitrator. Only if the parties cannot agree on the arbitrator, the dispute must be decided according to the Rules of Arbitration and Conciliation of the ICC.

[2]   "Employer B further stresses that the law applicable to the merits of the disputes arising under the two contracts is different, the law applicable to the Basic Agreement being fixed at the day of the signature of the Agreement. Employer B alleges that these differences – as well as the existence itself of an arbitration clause in the Purchase Contract, which is justified only if the parties did not intend to adopt the arbitration clause of the Basic Agreement – show that the parties intended to avoid application of the arbitration clause in the Basic Agreement to the disputes arising under the Purchase Contract. Since arbitration is an exception to the usual means of dispute resolution, an arbitration clause must be interpreted

strictly.

[3] "Employer B finally alleges that even if contractor's request were admissible, the arbitral tribunal can only decide on the basis of one of the two arbitration clauses and not on both clauses at the same time. In this case it should find that it cannot decide the dispute based on the Purchase Contract, since this arbitration clause was invoked after the arbitration clause in the Basic Agreement.

[4] "The arbitral tribunal finds that the differences alleged by employer B are non-existant or irrelevant in the context of the issue of admissibility or jurisdiction which the tribunal must decide. In fact, the arbitral tribunal was seized only after the amicable composition procedures under both contracts had been exhausted, according to their specific provisions. Hence, at this point the only clause still operable for each of the contracts valid is the arbitration clause referring to the Rules of Arbitration and Conciliation of the ICC as they have been put into operation here. The differences alleged by employer B as to the law applicable to the merits are minimal and apparently irrelevant as far as the solution of the dispute is concerned. They are not relevant since they concern the merits and not the issue of admissibility or jurisdiction.

[5] "It is beyond doubt that the parties intended to have their disputes settled by arbitration, that both the arbitration clauses and the parties are identical and that the claims are connected in such a manner that in the context of an international arbitration we must find that their joint examination – apart from allowing a better understanding of the facts of the case – is admissible in the light of the intention of the parties, as expressed in the arbitration clauses. In fact, the Purchase Contract has been concluded 'in application of Art. 4.3 of the Basic Agreement' and it refers in regard to the price of the purchase, to annex B 3 of the Basic Agreement.

[6] "Thus, contrary to what employer B contends, the mere fact that a new arbitration clause has been included does not show the unequivocal intention of the parties to rule out the arbitral procedure provided for in the Basic Agreement. On the contrary, the Purchase Contract falls squarely within the contractual provisions of the Basic Agreement.

[7] "It must be also mentioned that at the time of the drawing up of the Purchase Contract, employer B alleged that all its contractual obligations with the contractor had been terminated by employer B's June 1981 telex, confirmed by letter in July 1981. The parties disagreed on this point. Hence, it could be deemed advisable, in this legally confused situation, to provide for a specific clause in the case that only this contract would give rise to disputes. However, this would not rule out the possibility of hearing all disputes in one arbitration concerning the claims arising between the parties under a group of contracts concluded in the framework of one international commercial operation.

[8]   "Finally, the arbitral tribunal agrees with the parties' interpretation of the last part of Art. 6 of the Termination Agreement – whether it is terminated or not – i.e., that the parties agreed to have their disputes settled according to the arbitration clause contained in the Basic Agreement. Since the two clauses overlap perfectly, the arbitral tribunal finds that the contractor's request to have the disputes heard in one arbitration procedure is admissible. It also finds that it has jurisdiction in this ICC arbitration over all disputes between the parties, also those arising under the Purchase Contract."

II. Claim Against Employer A

[9]   "Contractor alleges that the solvency of employer A was an essential element of the obligation *intuitu personae* which contractor agreed to conclude with employer A. Contractor contends that the [Decrees which effected the succession of employer B for employer A] could not substitute employer B for employer A without contractor's consent.... In any case, contractor asserts employer A's liability for the period before 1 January 1982.

[10]   "The arbitral tribunal must ascertain, according to law X as in force on the day of the signing of the contract, whether the Decrees can be opposed to contractor or, if we approach the problem from another point of view, whether the new status of its counter-party, to which law X undoubtedly applies, can be opposed to contractor.

(. . . .)

[11]   "The 1980 Decrees ... are of a general nature and they pertain to internal public policy since they concern the organization of State X in a broad economic sense. It is true that the parties referred to law X in force on the day of the signing of the contract. However, the 1980 Decrees ... define the legal person competent to deal with the contractor and as such, since they concern the capacity of employer B, they can be invoked against contractor. The arbitral tribunal could only refuse to apply these provisions of public policy if they originated from an abuse of law tending to deprive contractor of its rights. Contractor does not raise this objection since it is clear here that the goal of the Decrees was not to damage contractor or to satisfy an illicit aim. Contractor alleges that employer B is less solvent than employer A, especially abroad. However, when employer B succeeded to employer A, contractor did not have any claims against employer A. Furthermore, contractor's objection must be further dismissed considering the context in which these developments took place.

[12]   "Contractor alleges that employer A is at least liable for the period before ... 1982, when the Decrees became effective ... and also because contractor's consent

for this succession, which amounted to a transfer of debts, was not obtained. The transferral of the activities of employer A to employer B involved the totality of the activities of employer A.... This objection made by contractor must be dismissed ... considering the generality of the economic reorganization measures taken by State X which eliminated the need for the express consent of the creditor. Employer A rightly alleges that contractor never objected to the substitution, but accepted it unambiguously.

(. . . .)

[13] "The tribunal finds that contractor by its behaviour accepted the substitution of employer B for employer A, and that therefore its claim against employer A is inadmissible."

III. Merits

A. The agreement of 22 September 1986 and the Termination Agreement of 1 October 1986

[14] "[After the meeting of 22 September 1986], employer B prepared the text of a Termination Agreement. Contractor added the following words to the draft submitted by employer B: 'in case the amounts mentioned in Arts. 2 and 3 are not paid according to Art. 5 [i.e., before 20 December 1986], the parties reserve all rights under the provisions of the Basic Agreement.' Art. 7 of the Termination Agreement states, as usual, that the agreement will enter into force only when approved by the competent authorities of state X and signed by the parties.

(. . . .)

[15] "The dispute between the parties firstly concerns the distinction between the minutes of the meeting in September 1986 and the Termination Agreement of 1 October 1986. Contractor makes a distinction between the two agreements and alleges that employer B had the power to sign the former, which is a agreement containing a resolutory condition, i.e., payment before 20 December 1986. Employer B considers that only the Termination Agreement of 1 October 1986 is an agreement, under the suspensive condition of approval by the competent authorities of State X.

[16] "In attempting to ascertain the intention of the parties, the arbitral tribunal holds that their agreement materialized definitively in the Termination Agreement, and that this agreement, foreseen in the meeting in September 1986, is the final expression of their intentions. However, it can only be interpreted by taking into consideration the facts that preceded its drawing up. Contractor, accustomed to business relationships with employer B and other businesses subject to the same restrictions by State X, cannot allege that the representative of employer B had the

power to sign in September 1986, when at the same time the parties provided for the conclusion of a Termination Agreement in which their intentions were to be laid down, an agreement which was to be submitted for approval to the competent authorities. Hence, the arbitral tribunal holds that the approval by the authorities of State X was a suspensive condition of the agreement between the parties.

[17] "The second issue between the parties is whether or not their agreement contains a resolutory condition in the sense that the agreement would be terminated if the amount agreed upon by the parties was not paid before 20 December 1986. Employer B alleges that, even if this resolutory condition existed, it could not have any effect before the agreement entered into force, i.e., after the approval of the Termination Agreement by the authorities of State X. We must therefore ascertain whether the parties intended the payment of the amount before 20 December 1986 to be a resolutory condition of their intentions as expressed in the Termination Agreement. We must consider the letter of the expression of their intentions and the circumstances preceding its adoption by the parties.

[18] "Contractor alleges that since 1984 it awaited payment of the amounts involved and that it frequently requested payment, also by means of its legal counsel. Contractor maintains that in order to reach a speedy solution of the dispute it had made all possible concessions, and this while employer B did not contest the existence or the quantum of the debt. Contractor alleges that it was in this spirit that it accepted the agreement in September 1986, on the resolutory condition of payment before 20 December 1986, as expressed in the minutes of the September 1986 meeting. Employer B does not deny this fact.

[19] "When employer B prepared the text of the Termination Agreement, it mentioned the date of 20 December 1986 as the last day on which the payment had to be made. However, it omitted to make this condition a resolutory condition. Before signing the agreement, contractor inserted the sentence mentioned above, the parties having agreed that the mention of the 'provisions of the Basic Agreement' refers to the arbitration mechanism contained in the latter. Employer B alleges however ... that the clause thus inserted at Art. 6 of the Termination Agreement requires the common intention of the parties in order to be put into operation. This interpretation, which employer B does not further explain, must be dismissed since it is at odds with the sentence, which in this case would be meaningless.

[20] "We find that, even if the expression 'resolutory clause' does not appear [in the last sentence of Art. 6], this sentence has an unambiguous meaning. Hence, the arbitral tribunal finds that, in the light of this provision and the circumstances preceding the drawing up of the Termination Agreement, the parties included in their agreement a resolutory condition which began to operate on 20 December 1986 if employer B failed to pay, in case contractor chose to apply it.

Yearbook Comm. Arb'n XV (1990)

[21] "The cumulative effect of the suspensive and the resolutory condition – each of them expressing the intention of one of the parties – cannot be an obstacle to the coming into operation of the resolutory condition if the suspensive condition is not invoked, insofar as it cannot be alleged that payment could only take place after approval of the Agreement by the authorities of X and that by accepting the time limit of 20 December 1986, employer B knew that the suspensive condition was subject to the same limit. If this were not so, this time limit would be meaningless.

[22] "Employer B cannot rely on a letter by contractor, sent in January 1987, in which contractor grants employer B an extension of the time limit until the end of the month to pay its debt, to allege that contractor thereby renounced the resolutory condition, or that the condition did not exist. This letter is, on the contrary, a confirmation of contractor's intention to execute the agreement.

[23] "The arbitral tribunal also finds that employer B cannot allege that contractor's attitude in the following months was ambiguous, in the sense that contractor waited until after the second payment made by employer B in June 1987 to initiate arbitration proceedings. Contractor made clear by its letter in May 1987 that it considered the agreement to have been terminated, and employer B was well aware of the situation when it paid the amount which it deemed to owe contactor.

[24] "The arbitral tribunal finds that the agreement between contractor and employer B is terminated and that it must ascertain the consequences of this finding when deciding and quantifying the claims.

B.   The Basic Agreement of 14 March 1978

[25] "Contractor asks the arbitral tribunal ... to declare that the Basic Agreement between the parties has been terminated due to breach of contract by employer B, and claims damages for this reason."

[26] "The arbitral tribunal examined the nature of the Basic Agreement, finding that it clearly aimed at a long-term relationship, and held that

> 'the Basic Agreement was not formally terminated according to the contractual provisions. We must ascertain whether it expired with the approval of contractor, as alleged by employer B.'

(. . . .)

[27] "The relationship between the parties changes [in the course of the contract]. In April 1979, i.e., after the entrance into force of the Basic Agreement in 1978, contractor submitted to employer A a proposal for [a construction contract] which does not mention the Basic Agreement, even though the project

fell within the framework of the Basic Agreement. The contractual provisions of the project did not fit within the contractual scheme provided by the Basic Agreement. Contractor alleges that this proposal fell under a previous agreement. However, it is curious that no mention is made of the Basic Agreement, which should have rendered useless or obsolete any previous project between the parties which had not yet come to a decisive stage.
(. . . .)

[28] "When drawing up the Technical Contract, which was signed by contractor in January 1982 and at that date only initialled by employer B, contractor completely detached itself from the Basic Agreement to which no reference is made, while this Technical Contract is the direct result of the decisions taken by employer B concerning the execution of the Basic Agreement.

[29] "The arbitral tribunal holds that contractor, by its attitude after the signing of the Basic Agreement, showed that it chose not to apply that Agreement, which it could have done, but preferred to put its relationship with employer B on a more commercial level, which it thought would be more profitable.

[30] "As far as damages are concerned, contractor only alleges a loss of profit, but does not justify any expense incurred for research or maintainance necessitated by the Basic Agreement. We must further note that in 1984, the claims made by contractor do not mention damages and that only in July 1986 did contractor first request damages.

[31] "The arbitral tribunal holds that the parties unambiguously expressed their intention to consider their Basic Agreement to have expired, without either of them being responsible. The termination of the contract cannot be ascribed to the fault of employer B; contractor's claim for damages must be dismissed."

C.   The allocation of the amounts received by contractor

[32] "It is clear that employer B paid the sums it thought it should pay. Hence, ... the payments it made specifying their application cannot be applied to another purpose by the creditor. The arbitral tribunal holds that the sums paid by employer B apply to the principal amounts as resulting from the annex to the Termination Agreement of 1 October 1986."

D.   Application Contract no. 1 and Purchase Contract

[33] The arbitral tribunal reasoned that these amounts are not disputed, nor is it disputed that employer B paid the amounts. The only point at issue is whether there is interest due. The arbitral tribunal found that interest was due starting from the day on which contractor first requested the interest, i.e., 9 April 1984.

Final award in case no. 6076 of 1989

Parties: Claimant: Seller (Netherlands)
                            Respondent: Buyer (Italy)

Place of
arbitration: Paris, France

Published in: Unpublished

Subject matters: - applicable law to the contract
                            - Uniform Law on the International Sale of Goods, 1 July
                            1964
                            - avoidance of sales confirmations
                            - mitigation of damages

Facts

On 20 November 1985, a Dutch seller (claimant) concluded through its agent a contract for the sale of a specified type of product with an Italian buyer (respondent). Deliveries took place in February and March of 1986. On 9 June 1986, parties contracted for the delivery of the same product. After the first delivery under the June 1986 contract, in September 1986, buyer cancelled the remainder of the contracts, alleging that the product did not meet the agreed upon specifications.

Claimant invoked breach of contract and on 4 November 1987 initiated ICC arbitration, seeking compensation for the difference between the contract price and the resale price. He also sought damages regarding other retailed costs for storage, insurance and loss of interest. Respondent counterclaimed for damages arising from storage and production costs as well as loss of reputation.

The arbitrator, applying the 1964 Hague Sales Convention to the substance of the dispute, rejected respondent's counterclaims and awarded the claimant damages for breach of contract.

236

Excerpt

A.   *Applicability of the Uniform Law on International Sales*

[1]   "On 20 November 1985 and 9 June 1986, dates at which the contracts of sale of [a certain product] were concluded between claimant and respondent, both Italy[1] and the Netherlands were parties to the Hague Convention of 1 July 1964 relating to a Uniform Law on the International Sale of Goods (ULIS).

[2]   "ULIS entered into force in Italy on 22 August 1972; Italy made the proviso allowed by Art. IV of the Hague Sales Convention.[2]

[3]   "The Dutch [implementing law] (dated 1 December 1971), entered into force on 18 August 1972, added the following provision (as paragraph 1, hereafter quoted in English translation) to ULIS, Art. 2.

'Without prejudice to the provisions contained in Art. 1, the present law shall also apply if, by virtue of any rule of private international law, Dutch law applies to an international sale of goods in the sense of the present law.'

The Netherlands made the provision allowed by Art. III of the Hague Sales Convention.[3]

---

1.   The arbitrator added in a footnote:

"Italy ratified the United Nations Convention on Contracts for the International Sale of Goods (Vienna, 1980), which entered into force on 1 January 1988; by virtue of Art. 99 of the Vienna Convention, Italy denounced the 1964 Hague Sales Convention."

2.   Art. IV of the Hague Convention relating to a Uniform Law on the International Sale of Goods of 1 July 1964 (ULIS) reads:

"1.   Any State which has previously ratified or acceded to one or more Conventions on conflict of laws in respect of the international sale of goods may, at the time of the deposit of its instrument of ratification of or accession to the present Convention, declare by a notification addressed to the Government of the Netherlands that it will apply the Uniform Law in cases governed by one of those previous Conventions only if that Convention itself requires the application of the Uniform Law.

2.   Any State which makes a declaration under paragraph 1 of this Article shall inform the Government of the Netherlands of the Convention or the Conventions referred to in that declaration."

3.   Art. III of the Hague Convention relating to a Uniform Law on the International Sale of Goods of 1 July 1964 (ULIS) reads:

"By way of derogation from Article 1 of the Uniform Law, any State may, at the time of the deposit of its instrument of ratification of or accession to the present Convention declare by a notification
→

[4]   "Each of the aforementioned contracts (...) provides:

'This contrat [sic] is to be governed by Dutch law'
'Conditions .... Further on the Incoterms 1953 plus addenda 1967'.

[5]   "The fact that the Netherlands made the proviso allowed by Art. III of the 1964 Hague Sales Convention is of no relevance to the present case, as both Italy and the Netherlands are contracting states.

[6]   "The proviso allowed by Art. IV of the 1964 Hague Sales Convention and made by Italy is irrelevant for the present dispute as the aforementioned contracts provide for the application of the Dutch Law (Convention on the Law Applicable to the International Sales of Goods, The Hague, 15 June 1955, Art. 2).[4]

[7]   "Legal writers and modern jurisprudence generally admit that if the parties designate the applicable law of a contracting state, ULIS is applicable, failing obvious arguments in favour of the contrary (Doelle, H., *Kommentar zum Einheitlichen Kaufrecht* (München, C.H. Beck, 1976) 21; Van der Velden, F.I.A. *De eenvormige koopwet van 1964* (Deventer, Kluwer, 1979) 26; Paul van Hooghten, 'Overzicht van de Belgische Rechtspraak in verband met het Verdrag houdende een Eenvormige wet inzake de internationale koop van roerende lichamelijke zaken, ondertekend te Den Haag, op 1 juli 1964', Revue de Droit Commercial Belge (T.B.H.) 1988, 168-177; Jean-Pierre Plantard, 'Un nouveau droit uniforme de la vente internationale: la convention des Nations Unies du 11 avril 1980', Journal du droit international, 1988, n° 2, 321; Oberlandesgericht Hamm 16 March 1981, E.T.L. 1981, 735; Landgericht Bonn, 21 April 1982, Revue de droit uniforme 1982, 397).

[8]   "In the present case it must be considered that parties had no intention to

---

addressed to the Government of the Netherlands that it will apply the Uniform Law only if each of the parties to the contract of sale has his place of business or, if he has no place of business, has habitual residence in the territory of a different Contracting State, and in consequence may insert the word 'Contracting' before the word 'States' where the latter word first occurs in paragraph 1 of Article 1 of the Uniform Law."

4.   Art. 2 of the Hague Convention on the Law Applicable to the International Sales of Goods of 15 June 1955 reads:

"A sale shall be governed by the domestic law of the country designated by the Contracting Parties.

    Such designation must be contained in an express clause, or unambiguously result from the provisions of the contract.

    Conditions affecting the consent of the parties to the law declared applicable shall be determined by such law."

exclude the application of ULIS (Art. 3 ULIS).[5] The fact that the applicability of ULIS is not challenged by the parties appears therefore as the most significant element. Furthermore, the aforementioned contracts do not exclude, either expressly or by implication, the applicability of ULIS (Art. 3 ULIS). A reference in a contract to trade terms (Art. 9(3) ULIS)[6] like ICC's Incoterms should not be taken as an exclusion of ULIS (Honnold, *Uniform Law for International Sales* (1981, Kluwer, Deventer) (Nl n° 76). It must be emphasized that none of the articles of ULIS referred to in the present dispute is inconsistent either with the provisions of Incoterms 1953 plus addenda 1967 to which the contracts dated 20 November 1985 and 9 June 1986 refer or with the specific contents of said contracts.

[9]   "ULIS applies to the aforementioned contracts for the following reasons:
-   claimant and respondent have their places of business in the territories of different contracting states (art. 1(1) ULIS);[7]
-   the contracts involve the sale of goods 'which will be carried from the territory of one State to the territory of another' (Art. 1(1)(a) ULIS);
-   the acts constituting the offer and the acceptance have been effected in the territories of different states (Art. 1(1)(b) juncto Art. 1(4) ULIS);[8]

---

5. Art. 3 of the Uniform Law on the International Sale of Goods of 1 July 1964 (ULIS) reads:

"The parties to a contract of sale shall be free to exclude the application thereto of the present Law either entirely or partially. Such exclusion may be express or implied."

6. Art. 9(3) of the Uniform Law on the International Sale of Goods of 1 July 1964 (ULIS) reads:

"3.   Where expressions, provisions or forms of contract commonly used in commercial practice are employed, they shall be interpreted according to the meaning usually given to them in the trade concerned."

7. Art. 1(1) of the Uniform Law on the International Sale of Goods of 1 July 1964 (ULIS) reads in pertinent part:

"1.   The present Law shall apply to contracts of sale of goods entered into by parties whose places of business are in the territories of different States, in each of the following cases:
(a)   where the contract involves the sale of goods which are at the time of the conclusion of the contract in the course of carriage or will be carried from the territory of one State to the territory of another;
(b)   where the acts constituting the offer and the acceptance have been effected in the territories of different States;
(c)   where delivery of the goods is to be made in the territory of a State other than that within whose territory the acts constituting the offer and the acceptance have been effected."

8. Art. 1(4) of the Uniform Law on the International Sale of Goods of 1 July 1964 (ULIS) reads in pertinent part:

"4.   In the case of contracts by correspondence, offer and acceptance shall be considered to have been effected in the territory of the same State only if the letters, telegrams or other documentary communications which contain them have been sent and received in the territory of that State."

- the contracts provide for the application of the Dutch law. By virtue of the provision quoted in [3] above the applicability of Dutch law implies the applicability of ULIS. ULIS must therefore be considered as applicable to the present dispute.

(. . . .)''

B.   *Notice of Lack of Conformity*

[10]   "Art. 49 ULIS provides as follows:

'1. The buyer shall lose his right to rely on lack of conformity with the contract at the expiration of a period of one year after he has given notice as provided in Art. 39, unless he has been prevented from exercising his right because of fraud on the part of the seller.'
2. After the expiration of this period, the buyer shall not be entitled to rely on the lack of conformity, even by way of defence to an action....'

It must be underlined that the aforementioned period of one year is of strict application.[9]
[11]   "It appears from the file that several notices of lack of conformity were given by respondent during the year 1985. It must be emphasized that with respect to all the notices dated 1985, the period of one year referred to in Art. 49(1) ULIS had lapsed long before the present disputes arose. By application of Art. 49 ULIS it is clear that respondent is not entitled to rely on lack of conformity of the [product] to which the notices dated 1985 relate, either by way of defence to claimant's claims or as a ground for its counterclaim.
[12]   "The same conclusion holds for the complaints dated 19 February 1986 (...). Moreover, it appears from respondent's letter dated 3 April 1987 (...) that the complaints contained in the notice dated 19 February 1986 have been settled amicably: Claimant sent a credit-note to respondent dated 20 May 1986 (...).
[13]   "With respect to the notice of lack of conformity dated 23 April 1986 (...), the following points have to be emphasized:
- the said notice doesn't fulfil the conditions set forth by Art. 39(2) ULIS: 'In giving notice to the seller of any lack of conformity, the buyer shall specify its nature *and invite the seller to examine the goods or to cause them to be examined by his agent'*,
- Notwithstanding the complaints, respondent kept the delivered [product] to which the notice dated 23 April 1986 refers; respondent specified, however, the

---

9. Y. Loussouarn and J.D. Bredin, *Droit du Commerce International* (Paris, 1969, Sirey) nr. 606.

conditions to be fulfilled for the acceptance of further deliveries;

It may be assumed that the complaints made in the aforementioned notice were made with good cause (...); however, it doesn't appear from the file that the said complaints have been settled amicably;

Furthermore, respondent didn't exercise buyer's right to remedies as provided in Art. 41 ULIS,[10] within the time limit of one year fixed by Art. 49 ULIS. It must be emphasized that respondent's letter dated 3 April 1987 (...) can't be considered as the exercise of buyer's rights provided in Art. 41 ULIS with respect to the [product] to which the notice dated 23 April 1986 relates.

14] "The declaration of avoidance contained in respondent's letter dated 3 April 1987 exclusively relates to the last 6 of the 7 confirmations dated 9 June 1986. Paragraph 4 of the aforementioned letter relates to the notice of lack of conformity dated 23 April 1986 without any reference to the remedies provided in Art. 41 ULIS.

15] "It appears from the foregoing that, with respect to the notice of lack of conformity dated 23 April 1986, the period of one year fixed in Art. 49 ULIS had lapsed before the present proceedings commenced. By virtue of Art. 49 ULIS, it follows that respondent has lost its right to rely on lack of conformity of the [product] to which the said notice relates, either by way of defence to claimant's claims or as a ground for its counterclaim against claimant.

16] "Moreover, it must be stressed that notwithstanding the different notices of lack of conformity given in 1985 and in the early 1986, respondent signed both the confirmation of sale [of the agents] and the seven confirmations of sale from claimant dated 9 June 1986 (...) without making any reserve as to the aforementioned notices, in particular those dated 19 February 1986 and 23 April 1986. In its letter dated 3 April 1987 respondent invokes a.o. the said notices to justify its refusal to take further deliveries under the agreement dated 9 June 1986. This appears, at least, as an incoherent position."

C. *Right to Rely on Lack of Conformity*

17] "By letter dated 25 September 1986 addressed to [agents], respondent

---

10. Art. 41 of the Uniform Law on the International Sale of Goods of 1 July 1964 (ULIS) reads:

"1. Where the buyer has given due notice to the seller of the failure of the goods to conform with the contract, the buyer may, as provided in Articles 42 to 46:
(a) require performance of the contract by the seller;
(b) declare the contract avoided;
(c) reduce the price.
2. The buyer may also claim damages as provided in Article 82 or in Articles 84 to 87."

approved the [product] delivered on 10 September 1986 (...).

[18] "Furthermore, in its letter dated 20 October 1986 addressed to [agents] respondent states:

'Therefore, notwithstanding the fact that the last consignment delivered to us was of considerably better quality compared with previous ones and homogeneous in colour,...'

[19] "It must be emphasized that no specific complaints about lack of conformity of the September 1986 delivery are contained in respondent's letter dated 4 April 1987 addressed to [agents].

[20] "In his answer to the Request for Arbitration, respondent declares as follows (...):

'*At first sight*, this delivery (= the September 1986 delivery), seemed to be better than the previous ones. In fact, in October 1986 some of the customers ... presented serious complaints to respondent *as to the old deliveries*.'

It must be considered that this last sentence does not relate to the September 1986 delivery, as it refers clearly to 'the old deliveries'. It appears from the foregoing and from ... its Answer that respondent submits that the approval dated 25 September 1986 was only a 'prima facie' approval. Furthermore, respondent states ... that the aforementioned approval doesn't relate to the entirety of the September 1986 delivery.

[21] "The aforementioned statements have to be rejected as they are inconsistent with the content of the letter dated 25 September 1986: not only was the delivery approved ('the consignment delivered to us on 10 September 1986 conforms to our requests'), but it was also set as the standard for further deliveries ('all consignment which are to be delivered in the future should be of superior quality, equal to those which we have already received').

In view of this explicit approval – made by an experienced buyer – it must be considered that the quality of the September 1986 delivery had been duly examined by respondent in accordance with Art. 38(1) ULIS[11] and found to be satisfactory.

[22] "Assuming that the September 1986 delivery was defective, but that the defect was of such a kind that it could not have been revealed by the examination of

---

11. Art. 38(1) of the Uniform Law on the International Sale of Goods of 1 July 1964 (ULIS) reads:

"1. The buyer shall examine the goods, or cause them to be examined, promptly."

he goods provided for in Art. 38(1) ULIS, respondent should have given notice hereof 'promptly after its discovery' (by virtue of Art. 39(1) ULIS).[12] It doesn't appear from the file that such notice has been given. Moreover, the period of two years within which the buyer has to give the seller notice of the defect (Art. 39(1) ULIS) has already lapsed.

23] "For the reasons stated above, the conclusion must be that respondent lost his right to rely on lack of conformity of the [product] delivered in September 1986."

D. Avoidance of Confirmations

24] "In its letter dated 3 April 1987, sent to [agents], respondent declares that he *will not take delivery of the 286 tons* which in the opinion of claimant are still to be delivered, for *the exclusive reason* of non conformity of the delivered [product] to the sample bale in their possession, its inferior quality and non suitability to his production.

25] "It appears from [19] above that the aforementioned letter doesn't contain specific complaints about the lack of conformity of the September 1986 delivery, [the] only delivery which was made in performance of the agreement dated 9 June 1986 and has been explicitly approved by respondent (see: [20] above).

26] "Respondent's declaration of avoidance dated 3 April 1987 was exclusively based on complaints relating to deliveries made in performance of previous contracts; ... only the complaints dated 19 February 1986 and 23 April 1986 referred to in paragraphs 3 and 4 of the aforementioned declaration relate to the agreement dated 20 November 1985.

27] "ULIS does not entitle a buyer to avoid a contract of sale for lack of conformity of goods delivered in performance of another contract (see: Art. 43 ULIS: '...if the failure of the goods to *conform to the contract...*').

28] "Assuming that the confirmations dated 9 June 1986 are to be considered

---

12. Art. 39(1) of the Uniform Law on the International Sale of Goods of 1 July 1964 (ULIS) reads:

"The buyer shall lose the right to rely on a lack of conformity of the goods if he has not given the seller notice thereof promptly after he has discovered the lack of conformity or ought to have discovered it. If a defect which could not have been revealed by the examination of the goods provided for in Article 38 is found later, the buyer may nonetheless rely on that defect, provided that he gives the seller notice thereof promptly after its discovery. In any event, the buyer shall lose the right to rely on a lack of conformity of the goods if he has not given notice thereof to the seller within a period of two years from the date on which the goods were handed over, unless the lack of conformity constituted a breach of a guarantee covering a longer period."

only as modifications of the contracts dated 20 November 1985 – quod non – (se [*G*], hereafter), only the complaints dated 10 February 1986 and 23 April 1986 (se *A*, above) could be relevant (see, however the conclusion under [*B*] above). Th question is also to be considered whether those complaints were a case o fundamental breach as defined in Art. 10 ULIS.[13] For the reasons stated in [13]-[16 above they can't be considered as such. Assuming, however, they were, it must b emphasized that those complaints were not promptly followed by avoidance (Art 41(1)(b) ULIS); it follows that respondent, by virtue of Art. 43 ULIS ('... The buye shall lose his right to declare the contract avoided *if he does not exercise it promptl after giving the seller notice* of the lack of conformity or,...') lost his right o avoidance long before the declaration of avoidance dated 3 April 1987.

[29]   "Furthermore, the existence of a right of avoidance still available on 3 Apri 1987, would also be inconsistent with respondent's viewpoint that th confirmations dated 9 June 1986 were only modifications of the contracts dated 20 November 1985:

- respondent signed the confirmations dated 9 June 1986 without making any reserve (see: [16] above);

- an agreement to modify an existing contract necessarily implies a waiver of any right to avoid the modified contract for a breach committed prior to it modification.

- Prior to the agreement of 9 June 1986, respondent declared as follows in a lette dated 14 March 1986 sent to [agents] (...): 'Hence, we deem it fit to pay you more, both because there is a contract *and because you have proved your seriousness*, and because we as a rule do not change *a supplier who perform. well*'. By this letter, respondent thus confirms the 'seriousness' of claimant.

[30]   "It appears from the foregoing that respondent was not entitled to avoid the last six of the seven confirmations dated 9 June 1986, regardless whether they should be considered as totally new contracts or only as modifications of the contracts dated 20 November 1985.

[31]   "Finally, it appears interesting to mention the other following elements of the case, which could clarify the context in which respondent refused to take further deliveries under the 9 June 1986 agreement:

- By letter dated 9 July 1986 sent to [agents], respondent informs [agents] about

---

13. Art. 10 of the Uniform Law on the International Sale of Goods of 1 July 1964 (ULIS) reads:

"For the purposes of the present Law, a breach of contract shall be regarded as fundamental wherever the party in breach knew, or ought to have known, at the time of the conclusion of the contract, that a reasonable person in the same situation as the other party would not have entered into the contract if he had foreseen the breach and its effects."

the fact that the most important Italian producer of [the product] is lowering his prices (notwithstanding the contract) and asks [agents] to do the same;
- By letter dated 10 July 1986 addressed to [agents], respondent asked to carry the first delivery expected early September and as from then to suspend subsequent deliveries until further notice: 'Because of problems of storage and reduction in sales...'
- By letter dated 20 October 1986 sent to [agents] (...) respondent states as follows:

'By the way, we inform you that in accordance with the present quotations, [the product], has been offered to us these days at Lit. ... per kg. It is up to you to consider whether this could be a reason for you to reduce your price'.''

E. Damages

[24] "By letter of 16 March 1987, addressed to respondent, claimant gave notice of default (...), granting to respondent a grace period of one month – until 15 April 1987 – for making a proposal to take delivery of the outstanding balance of 286 tons [of the product] at the price agreed in the contract dated 9 June 1986. In the said letter, claimant made its position quite clear: the outstanding balance would be closed out unless before 15 April 1987 respondent should make a proposal for taking delivery at the contracted price. In its answer dated 3 April 1987, respondent (...) wrongfully avoided the last six of the seven confirmations dated 9 June 1986 (see: [D], above).

[25] "After this wrongful repudiation the conditional avoidance which had been declared in claimant's letter to respondent dated 16 March 1987 became operative. Claimant was entitled to avoid the contract for the following reasons which are concurrent:
- in the existing circumstances there were good grounds for fearing that respondent would not pay the price if claimant should attempt to perform the contracts by sending [the product] to Italy (Art. 66(1) ULIS).[14]
- respondent had neither taken delivery nor even declared its willingness to take

---

14. Art. 66(1) of the Uniform Law on the International Sale of Goods of 1 July 1964 (ULIS) reads:

"1. Where the buyer's failure to take delivery of the goods in accordance with the contract amounts to a fundamental breach of the contract or gives the seller good grounds for fearing that the buyer will not pay the price, the seller may declare the contract avoided."

delivery within the additional period granted in claimant's letter of 16 March 1987 (Art. 66(2) ULIS).[15]

[26]   "As claimant was entitled to avoid the unperformed contracts, respondent incurred a liability to pay damages by virtue of Art. 68(1) ULIS which provides as follows:

'Where the contract is avoided because of the failure of the buyer to accept delivery of the goods..., the the [sic] seller shall have the right to claim damages in accordance with articles 84 to 87.' "

The arbitrator held that the principal amount claimed by claimant for damages resulting from breach of contract and the additional costs for storage and interest were well founded whereas the costs of insurance was not sufficiently proven and thus not to be taken into account.

F.   New Contracts

[29]   "The confirmation of sale dated 9 June 1986 sent by [agents] to respondent and signed by the latter (...) contains the following special condition: 'This contract *cancels and substitutes* the balance of contract N° [xyz] not delivered at this date.' [xyz] refers to [agents'] confirmation of sale dated 20 November 1985 (...).

[30]   "It appears clearly from this explicit mention that it was the intention of the parties to cancel the contracts dated 20 November 1985 rather than to modify them.

[31]   "Furthermore, it must be emphasized that the differences between both contracts are not limited only to terms of delivery or quantity. This is a further reason why the agreement dated 9 June 1986 is to be considered as a totally new contract.

(. . . .)

[32]   "The intention of the parties to cancel the contracts dated 20 November 1985 is also confirmed in the following letters:
-   letter dated 14 March 1986 sent by respondent to [agents] (...):

---

15. Art. 66(2) of the Uniform Law on the International Sale of Goods of 1 July 1964 (ULIS) reads:

"2.   Where the failure to take delivery of the goods does not amount to a fundamental breach of the contract, the seller may grant to the buyer an additional period of time of reasonable length. If the buyer has not taken delivery of the goods at the expiration of the additional period, the seller may declare the contract avoided, provided that he does so promptly."

'We ask you, therefore, to send us *a new proposal* by claimant, which is more favourable *than the previous one…*'

letter dated 26 May 1986 sent by respondent to [agents]:

'We ask you, therefore, to send us before September/December a *new offer* as amended'.

letter dated 11 July 1986 from [agents] to respondent (…):

'The contract we are talking about is already the product of renegotiation of the price of an *old contract*'.

33] "The question is to be considered whether the agreement of 9 June 1986 onstitutes either one independent contract or 7 independent contracts. Although ach of the confirmations sent by claimant to respondent has been drafted as a eparate contract, it must be stressed that they are identical but for the clauses with espect to 'quality' and 'delivery'.

34] "As the goods to which these confirmations refer are specified in [the gents'] confirmation dated 9 June 1986 and taking into account the fact that the rice is calculated on the basis of the total quantity of [the product] sold (…), the onclusion must be that the agreement of 9 June 1986 is one independent and idivisible contract with successive deliveries."

G. Resale "in a reasonable manner"

'he arbitrator rejected respondent's allegation that claimant made a very bad argain in reselling the product, and thus not in accordance with Art. 85 ULIS.[16]

35] "Respondent's position that the price of DM … per kg in April 1987 relates o a second choice [product] doesn't hold as the [product] resold to [company X] vas the outstanding quantity of [the product] under the agreement of 9 June 1986, nd taking into account the fact that the September 1986 delivery under this greement was explicitly approved by respondent (see: [C], above).

36] "In the market of [the product, there] is a broad spectrum of prices which are etermined by factors such as the origin of the product and its brand.

---

6. Art. 85 of the Uniform Law on the International Sale of Goods of 1 July 1964 (ULIS) reads:

"If the buyer has bought goods in replacement or the seller has resold goods in a reasonable manner, he may recover the difference between the contract price and the price paid for the goods bought in replacement or that obtained by the resale."

It is, for instance, well known within the trade that the prices of [the product] of East-European origin are generally lower than the prices at which the leading western brands are sold in the market. It must be underlined that the origin of the [product] was not specified in the contracts dated 20 November 1985 and 9 June 1986. However, respondent knew that the delivered [product] was of East-European origin (...).

[37] "As there are so many different types and brands of [the product] and as the price is determined by factors such as the origin of the [product], it is unrealistic to compare the price obtained by the resale to [company X] with the prices invoiced to respondent....

[38] "However, as the prices of the different types and brands of [the product] follow a common pattern, it is a more realistic approach to compare the price at which claimant sold to respondent in June 1986 with the price at which claimant resold in April 1987 to [company X], and then to compare both prices with the general trend in the market for [the product].

(. . . .)

[39] "It appears from the foregoing that claimant resold the [product] at an even better price than the one to be expected on the basis of the general trend in the market.... It follows that respondent's submission that claimant resold at a price far below the current price as it was on 15 April 1987 is not only in contradiction with the general trend in the market as indicated above, but it is also inconsistent with respondent's statements that the contractual price was far above the market price.

(. . . .)

[40] "For the reasons stated above, the conclusion must be that claimant sold the [product] to [company X] 'in a reasonable manner' in accordance with Art. 85 ULIS, at a price which was in accordance with the current price on 15 April 1987."

Final award in case no. 6281 of 26 August 1989

Parties: Claimant: Egyptian company (buyer)
                            Defendant: Yugoslav company (seller)

Place of
arbitration: Paris, France

Published in: Unpublished

Subject matters: - applicable law to contract
                            - frustration of contract
                            - ''purchase in replacement''
                            - calculation of interest

Facts

On 20 August 1987, the parties concluded a contract for the sale of 80,000 metric tons of steel bars at an average price of US$ 190.00 per metric ton. The goods were delivered in accordance with the contract between 15 September 1985 and 15 January 1988 to a suitable Yugoslav port.

Claimant had the option to increase the quantity to 160,000 metric tons at the same price and conditions, provided it declared its option to purchase the additional 80,000 metric tons at the latest by 15 December 1987 and opened its letter of credit for the first delivery at the latest by 31 December 1987.

On 26 November 1987, claimant informed defendant that it would exercise the option and would open the L/C during the second half of December 1987. On 9 December 1987, defendant requested a meeting to be held that month, to discuss the prices for the additional quantity of the goods. Claimant insisted on the originally agreed price but was prepared to discuss future business transactions. At the meeting held on 28 December 1987, defendant requested US$ 215.00 per metric ton for the additional deliveries, but claimant did not agree.

In its letter of 31 December 1987, claimant stated that defendant's behaviour was a breach of contract and requested defendant to announce the beneficiaries of the future letters of credit. If defendant did not agree by 6 January 1988, claimant would hold defendant liable for any and all damage, caused by breach of contract. This period was extended to 25 January 1988.

On 26 January 1988, claimant bought 80,000 metric tons of the same type of steel bars from a Romanian company at a price of US$ 216.00 per metric ton. Claimant alleged that shipping costs from Romania to Egypt were US$ 2.00 to US$ 2.50 per metric ton lower than from Yugoslavia to Egypt.

Claimant initiated arbitration under the arbitration clause in the contract which provided for arbitration at the International Chamber of Commerce, claiming compensation for the loss due to the price difference. The sole arbitrator held that claimant was entitled to damages due to defendant's failure to deliver the additional quantity of goods at the original price.

Excerpt

[1]   The arbitrator decided that Yugoslav law was applicable:

[2]   "It should be determined, first and foremost, in connection with the alleged unreasonableness, due to an increase in world-market prices, which legal provisions should be applied to evaluate the sales contract and, thus also, this central issue. At any rate, the Vienna United Nations Convention on Contracts for the International Sale of Goods of 11 April 1980, cannot be applied as such. The Convention is in force, both in Egypt and in Yugoslavia, as well as in France; yet, according to Art. 100(2) it applies to such sales contracts only that were concluded after the day the Convention went into force, i.e., 1 January 1988. The present sales contract was concluded on 20 August 1987.

[3]   "The question, which law applies, must therefore be examined on the basis of the rules on international private law.

[4]   "According to Egyptian international private law, the law of that country applies, where the contract is signed, unless the parties agree otherwise, and, in addition, if they have their principal offices in different states (Art. 19 of the 1949 Civil Code).

[5]   "According to Yugoslav international private law, the law of that country applies, where the seller had his principal office at the time when he (or the other party) received the offer, if there is no agreement on applicable law between the parties (Bill on International Private Law of 15 February 1982, Sluzbeni list No. 43/1982).

[6]   "France is a member of the Convention on the Law Applicable to the International Sales of Goods, done at The Hague on 15 June 1955. Art. 3(2) of the above Convention states that if parties have not chosen another law, the contract is governed by the internal law of the state, where the seller has his habitual residence at the time at which he received the order....

[7]   "Since the principal office and the habitual residence of the seller at the time in question was Yugoslavia, and since the sales contract was concluded in

Yugoslavia, all applicable rules on international private law refer to Yugoslav substantive law.

[8]   "Paragraphs 1 and 2 of [Art. 133 of] the Yugoslav Law on Obligations of 1978 read as follows (in an unofficial translation):

'(1)   In case of circumstances occurring after the conclusion of the contract, which are of the nature to render the contractual performance of one of the parties difficult or to prevent the scope of the contract to be attained, both to such an extent that it becomes obvious that the contract ceases to correspond to the expectations of the parties and that it would be generally considered unjust to maintain it in force in the unchanged form, the party whose performance has been rendered difficult or which is prevented to attain the scope of the contract by the changed circumstances, can request that the contract be rescinded.

(2)   The rescission of the contract cannot be claimed if the party, which invokes the changed circumstances, should have taken these circumstances into account at the time of the conclusion of the contract or could have escaped or overcome such circumstances.'

The above definition corresponds to that of a 'frustration' according to Anglo-American law or of a *Wegfall der Geschäftsgrundlage* according to German and Austrian law. Yugoslav commentaries (Blagojevic-Krulj; Vizner) speak of a *clausula rebus sic stantibus*, mainly because of the historical development of Yugoslav law. After all, a 'genuine' *clausula rebus sic stantibus* would sustain (in a positive sense) legal relationships only for as long as there are no changes at all, giving no consideration to predictability and applicability. Such a concept cannot be found in the law of obligations, nor the commercial law, of any country (except, as the most, for unlimited obligations, such as rent and lease relationships, but mainly for support obligations). Otherwise, any business transaction would be exposed to uncertainty, or even be rendered impossible altogether, whenever the mutual covenants are not performed at the time at which the contract is concluded.

[10]   "In addition to Art. 133 of the Law of Obligations, Usage No. 56 continues to be in force under Yugoslav law, which lists 'economic events, such as extremely sudden and high increases or decreases of prices' as one of the reasons resulting in a frustration."

[11]   The arbitrator subsequently examined whether the increase on the steel price from US$ 190.00 to US$ 215.00 per metric ton was an extreme sudden and an extremely high price increase (Art. 133(1)) and, if so, whether defendant should have taken such a development into consideration at the time when the contract was concluded (Art. 133(2)).

[12] "The world market prices of products, such as steel, fluctuate, as is known from experience. At the time, when the contract was concluded, steel prices had begun to go up slightly – a trend that continued between the conclusion of the contract and the exercise of the option, and became even more pronounced towards the end of 1988.

[13] "In the opinion of Blagojevic-Krulj, Comments on the Law of Obligations, p. 351, the court must assess the issue, at which amount of damage contract performance is still, or no longer, reasonable, if one of the parties possibly suffers a damage when performing contractual obligations without change of contract. At any rate, such damage must exceed a reasonable entrepreneurial risk. In the present case, the increase in world market prices, i.e., from US$ 190.00 to US$ 215.00, amounts to slightly less than 13.16 %. Having to sell a product at the agreed price, instead of at a price that is higher by 13.16 %, is well within the customary margin.

[14] "Furthermore, the development was also predictable. A reasonable seller had to expect that steel prices might go up further, perhaps even more dramatically than in actual fact. Whether defendant was a reasonable seller when granting the option 'at the same price' for a relatively long period, given these circumstances, is a matter beyond Arbitrator's terms of reference. In any event, even Yugoslav law precludes that a seller entices a buyer to sign a first contract, containing the option 'at the same price', while having the mental reservation that he can invoke Art. 133 of the Law on Obligations if prices should continue to go up...."

[16] The arbitrator examined the nature of the damages:

[17] "Defendant maintains that claimant's buying 80,000 metric tons of steel from the Romanian firm ... cannot be interpreted as a purchase in replacement, since defendant was not informed in advance of claimant's specific purchasing intention, since, moreover, defendant had offered the steel at a lower price, i.e., US$ 215.00 per metric ton, and since, in addition, defendant's steel was of a better quality.

[18] "First of all, the legal interaction between Arts. 262 and 525 of the Yugoslav Law on Obligations must be defined clearly. Art. 262 grants every contracting party the right to claim compensation for the damage accruing to him, which is due to non-performance, deficient or delayed performance of the obligations by the other party. Art. 525, dealing with purchases in replacement, operates as a relief for the aggrieved party, when bringing evidence for the damage suffered. If one were to assume that damages are not due in case of non-compliance with the obligation to give notice according to Art. 525, then no sanctions could be imposed on the non-delivery of goods, for which there is no equivalent, nor on the non-delivery of goods, where it is no longer possible, in due time, to procure an equivalent by purchase in replacement.

19]   "Neither of the parties contested that the world market price for steel (of the grade of the delivery) had gone up to a minimum of US$ 215.00 per metric ton at the time when the option was exercised. If defendant states, however, that, given these premises, claimant would have been best advised at that price to buy defendant's steel, then the only reaction to that can be that claimant would have been foolish to do so. By invoking defendant's obligation to damages, in case of non-delivery at the agreed price, claimant wanted to balance the difference in price. If claimant had bought from defendant, claimant would have been in a much more difficult position, since defendant would have maintained that the price had changed due to novation.

20]   "Claimant maintains that he actually obtained a cheaper deal, in the final analysis. He paid US$ 216.50 per metric ton but saved US$ 2.00 to US$ 2.50 per metric ton in freight costs. Claimant must accept that this argument is also applied against him – with the higher amount of US$ 2.50, in case of doubt. His damage is therefore less than the difference in world market prices. It amounts only to the difference between US$ 190.00 and US$ 214.00, i.e., US$ 24.00 per metric ton. Defendant claims that claimant had to pay a higher import duty on the Romanian goods than he would have to pay on Yugoslav goods, which is irrelevant since claimant did not claim any additional damage, arising from the purchase in replacement. It is also of no relevance whether the steel supplied by [the Romanian firm] was of lower quality than the steel which defendant would have delivered. For the claimant, the steels were of equivalent quality.

[21]   "It is also of no significance whether Art. 525 must be interpreted to mean that the infringing party must be informed in advance of an actual purchase in replacement. The claim for damages, however, arising from the purchase in replacement, is slightly less than the difference in world market prices at the time in question, when taking account of the lower freight costs. According to Art. 262 of the Law on Obligations, claimant cannot claim more than the amount of his actual damage.

[22]   "It should be remarked in passing that the outcome would have been the same, if Arts. 74 to 77 of the Vienna Sales Convention had been considered, which has 19 member states so far and which one will soon be able to call universal law, on account of the large number of ratifications and accessions that are intended in the near future.

[23]   "The above result is by no means surprising....

[24]   "Accordingly, defendant shall reimburse claimant for a damage of 80,000 x US$ 24.00 = US$ 1,920,000."

[25]   The arbitrator then established the amount of interest.

[26]   "According to Art. 277(1) of the Yugoslav Law on Obligations, interest is due to the creditor on the amount of damages, as of the date at which the debtor

begins to default. Defendant did not default by refusing to deliver at the agreed price, nor by claimant's conclusion of a purchase-in-replacement contract, nor on the date at which payment was due to the new supplier. Defendant's default begins on every day at which he should have delivered but did not deliver. According to the sales contract, the 80,000 metric tons of steel under the option should have been delivered in five part shipments of more or less equal quantity between January and May 1988. Defendant was therefore in default for one fifth of the amount on 1 February, 1 March, 1 April, 1 May and 1 June 1988. For the sake of mathematics, interest can be calculated as though defendant defaulted on a total delivery, which would have been due on the date of the third shipment, i.e., on 1 April 1988.

[27] "As mentioned before, the interest rate amounted and amounts to 6.25 to 8.25 %. No prediction can be made, on how the interest rate will develop. Since there is a time delay between issuing the Arbitral Award and voluntary or enforced performance, the Arbitral Award must also fix an interest rate for the future, i.e., until the voluntary or enforced performance of the award. With a view to the mean value of the development so far, an interest rate of 7.25 % is appropriate...."

Sentences arbitrales de la CCI

initialement publiées au *Journal du droit international* (Clunet)

1986 - 1990

I. — Capacité de compromettre pour une entreprise publique syrienne. — Autorisation du Conseil d'Etat Syrien. — Condition préalable (non).

II. — Contrat. — Nullité. — Règles syriennes relatives au boycottage d'Israël. — Ordre public syrien. — Ordre public international.

III. — Règlement C.C.I. — Opinions dissidentes des deux coarbitres.

Sentence rendue en 1984 dans l'affaire 3881.

Aux termes d'un contrat passé le 2 juillet 1978 entre une société suisse et une société ouest-allemande d'une part (demanderesses) et un établissement public — entreprise syrienne, d'autre part (défenderesse), la demanderesse allemande devait fournir à l'entreprise syrienne le know how, l'assistance technique et la supervision de la direction technique et de l'entretien d'une nouvelle usine en Syrie. La demanderesse suisse (agent général des Syriens) garantissait la qualité des produits avec l'assistance et sous la marque de « X » et s'engageait à rétribuer cette dernière en échange des sommes que l'entreprise syrienne s'engageait à lui verser.

L'entreprise allemande s'engageait, selon les modalités du contrat, à mettre ses experts à la disposition de la partie syrienne pendant la durée du contrat. La durée du contrat était de deux ans et son entrée en vigueur devait se situer trois mois après sa signature et son approbation. La durée du contrat pouvait être prolongée.

Le contrat était soumis au droit syrien et les litiges éventuels devaient être portés devant un Tribunal arbitral conformément aux règles et à la procédure d'arbitrage de la Chambre de Commerce Internationale, Paris ; l'arbitrage devrait se dérouler à Damas (Syrie) et la sentence arbitrale serait sans appel *(final)* et obligatoire *(binding)* pour toutes les parties (article 14).

Par télex du 11 septembre 1978, adressé à l'entreprise syrienne, l'entreprise allemande protestait contre le non-paiement de l'équivalent d'environ 30.000 U.S. dollars et déclarait qu'en raison de ce retard, elle était obligée de retarder l'envoi de ses experts.

Par lettre du 20 mai 1979 l'entreprise syrienne informait l'entreprise suisse que leur Conseil d'Administration avait annulé :

a) le contrat d'agence du 11 juin 1977 conclu entre l'entreprise syrienne et la société « G » S.A. de Genève, à laquelle la demanderesse suisse s'était substituée en tant qu'agent des Syriens, parce que « G » ne s'était pas acquittée de ses obligations contractuelles ;

b) le contrat du 2 juillet 1978 en raison de difficultés qui en rendent l'exécution impossible.

Par lettre du 20 mai 1979, l'entreprise syrienne informait la demanderesse allemande que leur Conseil d'Administration avait décidé d'annuler *(to cancel)* le
contrat avec les Allemands et les Suisses parce qu'ils faisaient face à des difficultés
qui en rendaient l'exécution impossible. Plus particulièrement, la demanderesse
suisse ne s'était pas acquittée de ses obligations en tant qu'agent *(sale agents)* de
l'entreprise syrienne.

Les efforts pour trouver une solution amiable n'ayant pas abouti, les entreprises
allemande et suisse ont, le 18 avril 1980, adressé à la C.C.I. une demande d'arbitrage dans laquelle elles désignaient comme arbitre un avocat syrien.

Les demanderesses allèguaient que l'entreprise syrienne n'avait pas exécuté ses
obligations, qu'elle avait résolu le contrat abusivement, et elles réclamaient un
certain montant en dommages et intérêts ainsi que la réparation de l'atteinte à leur
réputation commerciale du fait de l'inexécution du contrat.

L'entreprise syrienne désigna un avocat syrien comme coarbitre. Le président
du Tribunal arbitral, un avocat grec, fut nommé par la Cour d'arbitrage de la
C.C.I. Conformément à la clause compromissoire Damas était confirmé comme
lieu d'arbitrage.

Devant les arbitres la défenderesse soutint, en outre, que la « demanderesse »
avait violé les prescriptions des lois syriennes relatives au boycottage d'Israël, du
fait qu'a été attestée l'existence de relations entre ladite demanderesse et Israël. La
défenderesse insista sur les relations de l'entreprise allemande avec des entreprises
ayant leur siège dans l'Etat d'Israël.

Les questions litigieuses qui ont été définies dans l'acte de mission signé par le
Tribunal arbitral et par les avocats représentant les parties sont, entre autres :

L'autorisation du Conseil d'Etat syrien est-elle une condition préalable de
la capacité de la défenderesse à compromettre, et à participer à la présente
instance arbitrale ?

La défenderesse a-t-elle résilié le contrat passé avec les demanderesses le
2 juillet 1978 ? Si oui, cette résiliation engage-t-elle sa responsabilité envers
les demanderesses ?

Dans la sentence rendue par le président du Tribunal uniquement, le Tribunal
arbitral statua :

(Sur la capacité de l'entreprise syrienne de participer à l'arbitrage).

« *Conformément à l'article 8, alinéa 3 du règlement de la Cour d'arbitrage de la
C.C.I., il appartient à l'arbitre de prendre toute décision sur sa propre compétence.
La même règle existe dans la loi syrienne (Cass. 8 fév. 1973,* M. *1973, p. 15,
n° 13 — aussi J. El-Hakim, « Arbitration in Syria » dans* Yearbook Commercial
Arbitration, *Vol. VII, p. 45).*

« *La compétence des arbitres découle de la convention d'arbitrage. Si une des
parties à la convention n'avait pas la capacité de compromettre, il n'existe pas de
convention d'arbitrage valable.*

« *L'article 44 du Code du Conseil d'Etat Syrien (loi 55 du 21 février 1959) dispose
que les Ministères et les services publics doivent demander et obtenir l'autorisation
du Conseil d'Etat avant de conclure ou d'accepter un contrat ou une clause arbitrale.*

« *Mais la défenderesse n'est pas un Ministère ou un service public, elle est un établissement public, régi par le décret législatif Syrien n° 18 du 15 février 1974, comportant la loi sur les établissements, les sociétés publiques et les entreprises de caractère économique. Dans ses relations avec les tiers, la défenderesse est réputée commerçant et elle exerce toutes les activités en découlant (article 2-B du décret législatif) ; les marchés, conclus et les opérations effectuées par elle sont dispensés de l'approbation du Conseil d'Etat (article 35 du décret législatif) ; les lois et les dispositions contraires au décret législatif n° 18 de 1974 sont abrogées en vertu de l'article 41 dudit décret législatif.*

« *La circulaire n° 49/B-2333/15 du 1-4-1982 de M. le Président du Conseil des Ministres :*

a) est postérieure à la conclusion (2-7-1978) et à la ratification (3-8-78) du contrat litigieux et,

b) surtout, en droit syrien comme ailleurs, une circulaire ne peut pas déroger aux dispositions d'un décret législatif.

En conséquence, la défenderesse ou les demanderesses n'ont pas besoin de demander au Conseil d'Etat Syrien de ratifier la clause compromissoire qui est valable en droit syrien et engage les parties. Les arbitres, nommés conformément au règlement de la Cour d'arbitrage de la C.C.I. auquel renvoie la clause compromissoire, sont compétents pour instruire la cause et pour statuer sur le litige.

(Sur le boycottage d'Israël).

« *La défenderesse a soulevé une question d'ordre public syrien. Elle a notamment prétendu, que la "demanderesse" aurait violé les prescriptions des lois syriennes relatives au boycottage d'Israël, du fait qu'il aurait été attesté l'existence de relations entre ladite demanderesse et Israël. Les demanderesses, qui sont deux et non une, ont démenti catégoriquement cette assertion.*

« *Dans un mémoire, la défenderesse déclare que l'agent suisse a des relations d'affaires avec Israël et y a même un agent en la personne de la société israélienne "Y".*

« *Elle a, en même temps, produit la traduction de la lettre n° 1718 du 5-6-1983 de l'office de boycottage d'Israël du Ministère de la défense de la République Arabe Syrienne.*

« *Le Tribunal arbitral considère :*

1) Aux termes de l'article 1 de la loi syrienne n° 286 de 1956, il est prohibé d'avoir des relations d'affaires avec les sociétés ou établissements nationaux ou étrangers, ayant des intérêts, succursales ou agences générales en Israël.

« *Si la défenderesse avait contracté des relations d'affaires (contrat du 2 juillet 1978) avec une société allemande ayant des intérêts, succursales ou agences générales en Israël, en violation de la loi syrienne n° 286 de 1956, c'est elle (la défenderesse) qui devrait en supporter les conséquences, tant sur le plan de sa responsabilité contractuelle que sur le plan de ses responsabilités envers l'Etat.*

« *Par ailleurs, l'interdiction de traiter avec une entreprise quelconque ne peut exister qu'une fois que cette entreprise a été placée sur la liste noire et que cette décision ait été communiquée au Ministère de l'économie et du commerce extérieur avant la conclusion du contrat "litigieux" (qui remonte à plusieurs années). Or, il est impensable que les autorités Syriennes aient pu ratifier le contrat litigieux (télex de "Z" du 15-7-1978 et lettre du 16-7-1978) en l'existence d'une telle mesure.*

2) D'après la lettre nº 1718/5-6-1983 du Ministère Syrien de la Défense nationale, la société "Z A.G." avait nommé, non une succursale ou une agence générale, mais un agent commissionnaire, c'est-à-dire une agence commune, qui, en plus, n'a pu rien vendre des produits de la société allemande "Z" A.G. Donc, cette dernière n'a pas eu d'intérêts en Israël.

3) Ainsi qu'il résulte de la lettre précitée du Ministère Syrien de la Défense nationale, la société (demanderesse) est une société tout à fait différente de la société "Z A.G.".

D'après cette lettre, "Z A.G." :

a) est une société anonyme (Aktien Gesellschaft) ;

b) elle a été fondée en 1883 ;

c) elle est une industrie de textiles.

« *Elle ne pouvait donc pas provenir de la société (demanderesse) depuis une date bien récente.*

« *En plus, la demanderesse est une société à responsabilité limitée GmbH : Gesellschaft mit beschränkter Haftung) avec un capital très inférieur à celui d'une société anonyme ; son activité n'est pas celle d'industriel, mais de commerçant et consultant et, ce qui est plus important, elle continue à exister bien après le 5 juin 1983, date de lettre du Ministère de la Défense nationale.*

« *Les arbitres estiment donc qu'une erreur, justifiée par la ressemblance des initiales des deux entreprises, a conduit le Ministère de la Défense nationale à supposer que la société à responsabilité limitée (demanderesse) est devenue avant le 5 juin la société anonyme industrielle "Z A.G." qui, d'ailleurs, d'après les renseignements contenus dans cette même lettre, existait comme société anonyme depuis 1883.*

« *En conséquence, l'exception de nullité du contrat du 2 juillet 1978, exception fondée sur la prétendue violation par la demanderesse de la loi syrienne 286 de 1956 doit être rejetée.* »

La sentence prononcée par le président du Tribunal fut signée par les trois arbitres, la signature des deux coarbitres étant suivie par la mention « dissident ». Dans deux opinions dissidentes séparées, chacun des coarbitres exprimait pourquoi il n'avait pas pu suivre la décision du président en ce qui concerne les montants alloués aux demanderesses, l'un d'eux trouvant qu'ils excédaient le dommage réel, l'autre que les montants étaient inférieurs.

OBSERVATIONS. — La Cour d'arbitrage de la C.C.I. reçoit chaque année — grosso modo — 300 requêtes d'arbitrage. Les statistiques traditionnelles de la C.C.I. qui sont publiées sur le nombre d'affaires d'arbitrage démontrent certaines tendances en ce qui concerne la participation à l'arbitrage des parties du vieux continent, des pays industrialisés, en voie d'industrialisation ou en voie de développement.

Moins connue dans ses détails est la répartition des parties entre parties privées d'une part et Etats ou entreprises publiques d'autre part. L'inventaire des nouvelles requêtes d'arbitrage introduites par ou contre un Etat ou une entreprise publique et soumises dans les années 1983, 1984 et dans les 6 premiers mois de l'année 1985 révèlent des chiffres intéressants.

Compte tenu de l'aspect confidentiel de l'arbitrage C.C.I., il n'est pas possible de fournir d'une façon détaillée le nombre d'affaires pour chaque pays, mais seulement un chiffre global par continent. Aussi faudrait-il traiter ces chiffres avec prudence, car dans beaucoup de cas il est difficile de dire avec certitude s'il s'agit d'une entreprise étatique, para-étatique ou privée. Avec ces réserves, voici les données en question :

CONTINENT	1983	1984	1985 (6 mois)
Afrique du Nord	18	16	9
Afrique	4	6	5
Europe de l'Est	31	27	11
Europe de l'Ouest	20	22	12
Amérique du Nord	2	1	0
Amérique du Sud	0	0	1
Moyen-Orient	19	11	1
Extrême-Orient	2	1	3
Total	96	84	42

Une première observation à partir de ces statistiques est le nombre important de parties étatiques et para-étatiques, il atteint presque un sixième de la totalité des parties à l'arbitrage C.C.I. pendant cette période. En d'autres termes, l'on trouve une partie étatique dans presque un tiers des affaires.

Nonobstant cette participation considérable des Etats et des entreprises publiques à l'arbitrage C.C.I., c'est plutôt rarement qu'une telle partie soulève l'exception d'incompétence des arbitres sur le fondement de la qualité étatique ou publique de la partie même.

I. — Grâce à l'existence du décret législatif syrien dans l'espèce , la vraie qualité de la défenderesse a pu être établie en application des normes syriennes, la loi syrienne étant la loi applicable selon le contrat.

Les arbitres n'ont pas été obligés d'examiner la question épineuse, vivement débattue dans la doctrine, de savoir si la capacité de compromettre doit être décidée selon la nature de l'acte entrepris par la partie — c'est-à-dire *jure imperii* ou *jure gestionis* — ou bien en application de la doctrine selon laquelle toute partie, et surtout un Etat souverain, est souveraine pour s'engager valablement par des accords à soumettre les futurs différends à l'arbitrage (voir : Gillis Wetter dans *Journal of International Arbitration* 1985, page 7. Dans son article M. Wetter discute quatre affaires C.C.I., notamment 1803, 2321, 3493, 3879 dans lesquelles l'exception de souveraineté avaient été évoquée dans des formes variées).

II. — Les échanges économiques entre le monde arabe et les Etats occidentaux sont influencés par la mise à l'index des entreprises qui ont des relations avec l'Etat d'Israël. Proposées par un organisme institué en 1951, le Bureau Central pour le boycottage d'Israël, des mesures ont été introduites dans la législation interne des pays membres de la Ligue Arabe (Jean-Louis Bismuth, *Le boycottage dans les échanges économiques internationaux au regard du droit*, Economica, Paris, 1980, page 11, note 30). La loi syrienne est citée dans l'espèce.

Même si le boycottage arabe d'Israël a été qualifié de tigre de papier (Lionel Stoléru dans *le Monde*, 13 mai 1986), les pratiques de mise à l'index arabe « sont incompatibles avec l'esprit du droit et plus particulièrement avec deux principes juridiques fondamentaux animant tant le droit interne (français) que l'ordre juridique communautaire : le principe de liberté du commerce et celui de non discrimination » (note établie en 1984 par le Mouvement de la Liberté du commerce). Les textes qui font autorité en la matière sont contenus dans le document « Principes généraux pour le boycott d'Israël, juin 1972 », émis par le secrétariat général de la Ligue des pays Arabes, Bureau Central du boycott d'Israël, à Damas. Le boycott frappe essentiellement les activités d'implantation et de transfert de technologie, mais non la simple exportation de marchandises (matières premières, biens de consommation ou d'équipement).

Deux pays européens, les Pays-Bas et la France (loi 77-574), ont légiféré pour contrecarrer la pratique des pays de la Ligue Arabe. Au sein de la C.E.E. une législation anti-discriminatoire a été proposée. Une telle législation « est considérée, à juste titre, comme "force majeure" par la presque totalité des pays arabes. Ceci protège les opérateurs des pressions extérieures et permet la non-application du boycott contre les entreprises, personnes ou institutions dans des pays tiers, étrangers au conflit israélo-arabe ayant cette législation » (note présentée par M. Zvi Tenney, Directeur du département C.E.E. au Ministère des affaires étrangères à la commission de coopération C.E.E. - Israël du 7 février 1984).

C'est grâce à la constatation de l'identité des sociétés en cause que l'exception de nullité du contrat, sur le fondement d'une prétendue violation des prescriptions syriennes relatives au boycottage d'Israël, a pu être dissipée. Les arbitres n'ont pas été obligés de considérer la conformité d'une telle législation nationale avec un ordre public étranger ou international.

L'arbitre international doit en premier lieu appliquer la loi convenue par les parties comme étant la loi applicable au fond du litige. Selon le règlement C.C.I., article 13,5, l'arbitre est également tenu de prendre en considération les stipulations du contrat et les usages du commerce. Pourtant l'arbitre doit en plus tout faire pour assurer que la sentence arbitrale sera exécutoire, voir article 26 du Règlement. Ces dispositions peuvent mener à une situation de conflit dans la mesure où l'application stricte du droit applicable risquerait de rendre la sentence inexécutoire dans un pays autre que celui dont la loi est applicable ou du pays où se déroule l'arbitrage.

Il est concevable qu'un certain nombre de pays s'opposeraient à l'exécution d'une sentence fondée sur des règles de boycottage d'Israël en invoquant l'article v 2 B) de la convention de New York selon lequel la reconnaissance ou l'exécution de la sentence serait contraire à l'ordre public de ce pays. Dans quelle mesure les arbitres doivent-ils anticiper une telle difficulté et se laisser guider au stade de la rédaction de la sentence ?

Le dilemme de l'arbitre pourrait être plus difficile si la loi syrienne non seulement était la *lex contractus* choisie par les parties, mais si le contrat contenait une clause de boycottage, par laquelle l'entreprise s'engageait à ne pas avoir des relations défendues avec Israël ou d'autres entreprises figurant sur la liste. Dans ce dernier cas le boycott serait une obligation contractuelle, donc couvert par la volonté des parties et aussi conforme à la loi par elles choisie. On se demande si dans ce cas un arbitre peut, au nom d'une notion d'ordre public « véritablement » international, se refuser à donner effet à l'accord des parties exprimé par la clause de boycott. Ceci d'autant plus que le Règlement d'arbitrage de la C.C.I. dispose que l'arbitre doit tenir compte « dans tous les cas » des stipulations du contrat (règlement C.C.I., article 13-5).

Rappelons enfin l'affaire Gotaverken *(Yearbook International Arbitration,* VI, page 137) dans laquelle la loi libyenne sur le boycott avait été invoquée par une partie pour justifier la non-réception des navires commandés. Dans cette affaire-là les arbitres ont entrepris la recherche du droit applicable et sont parvenus à une loi autre que la loi libyenne (droit suédois) et ils ont conclu que la loi libyenne de boycott n'était pas applicable. Les arbitres n'ont pas eu à discuter le point de savoir si la loi sur le boycott était une loi de police qui s'imposerait ou si son application poserait des problèmes concernant l'ordre public international.

III. — La sentence est un des rares exemples dans l'arbitrage C.C.I. de sentence rendue par le président du Tribunal arbitral seul. Dans l'espèce les trois arbitres ont tous signé la sentence. Avant de communiquer aux parties les opinions dissidentes, la Cour examine — en l'absence d'un accord des parties dans l'acte de mission ou ailleurs, ou d'un accord des arbitres sur ce point — la question de savoir si la notification est conforme à la loi du lieu de l'arbitrage et, éventuellement, à celle du lieu d'exécution de la sentence quand il peut être déterminé, et si elle violerait l'ordre public de ce pays, à savoir le principe du secret du délibéré des arbitres. La communication d'opinions dissidentes ne pose aucun problème dans les pays de *Common Law* et beaucoup d'autres pays. Un groupe de travail de la Cour étudie actuellement ce problème.

S. J.

I. — **Clause compromissoire.** — Validité. — Règlement d'arbitrage de la C.C.I. — Application des usages du commerce international.

II. — **Clause compromissoire.** — Autonomie juridique. — Portée. — Nécessité d'un accord spécial à la clause compromissoire (non).

III. — **Arbitrage international.** — Détermination du droit international privé applicable (non).

IV. — **Capacité de compromettre.** — Application de la loi personnelle des parties.

V. — **Ordre public international.** — Etat. — Aptitude à compromettre. — Bonne foi. — Devoir d'information.

VI. — **Usages du commerce international.** — Incompétence du président d'une société. — Inopposabilité aux tiers. — Contrainte.

Sentence rendue dans l'affaire n° 4381 en 1986.

Une société iranienne (défendeur) et une société française (demandeur) s'étaient associées au sein d'une société en participation dont l'objet était d'assurer en Iran, conjointement et solidairement, un projet de construction déterminé. Une fois réalisé ce projet, les parties se virent confier l'exécution d'un nouveau projet. Elles commencèrent les travaux sans avoir pu se mettre d'accord sur le texte d'un nouvel accord d'association. Cependant, certaines divergences étant intervenues entre les parties, le Président du Conseil d'Administration et Directeur Général du défendeur, par lettre adressée au Ministère de l'énergie, son ministère de tutelle, indiqua que des dispositions de l'accord de société en participation créée pour le premier projet régissaient les relations des parties pour la réalisation du nouveau projet. Le demandeur prit acte par lettre de cet accord sous réserve d'amendements mineurs. Compte tenu des divergences intervenues entre les parties, la société française introduisit en 1982 une action en arbitrage devant la Cour d'arbitrage de la C.C.I. sur la base de la clause d'arbitrage contenue dans l'accord de société en participation. La société iranienne déclina la compétence de la Cour d'abitrage en invoquant essentiellement trois moyens :

a) La lettre de son Président et Directeur Général se référant à l'accord de société en participation serait dépourvue de valeur contractuelle en raison de l'incompétence de ce dernier et, ayant, entre autres, été rédigée sous la contrainte ;

b) Compte tenu de l'autonomie juridique de la clause d'arbitrage, la référence globale que cette lettre faisait à l'accord de société en participation ne pouvait valoir acceptation de la clause d'arbitrage que celui-ci contenait ;

c) En tant qu'entreprise d'Etat, elle n'avait pu valablement conclure une convention d'arbitrage sans autorisation des instances compétentes de l'Etat.

La clause d'arbitrage était libellée comme suit :

« Tout litige qui pourrait surgir entre les parties au sujet de l'application et de l'interprétation du présent accord et qui ne pourrait faire l'objet d'un règlement amiable entre les parties, sera soumis à l'arbitrage. La commission d'arbitrage comprendra trois arbitres, l'un choisi par (...), l'autre choisi par (...) et le tiers arbitre désigné sur requête du Président du Tribunal civil de Téhéran par l'un des comités nationaux de la Chambre de Commerce Internationale de Suisse, Suède ou Danemark et choisi parmi leurs membres.

La commission d'arbitrage réglera le litige en fonction des dispositions du présent accord et des conditions du contrat avec le maître de l'ouvrage et conformément aux règles d'arbitrage de la Chambre de Commerce Internationale pour autant que ces règles ne sont pas contraires aux règles d'arbitrage iraniennes ou françaises. Sa décision sera finale et liera les parties.

Si le gérant désire demander l'arbitrage conformément à la clause d'arbitrage du contrat 384-3 avec le maître de l'ouvrage, il devra en informer préalablement (...) au cours d'une réunion du comité de direction provoquée à cet effet ».

Chacune des parties désigna un arbitre. Par décision du 14 mars 1983, le Président du Tribunal commun de Téhéran, sollicité par la C.C.I. en vertu de la procédure particulière prévue par la clause d'arbitrage, choisit le comité suédois de la C.C.I. comme autorité de désignation du Président du Tribunal arbitral, de façon à ce que l'arbitrage puisse avoir lieu. Le Tribunal iranien évoqua la difficulté relative à l'opposabilité de la clause d'arbitrage à une entreprise d'Etat iranienne, mais estima que les principes de la loi constitutionnelle iranienne étaient suffisamment clairs pour que l'arbitrage tranche la question.

Le Tribunal arbitral, ainsi composé et siégeant à Stockholm rechercha tout d'abord les sources du droit applicable à la validité de la clause d'arbitrage.

« *Considérant que la question de l'incompétence et, partant, celle de l'irrecevabilité soulevées par le Défendeur posent au Tribunal la question de la validité de la Convention d'arbitrage ; que ce sont les sources de droit propres à déterminer la validité de la Convention d'arbitrage et la compétence du Tribunal d'arbitrage qu'il convient de définir.*

Considérant qu'il convient de définir ces sources de droit, compte tenu d'abord des indications à cet égard que pourrait contenir la convention d'arbitrage en question, sauf en ce qui concerne la capacité de chacune des parties à compromettre qui est soumise à la loi personnelle de la partie.

Considérant qu'aux termes de la Convention d'arbitrage de l'accord d'association du... un litige entre les parties serait réglé par une commission d'arbitrage en fonction des dispositions de cet accord et des conditions du contrat avec le maître de l'ouvrage et conformément aux règles d'arbitrage de la Chambre de Commerce Internationale, pour autant que ces règles ne soient pas contraires aux règles d'arbitrage iraniennes ou françaises.

Considérant qu'il appartient aux parties de préciser si elles souhaitent que le droit qu'elles choisissent soit appliqué à la fois au contrat, à la convention d'arbitrage et, éventuellement, à la procédure arbitrale, ce qui découle de plusieurs sentences arbitrales — à titre d'exemple il convient de se référer ici aux sentences rendues en 1983, dans l'affaire n° 3880 (cf. Clunet, 1983, p. 897) et en 1982, dans l'affaire n° 4131 (cf. Clunet 1983, p. 889) — et que de telles précisions font défaut dans la Convention d'arbitrage qui est ici mise en cause.

Considérant par conséquent que les sources de droit figurant dans la Convention d'arbitrage semblent être de nature à pouvoir s'appliquer tant au fond d'un éventuel litige qu'à la procédure à appliquer lors d'une instance arbitrale mais que ladite convention d'arbitrage ne renferme aucune précision quant aux sources de droit applicables à la validité de la Convention d'arbitrage.

Considérant que, vu les constatations ci-dessus, il incombe au Tribunal d'arbitrage de choisir les sources de droit applicables pour la détermination de la validité de la Convention d'arbitrage, sans qu'il lui soit nécessaire d'établir le droit international privé applicable (cf. la sentence C.C.I. rendue en 1983 dans l'affaire n° 3880 : Clunet 1983, p. 897) à condition que ce choix ne soit pas contraire aux règles d'arbitrage iraniennes ou françaises.

Considérant que les parties se sont référées dans la présente affaire au règlement de la C.C.I. et qu'il est constant que ledit règlement, vu surtout son article 8, qui consacre notamment la complète autonomie de la clause compromissoire, confère à l'arbitre le pouvoir de prendre toute décision sur sa propre compétence, après que la Cour ait décidé que l'arbitrage aura lieu, sans lui prescrire d'appliquer pour ce faire une loi étatique quelconque (voyez alinéas 3 et 4 de l'article 8 ainsi que alinéas 3 et 5 de l'article 13 du règlement de la C.C.I.).

Considérant donc que le Tribunal prendra position quant à la validité de la clause compromissoire en question sur la base de la commune volonté des parties à la présente procédure, telle qu'elle résulte des circonstances qui ont entouré l'établissement, l'exécution et, finalement, la cessation des relations contractuelles entre les parties et en tenant compte également des usages conformes aux besoins du commerce international, dans la mesure où les sources de droit, ainsi précisées n'amèneraient pas à un résultat allant à l'encontre des règles d'arbitrage françaises ou iraniennes. »

Le Tribunal arbitral, statuant à la majorité, estima ensuite, dans les termes ci-après, que la clause d'arbitrage de l'accord de société en participation, s'appliquait aux relations nouées par les parties en ce qui concerne le nouveau projet :

« *Considérant qu'il convient de traiter d'abord la question si la convention d'arbitrage à l'article 15 de l'accord d'association en date du... a été adoptée par les parties pour s'appliquer aux différents entre elles relatifs (au nouveau projet) et, dans l'affirmative, si cette convention serait applicable au présent litige entre les parties.*

Considérant qu'à cet égard il convient d'examiner en premier lieu la validité et la valeur contractuelle tant de la lettre du... que de la convention d'arbitrage en question dans l'optique de la correspondance et d'autres relations, entre les parties ainsi que le comportement des parties antérieurement aussi bien que postérieurement à la lettre du..., le tout étant ensuite à revoir compte tenu des dispositions de l'article 139 de la constitution de la République Islamique d'Iran, à condition que cet article soit applicable dans la situation en cause...

... Considérant que, même s'il ressort des pièces versées au dossier par les parties que celles-ci avaient bien l'intention d'aligner leur coopération concernant (le nouveau projet) sur l'accord de (société en participation), il ne ressort pas des pièces versées au dossier que les parties se sont mises d'accord sur une convention d'arbitrage avant la lettre concernant leur coopération relative au (nouveau projet) (cf. à titre d'exemple, la sentence C.C.I. en 1983 dans l'affaire n° 4392, Clunet 1983, p. 907).

Considérant, par contre, qu'il découle de la lettre en date du... du défendeur à l'intention du Ministre de l'énergie que le défendeur considérait l'accord de (société en participation) comme applicable aux relations contractuelles entre les parties en ce qui concerne le (nouveau projet), qu'il est constant qu'une copie de cette lettre a été transmise au demandeur par les soins du défendeur, que les prétentions du défendeur selon lesquelles la lettre en date du... aurait été rédigée sous la contrainte, n'ont pas été prouvées et ne seraient d'ailleurs pas de nature à priver ladite lettre de sa valeur contractuelle, qu'il serait contraire au principe de la bonne foi dans les relations contractuelles internationales de priver la lettre de sa valeur contractuelle en raison d'une défaillance dans la compétence du directeur général, Président du Conseil d'Administration (du défendeur) étant donné que le défendeur n'a pas prouvé que (le demandeur) avait connaissance de ladite incompétence et que, selon les sources de droit invoquées ci-dessus, une défaillance de cette nature n'est de toute façon pas opposable aux tiers, que pleine valeur contractuelle doit par conséquent être accordée à cette lettre, dont la teneur quant à l'application de l'accord de (société en participation) a aussitôt été acceptée par le demandeur, par sa lettre..., ayant également pleine valeur contractuelle...

Considérant que, compte tenu des termes des lettres en date du... mentionnées ci-dessus, le Tribunal trouve mal fondé le moyen du défendeur, dit de l'autonomie de la convention d'arbitrage, prétendant que les manifestations de volonté exprimées dans les lettres des... ne viseraient pas de façon suffisamment claire et sans équivoque la convention d'arbitrage faisant partie de l'accord de (société en participation) (cf. sentence C.C.I., en 1982, dans l'affaire n° 4131, Clunet 1983, p. 899, et sentence C.C.I. en 1975, n° 1434, Clunet 1976, p. 978, et concernant le principe de l'autonomie J. Robert, L'arbitrage droit interne, droit international privé 282-286).

Considérant que les différends qui seraient dorénavant aux dires du défendeur intervenus entre les parties concernant l'interprétation de cet accord quant à la façon dont devait s'appliquer l'article XVI de (l'accord de société en participation) ne sont pas de nature à nuire à l'accord des volontés relatif à la convention d'arbitrage, vu le principe dit de l'autonomie de ladite convention, dont il s'ensuit que la question de la validité de celle-ci est à considérer indépendamment de celle de la validité de la convention au fond, et que des circonstances pouvant entacher la validité de la convention au fond n'entraînent donc pas — sans indication spécifique dans ce sens — l'invalidité de la convention d'arbitrage.

Considérant que, quant à la question de savoir s'il y a eu accord des volontés pour appliquer la convention d'arbitrage du... tant à des conflits futurs qu'aux différends déjà surgis entre les parties, il convient d'abord de constater qu'une interprétation dans ce sens du comportement et des expressions de volonté des parties paraît la plus vraisemblable, vu que les négociations entre les parties à l'époque concernaient presque exclusivement des différends déjà existants et compte tenu de la rédaction de la lettre du..., faisant allusion à une application de fait déjà intervenue concernant le nouveau projet) de l'accord de (société en participation), application qui fut ainsi confirmée avec effet rétroactif, et qu'il n'y a pas de raison de penser que la lettre du... doive s'interpréter de façon différente quant au champ d'application qu'elle accordait à la convention d'arbitrage, d'autant plus que les maints projets de conventions d'arbitrage échangés par les parties permettent de conclure qu'il y avait accord entre elles pour soumettre leurs différends à l'arbitrage et qu'il ne s'agissait à l'époque ici évoquée que d'en trouver une formule qui conviendrait aux deux parties, ce qu'elles ont réalisé par l'échange des lettres des...

Considérant que la convention d'arbitrage de l'accord (de société en participation) doit donc, en ce qui concerne l'accord actuellement en vue, s'interpréter en conjonction avec la teneur de l'échange des lettres entre les parties qui vient d'être évoquée, et qu'il faut en conclure qu'il y avait accord des volontés entre les parties pour appliquer la convention d'arbitrage ainsi conclue tant aux conflits futurs qu'aux différends déjà survenus entre elles...

Considérant que, même s'il découle des pièces versées au dossier que (le défendeur) en sa qualité d'entreprise d'Etat, vu l'article 139 de la Constitution de la République Islamique d'Iran, n'a pas pu conclure de convention d'arbitrage sans y être autorisé par les autorités compétentes et qu'il est constant qu'une telle autorisation n'a pas été accordée, il faut néanmoins tenir compte du fait que le vice dont était par conséquent entachée la convention d'arbitrage n'avait pas été porté à la connaissance (du demandeur) lors de sa conclusion.

Considérant qu'il a été reconnu dans la jurisprudence arbitrale que l'ordre public international s'opposerait avec force à ce qu'un organe de l'Etat, traitant avec des personnes étrangères au pays, puisse passer ouvertement, le sachant ou le voulant, une convention d'arbitrage qui met en confiance le cocontractant et puisse ensuite, que ce soit dans la procédure arbitrale ou dans la procédure d'exécution, se prévaloir de la nullité de sa propre parole, et que (le défendeur) dans sa capacité de société d'Etat, a manifestement manqué à cette obligation de dévoiler les exigences du droit iranien relatives à la conclusion des contrats par des personnes publiques.

Considérant que c'est donc de bonne foi que (le demandeur) à donné son accord à la clause d'arbitrage, et qu'il faut par conséquent considérer l'inaptitude (du défendeur) à compromettre comme inopérante, en raison de sa non conformité avec l'ordre public international, dont la mise en jeu ne pourrait être exclue par l'application du droit iranien (cf. affaires C.C.I., n° 1526 de 1968 et 2521 de 1975 dans Clunet 1974, p. 915 et 1976, p. 997 et s. et l'affaire C.C.I., n° 1939 de 1971 dans P. Leboulanger, « Les contrats entre Etats et entreprises étrangères, 1985, ch. 460, affaire C.C.I., n° 3327 de 1981, Clunet 1982, p. 971, Leboulanger op. cit., ch. 4593-461 ; Derains, « Le statut des usages du commerce international devant les juridictions étrangères » : Rev. Arbitrage 1973, p. 122 et suiv., Bockstiegel Arbitration and state enterprises, 1984, p. 25, P. Lalive, « L'influence des clauses arbitrales » : actes du colloque de Louvain, Les contrats entre Etats et personnes privées étrangères, p. 4 ; Robert, L'arbitrage dans le commerce international, p. 250-253, 362-370, Oppetit, note concernant la sentence Framatome, Clunet 1984, p. 38-46 ; Fouchard, concernant la sentence Framatome dans Rev. Arbitrage 1984, p. 383 et s., et, dans le même sens, mais s'appuyant sur un raisonnement fondé sur la primauté de la liberté contractuelle ; A. Kassis, Théorie générale des usages du commerce, 1984, ch. 779-781). »

OBSERVATIONS. — I. — La sentence ici rapportée témoigne de ce que la publica tion de cette chronique, depuis 1974, a apporté en cohésion à la jurisprudence des arbitres du commerce international . En effet, la motivation des arbitres dans cette affaires s'appuie essentiellement sur des sentences arbitrales dont des extraits on déjà été publiés. Mais c'est peut-être en ce qui concerne la détermination des sources de droit applicable à la clause d'arbitrage que l'on perçoit le mieux le souc des arbitres de se rattacher à un précédent arbitral. Ce précédent est la sentence rendue sous l'égide de la Chambre de Commerce Internationale dans l'affaire n° 4131, en 1982 (*cf. Clunet* 1983, p. 899), à laquelle référence est faite, parm d'autres dont l'influence sur les auteurs de la sentence ici rapportée est cependant bien moindre. Non seulement le raisonnement, mais encore la terminologie de deux décisions sont quasiment identiques. Tout d'abord la référence à la notion de sources de droit lorsqu'il s'agit simplement de déterminer le droit applicable à la clause d'arbitrage est trop caractéristique de la sentence de 1982 pour n'être qu'une coïncidence.

Ensuite, la formule de la sentence ici rapportée selon laquelle « *le Tribuna* *prendra position quant à la validité de la clause compromissoire en question sur la* *base de la commune volonté des parties à la présente procédure, telle qu'elle résulte* *des circonstances qui ont entouré l'établissement, l'exécution et, finalement, la cessa-* *tion des relations contractuelles entre les parties et en tenant compte également des* *usages conformes aux besoins du commerce international* » fait plus qu'évoquer celle de la sentence de 1982... « *Le Tribunal arbitral déterminera la portée et les* *effets des clauses compromissoires dont il s'agit, et en déduira sa décision relative à* *l'exception d'incompétence, en se fondant sur la commune volonté à la présente* *procédure, telle qu'elle résulte des circonstances qui ont entouré la conclusion et* *caractérisé l'exécution puis la résiliation des contrats où elles figurent, et en tenant* *également compte, à l'exemple notamment de la jurisprudence française relative à* *l'arbitrage international, des usages conformes aux besoins du commerce internatio-* *nal...* ». La seule différence importante entre les deux rédactions est l'absence de référence à l'exemple de la jurisprudence française dans la sentence ici rapportée, référence qui n'aurait eu aucune raison d'être dans une décision rendue à Stokcholm, mais qui, dans la sentence de 1982 exprimait sans doute un sentiment de prudence des arbitres qui, statuant à Paris, ne pouvaient exclure l'éventualité d'un recours contre leur sentence devant la Cour d'appel de Paris. Prudence justifiée d'ailleurs puisqu'effectivement, la Cour d'appel de Paris rejeta une action en annulation de la sentence le 21 octobre 1983 (*cf.* Paris, 21 oct. 1983 : *Rev. Arbitrage* 1984, 98, note A. Chapelle).

Mais c'est probablement le fait que la sentence ici rapportée, comme celle de 1982, se fonde sur les dispositions du règlement d'arbitrage de la C.C.I. pour décider que la validité de la clause d'arbitrage doit être appréciée en fonction de la volonté des parties et des usages conformes aux besoins du commerce internatio- nal qui retient l'attention. La répétition de cette motivation révèle qu'une règle de jurisprudence arbitrale est peut être en train de s'établir. Le raisonnement suivi dans les deux sentences et exprimé sous des formes voisines peut être résumé ainsi : compte tenu de l'autonomie de la clause compromissoire, celle-ci peut être régie par des sources de droit qui lui sont propres, cette autonomie est confirmée par le règlement d'arbitrage de la C.C.I., dans son article 8 (4) ; l'article 8 (3) du même texte donne à l'arbitre le pouvoir de « prendre toute décision sur sa propre compé- tence », sans lui prescrire d'appliquer pour ce faire une loi étatique quelconque ; par conséquent, sauf stipulation contraire, la référence au règlement d'arbitrage de la C.C.I. donne aux arbitres le pouvoir d'apprécier la validité et la portée de la clause d'arbitrage indépendamment du droit régissant le contrat et sans recours à un droit étatique. C'est donc une présomption que posent les arbitres dans ces deux affaires : dans l'arbitrage de la C.C.I., la validité, la portée et les effets de la clause d'arbitrage sont régis par la volonté des parties et les usages du commerce international, sauf stipulation contraire des parties.

On ne peut que se féliciter de l'émergence d'une telle présomption et souhaiter qu'elle se renforce. En effet, elle a le mérite d'accentuer le détachement de l'arbitrage international des dispositions nationales sur l'arbitrage longtemps et encore trop souvent élaborées en fonction de préoccupations exclusivement internes. Son développement risque cependant de se heurter au texte de l'article V (1) (a) de la Convention de New York de 1958 qui soumet la validité de la convention d'arbitrage à « la loi à laquelle les parties l'ont subordonnée ou à défaut d'une indication à cet égard » à « la loi du pays où la sentence a été rendue ». Les arbitres sont ainsi tenus de respecter les exigences de l'ordre public du pays où ils siègent s'ils veulent que leur sentence soit susceptible d'être exécutée sur la base de la Convention de New York chaque fois que les parties n'ont pas indiqué le droit applicable à la clause compromissoire et il ne semble pas que la Convention de New York se contente d'un choix implicite (cf. A. J. Van Den Berg, The New York Arbitration Convention of 1958, p. 293).

Cette solution de la convention de New York est d'ailleurs tout à fait criticable chaque fois que le lieu de l'arbitrage n'a pas été choisi par les parties elles-mêmes dans la clause compromissoire. Ce n'est en effet que dans cette dernière hypothèse que le lieu de l'arbitrage peut exprimer une volonté localisatrice des parties (cf. les sentences rendues dans l'affaire n° 4504, infra p. 1118). Par contre, quand le lieu de l'arbitrage est fixé par une institution d'arbitrage, par exemple la Cour d'arbitrage de la C.C.I. sur la base de l'article 12 de son règlement, ou, dans le cas de certains arbitrages ad hoc, par les arbitres eux-mêmes, le lieu de l'arbitrage ne peut être considéré comme un indice de la volonté des parties de localiser la clause d'arbitrage dans un système juridique plutôt qu'un autre.

Quoi qu'il en soit, cette disposition regrettable de la Convention de New York doit inciter les parties, et, en leur absence, les institutions d'arbitrage ou les arbitres, à la plus grande prudence lors du choix du lieu de l'arbitrage.

Dans l'espèce qui a donné lieu à la sentence ici rapportée, les arbitres pouvaient ne pas se soucier des dispositions de la convention de New York. En effet, l'Iran n'est pas partie à cette convention, et, si la France l'est, il est toujours possible d'exécuter une sentence rendue à l'étranger sur la base, plus libérale, des dispositions des articles 1498 et suivants du nouveau Code de procédure civile (cf. Cass. civ. I, 9 oct. 1984 : Rev. Arbitrage, 1985, p. 431, note B. Goldman). C'est sans doute pour cela que les arbitres ont pris soin de préciser qu'ils veilleraient à ce que leur décision quant à la validité de la clause d'arbitrage ne conduise pas à un résultat « allant à l'encontre des règles d'arbitrage françaises ou iraniennes », après avoir pourtant relevé auparavant que la référence cumulative des parties à leurs règles d'arbitrage nationales ne s'appliquaient pas à la validité de la clause d'arbitrage.

II. — Selon le défendeur, l'autonomie juridique de la clause compromissoire aurait pour effet qu'une référence générale à l'accord dans lequel elle est contenue n'emporterait pas approbation de cette clause. Puisqu'au-delà de leur coexistence dans un même document le contrat et la clause compromissoire sont des actes juridiques autonomes, la manifestation de l'accord des parties sur le contrat n'implique pas un accord sur la clause compromissoire.

Le principe d'autonomie de la clause compromissoire, invoqué par ailleurs dans la sentence ici rapportée pour justifier la solution adoptée en ce qui concerne sa validité, ne fait plus l'objet de contestations sérieuses en France et dans le monde (cf. Affaire Gosset, Cass. civ. I, 7 mai 1963 : D. 1963, 545, note Robert ; J.C.P. 63, II, 13045, note Goldman ; Clunet 1964, 82, note Bredin ; Rev. crit. dr. int. pr. 1963, 616, note Motulsky et ses développements dans les affaires Hecht : Clunet 1972, 843, note B. Oppetit ; Rev. trim. dr. com. 1973, 419, note Y. Loussouarn, et Menicucci, Paris 13 déc. 1975 : *Rev. crit. dr. int. pr.* 1976, 510 ; *Clunet* 1977, 106, note E. Loquin et parmi les sentences les plus récentes, celles rendues dans l'affaire n° 4131 en 1983 : Clunet 1983, p. 899, dans l'affaire n° 4504 en 1985 et 1986 : *infra* p. 1118 ; pour le droit comparé, *cf.* P. Sanders, « L'autonomie de la clause compromissoire » *in Hommage à F. Eisemann,* p. 31).

Déduire de ce principe bien établi que le consentement à la clause compromissoire doit se manifester d'une façon autonome du consentement au contrat principal serait lui donner une portée bien excessive. En effet, l'existence de deux actes juridiques autonomes n'est pas incompatible avec le fait qu'ils soient l'objet d'un seul échange des consentements. C'est d'ailleurs ce double objet de l'échange des consentements lorsqu'est conclu un contrat contenant une clause compromissoire, qui avait permis à certains de relever que le vice du consentement pourrait être l'une de ces « circonstances exceptionnelles », dans lesquelles, selon l'arrêt Gosset, le principe d'autonomie de la clause compromissoire ne jouerait pas, la nullité du contrat affectant aussi la clause compromissoire (*cf.* en ce sens, B. Goldman, *Rep. dr. int. pr. V°* Arbitrage (droit international privé), n° 57, qui souligne judicieusement qu'il s'agit en réalité dans ce cas de nullités convergentes). Ce n'est finalement que si, selon le droit qui lui est applicable, la conclusion de la clause compromissoire donne lieu à un formalisme particulier (exigence de l'écrit, nécessité de parapher spécialement la clause) qu'un échange de consentement englobant indistinctement la clause compromissoire et le contrat ne sera pas suffisant. Or, dans l'espèce ici rapportée, ni les usages du commerce international, ni les droits français et iranien n'exigeaient le respect d'un formalisme quelconque.

III. — Pour affirmer sa liberté de déterminer les sources de droit applicable à la clause d'arbitrage « *sans qu'il lui soit nécessaire d'établir le droit international privé applicable* » le Tribunal arbitral se réfère à la sentence C.C.I. rendue dans l'affaire n° 3880 en 1983 (*cf. Clunet* 1983, 897). Celle-ci soulignait que des arbitres pouvaient désigner le droit applicable à un contrat de vente « *sans qu'il soit nécessaire d'établir quel droit international privé serait applicable* ». Là encore, on constate le souci des arbitres, dans la sentence ici rapportée de puiser, non seulement leur solution, mais encore leur terminologie, dans la jurisprudence arbitrale. Quant à la solution elle-même, elle est classique. La liberté de l'arbitre de déterminer le droit applicable sans se référer à un système de droit international privé préalablement établi est la conséquence de l'absence de *lex fori* de l'arbitre international (*cf.* récemment P. Lalive, « L'ordre public transnational (ou réellement international) et l'arbitrage international » : *Rev. Arbitrage* 1986, p. 329 ; Y. Derains, « L'ordre public et le droit applicable au fond du litige dans l'arbitrage international » : *Rev. Arbitrage* 1986, p. 375 ; voir aussi les observations sous la sentence rendue dans l'affaire n° 4132 en 1983, et les références *Clunet* 1983, 891).

De plus, la décision des arbitres vient une fois encore confirmer que l'article 13 (3) du règlement d'arbitrage de la C.C.I., qui oblige l'arbitre à appliquer « la loi désignée par la règle de conflit qu'il jugera appropriée en l'espèce » vise bien une règle de conflit de lois, qui peut éventuellement être définie par l'arbitre lui-même, et non pas un système de conflit de lois. Cependant, force est de constater que cette disposition du Règlement d'arbitrage de la C.C.I., inspirée de l'article VII (1) de la convention européenne sur l'arbitrage commercial international de 1961, n'est plus vraiment adaptée à la pratique actuelle de l'arbitrage international tant en raison de sa référence conflictualiste, passablement artificielle, que de son apparente volonté de limiter le pouvoir des arbitres d'appliquer une loi, alors que l'application par les arbitres statuant sous l'égide de la C.C.I. de règles de droit anationales est fréquente, (*cf.* cette chronique, l'affaire n° 4761

p. 1136 et surtout B. Goldman, « La *lex mercatoria* dans l'arbitrage et les contrats internationaux : réalités et perspectives » : *Clunet* 1979, p. 475).

Il faut espérer qu'il sera remanié à l'occasion d'une prochaine révision du règlement d'arbitrage de la C.C.I. de façon à ce qu'il reflète, sans besoin d'interprétation, la pratique véritable des arbitres statuant sous l'égide de la C.C.I., tout comme les dispositions de l'article 1496 du nouveau Code de procédure civile français reflète la pratique arbitrale internationale : « l'arbitre tranche le litige conformément aux règles de droit que les parties ont choisies ; à défaut d'un tel choix, conformément à celles qu'ils estiment appropriées ». A cet égard, on ne peut que regretter que la loi modèle adoptée par la commission des Nations Unies pour le droit commercial international (C.N.U.D.C.I.) le 21 juin 1985 ait préféré une rédaction voisine de celle de l'article 13 (3) du Règlement d'arbitrage de la C.C.I. qui, sans interdire à la liberté des arbitres en matière de détermination du droit applicable de continuer à se développer (la jurisprudence arbitrale de la C.C.I. le prouve) n'a pas pour effet de la favoriser.

IV. — Le Tribunal arbitral affirme que la capacité de chacune des parties à compromettre est soumise à la loi des parties. C'est là la solution consacrée par la convention de New York de 1958 qui admet (art. 5, 1-a) le refus de reconnaissance ou d'exécution de la sentence si la partie contre laquelle celle-ci est invoquée apporte la preuve que les parties à la convention d'arbitrage étaient, « en vertu de la loi à elles applicable », frappées d'une incapacité.

Cette solution a donné lieu à un important débat, en France, lorsque l'une des parties est une personne morale de droit public. Une hésitation s'est en effet manifestée en ce qui concerne le point de savoir si l'aptitude des personnes morales de droit public à compromettre était une question de capacité, se rattachant au statut personnel de cette personne morale, ou une question de nature contractuelle, soumise à la loi d'autonomie. Le problème a été tranché par la Cour de cassation, dans son arrêt Galakis (Cass. 2 mai 1966 : *D*. 1966, 575, note J. Robert ; *Clunet* 1966, 648, note Level : *Rev. crit. dr. int. pr*. 1967, 533, note Goldman) créant une règle matérielle propres aux opérations du commerce international et autorisant l'Etat à compromettre.

La jurisprudence des arbitres du commerce international a hésité, semble-t-il, à considérer que la loi de l'Etat devait être appliquée en tant que statut personnel. On renverra aux sentences n° 1526, de 1968 (*Clunet* 1974, 915) et n° 2521 de 1975 (*Clunet* 1976, 997) où c'est plus en tant que loi que les parties avaient déclarée applicable au fond du litige qu'en tant que loi personnelle que les arbitres avaient appliqué la loi de l'Etat (en ce sens *cf*. les observations sous ces sentences et, plus récemment, P. Leboulanger, « *Les contrats entre Etats et entreprises étrangères* », note 120, p. 264). L'application par les arbitres de la loi de l'Etat en tant que loi personnelle paraît à la fois plus conforme aux qualifications classiques du droit international privé, selon lequel la capacité de contracter s'apprécie selon la loi personnelle et au réalisme. L'application de la loi du contrat risque en effet de fixer l'étendue des pouvoirs de l'Etat et des personnes morales de droit public en fonction d'une loi étrangère, conçue à partir de considérations propres au rôle et à la structure de l'Etat dans le pays d'origine de la loi régissant le contrat, alors que le rôle et les structures de l'Etat partie à l'arbitrage n'est pas comparable. Mais la conséquence de cette qualification de l'aptitude de l'Etat à compromettre en tant qu'institution du statut personnel suppose que l'ordre public international puisse, chaque fois qu'il en est besoin, intervenir pour éviter que l'Etat ou les personnes morales de droit public n'invoquent utilement leur loi personnelle pour se soustraire à leurs engagements (en ce sens *cf*. P. Lalive, *op. cit. loc. cit*.).

V. — La sentence ici rapportée fournit un exemple d'une telle intervention de l'ordre public international. Les arbitres jugent en effet comme inopérante l'inaptitude à compromettre invoquée par l'entreprise d'Etat iranienne « *en raison de sa non conformité avec l'ordre public international dont la mise en jeu ne saurait être exclue par l'application du droit iranien* ».

La notion d'ordre public international, ou transnational, étant régulièrement mise en doute, sinon contestée, il est toujours utile de souligner que la pratique arbitrale internationale en confirme l'existence.

Le problème de l'aptitude de l'Etat à compromettre constitue un domaine où son intervention est la plus fréquente, même si c'est loin d'être le seul, ainsi que l'a montré P. Lalive dans son étude précitée. Cependant, la sentence ici rapportée se garde bien d'affirmer, de façon générale, que l'inaptitude à compromettre de l'Etat ou des entreprises publiques serait contraire à l'ordre public international. On voit d'ailleurs mal au nom de quel principe supérieur le législateur national devrait être tenu d'autoriser l'Etat et les personnes morales de droit public à recourir à l'arbitrage. En réalité, ce que la pratique arbitrale internationale dénonce comme étant contraire à l'ordre public international, c'est le fait pour l'Etat ou la personne morale de droit public de conclure une clause d'arbitrage sans révéler son inaptitude puis d'invoquer celle-ci pour ne pas respecter son engagement. C'est l'acte d'invoquer une inaptitude non dévoilée au contractant étranger lors de la conclusion de la convention d'arbitrage qui est contraire à l'ordre public international, et non pas cette inaptitude elle-même. Et, dans son souci de s'appuyer le plus fermement possible sur des précédents arbitraux, la sentence ici rapportée cite mot pour mot la sentence rendue dans l'affaire n° 1939, dès 1971 (*Cf. Clunet* 1975, 919) :

« *L'ordre public international s'opposerait avec force à ce qu'un organe étatique, traitant avec des personnes étrangères au pays, puisse passer ouvertement, le sachant et le voulant, une clause d'arbitrage qui met en confiance le cocontractant et puisse ensuite, que ce soit dans la procédure arbitrale ou dans une procédure d'exécution, se prévaloir de la nullité de sa propre parole.* »

Un tel comportement de l'Etat ou de la personne morale de droit public est incompatible avec l'ordre public international, ceci parce qu'il est normalement condamnable et parce qu'il sape la confiance nécessaire à la sérénité du commerce international, dont l'arbitre est le protecteur naturel (*cf.* sur ce point, P. Lalive, *op. cit. loc. cit.*).

Dans un contexte légèrement différent, ce principe a été confirmé dans la sentence Framatome rendue dans l'affaire n° 3896 en 1982 (*Clunet* 1984, 58) également mentionnée par les arbitres « *... un principe général, aujourd'hui universellement reconnu tant dans les rapports interétatiques que dans les rapports internationaux privés (que ce principe soit considéré comme d'ordre public international, comme appartenant aux usages du commerce international ou aux principes reconnus tant par le droit des gens que par le droit de l'arbitrage international ou la* « *lex mercatoria* ») *interdirait de toute façon à l'Etat iranien — même s'il en avait eu l'intention, ce qui n'est pas le cas — de renier l'engagement d'arbitrage qu'il aurait souscrit lui-même ou qu'un organisme public comme l'A.E.O.I. aurait souscrit précédemment* ». On peut discuter sur le point de savoir si ce principe se rattache aux notions de bonne foi, d'abus de droit, de « *venire contra factum proprium* », et même au concept de l'« estoppel » (*cf.* E. Gaillard, « L'interdiction de se contredire au détriment d'autrui comme principe général du droit du commerce international (le principe de l'estoppel dans quelques sentences arbitrales récentes) » : *Rev. Arbitrage* 1985, 241), mais il est aujourd'hui incontestable qu'il fait partie de l'ordre public international.

On ajoutera également que dans la sentence ici rapportée, l'aptitude de l'entreprise d'Etat iranienne à compromettre n'était pas réellement en cause. En effet l'aptitude des entreprises d'Etat iraniennes à compromettre est d'autant moins douteuse que l'article 139 de la Constitution de la République Islamique d'Iran, approuvée par référendum du 15 novembre 1979, en organise les modalités d'exercice. Il est libellé comme suit, dans sa traduction française : « l'entente concernant les actions en justice s'appliquant aux biens publics et gouvernementaux ou le recours à l'arbitrage, devra, dans chaque cas, être approuvé par le conseil des Ministres et porté à la connaissance de la Chambre. Dans le cas où l'action est engagée par l'étranger et dans les importants cas intérieurs, l'approbation de la Chambre doit être également requise. La loi déterminera les cas importants ».

Le problème posé aux arbitres n'était donc pas tant celui de savoir si l'entreprise d'Etat iranienne était apte à compromettre, ce qui n'était pas douteux, mais de tirer les conséquences de ce qu'elle n'avait pas, à l'insu de son contractant étranger, respecté les formalités indispensables à la conclusion d'une convention d'arbitrage, selon la Constitution de la République Islamique d'Iran (pour un problème voisin, mais où les arbitres ont constaté qu'en l'espèce aucune formalité n'était nécessaire, cf. la sentence rendue dans l'affaire n° 3881, *supra* p. 1096). Parmi les précédents arbitraux évoqués par les arbitres, certains ne concernaient qu'indirectement la question, s'agissant de l'inaptitude même à compromettre où, comme la sentence Framatome (*Clunet* 1984, 58) s'appliquant à la question de savoir si l'article 139 de la Constitution de la République Islamique d'Iran pouvait être invoqué à l'égard de conventions d'arbitrage conclues avant 1979. C'est la sentence rendue en 1981, dans l'affaire n° 3327 (*Clunet* 1982, 971), sur laquelle se fondent également les arbitres, qui constituait le précédent le plus pertinent. Il s'agissait là aussi d'un cas où un Etat cherchait à se réfugier derrière le défaut d'une approbation prétendûment prévue par sa Constitution pour nier la validité d'un accord qu'il avait conclu. Après avoir relevé que l'exigence de cette approbation ne leur paraissait pas démontrée les arbitres indiquèrent « *que quoi qu'il en soit, une telle exigence non prévue conventionnellement ne pouvait autoriser la défenderesse à s'en prévaloir pour ne pas s'estimer liée* ». Ainsi le principe selon lequel un Etat ou une personne morale de droit public ne peut invoquer son inaptitude à compromettre pour se soustraire à une clause d'arbitrage conclue en parfaite connaissance de cause trouve-t-il son prolongement dans la règle d'après laquelle le même Etat ou la même personne morale de droit public jouissant de l'aptitude à compromettre, ne saurait renier son engagement de participer à l'arbitrage en invoquant que les formalités qui conditionnent, dans son droit national, l'exercice de cette aptitude n'ont pas été remplies. Elle ne le pourrait que si les parties avaient fait de l'accomplissement de ces formalités des conditions contractuelles. L'ordre public international s'oppose donc de la même façon à ce qu'un Etat ou une personne morale de droit public cherche à tirer avantage de règles particulières de son droit national, soit qu'elles lui interdisent de compromettre, soit qu'elles entourent son aptitude à compromettre de conditions d'exercice, lorsqu'il a conclu une clause d'arbitrage au mépris de ces règles.

Dans la sentence ici rapportée les arbitres se réfèrent à l'obligation qu'avait le défendeur de « dévoiler les exigences du droit iranien relatives à la conclusion des contrats par des personnes publiques ». Ceci rejoint l'idée que les procédures d'habilitation et d'autorisation des agents de l'Etat ou des entreprises publiques ne sont opposables au contractant étranger dans un contrat international que si l'organisme d'Etat a précisé contractuellement ces autorisations ou approbation (cf. Ph. Kahn, « Souveraineté de l'Etat et règlement du litige. Régime juridique du contrat » : *Rev. Arbitrage* 1985, 65). Il est vrai que la sentence ne va pas si loin, car elle semble se contenter d'une simple information, indiquer qu'elle doit être entrée dans le champ contractuel. Dans le même esprit, il a été suggéré que l'on pourrait admettre l'opposabilité du non respect d'exigences particulières du droit de l'Etat ou de l'entreprise publique s'il était établi que le contractant étranger, était au courant de ces exigences (en ce sens P. Lalive, *op. cit. loc. cit.* et, dans

273

une certaine mesure, la sentence Framatome précitée). Cette observation paraît justifiée si le cocontractant étranger, informé de certaines exigences du droit national de l'Etat ou de l'entreprise publique, ne pouvait légitimement supposer, lors de la conclusion du contrat ou de sa mise en vigueur, que ces exigences avaient été remplies. En effet, si l'on reconnaît avec Ph. Kahn (*op. cit., loc. cit.*) et la sentence ici rapportée, l'existence pour l'Etat ou ses agents d'une obligation d'informer son contractant de particularités du système applicable à l'Administration locale, on doit également admettre, au profit du contractant étranger, la présomption du respect de ce système par cet Etat ou son agent. La pratique contractuelle s'attache d'ailleurs généralement à renforcer cette présomption en prévoyant, parmi les conditions d'entrée en vigueur du contrat, une déclaration de chacune des parties selon laquelle les autorisations administratives requises dans leurs pays respectifs ont été obtenues, sans énumérer ces autorisations ni préciser leur nature.

D'ailleurs, on notera que la sentence rattache plus la bonne foi du demandeur à son ignorance du vice entachant la convention d'arbitrage qu'au fait qu'il n'avait pas été informé des exigences particulières du droit iranien.

VI. — Les arbitres rejettent l'affirmation du défendeur selon laquelle la lettre de son Président et Directeur Général indiquant que l'accord de société en participation créée pour le premier projet régissait les relations des parties pour la réalisation du second aurait été rédigée sous la contrainte. C'est là une question d'appréciation des faits dans laquelle les arbitres sont souverains. On ne suivra pas par contre les arbitres lorsqu'ils semblent affirmer que même s'il avait été prouvé que la lettre en question avait été rédigée sous la contrainte, elle n'en serait pas moins opposable à la société au nom de laquelle elle a été émise. Dans cette hypothèse, il y aurait là un véritable vice du consentement. Mais, en réalité, il apparaît que ce n'est pas tant la contrainte qu'invoquait le défendeur, mais le manque de compétence de son ancien président. Et, cette incompétence, bien difficile à apprécier d'ailleurs, ne saurait suffire à dégager une société des obligations contractées en son nom par un président mal choisi. Il ne s'agit pas d'une incapacité et, à cet égard, le fait, relevé par les arbitres, que le cocontractant ignorait l'incompétence alléguée de la personnalité avec laquelle elle traitait, semble un *obiter dictum* sans conséquences juridiques bien définies.

Y. D.

I. — **Clause compromissoire.** — Arbitrage international. — Droit français. — Exigence de forme. — Ecrit (non). — Règlement d'arbitrage de la C.C.I.

II. — **Acte de mission.** — Article 13 du règlement de la C.C.I. — Complément de la clause compromissoire.

III. — **Clause compromissoire contenue dans le contrat principal.** — Avenant. — Article 1443 du N.C.P.C.

Sentence rendue en 1986 dans l'affaire n° 5117.

Le Tribunal arbitral, statuant à Paris, était saisi d'un litige opposant deux sociétés française et mexicaine, demanderesses, à deux sociétés française et mexicaine également, défenderesses. Le litige portait sur l'exécution de deux contrats pour l'étude, la préfabrication et le montage au Mexique de tuyauteries. Ces deux contrats contenaient une convention d'arbitrage identique prévoyant l'arbitrage de la C.C.I. à Paris, la législation française étant applicable. Ils furent suivis, en cours de réalisation, de commandes relatives à des travaux de préfabrication, de montage et de mise en place de réservoirs. Les défenderesses déclinèrent la compétence des arbitres concernant deux de ces commandes, portant les numéros 021 et 053 au motif qu'elles ne contenaient pas de clause compromissoire, et que l'article 1443 du nouveau Code de procédure civile français (N.C.P.C.), exige sous peine de nullité la forme écrite pour la clause compromissoire. Les demanderesses répondaient que les exigences de l'article 1443 N.C.P.C. ne s'appliquaient qu'à la clause compromissoire figurant dans la convention principale et non pas à celles qui en procédent « dans le temps et dans l'espace ».

Le Tribunal arbitral statua sur sa compétence dans les termes suivants :

« Le Tribunal arbitral ayant entendu les parties considère :

— que la défenderesse décline la compétence du Tribunal arbitral en fondant son exception sur l'application de l'article 1443 du nouveau Code de procédure civile, inclus dans le titre I de ce même Code. S'agissant d'un arbitrage international soumis à la loi française et relevant en conséquence du titre V du Code, la question de l'applicabilité d'une disposition contenue dans le titre I du Code doit être tranchée suivant le régime institué par les articles 1494 et 1495 du titre V ;

— que l'article 1495 ne maintient en vigueur les dispositions du titre 1er du Livre IV qu'à défaut de convention particulière et sous réserve de l'article 1494 ; qu'en l'espèce les parties ont passé une convention particulière : la clause compromissoire les soumettant au règlement de la Cour d'arbitrage de la Chambre de Commerce Internationale ;

— que ledit règlement que les parties ont choisi d'adopter ne fait preuve d'aucune exigence particulière quant à la forme que devrait revêtir une convention d'arbitrage et qui soit comparable à l'article 1443 du nouveau Code de procédure civile, puisque le règlement dans son article 8-3 prévoit qu'il appartiendra à l'arbitre de prendre toute décision sur sa propre compétence au vu d'une convention d'arbitrage dont la Cour aurait constaté prima facie l'existence, mais qu'en l'absence de règle de décision précise prévue par le règlement, l'arbitre devra chercher celle-ci dans la convention elle-même, ou, comme l'article 1494 du N.C.P.C. l'y invite, par référence à une loi ;

— que par ailleurs le règlement laisse les parties libres de convenir de règles applicables à la procédure et en particulier de celles suivant lesquelles l'arbitre devrait prendre sa décision et que les parties ont signé un acte de mission le 25 août 1985 complétant la convention d'arbitrage. »

« — que ledit acte de mission, exposant sommairement le litige, se réfère expressément aux mémoires écrits pour la demande d'arbitrage que l'acte se borne à résumer, et que, dans les dits mémoires l'une et l'autre parties ont fondé l'exception d'incompétence et la défense à cette exception sur la règle posée par l'article 1443 du N.C.P.C., ne se séparant que sur son interprétation ;

— que le Tribunal arbitral qui a reçu mission de se prononcer sur l'exception d'incompétence ainsi formulée ne saurait, sauf à trahir la commune volonté des parties telle qu'elle s'est exprimée dans leur soumission à l'arbitrage et a été retenue par l'acte de mission, choisir de régler la procédure suivant l'article 1494 en adoptant une autre loi que celle qui lui a été désignée ;

— qu'en conséquence l'article 1443 doit être appliqué à la résolution du litige sur la compétence. »

275

« *Le Tribunal arbitral au vu de ce qui précède considère :*

— que l'article 1443 du N.C.P.C. est d'interprétation stricte ; qu'en l'absence de clause compromissoire écrite dans la convention ou d'une référence à une clause compromissoire, la volonté des parties de soumettre leurs différends à l'arbitrage ne peut ni se présumer ni être prouvée par tout moyen, et que l'on se heurte à l'exigence d'une formalité substantielle, la jurisprudence antérieure de la Cour de cassation se trouvant écartée par la loi ;

— que le terme "convention principale" employé dans l'article 1443 doit s'entendre comme désignant l'ensemble des stipulations qui définissent les obligations des parties par opposition à la clause particulière de règlement des litiges, celle-ci pouvant être soit stipulée dans cette "convention principale", soit au contraire inscrite dans un autre document auquel "la convention principale" se réfère ;

— qu'il n'est conforme ni à la lettre ni à l'esprit du texte invoqué de définir la "convention principale" par opposition à d'autres conventions qui pourraient en procéder "dans le temps ou dans l'espace" ; qu'on ne peut donc sur la base de cette prétendue distinction raisonner a contrario *pour établir pour ces dernières le principe de liberté de preuve en matière commerciale.* »

« *— mais que, cependant, lorsqu'il s'agit de déterminer quel est le champ des obligations défini par ladite "convention principale", ou encore de juger de la valeur de la référence à un document contenant la clause compromissoire, la liberté de preuve n'est nullement limitée par l'article 1443 suivant l'article 109 du Code de commerce ; qu'il est dès lors légitime d'en user, sauf à s'enfermer dans un formalisme étroit étranger à l'inspiration générale des titres I et II du Livre IV du N.C.P.C. Car, en l'espèce, la commande d'origine... obéit à la qualification de contrat d'entreprise, dont le caractère évolutif est un aspect essentiel à raison de son exécution progressive et des modifications auxquelles il peut être sujet, par la découverte de difficultés ou la définition de besoins nouveaux au cours de sa réalisation.*

« *La clause dite "modifications" dont la stipulation est habituelle dans ce type de contrats prévoit conformément à ce principe que : (une des défenderesses) se réserve le droit de demander à (une des demanderesses) des modifications relatives aux travaux, que ce soit pour les étendre ou les diminuer. Toutes ces demandes de modifications, pour être opposables... devront faire l'objet d'un avenant ;*

« *— que la commande 021 passée par... est une convention entre les mêmes parties que la commande d'origine nº 49, portant sur la réalisation du même ouvrage, destinée à être exécutée concurremment avec les travaux de la première commande, que ces deux commandes devaient faire l'objet tant pour le Maître de l'Ouvrage que pour l'entrepreneur d'une gestion globale, et qu'il est contingent d'observer qu'un autre entrepreneur aurait pu en être chargé, cela en fait n'ayant pas été le cas ;*

— que la commande 021 se borne à l'énoncé des mentions indispensables d'objet, de prix, de délais et pénalités et durée de garantie et ne comprend pas de conditions générales d'achat : qu'elle revêt ainsi un caractère particulièrement elliptique. »

« *— qu'il résulte de ce qui précède que ladite commande 021 est insusceptible de jouir d'une véritable autonomie et doit donc être qualifiée d'avenant à la commande d'origine nº 49, qui a la nature d'un contrat d'entreprise, et plus particulièrement par application de la clause dite "modifications" stipulée dans ce contrat 49 ;*

« *— qu'en conséquence la commande 021 est devenue partie intégrante de la commande d'origine qui s'en est trouvée modifiée dans son objet et que, la clause compromissoire étant stipulée dans cette "convention principale" dont un tel avenant ne peut être dissocié, il est satisfait directement à l'exigence de l'article 1443 sans qu'il soit besoin de chercher une quelconque référence à ladite clause ;*

« *— que le même raisonnement pourrait être développé au sujet de la commande 053 mais qu'il faut observer que le texte de cette commande stipule :*

« "les hacemos el siguiente pedido bajo nuestras condiciones generales y bajo las condiciones particulares abajo citadas".

« *et que la distinction apparaît ainsi clairement entre "conditions générales" et les "conditions particulières ci-dessous"* ;

« *— qu'en l'absence au dossier de toutes autres "conditions générales" de (une des défenderesses) qui auraient dû être communiquées à (une des demanderesses) il ne peut s'agir ici sous le terme "conditions générales" que d'une référence expresse aux conditions régissant la commande d'origine n° 49 qui serait alors au regard de l'article 1443 le "document" comprenant la clause compromissoire auquel se réfère la commande 053, si cette dernière revêtait à son tour la forme d'une "convention principale."*

« *— qu'il est dès lors pour la commande 053 satisfait aux exigences de l'article 1443 : soit directement par intégration de la commande 053 dans la commande d'origine ; soit, par l'alternative de la formalité exigée par l'article 1443, par la référence à un document contenant la clause compromissoire.* »

OBSERVATIONS. — I. — Le litige soumis aux arbitres mettait indiscutablement « en cause des intérêts du commerce international », au sens de l'article 1492 N.C.P.C. En effet, il découlait de conventions conclues entre des parties françaises et mexicaines et concernait des prestations à réaliser pour une part en France (l'étude, la fabrication) et pour une autre au Méxique (le montage, la mise en place). Les dispositions du droit français propres à l'arbitrage international trouvaient donc lieu à s'appliquer, c'est-à-dire les dispositions du titre V du Livre IV du N.C.P.C. Or ces dispositions ne contiennent aucune exigence quant à la forme des conventions d'arbitrage, l'article 1493 N.C.P.C. se contentant d'indiquer que « directement ou par référence à un règlement d'arbitrage, la convention d'arbitrage peut désigner le ou les arbitres ou prévoir les modalités de leur désignation ». On en déduit habituellement qu'en matière d'arbitrage international, le droit français n'exige pas la forme écrite pour la convention d'arbitrage (*cf.* entre autres Ph. Fouchard ; *Clunet* 1982, 385 ; P. Bellet et E. Mezger : *Rev. crit. dr. int. pr.* 1981, 622 ; R. Bourdin, *in Droit et pratique de l'arbitrage international en France* V° « La convention d'arbitrage international en droit français depuis le décret du 12 mai 1981 », p. 21 ; M. de Boisseson, *Le droit français de l'arbitrage,* n° 490 ; Y. Derains ; *Yearbook Commercial Arbitration,* 1982, p. 6). Telle est bien également l'opinion exprimée dans la sentence ici rapportée. Elle explique en effet qu'en vertu des dispositions de l'article 1495 N.C.P.C., l'article 1443 du même Code, qui exige que la clause compromissoire soit conclue par écrit, ne s'applique qu'à défaut de convention particulière et sous réserve de l'article 1493 précité et de l'article 1494, ce qui laisse aux arbitres et aux parties la maîtrise de la procédure (en ce sens *cf.* M. de Boisseson, *op. cit.,* n° 499).

Les arbitres estiment qu'en l'espèce il existe une convention particulière, le règlement d'arbitrage de la C.C.I. qui n'a aucune exigence quant à la forme des conventions d'arbitrage, laissant aux arbitres le soin de prendre toute décision sur leur propre compétence, à la lumière de la convention elle-même ou par référence à une loi. On notera que les arbitres tiennent ici un raisonnement voisin de celui qui apparaît dans les sentences n° 4131 de 1982 (*Clunet* 1983, 889) et n° 4381 de 1986 (1103), sans en tirer toutes les conséquences puisqu'ils envisagent l'application d'une loi et non pas des usages du commerce international. Ceci vient sans doute d'une interprétation selon laquelle l'article 1494 du N.C.P.C. inviterait les arbitres à se référer à une loi lorsqu'il s'agit d'apprécier leur propre compétence. Il ne semble pourtant pas que cet article, qui vise la procédure à suivre dans l'instance arbitrale, puisse être invoqué à l'occasion de la forme de la convention d'arbitrage.

II. — Cependant, ce n'est pas par le biais de l'article 1494 N.C.P.C. que les arbitres décident finalement d'appliquer l'article 1443 du même Code, qu'ils avaient pourtant déclaré d'emblée étranger à l'arbitrage international. Ils s'estiment liés par les conclusions des parties, ceci parcequ'elles figurent dans des mémoires visés à l'acte de mission. Or celui-ci complète la convention d'arbitrage. Les arbitres en déduisent qu'il y a accord des parties pour soumettre leur convention d'arbitrage à l'article 1443 N.C.P.C., les parties ne se séparant que sur son interprétation.

Cette approche est à la fois justifiée et trop limitative. Il est exact que l'acte de mission visé à l'article 13 du règlement d'arbitrage vient compléter la convention d'arbitrage, tout au moins lorsqu'il est signé par les parties (sur l'acte de mission, cf. les observations sous la sentence n. 4504, p. 1118). Il définit les questions en litige et précise les conditions dans lesquelles le litige sera résolu. Cependant, en ce qui concerne un accord des parties sur le droit applicable, qu'il s'agisse du droit applicable au fond du litige, à la procédure ou à la convention des parties, il est indifférent que cet accord soit absorbé par l'acte de mission, directement ou indirectement.

L'important est que cet accord existe. Aussi, qu'il en soit fait état dans la convention d'arbitrage, dans l'acte de mission, qu'il résulte des conclusions des parties ou de déclarations à l'audience, les arbitres doivent le respecter dans les limites de l'ordre public international.

III. — Pour échapper à la nullité que l'article 1443 N.C.P.C. fait peser sur la clause compromissoire non écrite, les demanderesses semblaient procéder à une exégèse bien difficile à suivre du premier alinéa de cet article. Il est libellé comme suit :

« La clause compromissoire doit, à peine de nullité, être stipulée par écrit dans la convention principale ou dans un document auquel celle-ci se réfère. »

A en croire les demanderesses, la « convention principale » visée au texte aurait été constituée par les contrats principaux dans lesquels figuraient des clauses compromissoires écrites, par opposition aux commandes ultérieures. Il n'est pas surprenant que les arbitres prennent soin de corriger cette interprétation audacieuse en rappelant que dans l'article 1443 le contrat principal est l'ensemble des droits et obligations des parties susceptibles de donner lieu à des litiges qui seront résolus au moyen de la clause compromissoire. Ils parviennent par ailleurs au même résultat que les demanderesses, à savoir la constatation de leur compétence, par une analyse rigoureuse de ce qu'il faut entendre par contrat principal au sens de l'article 1443 N.C.P.C. Ce n'est pas seulement le document signé en même temps que la clause compromissoire, mais un acte juridique qui, loin d'être figé est susceptible d'être amendé ou complété par les parties. Les amendements ou compléments font partie du contrat principal et il n'est pas besoin qu'il reproduisent à nouveau la clause compromissoire initialement conclue pour lui être soumis. Il en irait bien évidemment tout autrement si un avenant au contrat d'origine prévoyait une autre modalité de solution des litiges. Il conviendrait alors, par une interprétation des textes contractuels, de déterminer si les parties ont voulu modifier la clause compromissoire d'origine, ou si le soi-disant avenant doit être considéré comme un contrat qui, bien qu'accessoire au contrat principal, jouit d'une totale autonomie juridique (*cf.* par exemple la sentence rendue en 1983 dans l'affaire 4392 : *Clunet* 1983, 907).

Y. D.

I. — **Acte de mission.** — Article 13 du règlement C.C.I. — Contenu et ffet de l'acte de mission.

II. — **Existence « prima facie » d'une clause d'arbitrage.** — Article 8- du règlement C.C.I.

III. — **Clause compromissoire.** — Autonomie juridique. — Application u droit régissant le contrat principal (non). — Application de la *lex fori* oui).

IV. — **Sociétés d'un même groupe.** — Clause compromissoire. — Opposabilité à la filiale n'ayant pas signé (non). — Article 6 du concordat uisse.

V. — **Demande reconventionnelle.** — Note en réponse déposée dans le lélai prescrit. — Article 5-2 du règlement C.C.I.

Sentences intérimaires rendues en 1985 et 1986 dans l'affaire 4504.

Suivant un contrat conclu en avril 1979 (« le contrat »), un producteur de pétrole demanderesse dans l'arbitrage) s'est engagé à rendre à une société (première léfenderesse à l'arbitrage) certaines quantités de condensats par an à un prix léterminé par l'application d'une formule de fixation. Après des difficultés entre es parties l'une d'elles avait résilié le contrat dans un délai prévu par le contrat. Dans l'arbitrage la demanderesse réclamait le paiement du solde du prix des ivraisons restant dû, en dirigeant sa demande contre non seulement son partenaire contractuel mais également contre une deuxième société du même groupe de ociétés (la 2ᵉ défenderesse à l'arbitrage).

Finalement la demanderesse concluait que les deux défendeurs soient condamnés à payer solidairement des dommages et intérêts. Dans une demande reconvention-nelle la première défenderesse, se référant à deux autres contrats conclus avec la demanderesse en octobre 1978 et décembre 1979, réclamait des dommages et ntérêts.

Trois arbitres siégeant à Genève — lieu d'arbitrage convenu entre les parties — devaient résoudre le différend. L'acte de mission, signé par les arbitres et toutes es parties, disposait entre autres :

« *Exposé sommaire des prétentions des parties.*

Le présent exposé, basé sur la requête aux fins d'arbitrage de... (demanderesse), sur la réponse et demande reconventionnelle de... (1ʳᵉ défenderesse) sur la note en réponse sur les demandes reconventionnelles déposées par... (demanderesse), ainsi que sur la duplique du conseil des deux défenderesses, constitue une simple indication des positions des parties destinée à situer le litige. Cet exposé n'a aucun caractère exhaustif et le Tribunal arbitral se référera toujours aux mémoires écrits et aux exposés verbaux des parties, et non au seul acte de mission pour connaître les moyens de fait et de droit invoqués par les parties. »

La première question à trancher par les arbitres fut de décider si la clause compromissoire figurant dans le contrat passé entre la demanderesse et la première défenderesse était opposable à la deuxième défenderesse qui, elle, n'avait pas signé ce contrat. Les arbitres abordèrent le problème dans les termes suivants :

« *Etant donné que la Cour d'arbitrage a décidé que l'arbitrage aurait lieu dans les conditions de l'article 8-3 du règlement de la Cour d'arbitrage de la Chambre de Commerce Internationale, il appartient au seul Tribunal arbitral de définir la portée de la clause compromissoire insérée dans le contrat. Il déterminera ainsi si (2e défenderesse) a qualité de partie au présent arbitrage, sans considération aucune de la décision préjudicielle de la Cour d'arbitrage qui n'a que valeur d'injonction au Tribunal arbitral d'examiner cette question. La demanderesse ne saurait donc s'en prévaloir de quelconque façon.*

« *D'ailleurs, l'article 8-3 du règlement C.C.I. est on ne peut plus clair à ce sujet : la décision de la Cour ne préjuge en rien la recevabilité ou le bien-fondé des moyens relatifs à l'existence ou à la validité de la convention d'arbitrage. Elle a pour seul et unique effet de transférer au Tribunal arbitral la mission de statuer sur sa propre compétence à l'égard de (2e défenderesse) sous réserve de la décision de l'autorité judiciaire de recours qui peut librement revoir cette compétence (Tribunal cantonal Vaudois, 21 mars 1978, BMW A.G.).*

« *En vertu du principe de l'autonomie, la clause compromissoire peut être soumise, dans les arbitrages internationaux, à une loi différente de la loi qui régit le contrat principal (Jolidon, commentaire du concordat suisse sur l'arbitrage, Berne 1984, ad. art. 4, n° 81). C'est la conséquence de la séparabilité de la clause arbitrale dudit contrat.*

« *Le fait que tout litige entre les parties signataires de la clause arbitrale doit être résolu en application du droit (du pays du demandeur) (art. 16-1 du contrat), ne signifie pas nécessairement que celui-ci régit aussi la portée de la clause compromissoire comme la demanderesse le soutient car il ne s'agit pas de l'application du droit de fond.*

« *Pour déterminer la portée de la clause, il convient en premier lieu de qualifier celle-ci et partant, de déterminer la loi applicable à cette qualification. En l'absence de toute détermination des parties à cet égard, le Tribunal arbitral est d'avis que la qualification de la clause compromissoire ne peut être faite qu'en application de la lex fori, à savoir le droit suisse.*

« *La pratique judiciaire suisse, et notamment le Tribunal fédéral, considèrent que les clauses arbitrales ne sont pas de nature privée mais des contrats de procédure soumis au droit public. En tant que telle, la validité de la convention d'arbitrage est soumise à la loi de procédure du siège du Tribunal arbitral (A.T.F. 57, I, 295 — J.T. 1930, I, 26 ; A.T.F. 76, I, 338 — J.T. 1951, I, 239 ; A.T.F. 96, I, 334 — J.T. 1972, I, 27 ; Dutoit, Knoepfler, Lalive, Mercier, Répertoire de droit international privé suisse, Berne 1972, p. 262, n 87).*

« *En l'espèce, la clause arbitrale mentionne "Genève" comme siège du Tribunal arbitral. Elle doit par conséquent être appréciée au regard du concordat suisse sur l'arbitrage des 27 mars/27 août 1969, auquel le canton de Genève a adhéré en 1971, et dont le champ d'application s'étend, selon l'article 1, alinéa 1, à toute procédure par devant un Tribunal arbitral dont le siège se trouve sur le territoire de l'un des cantons concordataires.*

« *L'alinéa 1 de l'article 1 C.I.A. n'étant pas de droit impératif, l'alinéa 2 dudit article aurait permis aux parties, dont il confirme l'autonomie, de convenir, dans les limites de l'alinéa 3, de l'application des dispositions d'un Code de procédure étranger au C.I.A. (Jolidon, ad. art. 1, n° 1).*

« *Or, en l'occurrence, les parties sont seulement convenues, à l'article 16-1 du contrat, que le contrat de droit matériel est régi par le droit (du pays du demandeur) en application duquel le Tribunal arbitral statuera sur le fond. Le concordat suisse sur l'arbitrage — et singulièrement les dispositions de droit impératif de ce concordat, auxquelles il ne peut, par définition, être dérogé — est donc applicable à la présente procédure, ainsi d'ailleurs que le confirme l'acte de mission, sous lettre G relative aux règles applicables à la procédure.*

« *Or, le concordat suisse sur l'arbitrage stipule expressément à son article 6, alinéa 1, qui est une disposition impérative que tout Tribunal arbitral siégeant à Genève doit respecter, que la convention d'arbitrage doit être passée en la forme écrite.*

« *Etant donné que le concordat ne donne aucune précision à cet égard, l'exigence de la forme écrite doit être déterminée en fonction des dispositions y relatives du Code fédéral Suisse des obligations (art. 13 et ss C.O.) appliquées par analogie (commentaire Jolidon, ad. art. 6, n° 2 ; Arrêt semaine judiciaire S.J. 1980, p. 443).*

« *L'article 13, alinéa 1 C.O. dispose que "le contrat pour lequel la loi exige la forme écrite doit être signé par toutes les personnes auxquelles il impose des obligations". Si la convention arbitrale n'est pas passée en la forme écrite, nul ne peut être contraint de se soumettre contre son gré à une procédure arbitrale (A.T.F. 102, I a 582 ; S.J. 1980, p. 443, notamment 444 in fine).*

« *L'exigence de la forme écrite est respectée si la convention d'arbitrage est formulée dans un document unique, ou si elle résulte de plusieurs documents se référant les uns aux autres, tels un échange de lettres signées ou même un échange de télégrammes, pour autant que l'original porte la signature manuscrite de l'expéditeur (commentaire Jolidon, ad. art. 6, n° 2).*

« *Force est de constater en l'espèce que seules (1re défenderesse) et la demanderesse ont signé la clause compromissoire contenue à l'article 16-1 du contrat. (2e défenderesse) ne l'a pas signée et la demanderesse n'a pas produit de documents tels que lettres ou télégrammes attestant l'existence d'une convention arbitrale liant les deux sociétés et satisfaisant à l'exigence écrite de l'article 6, alinéa 1, C.I.A. qui, étant impératif, doit être appliqué en toutes circonstances.*

« *Cela étant, bien que... (demanderesse) reconnaisse que... (2e défenderesse) n'a pas signé la clause compromissoire sur laquelle est fondée sa requête aux fins d'arbitrage, elle considère néanmoins que ladite clause compromissoire est opposable à... (2e défenderesse). Elle tire notamment argument de l'existence de ce que... (1re défenderesse) et... (2e défenderesse) appellent des "liens institutionnels" unissant les deux sociétés. La demanderesse considère que... (les défenderesses) :*

« *"ne forment qu'une seule et même identité" étant donné qu'elles appartiennent au même groupe. ...(2e défenderesse) est dans la dépendance totale de... (1re défenderesse) dont elle est une filiale à 100 % et dont elle est co-locataire des bureaux. ... (1re défenderesse) a deux représentants légaux dont l'un serait simultanément le représentant légal de... (2e défenderesse). Les défenderesses se sont opposées à cette interprétation des faits arguant de ce qu'elles sont des entités juridiques nettement distinctes l'une de l'autre.*

« *Sans nullement nier l'existence — d'ailleurs admise de part et d'autre — de liens unissant .... (les défenderesses), le Tribunal arbitral doit constater que... (les défenderesses) sont des sociétés de droit (d'un pays du continent américain).*

« *Elles constituent ainsi bel et bien deux entités distinctes, dotées chacune d'une personnalité juridique autonome, capables de s'obliger séparément sans que les engagements de l'une aient des effets pour l'autre.*

« *Une autre constatation serait en contradiction avec les faits. La thèse des défenderesses sera donc admise sur ce point, l'argument de la demanderesse tiré de la prétendue confusion entre les deux sociétés défenderesses ne résistant visiblement pas à l'examen.*

« *La demanderesse affirme en outre que, par son comportement après la signature du contrat, 2e défenderesse s'est comportée à tout moment comme si elle en avait été signataire et qu'elle l'aurait ainsi ratifié, ce que contestent avec autant de véhémence les défenderesses.*

« *La demanderesse insiste particulièrement sur le rôle joué par M. A., président de 2ᵉ défenderesse, dans la négociation et l'exécution du contrat, ainsi que dans la négociation de l'Avenant n° 1 audit contrat.*

« *A cet égard, le Tribunal arbitral constate d'emblée que l'Avenant n° 1 au contrat, ainsi que la signature de M. A., indique clairement que ce dernier l'a signé pour le compte de la 1ʳᵉ défenderesse et qu'il était dûment habilité à cet effet. L'impression d'une confusion entre les deux sociétés n'a ainsi pas pu naître à cette occasion.*

« *Dans ces conditions, on ne saurait admettre que M. A. ait, par cette signature, engagé la 2ᵉ défenderesse quelles que soient d'ailleurs les fonctions qu'il ait pu exercer à ce moment-là dans chacune des deux sociétés défenderesses. La façon dont cet Avenant a été rédigé interdit à elle seule déjà une autre constatation.*

« *Quant à l'intervention de M. A. dans l'exécution du contrat lui-même, elle est attestée par une série de télex et de lettres signées par M. A.*

« *Pourtant, une interprétation systématique du contenu de ces télex et lettres fait clairement apparaître que leur auteur agissait effectivement au nom et pour le compte de la 1ʳᵉ défenderesse.*

« *En effet, ainsi que l'explique la demanderesse, les télex en question étaient adressés par M. A. à la demanderesse dans le cadre des négociations en vue de la détermination du prix de vente à payer pour chaque baril de condensat livré en exécution du contrat.*

« *Comme on sait que, bien qu'elles fussent libellées au nom (d'une troisième société du groupe auquel les deux défenderesses faisaient parties) et envoyées à l'adresse de la 2ᵉ défenderesse, les factures de condensat étaient effectivement payées par la 1ʳᵉ défenderesse — à partir d'un compte bancaire ouvert au nom de la 1ʳᵉ défenderesse —, l'acheteur au sens du contrat, il est manifeste que M. A. est intervenu au nom et pour le compte de la 1ʳᵉ défenderesse qui était seule et directement intéressée par le résultat des négociations conduites par M. A.*

« *Aussi doit-on admettre que quand M. A. utilise des expressions telles que : "ma société", "notre société", "notre contrat", il se réfère à la 1ʳᵉ défenderesse et au contrat conclu par cette société avec la demanderesse.*

« *Le même raisonnement peut être tenu pour l'expression "nos prétentions" que M. A. utilise dans ses deux lettres adressées à la demanderesse.*

« *Les prétentions en question ne peuvent être que celles de la 1ʳᵉ défenderesse qui, par télex du..., a informé la demanderesse qu'elle allait retenir une somme sur le montant de la dernière facture de la demanderesse. C'est en tout cas ce qui ressort du télex du 31 juillet adressé par la demanderesse à la 1ʳᵉ défenderesse : "We have been quite surprised by the content of your a/m telex which informs us of your intention to make a compensation against our last invoice of U.S.$..."*

« *Le début de la lettre du 25 août 1981, libellée ainsi : "You have asked (la 1ʳᵉ défenderesse)", indique clairement que M. A. s'adresse à la demanderesse en tant que mandataire de la 1ʳᵉ défenderesse.*

« *Il en va de même pour la lettre du 10 juin 1982 où M. A., bien que s'exprimant à la première personne du pluriel ("nous", "nos prétentions") précise qu'il s'agit bien des prétentions de la 1ʳᵉ défenderesse : "... you have not been informed of the status of this deduction and (1ʳᵉ défenderesse) claims (against la demanderesse...)"*

« *Le Tribunal arbitral reconnaît néanmoins que M. A., par la façon dont il s'est exprimé dans ses télex et lettres qu'il a signés tantôt à titre personnel, tantôt en tant que président de la 2ᵉ défenderesse, s'est comporté d'une manière telle dans ses rapports avec la demanderesse qu'il y a eu immixtion de la 2ᵉ défenderesse dans l'exécution du contrat signé par la 1ʳᵉ défenderesse.*

« *On ne peut toutefois pas déduire des interférences de la 2ᵉ défenderesse dans l'exécution du contrat, que cette société a ratifié ledit contrat, ce d'autant qu'au vu des pièces produites, le fait que M. A. agissait pour le compte de la 1ʳᵉ défenderesse était ou devait être clairement reconnaissable par la demanderesse.*

« *Quoi qu'il en soit, les interférences de la 2ᵉ défenderesse dans l'exécution du contrat n'ont en elles-mêmes pas de portée juridique et ne sont pas de telle nature à pouvoir emporter ratification du contrat.*

« *Pour étayer sa thèse, la demanderesse se réfère enfin à la jurisprudence des Tribunaux arbitraux institués sous l'égide de la Cour d'arbitrage de la Chambre de Commerce Internationale et ayant eu à statuer sur des exceptions d'incompétence. Les défenderesses contestent que l'on puisse s'y référer en l'occurrence.*

a) Dans l'affaire n° 1434 dans laquelle la sentence a été rendue en 1975 (Clunet 1976, n° 4, p. 978 et ss.), un Tribunal arbitral devait trancher si la clause compromissoire contenue dans deux contrats était opposable aux seuls signataires du contrat ou à l'ensemble des sociétés du groupe.

L'un des deux contrats avait été signé par M. A. comme "représentant l'organisation A", ce dernier terme étant utilisé à plusieurs reprises dans le contrat, avec celui de "groupe A" utilisé comme son synonyme.

« *Cet état de fait diffère manifestement du cas d'espèce où il n'est nullement question du groupe A. dans le contrat signé par M. D. agissant pour le compte de la 1ʳᵉ défenderesse et non en tant que représentant du groupe A.*

« *La référence de la demanderesse à cette sentence n'est donc pas pertinente.*

b) Il en va de même pour la sentence rendue dans l'affaire n° 2375 en 1975 (Clunet 1976, p. 973 et s.).

« *Dans celle-ci, un Tribunal arbitral était saisi d'une demande formée par la société X. contre une société Y., première défenderesse, et la société mère Z, deuxième défenderesse. La demande était basée sur un protocole passé entre la société W qui en son temps contrôlait X et la seconde défenderesse Z. Le protocole passé entre les deux sociétés mères W et Z engageaient tant elles-mêmes que leurs filiales respectives X et Y. En outre, l'article 3 du protocole intégrait à la convention une lettre de Y à X soulignant l'appartenance de la filiale Y au groupe Z.*

« *Cette affaire est à l'évidence différente du cas d'espèce où la clause compromissoire n'est pas contenue dans un contrat qu'aurait signé la société mère engageant ses filiales. La 1ʳᵉ défenderesse a en outre toujours agi en tant que telle sans jamais faire référence à son appartenance au groupe.*

c) Dans l'affaire n° 4131 dans laquelle la sentence a été rendue en 1982 (Clunet 1983, p. 899 et s./Yearbook on Commercial Arbitration IX, 1984, p. 131 et ss.), les clauses compromissoires dont les demanderesses, au nombre de quatre, se prévalaient, figuraient dans des contrats qui n'avaient pas été signés par deux d'entre elles, X France et X U.S.A. Les deux sociétés soutenaient pouvoir les invoquer, en raison tant des circonstances dans lesquelles les contrats en cause avaient été conclus et exécutés, que du fait qu'elles faisaient partie d'un groupe dont X U.S.A. était la société mère et les trois autres, ses filiales.

« *Examinant les circonstances de la négociation, de l'exécution et de la résiliation des contrats dans lesquels figuraient les clauses compromissoires invoquées, le Tribunal arbitral siégeant à Paris est arrivé à la conclusion que dans l'esprit de la défenderesse, le partenaire de la société dans le contrat était le groupe X, sans que l'on attache une signification effective au choix de tel ou tel membre du groupe pour signer ce contrat.*

« *Bien que l'on puisse admettre qu'en l'espèce il était indifférent à la demanderesse de conclure un contrat avec telle filiale (du groupe) plutôt qu'avec telle autre, et quelles que soient d'ailleurs les raisons qui ont incité (le groupe) à choisir la 1re défenderesse plutôt qu'une autre filiale pour signer le contrat, il n'en demeure pas moins que la demanderesse était pleinement consciente qu'en signant ce contrat, elle s'engageait avec la 1re défenderesse seulement et non pas avec la 2e défenderesse, ni non plus avec la société mère qui n'a pas été mise en cause dans le présent arbitrage.*

« *La preuve en est fournie par le fait que la demanderesse a, avant la conclusion du contrat pour la vente et l'achat de pétrole brut d'octobre 1978, ainsi qu'avant la conclusion du contrat pour la vente et l'achat de produits raffinés de décembre 1979, demandé et obtenu que l'exécution des obligations contractées par la 1re défenderesse, également signataire des deux contrats précités, soit garantie par la société mère.*

« *Dans ces conditions, on ne saurait considérer d'une part que la demanderesse était dans l'erreur sur la personne de son cocontractant au moment de la conclusion du contrat, ni d'autre part que (le groupe) a commis un abus de droit en faisant signer le contrat par sa filiale (1re défenderesse).*

« *Toujours à propos de la sentence rendue dans l'affaire 4131 en 1982, le Tribunal arbitral constate que la société X France a résilié le contrat dont elle n'était pas signataire dans les termes suivants : "... il est préférable de résilier le contrat qui nous lie actuellement... nos deux sociétés reprennent leur entière et complète liberté".*

« *Dans le télex par lequel il a résilié le contrat, M. A. parle bien de "sa société" et de "notre contrat", mais comme il écrit que sa société n'est pas d'accord de payer le prix indiqué par la demanderesse et que, comme déjà dit, c'est (1re défenderesse) et non (2e défenderesse) qui a payé les factures de condensat, on doit bien admettre qu'il a résilié le contrat pour le compte de la 1re défenderesse.*

« *A propos de la notion de "groupe de sociétés" et de la théorie de "la réalité économique" dont font état les cas de jurisprudence invoqués par la demanderesse, le Tribunal arbitral relève que la question de la portée de la clause d'arbitrage notamment lorsqu'une société négocie un contrat, ne le signe pas, mais confie cette tâche à une filiale, a été abordée par un colloque d'arbitres tenu à Paris le 5 octobre 1982 dans le cadre de l'institut du droit et des pratiques des affaires internationales (Revue de l'arbitrage, 1982, p. 495 à 497). Les arbitres se sont demandés si, en cas de litige entre cette filiale et son cocontractant, ils ont la possibilité de considérer que la clause lie aussi la société mère.*

A cet égard, on peut déjà s'étonner que la demanderesse invoque la notion du Groupe de Sociétés, alors même qu'elle n'a pas dirigé sa requête aux fins d'arbitrage contre la Société Mère.

« *S'il est vrai que certains arbitres se sont déclarés favorables à la notion de groupe, le colloque a relevé que le Tribunal fédéral suisse, dans l'arrêt Cartier du 10 octobre 1979 (arrêt non publié) s'est prononcé par une interprétation restrictive de la clause compromissoire, l'engagement d'un seul signataire n'étant pas suffisant pour attraire l'ensemble des sociétés du groupe devant un Tribunal arbitral.*

« *Dans l'affaire Cartier, un contrat avait été signé entre une société A demanderesse et deux sociétés B et B' représentées par une seule et même personne, l'actionnaire principal. Invoquant la clause d'arbitrage contenue dans ce contrat, la société A avait dirigé sa requête aux fins d'arbitrage contre le groupe de sociétés auquel appartenaient B et B' et auquel il était d'ailleurs fait allusion dans le contrat.*

« *Aussi bien le Tribunal arbitral saisi de cette affaire que l'instance cantonale de recours au sens de l'article 36 C.I.A. ont accédé à la demande.*

« *Le Tribunal fédéral suisse a pour sa part relevé qu'un groupe de sociétés n'a pas la personnalité juridique (commentaire Jolidon, ad. art. 4, n° 34, p. 121) et a retenu que seules les sociétés A et B pouvaient être liées par la clause d'arbitrage, mais qu'en revanche tel n'était pas le cas pour les autres sociétés du groupe, "nonobstant l'interpénétrabilité et l'imbrication des sociétés dominées par un seul homme" (Dutoit, Knoepfler, Lalive et Mercier, n° 75).*

« *Eu égard à la pratique suisse, manifestement plus rigoureuse que la pratique d'autres pays en matière d'interprétation de la clause compromissoire, le Tribunal arbitral ne saurait s'écarter en l'occurrence de l'article 6, alinéa 1 C.I.A. En effet, la seule hypothèse où il peut être dérogé à l'exigence impérative de la forme écrite de l'article 6, alinéa 1 C.I.A. est réalisée quand une partie accepte la compétence du Tribunal arbitral par actes concluants en entrant en matière sans réserve devant un Tribunal arbitral, alors même que les parties ne seraient pas liées par une clause compromissoire valable (Tribunal cantonal du canton de Vaud, arrêt non publié du 29-11-1977 dans la cause I. c/A., consid. 4).*

« *Or, il n'y a rien de tel en l'occurrence, aucune pièce n'étant notamment produite de laquelle on pourrait inférer même un commencement d'acte concluant tendant à accepter la qualité de partie au présent arbitrage.*

« *Etant donné que la 2ᵉ défenderesse a soulevé l'exception d'incompétence du Tribunal préalablement à toute défense sur le fond conformément à l'article 8, alinéa 2 C.I.A. et qu'il est constant qu'elle n'est pas liée à la demanderesse par une clause compromissoire passée en la forme écrite selon l'article 6, alinéa 1 C.I.A., le Tribunal arbitral ne saurait en aucune façon la considérer comme étant partie au présent arbitrage.* »

Dans la deuxième sentence intérimaire les arbitres étaient appelés à trancher une question de procédure, à savoir si un mémoire en réponse à une demande reconventionnelle avait été déposé dans le délai prévu du règlement C.C.I., et s'il avait été formé devant l'institution compétente.

Rappelons les dates principales :

— le 20 septembre 1982 la demanderesse adresse sa demande d'arbitrage à la C.C.I. ;

— le 6 mars 1983 la 1ʳᵉ défenderesse remet sa réponse et présente une demande reconventionnelle ;

— le 19 avril 1983 la Cour d'arbitrage constitue le Tribunal arbitral ;

— le 29 avril 1983 la Cour d'arbitrage transmet le dossier au tribunal arbitral ("saisine") ;

— le 26 septembre 1983 la demanderesse adresse au Tribunal arbitral une note en réponse aux demandes reconventionnelles ;

— le 23 février 1984 les arbitres et les parties signent l'acte de mission ;

— le 28 mai 1985 la 1ʳᵉ défenderesse prétend que la note du 26 septembre 1983 est irrecevable ;

— le 17 juin 1985 la demanderesse soumet une note en réponse au mémoire sur exception d'irrecevabilité.

Dans sa note du 26 septembre 1983 la demanderesse concluait à l'incompétence des arbitres pour les demandes reconventionnelles fondées sur d'autres contrats que celui d'avril 1979 et — en admettant la compétence des arbitres pour connaître des demandes reconventionnelles découlant du contrat d'avril 1979 — concluait à ce que le Tribunal rejette ces demandes, mal fondées selon la demanderesse.

La 1ʳᵉ défenderesse pour sa part considérait dans sa note du 28 mai 1985 qu'aucune question de compétence ne se posait, que les contestations de la demanderesse posaient en effet une question d'organisation de la procédure d'arbitrage, qu'il en résultait que la note en réponse du 26 septembre était irrecevable pour ne pas avoir été déposée dans le délai de trente jours prévu aux articles 5-2 et 4-1 du règlement C.C.I. et pour ne pas avoir été formée devant l'institution compétente, « la question de l'organisation de l'arbitrage relevant de la compétence exclusive de la Cour d'arbitrage ». La 1re défenderesse concluait, entre autres, que la demanderesse était forclose pour toutes les demandes exprimées dans sa note du 26 septembre 1983 et que le Tribunal ordonne la continuation de la procédure sur les trois contrats (et non seulement celui d'avril 1979).

Les arbitres déclarèrent recevable la note de la demanderesse du 26 septembre dans les termes suivants :

« *Pour ce qui est des délais, l'article 5-2 du règlement de la Cour d'arbitrage de la C.C.I. dispose que : "La partie demanderesse peut, dans un délai de trente jours à partir de la communication de cette demande reconventionnelle, présenter une note en réponse".*

« *Selon la 1re défenderesse, cette disposition doit être examinée en relation avec l'article 4-1, c'est-à-dire que les dispositions relatives à la réponse à la demande principale devraient s'appliquer également à la réponse à la demande reconventionnelle. En vertu de l'article 4-1 : « La partie défenderesse doit, dans un délai de trente jours au plus à dater du reçu de cette communication (une copie de la demande), se prononcer sur les propositions qui auront été formulées concernant le nombre des arbitres et leur choix en faisant éventuellement une désignation d'arbitre, de même qu'exposer ses moyens de défense et fournir ses pièces."*

« *La partie défenderesse pourra exceptionnellement demander au secrétariat un nouveau délai pour exposer ses moyens de défense et fournir ses pièces. Toutefois, la demande de nouveau délai devra contenir la réponse de la partie défenderesse aux propositions qui auront été formulées concernant le nombre des arbitres et leur choix, ainsi qu'éventuellement une désignation d'arbitre. A défaut, le secrétariat saisira la Cour qui procèdera à la mise en œuvre de l'arbitrage conformément au règlement. »*

« *Pour la 1re défenderesse, l'article 4-1 du règlement de la Cour d'arbitrage de la C.C.I. établit une différenciation entre les questions qui intéressent l'instance arbitrale proprement dite pour lesquelles le délai de réponse est « relativement flou, puisque prorogeable » et les questions qui concernent la mise en place et l'organisation de l'arbitrage qui doivent impérativement être résolues dans le délai de trente jours.*

« *Or, contrairement à la demanderesse qui affirme que, dans sa note en réponse, elle a incontestablement soulevé une exception d'incompétence à l'encontre d'une partie de la demande reconventionnelle présentée par la 1re défenderesse, celle-ci soutient qu'aucune question de compétence ne se pose en l'espèce, la contestation de la demanderesse concernant en fait une question d'organisation de l'arbitrage, au sujet de laquelle elle aurait dû par conséquent faire valoir ses arguments dans le délai de trente jours suivant le dépôt de la demande reconventionnelle de la 1re défenderesse.*

« *Pour sa part, la demanderesse conteste que l'article 5-2 du règlement de la Cour d'arbitrage de la C.C.I. doit être interprété en relation avec l'article 4-1. Selon elle, le raisonnement de la 1re défenderesse repose sur le postulat totalement faux que la note en réponse de la demanderesse viserait une question d'organisation de l'arbitrage.*

« *La demanderesse tire en outre argument du texte même des articles 4-1 et 5-2 du règlement. Alors que l'article 4-1 prévoit que le défendeur principal a l'obligation ("doit") de répondre à la demande d'arbitrage dans un délai de trente jours, l'article 5-2 offre une faculté ("peut") de répondre au défendeur reconventionnel.*

« *La demanderesse relève enfin qu'il n'existe pas de cas dans la jurisprudence en matière d'arbitrage sous l'égide de la C.C.I. où une note en réponse aurait été déclarée irrecevable motif pris que cette note aurait été déposée plus de trente jours après la communication de la demande reconventionnelle.*

« *Le Tribunal arbitral constate, comme l'a d'ailleurs relevé la demanderesse, que la 1ʳᵉ défenderesse s'est servi du contenu de la note en réponse pour démontrer qu'il y avait un lien entre l'article 4-1 et l'article 5-2 du règlement de la Cour d'arbitrage de la C.C.I. En effet, lorsqu'elle affirme que la note en réponse soulève une question d'organisation de l'arbitrage, la 1ʳᵉ défenderesse qualifie le contenu de la note.*

« *La demanderesse procède d'ailleurs de la même manière quand elle affirme que dans sa note elle a soulevé devant le Tribunal arbitral une exception d'incompétence à l'encontre d'une partie de la demande reconventionnelle.*

« *Au contraire des parties, le Tribunal arbitral considère que la question de la recevabilité, notion relevant du droit de la procédure, doit, par définition, être tranchée avant d'entrer en matière sur le fond dont l'examen relève du droit matériel.*

« *La recevabilité peut en effet se définir comme la qualité d'une écriture à l'encontre de laquelle il n'existe aucun moyen de forme ou d'incapacité mettant obstacle à l'examen du fond du droit. Des dispositions sont aménagées pour examiner les problèmes de recevabilité d'une écriture qui, par une solution d'entrée de cause, permettent d'éviter de procéder inutilement sur la cause au fond au cas où, pour des questions de pure forme, le juge ne pourrait pas se prononcer sur le fond.*

« *S'agissant en l'occurrence d'une note en réponse à une demande reconvention- nelle, sa recevabilité est réglementée par l'article 5-2 du règlement de la Cour d'arbi- trage de la C.C.I. C'est par conséquent sur la seule base de cet article que le Tribunal arbitral décidera si la note en réponse incriminée est recevable sous l'angle des délais.*

« *Dans l'analyse de l'article précité, le Tribunal arbitral a été sensible à l'argument invoqué par la demanderesse et tiré du texte même de l'article. L'article 5-2 prévoit un délai de trente jours, sans autre précision. Il est en cela manifestement moins contraignant que l'article 4-1 qui oblige le défendeur à répondre dans le délai de trente jours "au plus", est-il précisé.*

« *Le Tribunal arbitral considère dès lors que le délai de trente jours prévu par l'article 5-2 n'est pas un délai de déchéance comme celui de l'article 4-1 qui ne peut être renouvelé qu'exceptionnellement et sur demande par le secrétariat de la Cour d'arbitrage.*

« *Vu la formulation concise et relativement peu contraignante de l'article 5-2, il y a en effet tout lieu d'admettre que le délai de trente jours institué par cet article n'est pas impératif, mais qu'il est bien plutôt un simple délai d'ordre.*

« *Le Tribunal arbitral fait remarquer par ailleurs qu'il y a fort à croire que si la demanderesse avait demandé au secrétariat de la Cour d'arbitrage ou, une fois saisi du dossier, au Tribunal arbitral de céans, un nouveau délai pour présenter une note en réponse, comme l'article 4-1 le permet pour les réponses à la demande principale, il n'aurait guère pu lui être refusé.*

« *Il aurait été excessif de priver une partie du droit de réponse à cause de l'échéance d'un délai dont il n'est pas établi qu'il a un caractère impératif. Cette solution doit d'autant plus être admise qu'il n'en résultera aucun inconvénient pour l'examen du fond du litige.*

« *Pour ces raisons, le Tribunal arbitral considère comme recevable la note en réponse de la demanderesse au regard des délais. Il reste par conséquent à examiner encore si elle est recevable au regard de ce que la 1ʳᵉ défenderesse appelle les règles de compétence d'attribution fixées par le règlement de la Cour d'arbitrage de la C.C.I.*

« *Pour contester la recevabilité de la note en réponse sous cet aspect, la 1ʳᵉ défende- resse se fonde là encore sur la qualification qu'elle a donnée du contenu de la note.*

La note en réponse pose seulement un problème d'organisation de l'arbitrage, selon elle, et la Cour ayant pouvoir général d'organisation de l'instance arbitrale, la 1ʳᵉ défenderesse estime que le Tribunal arbitral ne peut en connaître, la question de l'étendue de la saisine des arbitres étant du ressort exclusif de la Cour d'arbitrage.

« *La demanderesse considère quant à elle que, le Tribunal arbitral ayant été constitué le 19 avril 1983, c'est à bon droit que le 26 septembre 1983, elle a adressé sa note en réponse à ce Tribunal et non au secrétariat de la Cour d'arbitrage.*

« *Le Tribunal arbitral, estimant encore une fois qu'il ne lui appartient pas de qualifier le contenu de la note en réponse à ce stade, ne peut que suivre sur ce point l'avis de la demanderesse et considérer que s'agissant d'un mémoire d'une partie, une note en réponse en l'occurrence, elle devait être adressée au Tribunal arbitral du moment que celui-ci avait été saisi du dossier de l'affaire, au sens de l'article 9 du règlement de la Cour d'arbitrage de la C.C.I., en date du 29 avril 1983.*

« *Eu égard aux développements qui précèdent, le Tribunal arbitral considère donc comme recevable la note en réponse de la demanderesse du 26 septembre 1983.* »

OBSERVATIONS. — I. — Selon l'article 13 (1) du règlement de la Cour d'arbitrage de la C.C.I., l'arbitre doit établir sur pièces ou en présence des parties, en l'état des derniers dires de celles-ci, un acte précisant sa mission.

L'Acte de mission apparaît comme l'une des caractéristiques de l'arbitrage de la C.C.I. On ne retrouve pas cette institution dans les règlements des centres d'arbitrage internationaux les plus connus (comme, pour n'en citer que quelques uns : l'American Arbitration Association, l'Institut d'Arbitrage de la Chambre de Commerce de Stockholm, ou la London Court of International Arbitration).

L'acte de mission a traditionnellement fait l'objet de critiques, en particulier lors de la révision de 1975 du règlement d'arbitrage de la C.C.I., où après de longues discussions, il a été décidé, à une légère majorité, d'en maintenir l'exigence (note interne C.C.I. du 10 mai 1982).

La pratique de l'arbitrage de la C.C.I. révèle de la part de certains arbitres des attitudes opposées en ce qui concerne l'acte de mission : certains arbitres estiment qu'il s'agit pour eux d'un instrument d'une utilité essentielle, d'autres le réduisent à sa plus simple expression.

Si dans le passé certains arbitres et certaines parties ont parfois pu recueillir l'accord (tacite) de la Cour d'arbitrage pour convenir de renoncer purement et simplement à l'établissement de l'acte de mission, la pratique actuelle de la Cour depuis quelques années est d'exiger l'établissement dans toutes les affaires de l'acte de mission conformément à l'article 13 du règlement. Aujourd'hui aucune affaire ne peut être examinée sur le fond sans qu'un acte de mission ait été communiqué à la Cour d'arbitrage ou approuvé par elle (article 13-2, alinéa 2).

La pratique de la Cour d'arbitrage révèle également de la part des parties des attitudes contrastées concernant l'effet de l'acte de mission. On peut craindre que des incertitudes et hésitations sont à l'origine des retards dans son établissement.

Un nombre important de parties ont peine à comprendre que l'acte de mission expose le point de vue respectif des parties, mais n'emporte aucun accord de l'une sur le contenu de l'exposé de l'autre. Ce malentendu explique que dans de nombreux cas la signature de l'acte de mission soit difficile à obtenir. Ces difficultés, d'ordre psychologique, sont accrues par les dispositions de l'article 16 du règlement interdisant la présentation de demandes nouvelles après la signature de l'acte de mission, car les parties craignent souvent, à juste titre, de se lier définitivement par la formulation de leurs demandes dans l'acte de mission.

L'acte de mission dans l'affaire ci-dessus présentée montre que l'incertitude des parties peut inclure d'autres sujets que la formulation des demandes, notamment les moyens de faits et de droit que pensent invoquer les parties. Les parties ont pris la peine de préciser dans l'acte de mission que l'arbitre doit se référer aux mémoires écrits et aux exposés oraux produits au cours de la procédure et non au seul acte de mission.

L'acte de mission dans une autre affaire, 5302, entre deux parties de nationalité américaine, écarte d'autres malentendus qui risqueraient de se produire, en stipulant que l'acte de mission n'empêche pas la présentation d'arguments ou l'introduction de preuves : « *These Terms of Reference are designed to enable the parties and the Arbitral Tribunal to focus on the issues in this arbitration ; they are not to be understood as foreclosing the making of arguments or introduction of evidence not expressly referred to herein* ».

(Traduction : « Cet acte de mission est rédigé dans le but de donner aux parties et au Tribunal arbitral la possibilité de se concentrer sur les questions de cet arbitrage ; l'acte de mission ne doit pas être interprété comme excluant toute future présentation d'arguments ou de preuves qui n'y est pas mentionnée »).

Ces deux exemples montrent qu'il serait souhaitable, lors d'une prochaine révision du règlement, de préciser que l'acte de mission ne limite aucunement le pouvoir des parties, après sa signature, de présenter des arguments ou des preuves. Aussi serait-il souhaitable qu'apparaissent plus clairement quels sont les différents composants d'un acte de mission.

L'acte de mission en premier lieu identifie les arbitres, les parties et leurs conseils [article 13-1 a), b) et e)] : il s'agit d'une constatation de pur fait qui habilite en même temps pour toute la durée de l'arbitrage les mandataires et représentants des parties.

L'acte de mission, établi par application de la clause compromissoire, peut en même temps constater l'accord des parties, adapter, modifier ou compléter les stipulations de celle-ci. C'est le cas pour le siège de l'arbitrage [article 13-1 f)]. Ce peut être le cas aussi si les parties tombent d'accord sur la loi de procédure, la loi de fond, les pouvoirs d'amiable compositeur ou la langue de l'arbitrage. Sur tous ces points les arbitres doivent constater explicitement ces accords qui ont pour effet de compléter ou modifier la clause compromissoire et à ce titre s'imposeront à eux. Ces accords des parties font donc corps avec la clause compromissoire et ont la même autorité.

L'acte de mission expose les prétentions des parties et en conséquence des points litigieux à résoudre [article 13-1 c) et d)].

Il s'agit ici de l'œuvre des arbitres qui ne requièrent pas juridiquement l'accord des parties, même si leur signature est évidemment souhaitable et est, en fait, exigée en principe par l'article 13-2.

Les arbitres sont ici tenus au respect des mémoires des parties qu'ils ne peuvent évidemment pas dénaturer.

Enfin, l'acte de mission contient souvent, au titre semble-t-il de l'article 13-1 h), des décisions diverses du Tribunal arbitral, portant par exemple sur la langue de l'arbitrage ou la procédure arbitrale qui pourraient fort bien faire l'objet d'une ordonnance séparée ou même être incluses, ou reprises dans la sentence au titre des articles 11 et 15-3. Dans ce domaine dans lequel les parties n'ont rien décidé, ou ne sont pas tombées d'accord, la décision appartient aux arbitres en vertu du règlement. L'accord des parties est indifférent.

II. — L'article 8-3 du règlement d'arbitrage C.C.I. dispose :

« Lorsqu'une des parties soulève un ou plusieurs moyens relatifs à l'existence ou à la validité de la convention d'arbitrage, la Cour, ayant constaté *prima facie* l'existence de cette convention, peut décider, sans préjuger la recevabilité ou le bien-fondé de ces moyens, que l'arbitrage aura lieu. Dans ce cas, il appartiendra à l'arbitre de prendre toute décision sur sa propre compétence. »

Cette fonction de la Cour d'arbitrage de décider sur l'existence *prima facie* d'une convention d'arbitrage apparaît comme une autre des caractéristiques de l'arbitrage C.C.I. La raison d'être de cet article doit être le désir général de trouver un moyen efficace pour débloquer des situations dans lesquelles le choix entre diverses juridictions risque de retarder la mise en route de la procédure, et par conséquent le règlement d'un litige. Le pouvoir de la Cour de déclencher un arbitrage est lourd de conséquences puisqu'elle place la partie qui met en question la validité ou l'existence de la clause arbitrale devant un problème aussi bien pratique que juridique. Doit-elle participer à un arbitrage, dont elle refuse l'existence, pour défendre sa thèse et par là-même engager des frais importants qui ont peu de chances d'être remboursés ? Si la partie accepte d'y entrer, risque-t-elle à un moment donné d'être considérée comme partie prenante à la procédure et d'avoir accepté, par son comportement, de participer à l'arbitrage ? Il paraît utile de se poser ces questions puisque ce moyen d'irrecevabilité est souvent invoqué devant la Cour d'arbitrage de la C.C.I., et puisque la Cour la rejette dans une majorité des cas, permettant ainsi aux arbitres de décider de leur propre compétence et forçant les parties à se présenter devant les arbitres.

En ce qui concerne le risque d'être censé avoir accepté l'arbitrage que court une partie en s'engageant dans la procédure arbitrale pour exprimer ses arguments d'irrecevabilité, la décision de la Cour d'appel de Paris (Paris, 12 juill. 1984) dans l'affaire dite « des Pyramides » peut soulager les esprits hésitants *(Rev. Arbitrage* 1986, p. 75).

Il apparaît d'après cette décision de la Cour d'appel qu'une partie peut non seulement présenter ses arguments à l'appui de la non-existence d'une convention d'arbitrage *in limine litis,* mais également signer l'acte de mission de l'arbitre et ensuite plaider l'affaire sur le fond, sans rique d'être censée avoir renoncé à sa position. La décision admet qu'une partie qui conteste la compétence de l'arbitre a un intérêt légitime à s'engager sur le fond afin de tempérer les dommages et intérêts auxquels elle risquerait d'être condamnée si elle n'était pas présente. Donc, dans le cas où la compétence arbitrale est contestée, la signature d'un acte de mission ne constitue pas une convention d'arbitrage, contrairement au cas où ce moyen d'irrecevabilité n'est pas invoqué (voir aussi commentaires sur l'affaire des Pyramides dans *International Construction Law Review,* January 1985, p. 180).

III. — On sait que la tendance des arbitres internationaux est d'écarter le système de conflit de lois du lieu de l'arbitrage pour déterminer le droit applicable au fond du litige, sauf peut-être en Suisse (voir commentaire sur l'affaire n° 4434 dans *Clunet* 1983, p. 893).

En est-il de même quand il s'agit de déterminer le droit applicable pour qualifier la portée de la convention d'arbitrage en l'absence d'une indication des parties sur ce point ? Il est acquis, et les arbitres le constatent dans l'affaire en question, que la clause compromissoire peut être soumise à une loi différente de la loi qui régit le contrat principal ; mais comment trouver cette loi ?

En l'espèce le Tribunal arbitral n'a pas retenu la solution choisie par les trois arbitres siégeant à Paris dans l'affaire Dow Chemical (*Clunet* 1983, p. 899 ; *Rev. arbitrage* 1984, p. 98, où est publié la décision de la Cour d'appel de Paris confirmant la sentence arbitrale) qui se sont considérés libres de fonder la validité de la convention d'arbitrage sur la seule volonté des parties sans recourir à l'application d'une loi de conflit étatique. La solution dans l'affaire Dow Chemical peut être considérée comme une manifestation d'un mouvement vers plus de détachement en faveur des principes généraux du droit par rapport aux droits nationaux et, comme la preuve du pouvoir de l'arbitre de se dégager des voies nouvelles en matière de conflit de loi (*cf.* également la sentence rendue dans l'affaire n° 4381 supra, p. 1103).

Il ne faut pas penser que les arbitres dans le cas d'espèce ont été dépourvus d'alternatives à la *lex fori* et ont été obligés d'accepter la loi suisse pour qualifier la clause compromissoire. Ils auraient pu appliquer les principes généraux du droit et les usages du commerce international pour écarter une loi étatique et chercher la volonté commune des parties et leur comportement avant, pendant et après l'exécution des contrats pour constater ou rejeter l'existence d'une clause arbitrale.

Ne doit-on pas interpréter leur choix de la *lex fori* comme l'exercice de leur libre choix plutôt que l'application d'une règle obligatoire en Suisse, même si l'expression des arbitres est très prudente (« *le Tribunal arbitral est d'avis que la qualification... ne peut être faite qu'en application de la* lex fori... ») ?

Il n'est pas exclu que les arbitres ont fait leur choix en prévoyant les effets sur la convention du choix de tel ou tel droit national et en sachant que le Concordat impose impérativement que la clause arbitrale soit écrite. Qualifier la convention arbitrale non-écrite comme existant selon un droit non-suisse risquerait de produire un conflit avec le Concordat dans le cas où la sentence serait attaquée en nullité pour absence de convention arbitrale en bonne et due forme. Quoi qu'il en soit, en se référant à la *lex fori* dans un cas où les parties ont elles-mêmes fixé le lieu d'arbitrage, la décision des arbitres doit mieux correspondre à l'attente des parties qui — on peut le présumer — ont choisi le lieu d'arbitrage en Suisse en connaissance des pratiques propres aux arbitres qui y siègent.

IV. — Tout comme dans l'affaire Dow Chemical, les arbitres examinent dans la présente affaire non seulement le statut juridique de chacune des défenderesses, mais aussi le comportement des deux sociétés pour voir si la condition de forme écrite exigée par le Concordat est remplie. Eu égard à la condition posée dans l'article 6-1 du Concordat, à savoir que la convention d'arbitrage doit être passée en la forme écrite, la seule volonté des parties n'a pas pu jouer le même rôle important que dans l'affaire Dow Chemical. Après avoir constaté que la 2ᵉ défenderesse n'a jamais ratifié le contrat, montré ou exprimé une volonté de le faire, la condition de forme écrite ne peut guère aboutir à un autre résultat que celui trouvé en l'espèce. La tâche des arbitres aurait été plus difficile en l'absence toujours d'une signature de la 2ᵉ défenderesse mais en présence de faits démontrant de la part de la 2ᵉ défenderesse une volonté d'exécuter et/ou une participation dans l'exécution du contrat signé par la société mère. Le rapprochement des deux sociétés sous l'influence de la théorie de « la réalité économique du groupe » ou des « liens institutionnels » se feraient dans tel cas peut-être plus facilement. Ne doit-on pas constater que le choix du lieu d'arbitrage ne manque toujours pas d'intérêt pour déterminer la portée de la clause compromissoire. Dans ce contexte la Suisse offre, grâce à l'exigence dans son Concordat de la forme écrite, un avantage de prévisibilité.

V. — Il est rare — d'après ce qu'on peut constater en étudiant les dossiers d'arbitrage C.C.I. — que les parties soulèvent des questions concernant le délai dans lequel elles doivent soumettre une demande reconventionnelle et une note en réponse.

Certaines conditions nécessaires à la mise en route d'une affaire litigieuse dans les plus brefs délais sont précisées à l'article 4 du règlement C.C.I. Une des premières décisions à prendre par la Cour d'arbitrage est celle de constituer le Tribunal arbitral. Pour ce faire, la Cour d'arbitrage doit connaître les moyens de défense de la défenderesse parce qu'ils peuvent être décisifs pour déterminer les qualités et l'experience de l'arbitre que va nommer la Cour. C'est pourquoi c'est seulement exceptionnellemei : que le secrétariat de la Cour prolonge un délai pour répondre à la requête d'arbitrage. La Cour a évidemment pour les mêmes raisons intérêt à connaître des demandes reconventionnelles le plus vite possible, et avant de constituer le Tribunal arbitral. La situation est différente une fois que les arbitres ont été nommés. C'est alors à eux d'organiser l'échange de mémoires entre les parties en assurant une bonne administration et en tenant compte des délais prescrits pour rédiger l'acte de mission et rendre la sentence. Dans cette perspective le délai de l'article 5-2 est, comme l'ont trouvé les arbitres en l'espèce, un simple délai d'ordre.

Au contraire des article 4-1 et 5-1, qui précisent que la partie doit saisir le secrétariat de la Cour, l'article 5-2 n'indique rien quant à qui — le secrétariat ou les arbitres — la partie doit adresser sa note en réponse. N'est-ce pas là encore une indication que l'article 5-2 n'exprime qu'une recommandation ?

Finalement on pourrait discuter dans ce contexte de l'effet des articles 13 et 16 sur le problème posé par la 1re défenderesse. L'article 16 dispose que « les parties peuvent formuler devant l'arbitre de nouvelles demandes, *reconventionnelles ou non,* à condition que ces demandes restent dans les limites fixées par l'acte de mission ou qu'elles fassent l'objet d'un addendum... signé par les parties... ». L'article 13 précise que l'acte de mission sera établi « en l'état des derniers dires » des parties. Dans la pratique de l'arbitrage C.C.I. ces dispositions sont généralement ainsi comprises, qu'elles offrent plusieurs occasions aux parties de préciser leurs demandes reconventionnelles et réponses là-dessus :

— simultanément avec la réponse à la requête, une demande reconventionnelle peut être formulée ;

— la demanderesse dispose d'un délai d'au moins 30 jours pour y répondre ;

— devant les arbitres, lors de la rédaction de l'acte de mission, les parties peuvent modifier leurs demandes et prises de position. Avec la signature de l'acte de mission, les parties se lient par la formulation de leurs demandes dans cet acte.

Après la signature de l'acte de mission, des demandes principales et/ou reconventionnelles peuvent toujours être introduites, même contre la volonté d'une partie, sous la seule condition de rester dans les limites fixées par l'acte de mission. Au-delà de ces limites, il faut l'accord de l'autre partie et du Tribunal arbitral.

On constate qu'il n'existe aucune disposition, ni même de recommandation, dans le règlement d'arbitrage, en ce qui concerne le délai dans lequel une note doit être présentée en réponse à une demande reconventionnelle formulée lors de l'établissement de l'acte de mission ou après. C'est donc la tâche des arbitres d'en fixer un.

S. J.

I. — **Droit applicable.** — Recherche de la règle de conflit appropriée. — Application cumulative des systèmes de conflits intéressés au litige (non).

II. — **Droit applicable.** — Agence commerciale. — Principes généraux du droit international privé. — Droit du lieu de conclusion (non). —

Droit du lieu d'exécution. — Droit du lieu de résidence du débiteur de la prestation caractéristique.

III. — Droit applicable. — Application du droit validant le contrat. — Attente légitime des parties.

IV. — Clause compromissoire. — Clause de prorogation de for (subsidiaire).

Sentence rendue dans l'affaire n° 4996 en 1985.

Le Tribunal arbitral, siégeant à Lausanne, était appelé à se prononcer sur les conséquences de la rupture d'un contrat d'agence liant une société italienne, défenderesse, à son agent en France, demanderesse. Le contrat qui contenait une clause d'arbitrage de la C.C.I. prévoyait également la compétence des tribunaux du lieu du siège social de la société italienne à titre subsidiaire.

Les parties n'ayant pas prévu le droit applicable au contrat, il appartenait au Tribunal arbitral de le déterminer. Il le fit dans les termes suivants :

— *« Comme ledit contrat ne contient pas de disposition sur le droit applicable, il faut se référer à l'article 13, alinéa 3, du règlement de la Cour d'arbitrage de la C.C.I. ainsi libellé : "Les parties sont libres de déterminer le droit que l'arbitre devra appliquer au fond du litige. A défaut d'indication par les parties du droit applicable, l'arbitre appliquera la loi désignée par la règle de conflit qu'il jugera appropriée en l'espèce".*

— *« Or, en l'occurrence, il s'agit d'un contrat rédigé et conclu en Italie, en langue italienne et contenant, à titre subsidiaire par rapport à la clause arbitrale de l'article 19, une clause de prorogation de for en faveur des tribunaux italiens (art. 21). Toutefois, ce contrat a été exécuté entièrement en France. Dans ces conditions, il faut examiner si c'est la règle de conflit italienne ou française qui apparaît la plus appropriée dans le cas présent.*

« Face aux arguments existant tant en faveur de l'application du droit international privé italien que du droit international privé français, une façon de résoudre le problème consiste à se demander si l'application cumulative du droit international privé italien et français donnerait compétence en l'espèce à une loi interne unique, qui serait alors retenue (cf. à ce sujet, Y. Derains, "L'application cumulative par l'arbitre des systèmes de conflits de lois intéressés au litige. A la lumière de l'expérience de la Cour d'arbitrage de la C.C.I." : Rev. Arbitrage 1972, p. 99 s.).

— *« En Italie, selon l'article 25 de la loi d'introduction au Code civil italien, les obligations nées d'un contrat sont régies par la loi nationale des contractants si elle leur est commune ; sinon par la loi du lieu de conclusion du contrat. En tout état de cause on tiendra compte d'une volonté contraire des parties. Ainsi donc, en l'occurrence, c'est le droit interne italien qui devrait s'appliquer au contrat litigieux. Dans la mesure où l'on qualifie ce dernier, en droit italien, de contrat d'agence, en ce qui concerne l'activité exercée par l'agent français comme représentant exclusif de la société italienne, on soulignera que, selon la doctrine (cf. R. Baldi, Il contratto di agenzia, 2ᵉ éd. Milan 1977, Giuffré, p. 312 s.) et la jurisprudence italienne (cf. Cour d'appel de Turin, 16 oct. 1974 : Mass. giur. lav. 1975, p. 237) le contrat d'agence est également soumis aux circonstances de rattachement prévues par l'article 25 précité. Il importe de remarquer qu'en droit international privé italien — contrairement au droit international privé français par exemple — le fait que les parties ont soumis par clause compromissoire la solution d'un litige éventuel aux juges d'un pays donné ne constitue pas un indice permettant de déduire la soumission*

293

*du litige à la loi interne de ce même pays (*cf. *Cour de cassation 27 déc. 1948 :* Giur. it. *1950 I, 1, 121 et E.* Vitta, Diritto internazionale privato, *vol. III, 1975, Turin, p. 260).*

— « En France, *on notera que, dans un arrêt du 24 janvier 1978 (*Rev. crit. dr. int. pr. *1978, 689), la Cour de cassation n'a pas sanctionné — mais n'a pas approuvé explicitement non plus — le Tribunal de commerce de la Seine d'avoir appliqué le droit français à une convention de représentation commerciale à exécuter en Allemagne, mais conclue à Paris, rédigée en langue française et contenant une clause attributive de compétence au Tribunal de commerce de la Seine, cette clause n'étant que subsidiaire par rapport à une clause compromissoire en faveur de la Cour d'arbitrage de la C.C.I. ».*

« *A suivre cet arrêt, il faudrait donc admettre qu'en l'occurrence le droit international privé français renvoie au droit interne italien. On ne saurait nier toutefois, ainsi que le souligne le commentateur de cette décision, que "la doctrine et la jurisprudence (françaises) sont en effet unanimes pour soumettre le mandat à la loi du lieu où doivent être exécutés les actes à accomplir par le mandataire ou, de façon plus précise, à la loi qui régira ces actes. C'est en effet ainsi que se localise le mieux la prestation caractéristique du contrat, et cette loi aura encore le plus souvent l'avantage d'être aussi celle régissant les rapports avec les tiers (Rouen, 31 mai 1950 :* Clunet *1950, p. 603 ;* Paris, 21 mai 1957 ; Clunet *1958, p. 128, note Franceskakis ; Batiffol, Les conflits de lois en matière de contrats, n°s 304 à 320 ; Batiffol et Dayant, Rép. Dalloz dr. int. v^o Mandat n° 2 ; Loussouarn et Bredin, Droit du commerce international, n° 641 ; P. Mayer, Droit international privé, n° 695)" (*Rev. crit. dr. int. pr. *1978, p. 694).*

« *Certes, la doctrine et la jurisprudence françaises ont retenu fréquemment, avec d'autres éléments, la clause attributive de juridiction comme un indice de la volonté des parties de se soumettre au droit du pays dont les tribunaux ont été déclarés compétents (*cf. *Batiffol/Lagarde, droit international privé, t. II, 7e éd. 1983, Paris, n° 589). Mais il faut remarquer qu'en l'espèce, comme dans l'affaire précitée jugée par la Cour de cassation, cet indice perd de sa valeur, puisque, dans la convention du 1er septembre 1981, la clause attributive de juridiction aux tribunaux italiens (art. 21) n'intervient qu'à titre subsidiaire après la clause compromissoire en faveur de la C.C.I. (art. 19).*

« *A la lumière de ce qui précède, on concluera que, dans le cas présent, le droit international privé français soumet le contrat litigieux à la loi du pays où le contrat doit être exécuté, à savoir au droit français.*

« *Ainsi donc l'application du droit international privé italien d'une part et du droit international privé français de l'autre ne conduit pas à l'application d'une loi interne unique. Quelle règle de conflit de lois convient-il, dans ces conditions de considérer la plus appropriée en l'espèce ? »*

— « *Parmi les indices plaidant en faveur du rattachement au droit international privé italien figurent le lieu de conclusion du contrat en Italie, la rédaction du contrat en italien et en Italie ainsi que la clause (subsidiaire) de prorogation de for mais dont le droit international privé italien ne fait pas un indice de la volonté des parties quant au droit applicable. Ces trois derniers éléments n'apparaissent pas d'un grand poids de telle sorte que finalement seul le lieu de conclusion du contrat en Italie constitue un indice sérieux de rattachement au droit international privé italien. Or, au lieu de conclusion en Italie s'oppose le lieu d'exécution du contrat en France.*

« *En droit international privé comparé, la loi du lieu d'exécution du contrat (éventuellement sous la forme de la loi du domicile ou de la résidence habituelle du débiteur de la prestation caractéristique) l'emporte de plus en plus sur la loi du lieu de conclusion du contrat (*cf. *Batiffol/Lagarde, op. cit. t. II, n°s 580 s.). De même, sur le plan conventionnel, la convention de La Haye, du 15 juin 1955 sur la loi* *applicable aux ventes à caractère international d'objets mobiliers corporels soumet, à défaut de loi désignée par les parties, une telle vente à la loi interne du pays où le vendeur à sa résidence habituelle au moment de la réception de la commande (art. 3). La convention de La Haye, du 14 mars 1978 sur la loi applicable aux contrats d'intermédiaires et à la représentation retient, pour les relations entre représenté et intermédiaire, à défaut de loi choisie par les parties, la loi de l'Etat dans lequel l'intermédiaire a son établissement professionnel (art. 6). De même la convention de Rome, du 29 juin 1980, sur la loi applicable aux obligations contractuelles soumet, à défaut de choix exprès, le contrat à la loi du pays avec lequel il présente les liens les plus étroits, étant admis que "le contrat présente les liens les plus étroits avec le pays où la partie qui doit fournir la prestation caractéristique a, au moment de la conclusion du contrat, sa résidence habituelle ou son établissement principal" (art. 4, § 2).*

« *En l'espèce, non seulement le lieu d'exécution du contrat se trouve en France, mais encore le domicile du débiteur de la prestation caractéristique (dans sa partie relative à l'activité d'agent de l'agent français) est localisé en France.*

« *En conclusion, on admettra que la règle de conflit la plus appropriée en l'espèce est celle qui rattache le contrat du 1ᵉʳ septembre 1981 à la loi du lieu d'exécution du contrat et de la résidence habituelle du débiteur de la prestation caractéristique, à savoir au droit français. On n'omettra pas toutefois de se demander si le droit interne italien conduirait en l'occurrence à une autre solution que le droit français quant au fond* ».

Par ailleurs, ayant relevé qu'en droit italien, le contrat d'agence doit être inscrit à peine de nullité, le Tribunal arbitral ajouta :

« *Si l'on appliquait le droit italien au contrat litigieux, on pourrait se demander comment exiger d'un agent français exerçant son activité en France et résidant en France qu'il se fasse immatriculer dans le registre italien, à supposer que cela soit possible. On risquerait alors de soumettre le contrat litigieux à un droit qui le déclarerait nécessairement nul pour violation d'une disposition vraisemblablement impossible à satisfaire. Il y a là une raison supplémentaire et importante d'appliquer en l'espèce le droit français à ce contrat.* »

OBSERVATIONS. I. — La sentence rendue dans l'affaire n° 4381 (*supra*, p. 1103) rappelle que l'arbitre peut déterminer le droit applicable sans se prononcer préalablement sur le droit international privé applicable. On a noté que c'était là une approche caractéristique d'une tendance importante des arbitres du commerce international. La sentence ici rapportée se rattache à une autre tendance qui préfère déterminer le droit applicable par l'intermédiaire d'un des systèmes de conflit de lois des pays intéressés au litige. La sentence rendue en 1983 dans l'affaire n° 4434 en constituait un bon exemple (*Clunet* 1983, 893). L'arbitre unique, siégeant à Lausanne également, s'exprimait ainsi : « Les règles de droit international privé qui peuvent entrer en ligne de compte sont celles du droit français et du droit belge, étant donné que l'objet ne présente des liens de rattachement qu'avec ces deux ordres juridiques, et éventuellement celles en vigueur dans le pays du siège de l'arbitrage. En ce qui concerne ces dernières, il est maintenant admis par une grande partie de la doctrine et de la jurisprudence arbitrale que l'arbitre n'a pas à prendre en considération les règles de conflit de lois d'un ordre juridique, qui n'a d'autre lien avec le litige que la localisation sur son territoire de l'arbitrage ». Cependant, avant de choisir entre le droit international privé des pays de l'une et l'autre des parties, à savoir le droit international privé français et le droit international privé italien, le Tribunal arbitral recherche si ces systèmes n'aboutissent pas l'un et l'autre à l'application d'un seul et même droit. Pour ce faire, il invoque un procédé de détermination du droit applicable auquel les arbitres recourent fréquemment : l'application cumulative des systèmes de conflit de lois intéressés au litige (*cf.* en plus de la référence citée par le Tribunal arbitral P. Lalive, « Les règles de conflit de lois en Suisse » ; *Rev. Arbitrage* 1976, 155, qui a pu constater que ce procédé était l'un des trois les plus souvent utilisés dans la jurisprudence arbitrale).

Cependant, le Tribunal arbitral constate que l'application du droit international privé italien d'une part et du droit international privé français de l'autre ne conduira pas à l'application d'un droit interne unique. Ainsi se confirme, aux yeux des arbitres, la nécessité de choisir, entre la règle de conflit française et la règle de conflit italienne, celle qui est la plus appropriée en l'espèce.

Cette démarche mérite d'être soulignée car il est tout à fait exceptionnel que des arbitres utilisent le procédé d'application cumulative des règles de conflit de lois intéressées au litige lorsque celui-ci aboutit à un échec. En effet, le procédé d'application cumulatative vise à établir que le droit déclaré par l'arbitre comme approprié pour régir les relations juridiques des parties est reconnu comme compétent par la communauté de systèmes juridiques à laquelle appartiennent celles-ci. C'est donc essentiellement une justification a posteriori du caractère approprié d'un droit interne. Au contraire, dans la sentence ici rapportée, le procédé n'a d'autre objet que d'expliquer qu'il est indispensable de choisir la règle de conflit de lois appropriée parmi celles qui sont intéressées au litige, c'est-à-dire celles des Etats où les parties ont leur résidence habituelle. Certains s'étonneront sans doute d'une telle approche, en relevant que le texte de l'article 13 (3) du règlement d'arbitrage de la C.C.I. qui invite l'arbitre à appliquer « la loi désignée par la règle de conflits qu'il jugera appropriée en l'espèce » dispensait le Tribunal arbitral de l'obligation d'établir qu'il ne pouvait se passer de rechercher la règle de conflit appropriée. On y verra surtout une nouvelle confirmation du caractère inadapté de ce texte (*cf.* les observations sous la sentence rendue dans l'affaire n° 4381, p. 1103) dont la lettre paraît obliger les arbitres à démontrer que la règle de conflit qu'ils appliquent est appropriée, alors qu'en réalité, c'est le caractère approprié de l'application au fond du litige d'un droit plutôt qu'un autre qui est en cause. Heureusement, l'examen de la jurisprudence arbitrale montre que nombreux sont les arbitres qui ont donné à cet article l'interprétation que son esprit imposait.

II. — La démarche du Tribunal arbitral se présente tout d'abord comme une évaluation des indices de rattachement prévalant en droit international privé italien et en droit international privé français à la lumière des principes généraux du droit international privé, tels que les expriment les conventions internationales les plus récentes. Mais cette analyse n'est pas poursuivie jusqu'au bout et les arbitres ne décident pas d'appliquer le droit international privé français, ou le droit international privé italien. Ils déclarent que « *la règle de conflit la plus appropriée en l'espèce est celle qui rattache le contrat... à la loi du lieu d'exécution du contrat et de la résidence habituelle du débiteur de la prestation caractéristique, à savoir le droit français* ».

Or, cette règle de conflit n'est pas exactement la règle de conflit française, même s'il est vrai que la recherche de la localisation du contrat d'agence commerciale aboutit le plus souvent à cette solution, que commande, également, la convention de Rome du 19 juin 1980.

C'est qu'au-delà d'une analyse un peu artificielle, les arbitres évaluent en réalité divers indices de rattachement pour décider de celui ou de ceux qui s'imposent compte tenu des principes généraux du droit international privé. A cet égard, l'affirmation de la supériorité du lieu d'exécution sur le lieu de conclusion permet à nouveau de rapprocher la sentence ici rapportée de celle précitée, rendue dans l'affaire n° 4434. L'arbitre s'y exprimait en effet ainsi : « Les deux principaux indices objectifs du rattachement d'un contrat sont la loi d'exécution et la loi de conclusion de celui-ci. Le premier critère a toutefois une valeur prépondérante par rapport au second, qui a souvent un caractère fortuit ».

On notera enfin l'accumulation des justifications recherchées par les arbitres pour motiver leur décision d'appliquer le droit français. En effet, si le droit français est appliqué en tant que droit du lieu d'exécution du contrat, c'est aussi en tant que droit du lieu de résidence du débiteur de la prestation caractéristique, ce qui est une référence à la convention de Rome du 19 juin 1980 (art. 4, § 2). Mais comme si ceci ne suffisait pas, le Tribunal arbitral évoque également la convention de La Haye du 14 mars 1978, ce qui est compréhensible compte tenu de la nature du contrat, et la convention de La Haye du 15 juin 1955, ce qui l'est moins. Il semble bien qu'en réalité les arbitres s'efforcent de démontrer que l'application du droit français, plus que du droit international privé français, rencontre une sorte de consensus international, dont le droit international privé italien, il est vrai, est exclu et qu'à ce titre, cette application est appropriée.

III. — Le Tribunal arbitral pousse le souci de justification si loin qu'il ajoute que l'application du droit italien au contrat litigieux aurait pour conséquence la nullité de ce dernier. Il estime qu'« il y a là une raison supplémentaire et importante d'appliquer en l'espèce le droit français à ce contrat ». L'application par les arbitres du droit validant le contrat plutôt que de celui qui l'annule est fréquent (*cf.* par exemple, la sentence rendue dans l'affaire n° 4145 en 1984 : *Clunet* 1985, p. 985). On peut même penser que les arbitres, qui s'attachent à répondre à l'attente légitime des parties ne devraient jamais appliquer à un contrat un droit qui l'annule, à moins évidemment que les parties aient expressément choisi de soumettre leur contrat à ce droit (*cf.* sur ce point, Y. Derains, « L'ordre public et le droit applicable au fond du litige dans l'arbitrage international » : *Rev. Arbitrage* 1986, p. 375).

Cependant, force est de remarquer qu'en l'espèce, il n'était pas du tout établi que le droit italien aurait conduit à l'annulation du contrat. En effet, ainsi que l'a relevé une sentence arbitrale rendue dans l'affaire n° 4667 en 1985 :

« La Cour de cassation italienne (Cass. Sez. Lav. 21 janv. 1984, n° 526) a décidé que l'inscription prévue à l'article 3 de la loi du 12 mars 1968 ne s'applique qu'aux seuls agents de commerce résidant sur le territoire de l'Etat italien et n'est pas applicable à ceux qui, même citoyens italiens, agissent à l'étranger ; qu'à fortiori la loi du 12 mars 1968 ne saurait être applicable à un agent non italien résidant hors d'Italie ».

IV. — Le contrat à l'origine du litige soumis aux arbitres comprenait, à côté d'une convention d'arbitrage, une clause d'attribution de compétence aux tribunaux du siège de la société italienne, applicable à titre subsidiaire. Cette dualité de dispositions relatives à la solution des litiges n'est malheureusement pas tout à fait exceptionnelle. Elle est de nature à créer des difficultés d'interprétation car on peut toujours s'interroger sur les rôles respectifs des deux clauses, le caractère subsidiaire de l'un par rapport à l'autre n'étant pas nécessairement évident. De plus sa signification n'est pas très claire. Sauf stipulation des parties permettant une autre interprétation, on considère généralement que ces clauses offrent une option au demandeur qui, selon qu'il choisit l'arbitrage ou le recours aux tribunaux, lie le défendeur par sa décision. Il en va de même des conventions d'arbitrage qui prévoient deux lieux d'arbitrage : « Paris ou Genève », « Londres ou Zurich ». Là encore le choix du demandeur doit être considéré comme déterminant. Mais il n'en reste pas moins que des dispositions contractuelles de ce type sont à proscrire.

Y. D.

I. — Règlement de la C.C.I., articles 11, 17, 21. — Règles de procédure autres que celles du lieu de l'arbitrage. — Sentence partielle. — Sentence d'accord parties.

II. — Lex Mercatoria. — Principes généraux du droit. — Référence à la *lex mercatoria* pour combler des lacunes d'un droit national. — Ordre public international.

Sentence partielle rendue en 1984 dans l'affaire 4761.

Dans un litige de construction opposant une partie italienne à une partie libyenne, l'Acte de Mission des arbitres disposait en ce qui concerne droit et procédure applicables que le Tribunal devait « statuer par une sentence partielle sur le droit applicable au fond du litige, que la procédure serait régie par le règlement de la Cour d'arbitrage de la C.C.I., ainsi que par les décisions que le Tribunal arbitral pourrait prendre, de cas en cas, en s'inspirant de la loi de procédure civile genevoise et que le droit au fond du litige devra être prouvé par les parties comme un fait, à moins qu'il ne soit connu des arbitres. »

L'Acte de Mission était signé par les deux parties ainsi que par les trois arbitres (président : suisse, co-arbitres : français, proposé par la demanderesse italienne et italien, proposé par la défenderesse libyenne). Le lieu de l'arbitrage était Paris.

Lors d'une première audience du Tribunal arbitral les parties se mettent d'accord sur le droit applicable. Dans une sentence partielle d'accord parties les arbitres décident :

« *1° Le droit libyen est en principe applicable à tous les aspects du litige, en ce qu'il n'est pas contraire à l'ordre public international et aux principes de la bonne foi.*

2° Dans l'hypothèse où le droit libyen n'aurait pas été prouvé conformément à l'article 8 de l'acte de mission, le Tribunal arbitral appliquera la lex mercatoria, *soit les principes généraux du droit.*

3° La lex mercatoria *s'appliquera également si le droit libyen tel qu'il a été établi pour l'une ou l'autre des parties était manifestement lacunaire ou incomplet sur un ou plusieurs aspects du litige. »*

OBSERVATIONS. — I. — La sentence ici présentée est d'un type peu fréquent dans les arbitrages C.C.I. Bien que le règlement de la C.C.I. connaisse des sentences d'accord parties (voir article 17) et des sentences partielles dont le règlement fait mention dans son article 21 sans pour autant en fixer des règles plus précises, il est rare de voir une combinaison des deux types de sentences comme celle-ci, libellée « sentence partielle d'accord parties ».

Deuxièmement il faut noter l'accord des parties, établi déjà dans l'acte de mission, pour autoriser les arbitres à prendre subsidiairement des décisions d'ordre procédural en s'inspirant de la loi de procédure civile genevoise, bien que le lieu d'arbitrage fût fixé à Paris. Notons que ni le règlement de la C.C.I. ni le nouveau Code de procédure civile français ne l'empêchent, l'article 11 du règlement C.C.I. envisageant une détermination des règles de procédure sans nécessité de se référer à une loi interne de procédure et l'article 1494 du N.C.P.C. laissant libre choix aux parties de soumettre l'arbitrage à la loi de procédure qu'elles déterminent.

II. — En limitant le champ d'application d'un droit national, en l'espèce libyen, aux aspects qui ne soient pas contraires à « l'ordre public international » et aux principes de la bonne foi, les parties confirment la tendance qu'on observe depuis un certain temps, notamment de ne pas limiter le droit applicable à celui d'un seul système national, mais de prendre en compte d'autres règles de nature impérative ou suprême, dont le non-respect risquerait de mettre en danger la possibilité d'obtenir la reconnaissance ou l'exécution de la sentence qui doit suivre. Notons que les parties se réfèrent à un « ordre public international » sans pour autant préciser s'il s'agit d'un ordre public international d'un pays individuel ou de celui de plusieurs pays. Dans la dernière hypothèse l'ordre public international pourrait ne pas être identique dans divers pays et serait à préciser par une instance judiciaire nationale au moment où la reconnaissance et/ou l'exécution de la sentence sera demandée dans un pays spécifique.

La deuxième limitation à l'application du droit libyen — respect des principes de la bonne foi — peut paraître moins évidente. On pourrait être tenté de penser que c'est extraordinairement rare de trouver un droit national qui ne reconnaîtrait pas les principes de la bonne foi, principe fondamental d'une majorité — sinon tous — de systèmes de droit et que, par conséquent, le risque de conflit entre un droit national et les principes de la bonne foi soit extrêmement réduit.

Par contre des lacunes peuvent exister dans un droit national et celui-ci peut être incomplet. C'est le cas de figure envisagé par les parties dans le troisième alinéa de la sentence d'accord parties où les parties décident que dans un tel cas les arbitres devront appliquer la *lex mercatoria*.

Il n'est nullement universellement admis que la *lex mercatoria* soit du droit positif. La Cour d'appel de Vienne l'a qualifié de « droit mondial d'une validité incertaine » (affaire Norsolor, voir Goldman : *Rev. Arbitrage* 1983, p. 383). La Cour de cassation d'Italie a affirmé (Goldman, *op. cit.*, p. 404) que la *lex mercatoria* est un ensemble de règles de droit — complet ou non, disparate ou non — qui relève d'un ordre juridique spécifique propre. Les parties semblent prendre position sur le problème de savoir si la *lex mercatoria* est du droit ou non, en donnant leur propre interprétation, la qualifiant de « principes généraux du droit ».

En attendant le développement de la doctrine et de la jurisprudence internationale sur la définition de la *lex mercatoria,* suffit-il de dire que la définition donnée par les parties risque de limiter l'action de l'arbitre à un ensemble de règles *de droit,* alors que le règlement C.C.I. article 13-5 dispose et ce déjà sans l'accord des parties, que l'arbitre doit toujours tenir compte des usages du commerce.

Malgré le vif intérêt pour ce qu'on appelle *lex mercatoria* dans les milieux à travers le monde où l'on discute de l'arbitrage international, on constate que par rapport au nombre total d'affaires soumises à l'arbitrage selon le règlement de la Cour d'arbitrage de la C.C.I., la *lex mercatoria* ne fait son apparition que rarement. Le nombre important de sentences reproduites dans ce *Journal* depuis le commencement des chroniques C.C.I. ne saurait donc donner l'impression que la majorité des arbitrages C.C.I., ou même une grande partie, font état de la *lex mercatoria*. La sentence en l'espèce est pour ce motif digne d'intérêt.

Puisque deux parties sont convenues de l'application éventuelle d'une *lex mercatoria,* admettons au moins que la *lex mercatoria* peut prétendre qu'elle existe (voir commentaire par Denis Thompson dans *The Journal of International Arbitration,* vol. 2, n° 2, June 1985, p. 76 à propos de l'affaire Norsolor).

Espérons que dans une chronique ultérieure, nous aurons l'occasion d'examiner l'application sur le fond que feront les arbitres de leur pouvoir selon cette sentence d'accord parties.

S. J.

Mesures provisoires. — Pouvoir de l'arbitre d'ordonner des mesures provisoires. — Pouvoir de l'arbitre de modifier une mesure ordonnée par une autorité judiciaire ordinaire (non). — Article 8-5 du règlement C.C.I. — Article 26 du concordat suisse sur l'arbitrage.

Sentence partielle rendue en 1985 dans l'affaire 4998.

Dans une affaire opposant une société française (demanderesse dans l'arbitrage) à — entre autres — une société marocaine (défenderesse), les trois arbitres, siégeant à Genève, lieu d'arbitrage contractuel, étaient saisis d'une requête urgente de la défenderesse marocaine. Celle-ci prétendait que la demanderesse avait pratiqué des saisies à son encontre au Maroc, auprès de diverses banques et sociétés.

La défenderesse demandait au Tribunal arbitral (entre autres) :

— de prendre acte que la société (défenderesse) en garantie du solde de la créance alléguée, offre une garantie bancaire à première demande exécutoire sur simple présentation de la décision finale du Tribunal arbitral ;

— d'ordonner, une fois remise la garantie bancaire, la mainlevée immédiate des quatre saisies pratiquées au Maroc à l'encontre de la Défenderesse ;

— de prendre acte que la défenderesse entend faire valoir le préjudice qui résulte pour elle de ces saisies abusivement pratiquées.

La demanderesse acceptait en principe la proposition de garantie de la défenderesse.

Les arbitres statuaient ensuite :

« *Les parties ont engagé des négociations au sujet de la garantie bancaire qui serait donnée relativement aux prétendus frais de pilotage. Elles n'ont cependant pu se mettre d'accord sur un texte définitif.*

« *Sur l'invitation du Tribunal arbitral , chaque partie lui a présenté un projet de garantie. Bien que les divergences entre les deux textes ne paraissent pas être de nature à empêcher un accord, elles ont pourtant eu cet effet.*

« *Le Tribunal arbitral entend statuer sans plus attendre sur la demande de la défenderesse.*

« *La requête adressée au Tribunal arbitral par la défenderesse vise la modification des mesures provisionnelles ordonnées par les tribunaux du Maroc sur demande de la demanderesse. En effet, la requérante souhaite que les saisies-arrêts effectuées sur ses comptes bancaires soient remplacées par une caution bancaire, qui garantirait les créances alléguées par la demanderesse couvertes par les saisies-arrêts.*

« *Dans certaines législations, il est permis de remplacer, à la demande de la partie intéressée, les saisies par des cautions bancaires. La défenderesse n'a pas allégué l'existence en droit marocain d'une disposition de ce genre, mais cette omission ne tire pas en conséquence, car le Tribunal arbitral est incompétent pour ordonner ladite modification.*

« *Les arbitres ne peuvent au mieux que* proposer *des mesures conservatoires ou provisionnelles* (cf. *sur ce point Pierre Lalive*, Répertoire de droit international suisse, l'arbitrage international, *vol. 1, Berne 1982, p. 290) ; pour ces mesures, la juridiction arbitrale comme telle est exclue (Pierre Jolidon*, commentaire du concordat suisse sur l'arbitrage, *Berne 1984, p. 383).*

« *L'article 8-5 du règlement de la Cour d'arbitrage de la C.C.I. et l'article 26 du concordat suisse sur l'arbitrage visent directement la compétence des arbitres pour ordonner des mesures provisionnelles, mais il est évident qu'il serait plus grave encore de modifier une mesure déjà ordonnée par une autorité judiciaire ordinaire. Le Tribunal arbitral déboute donc la défenderesse de sa demande urgente. Par ailleurs, comme il prévoit de rendre prochainement sa sentence au fond, il n'estime pas nécessaire de proposer aux parties la modification des mesures provisionnelles opérées.* »

OBSERVATIONS. — Il est acquis dans un certain nombre de pays que la saisine d'un Tribunal étatique pour demander des mesures provisoires et conservatoires ne vaut pas renonciation à la clause arbitrale (voir cette chronique, affaires 4126 et 4156 : *Clunet* 1984, p. 934, 937 avec références à la doctrine). Pourtant, dans d'autres pays, par exemple aux Etats-Unis, les tribunaux ne semblent pas encore avoir pris une position unanime en ce qui concerne les arbitrages internationaux pour lesquels s'applique la convention de New York.

Certains tribunaux américains ont considéré qu'ordonner des mesures conservatoires est contraire à la convention de New York (Charles N. Brower, W. Michael Tupman : 'Court ordered provisional measures under the New York Convention', dans *American Journal of International Law,* January 1986, Vol. 80, p. 24). En effet la convention de New York prévoit, dans son article VI, la possibilité de poser comme condition pour l'exécution d'une sentence la fourniture des sûretés convenables ; donc une mesure de sécurité *après* que la *sentence* ait été rendue. Par contre la convention de New York ne prévoit rien en termes de sécurité *avant ou pendant l'arbitrage* propre (voir affaires I.T.A.D. Associates v. Podar Brothers et Cooper v. Ateliers de la Motobécane S.A. p. 30 dans l'article Brower, Tupman cité).

Le règlement de la C.C.I. ne prévoit pas, dans son article 8-5 ou ailleurs, expressément un pouvoir des arbitres d'ordonner des mesures conservatoires ou provisoires ; il en reconnaît pourtant la possibilité (« … sans préjudice du pouvoir réservé à l'arbitre à ce titre »). Seule la faculté pour les parties de s'adresser aux autorités judiciaires « avant et exceptionnement après » la saisine de l'arbitre est expressément prévue.

Les arbitres statuant selon le règlement C.C.I., face à une demande urgente de mesures provisoires, doivent examiner si les règles de procédure applicables selon l'accord des parties, ou étant de nature impérative sur le lieu d'arbitrage, permettent l'ordonnance de mesures provisoires. Le concordat suisse limite, comme on le voit dans l'affaire en l'espèce, l'étendue du pouvoir de l'arbitre à faire des recommandations et exclut la prise de décisions contraignantes. Il est exclu que les arbitres fassent exécuter les ordonnances qu'ils rendent, l'exécution étant réservée aux autorités nationales dans chaque cas.

La question posée dans l'espèce est de savoir si un Tribunal compétent peut prendre une décision de nature intérimaire qui va à l'encontre ou qui modifie une décision déjà prise par une autorité étatique. On pourrait d'une manière générale penser que si l'utilité de pouvoir saisir un juge étatique pour une mesure conserva-

301

toire est nécessaire avant la mise en place d'un Tribunal arbitral, rien n'empêcherait les arbitres une fois saisis de l'affaire, et étant compétents pour trancher le différend sur le fond, de prendre toute décisions de nature intérimaire qu'ils trouvent bon après avoir entendu les parties, et même de modifier une ordonnance prise en référé. L'exécution serait bien entendu toujours réservée aux organes étatiques.

Le concordat exclut évidemment toute modification, par les arbitres de la décision prise par une autorité judiciaire, puisque l'article 26 du Concordat donne compétence exclusive aux autorités judiciaires. M. Franz Laschet, ancien membre de la Cour d'arbitrage, semble être du même avis et pas seulement pour les cantons concordataires (Franz Laschet, « Schiedsgerichtsbarkeit und einstweiliger Rechtsschutz » : *Zeitschrift für Zivilprozessrecht* 99. Band, Heft 3, 1986, p. 282). Pourtant, ne serait-il souhaitable *de lege ferenda* et plus conforme aux vœux des parties ayant choisi l'arbitrage comme mode de règlement des litiges que les arbitres aient compétence pour prendre la relève des autorités judiciaires, même en modifiant leurs décisions ?

S. J.

I. — **Contrat.** — Contrat de Construction, — Révision du prix stipulé au forfait. — Abandon du chantier. — Droit libyen et *Lex Mercatoria.* — Obligation de coopérer de bonne foi.

II. — **Lex Mercatoria** — Théorie de l'imprévision. — Application. — Obligation du créancier de prendre toutes les mesures pour réduire son préjudice.

Sentence rendue dans l'affaire 4761 en 1987.

Dans cette chronique (1986 p. 1137) nous avons rapporté sur la sentence partielle d'accord parties qui fut rendue par le Tribunal Arbitral, siégeant à Paris, dans un différend dans le domaine de construction entre une partie italienne et une partie libyenne.

La demanderesse est un consortium — personne juridique de droit italien formé de deux sociétés italiennes, créée en vue d'exécution des travaux de Génie Civil en Libye. La défenderesse est une société par actions de droit libyen, dont l'activité consiste dans la réalisation de travaux de construction et de Génie Civil en Libye.

En 1978, la défenderesse s'était vu confier l'achèvement des travaux de construction de certains bâtiments pour un Maître d'Ouvrage libyen. La défenderesse a sous-traité à la demanderesse les travaux qu'elle devait exécuter dans le cadre du contrat principal tels que : gros-œuvre, installations électriques, chauffage, sanitaires, etc...

Les parties avaient stipulé un prix à forfait fixé dans le contrat, qui disposait que le prix de l'ouvrage « sera fixe pour toute la durée de la période du contrat et ne sera sujet à aucune révision ».

Le contrat était expressément soumis au droit libyen. Le délai d'exécution était fixé à 24 mois. Un acompte serait versé contre émission d'une garantie de remboursement d'acompte et d'une garantie d'achèvement.

Dès le début des travaux, le chantier subit d'importants retards, tels que :

— retard dans la concession, par l'administration des douanes libyennes, des permis d'importation des matériaux et de l'outillage nécessaires pour la réalisation de l'ouvrage ;

— retard dans la concession, par l'autorité administrative libyenne, des visas d'entrée pour les travailleurs étrangers ;

— non conformité des plans ;

— obligation de démolir certaines constructions ;

— mauvaises conditions climatiques ;

— difficultés d'approvisionnement de certaines matières premières tels le ciment et le sable.

Considérant ces difficultés, la défenderesse demanda au Maître de l'Ouvrage de différer de huit mois la date de la délivrance de l'ouvrage.

Par ailleurs et toujours dans cette même lettre, la défenderesse demandait au Maître de l'Ouvrage d'approuver une majoration de 30 % du prix de l'ouvrage, au motif que le prix du bois, du ciment et du sable avait augmenté depuis la conclusion du contrat dans des proportions considérables.

Au premier mai 1980, environ 10 % seulement de la valeur totale des travaux avait été exécuté, ce qui illustre bien les difficultés rencontrées sur le chantier.

Les parties se rencontrèrent à plusieurs reprises, notamment en octobre 1980, avec des représentants du Maître de l'Ouvrage, aux fins de rechercher une solution susceptible de résoudre les difficultés afférentes à l'exécution des travaux.

Ces réunions débouchèrent sur la conclusion, en date du 28 octobre 1980, d'un avenant au contrat du 22 octobre 1978.

Cet avenant prévoyait en substance ce qui suit :

— le délai de livraison de l'ouvrage était reporté au 15 juin 1982, soit de vingt-et-un mois à compter du 15 octobre 1980 ;

— la défenderesse acceptait le principe d'une révision du prix du contrat, sous réserve de son approbation par le Maître de l'Ouvrage ;

— la défenderesse acceptait de procurer à la demanderesse des facilités de trésorerie pour lui permettre de poursuivre les travaux.

Par acte séparé du même jour, la défenderesse s'engageait à donner, dans un délai qui ne devait pas dépasser deux mois, une « réponse officielle » au sujet de la détermination d'une augmentation éventuelle du prix du contrat, dont le principe avait été admis avec certaines réserves par l'avenant du 28 octobre 1980.

Après la conclusion de l'avenant d'octobre 1980, les travaux se poursuivirent. Cet avenant ne résolut pas tous les problèmes rencontrés sur le chantier et en 1981, la demanderesse insistait sur la nécessité d'une révision du prix. La défenderesse adressait au Maître de l'Ouvrage des invitations d'accorder une augmentation du prix du contrat de 45 %.

Malgré l'absence de toute « réponse officielle » quant à l'augmentation éventuelle du prix de l'ouvrage, promise par la défenderesse dans l'acte séparé signé le même jour que l'avenant au contrat en date du 28 octobre 1980, la demanderesse poursuivait l'exécution des travaux.

En décembre 1981, les parties établissaient un protocole d'accord qui précisait entre autres, que la détermination de l'augmentation du prix du contrat serait effectuée et payée le 31 décembre 1982 au plus tard. Le protocole d'accord déboucha sur un nouvel avenant au contrat en janvier 1982. Jusqu'en juillet 1982, le nombre de personnes employées par la demanderesse sur le chantier était légèrement supérieur au chiffre que les parties avaient arrêté dans l'avenant en janvier 1982. En revanche, la défenderesse ne quantifia ni ne paya un montant quelconque à la demanderesse au titre de la révision du prix ; en effet le Maître de l'Ouvrage n'avait jamais accepté la révision du prix contractuel

Malgré l'absence d'une détermination de l'augmentation du prix et autres conditions convenues, la demanderesse n'en poursuivit pas moins son activité sur le chantier, car la défenderesse l'avait assurée que la carence était exclusivement due à des lenteurs bureaucratiques.

En juillet 1982, profitant de la période des vacances, la demanderesse procéda à l'évacuation de son personnel du chantier. Elle estimait qu'elle n'était plus tenue d'exécuter ses prestations dès lors que la défenderesse était en demeure dans l'exécution des obligations qu'elle avait souscrites de par l'avenant de janvier 1982. Cette décision n'a été précédée d'aucune mise en demeure formelle car la demanderesse craignait, si elle avait fait connaître ses intentions par écrit des mesures de représailles de la défenderesse dirigées notamment contre le ouvriers employés sur le chantier. (Ces craintes se sont vérifiées par la suite puisque deux personnes restées sur place sont demeurées contre leur gré en Libye, l'une durant dix mois, l'autre durant dix-huit mois).

La demanderesse avait achevé un peu moins de 20 % de l'ouvrage lorsqu'elle a quitté le chantier.

Le certificat de paiement a été signé non seulement par les représentants des parties mais aussi par le Maître de l'Ouvrage. Tous les paiements mentionné dans le certificat ont été effectués sans réserve.

Après la rupture du mois de juillet 1982, les parties eurent en décembre divers entretiens pour sortir de l'impasse.

C'est alors que la défenderesse avait fait appel aux deux garanties émises dans le cadre du contrat du 22 octobre 1978. Les banques ont effectué le paiements qui ont été débités du compte de la demanderesse.

Après des tentatives de conciliation, la défenderesse adressa, en juillet 1983 une lettre à la demanderesse dans laquelle elle déclarait résilier le contrat de sous-traitance aux torts de la demanderesse. Après quoi la demanderesse a déposé une requête d'arbitrage auprès de la CCI, demandant une déclaration de résiliation du contrat pour faute grave de la défenderesse, restitution des sommes retirées en vertu des garanties bancaires et condamnation de tous les dommages subis. Les parties se mettaient d'accord sur le montant de la créance de la défenderesse à l'égard de la demanderesse qui se composait de frais pour le matériel et les fournitures achetés par la défenderesse pour le compte de la demanderesse, avance de trésorerie et frais anticipés.

Dans une sentence partielle rendue d'accord parties en 1984, le Tribunal Arbitral statua sur le droit applicable (V. *Clunet* 1986, 1137) que le droit libyen est en principe applicable au litige, avec la possibilité pour les arbitres d'appliquer a *Lex Mercatoria* dans le cas où le droit libyen n'aurait pas été prouvé ou s'il ètait lacunaire ou incomplet.

Dans la sentence finale, les arbitres déclarent, sous la rubrique « droit et liscussion », qu'ils statueront en appliquant à titre principal la législation ibyenne et, à titre subsidiaire, la *Lex Mercatoria* et les principes généraux du lroit.

Extrait de la sentence :

« *Chacune des parties a, par une déclaration de volonté, mis un terme à la convention du 22 octobre 1978 en invoquant l'existence d'une série de violations contractuelles de son partenaire, justifiant la résiliation anticipée du contrat et le paiement de dommages et intérêts en réparation du préjudice subi.* »

Après avoir constaté que les parties avaient conclu des avenants au contrat après les premières difficultés rencontrées sur le chantier et qu'il n'y avait alors pas lieu à examiner dans quelle mesure certains griefs étaient imputables à la demanderesse, les arbitres continuaient :

« *Reste alors le grief de l'abandon abrupt du chantier en juin/juillet 1982 : cette circonstance constituerait certes un motif de résiliation de la convention de sous-traitance aux torts de la demanderesse, à moins qu'elle ne soit justifiée par un comportement fautif de la défenderesse, ce qui conduit le Tribunal Arbitral à examiner les griefs que fait valoir la demanderesse à l'encontre de cette dernière.*

La demanderesse soutient qu'elle était en droit de quitter le chantier en juin/juillet 1982 et de résilier le contrat du 22 octobre 1978, aux torts de la défenderesse, en avançant à l'encontre de sa partie adverse les griefs suivants :

— inexécution de l'obligation souscrite par la défenderesse dans les avenants des 28 octobre 1980, 11 décembre 1981 et 14 janvier 1982 de fixer l'augmentation du prix de l'ouvrage et de payer la somme due à ce titre.

Il n'est pas contesté que la défenderesse n'a ni déterminé, ni a fortiori payé un montant quelconque au titre d'augmentation du prix stipulé dans le contrat.

Pour sa défense, la défenderesse allègue, d'une part, que cette révision du prix du contrat était soumise à la condition de son approbation par le Maître de l'Ouvrage, laquelle n'aurait jamais été donnée, d'autre part, que le droit libyen exclut le principe même de la révision du prix fixé à forfait, de sorte que l'engagement qu'elle aurait pu prendre à cet effet serait dépourvu de toute efficacité juridique.

Pour ce qui a trait à ce premier argument, le Tribunal Arbitral constate que s'il est vrai que l'avenant du 28 octobre 1980 subordonnait l'accord de la défenderesse quant au principe d'une révision de prix du contrat à l'approbation du Maître de l'Ouvrage, cet engagement est souscrit sans réserve ni condition dans les avenants ultérieurs.

Bien plus, l'avenant du 14 janvier 1982 précise que le principe d'une révision du prix du contrat "a déjà été approuvé depuis longtemps par le Maître de l'Ouvrage".

Dès lors que le contrat principal conclu entre le Maître de l'Ouvrage et la défenderesse doit être réputé indépendant des rapports juridiques liant cette dernière à la demanderesse et que dans les avenants des 11 décembre 1981 et 14 janvier 1982, la défenderesse a pris un engagement inconditionnel de procéder à la détermination de l'augmentation du prix du contrat qu'elle s'obligeait à payer dans un délai déterminé, la position qu'a pu prendre le Maître de l'Ouvrage quant au principe de la révision du prix contractuel, est sans incidence sur la solution du présent litige.

Reste le second argument tiré de la législation libyenne : à cet égard, le Tribunal Arbitral relève qu'il est vrai que l'article 657 ch. 1 du Code civil libyen exclut en principe toute révision du prix contractuel lorsque celui-ci a été fixé à forfait, le chiffre 4 de cette même disposition confère au juge le pouvoir d'augmenter le prix ou de résilier le contrat en cas de bouleversement des bases économiques de la convention dû·à la survenance a événements exceptionnels et imprévisibles à la conclusion du contrat.

Ce faisant, le droit libyen, à l'image d'autres droits nationaux tels le droit allemand et le droit suisse ou encore de la Lex Mercatoria *(Cf. sentence CCI, 1512, Clunet 1974, 905 ; sentence CCI 2291, Clunet 1976, 999), donne effet à la théorie de l'imprévision qui procède du principe que la règle "pacta sunt servanda" trouve sa limite dans le principe supérieur de la bonne foi.*

Dans cette perspective, le Tribunal Arbitral observera encore que le droit libyen, tout comme le droit suisse et le droit allemand, prescrit non seulement aux parties d'exécuter leurs obligations conformément aux règles de la bonne foi (Cf. art. 148 ch. 1 du Code civil libyen), mais encore interdit l'abus de droit (Cf. art. 5 du Code civil libyen).

L'article 657, ch. 4 du Code civil libyen ne constitue ainsi qu'un cas d'application de ces deux principes — au demeurant interdépendants —, car il est manifestement contraire à la bonne foi et, partant, abusif de maintenir des obligations imposées au débiteur par le contrat si les circonstances existant lors de sa conclusion se sont modifiées à un point tel que l'économie de ce contrat se trouve bouleversée.

Quant au Décret/Loi promulgué par le comité populaire de la Jamahirya arabe libyenne populaire et socialiste en date du 6 mai 1980, également invoqué par la défenderesse à l'appui de sa thèse, il ne modifie en rien les considérations qui précèdent. Certes, l'article 104 dudit décret exclut toute augmentation d'un prix fixé à forfait ; toutefois, l'article 114 apporte un tempérament à cette règle en prévoyant une norme corrective en tous points identiques à celle prévue à l'article 657 ch. 4 du Code civil libyen.

En conséquence, et contrairement à ce qu'a soutenu la défenderesse, le droit libyen n'interdit nullement l'adaptation ou la révison d'un prix stipulé à forfait, en cas de survenance de circonstances extraordinaires et imprévisibles ; bien plus, dans de telles circonstances, il autorise expressément le juge à augmenter le prix fixé dans le contrat ou à résilier la convention, et ne se distingue par là en rien d'autres systèmes juridiques, tel le droit suisse ou le droit allemand, qui reconnaissent expressément la théorie de l'imprévision.

Il en résulte qu'un accord, tel l'avenant du 14 janvier 1982 qui, de par son article 7, consacre l'engagement d'une partie de procéder dans un délai déterminé à une révision du prix du contrat et à payer le montant de l'augmentation n'est ni illicite, ni illégal et, partant doit déployer, au plan juridique, tous ses effets.

La défenderesse a également soutenu, à titre subsidiaire, qu'un tel engagement ne pouvait l'obliger, car, si les parties avaient admis le principe de l'augmentation, elles ne s'étaient pas encore mises d'accord sur son montant qui, lors de la conclusion de l'avenant, n'était ni déterminé, ni déterminable.

La défenderesse paraît ainsi en déduire que l'accord des parties n'était pas parfait, puisqu'il ne portait pas sur un élément essentiel de la convention, à savoir le montant de l'augmentation. A cela, la demanderesse a rétorqué que l'accord sur le "quantum" de l'augmentation résultait déjà implicitement de la lettre adressée par la défenderesse au Maître de l'Ouvrage en date du 4 juin 1981 dont copie avait été communiquée à la demanderesse, et par laquelle elle réclamait au Maître de l'Ouvrage une augmentation de 45 % du prix du contrat.

Il n'est pas nécessaire de décider si la susdite lettre consacre un accord implicite des parties sur l'augmentation du prix, dès lors qu'il est patent, au regard des pièces produites dans la présente cause, notamment du rapport sur l'évolution du coût de matériaux, de la main-d'œuvre, du transport et des autres services, que l'augmentation du prix était objectivement déterminable sur la base des statistiques existantes et, de la sorte, était soustraite à une fixation arbitraire et artificielle par l'une des parties, ce qui aurait pu rendre l'accord illégal ou à tout le moins inefficace.

En d'autres termes, et à supposer que la défenderesse ait procédé à la détermination de l'augmentation du prix contractuel comme elle s'y était obligée, mais que la demanderesse n'ait pas accepté cette détermination, le litige aurait pu être soumis à un Tribunal Arbitral qui aurait fixé ladite augmentation en fonction de données objectives résultant de statistiques et autres moyens d'analyses économiques.

*En réalité, lorsque la défenderesse allègue que l'accord ne portait que sur le principe d'une augmentation, elle se trompe sur la nature de son engagement : l'article 7 de l'avenant du 14 janvier 1982 lui imposait en effet l'obligation de procéder, dans un certain délai, à la détermination de l'augmentation du prix du contrat, soit une obligation de faire, c'est-à-dire de négocier, ou plus exactement de coopérer de bonne foi pendant l'exécution du contrat. (Cf. Morin, Le devoir de coopération dans les contrats internationaux in : D.P.C.I. 1980, n° 1, p. 9 s ; S. Jarvin, L'obligation de coopérer de bonne foi, dans l'*Arbitrage Commercial International, apport de la jurisprudence arbitrale, *colloque de Paris, 7 et 8 avril 1986).*

En refusant d'entreprendre une démarche quelconque en vue de déterminer le "quantum" de l'augmentation du prix contractuel, la défenderesse a violé cette obligation et, partant, a engagé sa responsabilité.

Le Tribunal Arbitral décide donc que le deuxième grief allégué par la demanderesse est bien fondé.

Le Tribunal Arbitral doit maintenant fixer le montant des dommages et intérêts compensatoires qui seront alloués à la demanderesse, et il procédera à cette détermination en se fondant sur les principes exposés aux articles 224 s du Code civil libyen : au nombre de ces principes, il faut tout d'abord citer celui qui prescrit que l'étendue de la réparation doit être déterminée d'après les circonstances et la gravité de la faute du débiteur (art. 224 ch. 1 du Code civil libyen). Or, dans le cas d'espèce, la défenderesse a certes souscrit d'une façon quelque peu imprudente à des engagements qu'elle n'a pas été en mesure de tenir. Ce faisant, elle n'a toutefois nullement cherché à nuire à la demanderesse, mais a tenté de conserver coûte que coûte sa collaboration dans l'espoir de terminer la construction des deux bâtiments. Le fait qu'en cours d'exécution des travaux la défenderesse ait consenti à la demanderesse, sans y être obligée par le contrat d'importants crédits, constitue la meilleure preuve de cette attitude qui, si elle doit être sanctionnée, ne saurait l'être trop lourdement

*Le Tribunal Arbitral rappelera également la disposition du droit libyen qui oblige le créancier à prendre toutes les mesures en son pouvoir pour réduire l'ampleur de son préjudice (art. 224 ch. 2 du Code civil libyen ; en ce qui concerne la *Lex Mercatoria, Cf. *sentences CCI 2103 et 2142, Clunet 1974, 902, 2478, Clunet 1975, 925 ; 2291, Clunet 1976, 989 ; 2520, Clunet 1976, 992 ; 3344, Clunet 1982, 978 qui appliquent cette même règle).* »

OBSERVATIONS

I et II. — La sentence ici rapportée est surtout digne d'intérêt parce que ce sont les parties — et non seulement les arbitres, comme c'est souvent le cas — qui ont choisi l'application de la *Lex Mercatoria*.

La *Lex Mercatoria* ne devrait, selon la sentence intérimaire, trouver application que dans le cas où le droit libyen serait contraire à « l'ordre public international » ou encore aux « principes de la bonne foi ». De plus, la *Lex Mercatoria* trouverait application si le droit libyen n'avait pas été prouvé ou était lacunaire.

On constate que la *Lex Mercatoria* joue un rôle plutôt modeste dans cette affaire. Car c'est après des analyses détaillées de la loi libyenne que les arbitres arrivent à leurs conclusions sur le fond : d'une part, que le droit libyen donne effet à la théorie de l'imprévision, d'autre part, que ce même droit oblige le créancier à prendre toutes les mesures en son pouvoir pour réduire l'ampleur de son préjudice. On ne se trouve pas dans une situation où le droit libyen n'est pas prouvé ou est lacunaire. Le seul obstacle à son application serait sa contradiction avec l'ordre public international et les principes de bonne foi. Par référence aux solutions identiques dans les droits allemand et suisse, on doit comprendre que les arbitres écartent une quelconque contradiction du droit libyen avec l'ordre public international. Et au moins pour la théorie de l'imprévision, il est dit conforme aux principes de la bonne foi.

Que reste-t-il alors de la *Lex Mercatoria* ? Apporte-t-elle quelques éléments supplémentaires que l'on ne trouve pas dans le droit libyen ? Si des références à la *Lex Mercatoria* figurent dans la sentence — ce qui à notre avis ne serait pas nécessaire une fois que le droit libyen a été prouvé — est-ce pour donner du relief à l'ordre public international ? Si par hasard le droit libyen ne se conformait pas à ce que l'on appelle *Lex Mercatoria*, devrait-il alors céder la place à la *Lex Mercatoria*, étant entendu que la dernière représente l'ordre public international ? Ce serait donner une primauté à la *Lex Mercatoria* sur le droit libyen qui à notre avis serait dangereuse. D'abord parce que les parties sont convenues de l'application du droit libyen en premier lieu. Deuxièmement parce que la *Lex Mercatoria* doit rester l'expression des usages du commerce international mais ne peut être élevée à un rang supérieur à moins que les parties l'aient explicitement voulu.

La hiérarchie ne doit pas être inversée. Si la Court of Appeal d'Angleterre a récemment reconnu que la *Lex Mercatoria* n'est pas contraire à l'ordre public (Bulletin de l'association suisse de l'arbitrage n° 2, 1987, page 165 et ss), elle ne doit pas être confondue avec la notion d'ordre public.

S. J.

I. — **Conditions de la Fédération Internationale des Ingénieurs Conseils (FIDIC).** — Article 67. — Délai pour soumettre une demande d'arbitrage.

II. — **Procédure.** — Injonction par un tribunal étatique d'arrêter la procédure d'arbitrage — Forme requise pour une injonction — Effets d'un injonction sur les arbitres siégeant dans une autre juridiction.

Sentence partielle rendue dans l'affaire 4862 en 1986.

Un différend dans le domaine des travaux publics opposait une joint-venture de trois firmes européennes de nationalités différentes à une entité publique de la République Arabe du Yémen. Le constructeur européen qui devait entreprendre la construction d'une route demandait, dans une requête d'arbitrage, le remboursement des frais supplémentaires. Le contrat, à prix fixe, était régi par les conditions FIDIC, 2ᵉ édition. L'ingénieur, une firme d'ingénieurs conseils, avaient, en août 1978, pris une décision sous l'article 67 des conditions FIDIC, en approuvant une partie de la demande du constructeur pour des frais supplémentaires, et en en rejetant la plus grande partie. Avant cette décision sur les frais supplémentaires, l'ingénieur avait délivré le Certificat de Réception Définitive, en avril 1978, pour lequel le paiement fut effectué en juillet 1978.

Par une lettre d'octobre 1978, le constructeur informait l'ingénieur qu'il n'acceptait pas sa décision et lui signifiait formellement selon l'article 67 qu'il exigeait que les questions en litige soient soumises à arbitrage. Le constructeur ajoutait qu'il espérait toujours qu'une solution à l'amiable pourrait être trouvée et que par conséquent, il ne prenait aucune initiative encore pour commencer l'arbitrage.

En juin 1981, le constructeur écrivait au secrétariat de la Cour d'Arbitrage de la CCI pour annoncer qu'il avait un différent avec le Maître de l'Ouvrage, que ce différend n'avait pas été résolu et qu'il était en train de préparer une requête en bonne et due forme qu'il avait l'intention de soumettre dans le cas où une solution à l'amiable ne pourrait être trouvée.

Le 21 décembre 1983, le secrétariat de la Cour d'Arbitrale de la CCI recevait une requête d'arbitrage complète, accompagnée d'une avance sur les frais de 450 $ en complément de la requête de juin 1981 et le paiement à l'époque de 50 $.

En mai 1984, le Maître de l'Ouvrage présentait une réponse limitée à l'exception de prescription de la requête d'arbitrage selon le droit de la République du Yémen. La défenderesse exposait aussi qu'elle avait commencé, le 13 mai 1984, une procédure contre le constructeur devant un Tribunal de Commerce au Yémen en demandant, entre autre, que ce tribunal déclare que la requête d'arbitrage à la CCI était en contradiction avec les lois du Yémen à cause de la prescription.

La Cour d'Arbitrage de la CCI décidait de l'existence *prima facie* d'une convention d'arbitrage et mettait l'arbitrage en marche. Un tribunal de trois arbitres (président libanais, co-arbitres allemand et britannique) était constitué et le siège de l'arbitrage fixé par la CCI à Paris.

Participaient aux réunions, pour établir l'Acte de Mission, les trois arbitres et la demanderesse, alors que la défenderesse, en invoquant l'injonction par le Tribunal de Commerce de Sana'à, refusait de participer pour ne pas violer l'injonction.

L'Acte de Mission était signé par les arbitres et la demanderesse et approuvé par la Cour d'Arbitrage de la CCI en mars 1986 (art. 13.2 du règlement CCI).

Les arbitres tranchaient ensuite certaines questions avant-dire droit dans les termes suivants (sentence en langue anglaise) :

Sur le délai pour conserver le droit d'aller en arbitrage selon l'article 67 des conditions FIDIC.

Attendu que la demanderesse avait en effet rempli toutes les conditions de l'article 67 afférentes à la présente affaire à savoir (1) qu'elle avait en effet informé l'ingénieur le 24 mai de sa non acceptation de l'évaluation par l'ingénieur de ses demandes — définissant ainsi le "différend", (2) que le 24 mai 1978 elle avait en effet demandé à l'ingénieur une décision aux termes de l'article 67 sur le montant desdites demandes, et (3) que le 19 octobre 1978, elle avait en effet avisé l'ingénieur 66 jours après l'émission le 14 août 1978 par ce dernier de sa décision aux termes de l'article 67 d'exiger que le différend soit soumis à l'arbitrage, c'est-à-dire, bien dans le délai de 90 jours accordé pour la notification d'un tel dissentiment,

Attendu que rien dans l'article 67 ne pourra être interprété comme obligeant une partie dissidente de déposer effectivement auprès de la Cour d'Arbitrage de la CCI une demande d'arbitrage (telle qu'exigée par le règlement de la CCI) dans le délai de 90 jours suivant la réception de la décision de l'ingénieur, les mots "exige que la ou les questions en litige soient soumises à arbitrage" signifiant clairement que la partie dissidente souhaite établir qu'elle opte pour l'opportunité qui lui est offerte par l'article 67 de faire régler le différend par voie d'arbitrage sous l'égide de la CCI, plutôt que d'être liée de façon permanente par la décision de l'ingénieur qu'elle rejette,

Attendu que la phrase citée prétend en réalité exprimer l'intention sérieuse de la partie dissidente de demander l'arbitrage et qu'elle doit donc être interprêtée comme la notification par celle-ci qu'elle déposera une demande d'arbitrage à un moment donné, et qu'entre temps elle atteint le but important d'éviter que la décision de l'ingénieur devienne de façon permanente définitive et obligatoire,

Attendu que si le contraire est vrai, c'est-à-dire, au cas où le texte de l'article serait interprété comme signifiant qu'une demande d'arbitrage doit effectivement être déposée dans les ⁰⁰ jours de la réception par la partie dissidente de la

décision de l'ingénieur, l'on pouvait imaginer qu'il y aurait dans beaucoup d'affaires plusieurs demandes d'arbitrages déposées, toutes relatives au même contrat, lesquelles devraient éventuellement être résolues alors selon des calendriers différents se chevauchant les uns sur les autres, avec éventuellement des arbitres différents nommés dans les différents cas, le tout à grand coût et supplice pour tous concernés, une situation que ni les auteurs du texte de l'article 67, ni même les parties lors de la signature du contrat ne pourraient imaginer,

Attendu qu'un des spécialistes de premier plan en la matière, I.N. Duncan Wallace, Q.C., dans un article bien documenté sur ce sujet même, dans le numéro de juillet 1985 de L'International Construction Law Review, *a également conclu que la seule action exigée pour empêcher la décision de l'Ingénieur de devenir obligatoire de façon permanente était pour la partie dissidente de faire connaître, dans le délai stipulé dans l'article, son exigence « que la question en litige soit soumise à l'arbitrage », la demande d'arbitrage elle-même étant déposée à une date ultérieure,*

Attendu que l'argument évoqué par le défendeur — que la demanderesse a violé les termes de l'article 67 en conditionnant sa demande de se soumettre à l'arbitrage sur l'impossibilité pour lui de parvenir à une solution par voie de négociations — n'a aucun fondement légal, la demanderesse ayant déclaré immanquablement et constamment qu'en cas d'échec dans les négociations, elle ne serait laissée avec aucun autre choix que de déposer une demande d'arbitrage,

Le Tribunal juge à l'unanimité que la demanderesse a correctement obéi aux exigences de l'article 67 du Contrat et qu'en conséquence le fait que sa demande

d'arbitrage n'avait pas été déposée dans les 90 jours de la réception par elle de la décision de l'Ingénieur ne rend pas l'arbitrage nul et sans effet.

Les effets sur l'arbitrage de la procédure devant le Tribunal de Sana'à.

Attendu que les parties au présent litige ont clairement accepté, à l'article 67 du Contrat, que les litiges ou les différends de quelque nature que ce soit doivent en premier lieu être soumis à l'Ingénieur et après à l'arbitrage de la CCI,

Attendu que le défendeur n'a pas contesté la validité de l'article 67,

Attendu que le procès introduit par le défendeur devant le Premier Tribunal de Commerce de la République Arabe du Yémen (« RAY ») a commencé le 13 mai 1984, soit presque 5 mois après le dépôt de la Demande d'Arbitrage par la demanderesse et un jour avant le dépôt par le défendeur auprès de la CCI de ses Objections Préliminaires,

Attendu que la lettre nº 515, en date du 24 octobre 1984, adressée par le Président du Premier Tribunal de Commerce de Sana'à aux « Président et Membres de la Chambre d'Arbitrage International à Paris » ne peut être interprétée comme une injonction notifiée à la Cour d'Arbitrage de la CCI afin de bloquer la procédure d'arbitrage et de même elle ne peut être interprêtée comme une injonction au Tribunal Arbitral lorsqu'elle lui est notifiée par le défendeur le 26 juin 1986,

Attendu que les lettres ultérieures, nº 61 et 63, envoyées le 13 février 1985 par le même Président du Premier Tribunal de Commerce de Sana'à à la demanderesse et au défendeur respectivement, ne sont pas non plus des injonctions notifiées à la Cour d'Arbitrage de la CCI et de même elles ne sont pas des injonctions au Tribunal (Arbitral) lorsqu'elles lui sont notifiées par le défendeur le 10 février 1986,

Attendu qu'en tout état de cause lesdites lettres ne sont pas des injonctions d'un tribunal yéménite, mais des lettres adressées par le Président du Tribunal demandant aux parties de s'abstenir de procéder à l'arbitrage en attendant la décision du Tribunal RAY,

Attendu que dans cette affaire une décision provisoire a été rendue le 9 février 1985 par le Premier Tribunal de Commerce, laquelle décision n'a pas été communiquée au Tribunal Arbitral par le défendeur, mais portée à sa connaissance dans les documents produits par la demanderesse le 30 juillet 1986,

Attendu que cette décision n'a rien à voir avec le présent arbitrage, réfutant purement et simplement deux des Objections Préliminaires faites par la demanderesse dans le présent cas (la défenderesse devant le Tribunal RAY) relativement à la compétence du Tribunal RAY,

Attendu qu'en tout état de cause un appel a été interjeté devant une cour supérieur RAY contre ces décisions,

Attendu qu'il n'y a rien dans l'affaire instituée devant le Tribunal RAY qui pourrait éventuellement affecter la compétence du présent Tribunal,

Attendu que le présent Tribunal n'accepte pas qu'il a refusé d'obéir à une ordonnance ou une décision quelconque rendue par le Tribunal RAY,

Le Tribunal décide à l'unanimité :

1. Que la procédure pendante devant le Tribunal RAY n'a aucun effet sur le présent arbitrage.

2. Que le Tribunal RAY n'a rendu aucune ordonnance formelle ayant pour effet de renvoyer ou d'arrêter la procédure du présent arbitrage ;

3. Que les lettres émanant du Président du Premier Tribunal de Commerce de Sana'à ne sont pas des injonctions adressées au présent Tribunal ou à la Cour d'Arbitrage de la CCI, et en conséquence elles n'ont aucun rapport avec le présent arbitrage ;

4. Que ce Tribunal ne considère pas qu'il a refusé d'obéir à une ordonnance ou décision quelconque rendue par le Tribunal RAY ;

5. Que ce Tribunal considère qu'il est compétent pour entendre et résoudre le présent arbitrage ;

6. Que toutes les autres questions, y compris coûts, seront traitées ultérieurement.

OBSERVATIONS. — I. — L'article 67 des conditions FIDIC institue un stade pré-contentieux. L'Ingénieur doit faire connaître sa décision dans un délai de quatre-vingt-dix jours à compter de sa saisine. A compter de cette décision, — ou à compter de l'expiration de ce délai de quatre-vingt dix jours si l'Ingénieur ne se prononce pas —, les deux parties, l'entrepreneur ou le Maître de l'Ouvrage, ont un nouveau délai de quatre-vingt dix jours pour exiger que la ou les questions en litige soient soumises à l'arbitrage. La juridiction arbitrale est la Cour d'Arbitrage de la CCI, explicitement désignée.

A défaut, la décision de l'Ingénieur est réputée définitive et s'impose aux deux parties, sauf fraude ou irrégularité. La demande d'arbitrage qui serait présentée hors délai ne serait plus recevable, dans la mesure où elle aurait pour objet de remettre en cause la décision de l'Ingénieur.

Le non respect par une partie du délai de quatre-vingts-jours est, comme on le voit, lourd de conséquences. Il est donc important de connaître les conditions exactes qui doivent être remplies par une partie pour qu'elle soit censée avoir exigé que le différend soit soumis à l'arbitre. Est-il nécessaire que dans les quatre-vingt-dix jours une requête d'arbitrage soit soumise à la Cour d'Arbitrage de la C.C.I. à Paris ou est-il suffisant que la partie notifie à l'Ingénieur son intention d'aller en arbitrage ?

Dans le dernier cas, la requête d'arbitrage serait soumise à la C.C.I. à une date ultérieure. Cette question a été posée à plusieurs reprises dans des arbitrages C.C.I. ces dernières années. Les arbitres y ont donné des interprétations opposées.

Regardons d'abord le libellé de la clause 67 dans la 2ᵉ édition des conditions FIDIC dans sa version française.

« Règlement des litiges

67. Tout litige ou différend relatif au Marché survenant entre le Maître de l'Ouvrage ou l'Ingénieur, d'une part, et l'entrepreneur, d'autre part, soit en cours d'exécution ou après achèvement, soit avant ou après résiliation, abandon ou interruption du Marché, sera tout d'abord soumis à l'Ingénieur qui décidera et, dans les 90 jours après que son intervention aura été requise, signifiera par écrit sa décision au Maître de l'Ouvrage et à l'Entrepreneur. Sous les réserves formulées ci-après, cette décision sur tout point litigieux soumis à l'Ingénieur sera définitive et liera le Maître de l'Ouvrage et l'Entrepreneur jusqu'à achèvement des travaux. L'Entrepreneur devra s'y conformer immédiatement et poursuivre l'exécution avec toute la diligence voulue, sans tenir compte des demandes d'arbitrages éventuelles formulées par lui-même ou le Maître de l'Ouvrage. Si, dans les 90 jours qui suivront la signification de la décision de l'Ingénieur aux deux parties, ni le Maître de l'Ouvrage, ni l'Entrepreneur ne formulent de demande d'arbitrage, cette décision demeurera définitive et liera le Maître de l'Ouvrage et l'Entrepreneur.

Si, dans les 90 jours après avoir été requis d'intervenir, l'Ingénieur ne signifie pas sa décision, ou si le Maître de l'Ouvrage ou l'Entrepreneur n'en est pas satisfait, le Maître de l'Ouvrage ou l'Entrepreneur pourra, dans les 90 jours qui suivront la signification (ou dans les 90 jours qui suivront l'expiration de la période de 90 jours indiqués en premier lieu) exiger que la ou les questions en litige soient soumises à arbitrage suivant les modalités indiquées ci-après.

Tous litiges ou différends pour lesquels la décision (éventuelle) de l'Ingénieur n'est pas devenue définitive et opposable aux parties, devront être réglés définitivement conformément aux Règles de Conciliation et d'Arbitrage de la Chambre de Commerce Internationale par un ou plusieurs arbitres désignés conformément auxdites règles.

Le ou lesdits arbitres aura ou auront entière faculté de remettre en cause, revoir et réviser toute décision, opinion, directive, attestation ou évaluation de l'Ingénieur ; et ni l'une ni l'autre des parties ne sera limitée dans la procédure devant le ou lesdits arbitres, aux preuves ou arguments présentés à l'Ingénieur pour obtenir sa décision.

Aucune décision donnée par l'Ingénieur conformément aux dispositions qui précèdent ne le disqualifiera pour témoigner devant le ou les arbitres sur une question concernant le litige ou le différend soumis à l'arbitrage. Le ou les arbitres ne devront procéder à l'arbitrage qu'après l'achèvement ou le prétendu achèvement des travaux, à moins du consentement écrit du Maître de l'Ouvrage et de l'Entrepreneur, restant entendu toutefois :

(1) Que la procédure arbitrale pourra être ouverte avant l'achèvement réel ou prétendu à l'occasion du refus de la part de l'Ingénieur de payer un décompte ou de restituer en totalité ou en partie la retenue de garantie, auxquels l'Entrepreneur prétend avoir droit conformément aux conditions stipulées à la 2ᵉ partie, article 60, ou à l'occasion de l'exercice par l'Ingénieur de la faculté qui lui est donnée de délivrer un certificat en vertu de l'article 63 (1) ou à l'occasion d'un différend prenant naissance en vertu de l'article 71.

(2) Que la délivrance d'un certificat de réception provisoire en vertu de l'article 48 ne constituera pas une condition préalable à l'ouverture d'une procédure arbitrale.

C'est premièrement dans l'affaire C.C.I. 3790 (*Clunet* 1983, 910) que trois arbitres ont donné — dans un *obiter dictum* — une interprétation en faveur de la nécessité de déposer la requête auprès de la C.C.I. dans les 90 jours (p. 911, 912).

Dans l'affaire 4707, rendue en 1986, l'arbitre unique jordanien, siégeant à Amman et appliquant la loi des Emirats sur la 2ᵉ édition des conditions FIDIC, décidait qu'une requête d'arbitrage devait être présentée à la C.C.I. dans le délai de 90 jours afin d'empêcher la décision de l'Ingénieur de devenir définitive.

Dans une troisième affaire, numéro 5029, rendue également en 1986, trois arbitres de nationalités différentes, siégeant à La Haye, appliquant la loi d'Egypte sur la 3ᵉ édition des conditions FIDIC, arrivaient à une décision diamétralement opposée et décidaient qu'une simple notification à l'Ingénieur de l'intention d'aller en arbitrage suffit pour empêcher que la décision de l'Ingénieur ne devienne définitive. Les deux dernières affaires sont publiées dans « *International Construction Law Review* » (Vol. 3, Part. 5, octobre 1986, p. 470 et suivantes).

Venait ensuite l'affaire en espèce numéro 4862 sur l'interprétation de la 2ᵉ édition FIDIC, qui a été décrite plus haut.

Finalement, dans une sentence rendue en 1987 — dans l'affaire numéro 5634 (non publiée) — trois arbitres de nationalités irlandaise et britannique, siégeant à Paris et appliquant la loi de l'Angleterre sur une clause inspirée par la 3ᵉ édition des conditions FIDIC, décidaient qu'il n'est pas nécessaire de soumettre une requête à la C.C.I. mais simplement de notifier la décision àl'Ingénieur dans les 90 jours.

Les arguments avancés pour et contre la nécessité de soumettre une requête d'arbitrage à la C.C.I. dans les 90 jours se résument ainsi :

Arguments pour :

La détermination de ces délais fixes de 90 jours a pour objet de donner des moyens pour le prompt règlement de demandes. Le but de l'article échouerait complètement s'il devrait être interprété dans un sens conduisant à retarder ou à entraver le règlement des litiges. L'intention de l'article est sûrement de rendre l'arbitrage toujours possible dès lors que la décision de l'ingénieur ne devenait pas définitive et obligatoire. Sinon, quelques affaires ne seraient éventuellement jamais résolues, et cela ne pouvait pas être l'intention de l'article. Il résulterait de l'adoption du point de vue que l'envoi d'un simple télex à l'Ingénieur, sans réellement commencer une procédure d'arbitrage devant l'organisme désigné au contrat, n'ait rendu la décision de l'ingénieur nulle et sans effet, une situation absurde et inacceptable entièrement incompatible avec l'article 67 puisqu'il n'y aura pas de décision obligatoire et que l'affaire ne fera pas non plus l'objet d'un arbitrage. Les rédacteurs de l'article 67 n'auraient pas pu envisager une telle situation.

Si l'une des parties peut « exiger » l'arbitrage sans réellement le commencer, quelle est la situation de l'affaire après que l'arbitrage a été « exigé », mais avant qu'il n'ait commencé ? La décision sur l'affaire ne serait ni définitive et obligatoire ni soumise à l'arbitrage. De plus, quand commencerait l'arbitrage ? Il n'y aurait aucun délai limite du tout. Ceci n'est pas en accord avec un article dont le but est de promouvoir le prompt règlement définitif de différends.

Le mot dans l'article est « exiger », et non « demander », ce qui implique que l'arbitrage aura certainement lieu. Donc, puisque l'Ingénieur ne peut pas commencer la procédure d'arbitrage, comment cet objectif peut-il être atteint par une simple notification à l'Ingénieur ou à l'autre partie ?

L'article 67 prévoit que « le Maître de l'Ouvrage ou l'Entrepreneur pourra, dans les 90 jours... exiger que la ou les questions en litige soient soumises à arbitrage suivant les modalités indiquées ci-après ». Il est prévu à la phrase suivante de l'article que l'arbitrage devrait se dérouler conformément aux Règles de la CCI lesquelles exigent que la partie désirant avoir recours à l'arbitrage de la CCI doit adresser une « demande d'arbitrage » à la CCI. La date de réception de la Demande par le Secrétariat de la Cour est réputée être la date d'introduction de la procédure (article 3.1). C'est en vertu de la demande d'arbitrage adressée à la CCI qu'il sera « exigé » de l'autre partie d'arbitrer (en réalité, obligé d'arbitrer) et qu'il y aura un moyen sûr de régler définitivement le litige.

Interpréter « exiger » comme nécessitant qu'une demande d'arbitrage soit adressée à la CCI serait compatible avec le but de l'article 67, à savoir le règlement rapide et prompt de demandes.

Arguments contre :

Au cours de la longue période de construction aux termes d'un contrat de génie civil, où les parties sont devenues *at arm's length* (distantes), les décisions de l'Ingénieur relatives à plusieurs questions litigieuses différentes pourront être prises et contestées — par exemple au sujet de dimensions, de variation dans les évaluations, de réclamations afférentes aux conditions physiques, de prorogations de délais, d'informations tardives, de difficultés de propriété ou de droit de passage ou de problèmes désignés de sous-traitance. Si une demande formelle adressée à la CCI était exigée afin d'éviter des décisions obligatoires, il serait nécessaire de commencer à des époques différentes plusieurs arbitrages tout à fait différents conformément aux délais limites assez urgents de la Cour figurant dans le règlement, entraînant une multiplication de demandes et de réponses formelles et (dans le cas de la Deuxième Edition) un embargo sur l'instruction de l'affaire jusqu'à ce que les travaux soient achevés. Le souhait commercial net des parties envisageant l'arbitrage dans un contrat de construction est de différer la décision finale le concernant jusqu'à ce que le résultat de toutes les diverses demandes et demandes reconventionnelles soit connu, ce qui le sera vers la fin du contrat à l'époque du certificat final ou du certificat de maintenance, au stade où ont normalement lieu les négociations sur la demande finale. C'est à ce stade que les parties souhaiteront revoir la situation, avant de décider enfin d'encourir des frais considérables et d'autres désavantages et risques possibles d'un arbitrage de grande envergure. Le point de vue opposé exigerait des demandes formelles fréquentes, le paiement de plusieurs provisions initiales peut-être importantes, des délais séparés pour la production séparée de réponses, et la possibilité, non pas entièrement théorique, de la nomination d'arbitres différents, selon les différents types de litiges tels qu'ils émergent l'un après l'autre.

Nous pensons que les difficultés envisagées avec la solution qui demande qu'une requête d'arbitrage soit présentée à la C.C.I. dans le délai de 90 jours, sont quelque peu exagérées. Il est vrai d'abord, que chaque requête d'arbitrage à la C.C.I. coûte, à partir du 1er juillet 1986, 2 000 $ payables par la demanderesse au lieu de 500 $ payables à moitié par les deux parties. Des requêtes d'arbitrage répétées pourront peser plus lourdement sur le *cash flow* de la demanderesse par rapport à une seule demande faite en fin de contrat.

Mais plus important à notre avis est l'intérêt de clarté à tout moment entre Maître de l'Ouvrage et Entrepreneur sur quelques décisions de l'Ingénieur qui soient contestées ou acceptées définitivement.

Même dans le cas où plusieurs demandes d'arbitrage seraient soumises à la C.C.I. dans un délai plus ou moins bref, les parties auront la possibilité de nommer les mêmes arbitres qui pourront, avec l'accord des parties, coordonner les multiples requêtes dans une seule procédure. A moins que les premières demandes d'arbitrage ne soient au-delà du stade de l'Acte de Mission quand les demandes suivantes seront présentées, la Cour d'Arbitrage pourra user de son droit de joindre les affaires (article 18 du Règlement Intérieur). Des tentatives de transactions pourront être menées entre les parties indépendamment du fait qu'une ou plusieurs demandes d'arbitrage aient été faites. Les parties pourront conjointement prolonger les délais prévus dans le règlement pour rendre la sentence si elles désirent traiter les premières requêtes d'arbitrage simultanément avec les dernières.

La solution qui préconise la simple notification de l'intention d'aller en arbitrage peut peser très lourd sur une partie qui risque de vivre dans l'incertitude pendant des années et des années, dans le pire des cas, avant de savoir définitivement si son partenaire, ayant fait la notification, va se décider ou non pour une procédure d'arbitrage. Car ni les conditions FIDIC, ni les arbitres dans les affaires référées, ne précisent dans quel délai une requête d'arbitrage doit être présentée suivant une notification de l'intention dans les 90 jours. On peut se demander si la limite sera le délai de prescription, qui, bien entendu, varie avec le droit applicable. Et l'on ne connaît pas toujours à l'avance le droit applicable pour un différend relevant du Commerce International, comme cette chronique de 1974 le montre.

En septembre 1987 la FIDIC à présenté une 4ᵉ édition des conditions y inclus la clause 67 dans laquelle la question ici rapportée sera résolue. Cette nouvelle rédaction sera la bienvenue pour les praticiens internationaux de la construction.

L'expérience nous montre pourtant que les éditions précédentes parviennent à survivre et à « remonter à la surface » dans beaucoup de contrats longtemps après la date à laquelle elles ont été remplacées par une édition nouvelle. D'ou l'intérêt de rapporter ici les décisions arbitrales sur les 2ᵉ et 3ᵉ éditions FIDIC. Que la jurisprudence arbitrale ici rapportée mette les parties en garde et les incite à prendre les précautions nécessaires à la rédaction de leur contrat s'il est inspiré par la clause FIDIC des 2ᵉ et 3ᵉ éditions, ou d'agir rapidement quand un différend basé sur la décision de l'Ingénieur surgit.

II. — Depuis quelques années, les cas sont devenus plus fréquents dans l'arbitrage C.C.I., dans lesquels une juridiction étatique ordonne des mesures pour suspendre ou arrêter un arbitrage en cours. Dans la plupart de ces cas, c'est un tribunal du lieu de résidence de l'une des parties qui, saisi d'une demande de la partie à l'arbitrage, ordonne l'autre partie, et/ou les arbitres, et/ou même la Cour d'Arbitrage de la C.C.I. d'interrompre leurs activités en attendant qu'une décision soit prise par le tribunal judiciaire. Des exemples en ont été donnés dans les observations de l'affaire numéro 5269 (citée p. 1029). Malheureusement mais indéniablement, on doit y voir une preuve de la « procéduralisation » de l'arbitrage commercial international moderne. C'est par préférence la mise en question de l'existence et de la validité de la convention d'arbitrage qui a donné lieu à de telles demandes. Lorsque la validité de la convention d'arbitrage est contestée devant un Tribunal Arbitral, on admet généralement que celui-ci est compétent pour examiner cette prétention et pour statuer sur la validité de la convention et décider s'il est compétent ou non. Il est aussi admis selon la loi de plusieurs Etats, ou au moins sous-entendu qu'une partie à une convention d'arbitrage est autorisée à agir en justice pour obtenir un jugement déclaratif ayant pour effet de déclarer la convention d'arbitrage nulle et non avenue.

Pourtant, si une question de validité de la convention d'arbitrage est soulevée par la défenderesse devant un Tribunal Arbitral, est-il conforme à l'esprit de l'arbitrage international d'engager une action sur le même problème et parallèllement devant un tribunal judiciaire ?

Une partie qui espère que les arbitres vont s'abstenir d'étudier la question et ne vont pas statuer sur leur compétence au moment où les juges se sont prononcés peut facilement mettre des bâtons dans les roues de la procédure arbitrale en entamant une action en justice. Les arbitres qui attendent la décision de l'instance judiciaire et qui s'abstiennent de leur droit d'exercer la compétence jusqu'à la décision du tribunal judiciaire, agissent-ils conformément à l'intérêt général de résolutions rapides des différends commerciaux internationaux ?

Si l'on admet que c'est conforme à l'esprit de l'arbitrage international pour une partie qui a signé une convention arbitrale de contester sa validité ou son existence devant un tribunal judiciaire (et j'en doute), on peut se demander si c'est également de « bonne manière » de la part d'une partie que de demander à une juridiction étatique d'ordonner la suppression de l'arbitrage en attendant le jugement.

La convention de New York ouvre dans son article II.3 la possibilité pour une partie de saisir un tribunal judiciaire sur un problème concernant une question au sujet de laquelle les parties ont conclu une convention d'arbitrage, mais elle ne va pas plus loin, et ne prévoit pas la possibilité d'injonctions pour le temps pendant lequel le tribunal judiciaire examine l'exception de caducité de la convention d'arbitrage.

Si la partie se contente de saisir le tribunal judiciaire sans demander une injonction, le risque existe que les deux tribunaux, judiciaire et arbitral, arrivent à des conclusions différentes, l'une déclarant que la convention est nulle, l'autre qu'il est compétent pour connaître le différend.

Il est concevable que le Tribunal Arbitral choisisse de ne pas attendre le jugement du tribunal judiciaire, même si c'est l'avis de quelques uns qu'il doit le faire (Nordenson dans 60 ans après — regard sur l'avenir, I.C.C. Publishing S.A. Paris 1984, p. 317). Si le tribunal ne se soumet pas à la décision du tribunal judiciaire qui a trouvé la convention nulle, et l'on peut avoir des doutes sur son obligation de la faire quand il réside dans un autre pays que le tribunal judiciaire, la partie risque d'être très gênée dans la suite. On comprend alors mieux son attitude quand il demande une injonction pour éviter que deux juridictions se penchent sur le même problème en même temps.

Quelle attitude les arbitres doivent-ils prendre vis-à-vis d'une injonction émanant d'une juridiction étrangère ? Sont-ils liés par toute injonction, et quelle est la position de la C.C.I. à cet égard ?

L'attitude de la Cour d'Arbitrage varie selon les cas. Elle examine attentivement la mesure dans laquelle une injonction a des effets contraignants pour les arbitres, ou l'un d'entre eux, ou sur l'une ou l'autre des parties, avant de faire des recommandations. La décision finale reste bien entendu celle des arbitres et la Cour ne possède pas de pouvoirs contraignants pour forcer un Tribunal Arbitral à poursuivre une affaire en présence d'une injonction émanant d'une juridiction dont ils dépendent. Le cas en l'espèce est un exemple sur la méthode que prennent les arbitres. Le dispositif laisse penser — *a contrario* — que si une injonction en bonne et due forme avait été prise par le tribunal de Sana'à et présentée aux arbitres, ils se seraient inclinés devant une telle décision.

La Cour d'Arbitrage de la CCI refuse en principe d'accepter que des injonctions soient ordonnées contre elle ou contre l'organisation C.C.I. Chaque fois que cela est arrivé, la Cour d'Arbitrage a systématiquement attiré l'attention de la juridiction étrangère sur le fonctionnement de l'arbitrage CCI en expliquant le rôle de la Cour qui est de nature administrative et celui des arbitres, de nature juridictionnelle. De l'avis de la Cour d'Arbitrage, il est dépourvu de sens de mettre en demeure l'institution CCI dont la tâche est d'organiser l'arbitrage mais pas de trancher le différend entre les parties.

S. J.

―――――――――

Droit applicable. — Amiables compositeurs. — *Lex Mercatoria* (non). — Choix d'un droit national au profit des usages du commerce international. — Application cumulative des systèmes de conflits intéressés au litige (oui).

Sentence rendue dans l'affaire 5118 en 1986.

Trois arbitres siégeant à Paris, étaient appelés à trancher un différend entre une demanderesse italienne et deux défenderesses tunisiennes. A l'origine du différend on trouve deux contrats d'agence pour la vente exclusive en Italie de produits d'origine tunisienne.

L'une des questions à résoudre par les arbitres était celle du droit applicable au contrat. Ils le déterminaient dans les termes suivants :

« *Dans leurs requêtes respectives introductives d'arbitrage, les parties n'ont pas revendiqué l'application d'un droit national particulier. Dans l'acte de mission signé par les parties, il est prévu que les règles de droit applicables aux conventions liant les parties seront déterminées par le Tribunal Arbitral. Dans son mémoire, la demanderesse estime que les parties ont entendu soustraire leurs relations contractuelles à l'application de tout droit étatique et que la* Lex Mercatoria *doit être seule déclarée applicable. Une trace de cette volonté des parties apparaîtrait dans les contrats de base liant celles-ci, où, en ce qui concerne les cas de force majeure, il est fait référence au sens de celle-ci "dans la pratique du commerce international". La demanderesse ajoute que la volonté des deux parties de soumettre le litige aux arbitres en leur accordant le pouvoir d'amiable composition exclut qu'un droit de fond prévale dans la cause.*

Subsidiairement, la demanderesse affirme que si un système de droit devait être adopté, ce serait le droit italien où devaient être effectuées les livraisons de marchandises et d'où émanaient les paiements. La demanderesse, cependant, dans un autre mémoire, invoque, dans un domaine particulier, l'application de la loi tunisienne.

Les deux sociétés défenderesses dans ce domaine revendiquent, dans leur mémoire, l'application de la loi tunisienne. Celle-ci, en matière de ventes internationales, est applicable, selon les défenderesses, par application de la convention de La Haye du 15 juin 1955, aussi bien que par application des règles de conflit tunisiennes et italiennes.

Il convient de remarquer que le pouvoir d'amiable composition conféré au Tribunal Arbitral n'exclut en aucune manière une appréciation des droits respectifs des parties au regard d'un système de droit déterminé. C'est à partir de cette appréciation des droits respectifs des parties que le Tribunal Arbitral, amiable compositeur, aura à déterminer s'il entend faire usage de ce pouvoir que lui ont conféré les parties pour, dans sa sentence, adopter une solution plus conforme à l'équité qu'une application stricte des règles de droit.

Il y a lieu de noter en second lieu que dans l'affaire soumise au Tribunal Arbitral, la convention des parties est souveraine car les règles de droit d'origine nationale susceptibles de recevoir application, y compris les règles d'interprétation, se trouvent supplétives de volonté et non pas impératives si bien que l'incidence sur le litige de l'application du droit tunisien ou du droit italien est faible, voire nulle. Si ce n'est sur le point particulier, comme il sera indiqué plus loin, de la référence à déterminer pour le taux d'intérêt légal applicable aux créances commerciales, l'ensemble des autres points en litige peut être indifféremment régi par la loi italienne ou la loi tunisienne, puisque celles-ci laissent les parties souveraines et qu'il appartient au tribunal d'interpréter leurs conventions.

Les parties, dans les documents contractuels, s'étant abstenues de toute référence à une loi de fond applicable, le Tribunal Arbitral estime, à la majorité, devoir, sur le point susvisé, seul en question, en application des règles de la Cour d'Arbitrage, déterminer la loi applicable par l'intermédiaire du choix d'une règle de conflit appropriée, dès lors qu'une volonté claire des parties n'a pas écarté l'application d'un droit national au profit des usages du commerce international.

S'agissant de contrats tous signés à Tunis, entre sociétés publiques tunisiennes vendeuses de marchandises, et une société italienne acquéreuse venant prendre livraison à Gabès, ou en tout cas dans un port tunisien, la règle de conflit tunisienne conduit à l'application du droit tunisien et il en est de même de la règle de conflit italienne qui prévoit en pareil cas l'application du droit du vendeur et du lieu de conclusion du contrat.

Il faut noter qu'en outre c'est la solution de la coutume internationale et cette solution se trouve consacrée par aussi bien la convention du 15 juin 1955 susvisée que par d'autres conventions internationales ayant même objet, bien qu'il faille préciser qu'aucune de ces conventions n'est applicable au litige puisque la Tunisie n'a pas ratifié ces conventions.

Dans la mesure, limitée, où l'application d'un droit national est requise dans la présente sentence, le Tribunal Arbitral appliquera donc la loi tunisienne. »

OBSERVATIONS. — Le « conflictualisme » n'est pas mort ; il vit et se porte bien dans beaucoup d'affaires d'arbitrage soumises au Règlement C.C.I. La décision des arbitres consacre l'application stricte de l'article 13 (3) du Réglement d'Arbitrage de la C.C.I. qui oblige l'arbitre à chercher la loi sur le fond désignée « par la règle de conflit qu'il jugera appropriée en l'espèce ».

C'est donc une interprétation et une application classique que donnent les arbitres au Règlement C.C.I. qui, dans ce domaine, n'est pas aussi progressiste que la nouvelle loi française sur l'Arbitrage International (voir observations dans *Clunet* 1986, 1109, 1110).

Rechercher le droit sur le fond en cumulant les règles de conflit italienne et tunisienne est, comme approche conflictualiste, également reconnue et établie. Nous verrons ultérieurement si la révision du Réglement C.C.I., qui doit être entreprise dans les prochaines années, va introduire une modification sur ce point. En attendant, on ne peut guère reprocher aux arbitres d'appliquer le Réglement dans sa version actuelle à la lettre dans l'intérêt de rendre le choix du droit applicable plus prévisible que ce ne serait le cas s'ils créent leur règle

de conflit eux-mêmes et cas par cas. Mais, comme on le sait, tous les arbitres ne se considèrent pas contraints de choisir une loi nationale et la Cour d'Arbitrage n'a pas l'habitude d'émettre des objections contre une approche plus libérale, comme celle consistant à appliquer des règles anationales, là où les arbitres donnent une motivation solide qui explique leur choix. La révision prochaine du Réglement sera la bienvenue pour clarifier une situation actuellement un peu ambiguë.

L'intérêt que suscite la sentence n'est pas moindre en ce qui concerne la manière dont les arbitres écartent l'application d'une *Lex Mercatoria* ou les usages du commerce international. Là encore, on doit se rappeler l'article 13 (3) du Réglement C.C.I. qui oblige les arbitres à examiner si une indication a été donnée ou faite par les parties en ce qui concerne le droit applicable.

Les arbitres constatent qu'aucune volonté claire des parties n'a pu être démontrée pour l'application de la *Lex Mercatoria* et que par conséquent, c'est un droit national qu'ils doivent appliquer. Encore une interprétation classique de l'article 13 (3) du Réglement CCI, et qui rejette la thèse selon laquelle le recours à l'arbitrage international serait en soi un indice révèlateur de la volonté des parties de voir le litige résolu suivant le droit propre à cette communauté, à savoir la *Lex Mercatoria*. Car il n'est pas équivalent à une indication du droit applicable, voire *Lex Mercatoria*, que de s'être abstenu de toute référence à une loi de fond applicable.

S. J.

Compétence arbitrale. — Arbitrage international concernant une partie égyptienne. — Code de procédure civile égyptien article 502 (3). — nécessité de nommer l'arbitre dans la convention d'arbitrage (non). — Ordre public égyptien.

Sentence intérimaire rendue en 1986 dans l'affaire 5269 (original en langue anglaise).

Dans une sentence intérimaire, les trois arbitres (un Français nommé par la demanderesse, un Egyptien nommé par la CCI aux lieu et place de la défenderesse qui s'est abstenue de le faire, un Suisse, président du Tribunal Arbitral, nommé sur proposition des deux coarbitres), siégeant à Paris, étaient invités à se prononcer sur leur propre compétence.

Extrait de la sentence intérimaire :

Les faits

1. La demanderesse, la société française, a signé un contrat avec une société égyptienne pour la construction des gros travaux. Aux termes d'un accord du 4 février 1983, les Travaux de Génie Civil furent confiés en sous-traitance à la défenderesse, la société égyptienne.

2. L'article XIV de l'accord contient une clause d'arbitrage ainsi conçue :

« XIV — réglement des litiges

14.1. Tout litige ou différend résultant du contrat ou s'y rapportant, qui ne pourra pas être réglé par accord amiable entre les parties, sera réglé définitivement selon les règles et procédures d'arbitrage de la Chambre de Commerce Internationale à Paris (CCI) par un Comité d'arbitrage de trois arbitres. La société française et l'entrepreneur (la société égyptienne) nommeront chacune un arbitre et les deux arbitres en nommeront un troisième. Si les deux arbitres n'en nomment pas un troisième dans les trente (30) jours, celui-ci sera nommé par la CCI.

14.2. Le Comité d'arbitrage siègera à Paris.

14.3. La sentence arbitrale sera définitive et sans appel et règlera la question des frais de l'arbitrage et toutes matières s'y rapportant. »

L'article XV de ce même accord stipule que le contrat « est régi par le droit égyptien ».

3. Se fondant sur la clause d'arbitrage, la demanderesse a présenté une requête d'arbitrage au Secrétariat de la Cour d'Arbitrage de la CCI le 10 avril 1985. Cette requête était dirigée contre la défenderesse. Elle contenait les informations requises par l'article 3.2. du Règlement de la CCI. Elle se terminait par la nomination de M. B. comme arbitre choisi par la demanderesse.

4. Dans le délai de 30 jours prévu à l'article 4.1 du Règlement de la CCI, la défenderesse écrivit une lettre présentée comme une « réponse définitive ». Cette lettre, datée du 10 mai 1985, fut envoyée au Secrétariat de la Cour d'Arbitrage de la CCI. Elle disait en substance que certains aspects de la procédure d'arbitrage de la CCI sont contraires à des règles égyptiennes d'ordre public et que c'était la raison pour laquelle la défenderesse s'était abstenue jusque là « de prendre aucun engagement concernant la demande d'arbitrage ».

5. Il faut faire renvoi aux arguments juridiques avancés par la défenderesse pour refuser de prendre aucune part active dans la procédure. En fait la défenderesse ne nomma pas d'arbitre. M. Z. fut nommé par la Cour d'Arbitrage de la CCI, conformément à l'article 2.4 du Règlement de la CCI. La constitution du Tribunal Arbitral fut complétée le 3 novembre 1985 par la nomination par la Cour d'Arbitrage de la CCI, sur proposition commune des deux coarbitres, de M. G.

6. Bien que dûment mise en demeure, la défenderesse ne se présenta pas non plus à la première session du Tribunal Arbitral. Cette session eut lieu à Paris le 16 janvier 1986 aux fins de rédaction de l'Acte de Mission du Tribunal Arbitral. L'Acte de Mission, approuvé par la Cour d'Arbitrage de la CCI le 4 mars 1986 fut envoyé aux parties dès le lendemain. Un délai de 15 jours était accordé à la défenderesse pour le signer. La défenderesse accusa réception de l'Acte de Mission mais ne le signa pas et le retourna au Secrétariat de la Cour d'Arbitrage de la CCI.

7. Le 18 novembre 1985, la défenderesse avait été invitée à envoyer au Secrétariat de la Cour d'Arbitrage de la CCI sa part de l'avance sur frais. Elle n'en fit rien. En conséquence, la demanderesse fut invitée à verser la part de la défenderesse (article 9.2 du Règlement d'Arbitrage de la CCI). Le dépôt correspondant fut versé par la demanderesse le 28 avril 1986, ce qui fit que l'acte de mission entra en vigueur ce jour même (article 9.4 du Règlement d'Arbitrage de la CCI).

8. L'acte de mission stipule (page 6, dernier paragraphe) un examen séparé et préliminaire du problème de la compétence du Tribunal Arbitral et une sentence partielle sur ce sujet (article 8.3 du Règlement de la CCI). Un mémoire sur ce sujet fut présenté par le Conseil de la demanderesse le 28 mai 1986. Sa principale conclusion était que « le Tribunal arbitral est compétent pour trancher en dernier ressort le présent litige ». Une copie du mémoire fut adressée pour commentaires à la défenderesse le 30 mai 1986. La défenderesse ne répondit pas.

9. Dans la lettre d'envoi de son mémoire du 28 mai 1986, le conseil de la demanderesse, faisant référence à l'article 14.3 du Règlement de la CCI, demandait expressément au Tribunal Arbitral de se prononcer sur la question de compétence sur la seule base des documents pertinents.

Arguments juridiques de la défenderesse

Les arguments juridiques sur lesquels la défenderesse fonde ses objections à la compétence du Tribunal Arbitral sont les suivants :

— le droit égyptien régit la totalité de l'accord du 4 février 1983, y compris la clause d'arbitrage,

— dans le domaine de l'arbitrage comme dans toute autre partie du droit, il faut réserver l'ordre public (article 28 du Code civil égyptien),

— parmi les dispositions du Code de procédure civile égyptien, les articles 502 (sur le choix des arbitres), 509 (sur l'exécution des sentences arbitrales) et 512/513 (sur les recours en annulation de la sentence) doivent être considérés comme faisant partie de l'ordre public égyptien,

— ces mêmes dispositions du Code de procédure civile égyptien s'appliquent, que l'arbitrage en question soit national ou international,

— certaines des règles de la CCI sur l'arbitrage ne sont pas conformes aux dispositions du Code de procédure civile égyptien auxquelles il est fait référence,

— en conséquence, une sentence arbitrale rendue selon le Règlement de la CCI ne pourrait pas être exécutée en Egypte.

Arguments juridiques de la demanderesse

— En résumé, l'opinion de la demanderesse, exprimée dans le mémoire du 28 mai 1986, est que la clause d'arbitrage est valable en droit égyptien, en droit français et en droit international.

— Valable selon les lois égyptiennes puisque, aux termes de l'article 22 du Code civil égyptien, le problème de la validité d'une clause d'arbitrage doit être décidé selon le droit du pays où est rendue la sentence arbitrale.

— Valable selon le droit français qui est le droit du pays où l'arbitrage a lieu et où devra être rendue la sentence arbitrale.

— Valable selon les articles I, II et V de la Convention des Nations-Unies du 10 juin 1958 sur la Reconnaissance et l'Exécution des Sentences Arbitrales Etrangères (nommée ci-après « Convention de New York »), un traité international auquel sont parties l'Egypte et la France.

Selon la demanderesse, l'article 502 du Code de procédure civile égyptien n'est pas pertinent. Cet article ne relève pas de l'ordre public égyptien. Il ne saurait l'emporter sur les dispositions d'un traité international comme la Convention de New York. Les décisions contraires des tribunaux ont été renversées par la jurisprudence récente de la Cour de cassation égyptienne.

Le droit

1. Les parties sont convenues que tout litige ou différend résultant de leur contrat du 4 février 1983 ou s'y rapportant devra être tranché définitivement par arbitrage « selon les règles et procédures d'arbitrage de la Chambre de Commerce Internationale à Paris ». Elles ont choisi Paris comme lieu de l'arbitrage. La référence au Règlement de la CCI dans la clause d'arbitrage est d'une clarté parfaite. A l'époque de sa formulation, la défenderesse n'y a pas fait d'objection.

II. Même aujourd'hui la défenderesse ne suggère en aucune façon que l'actuelle procédure arbitrale pourrait être contraire au Règlement de la CCI, ni que le Règlement de la CCI lui-même pourrait être contraire au droit français ou à la Convention de New York. L'objection de la défenderesse à l'arbitrage considéré ici s'appuie entièrement sur quelques dispositions du Code de procédure civile égyptien de 1968, en particulier son article 502, paragraphe 3.

Aux termes de la disposition précitée, les arbitres doivent être mentionnés sous leur nom dans la clause d'arbitrage ou dans un accord séparé, à moins qu'une loi déterminée n'en décide autrement.

III. La principale question est donc de savoir si l'article 502, paragraphe 3 du Code de procédure civile Egyptien (CPCE) s'applique réellement au présent arbitrage. La défenderesse propose, apparemment sous forme d'alternative, quatre raisons de répondre à cette question par l'affirmative :

— Le Code de procédure civile égyptien ne fait aucune distinction entre les arbitrages nationaux et internationaux.

— Le droit égyptien régit dans sa totalité le contrat du 4 février 1983, y compris la clause d'arbitrage de l'article XIV.

— L'article 502, paragraphe 3 du CPCE est une disposition d'ordre public.

— Aucun Tribunal égyptien ne pourrait ordonner l'exécution d'une sentence arbitrale étrangère contraire à l'article 502, paragraphe 3 du CPCE.

Ces quatre raisons vont être examinées une à une.

IV. Il peut être vrai que le Code de procédure civile égyptien ne distingue pas entre arbitrages nationaux et internationaux. Certains Etats, dont la France, ont récemment promulgué deux Séries de règles (nationales) sur l'arbitrage, l'une pour les arbitrages nationaux, l'autre pour les arbitrages internationaux (voir par exemple, respectivement, les articles 1442 à 1491 et les articles 1492 à 1507 du nouveau Code de procédure civile français, qui ont fait l'objet du Décret n° 81-500 du 12 mai 1981). Mais la plupart des Etats, comme l'Egypte, n'ont qu'une seule série de règles (nationales) sur l'arbitrage. Cela ne veut pourtant pas dire que ces Etats vont nécessairement appliquer les mêmes règles à toutes les procédures et sentences arbitrales sans tenir compte, par exemple, du lieu de l'arbitrage. On peut au moins attendre d'eux qu'ils observent les dispositions des traités internationaux auxquels ils sont parties. Dans le cas présent le fait que le Code de procédure civile égyptien ne contienne pas de dispositions ayant pour objet spécifique les arbitrage internationaux est une chose. L'autre chose est que l'Egypte est partie à la Convention de New York, une Convention qui ne fait pas dépendre la reconnaissance et l'exécution d'une sentence arbitrale étrangère de conditions comme celles qui peuvent se trouver dans l'article 502, paragraphe 3 du CPCE.

V. L'article XV de l'accord du 4 février 1983 a déjà été cité. Il dit que « le contrat est régi par le droit égyptien ». La question de savoir si ceci s'applique seulement au fond de l'accord ou également à la clause d'arbitrage peut être

laissée ouverte. La loi égyptienne fait en tout cas dépendre la validité de la procédure arbitrale de la loi du pays où cette procédure doit avoir lieu (art. 22 du Code civil égyptien — Samir Saleh, l'Arbitrage commercial dans le Moyen-Orient Arabe, Londres, 1984, Chapitre 16 : Egypte, page 210). Dans l'affaire présente, c'est le droit français et celui-ci ne comporte aucune règle semblable à celle de l'article 502, paragraphe 3 du CPCE.

VI.   Quelques tribunaux égyptiens ont été ou sont encore d'avis que l'article 502, paragraphe 3 du CPCE non seulement représente une disposition obligatoire du droit national mais aussi fait partie de l'ordre public de l'Egypte et doit, à ce titre, l'emporter même sur toute règle du droit étranger normalement applicable. A présent, cependant, la doctrine juridique égyptienne est divisée à ce sujet (cf. Ahmed S. El-Kosheri, Quelques aspects particuliers des attitudes officielles égyptiennes vis-à-vis de l'Arbitrage commercial, dans (76) l'Egypte contemporaine — n° 400, avril 1985, pages 5-20) et dans des arrêts récents, la Cour de cassation égyptienne a exprimé une opinion différente, du moins en ce qui concerne les conventions arbitrales conclues hors d'Egypte. Dans ce contexte, il convient de se référer en particulier à l'arrêt de la Cour de cassation égyptienne du 26 avril 1982, dans l'affaire 714 de l'année judiciaire 47. Cet arrêt est résumé par le professeur El Kosheri dans l'article susmentionné (pages 118-119) et il l'a été aussi dans une contribution du même auteur à un séminaire tenu à Paris les 17, 18 décembre 1984, sous les auspices de l'Institut du Droit et des Pratiques du Commerce International. La conclusion de la Cour a été, essentiellement, qu'il était inacceptable de prétendre exclure l'application du droit étranger parce que ce droit ne serait pas conforme à l'article 502, paragraphe 3 du CPCE.

L'article 502, paragraphe 3 du CPCE contient lui-même une réserve. Il ne doit pas s'appliquer si des dispositions différentes de lois particulières ne comportent pas la même exigence. Une réserve de ce genre exclut la possibilité de se rallier à la prétention que l'article 502, paragraphe 3, faisant partie de l'ordre public, s'appliquerait à tout arbitrage, national ou international, conduit en Egypte ou ailleurs. Cette même prétention est églament inconciliable avec le fait que l'Egypte est liée par des traités internationaux, bilatéraux ou multilatéraux, impliquant qu'on ne saurait opposer une objection tirée de l'article 502, paragraphe 3 du CPCE à une sentence arbitrale étrangère. Or l'Egypte n'est pas seulement partie à la convention de New York mais aussi à la convention de Washington du 18 mars 1965 pour le règlement des litiges entre Etats et Nationaux d'autres Etats. Des clauses sur l'arbitrage figurent également dans plusieurs traités bilatéraux sur la protection de l'investissement, conclus par l'Egypte, par exemple avec la République Fédérale d'Allemagne, la France, la Suisse et les Etats Unis d'Amérique. Dans tous ces cas, la méthode de nomination des arbitres est différente de celle prescrite par l'article 502, paragraphe 3 du CPCE.

VII.   Une autre objection soulevée par la défenderesse est que même si la clause arbitrale de l'article XIV de l'accord du 4 février 1983 doit être considérée comme valable, un arbitrage régi par le règlement de la CCI serait néanmoins « vain » parce que l'article 502, paragraphe 3 du CPCE rendrait impossibles la reconnaissance et l'exécution de la sentence étrangère correspondante.

C'est bien sûr le devoir du Tribunal Arbitral de « faire tous ses efforts pour que la sentence soit susceptible de sanction légale » (article 26 du réglement de la CCI). Un autre fait, déjà mentionné, est que certains tribunaux égyptiens ont jugé que l'article 502, paragraphe 3 du CPCE était applicable même dans le cas de procédures arbitrales internationales conduites hors d'Egypte. Dans ces conditions — bien connues de la demanderesse — il est manifestement en dehors du pouvoir du Tribunal Arbitral de donner l'assurance qu'il n'y aurait pas de difficultés d'exécution en Egypte. Mais au point où nous en sommes, il n'est pas possible de prévoir avec certitude si la reconnaissance et l'exécution de la sentence seront recherchés en Egypte ou dans un autre pays. En tout cas la ferme conviction du Tribunal Arbitral est que s'il se fondait sur l'article 502, paragraphe 3 du CPCE, un refus de reconnaître et d'exécuter une sentence arbitrale rendue en France conformément au droit français et au Règlement de la CCI équivaudrait à une violation de la Convention de New York. Le Tribunal Arbitral s'interdit de fonder sa décision relative à sa propre compétence sur l'hypothèse qu'un tribunal égyptien voudrait commettre, ou approuver, une violation du droit que constitue une convention internationale. Il doit être au contraire assumé que tout tribunal égyptien voudrait tenir pleinement compte de l'évolution la plus récente de la jurisprudence de la Cour de cassation, et appliquer les engagements internationaux pris par l'Egypte qui a été l'un des premiers signataires de la Convention de New York.

VIII. Les parties, il faut le répéter, ont accepté une clause d'arbitrage prévoyant l'application du règlement de la Cour d'Arbitrage de la CCI. La requête d'arbitrage de la demanderesse a été présentée selon le règlement de la CCI. Dans une phase ultérieure, c'est également conformément au règlement de la CCI que le Tribunal Arbitral a été établi.

Il n'y a rien dans la façon dont a été nommé le Tribunal Arbitral qui serait contraire au droit français en tant que loi du pays où a lieu l'arbitrage. Il n'y a, dans la lettre écrite par la défenderesse le 10 mai 1985, rien qui puisse libérer les arbitres de la tâche qui leur a été confiée. Les objections soulevées par la défenderesse en référence à l'article 502, paragraphe 3 du CPCE sont sans effet car cet article ne porte pas sur l'affaire en cours.

Pour ces motifs,

le Tribunal Arbitral

1. Rejette les objections soulevées par la défenderesse contre la validité de la convention arbitrale.

2. Se déclare compétent pour juger le fond de l'affaire.

3. Fixe à la défenderesse un délai de trois mois à dater de la notification qui lui sera faite de la présente sentence pour soumettre un mémoire sur le fond.

4. Déclare qu'il n'y a pas encore à prendre une décision sur les coûts et frais de l'affaire.

OBSERVATIONS. — La situation actuelle en ce qui concerne l'arbitrage international en Egypte ou avec des parties égyptiennes est inquiétante, sinon alarmante.

On peut dire en général que les parties égyptiennes acceptent la clause d'arbitrage de la CCI et la procédure de nomination selon le règlement de la CCI, et cela lorsque la partie égyptienne est demanderesse mais également défenderesse. Cela comprend les affaires où la partie égyptienne est une autorité ou une entreprise publique, représentée par des conseils issus de l'administration qui représente l'Etat en justice.

Pourtant, dans plusieurs affaires portées devant la CCI, les parties égyptiennes ont contesté l'existence ou la validité de la convention d'arbitrage, tout en plaidant leur cause devant les arbitres chargés de trancher le litige. L'affaire 5269 en est un exemple. Les parties ont utilisé le cadre de l'arbitrage et les ouvertures qu'offrent les règles de l'arbitrage pour présenter leurs points de vue, maintenant ainsi l'affaire dans les frontières de l'organisation de l'arbitrage afin de respecter son caractère confidentiel.

Mais les choses ont changé vers la fin de 1983 quand une partie égyptienne a engagé un procès devant un tribunal égyptien. Cette affaire ne tarda pas à être suivie de plusieurs autres où la défenderesse cherchait à obtenir un jugement du tribunal interrompant et/ou invalidant la procédure arbitrale. Des attaques devaient suivre, non seulement contre l'autre partie à l'arbitrage mais aussi contre la CCI, sa Cour d'Arbitrage et ses comités nationaux. Ces nouveaux types d'action obligèrent la CCI à engager en Egypte des avocats locaux à ses propres frais (affaire CCI 4718, no. du rôle 433/1983, tribunal du Caire Sud, référé 11477/83, 14ᵉ Chambre civile ; affaire CCI 4974, no. du rôle 119/85, tribunal du Caire Sud ; affaire CCI 5472, tribunal du Caire Sud).

Dans les trois affaires qui viennent d'être citées, les tribunaux égyptiens n'ont pas pris de décision sur l'applicabilité de l'article 502 (3) du Code de procédure civile égyptien (CPCE). Dans les deux affaires intéressant des parties privées égyptiennes, les tribunaux égyptiens n'en auront pas non plus l'occasion car il y a eu retrait de l'arbitrage. Il reste à voir ce que le tribunal du Caire Sud décidera dans l'affaire restante où un ministère égyptien est engagé comme défenderesse.

Dans l'affaire dite Westland (publiée dans *Yearbook Commercial Arbitration*, Vol. XI p. 127 et au *Clunet* 1985, p.232) une société britannique avait engagé en 1980 un arbitrage contre des Etats arabes, dont l'Egypte, une société transnationale et une société égyptienne. Alors que l'arbitrage se déroulait à Genève, l'Etat Egyptien cita la CCI et les parties à son arbitrage à comparaître devant le Tribunal de Première Instance du Caire.

L'Etat Egyptien demandait qu'il soit dit que la CCI était incompétente pour juger le litige, l'annulation de la clause d'arbitrage, l'annulation de toutes mesures de procédure et décisions prises par la CCI et le paiement par la CCI et Westland d'un million de dollars à titre de dommages. Le Tribunal de Première Instance jugea la requête irrecevable, étant donné l'existence d'une clause d'arbitrage. La Cour d'appel du Caire cassa ce jugement et renvoya l'affaire au Tribunal de Première Instance qui, le 25 janvier 1986, apparemment condamna la CCI à payer la somme réclamée (un million de dollars).

La Cour d'appel du Caire a trouvé que les accords invoqués par Westland n'avaient été ni signés, ni souscrits par l'Etat Egyptien. Un tel accord ne pouvait lier que l'A.O.I. qui n'était pas dissoute et poursuivait ses activités en Egypte. En conséquence l'Egypte ne pouvait être partie à un arbitrage devant la CCI et la CCI était incompétente (Décision du 18 mai 1983, 12ᵉ Chambre civile).

La validité de la clause d'arbitrage de la CCI a été contestée devant des tribunaux égyptiens dans d'autres affaires et des ordonnances ont été sollicitées et accordées. Les arguments avancés sont invariablement l'article 502 (3) du Code de procédure civile égyptien et, dans certains cas, que les entreprises du secteur public ne peuvent pas consentir à l'arbitrage international (affaire CCI 4974, no. du rôle 119/85, Tribunal du Caire Sud ; aff. CCI 5029, no. du rôle 13029/1985, Tribunal du Cair Sud ; aff. CCI 5448, Tribunal du Caire Sud ; aff. CCI 5495, no. du rôle 8460/1986, Tribunal du Caire Sud). Le Tribunal du Caire n'a pas encore tranché ces quatre affaires.

Il est clair que la situation en Egypte s'est détériorée depuis quelques années par rapport au tableau idyllique que Mark S.W. Hoyle en a brossé en 1984, lorsqu'il a soutenu qu'une interprétation plus islamique des lois et procédures n'avait pas eu d'effet marqué et que les arbitrages pouvaient continuer sans être grandement affectés ; que le droit égyptien ne présentait pas de difficultés fondamentales pour les parties prenant des précautions raisonnables, y compris le recours à une clause d'arbitrage (An Introductory View of Arbitration in Egypt — dans *Arbitration*, november 1984, p. 166).

Au séminaire régional sur l'arbitrage qui s'est tenu au Caire en janvier 1986, le représentant de la CCI a exprimé les préoccupations de cette dernière et des milieux économiques internationaux et déclaré qu'à moins d'une confirmation que l'article 502 (3) du CPCE ne s'applique pas aux arbitrages soumis à des règles internationales, les entreprises internationales risquaient de marquer une très grande hésitation quant à la possibilité d'avoir recours à l'arbitrage avec des parties égyptiennes et à l'efficacité de l'arbitrage international en Egypte (V. *Arab Law Quarterly*, Vol. I no. 3 (1980) p. 298).

Le 7 février 1987, le Tribunal de Première Instance de Giza a rendu un jugement pouvant mettre fin aux difficultés que rencontre actuellement l'arbitrage international en Egypte. Le tribunal a décidé qu'une clause d'arbitrage de la CCI l'empêchait de juger une affaire soumise par une partie, et déclaré la requête « irrecevable » étant donné la présence d'une clause d'arbitrage. Ce faisant le tribunal s'est prononcé contre les arguments avancés dans l'affaire 5269 ainsi que par d'autres juristes depuis trois ou quatre ans, selon lesquels l'article 502 (3) du Code de procédure civile égyptien rendrait nulle et non avenue la convention d'arbitrage, à moins que les noms des arbitres ne figurent dans l'accord.

La décision du tribunal de Giza a été le premier jugement rendu dans un certain nombre d'affaires actuellement pendantes devant les tribunaux égyptiens et intéressant des parties à un arbitrage CCI.

La décision de Giza

(No. du rôle 10063, 1983, Tribunal de Première Instance de Giza ; décision rendue le 7 février 1987).

Le texte suivant est une traduction officieuse de l'original en langue arabe :

« *Le tribunal indique en premier lieu que l'arbitrage devient une méthode obligatoire de règlement des litiges dès lors que les parties se sont accordées à ce sujet. La convention arbitrale peut être comprise dans un contrat donné et est alors connue sous le nom de "clause compromissoire" ou peut être conclue à l'occasion d'un différend existant, sous forme de "compromis". Dans le premier cas l'application de la clause n'est qu'éventuelle car un différend peut se produire mais aussi ne se produire jamais.*

Considérant que l'arbitrage fait partie des « contrats consensuels » formés par l'échange d'une offre et de son acceptation, sans exiger aucune forme spéciale — qu'il s'agisse d'une clause compromissoire ou d'un compromis — les parties ont le droit de stipuler leur intention comme elles le jugent approprié — de même que dans tout autre contrat consensuel — sans être tenues d'employer certains termes. Ce qui compte par essence est que les parties exercent leur liberté d'exprimer une intention commune de s'abstenir de saisir les tribunaux judiciaires et de régler leurs différends en recourant à l'arbitrage.

Le paragraphe 3 de l'article 502 du Code de procédure civile égyptien indique que la convention d'arbitrage peut comporter deux phases dont la première est l'accord pour régler le litige par l'arbitrage, ou "promesse d'arbitrer", et la seconde l'accord sur la personne qui deviendra l'arbitre.

Considérant que la clause compromissoire implique l'accord des parties pour renoncer à saisir les tribunaux judiciaires, c'est-à-dire le tribunal initialement compétent pour juger le différend, les parties doivent donc être considérées comme ayant, d'une intention commune, exclu le recours aux tribunaux.

En conséquence l'action judiciaire perd l'une de ses conditions de recevabilité et le tribunal doit s'abstenir de se saisir de l'affaire.

La règle ci-dessus s'applique même si la clause compromissoire ne prévoit la détermination et la nomination des arbitres qu'après la naissance du litige relatif à l'exécution du contrat et si l'une des parties au litige ne se conforme pas par la suite à la clause d'arbitrage. Il est légalement établi que la situation est la même, que l'accord sur la personne des arbitres figure dans la convention d'arbitrage elle-même (clause compromissoire ou compromis) ou qu'elle fasse l'objet d'un accord indépendant. Il n'y a pas non plus de différence selon qu'un tel accord indépendant existe antérieurement au contrat ou qu'il soit conclu ultérieurement (Arbitrage obligatoire et librement consenti, par le D^r. Ahmed Aboul Wafi, 4e édition, p. 21 et ss.).

Considérant tout ce qui précède et que l'examen du contrat de bail daté du 21-03-1979, conclu entre les deux demandeurs en leur capacité et le premier défendeur, montre qu'il a été convenu dans l'article 18 dudit contrat ce qui suit :

"Tout litige survenant entre les parties au sujet de l'interprétation ou de l'exécution du contrat, et en particulier tout litige entre elles ayant trait au présent contrat directement ou indirectement sera réglé dans la ville de Port Saïd (RAE) conformément au système de conciliation et d'arbitrage de la Chambre de Commerce Internationale par trois arbitres, chaque partie nommant un arbitre et le troisième arbitre étant nommé selon ce système. La décision des arbitres sera définitive et engagera les parties."

Aux termes de l'article 8 du Règlement de la Cour d'Arbitrage de la CCI, Règlement selon lequel il est convenu d'aller à l'arbitrage, le refus de l'une des parties de participer à la procédure arbitrale ou son défaut de comparaître n'empêche par l'arbitrage de se poursuivre en dépit de ce refus ou défaut.

En raison de toutes les considérations ci-dessus, le tribunal décide de déclarer le recours irrecevable en raison de l'existence de la clause d'arbitrage.

Le tribunal condamne les deux demandeurs au paiement des frais et honoraires d'avocats, conformément à l'article 184 du Code de procédure et à l'article 187 de la loi no. 17/83 sur la défense.

Pour ces motifs

Le tribunal décide que les deux recours sont irrecevables en raison de l'existence de la clause d'arbitrage et condamne les deux demandeurs au paiement des frais et d'une somme de 10 livres pour honoraires de droit.

Le Greffier   *Le Président-juge du tribunal »*

On peut être surpris de voir que des arguments aussi prolongés et vifs ont été développés récemment au sujet de l'application de l'article 502 (3) du CPCE à propos de clauses d'arbitrage international, et que les tribunaux égyptiens de Première Instance ont jugé nécessaire d'arrêter des arbitrages, d'émettre des ordonnances contre des institutions arbitrales et des parties (même quand le lieu de l'arbitrage dans une affaire donnée se situait hors d'Egypte) plutôt que de débouter les requérants. Des commentateurs de la jurisprudence égyptienne ont exprimé leur surprise en observant qu'il est bien établi que l'article 502 (3) ne s'applique pas aux accords d'arbitrage internationaux et que ce n'est en tout cas pas une règle d'ordre public.

Dans la sentence intérimaire rendue dans l'affaire 5269, il est fait référence à la décision de la Cour Suprême égyptienne du 26 avril 1982 dans l'affaire Mabrouk Trading Import & Export c. The Arab Continental Navigation Co. et al. Aux termes d'une charte-partie pour le transport de ciment d'Alexandrie en Egypte à Tripoli en Libye, les litiges devaient être soumis à l'arbitrage à Londres. Un Tribunal de Première Instance et la Cour d'appel d'Alexandrie avaient rejeté la demande d'imposer l'arbitrage mais la Cour Suprême a renversé la décision. Voici l'essentiel de ses motifs (traduction officieuse) :

« I. La clause d'arbitrage comprise dans la charte-partie spécifie que les litiges seront soumis à l'arbitrage à Londres et le législateur a admis l'arbitrage à l'étranger et ne l'a pas considéré comme un manquement à l'ordre public.

II. L'appréciation de la validité de la clause d'arbitrage et de ses conséquences doit être faite selon les règles du droit anglais, qui est le droit du pays où l'arbitrage doit avoir lieu, à condition que ce droit ne viole pas l'ordre public égyptien. Lorsque l'arrêt considère cette clause comme nulle et non avenue parce que les noms des arbitres ne sont pas mentionnés conformément à l'article 502 (3) du Code de procédure civile Egyptien, il commet donc une erreur de droit en la faisant régir par le droit égyptien au lieu du droit anglais qui est le droit applicable.

III. Il n'y a pas de raison d'écarter les dispositions du droit anglais parce que celui-ci serait contraire à la procédure de l'article 502 (3), même dans l'éventualité d'une contradiction, puisque la loi étrangère applicable ne doit être écartée, aux termes de l'article 28 du Code civil, que si elle viole l'ordre public égyptien, c'est-à-dire contrevient aux fondements sociaux, à la politique, à l'économie ou à la morale et touche à l'intérêt public de la société ; il ne suffit pas qu'elle contredise une loi impérative.

IV. La procédure de l'article 502 (3) qui règle la nomination des arbitres dans une convention d'arbitrage ou un accord distinct, n'est pas d'ordre public et le fait d'y contrevenir n'est pas une raison suffisante pour écarter la loi étrangère applicable. »

La décision de la Cour Suprême dans l'affaire Mabrouk Trading semble signifier qu'un arbitrage devant avoir lieu hors d'Egypte est valable et ne viole pas l'ordre public égyptien ; la validité de la clause d'arbitrage dépend du droit du lieu de l'arbitrage pour autant que celui-ci ne viole pas l'ordre public égyptien ; l'article 502 (3) n'est pas d'ordre public ; ce qui est contraire à une loi impérative (obligatoire) n'est pas nécessairement contraire à l'ordre public égyptien.

Le 12 mars 1986, le Ministre égyptien de la justice a créé une commission d'éminents juristes égyptiens pour élaborer une loi sur l'arbitrage international. La Commission a présenté, au printemps 1987, un projet de loi qui paraît en partie inspiré de la loi modèle CNUDCI. Si ce projet de loi est adopté, prévoyant la liberté des parties de nommer les arbitres soit directement, soit par l'intermédiaire d'une institution, les difficultés actuelles relatives à la nomination des arbitres dans le contexte de l'arbitrage international et égyptien, pourront être évitées.

En résumé, la sentence rendue dans l'affaire 5269 est conforme à la décision de la Cour Suprême égyptienne dans l'affaire Mabrouk Trading. La décision du tribunal de Giza pourrait être le début de la fin d'une série d'affaires judiciaires contestant la validité de la clause d'arbitrage de la CCI. Mais, comme il a été fait appel du jugement de Giza, des doutes subsistent au sujet de l'efficacité d'une convention d'arbitrage dans le contexte égyptien. Le récent projet de loi égyptien sur l'arbitrage international pourra clarifier ces doutes.

S. J.

I. — **Clause compromissoire.** — Arbitrage international. — Article 8 (3) du règlement de la CCI. — Compétence de l'arbitre pour statuer sur sa propre compétence.

II. — **Clause compromissoire.** — Arbitrage international. — Droit applicable — Absence de choix par les parties. — Principes généraux du droit et usages du commerce international.

III. — **Contrat.** — Droit applicable. — Principes généraux du droit et usages du commerce international. — Contrat en formation. — Absence de signature. — Paraphe. — Portée. — Exécution.

IV. — **Contrat.** — Conclusion pour le compte d'une société à créer. — Principes généraux du droit et usages du commerce international. — Bonne foi.

V. — **Contrat.** — Apparence.

Sentence intérimaire rendue dans l'affaire n° 5065 en 1986 (l'original de la sentence est en langue anglaise).

Un arbitre unique, britannique, siégeant à Paris, était appelé à trancher un différend opposant un demandeur libanais, A..., à deux sociétés pakistanaises B... et C..., défenderesses, concernant la rupture par ces dernières d'un contrat relatif à la fourniture de conseils en architecture par le demandeur dans un projet de développement d'un stade.

Les parties défenderesses contestaient la compétence de l'arbitre en alléguant que le contrat produit par le demandeur et contenant une clause d'arbitrage n'avait pas d'effet obligatoire car il n'était pas signé mais seulement paraphé. La Cour d'Arbitrage de la Chambre de Commerce Internationale ayant estimé, en application de l'article 8 (3) de son Règlement qu'il existait *prima facie* une convention d'arbitrage, il appartenait à l'arbitre de se prononcer sur sa propre compétence. Il rappela tout d'abord qu'il avait effectivement ce pouvoir dans les termes suivants :

« *Avant d'examiner les faits, il serait utile de définir quelles sont les fonctions d'un arbitre lorsqu'il décide de sa propre compétence. Dans les cas où le recours à l'arbitrage n'est pas contesté, mais que c'est l'étendue des questions soumises à l'arbitrage qui est en cause, il est généralement accepté que l'arbitre a le pouvoir de décider de sa propre compétence sauf stipulation contraire des parties. Il en est toutefois tout à fait autrement lorsque c'est la question de la soumission à arbitrage elle-même qui est soulevée. La compétence arbitrale dépend exclusivement de l'accord des parties. En conséquence, il est logiquement impossible à l'arbitre de décider lui-même, de façon qui fasse autorité, de sa propre compétence, dans de telles circonstances. Une telle décision ne peut être prise que par un tribunal dont la compétence n'est pas dépendante de l'accord des parties. Face à une contestation relative à l'existence d'un quelconque accord concernant une soumission à arbitrage, le système d'arbitrage à le choix entre refuser de commencer toute procédure avant que la question n'ait été résolue par un tribunal approprié, qu'il soit national ou international, ou commencer la procédure "de bene esse", laissant les parties débattre de la question à la fois devant le Tribunal Arbitral, et si elles le désirent, devant tout tribunal auquel on demandera par la suite de faire exécuter la sentence.* »

330

Adopter la première solution signifie que le demandeur est privé des avantages qu'il a choisis en optant pour l'arbitrage et qu'il soutient avoir été acceptés par l'autre partie. Refuser de poursuivre une procédure d'arbitrage permet aux parties défenderesses de repousser la procédure et de refuser au demandeur exactement les avantages qu'il cherche à obtenir.

Adopter la deuxième solution et permettre à l'arbitrage de commencer ne signifie pas contredire l'argument logique qui veut que l'arbitre ne peut pas s'accorder lui-même compétence, mais permet simplement que la décision faisant autorité soit prise plus tard. L'arbitre doit lui-même prendre une décision préliminaire : lui semble-t-il qu'il y ait eu accord quant à sa compétence ? Le Règlement de la Cour d'Arbitrage de la Chambre de Commerce Internationale a adopté la deuxième solution et permet à l'arbitre, après qu'une décision administrative préliminaire ait été prise par la Cour, de prendre sa propre décision concernant sa compétence. Le demandeur qui réclame la continuation de la procédure d'arbitrage malgré la négation par l'autre partie de l'existence d'un accord de soumission à l'arbitrage prend le risque de supporter les coûts relatifs à la fois à la procédure d'arbitrage et à toute procédure ultérieure, mais obtient les avantages de l'arbitrage si ultérieurement les défendeurs acceptent la sentence du Tribunal Arbitral, ou si l'exécution de la sentence est ordonnée par une cour compétente. C'est toutefois le propre de telles procédures d'arbitrage que, pour éviter des injustices, les défendeurs aient la possibilité d'y prendre part sans être considérés s'être soumis à la juridiction de l'arbitre. Dans le cas présent, la première défenderesse a décidé de ne pas prendre part à la procédure, alors que la seconde a pris part à la procédure tout en réservant tous ses droits de contester la compétence de ce tribunal. L'objet de cette sentence préliminaire est de déterminer, en accord avec le Règlement de la Cour d'Arbitrage de la Chambre de Commerce Internationale, si le tribunal est persuadé qu'il y a eu accord de l'une ou l'autre, ou des deux défenderesses concernant la soumission à l'arbitrage. »

L'arbitre résuma ensuite les faits et les questions qui lui étaient soumises :

« Lorsqu'en 1980 B. voulut augmenter le nombre de sièges du stade qu'il possédait et dirigeait à..., il eut besoin de fonds pour ce faire et décida d'associer ces travaux au développement des terrains entourant le stade, les profits tirés de ce développement devant fournir le financement nécessaire. B., qui n'avait ni la taille ni l'expérience nécessaires pour planifier et contrôler de tels travaux de développement demanda à C... d'être le promoteur de ce projet. Etant donné que les deux sociétés avaient le même président ceci n'était pas surprenant, et il ne fait aucun doute d'après les preuves qui m'ont été apportées à la fois par des témoignages et des documents que C..., et donc ses dirigeants, agissaient à la fois pour le compte de cette dernière mais aussi pour le compte de B...

B... et C... nommèrent également MS... afin qu'il soit leur conseil et leur représentant spécial s'occupant et coordonnant le travail avec les architectes... Selon le propre témoignage de MS..., il était autorisé à signer des contrats pour le compte de B... et de C..., qu'il décrit comme remplissant le rôle de celui connu en France sous le nom de "Maître de l'Ouvrage". MS... était également chargé de mettre au point le contrat destiné aux architectes selon les instructions de MH... qui était à l'époque le Directeur Général de C... mais était également le bras-droit du Président commun de B... et de C... MH... n'occupait aucun poste officiel au sein de B..., mais étant donné que B... s'était en fait associé avec C... pour les travaux de développement et l'avait nommé pour agir en tant que Maître de l'Ouvrage, et étant donné que MH. était le Directeur Général de C..., il ne fait à mon avis aucun doute que MH. était investi d'une autorité apparente, et probablement réelle, lui permettant d'agir au nom de B... relativement au développement projeté...

Les travaux commencèrent donc avant que les négociations relatives au contrat des architectes soient terminées. Le 20 ou autour du 20 octobre 1980, les termes du contrat des architectes ont été acceptés par le demandeur et C... à l'exception de deux points. En effet, MH..., dans les réponses écrites qu'il m'a envoyées.. disait que le paraphe du "Contract Agreement" avait été apposé "dans l'intention d'indiquer que tous les termes étaient acceptés au nom de C... et également pour le compte du président de B...". Il semble que deux points étaient encore en suspens, ce pourquoi le "Contract Agreement" n'a été que paraphé et non signé de manière formelle. Le premier point était une question de double imposition, au sujet de laquelle on espérait que le paiement pourrait être effectué de telle façon que l'on puisse profiter des avantages d'un traité fiscal auquel le Pakistan était partie, plutôt que de risquer une double imposition.

Que cette question soit résolue était à l'avantage de B... et de C... car les termes du contrat concernant la rémunération des architectes prévoyaient le paiement des sommes dues en raison de la taxation en sus des pourcentages établis dans le contrat. Le second point qui a pu causer le fait que le contrat soit seulement paraphé est que B... et C... avaient l'intention de créer une société qui aurait inclus d'autres participants qui auraient fourni des fonds pour les travaux d'aménagements... »

« *L'intention de créer une société spéciale pour les travaux d'aménagements se traduit dans le titre même du contrat, étant donné que C... est déclarée agir "pour le compte et au nom" (le mot "de" est ensuite supprimé) de la société qui doit être créée. Les parties s'y réfèrent, en sa qualité à la fois de "propriétaire" et de "clients".*

Deux questions me semblent donc se poser : la première est de savoir si le fait que ce document fut seulement paraphé et tout-à-fait délibérément non signé dans sa forme définitive, signifie que les parties n'avaient pas l'intention d'établir un contrat formel qui les aurait liées, c'est-à-dire en d'autres termes, que leurs relations étaient "subject to contract" ; la seconde question est de savoir si C... agissait en tant que partie contractante, au moins jusqu'à ce que la nouvelle société soit formée ».

L'arbitre estima cependant qu'avant d'examiner ces deux questions, il devait se prononcer sur le droit applicable :

« *Quel droit régit les conséquences légales qui découlent de la négociation et du paraphage d'un contrat, ainsi que celles résultant du comportement ultérieur des parties. Tout d'abord, c'est une théorie bien connue que le droit auquel est soumis le contrat n'a pas nécessairement besoin d'être le même que celui qui régit la convention d'arbitrage, y compris la question de l'existence de cette convention. Dans le cas présent, les parties n'ont en fait pas choisi le droit qui devait régir le contrat lui-même. MS, qui a élaboré le projet de contrat sur les instructions de MH, pour le compte de B... et de C... et l'a négocié avec le demandeur, a déclaré que les parties avaient délibérément choisi de ne désigner aucun droit particulier, mais étaient prêtes à accepter celui choisi par la suite par l'arbitre, si une procédure devait intervenir. »*

« *Quel que soit le droit approprié pour régir le contrat lui-même, et qu'il s'agisse ou non d'un droit national, il me semble que quand l'existence même de la convention d'arbitrage est en jeu, alors que le prétendu contrat est à tout point de vue un contrat international, qu'aucune question de capacité des parties n'est en cause et qu'en plus les parties ont délibérément omis de choisir le droit applicable au contrat, le droit le plus approprié pour régir la question de l'existence de la convention d'arbitrage n'est pas celui d'un système national particulier mais les principes généraux du droit et les usages acceptés dans le commerce international, et en particulier le principe de bonne foi. Ces principes exigent, au nom de la justice, que toutes les parties prennent en considération l'intention commune de chacune d'entres elles, telle que révélée par les circonstances de la négociation et l'exécution ultérieure de tout accord apparent.* »

Il restait alors à l'arbitre à se prononcer sur le fond des problèmes qu'il y avait à trancher pour décider de sa compétence.

« *La première question est de savoir si les parties qui ont paraphé le "Contract Agreement" avaient ou non l'intention d'enregistrer un accord les liant. Pour soutenir l'argument selon lequel le paraphage était seulement une façon de montrer une intention (qui fut plus tard abandonnée selon C...) C..., qui a développé cet argument, déclare que l'accord était non daté, non timbré, non signé et paraphé par une personne qui n'avait aucune autorité pour donner valeur légale au document. Ce problème de pouvoir mis à part, il me semble que ces arguments ne font qu'un. Le contrat n'était ni daté ni dûment signé, ni timbré, comme l'exige pourtant la loi Pakistanaise (le Pakistan étant le lieu de la signature du contrat), car il était convenu que le document en question n'était pas la version finale du contrat. Mais cela ne me semble toutefois pas résoudre le problème.*

Quand les parties souhaitent qu'un document définitif et formel soit rédigé, elles peuvent ou non placer les négociations préalables, les documents préliminaires sous la condition exprimée par la clause "Subject to contract", par laquelle elles expriment formellement leur intention de ne pas créer de liens juridiques entre elles jusqu'à la signature du document final. Cette intention peut aussi être révélée par leur conduite. Il ne me semble pas qu'ici ce fut le cas. »

« *D'après le paragraphe 2 du procès-verbal le contrat entre le demandeur et C... tel que préparé par MS. agissant en tant que représentant du client a été approuvé dans son ensemble mais eu égard au problème de la double imposition, il a été décidé que la signature du contrat serait suspendue jusqu'à ce que soit trouvée une solution pour éviter toute double taxe s'ajoutant aux frais du demandeur, qui de toute façon devaient être payés par C... en plus des honoraires acceptés par le demandeur ; le procès-verbal relate également qu'il y a eu des discussions quant à la formation possible d'une société suisse. Le problème de la taxation a été soulevé dans un télex du 2 octobre avant la réunion, puis dans un télex en février 1981 et enfin lors de la réunion qui s'est tenue le 9 mai 1981. Ce fut le seul point resté en suspens mais le fait de parapher avait pour objet de montrer ce qui avait été décidé entre les parties. Il n'y eut pas d'accord exprès ou implicite comme quoi il n'y aurait aucun lien juridique entre les parties jusqu'à ce que la version définitive du contrat fût signée. Le demandeur voulait vraiment que les accord oraux passés entre les parties fussent actés et il est clair que MH... était prêt à le lui accorder. La procédure de paraphe tendait à exprimer leur accord, même s'il était entendu que sa forme pourrait être modifiée.*

Même si l'accord paraphé n'était pas "subject to contract", il se peut qu'aucun accord formel n'ait existé si restait en suspens une question dont l'importance pour l'accord était telle que les parties auraient exclu son entrée en vigueur tant qu'elle n'était pas résolue. Bien qu'il soit clair que les parties pensaient que ce point seul empêchait une signature définitive, il me semble que ce fut, en fait, pour des raisons de pure forme. Le problème de la taxation était vraiment mineur comparé à toutes les autres conditions du contrat. La raison pour laquelle la signature fut retardée, concernant une question qui était principalement dans l'intérêt de C... qui fournissait les fonds, était que l'accord devait être corrigé si, comme il était prévu, une société suisse était créée afin d'être l'architecte. Toutefois, l'importance de cette question ne me semble pas être telle que les parties n'envisageaient pas de créer de liens contractuels »...

« *J'ajouterai que l'argument suivant me fut avancé : étant donné que la clause d'arbitrage ne fut jamais discutée, elle ne pouvait pas faire partie du contrat. Pourtant il me semble, comme l'a dit MS..., que c'était une clause qui était acceptable sans avoir fait l'objet au préalable d'aucune discussion. C'était et c'est toujours une clause type dans un grand nombre de contrats internationaux. Il n'y a pas besoin de discuter ce qui est immédiatement admis. Par conséquent, je conclus que l'intention des parties était que le "Contract Agreement" constitue un acte des termes de leur accord, gouvernant leurs relations à partir de ce moment... »*

« *Reste le problème classique d'une personne morale existante contractant pour le compte d'une société à créer. Selon les principes généraux du droit commercial international et les usages, et de la bonne foi, il me semble que dans de telles circonstances la personne morale existante est personnellement tenue. C'est certainement le cas en droit anglais (Cf. Kelner v/ Baxeter (1866) L.R. 2.C.P. 174). C'est aussi maintenant d'une façon générale le droit de la Communauté Européenne de par la directive du 9 mars 1968, et avant cela, c'était déjà un principe du droit français. Ceci semble en parfait accord avec le principe de bonne foi. Lorsque les parties entendent clairement créer des relations juridiques pour la sécurité de leurs transactions, on ne peut que refuser une interprétation qui signifierait qu'il n'y a pas de contrat du tout en raison de l'inexistence d'une des parties et on doit accepter celle qui valide les actes des parties.*

Le principe de bonne foi ne permet pas qu'une partie puisse parapher un document contenant de toute évidence des conditions contractuelles et ensuite continuer pendant une longue période à bénéficier du travail d'une autre partie selon ces conditions et en même temps prétendre n'avoir aucune obligation parce que le contrat était conclu avec une société à créer, dont la création ne dépendait que d'elle seule. »

OBSERVATIONS. I. — Le principe du pouvoir de l'arbitre de statuer sur sa propre compétence est bien établi. On rappellera à cet égard la sentence rendue en 1983 dans l'affaire n° 3987 (*Clunet* 1984, p. 943) qui y voyait une « vieille question litigieuse de caractère théorique » et celle, plus ancienne, rendue en 1968 dans l'affaire n° 1526 qui indiquait que « c'est une règle admise en matière d'arbitrage international » (*Clunet* 1974, p. 915).

C'est pourquoi les justifications que lui donne l'arbitre peuvent paraître d'un caractère didactique excessif, d'autant plus que le principe est confirmé par le Règlement de la Cour d'Arbitrage de la CCI (art. 8 (3)). C'est probablement l'origine britannique de l'arbitre qui explique cette attitude, car il est de fait qu'en Angleterre, le pouvoir de l'arbitre de statuer sur sa propre compétence ne va pas de soi puisque la *Commercial Court* peut être saisie, même en cours d'arbitrage, pour statuer sur la validité d'une clause d'arbitrage (*Cf Yearbook Commercial Arbitration*, 1983, p. 24).

Par ailleurs, la distinction que paraît effectuer la sentence entre le pouvoir incontrôlé de l'arbitre de se prononcer sur l'étendue ou la portée d'une clause d'arbitrage et celui, soumis à la censure des tribunaux étatiques, de décider de l'existence de cette clause n'est pas convaincante. Vérifier le point contesté de savoir si les parties ont soumis telle ou telle question à l'arbitrage revient à s'assurer de l'existence d'une clause d'arbitrage en ce qui concerne ces questions. La Cour d'appel de Paris, dans un arrêt du 25 janvier 1972 (*Rev. Arb.* 1973, p. 158) n'a pas hésité à annuler une sentence arbitrale qui s'était prononcée sur un problème d'inexécution de contrat, au motif que la clause d'arbitrage ne visait que l'interprétation du contrat, sans pour autant remettre en cause le principe selon lequel l'arbitre a le pouvoir de statuer sur sa propre compétence. On en conclura donc que ce pouvoir s'exerce dans les mêmes limites, qu'il s'agisse de l'existence de la clause ou de son étendue, c'est-à-dire, dans les deux cas, sous le contrôle des tribunaux étatiques compétents.

C'est par contre à juste titre que la sentence rappelle que la partie qui conteste la compétence de l'arbitre n'est pas considérée avoir accepté cette compétence par le seul fait qu'elle s'est présentée devant l'arbitre. Beaucoup d'incertitudes subsistent à cet égard dans la pratique judiciaire de certains pays (Philippines par exemple). En ce qui concerne la France, la Cour d'appel de Paris, dans un arrêt du 12 juillet 1984 (*Rev. Arb.* 1986, p. 75) a confirmé la règle bien acquise selon laquelle une partie, qui a contesté la compétence de l'arbitre *in limine litis*, peut ensuite se défendre au fond sans être présumée avoir renoncé à son exception d'incompétence. On notera également que la sentence souligne que la décision par laquelle la Cour d'Arbitrage de la CCI, selon l'article 8 (3) de son Règlement, après avoir constaté « *prima facie* » l'existence d'une convention d'Arbitrage, invite l'arbitre à prendre toute décision sur sa propre compétence est une décision administrative. Il en va de même de la décision contraire de la Cour d'Arbitrage lorsque, par application de l'article 7 de son Règlement, elle informe la partie demanderesse de ce que l'Arbitrage ne peut avoir lieu lorsque « à son avis » il n'existe entre les parties « *prima facie* » aucune convention d'arbitrage. Cette qualification de la décision de la Cour d'Arbitrage, qui accepte ou refuse de constituer un Tribunal Arbitral pour statuer sur sa propre compétence a deux conséquences.

La première est quelle ne lie pas l'autorité juridictionnelle qui sera saisie ultérieurement. Ainsi, que la Cour d'Arbitrage ait constaté « *prima facie* » l'existence d'une clause d'arbitrage n'empêche pas que le Tribunal Arbitral constitué se déclare incompétent. De même, la constatation par la Cour d'Arbitrage qu'il n'existe pas « *prima facie* » de clause d'arbitrage n'est pas de nature à empêcher un tribunal étatique devant lequel l'affaire serait ensuite portée de se déclarer lui-même incompétent parce qu'il estimerait, contrairement à la Cour d'Arbitrage et probablement mieux informé, car son analyse ne se limiterait pas à un examen « *prima facie* », que les parties sont liées par une clause d'arbitrage.

Mais ici, une distinction semble s'imposer. En effet, il est douteux que la partie défenderesse qui avait soulevé une exception d'incompétence devant la Cour d'Arbitrage en invoquant l'absence de clause d'arbitrage, puisse ensuite opposer utilement la clause d'arbitrage à la même demanderesse, qui, acceptant la décision administrative de la Cour d'Arbitrage, l'aurait attraite devant un tribunal étatique. L'exception d'incompétence de la défenderesse devant la Cour d'Arbitrage devrait être interprétée comme une renonciation à la clause d'arbitrage et la saisine du tribunal étatique par la demanderesse comme une acceptation de cette renonciation. Par contre, si la partie défenderesse à l'arbitrage décide de porter le litige devant un tribunal étatique, la partie demanderesse à l'arbitrage pourra soulever une exception d'incompétence en se fondant sur la clause d'arbitrage, indépendamment de la décision administrative de la Cour d'Arbitrage et le tribunal ne sera pas évidemment lié par celle-ci. Enfin, cette décision administrative négative ne doit pas s'opposer à ce que la demanderesse à l'arbitrage saisisse le Président du Tribunal de grande instance de Paris, sur la base de l'article 1493 NCPC pour lui demander d'ordonner la constitution du Tribunal Arbitral, pour autant que le lieu d'arbitrage soit fixé en France ou que la procédure française soit applicable, l'article 7 du Règlement de la CCI n'étant pas une « clause contraire » au sens de l'article 1493 NCPC.

La deuxième conséquence de la qualification de décision « administrative » de l'acceptation ou du refus de la Cour d'Arbitrage de constituer un Tribunal Arbitral pour statuer sur sa propre compétence est qu'elle ne peut, en soi, faire l'objet d'aucun recours. Bien entendu, elle sera remise en cause indirectement par l'annulation d'une sentence arbitrale dans laquelle l'arbitre, nommé en vertu d'une telle décision, se serait déclaré compétent, ou, dans le cas d'une décision de rejet, selon l'article 7 du Règlement de la CCI, par la décision d'une autorité judiciaire qui estimerait, dans les conditions qui ont été envisagées plus haut, que les parties étaient, en réalité, liées par une clause d'arbitrage.

Mais, dans tous ces cas, ce n'est pas la décision de la Cour d'Arbitrage qui sera l'objet de l'attention de l'autorité judiciaire, mais la clause d'arbitrage elle même, une action en responsabilité à l'encontre de la CCI restant cependant possible, mais sans grandes chances de succès (*Cf.* P. Fouchard, « Les institutions permanentes d'arbitrage devant le juge étatique » *Rev. Arb.* 1987, p. 245).

Cette absence de recours doit inciter la Cour d'Arbitrage à la plus grande prudence, surtout avant de décider qu'il n'existe pas « *prima facie* » de clause d'arbitrage. En effet, dans les cas douteux, ceci revient à obliger la partie qui souhaite se prévaloir d'une clause d'arbitrage à en faire préalablement constater l'existence par une juridiction étatique dont la compétence sera souvent difficile à déterminer et selon des voies procédurales mal définies dans certains pays. Sans compter sur le risque, pour la Cour d'Arbitrage, de se trouver confrontée à deux décisions de tribunaux étatiques de pays différents, l'un estimant qu'il y a une clause d'arbitrage, l'autre qu'il n'y en a pas, et qu'il est compétent. Or, il n'est pas envisageable que la Cour d'Arbitrage soit en mesure de trancher un conflit de juridiction. C'est pourquoi, il est souhaitable pour les parties et le développement harmonieux de l'arbitrage, que la Cour d'Arbitrage renvoie à des arbitres le soin de décider de leur compétence chaque fois qu'il y a une possibilité sérieuse que les parties soient effectivement liées par une clause d'arbitage. Comme l'a relevé avec justesse P. Fouchard, l'attitude contraire irait à l'encontre « des principes modernes du droit de l'arbitrage, transfèrant à l'arbitre l'ensemble du contentieux de son investiture » (*Cf* P. Fouchard, *op. cit. loc. cit* p. 245).

II. — La décision de l'arbitre, en ce qui concerne le droit applicable à la clause d'arbitrage et plus particulièrement au problème de sa formation vient s'ajouter à la série de sentences qui, à défaut de choix par les parties d'un droit national, se réfèrent à des normes anationales : principes généraux du droit, usages du commerce international, etc... L'arbitre déclare en effet que le droit le plus approprié pour résoudre le problème de l'existence d'une clause d'arbitrage, s'agissant d'un contrat international, n'est pas un droit national particulier, mais les principes généraux du droit et les usages acceptés dans le commerce international, notamment le principe de bonne foi. Cette solution rappelle les sentences CCI rendues dans l'affaire n° 4131 en 1982 (*Cf. Clunet* 1983, p. 899) et dans l'affaire n° 4381 en 1986 (*Cf. Clunet* 1986, p. 1103). Ces deux sentences, comme celle ici rapportée, se référaient, à l'exclusion de toute loi nationale, aux usages du commerce international et à l'intention des parties, telle que révélée par les circonstances qui ont entouré la négociation et l'exécution des contrats. Cependant, dans les affaires n° 4131 et n° 4381, les arbitres justifiaient le recours à des normes anationales en se fondant sur les dispositions des articles 8 (3) et 8 (4) du règlement d'arbitrage de la CCI qui donnent à l'arbitre le pouvoir de « prendre toute décision sur sa propre compétence » sans lui prescrire d'appliquer une loi étatique quelconque. Les deux sentences en déduisaient que le règlement d'arbitrage de la CCI confère aux arbitres le pouvoir d'apprécier la validité et la portée d'une clause d'arbitrage, indépendamment du droit régissant le contrat et sans recours à un droit étatique.

On a pu y voir l'émergence d'une présomption selon laquelle, « dans l'arbitrage de la CCI, la validité, la portée et les effets de la clause d'arbitrage sont régis par la volonté des parties et les usages du commerce international, sauf stipulation contraire des parties » (*Cf. Clunet* 1986, p. 1108). La sentence ici rapportée semble confirmer cette analyse car elle ne prend même pas la précaution de s'appuyer sur les dispositions des articles 8 (3) et 8 (4) du règlement d'arbitrage de la CCI, comme si la solution qu'elle adopte allait de soi.

Il semble néanmoins qu'à cet égard une certaine prudence s'impose. Le détachement de la clause d'arbitrage de toute loi nationale en matière d'arbitrage international est incompatible avec les dispositions de droits nationaux qui, comme le concordat suisse sur l'arbitrage, s'appliquent de façon immédiate à toute procédure se déroulant sur le territoire qu'ils désignent comme leur champ d'application. Si ces droits contiennent des règles impératives sur la validité ou la forme, notamment écrite, des clauses d'arbitrage, l'arbitre qui siège sur le territoire qu'ils régissent devra les respecter.

Ainsi, un arbitre siégeant en Suisse, dans un canton concordataire doit respecter l'exigence de l'écrit que pose l'article 6 (1) du Concordat en matière de validité de la clause d'arbitrage (*Cf.* Sentences n° 4504, de 1985 et 1986 : *Clunet* 1986, p. 1118). Sinon, sa sentence risquera non seulement d'être annulée au lieu de l'arbitrage mais en plus se verra refuser l'exequatur sur la base de l'article V (1) de la Convention de New York de 1958 qui, à défaut d'indication par les parties du droit applicable à la clause d'arbitrage, soumet celle-ci au droit du pays où la sentence a été rendue.

Dans l'espèce qui faisait l'objet de la sentence ici rapportée, le problème ne se posait pas puisque Paris était le lieu de l'arbitrage et, qu'en matière internationale, le droit français permet le détachement de la clause d'arbitrage de tout système juridique national.

On relèvera également que la sentence prend soin de souligner que la capacité des parties n'est pas en cause. Elle rejoint en cela également la sentence précitée rendue dans l'affaire n° 4381, qui rappelait que la capacité de chacune des parties à compromettre est « soumise à la loi personnelle de la partie » (*Cf. Clunet* 1986, p. 1104).

III. — Bien que la sentence n'ait pas manqué de souligner que le droit auquel est soumis un contrat n'est pas nécessairement le même que celui qui régit la clause d'arbitrage qu'il contient, c'est en réalité les mêmes normes anationales qu'elle applique à l'une et à l'autre. Les parties n'ayant choisi aucun droit national, l'arbitre règle le problème de la formation du contrat à la lumière des principes généraux du droit, notamment du principe de bonne foi et des usages du commerce international. L'article 1496 NCPC en prévoyant qu'à défaut de choix par les parties, l'arbitre tranche le litige conformément aux règles de droit qu'il estime appropriées donnait expressément en l'espèce ce pouvoir à un arbitre siégeant en France, en matière d'arbitrage international. Mais, on doit noter que la pratique arbitrale bien établie (*Cf* entre autres les sentences rendues dans les affaires n° 4338 en 1984, *Clunet* 1985 p. 981, et 3627 en 1979, *Clunet* 1980, p. 962), selon laquelle les arbitres ne disposant pas des pouvoirs d'amiables compositeurs sont néanmoins autorisés à appliquer les normes anationales que l'on désigne communément comme *Lex Mercatoria*, continue d'être reconnue en droit comparé.

On en donnera deux exemples récents : l'alinéa 1er du Nouvel article 944 (10) du Code de procédure civile du Québec est libellé comme suit : « Les arbitres tranchent le différend conformément aux règles de droit qu'ils estiment appropriées et, s'il y a lieu, déterminent les dommages intérêts. » L'absence de référence à une loi est ici significative. Par ailleurs, une décision de la Cour of Appeals, en Angleterre, du 23 mars 1987 déclare, sous la plume de Sir John Donalson, Master of the Rolls : « *By choosing to arbitrate under the rules of the ICC, and, in particular, art. 13 (3), the parties have left proper law to be decided by the arbitrators and have not in terms confined the choice to national systems of law. I can see no basis for concluding that the arbitrator's choice of proper law — a common denominator of principles underlying the laws of the various nations governing contractual relations — is outwith the scope of the choice which the parties left to the arbitrators (Court of Appeals, Deutsche Schachtbau und Tiefbohrgesellschaft mbh v. The R'as al Khaimah National Oil company and Schell International Petroleum Co Ltd, 23 mars 1987 : Journal of Business Law 1987, 168).*

La solution que donne la sentence à la question de la formation du contrat n'est pas surprenante. Le problème posé était lui même classique : il s'agissait de savoir si les parties avaient quitté la phase de la négociation pour passer un contrat s'imposant à elles. Les paraphes apposés sur le texte d'un contrat non signé exprimaient-ils que le temps des pourparlers était déjà dépassé et que les parties étaient entrées dans un lien obligatoire ?

En réalité, la sentence n'attache pas une importance particulière aux paraphes eux mêmes. Si ceux-ci attestent un accord des parties sur un certain nombre de points, c'est le caractère essentiel ou accessoire de ces points par rapport à la relation contractuelle que les parties cherchent à bâtir qui permet de dire si l'accord révélé par les paraphes suffit à la formation d'un contrat. Or, l'arbitre constate qu'à l'exception de deux points qu'il considère mineurs en l'espèce — la solution d'un problème de double imposition et la création d'une société qui se substituerait à l'une des parties — il y avait accord sur les éléments essentiels du contrat. Il en déduit donc que ce dernier était effectivement formé. Le fait supplémentaire que le contrat ait reçu un commencement d'exécution dont avait bénéficié celles des parties qui en contestait l'existence vient, au nom du principe de bonne foi, conforter cette conclusion.

L'importance que semble attacher l'arbitre à l'absence de toute mention expresse de ce que les parties n'entendaient pas entrer dans un lien contractuel et à la clause « *subject to contract* », faisant défaut en l'espèce, est sans doute excessive. L'explication se trouve être à nouveau dans l'origine britannique de l'arbitre, le droit anglais reconnaissant une pleine efficacité à cette clause, même si les parties se sont mises d'accord sur les éléments essentiels du contrat. Ce n'est pas le cas en droit américain (*Cf.* B. Hanotiau, M. Demideleer et N. Gerryn, « Vers la conclusion du contrat : les éléments caractéristiques de la convention et les pouvoirs des négociateurs », *in Le contrat en formation*, Bruxelles 1987, p. 186 s) et il devrait en aller de même dans les droits continentaux : s'il y a accord sur les éléments essentiels de la négociation, la rédaction d'un contrat en bonne et due forme, à laquelle les parties s'obligent par la clause « *subject to contract* », n'est pas une condition d'existence de liens contractuels, mais un élément de la mise en œuvre de ces liens.

IV. — L'arbitre se fonde sur les principes généraux du droit et les usages du commerce international pour conclure qu'une partie agissant pour le compte d'une société qu'elle doit créer est tenue tant que cette société n'a pas vu le jour. Même si les sources de droit comparé invoquées ne sont pas nécessairement convaincantes, la solution doit être approuvée.

Admettre qu'une partie puisse conditionner l'entrée en vigueur d'un contrat à la création d'une société qu'elle est la seule à pouvoir créer reviendrait à pourvoir d'effet une condition purement potestative. Or, ceci serait incompatible avec le principe de bonne foi qui soutient l'ensemble de la décision de l'arbitre.

V. — La théorie de l'apparence et la bonne foi sont intimement liées. C'est pourquoi l'arbitre n'hésite pas à considérer que l'autorité apparente d'un dirigeant de société engage celle-ci. La solution n'est pas nouvelle dans la jurisprudence arbitrale. On en donnera pour exemple une sentence rendue en 1984, dans l'affaire n° 4667, où un tribunal arbitral était saisi du problème de l'opposabilité à une société italienne d'une clause d'arbitrage signée par son directeur commercial à l'issue d'une négociation où avait participé le directeur général de la société, alors que le signataire, contrairement à ce dernier, n'était pas habilité à conclure des accords d'arbitrage. Les arbitres estimèrent que la société italienne était tenue par la signature de son directeur commercial, notamment en raison de ses pouvoirs apparents :

« *Attendu par ailleurs, et d'une manière générale, que ladite théorie de la confiance, ainsi que le droit italien (article 1375 du Code civil) veulent que les conventions soient exécutées de bonne foi, ce qui est entre autre conforme à la position adoptée à l'égard des contrats par la majorité des systèmes de droit.*

Attendu enfin qu'en application de l'article 13, paragraphe 5 du règlement d'arbitrage de la CCI, les arbitres sont tenus de prendre en considération les usages du commerce.

Que selon ces usages, lorsqu'un directeur général est présent à une négociation, l'interlocuteur est fondé à croire que son représentant également présent dispose, lorsque le directeur général a quitté les lieux de la négociation après avoir vu l'ensemble des textes qui seront signés, d'un pouvoir de signature.

Que dans son discours introductif au 60ᵉ anniversaire de la Cour d'Arbitrage de la CCI, le Président de la Cour rappelait la nécessité de garantir la sécurité juridique des transactions et déclarait que... « La Cour note d'ailleurs, dans les projets de sentences qui lui sont soumis, le souci primordial des arbitres de faire respecter les engagements contractuels. C'est là une garantie fondamentale pour l'entrepreneur... « Que cette considération générale est partagée par la Cour de cassation italienne qui dans son arrêt n° 722 du 8 février 1982, a décidé que dans l'arbitrage commercial international, le droit dans lequel l'arbitrage se situe et opère est transnational, sans tenir compte des textes de lois des différents Etats, la *Lex Mercatoria* se réalisant par l'adhésion des opérateurs économiques aux valeurs de leur milieu et ce dans la conviction que lesdites valeurs ont force obligatoire ».

Y.D.

I. — **Clause compromissoire « pathologique ».** — Règlement de conciliation et d'interprétation de la Chambre de Commerce. — Interprétation.

II. — **Arbitrage international ou national.** — Compétence de la CCI pour trancher un différend entre deux parties françaises.

III. — **Clause compromissoire.** — Nullité partielle. — Effet de la chose jugée.

Sentence rendue dans l'affaire 5423 en 1987.

(Les noms des parties dans l'affaire sont rendus publics dans une procédure devant les tribunaux français ; sinon, ils n'auraient pas été reproduits dans cette chronique, eu égard au principe de la confidentialité qui est assurée aux parties dans un arbitrage CCI).

Les sociétés Datel-productions et King productions SARL ont conclu en 1985 un contrat ayant pour objet la coproduction d'un film. La clause compromissoire du contrat était ainsi libellée : « Tout différend, découlant du présent contrat sera tranché définitivement suivant le règlement de conciliation et d'interprétation de la Chambre de Commerce par un arbitre désigné conformément à ce règlement ; le lieu d'arbitrage sera Paris ; la loi applicable est la loi française. »

Le contrat comportait une clause résolutoire de plein droit en cas de manquement de l'une des parties à ses obligations.

Le film, achevé en août 1985, projeté dès septembre 1985, était intitulé : « Le Gaffeur ».

Par suite d'un incident relatif au règlement des apports, King faisait délivrer en juillet 1985 une sommation à Datel d'avoir à régler dans les 15 jours une certaine somme. Datel répondait à cet acte par une protestation à sommation et invoquait simultanément le recours à la procédure d'arbitrage prévu par le contrat. King assignait alors Datel en référé devant le Président du tribunal de grande instance de Paris, réclamant la constatation de l'acquisition de la clause résolutoire conventionnellement stipulée. Une décision rendue en août 1985 a dit qu'il n'y avait pas lieu à référé, le juge ayant trouvé que la clause compromissoire du contrat lui retirait compétence pour statuer en la matière.

King a introduit un appel devant la Cour d'appel de Paris, soulevant la nullité de la clause compromissoire. Selon King, la mise en œuvre de l'arbitrage se heurtait à une impossibilité pratique, car la « Chambre de Commerce et d'Industrie de Paris » selon elle désignée, n'a pas créé de « Règlement de conciliation et d'Interprétation ». Datel exposait que c'était la Chambre de Commerce Internationale qui était l'organisation visée par les parties dans la clause compromissoire. La Cour d'appel constatait que pour regrettable que soit l'imprécision de la dénomination « Chambre de commerce », sans indication d'adresse, il n'en résultait pas une nullité manifeste de la clause d'arbitrage ; la clause d'arbitrage interdisait la saisine du juge des référés et la juridiction de l'Etat était donc incompétente (*Rev. Arb.* 1986, p. 250). La Cour d'appel renvoyait les parties à saisir l'arbitre.

Datel a saisi la Cour d'arbitrage de la CCI le même mois d'octobre 1985 par une requête d'arbitrage.

King répondit à la demande de Datel en soulevant deux exceptions prises de :

1° la nullité de la clause compromissoire de la convention de 1985, par application des article 1443 et 1448 du Nouveau Code de procédure civile, au motif que la Chambre de Commerce et d'Industrie de Paris n'a pas créé de « règlement de conciliation et d'arbitrage », ainsi qu'il a été certifié à King par lettre de service juridique de cet organisme du 18 septembre 1985.

2° L'incompétence de la Cour d'Arbitrage de la CCI et de l'arbitre nommé par elle, s'agissant d'un conflit entre deux sociétés françaises relatif à des opérations commerciales situées en France.

Datel répliqua à la Cour d'Arbitrage, que cette exception n'était pas fondée, parce que les parties avaient eu manifestement l'intention de désigner la CCI par la dénomination « Chambre de Commerce ».

Après avoir constaté l'existence « *prima facie* » d'une convention d'arbitrage, la Cour de la CCI nommait un arbitre unique, dont la première tâche était de statuer sur sa compétence avant-dire droit.

Il le faisait dans les termes suivants :

« *L'arbitre constate qu'une des parties a soulevé des moyens relatifs à la validité de la convention d'arbitrage qui entrent dans les prévisions de l'article 8.3 du règlement CCI et qui, nonobstant la décision de la Cour d'Arbitrage constatant* prima facie *l'existence de la convention d'arbitrage, doivent conduire cet arbitre à statuer avant-dire droit sur sa propre compétence.*

L'exception prise de l'incompétence de la Cour d'Arbitrage de la CCI et de celle de l'arbitre nommé par elle, telle qu'elle est formulée par King, est à rejeter comme non fondée, car ladite cour a jugé qu'aucune disposition de son statut et de son Règlement ne lui interdit d'être saisie d'un arbitrage entre deux parties de même nationalité et qui ne mettant pas en cause des intérêts de commerce international, au sens de l'article 1492 du Nouveau Code de procédure civile français, n'est pas un arbitrage international.

Par contre, la question se pose de savoir si les parties ont voulu saisir la CCI de l'arbitrage prévu à leur convention. A cette question Datel répond par l'affirmative et King par la négative.

Le compromis d'arbitrage étant une convention (art. 1447 NCPC) et la convention faisant la loi des parties (art. 1101 C. civ.) il y a lieu de rechercher si le consentement des parties ou de l'une d'entre elle n'a pas été vicié par une erreur portant sur le sens des mots "Chambre de commerce".

Aux termes de l'article 1109 du Code civil "Il n'y a point de consentement valable, si le consentement n'a été donné que par erreur" et, selon l'article 1110 de ce Code, "l'erreur n'est une cause de nullité de la convention que lorsqu'elle tombe sur la substance même de la chose qui en est l'objet".

C'est à la partie qui invoque son erreur de prouver que celle-ci portait sur la substance de la chose et a déterminer son consentement (Cf. la chronique du prof. Malinvaud, au Dalloz *1972, p. 215). Cette preuve ne peut se faire que par des présomptions "abandonnées aux lumières et à la prudence des juges de fond" (art. 1353 c. civ.). L'erreur doit porter sur une « qualité convenue » (Cass. com. 20 oct. 1970 :* JCP. *71, II, 16916).*

En l'espèce, l'erreur est invoquée par King, qui soutient que les deux parties avaient eu en l'esprit, lors de la conclusion du compromis, la Chambre de Commerce et d'Industrie de Paris, communément appelée « Chambre de Commerce », et aucunement la CCI.

Datel soutient le contraire en alléguant seulement qu'il ne pouvait pas y avoir d'autre organisme possible puisque, seule, la CCI traite des arbitrages, ce qui n'est qu'une justification a postériori et ne prouve rien quant à l'intention du contractant lors de la conclusion de l'accord. Quoi qu'il en soit, cette erreur, si erreur il y a, porte effectivement, au sens de l'article 1110 du Code civil, sur la substance même de la chose qui était l'objet de la convention, puisque sans modalité applicable de désignation de l'arbitre, il ne saurait y avoir arbitrage.

L'appréciation du consentement relevant du pouvoir souverain du juge de fond (Cass. civ. I, 16 déc. 1964 : D. *65, 136 entre autres), l'arbitre constate qu'il y a présomption de ce que les deux parties ont voulu se soumettre à un arbitrage français, puisqu'elles ont d'ailleurs convenu que la loi française était applicable à cet arbitrage (art. 26, in fine, du contrat). Il ne saurait, dès lors, y avoir présomption d'une intention de saisir la CCI, alors d'ailleurs que cette solution conduit à l'application d'un tarif de frais et honoraires élevés, justifié par les nécessités de l'arbitrage international mais sans justification pour un arbitrage interne. C'est pour cette raison que King a refusé de verser les sommes demandées par la Cour d'Arbitrage de la CCI. Il n'est dès lors pas possible de présumer que les parties aient entendu adopter une voie de procédure contraire à leur intérêt et que rien ne pouvait leur suggérer, le litige ne présentant aucun élément de caractère international. Il ressort aussi des termes de la clause compromissoire que les parties ont voulu remettre la décision de désignation de leur arbitre à un organisme indépendant de l'une et de l'autre.*

341

Il en résulte que la clause compromissoire doit être tenue pour nulle et non avenue mais seulement en ce qui concerne les modalités de désignation de l'arbitre ; elle ne l'est aucunement en ce qui concerne le principe même du recours à l'arbitrage. En effet, cette nullité n'est encourue, selon l'article 1443, 2e alinéa, que lorsque la clause compromissoire ne prévoit pas les modalités de désignation des arbitres. Or, en l'espèce, la clause compromissoire prévoit ces modalités. King ne saurait dès lors, comme il le demande, être admis à porter le litige devant la juridiction de l'Etat, laquelle serait tenue, aux termes de l'article 1458 NCPC, de se déclarer incompétente, si elle était saisie.

Toutefois, l'incompétence de l'arbitre nommé par la CCI en application d'une modalité de désignation nulle de la clause compromissoire ne met pas les parties dans un « deadlock » ou situation sans issue ; il appartient à la plus diligente de mettre en œuvre la procédure de désignation d'un arbitre par le président du tribunal de grande instance prévue par l'article 1444 NCPC, aux termes duquel ce magistrat est saisi, comme en matière de référé (art. 1457 NCPC), lorsque, "le litige étant né, la constitution du tribunal arbitral se heurte à une difficulté du fait de l'une des parties ou dans la mise en œuvre des modalités de désignation".

Tel est le cas en l'espèce.

Par ces motifs,

— L'arbitre soussigné se déclare incompétent pour connaître du litige entre les sociétés Datel et King ;

— Renvoie les parties à se mieux pourvoir ;

— Dit que la Société Datel, demanderesse supportera les frais de la présente instance.

Ainsi fait et jugé à Paris (France)
Le

L'arbitre unique ».

OBSERVATIONS. — I. — Cette affaire enrichit notre expérience d'un autre exemple de clauses compromissoires mal rédigées, de désignation maladroite d'un organisme d'arbitrage. On doit déplorer le peu de soin que de nombreuses parties prennent pour rédiger les clauses d'arbitrage.

Il existe un nombre impressionnant d'institutions et de règlements d'arbitrage aujourd'hui, aussi bien au plan international que national. Les dénominations de ces institutions peuvent se ressembler et ne se distinguent parfois que par un seul petit mot. En suivant le libellé recommandé pour désigner la clause compromissoire de l'institution à laquelle on pense confier un arbitrage éventuel, on évite bien des difficultés et des malentendus.

Dans le cas d'espèce, les deux parties auraient pu économiser presque deux ans, maintenant perdus pour des questions de procédure et sans que la partie demanderesse n'ait avancé d'un pouce vers la solution du problème de fond qui la préoccupe.

On n'est pas nécessairement d'accord avec l'interprétation que donne l'arbitre à la volonté des parties en ce qui concerne la méthode pour résourdre les litiges éventuels. Il maintient que le principe même du recours à l'arbitrage est établi, même si la clause est nulle en ce qui concerne les modalités de désignation de l'arbitre. Il est vrai que l'on doit distinguer entre, d'un côté, les clauses pathologiques qui peuvent être considérées comme nulles et inopérantes dans leur totalité et, de l'autre côté, celles auxquelles on peut donner une validité limitée et une application restreinte. Tout dépend de la volonté réelle des parties.

Or, dans l'espèce, le libellé de la clause laisse penser que les parties ont voulu soumettre leurs différends éventuels à une institution, avec toutes les garanties que le choix d'une institution offre par rapport à un arbitrage *ad hoc*. La clause offre une très grande similitude avec la clause recommandée par la CCI dont elle a en commun la construction générale de la phrase ainsi que les mots choisis, sauf sur les points suivants :

a) La clause en espèce prévoit « tout différend » au singulier alors que la clause type CCI mentionne « tous différends » au pluriel ;

b) La clause en espèce désigne le règlement comme celui de « conciliation et d'interprétation » alors que la clause type de CCI désigne un règlement de « conciliation et d'arbitrage » ;

c) La clause en espèce prévoit « un arbitre » alors que la clause CCI en laisse aux parties le choix de « un ou plusieurs arbitres » ;

d) Le mot « internationale » fait défaut dans la désignation de la Chambre de Commerce.

Dans tous les autres aspects les deux clauses sont identiques et on ne se serait pas étonné d'une décision qui aurait accepté que la clause intentée fût celle de la CCI. On aurait plus facilement suivi le raisonnement de l'arbitre si la clause avait prévu, en premier lieu, la soumission des différends à l'arbitrage tout court et, en deuxième lieu, l'application du règlement de la Chambre de Commerce pour la nomination des arbitres (voir observations Derains dans l'affaire 3460. *Clunet* 1981 p. 939).

Une telle rédaction se concilierait plus facilement avec l'interprétation donnée par l'arbitre, à savoir que les parties avaient prévu le principe du recours à l'arbitrage, même si elles s'étaient trompées sur l'autorité de nomination de l'arbitre.

On ne doit pas, à notre avis, tirer des conclusions du fait qu'un organisme indépendant des parties devait nommer les arbitres, pour prétendre qu'un tribunal judiciaire puisse accomplir cette tâche. La clause prévoit une Chambre de Commerce, c'est-à-dire une institution privée et non un organe de l'Etat.

Face à la clause, il nous paraît que les alternatives sont plutôt tout ou rien, c'est-à-dire soit que la clause est une clause CCI, soit qu'elle est nulle et les parties libres de saisir les tribunaux judiciaires.

II. — On approuve entièrement le rejet de l'arbitre de l'exception d'incompétence de la Cour d'Arbitrage de la CCI au motif que le conflit opposait deux sociétés françaises relativement à des opérations commerciales situées en France. L'article 1ᵉʳ du Règlement Intérieur de la Cour d'Arbitrage de la CCI signale expressément que la Cour peut accepter d'être saisie de différends n'entrant pas dans le champ des différends ayant un caractère international intervenant dans le domaine des affaires s'il existe une Convention d'arbitrage lui attribuant compétence.

On est plus hésitant devant l'argument selon lequel il y a présomption que les parties ont voulu se soumettre à un arbitre français puisqu'elles étaient convenues que la loi française était applicable à l'arbitrage. Il existe un grand nombre d'affaires d'arbitrage CCI qui se déroulent entre parties d'une même nationalité, soient-elles françaises, allemandes, argentines ou nigériennes. Le choix d'une loi applicable n'est pas une indication d'un choix d'une institution ou de la nationalité d'une institution d'arbitrage. La chronique publiée dans ce *Journal* montre bien des exemples de litiges où les parties ont convenu de l'application du droit français dans un arbitrage selon le règlement CCI. Que le différend en espèce ne présente aucun élément de caractère international est plus convaincant pour penser, en l'absence d'une convention claire attribuant compétence à la CCI — que les parties n'ont pas envisagé un arbitrage de type international.

III. — Nous avons constaté dans cette chronique que les sentences dans lesquelles les arbitres se déclarent incompétents sont d'un intérêt tout particulier en raison de leur rareté (*Clunet* 1983 p. 909). La sentence dans l'affaire 5423 est d'un intérêt particulier pour une raison supplémentaire. Non seulement l'arbitre se déclare incompétent pour juger l'affaire mais en même temps décide que la clause compromissoire est en partie valable. C'est au moins le sens que nous voulons donner au passage de la sentence où l'arbitre statue que la clause compromissoire n'est aucunement nulle et non avenue pour ce qui concerne le principe même de l'arbitrage. Nous sommes confirmés dans cette opinion par le passage de la sentence qui interdit à la partie défenderesse de porter le litige devant la juridiction de l'Etat, laquelle serait tenue aux termes de l'article 1458 NCPC de se déclarer incompétente si elle était saisie.

La sentence invite à une réflexion de portée générale, à savoir : la compétence d'un arbitre qui se déclare incompétent pour connaître l'affaire peut-elle s'étendre à comprendre le pouvoir de se prononcer sur la validité comme telle de la clause compromissoire ? On pourrait voir une contradiction dans les deux décisions, puisque toute décision sur la validité de la clause supposerait a priori que l'arbitre considère qu'il a compétence pour s'occuper de l'affaire et les questions posées par les parties. La sentence ici rapportée ouvre une nouvelle dimension à la doctrine de la compétence.

Il nous semble que l'arbitre aurait pu se contenter de déclarer qu'il était incompétent et laisser l'affaire là. Dans ce cas, il aurait incombé aux parties, soit de saisir un tribunal judiciaire, soit une autre institution arbitrale de la requête. Un tribunal judiciaire pouvait soit statuer sur la validité de la clause arbitrale, soit, à la demande d'une partie, procéder à la nomination d'un arbitre. Une autre institution aurait pu nommer un arbitre qui devait se prononcer sur sa propre compétence.

Si l'arbitre, en espèce, ne limite pas son intervention à la simple constatation de son manque de compétence, c'est peut être dans le souci de rendre l'arbitrage plus efficace. Parce qu'en tranchant sur la validité de la clause comme telle, l'arbitre fait gagner du temps aux parties qui peuvent désormais orienter leurs efforts dans la direction indiquée par l'arbitre, notamment de demander à un tribunal judiciaire de nommer un arbitre. Ayant tranché sur la validité de la clause, l'arbitre évite aux parties l'étape supplémentaire de demander la confirmation par un tribunal étatique que la clause compromissoire existe et est bien valable.

Une autre question peut se poser à ce stade. Dans quelle mesure la sentence déclarant la clause arbitrale valable entraîne-t-elle l'effet de la chose jugée ? Un arbitre statuant sous les auspices d'un autre règlement que celui de la CCI serait-il lié par la sentence en ce qui concerne l'existence et la validité de la clause arbitrale ?

Il faut d'abord décider si la sentence de l'arbitre en espèce est finale, l'autorité de la chose jugée ne s'attachant pas aux sentences provisoires, simplement préparatoires ou « réservant le droit des parties à se pourvoir à nouveau » (Thierry Bernard, observations sur l'affaire Graimex C. Cargill : *Rev. Arb.* 1983, p. 344). Dans l'affirmative, l'article 1476 du NCPC consacre la solution de la chose jugée, une solution qui constitue un exemple d'une tendance internationale (observations Derains dans *Clunet* 1980, p. 982). Il n'appartient pas dans ce cas à un deuxième arbitre de vérifier la sentence rendue sur la validité de la clause par le premier arbitre. La partie insatisfaite de la sentence sur la validité n'a guère de possibilité de s'adresser immédiatement aux Tribunaux pour leur demander de statuer sur la nullité de la clause qu'elle allègue. L'article 1476 NCPC semble l'exclure et c'est seulement après que la sentence sur le fond sera rendue par le second arbitre qu'il sera possible de faire valoir qu'elle n'a pas à sa base une convention valable.

S. J.

Garantie de bonne fin. — Nature de celle-ci : caution accessoire ou garantie indépendante. — Intervention d'un expert comme condition pour appeler la garantie. — Refus de la banque de régler.

Sentence rendue dans l'affaire 5639 en 1987.

Par contrat en septembre 1982, une société européenne (le constructeur) s'est engagée envers un Maître d'Ouvrage d'un pays africain à réaliser un complexe portuaire de pêche et d'entretien de navires pour les sommes de plusieurs centaines de millions de francs.

Dans ce contrat, le constructeur s'est engagé à faire émettre par une banque européenne au profit du Maître de l'Ouvrage une caution bancaire de bonne fin d'un montant égal à 20 % du prix du contrat.

Par lettre en novembre 1984, une banque a garanti au Maître de l'Ouvrage la bonne fin des travaux, prestations et fournitures effectuées par le constructeur.

La banque a déclaré se porter caution solidaire des obligations contractuelles du constructeur à concurrence d'un montant représentant 20 % du marché, tout en précisant :

> « Nous paierons, tout en renonçant expressément au bénéfice de discussion et de division sur demande écrite de votre part accompagnée d'un rapport établi par un expert du centre international d'expertise de la Chambre de Commerce Internationale, tout ou partie du montant indiqué ci-dessus. »

Il était prévu au surplus que le montant de la garantie devait diminuer au fur et à mesure de la constatation de l'avancement des travaux.

Enfin, la banque terminait en soumettant la garantie aux règles uniformes pour les garanties contractuelles et tout litige relatif à son interprétation ou exécution à la Cour d'Arbitrage de la Chambre de Commerce Internationale.

Il est né en 1984, à l'occasion de l'exécution des travaux, entre le Maître de l'Ouvrage et le constructeur, une dispute qui a donné lieu le 10 septembre 1985 à une requête aux fins d'arbitrage en vue de faire établir si les parties avaient exécuté leurs obligations. Cette procédure arbitrale était toujours en cours au moment où les arbitres dans l'affaire d'espèce ont rendu leur sentence.

Le 10 octobre 1985, le Maître de l'Ouvrage a de son côté présenté une requête au centre international d'expertise technique de la Chambre de Commerce Internationale en vue de la nomination d'un expert dans le cadre de la caution bancaire émise en sa faveur.

Par décision du 12 novembre 1985, le président de ce centre, après avoir rappelé que l'expert n'était habilité qu'à faire des constatations, a désigné M. G., de nationalité Suisse, assisté de deux ingénieurs conseils. Dès le 27 novembre 1985, la banque a été avisée de cette désignation par le centre et l'expert a informé le constructeur de celle-ci à la même époque.

L'expert a commencé à procéder à sa mission, s'est transporté sur les lieux, a visité plusieurs autres installations en présence des dirigeants du constructeur, a interrogé les représentants de l'un et de l'autre, a finalement déposé son rapport en avril 1986.

Cet expert a conclu en évaluant le montant des réserves constatées sur l'ensemble des travaux d'une part à des dizaines de millions de francs. Il a au surplus décomposé ces réserves en trois catégories.

Par lettre du 21 avril 1986 le Maître de l'Ouvrage mettant en jeu l'acte susvisé a demandé à la banque le paiement par celle-ci du montant des sommes ainsi fixées par l'expert.

Par lettre du 2 mai 1986 la banque a répondu qu'elle ne remettait pas en question son engagement mais qu'elle s'étonnait devant cet appel alors qu'une procédure d'arbitrage était en cours pour fixer les obligations des parties.

Elle se disait au surplus obligée de faire des réserves sur les conditions dans lesquelles avait été établi le rapport de l'expert en ajoutant qu'il présentait des difficultés d'interprétation rendant impossible l'exécution de sa caution et qu'elle avait décidé de recourir à l'arbitrage.

Un Tribunal Arbitral composé de trois arbitres était constitué. Le lieu de l'arbitrage était Paris.

Au termes de sa requête en date du 22 mai 1986, la banque invitait les arbitres à dire :

1° « Si le rapport qui lui a été adressé par le Maître de l'Ouvrage, le 21 avril 1986, établi par M. G., correspond au rapport prévu par l'acte de caution.

a) Si, en effet, elle ne devait pas être avisée préalablement de la demande de nomination de cet expert.

b) Si le constructeur ne devait pas être partie au déroulement de la procédure d'expertise.

c) Si donc le rapport de M. G., fixant le montant de sommes estimées par lui nécessaires afin que le complexe réalisé par le Maître de l'Ouvrage puisse être considéré comme satisfaisant, est opposable au constructeur d'une part, et la banque d'autre part, lui permettant d'exécuter des engagements de novembre 1984.

2° Si, en conséquence, le rapport de M. G., doit s'interpréter comme étant celui qui est prévu par l'acte de caution.

3° Et donc si la banque doit payer les montants réclamés par le Maître de l'Ouvrage, malgré la contestation du constructeur sur l'appel de caution.

4° Subsidiairement, si elle ne doit pas surseoir à tout paiement en attendant l'issue du litige existant entre le Maître de l'Ouvrage et le constructeur actuellement soumis à la Cour d'arbitrage de la Chambre de Commerce Internationale. »

Par mémoire en juillet 1986, le Maître de l'Ouvrage a demandé au tribunal de constater :

1. *« Que l'engagement de la banque était subordonné à la seule production d'un rapport d'expertise établi par un expert du Centre International Technique de la Chambre de Commerce Internationale.*

2. Que le rapport G. correspond à ces exigences, les seules posées par la lettre de garantie.

3. Que les conclusions auxquelles l'expert G. est parvenu, chiffrant les non conformités réversibles et irréversibles qu'il avait contradictoirement constatées, étaient les éléments nécessaires mais suffisants à la mobilisation de la garantie par le Maître de l'Ouvrage.

4. Que l'engagement de la banque était indépendant de l'engagement du constructeur.

5. Qu'en conséquence, le refus opposé au Maître de l'Ouvrage est abusif et dilatoire.

6. Que l'expertise prévue par la lettre de garantie et mise en œuvre par le Maître de l'Ouvrage, est distincte et indépendante de toutes autres procédures d'arbitrage et/ou expertise. »

En outre, il s'est porté demandeur reconventionnel.

« Afin que soit constaté, par les arbitres, la mauvaise foi et le caractère manifestement dilatoire de la procédure d'arbitrage diligentée par la banque, dans le seul but de gagner du temps et de se soustraire à ses obligations. »

Un acte de mission a été établi et signé par les parties, précisant que le point litigieux soumis aux arbitres est celui de l'interprétation et de la portée de la lettre de garantie de novembre 1984.

Extrait de la sentence :

« La banque soutient :

1. — Que si la garantie donnée par elle doit être considérée comme une caution, son sort dépendrait de celui du litige principal opposant le Maître de l'Ouvrage et le constructeur et qui n'est pas encore résolu.

2. — Que si cette garantie est une garantie documentaire subordonnée à la production d'un rapport d'expert, ce rapport aurait été obtenu dans des conditions frauduleuses qui ne permettraient pas au Maître de l'Ouvrage de l'invoquer.

3. — Que ce rapport donnerait lieu à des difficultés d'interprétation rendant impossible l'exécution de la caution.

4. — Qu'elle ne peut payer les sommes réclamées, qu'il y a en tout état de cause lieu de surseoir, et qu'en l'absence de toute faute de sa part elle ne doit aucun dommage intérêt. »

« Le Maître de l'Ouvrage soutient de son côté que le rapport litigieux a été obtenu régulièrement, qu'il correspond aux exigences posées par la lettre de garantie, que celle-ci doit être mobilisée à hauteur des sommes retenues par l'expert, qu'elle est autonome et distincte du sort de toute autre procédure ; en conséquence, le refus de payer immédiatement, opposé par la banque, est fautif. Le maître de l'ouvrage demande à titre reconventionnel :

1. — Le paiement du montant des réserves évaluées par l'expert outre les intérêts de retard à compter du 21 avril 1986.

2. — Le remboursement des frais d'expertise, des frais et honoraires exposés à l'occasion de ce litige.

3. — Le versement de 1 500 000 francs en réparation du préjudice économique et matériel subi par lui.

Motifs du Tribunal Arbitral

A. Sur la demande principale.

1) Sur le point de savoir si les arbitres sont en présence d'une caution ou d'une garantie autonome.

La lettre de garantie est dans ses termes très équivoque. D'une part en effet la banque utilise les mots de :

"caution bancaire de bonne fin"
"caution solidaire"

"renonciation au bénéfice de discussion et de division", caractéristiques d'une caution.

Mais d'autre part, la banque s'engage à payer :

"sur une demande écrite de votre part accompagnée d'un rapport établi par un expert".

Certes, la banque relève trois autres traits, qui selon elle, caractérisaient une caution.

En premier lieu, en effet, selon la banque, si elle a promis de payer "tout ou partie" d'un montant indiqué dans sa lettre, c'est parce que ce paiement serait subordonné à la liquidation de la dette principale éventuellement due.

En second lieu, elle rappelle que la garantie devait se réduire progressivement au fur et à mesure des formalités constituant l'avancement des travaux.

En troisième lieu, dit la banque, l'insertion d'une clause arbitrale pour toute difficulté d'interprétation ou d'exécution révélerait que le jeu de la garantie n'était pas automatique.

Mais ces trois particularités ne caractèrisent en rien une caution plutôt qu'une garantie autonome.

Sur le premier point, l'engagement de payer tout ou partie découle simplement du fait que la créance invoquée par le Maître de l'Ouvrage pouvait être inférieure au montant de la garantie.

Sur le second point, le fait que la garantie se réduisait au fur et à mesure de l'avancement des travaux est entièrement indépendant du point de savoir si la garantie est autonome ou accessoire.

Enfin, sur le troisième point, l'insertion d'une clause d'arbitrage pour toute difficulté d'interprétation ou d'exécution n'implique pas que la garantie n'était pas autonome. Bien au contraire, si son jeu avait dépendu du sort de l'arbitrage entre le Maître de l'Ouvrage et le constructeur, point n'était besoin de prévoir un second arbitrage.

En réalité, la réduction de la garantie au fur et à mesure des travaux suffisait à susciter des difficultés rendant nécessaire le recours à des arbitres.

Il reste donc l'opposition entre les mots : "caution de bonne fin", "caution solidaire" et l'engagement de payer "sur demande".

Le Tribunal Arbitral, contraint de choisir entre ces termes contradictoires, et regrettant qu'une banque ait pu laisser subsister pareille contradiction, estime qu'il se trouve en l'espèce en présence d'une garantie bancaire, du genre documentaire, c'est-à-dire indépendante de l'obligation principale, et subordonnée à la seule production d'un document.

Aussi bien la banque, quand elle a refusé de payer le 2 mai 1986, n'a jamais allégué que son engagement était subordonné au sort d'un différend né entre le maître de l'ouvrage et le constructeur mais elle s'est contentée d'alléguer qu'il était « impossible » d'exécuter sa garantie.

On ne comprendrait pas d'autre part pourquoi la production d'un rapport aurait été imposé au Maître de l'Ouvrage si la banque n'avait été tenue à garantir qu'après la solution du litige entre le Maître de l'Ouvrage et le constructeur.

L'existence d'un rapport était de nature à empêcher un recours abusif, comme le constructeur l'a écrit à un sous-traitant en novembre 1984, sans être aussi astreignante pour le Maître de l'Ouvrage que la preuve "justifiée" de son dommage, comme la banque l'avait d'abord proposée.

Mais cette solution intermédiaire était quand même plus avantageuse pour la banque et par conséquent pour le constructeur, que l'immobilisation entre les mains de la banque, d'une certaine somme sous forme d'une "stand by letter of credit".

En fait, l'ambiguïté des termes utilisés réside dans le fait qu'il s'agit d'une solution de compromis entre :

— la caution "stricto sensu" proposée par la banque dans sa lettre en octobre 1984 dont il n'est pas contesté qu'elle ait été exclue ;

— et la garantie à première demande pure et simple sollicitée par le Maître de l'Ouvrage qui a été également exclue.

La banque a cependant continué à employer le terme de "caution" dans son sens général synonyme de garantie "lato sensu" et non dans son acception juridique spécifique.

Elle est en conséquence mal fondée à prétendre que la lettre du 9 novembre 1984 est une caution.

Le Tribunal Arbitral ayant retenu que la banque avait bien consenti au Maître de l'Ouvrage une garantie documentaire, décide en conséquence que le rapport de l'expert G. est bien la condition — posée par la banque elle-même — de sa mise en œuvre.

2) Sur le point de savoir si le rapport d'expertise a été obtenu dans des conditions frauduleuses ou irrégulières.

Cette question posée par la banque n'a d'intérêt qu'en tant qu'elle sous entend implicitement mais nécessairement la réponse qui vient d'être donnée sur le point précédent, savoir qu'il s'agit bien d'une garantie documentaire.

Le rapport à produire n'était nullement destiné à faciliter ou à hâter le sort du litige entre le maître de l'ouvrage et le constructeur, il était destiné, comme l'a écrit le constructeur, à empêcher tout recours abusif au jeu de la garantie de la part du Maître de l'Ouvrage, en soumettant au contrôle d'un technicien compétent et neutre, le montant des créances invoquées par le maître de l'ouvrage contre le constructeur et devait entraîner le jeu automatique de la garantie.

Ce rapport ne possède aucune autorité d'ordre juridique, à l'égard des arbitres et des parties, dans la procédure arbitrale dirigée contre le constructeur.

Il n'a pas a être contradictoire avec ce dernier, puisqu'il ne lui est pas opposable.

L'expert a été désigné conformément aux termes de la lettre de garantie et au règlement sur l'expertise technique, auquel se référait cette lettre.

Bien plus, non seulement la banque, mais le constructeur ont été informés de cette désignation, l'expert les a rencontrés et entendus, il a eu des réunions avec eux, s'est déplacé sur le site.

Il n'existe aucune irrégularité, encore moins de fraude, dans le sens où la jurisprudence sur les garanties bancaires l'entend.

En conséquence, le rapport ne peut être écarté.

3) Sur le point de savoir si les difficultés d'interprétation du rapport rendent impossible le jeu de la garantie.

C'est l'argument essentiel sur lequel s'est fondé la banque en refusant de payer.

La banque, depuis, a précisé que l'expert aurait fait des constatations inexactes, qu'il se serait livré à une appréciation erronée des termes du contrat et qu'il aurait abouti à des conclusions hypothétiques.

Sur ce point également, il faut tenir compte de ce qui vient d'être dit sur la nature de la garantie ; la production du rapport d'un expert désigné dans les conditions prévues, doit suffire en principe, à condition bien entendu que les conclusions de cet expert ne viennent pas contredire les allégations du Maître de l'Ouvrage. Il est certain qui si l'expert avait conclu qu'il n'y avait lieu à aucune réclamation, le maître de l'ouvrage n'aurait pas pu prospérer en sa demande.

Loin de là, l'expert après des recherches détaillées, a abouti à chiffrer d'une manière précise le montant des réclamations possibles du Maître de l'Ouvrage et c'est ce montant que le Maître de l'Ouvrage a repris dans sa demande.

En l'absence de toute erreur manifeste ou grossière de la part de l'expert, il n'est pas possible d'exercer un contrôle de fait ou de droit sur le travail de l'expert.

Celui-ci ne s'est pas livré à des hypothèses mais il a tenu à classer ses constatations et évaluations dans trois catégories différentes comme à ajouter par acquit de conscience que ses évaluations pouvaient être modifiées si l'état des choses venait à changer.

Ces appréciations ne sont pas dubitatives.

De même, il n'y a pas lieu de rechercher si le montant de la garantie a pu diminuer avec l'avancement des travaux, puisque la banque n'a présenté à ce sujet aucune demande ni faits précis de nature à confirmer ces allégations.

Il n'y a donc ni contradiction ni doute, ni difficulté rendant impossible l'exécution de la garantie et aucun sursis lié à l'exécution du contrat principal ne saurait être ordonné.

B. Sur la demande reconventionnelle

Il suit de ce qui précède que le Maître de l'Ouvrage est fondé à exiger l'exécution de la garantie promise, la banque est tenue au surplus de réparer le dommage qui résulte, directement pour le Maître de l'Ouvrage de son refus de payer.

Sur ce point, le Maître de l'Ouvrage est fondé à réclamer outre les sommes fixées par l'expert :

1. — Les intérêts de retard de ces sommes à compter de la mise en demeure adressée à la banque par lettre recommandée du 21 avril 1986, ces intérêts devant être calculés selon la loi française applicable, soit au taux de 9,5 % l'an.

2. — *La réparation du préjudice moral et matériel subi du même fait par le Maître de l'Ouvrage indépendamment du retard apporté dans l'exécution de la garantie.*

Le Tribunal Arbitral évalue celui-ci toutes causes et préjudices confondus — sous réserve de ce qui va être dit sur les frais d'expertise — à la somme de : un million trois cent mille francs français (1 300 000 FF).

Le Maître de l'Ouvrage n'est pas fondé à réclamer cependant le remboursement des frais de l'expertise qui lui incombait de toute manière.

Quant au frais d'arbitrage (frais administratifs de la CCI et honoraires d'arbitres) proprement dits, le tribunal estime équitable d'en faire supporter :

— *les trois quarts par la banque*

— *le quart par le Maître de l'Ouvrage.*

OBSERVATIONS. — Les contrats portant sur les travaux publics ainsi que sur les installations « clé-en-main », stipulent souvent qu'une tierce personne doit fournir des garanties ou cautions en faveur du Maître de l'Ouvrage pour la « bonne fin » des engagements du constructeur. Un problème courant consiste à trouver un moyen contractuel pour protéger le constructeur contre des manœuvres abusives de la part du Maître de l'Ouvrage, consistant à appeler la garantie sans que les défauts dans la performance du constructeur n'aient été démontrés. Contre l'appel en garantie de mauvaise foi des tribunaux de divers pays ont trouvé peu de protection en faveur du constructeur dans la situation où le constructeur, a accepté au moment de la conclusion du marché, que le bénéficiaire puisse appeler la garantie sur première demande et sans avoir à prouver une faute de la part du constructeur et encore moins produire une sentence arbitrale ou jugement d'un tribunal judiciaire donnant raison au Maître de l'Ouvrage.

L'affaire ici rapportée indique l'emploi que les praticiens du commerce international peuvent faire des services du Centre d'Expertise Technique de la CCI à cet égard. Il est déjà arrivé dans d'autres affaires du Centre d'Expertise Technique de la CCI, soumises ou non à l'arbitrage CCI, que les parties ont prévu le recours au Centre pour obtenir l'avis d'un expert comme une condition nécessaire pour appeler une caution.

Sans que l'avis du tiers devienne opposable au constructeur dans ses relations avec le Maître de l'Ouvrage, le fait même qu'un expert doive se prononcer sur l'état des ouvrages décourage le Maître de l'Ouvrage de faire un appel non fondé. Si l'expert ne trouve aucun défaut dans l'installation délivrée par le constructeur, il serait contraire à la bonne foi de la part du Maître de l'Ouvrage d'appeler la garantie. Si, par contre, l'expert constate des défectuosités, l'appel de la garantie ne saurait a priori être qualifié d'abusif ; tout dépend des circonstances de l'affaire en question.

On peut s'étonner d'ailleurs que la garantie en espèce n'a même pas posé comme condition pour l'appeler que, selon l'avis de l'expert, des défectuosités dans l'exécution de l'ouvrage étaient attribuables au constructeur. Une simple constatation de non conformité entre l'exécution réelle et les spécifications du contrat suffit.

L'intervention d'un expert, nommé par un organisme sans intérêt dans l'affaire, tel que le Centre d'Expertise Technique de la CCI, peut donc être utile afin de calmer les esprits des parties au contrat et empêcher des appels abusifs de la part d'un Maître de l'Ouvrage. Mais aussi faut-il que l'émetteur d'une garantie, une banque ou autre, exécute de bonne foi ses obligations conformément aux conditions stipulées dans la garantie émise par elle.

S. J.

I. — Clause compromissoire. — Détermination de la loi applicable à sa forme, à sa validité et au pouvoir de compromettre. — Nécessité d'autorisation écrite pour signer aux lieu et place de la société partie au contrat (oui).

II. — Clause compromissoire. — Formation du contrat. — Existence d'une convention d'arbitrage avant la conclusion du contrat (non). — Référence précontractuelle à une clause CCI dans les conditions générales d'une partie.

Sentence rendue dans l'affaire 5832 en 1988.

Ayant obtenu un marché pour la construction d'un ouvrage dans un pays du Moyen Orient, une société autrichienne (défenderesse) a reçu d'une entreprise du Liechtenstein (demanderesse) une offre pour la réalisation d'une partie des travaux. Plusieurs mois de négociations ont suivi et, en septembre 1982, la partie défenderesse a adressé à la demanderesse une « order letter » précisant les conditions contractuelles de son intervention et l'invitant à marquer son acceptation ou, au besoin, à indiquer les modifications souhaitées. Signée par deux dirigeants de la société autrichienne dûment autorisés, la « order letter » renvoyait à des conditions générales contenant une clause arbitrale CCI pour le règlement de différends. Peu de temps après (trois semaines) la partie demanderesse a conditionné son acceptation à l'introduction de certaines modifications laissant intacte la clause compromissoire. Finalement, en janvier 1983 les parties auraient conclu un accord constaté dans une commande et un procès verbal portant les signatures de deux employés de la société autrichienne ainsi que du représentant de la demanderesse.

Statuant sur sa compétence, le tribunal arbitral (siégeant à Zurich) devait examiner l'exception de la défenderesse autrichienne fondée sur le défaut d'autorisation des signataires du contrat de janvier 1983 rendant la clause arbitrale inopposable à son encontre. Mais, les arbitres devaient d'abord trouver la loi applicable à la clause d'abitrage :

Traduction de l'original anglais

« *Selon la doctrine et la jurisprudence suisses, une* convention d'arbitrage *n'est pas un contrat relevant du droit du fond mais du droit régissant la procédure... La question de savoir quelle loi est applicable à la convention d'arbitrage doit être tranchée selon les principes du droit procédural international suisse, applicable dans l'instance présente. D'après la doctrine suisse, unanime, la validité d'une convention arbitrale doit être déterminée en vertu de la lex fori qui est la loi du Canton de Zurich en tant que loi du siège du tribunal arbitral...*

En général, la forme *d'une convention d'arbitrage doit être conforme à la loi du siège du tribunal arbitral. Toutefois, dans une affaire internationale, cette forme peut aussi respecter la loi du lieu de la conclusion de l'accord, selon le principe* locus regit formam actus.

Selon la doctrine et la jurisprudence dominantes, la règle de rattachement citée ci-dessus est une solution alternative. D'après la loi applicable au siège du tribunal arbitral... une convention d'arbitrage doit être écrite. Peu importe que soit applicable, ou bien le ZPO du Canton de Zurich (§ 238 par. 1) en vigueur à la date où aurait pu être conclu le contrat, ou bien (le CIA) (art. 6 par. 1) actuellement applicable dans le Canton de Zurich...

Une autre question est de savoir si la convention d'arbitrage a été signée par des personnes autorisées *et, notamment, quel droit régit l'autorisation donnée* aux instances dirigeantes, employés ou représentants *d'une société. Selon le droit international privé et le droit de procédure suisses, cette dernière question ne relève pas, en général, de la* lex fori... *Si le représentant a agi en vertu des pouvoirs d'une instance dirigeante, l'existence et la portée de ses pouvoirs doivent être jugés en fonction du statut personnel de l'entité juridique en cause...*

... Si le représentant n'a pas agi en qualité d'instance dirigeante mais d'agent autorisé de la partie au litige, il faut séparer les questions relatives à l'existence du pouvoir et à sa portée. L'existence du pouvoir, c'est-à-dire le point de savoir si la convention arbitrale a été conclue par une personne autorisée à agir au nom du mandant, doit être décidée selon la loi du bureau ou du domicile enregistré du représentant... La question de la portée du pouvoir de représentation doit être tranchée selon la loi du lieu où le représentant a conclu la convention d'arbitrage avec le tiers, c'est-à-dire le lieu dit « de l'effet »...

La défenderesse *a son bureau enregistré à Vienne. Son (ses) représentant(s) ont fait usage à Linz de la procuration qui existait éventuellement. Le statut personnel de la défenderesse et le statut de l'effet sont donc identiques et le droit autrichien s'applique dans l'un et l'autre cas ».*

La solution en droit autrichien conduit les arbitres à exiger, pour la validité de la convention d'arbitrage, que l'autorisation pour signer soit donnée par écrit :

« ... *L'exigence formelle (selon la loi autrichienne) que la convention d'arbitrage doit être écrite s'étend aux relations entre le mandant et son mandataire si l'une des parties contractantes est représentée par une personne autre que son représentant légal. La doctrine et la jurisprudence... sont claires et sans équivoque : la convention d'arbitrage doit être entièrement couverte par les signatures données au nom des deux parties. Si la convention d'arbitrage n'est pas signée par la partie elle-même mais par un agent autorisé, l'autorisation de conclure une telle convention d'arbitrage fait partie de la convention elle-même et la complète de façon telle que la convention d'arbitrage ne peut pas être reconnue comme un accord valable sans un pareil pouvoir...*

L'octroi tacite, ou exprès mais oral, d'une procuration à l'agent, ou l'acceptation ultérieure de ses déclarations, ne suffit pas car cela viderait de son contenu l'objet des exigences formelles... Aucun autre résultat ne saurait — en droit autrichien — être obtenu par la preuve d'un « Auscheinsvollmacht » (pouvoir apparent), ni d'une approbation ultérieure de la convention d'arbitrage par la défenderesse. Ce serait aussi le cas si les dispositions de fond du contrat avaient fait l'objet d'une approbation informelle... Pour récapituler ce qui précède, on peut dire que selon la loi du fond autrichienne, qui est le droit applicable pour la défenderesse, l'autorisation de représenter une autre personne doit être écrite tant qu'aucune inscription à ce sujet n'a été faite au Registre du Commerce...

Les deux parties ont convenu que les personnes ayant signé l'Order letter du 20 septembre 1982 au nom de la défenderesse étaient autorisées à signer et avaient pouvoir de conclure une convention d'arbitrage au nom de la défenderesse. Toutefois, ce n'était pas le cas (des personnes) qui ont signé le procès-verbal de la réunion du 13 janvier 1983 au nom de la défenderesse... Il n'a pu y avoir une soumission valable à la clause d'arbitrage incluse dans les Conditions Générales de la défenderesse que si l'Order letter du 20 septembre 1982 formait, avec la confirmation de commande de la demanderesse du 11 octobre 1982, un accord obligatoire, mais non si cet accord a été conclu le 13 janvier 1983... Vu qu'un octroi tacite d'autorisation n'est pas valable en droit autrichien et qu'il n'y a pas eu de procuration écrite, on ne saurait conclure de la conduite de la défenderesse que la signature du document du 13 janvier 1983 a eu un effet juridique et obligatoire. »

Toutefois, au vu de l'existence d'un document précontractuel émanant de la société défenderesse incorporant par référence à des conditions générales une clause CCI, les arbitres retracent la formation du contrat afin de déterminer si, dès octobre 1982, un accord de volontés existait sur le recours à l'arbitrage :

« *Une soumission valable à la clause d'arbitrage incluse dans les Conditions Générales de la défenderesse n'a pu avoir lieu que si l'Order letter du 20 septembre 1982, formait avec la confirmation de commande par la demanderesse en octobre 1982 un accord obligatoire, mais non si cet accord a été conclu en janvier 1983...*

L'Order letter de septembre 1982 ne peut contenir une clause d'arbitrage valable que :

— si, jointe à la confirmation de commande, elle peut être considérée comme une convention d'arbitrage indépendante qui par elle-même, i.e. indépendamment des autres parties du contrat, aurait pu être, et a été conclue, ou

— si l'on admet qu'a été conclu — avec la confirmation de commande — un accord conditionnel parfait du fait de la réalisation de la condition, c'est-à-dire de la conclusion du contrat principal le 13 janvier 1983 ; ou enfin

— si l'offre — de conclure une convention d'arbitrage — contenue dans l'Order letter était restée valable alors que les discussions contractuelles se poursuivaient et avait été acceptée par la contrepartie le 13 janvier 1983. »

Ayant écarté les trois hypothèses posées, les arbitres examinent le résultat à la lumière du principe de la bonne foi avant de se déclarer incompétents pour aborder le fond sur la base de la convention d'arbitrage proposée par la défenderesse en septembre 1982.

« *Dans le cas présent... il n'y a pas de séparation entre les dispositions de fond du contrat et la convention d'arbitrage. Quand se pose la question de savoir si la clause d'arbitrage a une destinée juridique indépendante de celle du contrat principal, l'intention des parties doit être considérée comme décisive. Ni les déclarations des parties, ni les documents soumis au Tribunal arbitral ne permettent de conclure que les parties aient eu l'intention de conclure un accord indépendant sur le jugement par les arbitres de leurs relations mutuelles en échangeant l'Order letter et la confirmation de commande, donc avant d'être tombées d'accord sur le contenu du fond du contrat.*

... Une autre possibilité qu'il faut examiner, c'est si les parties ont convenu, les 20 septembre 1982 et 11 octobre 1982, de conclure une convention d'arbitrage à la condition *que le contrat principal serait conclu dans le futur. Si c'était le cas, les parties auraient été d'accord sur certaines parties du contrat, telles que la clause d'arbitrage, sous réserve de la condition d'un accord futur sur l'ensemble du contrat.*

Contrairement à cette hypothèse, la majorité du Tribunal arbitral estime qu'en général un contrat complet n'est conclu qu'au terme des négociations contractuelles.

C'est seulement à titre exceptionnel qu'on peut présumer certaines questions réglées d'avance, à la condition d'une conclusion ultérieure du contrat tout entier...

... Une dernière possibilité serait que l'offre de la défenderesse contenue dans l'Order letter du 20 septembre 1982 soit restée valable et ouverte *durant toute la période suivante des négociations entre les parties, et que la commande ait finalement été acceptée ferme le 13 janvier 1983, pour ce qui concerne la clause d'arbitrage.*

Selon l'article 1 du Code Suisse des obligations (CO) il est essentiel pour la conclusion d'un contrat que les parties se soient fait part de leurs intentions correspondantes mutuelles. A cet effet il est nécessaire qu'elles soient d'accord au moins sur les dispositions contractuelles objectivement et subjectivement importantes... C'est seulement si les parties sont d'accord sur toutes les dispositions contractuelles essentielles qu'un contrat peut être considéré comme conclu. Si les parties sont d'accord sur tous les points essentiels, il faut admettre qu'une réserve sur des dispositions secondaires ne fait pas obstacle au caractère obligatoire du contrat (art. 2, par. 1 CO).

Lors de la conclusion d'un contrat, les parties échangent mutuellement des déclarations d'intention. L'offre d'une partie à une autre qui n'est pas présente est valable tant que son auteur peut en attendre l'acceptation (si aucun délai n'a été convenu entre les parties, selon l'art. 5, par 1 CO), si son offre parvient à temps à l'autre partie et si l'acceptation est dûment renvoyée à temps. Si le délai s'écoule sans que l'offre soit utilisée, celle-ci cesse d'être valable à moins que l'intention contraire de l'auteur de l'offre puisse être présumée... L'acceptation doit s'accorder à l'offre pour que soit réalisée une déclaration d'intentions mutuelles et correspondantes ce qui est essentiel pour que le contrat soit conclu. Si la déclaration d'acceptation s'écarte de l'offre, elle n'est pas considérée comme une acceptation au sens de l'article 3 et suivants CO, mais constitue à son tour une nouvelle offre...

L'Order letter de la défenderesse, du 20 septembre 1982, a été suivie d'une confirmation de commande (probablement dans le délai pour une pareille acceptation selon l'art. 5 CO). La demanderesse a déclaré dans cette confirmation de commande qu'elle était d'accord avec la plupart des dispositions de l'offre, mais elle a aussi déclaré clairement et sans équivoque que cette « acceptation » ne pourrait être admise comme telle que si l'accord pouvait se faire sur les dispositions encore ouvertes du contrat. Selon les déclarations correspondantes des deux parties, les dispositions encore ouvertes du contrat devaient être considérées comme « essentiala negotii », si bien que l'article 2 CO ne saurait s'appliquer. On peut convenir avec les parties qu'à tout le moins les dispositions ouvertes visant le paiement d'avance, les conditions d'application de pénalités de retard et les dispositions sur les questions d'assurance étaient absolument des parties essentielles du contrat... Cela conduit à la conclusion qu'on ne peut pas dire que l'offre du 20 septembre 1982 fut fondamentalement acceptée sans changement par la demanderesse le 13 janvier 1983. La confirmation de la commande par la demanderesse, le 11 octobre 1982, constituait un rejet *de l'Order letter et — selon la doctrine mentionnée ci-dessus — une nouvelle (contre-) offre présentée à la défenderesse. L'offre initiale ne fut donc pas immédiatement acceptée - comme l'aurait exigé la loi — mais une contre-offre modifiée fut renvoyée à la défenderesse qui aurait pu l'accepter... Du fait du rejet de l'Order letter du 20 septembre 1982, toute l'offre de la défenderesse a cessé d'être valable y compris la convention d'arbitrage. Que les parties ne se soient plus considérées comme liées ressort du fait que la contre-offre ne fut pas acceptée non plus et que les parties poursuivirent leurs négociations contractuelles jusqu'au 13 janvier 1983...*

Aussi faut-il conclure que la défenderesse n'a pas souscrit à une convention *d'arbitrage d'une façon qui l'aurait juridiquement liée...*

... Enfin il faut examiner si ce résultat doit être considéré comme contraire au principe de la bonne foi.

Pour répondre à cette question, il faut commencer par examiner si s'applique le droit suisse ou l'autrichien. Le problème est de décider s'il y a invocation abusive d'un vice de forme pour un pouvoir et non s'il y a invocation abusive de défauts de la clause arbitrale en tant que telle. La loi *régissant le pouvoir est donc celle selon laquelle il faut décider si la défenderesse aurait ou non manqué au principe de la bonne foi ; or, c'est la loi autrichienne...*

Une référence au principe de la bonne foi est exclue dans les circonstances présentes. La raison de ce rejet est la rigueur des dispositions sur les formalités, stipulées afin d'assurer un moyen de preuve clair et simple et aussi de protéger les parties contre la renonciation aux garanties procédurales ; cette sévérité exclut toute possibilité d'alléguer une atteinte au principe de la bonne foi selon le droit autrichien.

Même si le droit suisse était applicable, on ne pourrait pas qualifier la clause d'arbitrage de valable au nom du principe de la bonne foi. Selon la doctrine et la jurisprudence prédominantes en Suisse, l'allégation d'un vice de forme peut être abusive dans certains cas, par exemple si les parties — sachant qu'il y a un vice de forme — exécutent le contrat d'une façon qui les engage en droit. *Mais une telle situation n'existe pas ici. »*

OBSERVATIONS :

I. — Tant la doctrine que la jurisprudence suisses citées par les arbitres admettent l'application de la *lex fori* pour apprécier la validité de la clause d'arbitrage (Straüli, Messmer, Wiget, *Kommentar zur ZPO,* Article 238, n. 6 ; Guldener, *Das Interkantonale und Internationale Zivilprozessrecht der Schweiz,* Zurich 1951 ; Tribunal fédéral 101 II 170, 96 I 340, 85 II 151 ; Schweizerische Juristenzeitung 71, 1975 ; Blätter für Zürcherische Rechtsprechung 48 (1949) N. 78). Solution contestable lorsque les parties n'ont pas elles-mêmes choisi le lieu de l'arbitrage, ce rattachement est également consacré par les conventions de New York de 1958 (article V.1.a) et de Genève de 1961 (articles VI.2.b et IX.1.a).

Mais d'autres règles de rattachement pourraient être considérées. Bien que reconnu par une partie de la doctrine (en France, cf. Robert, *L'arbitrage, droit interne, droit international privé*, p. 234, n. 269) la loi du lieu de conclusion du contrat ne saurait être retenue qu'en présence d'indices permettant d'établir de façon certaine la volonté des parties de soumettre leur convention à cette loi. Le lieu de conclusion du contrat est souvent aléatoire et toute tendance à y attacher une signification plus importante serait susceptible d'introduire un élément de rattachement artificiel. En l'espèce, cette règle, qualifiée de « *alternative solution* », est purement et simplement écartée par le tribunal arbitral.

En l'absence d'une loi d'autonomie, les arbitres n'ont pas eu à examiner si la loi de fond choisie par les parties pouvait également s'appliquer à la convention d'arbitrage. Naturellement, l'accord des parties sur le droit matériel permettrait aux arbitres de présumer que, malgré le principe de l'autonomie de la clause compromissoire, contrat et convention d'arbitrage sont soumis à la même loi (pour une solution différente, cf. sentences rendues dans l'affaire 4504 : *Clunet* 1986, 1118, observ. S. Jarvin).

Force est de constater la modernité de la nouvelle Loi fédérale suisse sur le droit international privé dont l'article 178 introduit une disposition qui met fin au débat sur la loi applicable à la validité de la clause d'arbitrage. Dès l'entrée en vigueur de cette loi la clause sera valable quant au fond « ... si elle répond aux conditions que pose soit le droit choisi par les parties, soit le droit régissant l'objet du litige et notamment le droit applicable au contrat principal, soit encore le droit suisse » (article 178.2). La loi suisse aura ainsi consacré le principe de l'autonomie de la volonté des parties et le caractère supplétif de la loi du for.

En l'espèce, les arbitres décident que la forme et la validité de la clause arbitrale doivent être appréciées à la lumière de la loi de Zurich (loi du for). Cela étant, le tribunal prend soin de préciser qu'il n'en va pas de même pour la détermination de la loi applicable au pouvoir de compromettre, celui-ci devant être apprécié selon la loi du mandant (existence du pouvoir) ou en application de la loi du lieu de l'acte (portée du pouvoir). Imposée par les règles du droit international privé suisse, cette démarche conduit les arbitres à l'application de la loi autrichienne à la fois pour l'existence et pour la portée du pouvoir. Cependant, une mise en garde est indispensable car la séparation de ces deux aspects est susceptible d'entraîner l'application des lois étatiques préconisant des résultats différents.

Dans la présente affaire la solution qui résulte de l'application du droit autrichien est sévère (en faveur de cette sévérité, cf. R. David, *L'arbitrage dans le commerce international*, Economica, 1982, p. 270-271). En l'absence d'une autorisation écrite habilitant les personnes qui ont signé le contrat de 1983 pour la société autrichienne, celui-ci ne saurait lui être opposable. Mais, le recours à la théorie de l'apparence, n'aurait-il pas permis de dégager un véritable accord justifiant l'attente légitime de voir le litige tranché par voie arbitrale ?

Ainsi contraints par la position qu'ils adoptent sur la capacité de compromettre, les arbitres procèdent à l'examen de la période de formation du contrat afin de déterminer si un accord de volontés pour un recours à l'arbitrage existait avant 1983.

II. — Il découle des relations précontractuelles entre les parties que déjà en septembre 1982 une offre, signée par des dirigeants sociaux de la société autrichienne dûment autorisés, incorporait par référence une clause CCI. Toutefois, les arbitres refusent d'y voir une convention d'arbitrage finale malgré une réponse émanant de la demanderesse communiquant son acceptation de l'offre sous réserve de certaines modifications qui ne portait pas sur le principe de l'arbitrage CCI pour la solution de différends. Mais, ces modifications, portaient-elles sur des éléments essentiels du contrat ? La sentence répond affirmativement :

« *Selon les déclarations correspondantes des deux parties, les dispositions encore ouvertes du contrat devaient être considérées comme « essentiala negotii ».* »

Dans ces conditions, les arbitres considèrent que la réponse à l'offre (i.e. « *acceptance* of the order is subject to modifications ») constitue en réalité une « *rejection* of the Order letter ». Cette interprétation vide les échanges précontractuels de signification (« with the *rejection* of the order... the entire offer of the defendant became invalid, including the arbitration agreement ») alors même que la réalité du commerce international semble favoriser un examen d'ensemble des rapports entre les parties (*Cf.* commentaire Y. Derains à la sentence 5065 rendue en 1985, *Clunet* 1987, 1039 et particulièrement B. Haniotiau, M. Demideleer et N. Gerryn, « Vers la conclusion du contrat : les éléments caractéristiques de la convention et les pouvoirs des négociateurs », *in Le contrat en formation*, Bruxelles 1987, ainsi que les observations de Ph. Kahn sur l'importance des échanges précontractuels dans « L'interpréaiton des contrats internationaux », *Clunet* 1981, p. 5 s.). On peut en outre constater que cette approche restrictive est également adoptée pour l'appréciation de la bonne foi, examinée sous l'angle d'une loi nationale (droit autrichien) et limitée au problème qualifié par les arbitres de « *abusive reliance on a defect in the form of the power of attorney* ».

Cette démarche des arbitres les conduit à se déclarer incompétents affirmant que la sévérité formelle du droit autrichien exclut la référence au principe de la bonne foi.

Justifié par l'absence d'un choix de loi applicable par les parties et par le souci de donner l'importance qu'elle mérite à la période de négociation, le recours à la bonne foi, en tant que principe général anational, aurait sans doute produit un résultat différent (*Cf.* E. Loquin, « L'application de règles anationales dans l'arbitrage commercial international *in L'apport de la jurisprudence arbitrale*, Les dossiers de l'Institut du Droit et des Pratiques des Affaires Internationales, Paris 1986, p. 98 et 99 ; « Les besoins du commerce international suscitent... la création de règles anationales qui, tenant compte des aléas des opérations commerciales internationales et de leurs coûts, imposent une coopération de bonne foi aux parties, qui dépasse par son ampleur celle normalement requise dans les opérations internes par les droits nationaux » ; et sentence rendue dans l'affaire 4381 en 1986, *Clunet* 1986, 1102).

G.A.A.

I. — **Contrat cadre.** — Contenu et portée. — Obligation de passer des commandes. — Obligation d'agir de bonne foi. — Application de la loi de l'Etat de New Hampshire.

II. — **Clause compromissoire.** — Arbitrabilité des demandes fondées sur la responsabilité délictuelle.

Sentence rendue dans l'affaire 5477 en 1988.

Après une longue période de pourparlers, une société italienne s'est engagée contractuellement à produire certains biens et à les vendre à une société américaine propriétaire de la marque. Conclu pour une durée initiale de 5 ans, le contrat était automatiquement renouvelable pour des périodes de 2 ans à défaut de notification de résiliation six mois avant son expiration. La société américaine, quant à elle, s'obligeait à établir une estimation annuelle de la production requise ainsi qu'à passer des commandes mensuelles selon un calendrier préalablement arrêté. Enfin, la société italienne était tenue de donner priorité aux commandes de la société américaine. Le contrat, par ailleurs soumis à la loi de l'Etat de New Hampshire, contenait la convention d'arbitrage suivante :

« *The parties hereto shall submit for arbitration all questions of difference which may at any time arise between them with respect to this agreement or to the application or construction of provisions thereof, and shall share the expenses of and abide by the decisions of such arbitration, which shall be conducted in accordance with the Rules of Conciliation and Arbitration of the International Chamber of Commerce located in Paris, France...* »

Dans sa requête d'arbitrage, la société italienne demande au tribunal arbitral la réparation du préjudice qu'elle aurait subi du fait de la tentative par la société américaine de mettre fin au contrat trois ans avant son terme. En revanche, considérant que la convention conclue ne serait qu'un contrat cadre, la société américaine considère qu'aucune obligation d'achat d'un minimum de produits ne saurait lui être opposable et qu'elle était en droit de manifester son intention de ne plus passer de nouvelles commandes. Par ailleurs, la société américaine introduit une demande reconventionnelle fondée sur la responsabilité contractuelle et délictuelle (concurrence déloyale et contrefaçons) de la demanderesse italienne.

Afin de placer le contrat dans le contexte des relations entre les parties et de lui attribuer une signification réelle, le tribunal arbitral déclara :

« *The Tribunal is not willing to hold that the contract was empty of contractual force as regards the placing of orders. It considers that (defendant), in addition to agreeing to place initial orders..., by necessary implication undertook an obligation to make an effort in good faith to satisfy a legitimate expectation on the part of (the claimant) that, unless the contract was terminated in accordance with its provisions, (claimant) would have a non-exclusive right to manufacture the existing models so long as market demand for them continued to exist and a fair opportunity to manufacture such new models, capable of being manufactured by (claimant), as (defendant) decided to introduce. The Tribunal is of the opinion that this interpretation of the contract is justified, indeed is called for, by the requirement of New Hampshire law concerning good faith.* »

Concernant la double nature de la demande reconventionnelle (contractuelle et délictuelle), les arbitres retiennent leur compétence :

« *The Tribunal considers that these claims are so closely interlinked that they are both within the jurisdiction of the tribunal conferred by (the arbitration agreement) of the contract. Indeed, in order to assess damages properly, and to avoid overlapping, it is unavoidable to consider both claims together. They depend upon the same set of facts and no objection was raised by either party to the jurisdiction of the Tribunal in respect of them. They are included in the Terms of Reference.* »

OBSERVATIONS :

I. — L'organisation de réalisations ponctuelles à partir d'un accord cadre est chose courante pour certaines opérations commerciales (*cf.* par exemple, l'affaire 5117 commentée par Y. Derains au *Clunet* 1986, 1113).

Lorsque les parties désirent définir les modalités d'échanges futurs dont le rythme et l'importance dépendent de circonstances à intervenir (par exemple, l'évolution du marché), le recours au montage contrat-cadre/contrats-d'application assure à la fois sécurité juridique et souplesse. Mais ce découpage des documents contractuels introduit des difficultés d'interprétation en ce qui concerne leur nature et leur portée.

Il n'est dès lors pas étonnant que les arbitres refusent d'admettre la thèse qui vide l'accord cadre de force contractuelle pour la passation de commandes (contrats d'application). Durant la vie du contrat et dans l'hypothèse où les conditions du marché seraient favorables, la société américaine était donc tenue de commander les produits dont la fabrication avait été confiée à son partenaire contractuel italien. Par conséquent, la défenderesse américaine aurait commis une faute contractuelle dommageable en notifiant à la demanderesse italienne son intention de ne plus passer commande des produits contractuels trois ans avant l'expiration du contrat. Notons au passage la référence des arbitres à l'obligation de bonne foi qui pèse sur les parties en application de la loi de New Hampshire et qui, cela va de soi, serait également applicable au titre de la *Lex Mercatoria* (*cf.* à ce sujet l'excellent article de Lord Mustill, « The New Lex Mercatoria : The First Twenty-five Years » : *Arbitration International,* July 1988).

II. — La nature contractuelle de l'arbitrage a souvent conduit les parties et les arbitres à s'interroger sur l'arbitrabilité de questions qui relèvent de la responsabilité délictuelle ou extra-contractuelle et qui échapperaient de ce fait à la clause arbitrale.

Deux approches différentes semblent permettre aux arbitres militant pour la solution arbitrale de retenir leur compétence.

Outre la non-objection des parties et l'incorporation des demandes fondées sur la responsabilité extra-contractuelle dans l'Acte de mission, le tribunal arbitral de la présente affaire fait appel à la notion de connexité des demandes (délictuelle et contractuelle) pour conclure qu'il est inévitable de cumuler leur examen. En effet, les arbitres considèrent que cette solution permet de « ... *assess damages properly, and ... avoid overlapping...* ».

En revanche, dans une affaire qui s'est déroulée en l'absence de la partie défenderesse dûment notifiée (sentence 5779 rendue en 1988), l'arbitre unique adopte une solution davantage rattachée au texte de la convention d'arbitrage libellée comme suit.

« *Any dispute arising under this agreement shall be settled under the Rules of Conciliation and Arbitration of the International Chamber of Commerce by a single arbitrator appointed in accordance with the Rules thereof.* »

Saisi de deux demandes de nature délictuelle, l'arbitre procède à l'examen de leur lien avec le contrat :

« *Each of (the) claims pertains directly to the performance of the contracts. The arbitrator finds that each of these claims is sufficiently related to the subject matter of the contracts to be considered as "arising under" them within the meaning of the contractual arbitration clauses... Hence, the arbitrator finds that he has jurisdiction to consider them.* »

Cette dernière solution semble par ailleurs consacrer l'importance que la pratique judiciaire américaine réserve au langage employé dans la clause compromissoire pour en apprécier la portée. Les practiciens anglo-saxons sont ainsi conduits à rédiger des conventions susceptibles de couvrir toutes les hypothèses (par exemple, « *disputes arising in connection with this agreement* » serait une formule plus large que « *disputes arising under this agreement* »). Il faudrait toutefois s'interroger sur l'opportunité d'une interprétation trop rigide de clauses plus ou moins type qui ne présentent pas d'éléments pathologiques.

G.A.A.

I. — **Droit applicable.** — Procédure arbitrale. — Choix des règles de procédure. — Règlement de la Cour d'arbitrage de la CCI. — Acte de mission. — Liberté de l'arbitre. — Droit applicable au fond. — Amiable composition. — Contrat. — Usages du commerce. — Règles communes aux droits nationaux concernés. — Attente légitime des parties.

II. — **Clause compromissoire.** — Aptitude d'une entreprise publique à compromettre (oui). — Bonne foi. — Compétence de l'arbitre. — Clause « pathologique ». — Effet utile des conventions. — Contestation des parties devant l'arbitre (non). — « Section internationale de la Chambre de Commerce de Paris ».

III. — **Exception de litispendance.** — Admissibilité (non). — Conflit de compétences judiciaire et arbitrale (non). — Caractère consensuel de l'arbitrage.

IV. — **Solidarité des débiteurs (oui).** — Notion de groupe de sociétés.

Sentence rendue dans l'affaire 5103 en 1988.

Le tribunal arbitral, siégeant à Paris, était saisi d'un litige opposant trois sociétés européennes du même groupe (A S.A., B S.A. et C Ltd., demanderesses) — ayant pour activité la transformation et la commercialisation de certains produits phosphatés — à quatre sociétés tunisiennes (défenderesses D, E, F et G groupées) productrices de ces biens. Le litige portait sur des difficultés dans les relations commerciales et financières entre demanderesses et défenderesses. Les arbitres étaient saisis par les demanderesses d'une demande d'indemnité pour rupture par les défenderesses de deux engagements financiers, et pour rupture des relations commerciales, ainsi que de dommages-intérêts en règlement de diverses difficultés au cours des livraisons antérieures. La position des parties défenderesses était elliptique. D'une part, elles soulèvent la nullité et la caducité des clauses compromissoires invoquées par les demanderesses et, subsidiairement, introduisent une demande reconventionnelle à leur encontre. Ayant saisi diverses juridictions françaises et tunisiennes parallèlement à l'arbitrage (à titre conservatoire et au fond) les défenderesses allèguent, en outre, qu'en ce qui concerne la demande reconventionnelle, seule la juridiction arbitrale est compétente. Sur ce point, les demanderesses (défenderesses reconventionnelles) opposent à la demande reconventionnelle l'exception de litispendance.

En application du règlement de la CCI (article 13.3) et du nouveau Code de procédure civile français (article 1494.2), les arbitres se sont d'abord prononcés sur le droit applicable :

« ... *En ce qui concerne le droit applicable à la procédure arbitrale, celle-ci a été soumise, comme le prévoyait l'acte de mission ... au règlement de la Cour d'arbitrage de la CCI et aux stipulations de cet acte de mission. En cas de lacune de ce règlement et de ces stipulations, et conformément aux dispositions de l'article 11 du Règlement et de l'article 1494, alinéa 2 du nouveau Code de procédure civile français, auxquelles les parties s'étaient expressément référées dans l'acte de mission, le Tribunal arbitral a déterminé lui-même les règles à suivre et pris les mesures nécessaires à l'instruction de l'affaire et à l'administration de la preuve...*

... Enfin, le Tribunal arbitral relève que les demanderesses, lorsqu'elles ont discuté de la compétence du tribunal arbitral, n'ont pas manqué de se référer à de nombreuses règles du droit international privé français en matière d'arbitrage et de conflits de juridiction, que ce soit d'ailleurs pour affirmer sa compétence ... ou pour la dénier en raison d'une prétendue litispendance... Le Tribunal arbitral, sans écarter a priori la référence, au moins subsidiaire, à certaines règles du droit français de l'arbitrage international, droit du lieu où se déroule la présente instance, examinera ci-dessous dans quelle mesure les règles invoquées sont pertinentes pour la solution des questions de compétence...

Il lui suffit de constater que la procédure arbitrale s'est déroulée en application de la volonté commune des parties, des dispositions du Règlement d'arbitrage de la CCI et des mesures prises par le Tribunal arbitral, sans que la détermination d'une loi nationale de procédure ait été sollicitée par une partie avant la dernière audience, ni que l'absence d'une telle désignation ait pu, en aucune manière, leur faire grief.

... En ce qui concerne le droit applicable au fond du litige, l'acte de mission ... stipulait que le Tribunal aurait à le déterminer conformément aux dispositions de l'article 13 § 3 du règlement d'arbitrage de la CCI et de l'article 1496 du nouveau Code de procédure civile français.

Le premier de ces textes confère aux parties la liberté de choisir le droit applicable, et, à défaut d'indication de leur part, confère à l'arbitre celle de le déterminer par application de la règle de conflit qu'il jugera appropriée en l'espèce. Le second est encore plus libéral, en ce qu'il n'impose pas le choix et l'application (par les parties, et à défaut par l'arbitre) d'une loi étatique mais plus largement de « règles de droit », et que l'arbitre applique celles qu'il juge appropriées sans avoir nécessairement à faire usage d'une règle de conflit. Enfin, les deux textes imposent à l'arbitre, dans tous les cas, de « tenir compte des usages du commerce ».

D'autre part, les parties ont expressément conféré au Tribunal arbitral des pouvoirs d'amiable compositeur... »

Saisi lors de la dernière audience d'une demande des demanderesses pour que soit prononcée une sentence sur le droit applicable afin « d'assurer le respect du contradictoire », le tribunal arbitral s'empresse d'indiquer :

« *Le Tribunal arbitral n'estime pas que le prononcé d'une sentence préalable sur le droit applicable au fond du litige soit nécessaire pour assurer le principe du contradictoire. Il constate en effet que chaque partie a pu, tout au long de la procédure, faire valoir ses moyens en se fondant sur les règles qui lui paraissaient pertinentes, sans qu'une discussion n'ait jamais surgi, ou un désaccord apparu, sur leur applicabilité en l'espèce. Le dernier mémoire des demanderesses ne cherche d'ailleurs pas à montrer l'utilité concrète d'une réouverture des débats sur le droit applicable au fond après le prononcé d'une sentence partielle. Dans ces conditions, le Tribunal arbitral se refuse à allonger encore une instance qui s'est poursuivie plus de deux ans, et détermine ici, par sa sentence finale et uniquement dans la mesure où cette détermination est utile à la motivation de sa sentence, les règles de droit applicables au fond du litige.*

... Les parties ayant invoqué tour à tour, mais assez sporadiquement, le droit tunisien ... et le droit français ... le premier étant celui de l'établissement des vendeurs et du lieu de la livraison, le second celui de l'établissement de deux des trois acheteurs et du lieu de l'arbitrage, le Tribunal arbitral tiendra compte de ces indices de localisation. Ces deux systèmes étant, en matière contractuelle, assez proches, le Tribunal arbitral statuera, en tant que de besoin, par application des règles communes aux droits français et tunisien des obligations et des contrats. C'est seulement lorsque, sur une question particulière, les solutions de ces deux systèmes sont différentes et qu'il est opportun de déterminer une règle de droit étatique applicable, que le Tribunal arbitral procédera à cette détermination. Mais à titre principal, il appliquera les stipulations contractuelles ; il tiendra compte des usages du commerce, et il fera usage, le cas échéant, de ses pouvoirs d'amiable compositeur.

De telles références coïncident avec les prévisions et l'attente légitime des parties. »

Sur sa compétence le tribunal arbitral a décidé comme suit :

« (La) première exception d'incompétence a été soulevée par les sociétés défende-resses, qui ont invoqué leur qualité d'entreprises publiques de droit tunisien pour dénier leur aptitude à soumettre leurs litiges à l'arbitrage, et pour prétendre que les clauses compromissoires insérées dans les contrats de vente étaient nulles...

Selon les défenderesses, les dispositions conjuguées des articles 251 et 260 du Code de procédure civile tunisien conduisent à cette solution. Le premier de ces textes impose la communication au Ministère public des dossiers des affaires « lors-que l'Etat ou les collectivités publiques sont intéressés, et le second décide qu'"on ne peut compromettre : ... 5) et dans les contestations qui seraient sujettes à commu-niquer au Ministère public, sauf disposition contraire de la loi".

... Cette exception, longuement combattue par les demanderesses ... doit être écartée. En effet, ni la jurisprudence (Trib. prem. inst. Tunis, 22 mars 1976, jugement devenu définitif : Rev. arb. *1976, 268, note F. Mechri ;* Clunet *1979, 661, obs. M. Charfi), ni la doctrine tunisiennes (Cf. Mechri et Charfi, notes préc. ;*

A. Mezghani, *Le cadre juridique des relations commerciales internationales de la Tunisie, C.E.R.P., Faculté de droit de Tunis, 1981, p. 376 s. ; L. Bouonoy, "Les personnes morales de droit public et l'arbitrage", in :* Les entreprises tunisiennes et l'arbitrage commercial international, *colloque CERP, Faculté de droit de Tunis, 1983, p. 247 s.) n'ont donné à ces textes une telle interprétation.*

D'une part, ils ne visent que l'Etat et les collectivités publiques, et non les entreprises publiques. De même que la Société Tunisienne de l'Electricité et du Gaz, dans l'arbitrage qui a donné lieu au jugement précité du Tribunal de Tunis, n'a pu s'en prévaloir puisqu'elle n'était pas une collectivité publique mais un établissement public, de même les sociétés défenderesses, qui sont des sociétés anonymes, soumises à ce titre au droit commercial, ne peuvent être qualifiées de "collectivités publiques" du seul fait de la participation de l'Etat tunisien à leur capital.

D'autre part, en invoquant la jurisprudence française qui, à partir de textes comparables, a écarté la prohibition interne dans les contrats commerciaux où les personnes morales de droit public agissent pour les besoins et dans des conditions conformes aux usages du commerce international (Cass. civ. I, 2 mai 1966, Gala-kis : D. *1966, 575, note Robert ;* Clunet *1966, 648, note Level ;* Rev. crit. dr. int. pr. *1967, 553, note Goldman), jurisprudence et doctrine tunisiennes estiment à leur tour que de telles prohibitions sont désuètes, contredites par l'attitude de la Tunisie et de la plupart des Etats à l'égard de l'arbitrage international, et qu'il serait contraire à la bonne foi qu'une entreprise publique, qui a dissimulé dans un premier temps l'existence de telles règles de droit interne, les invoque ultérieurement, si tel est son intérêt dans un litige déterminé, pour dénier la validité d'un engagement qu'elle a souscrit pourtant en parfaite connaissance de cause.*

La pratique, la doctrine et la jurisprudence arbitrale internationales condamnent aujourd'hui, de manière quasi-unanime, un tel comportement (Cf. notamment sentence CCI rendue en 1975, n° 2521 : Clunet 1976, 997, obs. Y. Derains, et les réf. ; Cf., à propos de la prohibition qui aurait visé l'Etat belge, sentence arbitrale rendue le 18 novembre 1983 par les arbitres : Cl. Reymond, prés., Böckstiegel et Franchimont : Journal des tribunaux, *31 mars 1984, p. 230 s. ; pour des références plus complètes de droit comparé et international, cf. K.H. Böckstiegel,* Arbitration and State Enterprises, *Kluwer et CCI, 1984) ... »*

Les deux parties ayant respectivement contesté la compétence des arbitres pour statuer sur les demandes principales ou sur la reconvention, le tribunal examine tour à tour les deux aspects de la question.

C'est ainsi que les arbitres constatent que pour une partie des demandes principales la clause attributive de juridiction insérée dans le contrat pertinent signalait le tribunal de commerce de Tunis comme seul compétent. Les arbitres se déclarent donc compétents uniquement pour les demandes ne concernant pas ce contrat.

Quant à la demande reconventionnelle, c'est une exception de litispendance que font valoir les demanderesses pour empêcher les défenderesses de soutenir les mêmes prétentions devant la juridiction tunisienne et devant les arbitres. La solution apportée par le tribunal arbitral retiendra sans doute tout l'intérêt des opérateurs du commerce international confrontés à des situations similaires :

... Ni les actions pénales ..., ni les procédures tendant à l'obtention de mesures provisoires ou conservatoires ... ne peuvent être considérées comme incompatibles avec la demande reconventionnelle présentée devant le Tribunal arbitral, ni contraires aux conventions d'arbitrage.

Les premières, même si elles permettent aux (défenderesses) de se constituer partie civile, ne sont pas dirigées contre les personnes morales que sont (les demanderesses) ; en outre, le préjudice dont les premières demandent réparation ne saurait résulter que des infractions pénales éventuellement établies ... Le Tribunal arbitral ne saurait donc, comme le lui demandent les défenderesses reconventionnelles ... se déterminer en fonction d'instances pénales étrangères au seul litige commercial dont il est saisi.

Quant aux secondes, pour une part, elles consistent en des mesures de séquestre judiciaire des biens personnels... et à ce titre ne concernent donc pas davantage les (demanderesses) ; pour une autre part, il s'agit essentiellement de référés-provision diligentés (avec succès pour certains d'entre eux) devant les juges français. Ils donnent lieu à des condamnations provisoires n'ayant pas autorité de chose jugée, et le règlement de la CCI (article 8 § 5), comme la jurisprudence française elle-même (cf. les arrêts ... de la Cour de Rouen et de la Cour de cassation, et les commentaires sous ces décisions de G. Couchez, : Rev. arb.*, 1986, 241, et* Rev. arb. *1987, 323 ;* adde *G. Couchez, "Référé et arbitrage — Essai de bilan ... provisoire" :* Rev. arb. *1985, 155, et les réf.) autorisent, à certaines conditions, de telles initiatives judiciaires malgré la présence d'une clause compromissoire, voire même après l'introduction de l'instance arbitrale.*

... Le Tribunal arbitral, tout en admettant que l'importance des créances commerciales incontestables que détenaient (les défenderesses) contre (les demanderesses) pouvait justifier des initiatives tendant à obtenir rapidement des paiements provisionnels, constate néanmoins que l'ensemble de ces actions, par leur dispersion et leur

nombre, n'ont pas contribué à faciliter et à accélérer l'instruction de l'affaire devant lui. En outre, le Tribunal arbitral relève que (les défenderesses), en ne portant pas "sans délai à la connaissance du Secrétariat de la Cour d'arbitrage", qui en aurait informé les arbitres, de telles demandes et les mesures prises en conséquence par les autorités judiciaires saisies, ne s'est pas conformé aux obligations qui découlent, en une pareille hypothèse, de l'article 8, § 5 du Règlement de la CCI.

... Reste alors la question posée par l'introduction des procédures commerciales, au fond, devant le Tribunal de première instance de Tunis. Ce faisant, (les défenderesses ont) provoqué une sérieuse et véritable difficulté. (Leur) attitude, ayant consisté à demander la même chose à deux juridictions différentes en prétendant devant chacune d'elles qu'elle était bien compétente (voire même seule compétente) pour prononcer les condamnations requises, n'est justifiée ni en fait ni en droit.

... Force est cependant de constater que l'exception de litispendance, telle qu'elle a été présentée par les défenderesses reconventionnelles ... ne saurait être retenue par le Tribunal arbitral.

... En effet, contrairement à ce que semblent prétendre (les demanderesses), les deux demandes (des défenderesses) n'ont pas été portées « devant les juridictions ... également compétentes ». La litispendance, à proprement parler, ne peut surgir qu'entre deux juridictions d'un même Etat ou de deux Etats différents, lorsque les règles de compétence de leur for les autorisent l'une et l'autre à connaître d'un même litige (sur l'admission récente de la litispendance internationale par la jurisprudence française, qui la subordonne cependant à la double compétence du juge français et du juge étranger, cf. Cass. civ. I, 26 nov. 1974 : Clunet 1975, 108, note A. Ponsard ; Rev. crit. dr. int. pr. 1975, 19, note D. Holleaux ; cf. A. Huet, J.-Cl. dr. int., fasc. 581-D, n° 110 s.). Cette situation de compétence concurrente ne peut surgir entre une juridiction arbitrale et une juridiction étatique, pour la raison que leur compétence respective ne dépend que d'un seul facteur ; l'existence, la validité et l'étendue de la convention d'arbitrage.

De deux choses l'une, en effet. Ou celle-ci est valable et attribue compétence, pour connaître d'une demande déterminée, aux arbitres : les tribunaux judiciaires doivent alors, si elle est invoquée devant eux, en le constatant, se déclarer incompétents. C'est ce que décide la Convention de New York du 10 juin 1958, dans son article II, § 3. Cette convention est applicable en l'espèce puisqu'elle a été ratifiée à la fois par la France et la Tunisie. Et le Tribunal, de son côté, dans les mêmes conditions, se reconnaîtra compétent. Ou bien au contraire la convention d'arbitrage n'a pas été invoquée par le défendeur, ou est nulle, ou ne vise pas le différend porté devant le juge judiciaire, et celui-ci se déclarera compétent par application des règles de son for, tandis que l'arbitre renoncera à connaître ce litige.

... Mais le Tribunal arbitral, en présence de l'incident soulevé devant lui, n'a aucune autorité pour, comme le lui demandent les demanderesses, "vérifier la compétence du Tribunal de première instance de Tunis initialement saisi" il s'immiscerait ainsi dans le fonctionnement de la juridiction étatique tunisienne. Mais il peut et il doit, comme tout juge, statuer sur sa propre compétence (conformément, d'ailleurs, aux prescriptions de l'article 8, § 3 du règlement d'arbitrage de la CCI), et vérifier si cette demande entre bien dans sa mission (Cf. M. de Boisséson, Le droit français de l'arbitrage, *n° 284 ;* J. Robert et B. Moreau, L'arbitrage, *n° 340).* »

Finalement, il est intéressant de noter que les arbitres, sans doute soucieux d'écarter toute possibilité de contestation ultérieure, examinent d'office la rédaction pathologique de la clause compromissoire libellée comme suit :

« *Tout différend pouvant surgir de l'interprétation ou de l'application des clauses de ce contrat sera réglé à l'amiable entre l'acheteur et le vendeur. Dans l'impossibilité d'une solution amiable, le différend sera soumis à l'arbitrage de la section internationale de la Chambre de Commerce de Paris. »*

A cet égard les arbitres s'expriment ainsi :

« ... Le Tribunal arbitral note... la mauvaise rédaction (des) clauses compromissoires, qui désignent comme institution permanente d'arbitrage "la Section Internationale de la Chambre de Commerce de Paris".

Cette dénomination défectueuse de la Chambre de Commerce Internationale est cependant sans conséquence, car, après que les demanderesses l'aient saisie, les défenderesses n'ont pas mis en doute, du moins devant le Tribunal arbitral, que c'était bien là l'institution d'arbitrage choisie par les parties. Certes (les défenderesses) ont bien fait valoir, à un certain moment, devant le Tribunal de première instance de Tunis, que la « Section internationale de la Chambre de Commerce de Paris... n'existe pas », mais ce moyen n'a jamais été avancé par les demanderesses devant le Tribunal arbitral. En outre, en demandant formellement et sans réserve que celui-ci se reconnaisse compétent sur ses demandes reconventionnelles (les défenderesses)..., ont confirmé que la maladresse de rédaction des contrats n'avait jamais entraîné dans l'esprit de ses représentants le moindre doute sur l'identité de l'organisme institutionnel choisi pour administrer l'arbitrage. Enfin, si une telle prétention avait été formulée, le Tribunal arbitral, dans le double souci de donner un effet utile à la stipulation contractuelle litigieuse, qui est une règle d'interprétation commune aux droits tunisien (article 518 du Code des obligations et des contrats) et français (article 1157 du Code civil), et de s'attacher plutôt à la commune intention des parties contractantes qu'au sens littéral des termes (en ce sens, les articles 515 du C.O.C. tunisien et 1156 du Code civil français), aurait jugé que cette désignation incorrecte de l'institution d'arbitrage ne privait ni de sens ni d'effet les clauses compromissoires. C'est en ce sens que se sont prononcées, dans des espèces voisines, de nombreuses sentences arbitrales (Cf. sentences CCI rendues en 1984, n° 4472 : Clunet *1984, 946, obs. S.J. ; n° 4023 :* Clunet *1984, 950, obs. S.J.,...). »*

Ayant décidé de cumuler ses décisions sur la compétence et sur la loi applicable au fond, le Tribunal arbitral s'est ensuite prononcé sur les demandes respectives des parties. En usant de leurs pouvoirs d'amiables compositeurs pour certains chefs, les arbitres font partiellement droit aux demandes principales et reconventionnelles prononçant ensuite la compensation entre les dettes réciproques résultant de la sentence. Pour la condamnation solidaire au paiement par les demanderesses des sommes finales, les arbitres font appel à la notion de groupe de sociétés :

« Les trois sociétés demanderesses, lors de la conclusion, l'exécution, l'inexécution et la renégociation de relations contractuelles entretenues avec (les défenderesses), apparaissent selon la commune volonté de toutes les parties à la procédure comme ayant été de véritables parties à l'ensemble de ces contrats. Cette analyse s'appuie, dans sa lettre et dans son esprit, sur une tendance remarquée et approuvée de la « jurisprudence arbitrale » favorable à la reconnaissance, dans de telles circonstances, de l'unité du groupe (Cf. sentence CCI rendue à Paris, le 22 sept. 1982, aff. Dow Chemical : Rev. arb. *1984, 137 et les réf. ; arrêt de la Cour d'appel de Paris du 21 oct. 1983, maintenant cette sentence :* Rev. arb. *1984, 98, note Chapelle ; I. Fadlallah, « Clauses d'arbitrage et groupe de sociétés »,* Communication au *Comité français de DIP du 24 avril 1985 :* Travaux du Comité, éd. CNRS, *1987, p. 105 s. ; en dernier lieu, Pau, 26 novembre 1986, Société Sponsor AB c/Lestrade, à paraître* Rev. arb.*, 1988, n° 1, note Chapelle, arrêt qui reprend exactement la formule de la sentence Dow Chemical).*

Le Tribunal arbitral estime qu'en l'espèce les conditions de la reconnaissance de l'unité du groupe sont remplies, les sociétés composant celui-ci ayant toutes participé, dans une confusion aussi réelle qu'apparente, à une relation contractuelle internationale complexe dans laquelle l'intérêt du groupe l'emportait sur celui de chacune d'elles. La sécurité des relations commerciales internationales exige qu'il soit tenu compte de cette réalité économique et que toutes les sociétés du groupe soient tenues ensemble et solidairement des dettes dont elles ont directement ou indirectement profité à cette occasion.

Au surplus, cette admission de la solidarité réciproque, active et passive, dans les rapports entre les sociétés appartenant à un même groupe est conforme aux positions prises expressément ou implicitement par toutes les demanderesses et défenderesses, à l'équité, et n'est contraire à aucune règle d'ordre public international des systèmes juridiques français et tunisien. »

OBSERVATIONS :

I. — La solution est classique. La procédure a été soumise, comme le prévoyait l'acte de mission, au règlement de la Cour d'arbitrage de la CCI et aux stipulations de cet acte de mission. En cas de lacune du règlement CCI, de ces stipulations et de l'article 1494.2 du NCPC (auquel les parties s'étaient expressément référées dans l'acte de mission), le Tribunal arbitral a déterminé lui-même les règles à suivre. Implicitement reconnue par l'article V.I.d de la Convention de New York de 1958, la liberté dont jouissent les parties pour fixer les règles de procédure est étendue à l'arbitre par l'article II du règlement CCI qui, depuis sa version de 1975, s'éloigne de la doctrine qui imposait aux arbitres l'application de la loi de procédure du lieu de l'arbitrage (sur cette évolution *cf.* Y. Derains, « Le lieu de l'arbitrage » ; *R.D.A.I.*, n° 2, 1986 ; K. H. Böckstiegel, « Les règles de droit applicables aux arbitrages commerciaux internationaux concernant des Etats ou des entreprises contrôlées par l'Etat » dans *Cour d'arbitrage de la CCI, 60 ans après, regard sur l'avenir*, Paris, 1984, p. 127 ; sentences CCI 1912 et 2879 respectivement dans *Clunet* 1974, 904 et 1979, 989 obs. Derains). Toutefois, certains pays restent attachés au principe de la compétence de la loi du lieu de l'arbitrage en matière de procédure arbitrale (par exemple la Suède, *cf. Arbitration in Sweden*, Stockholm, 1984, p. 45). D'autres, sans aborder la question en termes de conflits de lois, décident, par une règle d'application immédiate, que leur droit de procédure national régira tout arbitrage se déroulant sur leur territoire (*Cf.* en Suisse l'article premier du Concordat intercantonal sur l'arbitrage).

Naturellement, la liberté des parties ne saurait, sous peine de risque d'annulation de la sentence à intervenir, porter atteinte aux règles impératives de procédure de la loi du for.

En l'espèce, le Tribunal arbitral fait une exacte application des dispositions tant de l'acte de mission que du règlement CCI. Du bout des lèvres, il accepte l'idée de puiser éventuellement dans les règles de la *lex fori* (loi française). Le Règlement de la CCI permettant donc aux arbitres d'établir leurs propres règles de procédure, et ceux-ci étant amiables compositeurs, pourquoi le Tribunal arbitral s'est-il finalement senti obligé de désigner — de façon tout-à-fait subsidiaire, une loi de procédure nationale ? Faut-il voir ici un exemple de plus de la prudence des arbitres ? (*Cf.* sentence 3742 rendue en 1983, *Clunet* 1984, 910). En fait, sûrement parce qu'une partie le lui réclamait. Il fait, cependant, preuve d'une grande netteté.

En ce qui concerne la loi applicable au fond, on ne s'attardera pas sur la solution, elle aussi classique, donnée par les arbitres. Les parties ayant demandé aux arbitres de déterminer le droit applicable conformément aux articles 13.3 du règlement CCI et 1496 du NCPC, le Tribunal, rappelant ses pouvoirs d'amiable composition, décide d'appliquer à titre principal les stipulations contractuelles, en tenant compte des usages du commerce, comme l'y invitent d'ailleurs les textes précités. En tant que besoin, le tribunal statuera par application des règles communes aux droits français et tunisien des obligations et des contrats. Enfin, de façon tout-à-fait subsidiaire, les arbitres se réservent la possibilité de déterminer une règle de droit étatique, au cas où, sur une gestion particulière, les solutions de ces deux systèmes divergent.

En fait, le Tribunal arbitral semble souligner que d'une part, aucune des parties n'a sollicité l'application d'un droit déterminé, et d'autre part que ses pouvoirs d'amiable compositeur le dispensent de rechercher le droit applicable au fond du litige. On trouve dans la jurisprudence arbitrale des exemples d'une telle démarche :

« Considérant que les parties ne se réfèrent à aucun droit national et ne demandent pas au Tribunal arbitral de déterminer quel est le droit, application sera faite des usages commerciaux en vigueur en Europe, compte tenu des dispositions figurant au dos des commandes qui chargent les éventuels arbitres de statuer ex aequo et bono » (sentence 1850 rendue en 1972 : Clunet *1973).*

L'amiable composition a été, dans tel cas, « interprétée comme une renonciation générale à un système législatif déterminé » (E. Loquin, *L'amiable composition en droit comparé et international,* Thèse, Dijon, 1977, n. 570). Tel semble être ici exactement le cas, puisque les parties, selon la sentence, en n'insérant pas de disposition sur la loi applicable et en laissant au Tribunal le soin de se prononcer sur la question, auraient implicitement entendu soustraire le litige aux règles étatiques. La stipulation de la clause d'amiable composition le recours aux Incoterms et aux usages du commerce et la désignation de la Cour d'arbitrage de la CCI semblent conforter la thèse (sur le choix de l'arbitrage CCI cf. Y. Derains, « Le statut des usages du commerce international devant les juridictions arbitrales » : *Rev. arb.* 1973, 135).

Quant à l'application éventuelle par l'arbitre des règles communes aux droits des parties au litige, celle-ci est familière des lecteurs de cette chronique (V. notamment les différentes sentences sur le droit applicable publiées au *Clunet,* 1978). On sait que c'est une des trois méthodes dégagées par le Pr Lalive parmi les tendances dominantes (« Les règles de conflit de lois appliquées au fond par l'arbitre siégeant en Suisse » : *Rev. arb.* 1976, 155 ; les trois méthodes sont illustrées dans une sentence 2886 rendue en 1977 : *Clunet* 1978, 996).

L'application cumulative montre la volonté du Tribunal de souligner que la solution adoptée n'est pas propre à un système juridique particulier, mais aux deux systèmes intéressés au litige. On doit y voir un exemple de la prudence des arbitres, « corollaire de leur liberté de déterminer le droit applicable » (Y. Derains : *Clunet* 1978, 980 ; *cf.* aussi la sentence 2886 rendue en 1977 : *Clunet* 1978, 996). Mais, ne doit-on pas y voir, plutôt qu'une application cumulative, une application de la théorie de Rubino-Sammartano, dite du « tronc commun des lois nationales » ? (*Rev. arb.* 1987, 133).

Enfin le Tribunal arbitral conclut que « (de) telles références coïncident avec les prévisions et l'attente légitime des parties », consacrant une des idées de Y. Derains (« Attente légitime des parties et droit applicable au fond en matière d'arbitrage commercial international, » communication au *Comité français de droit international privé,* janvier 1985).

II. — Ayant introduit une demande reconventionnelle sur la base d'une clause compromissoire dont elles allèguent par ailleurs la nullité, les parties défenderesses sollicitent le Tribunal de se prononcer sur leur exception d'incompétence. Non sans relever cette contradiction, les arbitres rejettent l'argument tiré des articles 251 et 260 du Code de procédure civile tunisien qui interdirait aux entreprises publiques tunisiennes de compromettre. Fidèle au système cumulatif retenu pour le droit matériel, la décision des arbitres tient compte des droits tunisien et français ainsi que de la jurisprudence arbitrale.

En droit tunisien, l'interdiction vise exclusivement l'Etat et les collectivités publiques. Or, les sociétés défenderesses sont des sociétés anonymes soumises au droit commercial, échappant de ce fait aux restrictions du Code de procédure civile tunisien.

Plus attachée à une conception internationale (ou « anationale ») de l'arbitrage, la référence dans la sentence à la jurisprudence française conduit le Tribunal à appeler qu'il serait contraire à la bonne foi qu'une entreprise publique » ... qui a dissimulé dans un premier temps l'existence de ... règles de droit interne, les invoque) ultérieurement, si tel est son intérêt ... pour dénier la validité d'un engagement qu'elle a souscrit en parfaite connaissance de cause. »

Finalement, une telle attitude est condamnée par la pratique, la doctrine et la jurisprudence arbitrale qui considèrent que les principes d'estoppel et de *venire contra factum proprium* constituent des véritables principes généraux de droit (*cf.* K. H. Böckstiegel, *cit.,* p. 43).

Malgré les mises en garde et les critiques des auteurs de cette chronique depuis quelques années (par exemple *Clunet* 1981, 939 ; 1984, 946, 950 et 1987, 1048), les rédacteurs de clauses arbitrales ne semblent guère soigner les formules employées. La présente affaire nous fournit encore un exemple de maladresse dans la désignation de l'institution permanente d'arbitrage. Ceci est d'autant plus étonnant que le règlement CCI propose aux parties une clause type destinée à éviter les risques d'ambiguïté. Mais les statistiques recueillies récemment montrent que sur les 237 affaires soumises à la CCI en 1987, seulement *une* clause d'arbitrage adopte exactement la rédaction de la clause type alors qu'une mauvaise désignation de la CCI a été repérée dans seize conventions (*cf.* S.R. Bond, *How to draft an arbitration clause,* communication à la Conférence sur la validité de sentences arbitrales, Athènes, mars 1988).

Dans cette affaire les arbitres, soucieux de « donner un effet utile à la stipulation », se basent sur la commune intention des parties pour conclure qu'il s'agit bien d'une clause d'arbitrage CCI (*cf.* sentences 4145 dans *Clunet* 1985, 985, 2321 dans *Clunet* 1975, 939 et H. Scalbert & L. Marville, « Les clauses d'arbitrage pathologiques » : *Rev. arb.* 1988, 119).

III. — De la même manière que les parties renoncent à certaines voies de recours en faisant choix du règlement d'arbitrage CCI pour la solution de différends éventuels, elles écartent la possibilité d'invoquer les moyens de défense prévus par les lois étatiques de procédure pour résoudre les conflits de compétence judiciaire. En présence d'une clause compromissoire valide les parties ne sauraient donc s'opposer en instance arbitrale les exceptions de litispendance et de connexité au profit d'une juridiction étatique. En l'espèce, la condition d'admissibilité de l'exception de litispendance (i.e. l'existence de deux juridictions également compétentes parallèlement saisies du même différend) ne peut, par définition, être remplie. Les arbitres relèvent, à juste titre, qu'une « ... situation de compétence concurrente ne peut surgir entre une juridiction arbitrale et une juridiction étatique... ». En cas de contestation sur la validité ou sur l'existence de la clause compromissoire, les arbitres auront à statuer sur leur propre compétence. Le juge, quant à lui, devra se conformer à l'article II.3 de la Convention de New York.

Notons enfin le traitement réservé par les arbitres aux actions judiciaires visant à l'obtention de mesures provisoires. Déclarées conformes avec l'article 8.5 du Règlement CCI (*Clunet* 1984, p. 934, 937 et 952), les arbitres refusent d'y voir une violation de la convention d'arbitrage ou une incompatibilité avec la demande reconventionnelle. Cependant, le Tribunal ne manque pas de préciser que les parties défenderesses, en n'informant pas le Secrétariat de la Cour des mesures provisoires sollicitées, ne se sont pas conformées à l'obligation qui leur est imposée par l'article 8.5 du Règlement CCI. Les arbitres reconnaissent même que « ... l'ensemble (des) actions (des défenderesses), par leur dispersion et par leur nombre, n'ont pas contribué à faciliter et à accélérer l'instruction de l'affaire... ». Aux arbitres d'en tirer les conséquences et de prendre ces difficultés et ces retards en considération lors de leur décision sur la répartition des frais de l'arbitrage.

IV. — D'autres illustrations de cette chronique ont montré une tendance de la jurisprudence arbitrale à apprécier la portée et les effets de la clause arbitrale en fonction de la réalité économique du groupe de sociétés (*cf. Clunet* 1976, p. 973 et 978 : 1983, 899 ; 1984, 937 ainsi que Derains & Schaft, « Clause d'arbitrage et groupe de sociétés : *Journal du droit des affaires internationales,* 1985, p. 231). Or, dans cette sentence les arbitres font appel à la notion de groupe de sociétés afin d'ordonner la condamnation solidaire des défenderesses reconventionnelles. Facilitant ainsi la possible exécution forcée de la sentence, les arbitres estiment que les conditions justifiant l'appel à la notion sont en l'espèce remplies. Les trois défenderesses reconventionnelles faisant partie du groupe ont « toutes participé, dans une confusion aussi réelle qu'apparente, à une relation contractuelle internationale complexe dans laquelle l'intérêt du groupe l'emportait sur celui de chacune d'elles ». Toutefois des concepts tels que « relation contractuelle internationale complexe » ou « intérêt du groupe » doivent, pour constituer un point de repère dans la réflexion des arbitres, faire l'objet d'une analyse objective strictement attachée aux situations de fait dans chaque affaire.

Le Tribunal, une fois de plus faisant preuve de prudence, constate que la solution qui résulte de son analyse minutieuse des faits n'est contraire ni à l'ordre public international des systèmes juridiques tunisien et français ni à l'équité. Dans ces conditions, il est possible aux arbitres de prononcer la condamnation solidaire des défenderesses reconventionnelles.

G.A.A.

I. — **Usages du commerce international.** — Vente C & F. — Transfert des risques. — Faute du transporteur. — *Culpa in contrahendo* du vendeur.

II. — **Usages du commerce international.** — Préjudice. — Evaluation. — Obligation de minimiser les pertes.

III. — **Paiement.** — Intérêts compensatoires. — Point de départ.

IV. — **Paiement.** — Monnaie de compte. — Monnaie de paiement.

V. — **Arbitrage.** — Parties de même nationalité. — Vente à l'exportation. — Caractère international.

Sentence rendue dans l'affaire n° 5910 en 1988.

Un Tribunal arbitral composé de trois arbitres belges et statuant à Anvers selon le droit belge était saisi d'un différend opposant deux sociétés belges, dont l'une faisait partie d'un groupe japonais. Le litige était né de difficultés d'exécution d'un contrat de vente par lequel la demanderesse X avait acheté aux conditions C & F Karachi à la défenderesse Y un lot d'environ 500 tonnes métriques de zinc en vertu d'un contrat conclu à Bruxelles.

Le contrat prévoyait un embarquement au départ de « *any european port* » et « *per any outsider line* », à l'option du vendeur. Cependant, près d'un mois après la conclusion du contrat, X, répercutant sur Y les instructions que lui avait données son propre acheteur pakistanais lui indiqua que « la marchandise devait être chargée sur un navire de ligne *(regular liner vessel)* » se rendant directement à Karachi. Y transmit ces exigences nouvelles à son commissaire-expéditeur en lui signifiant : « ligne exigée : *regular liner goods vessel, sailing directly for Karachi* ».

Malheureusement, le navire choisi par le commissaire-expéditeur de Y ne devait pas atteindre Karachi. Parti de Anvers chargé du zinc vendu à X, il se rendit d'abord à Rotterdam où il demeura quelques jours puis à Dunkerque où il compléta sa cargaison en chargeant environ 12.000 tonnes de sucre. Il ne put cependant quitter Dunkerque, ayant été saisi par les créanciers de l'armateur du navire, pour y être vendu à l'encan après que la cargaison, y compris la marchandise vendue à X y ait été déchargée et entreposée en vertu d'une ordonnance rendue par le Président du Tribunal de commerce de Dunkerque.

L'acheteur pakistanais de X, ne recevant pas le zinc attendu décida de résilier son contrat. X indiqua à Y qu'elle la tenait responsable de tout dommage parce que le navire n'avait pas effectué le voyage Anvers/Karachi directement, tout en précisant que dans le souci « de minimiser le préjudice » elle s'efforcerait « d'arriver à un arrangement amiable avec son acheteur au Pakistan ». Ce à quoi elle parvint en versant à son acheteur une indemnité. Toujours en vue de réduire le dommage, la marchandise débarquée fût vendue par X avec l'accord de Y qui en racheta elle-même les 3/5.

Y, pour sa part, assigna X et son propre commissaire-expéditeur devant le Président du Tribunal de commerce d'Anvers en désignation d'un expert chargé de rassembler tous éléments permettant de vérifier si le navire pouvait ou non être considéré comme « *a regular goods vessel sailing directly from Karachi* ». L'expert désigné considéra que le navire ne répondait ni à l'une ni à l'autre de ces caractéristiques.

X demandait au Tribunal arbitral de condamner Y à réparer l'intégralité du préjudice qu'elle avait subi et qui comprenait, selon elle :

— la différence entre le prix du contrat et celui obtenu par la revente à Dunkerque,

— l'indemnité versée à l'acheteur pakistanais,

— les frais exposés à Dunkerque,

— les frais de livraison aux nouveaux acheteurs,

— des frais de voyage à Karachi.

X demandait également, outre des intérêts compensatoires, que les éléments du préjudice supportés en dollars et en francs français fussent convertis en francs belges au cours du change en vigueur, soit à la date du paiement, soit à la date où les débours résultant de l'inexécution du contrat avaient été effectués.

Y concluait au rejet de la demande en alléguant, entre autres que dans une vente C & F les risques postérieurs à l'embarquement sont à la charge de l'acheteur et qu'en tout état de cause le contrat ne l'obligeait pas à choisir un navire se rendant directement à Karachi. De plus, elle estimait que les seuls dommages-intérêts susceptibles d'être alloués à X se limitaient à la différence entre le prix contractuel et celui auquel cette dernière avait revendu la marchandise à l'acheteur pakistanais. Elle ajoutait qu'une conversion des sommes libellées en dollars et en francs français ne saurait intervenir qu'à la date d'exécution de la sentence.

Le Tribunal arbitral se prononça tout d'abord sur l'existence d'une faute de la part du vendeur Y eu égard aux usages régissant la vente C & F :

« ... Les parties sont, à juste titre, d'accord pour constater qu'en matière de vente C & F les obligations du vendeur sont les mêmes qu'en matière de vente CIF à cette différence que le vendeur n'est pas tenu d'assurer les marchandises.

Plus précisément, le vendeur C & F a pour obligation de transporter ou de faire transporter à ses frais la marchandise embarquée conformément aux conditions de transport convenues entre acheteur et vendeur, les risques du transport maritime étant toutefois à charge de l'acheteur à partir de l'embarquement.

Il est de doctrine et de jurisprudence constantes que lorsque les parties n'ont pas inséré dans leur contrat de stipulations expresses relatives aux conditions du transport, le vendeur doit affréter, respectivement réserver place, aux conditions d'usage du port d'embarquement sur un navire présentant les qualités requises par la nature particulière de la marchandise vendue.

Il est toutefois loisible aux parties de convenir d'exigences particulières en ce qui concerne le mode et les conditions de transport que le vendeur a, dès lors, l'obligation de respecter.

Selon X il avait été expressément convenu, par modification du contrat originaire, que le vendeur devait réserver place à bord d'un navire de ligne régulière se rendant directement d'Anvers à Karachi. Le vendeur n'aurait pas rempli cette obligation, provoquant ainsi le débarquement des marchandises et le préjudice allégué.

Y soutient au contraire qu'elle a correctement exécuté ses obligations du vendeur C & F et qu'aucune faute contractuelle ne saurait lui être reprochée. A cet égard elle fait valoir en premier lieu que le contrat de vente n'a pas été modifié de commun accord et que les instructions données postérieurement par X quant à l'embarquement à bord d'un navire de ligne régulière, se rendant directement à Karachi, n'étaient que l'expression d'un souhait, qu'elle s'est efforcée de réaliser mais dont le non-accomplissement ne constitue pas une inexécution du contrat. Elle fait valoir en second lieu que même s'il fallait admettre qu'elle s'était obligée quant aux conditions spéciales du transport, elle a, en exerçant toute diligence normalement exigée, correctement exécuté les obligations qui incombent au vendeur C & F en transmettant à son commissaire-expéditeur ... les instructions émanant de X et en concluant ... un contrat d'affrètement-transport par un navire qui présentait toutes les apparences d'un « regular liner vessel », devant se rendre directement à Karachi.

Elle fait valoir enfin qu'en agréant sans réserves les documents et notamment le connaissement, X a reconnu la bonne exécution par le vendeur de ses obligations et que, conformément aux principes de la vente C & F, les risques postérieurs à l'embarquement, notamment le non-accomplissement par le transporteur des obligations par lui souscrites, sont pour compte de l'acheteur.

Il importe de vérifier tout d'abord si Y a ou non effectivement accepté une modification du contrat originaire dans le sens ci-dessus indiqué.

A cet égard, il résulte des éléments du dossier et singulièrement des termes utilisés par X : « *goods should be shipped* » dans son télex du ..., tout comme de ceux utilisés dans le télex de Y au commissaire-expéditeur : « ligne exigée », de même que de la demande d'explication adressée par Y au commissaire-expéditeur le ... relevant que « le navire n'a pas effectué le voyage Anvers/Karachi directement comme convenu », que le vendeur et l'acheteur ont été d'accord de modifier les conditions du contrat originaire et de prévoir quant au transport de la marchandise deux conditions supplémentaires, acceptées par le vendeur et dont celui-ci devait procurer la mise en œuvre...

Les constatations auxquelles a procédé l'expert ... et les pièces du dossier font clairement apparaître non seulement que le navire ne faisait pas partie d'une ligne régulière... D'autre part, il est incontesté qu'après son départ d'Anvers le navire fait escale tant à Rotterdam qu'à Dunkerque...

A ce dernier égard aucun élément de conviction ne saurait être tiré de l'affirmation que, dans la pensée du transporteur, l'indication « *sailing directly for Karachi* » aurait simplement signifié que la marchandise ne serait pas transbordée. Cette interprétation n'a jamais été celle des parties ainsi qu'il résulte de la circonstance que la mention « *transhipment not allowed* » figurait déjà séparément tant dans les instructions de X que dans la transmission de celles-ci par le commissaire-expéditeur.

Etant établi dans les faits que le transporteur ... avec lequel Y a passé contrat à l'intermédiaire de son commissaire-expéditeur ... n'exploitait pas à proprement parler une ligne régulière et n'a jamais entendu se rendre directement à Karachi comme il s'y était cependant engagé, il importe en second lieu de vérifier si le vendeur C & F doit ou non être tenu pour responsable de cet état de choses à l'égard de son acheteur.

Il est exact que, dans un contrat de vente C & F les risques sont transférés à l'acheteur à partir de l'embarquement des marchandises et que, dès lors, les conséquences dommageables d'une exécution fautive, par l'armateur, du contrat d'affrètement-transport, sont, comme le soutien Y, pour le compte de l'acheteur. Il en va toutefois autrement lorsque le dommage est la conséquence d'une faute contractuelle du vendeur, notamment lorsque celui-ci n'a pas fait montre dans la conclusion du contrat d'affrètement-transport de la prudence et de la diligence que requéraient les obligations particulières auxquelles il s'était engagé envers son acheteur. A cet égard il ne lui suffit pas d'établir qu'il s'est adressé à des intermédiaires professionnels de bonne réputation.

Par ailleurs, il n'est pas contesté que le vendeur C & F est comptable non seulement de son propre comportement contractuel, mais également de celui du commissaire-expéditeur qu'il a chargé de conclure pour son compte le contrat d'affrètement-transport.

Les circonstances relevées dans la partie en fait font apparaître qu'en l'occurrence Y n'a pas correctement rempli les obligations qu'elle a souscrites.

En ce qui concerne le commissaire-expéditeur aucune information n'a été fournie aux arbitres quant aux démarches entreprises par ce commissaire-expéditeur en vue de la conclusion d'un contrat d'affrètement-transport avec un armement exploitant une ligne régulière sur Karachi, et il n'apparaît pas davantage que le commissaire-expéditeur en passant contrat avec le transporteur, aurait stipulé qu'il devait s'agir d'un navire effectivement intégré dans une ligne régulière qui, de surcroît, se rendrait directement à Karachi, pas plus qu'il n'apparaît que le commissaire-expéditeur ait simplement contrôlé si ces conditions étaient réalisées, alors qu'il incombe au vendeur C & F et donc à son mandataire de s'entourer de toutes les garanties souhaitables en vue de satisfaire aux obligations souscrites...

... Il y a lieu enfin de rejeter le moyen que Y entend tirer de l'agréation sans réserve des documents par X. Il va en effet de soi que cette agréation ne pouvait porter que sur les mentions apparaissant aux documents : or le connaissement était accompagné d'une attestation ... portant, contrairement à la réalité, qu'il s'agissait d'un navire de ligne régulière se rendant en droiture à Karachi.

De toutes ces considérations il résulte que la défenderesse doit réparation du préjudice subi par X à raison de l'interruption du voyage et de la non-délivrance des marchandises à Karachi ».

C'est dans les termes suivants que le Tribunal arbitral évalue ensuite le préjudice réparable subi par X :

« *Selon la défenderesse les dommages et intérêts susceptibles d'être alloués à X se limiteraient à la différence entre le prix d'achat qui lui a été payé par la demanderesse (US $ 457.000) et celui auquel cette dernière avait revendu la marchandise à son acheteur pakistanais (US $ 461.866,02), soit US $ 4.866,02, le surplus des dommages réclamés ayant selon elle une cause étrangère à la faute alléguée.*

Ce point de vue ne saurait être accepté.

En ne respectant pas les stipulations du contrat et en commettant des fautes qui exposaient la marchandise à des risques que son cocontractant avait expressément entendu éviter le vendeur, par application des articles 1150 et 1151 du Code civil, est tenu de supporter l'ensemble des pertes prévisibles qui sont la suite immédiate et directe de l'inexécution de la convention.

Dans les circonstances données et compte tenu des exigences précises de l'acheteur quant à l'acheminement direct de la marchandise, le dommage prévisible résultant immédiatement et directement de l'inexécution du contrat ne consiste pas seulement dans la perte du bénéfice du marché qui a été résilié du fait de la non-délivrance au destinataire pakistanais, mais comprend aussi le préjudice effectivement subi du fait que le destinataire lui-même acheteur de X a dû être indemnisé des frais qu'il a inutilement exposés, du fait d'autre part que la cargaison a dû être débarquée à Dunkerque et du fait enfin qu'elle a dû être réalisée au plus offrant, en accord avec Y afin d'éviter une perte plus considérable encore.

La demanderesse réclame en premier lieu la différence entre le prix qu'elle a dû rembourser à son acheteur pakistanais et celui réalisé à Dunkerque lors de la revente de la marchandise au plus offrant. Cette demande est justifiée pour les raisons qui viennent d'être indiquées.

Il résulte toutefois des pièces versées au dossier que le prix fait par X à son acheteur pakistanais ne s'élevait pas à US $ 461.866,02 (369.190,07 + 92.675,35), mais bien à US $ 459.015,67, la demanderesse ayant accordé une remise de US $ 2.850,35 sur une des factures.

Le produit de la réalisation à Dunkerque s'étant élevé à US $ 340.867,03, le préjudice subi de ce chef ne se monte qu'à US $ 118.148,64.

Quant aux indemnités versées par X à son acheteur pakistanais lors de la réalisation amiable du contrat, il s'agit d'une part des intérêts sur le montant de l'ouverture *de crédit couvrant le prix de vente, pour la période du 4 juin au 1ᵉʳ octobre 1985, soit US $ 23.892,19, et d'autre part des frais exposés par l'acheteur pakistanais dans le cadre du crédit documentaire, du coût de la licence d'importation, de la prime d'assurance et des intérêts sur l'ensemble desdits frais, soit US $ 21.225,54.*

Ces deux postes, qui forment un total de US $ 45.117,73, sont justifiés.

Il est également justifié d'allouer à la demanderesse les frais exposés par elle lorsqu'elle a délégué un représentant à Karachi qui y fit un bref séjour afin de réduire les prétentions de son acheteur, soit BF 93.378.

Sont également justifiés les débours exposés à Dunkerque, soit les frais portés en compte par le séquestre auquel le déchargement et triage de la marchandise avaient été confiés et d'autres dépenses connexes formant au total FF 122.340,16, ainsi que les frais se rapportant à la livraison des marchandises aux nouveaux acheteurs, soit FF 50.414,17 et BF 186.668 ».

Le Tribunal arbitral trancha comme suit le problème de la détermination de la date de conversion en francs belges des éléments du préjudice exprimés en dollars et en francs français.

« S'agissant de l'allocation de dommages et intérêts du chef de l'inexécution d'un contrat, la demanderesse doit être replacée dans la situation qui eût été la sienne si la défenderesse avait correctement rempli les obligations qui lui incombaient.

A cette fin il n'y a pas lieu de prévoir la conversion en francs belges des monnaies étrangères au cours du change en vigueur au jour de la conclusion du contrat, et pas davantage au jour du paiement, par la défenderesse, des dommages et intérêts alloués.

Il faut en revanche que cette conversion se fasse au cours du change en vigueur aux dates où la demanderesse, société de droit belge, a subi le préjudice dont la défenderesse lui doit réparation ».

Enfin, le Tribunal arbitral fixa ainsi le point de départ des intérêts compensatoires :

« Les intérêts compensatoires sur les sommes allouées à la demanderesse sont dus par la défenderesse à compter du 21 octobre 1985, date à laquelle X a mis Y en demeure de réparer le préjudice subi, sauf pour ceux des débours que la demanderesse n'a effectués qu'après cette date et sur lesquels les intérêts compensatoires ne sont dus qu'à compter de la date de leur paiement effectif ».

OBSERVATIONS :

I. — Même si les conclusions de la sentence relative à la faute du vendeur dans la conclusion du contrat de transport ne sont pas contestables, son analyse des relations des parties à une vente C & F (Coût et Fret) aurait gagnée à être nuancée sur certains points. Comme le soulignent les arbitres, les obligations du vendeur C & F sont les mêmes que celle du vendeur CAF (Coût, Assurance, Fret) en matière de conclusion du contrat de transport. On regrettera néanmoins qu'un Tribunal arbitral statuant en langue française préfère utiliser le sigle CIF (Cost, Insurance, Freight) plutôt que le terme CAF. Par contre, il n'est pas exact d'affirmer, comme le fait la sentence que *« le vendeur C & F a pour obligation de transporter ou de faire transporter à ses frais la marchandise embarquée conformément aux conditions de transport convenues entre acheteur et vendeur, les risques du transport maritime étant toutefois à la charge du vendeur à partir de l'embarquement ».*

S'il est exact que dans les ventes C & F et CAF l'acheteur supporte les risques à partir de l'embarquement, le vendeur n'a pas l'obligation de faire transporter la marchandise et encore moins de la transporter lui-même. En effet, l'obligation du vendeur en la matière se limite à conclure, à ses frais, un contrat de transport de la marchandise, aux conditions usuelles, par la route habituelle, par un navire de mer de type normalement employé pour la marchandise visée au contrat. L'article A (2) des Incoterms est très clair à cet égard, et l'on peut regretter que contrairement à beaucoup d'autres qui se fondent sur cette codification des usages même lorsque le contrat ne s'y réfère pas (*cf.* sentence CCI n° 3130 de 1980 : *Clunet* 1981, p. 931 ; sentence CCI n° 3894 de 1981 : *Clunet* 1982, p. 987), la sentence n'ait pas mentionné cette disposition :

« *Le vendeur doit :* ...

... conclure à ses propres frais, aux conditions usuelles, un contrat pour le transport de la marchandise par la route habituelle jusqu'au port de destination convenu, par un navire de mer (à l'exception des voiliers) du type normalement employé pour le transport de marchandise du genre visé au contrat ».

L'article 39 de la Loi française du 3 janvier 1969, relative à l'armement et aux ventes maritimes (J.O. *du 5 janvier 1969 ;* Dalloz *1969, p. 50) reflète de la même façon les usages internationaux :* « *dans une vente dite CAF (coût, assurance, fret) le vendeur s'oblige à conclure le contrat de transport et à mettre la marchandise à bord ainsi qu'à l'assurer contre les risques de ce transport* ».

Il en résulte que le vendeur a exécuté ses obligations relatives au transport à partir du moment où les conditions du contrat qu'il a conclu sont à l'abri des critiques de l'acheteur, tant à la lumière des usages que d'éventuelles dispositions particulières du contrat de vente. Par contre, le vendeur qui conclurait un contrat de transport à des conditions inhabituelles, dont la mise en œuvre serait de nature à causer un préjudice à l'acheteur engagerait sa responsabilité. La Cour d'Aix en Provence a ainsi reproché à un vendeur d'avoir accepté des « conditions draconniennes pour le déchargement de la marchandise, sanctionnées par des surestaries très élevées » (Aix, 29 avril 1976 : *Dr. mar. fr.* 1977, p. 49). C'est une « *culpa in contrahendo* » que peut reprocher l'acheteur au vendeur C & F ou CAF en matière de transport, et non pas une faute dans l'exécution du transport.

Le transport lui-même n'est pas une obligation du vendeur et le transporteur n'est pas son agent contrairement à ce que pourrait laisser entendre à tort la sentence lorsqu'elle indique que le vendeur « *a pour obligation de transporter ou de faire transporter* » la marchandise (*Cf.* en ce sens F. Eisemann et Y. Derains, « *La pratique des incoterms* », p. 137).

Le Tribunal arbitral ne s'y est d'ailleurs pas réellement trompé en précisant plus loin que « *les conséquences d'une exécution fautive par l'armateur du contrat d'affrètement transport sont ... pour le compte de l'acheteur* ». Il n'en irait pas ainsi si le transporteur exécutait une obligation du vendeur, pour le compte de celui-ci.

En l'espèce, il ne fait pas de doute que le vendeur ou du moins son agent, le commissaire-expéditeur, avait commis une faute dans la conclusion du contrat de transport. Les arbitres ont pu constater que les parties s'étaient mises d'accord postérieurement à la conclusion du contrat de vente pour que la marchandise soit transportée sur un navire de ligne régulière et se rendant directement à Karachi. Le vendeur ou son agent devait, en choisissant le navire s'assurer de ce que la première de ces deux conditions était respectée et exiger que la seconde le fût. Il s'agissait d'une obligation de résultat dans un cas, d'une obligation de moyens dans l'autre. Aucune des deux n'ayant été remplie, le vendeur était responsable du préjudice découlant de l'inexécution de ces obligations.

On doit d'ailleurs relever que les exigences de l'acheteur relatives au transport étaient parfaitement raisonnables. En effet, si dans les ventes C & F et CAF l'acheteur est un tiers au contrat de transport, il ne peut être indifférent aux conditions qui le régissent puisqu'il subit les conséquences directes de son exécution et des risques qui s'y attachent. C'est pourquoi il est fréquent que les contrats de vente C & F ou CAF soient extrêmement précis quant aux conditions du transport : ligne régulière ou non, responsabilité du transporteur, mode de chargement et de déchargement, vitesse du navire, navigabilité, etc...

L'argumentation de Y selon laquelle la formule « *sailing directly for Karachi* » signifiait simplement que la marchandise ne serait pas transbordée n'était cependant pas totalement fantaisiste. En effet, la pratique établit souvent une relation entre route directe et interdiction de transbordement (*cf.* F. Eisemann et Y. Derains, *op. cit.,* p. 136), l'interdiction de transbordement étant l'expression la plus courante de la volonté de l'acheteur de ce que la marchandise soit transportée directement au port de destination. Cependant, les arbitres ont pu relever à juste titre que l'interdiction des transbordements figurait déjà dans les instructions de X, indépendamment de l'exigence d'un voyage direct vers Karachi. C'est pourquoi les arbitres ne pouvaient que considérer qu'il s'agissait là d'une exigence supplémentaire, en vertu du principe d'interprétation dite de « l'effet utile » des dispositions contractuelles, consacré par la jurisprudence arbitrale (*cf.* Sentence CCI n° 1434 de 1976 : *Clunet 1976*, p. 982 ; Sentence CCI n° 3460 de 1980 : *Clunet* 1981, p. 939).

Le vendeur avait donc commis une faute en concluant un contrat de transport non conforme à l'accord des parties. Il prétendait cependant que cette faute n'était pas la cause de l'intégralité du dommage dont l'acheteur demandait réparation, dans le souci de ne rembourser que le gain manqué par ce dernier. On comprend que la sentence n'ait pas accepté ce point de vue car si la faute du vendeur était la cause du dommage, elle l'était de tous ses éléments, dans la mesure où, comme le souligne le Tribunal arbitral, il s'agissait d'un dommage prévisible et direct. C'est un principe bien établi que « le débiteur doit réparation du dommage et de tout dommage qui, sans sa faute, ne se serait pas immédiatement réalisé » (*cf.* Alex Weil et François Terré, *Droit civil, Les obligations,* n° 416, p. 440).

On peut simplement se demander s'il est certain que le dommage ne se serait pas réalisé au cas où la compagnie choisie aurait exploité une ligne directe Anvers/Karachi. Le navire n'aurait-il pu être saisi à l'occasion d'une escale technique ? C'est une question de probabilité dont les arbitres sont les seuls juges. La théorie des risques, telle que reçue par les usages de la vente internationale et notamment les Incoterms, aboutit aux mêmes conclusions. A partir du moment où le vendeur C & F ou CAF n'a pas embarqué la marchandise sur un navire correspondant aux exigences contractuelles les risques ne sont pas transférés à l'acheteur.

II. — L'obligation pour le créancier d'une obligation inexécutée de minimiser ses pertes est l'un des principes les mieux établis des usages du commerce international et de la *lex mercatoria* (*cf.* sentences CCI n° 2103 de 1972 : *Clunet 1974*, p. 902 ; n° 2142 de 1974 : *Clunet 1974*, p. 892 ; n° 2478 de 1974 : *Clunet 1975*, p. 925 ; n° 2139 de 1974 : *Clunet 1975*, p. 929 ; n° 2216 de 1974 : *Clunet 1975*, p. 917 ; n° 2291 de 1975 : *Clunet 1976*, p. 989 ; n° 2520 de 1975 : *Clunet 1976*, p. 992 ; n° 3344 de 1981 : *Clunet 1982*, p. 978 ; n° 4761 de 1987 : *Clunet 1987*, p. 1012 et plus généralement Y. Derains, « L'obligation de minimiser le dommage dans la jurisprudence arbitrale » : *R.D.A.I.,* 1987, p. 375 s.).

La présente sentence confirme que le principe appliqué par les arbitres dans ce domaine est bien le reflet d'une pratique suivie spontanément par les acteurs du commerce international. En effet, les arbitres relèvent tout d'abord que l'acheteur avait de lui-même conclu une transaction avec son propre créancier pour réduire le dommage que la faute du vendeur lui avait causé ; le montant de cette transaction et les frais s'y rattachant sont considérés par les arbitres comme devant légitimement lui être remboursés par le vendeur. La sentence souligne ensuite que dans le même souci de limiter son préjudice l'acheteur a vendu la marchandise avec l'accord du vendeur, ce dernier l'ayant partiellement rachetée.

On constate ainsi que l'obligation de coopération, autre règle de la *lex mercatoria* (*cf.* Sentence CCI n° 2291 de 1975 : *Clunet* 1976, p. 989) est intimement liée à celle de minimiser le dommage.

III. — On peut s'étonner de la facilité avec laquelle les arbitres octroient des intérêts compensatoires à l'acheteur. En effet, il est de principe que ceux-ci contrairement aux intérêts moratoires ne sont dus que si le débiteur en retard a causé par sa mauvaise foi, un préjudice indépendant du retard (art. 1153 C. civ.). Or, les arbitres ne se réfèrent pas expressément à la mauvaise foi du vendeur. Le souci d'indemniser totalement la victime d'une faute contractuelle est ici prédominant et en prise directe sur les réalités économiques. Une telle approche mérite d'être approuvée. Mais dans cet esprit pourquoi faire courir les intérêts à compter de la mise en demeure ? Les principes ne sont en effet pas en ce sens qui veulent que les sommes de caractère indemnitaire — ce qui est le cas — ne sont productrices d'intérêts qu'à compter de la date du jugement. Si les arbitres n'entendaient pas les respecter, et ce, à juste titre, il paraissait préférable, dans l'esprit même de leur volonté légitime d'indemniser totalement la créance, de faire courir les intérêts compensatoires à compter du jour où le préjudice avait été subi.

IV. — Seule la date de la conversion en francs belges des sommes allouées au vendeur faisait l'objet d'un débat entre les parties, et non pas le principe même de cette conversion. Cependant, si tel avait été le cas, il est probable que les arbitres se seraient prononcés en faveur de la conversion. Tout d'abord en raison de leur détermination de replacer la partie victime de l'inexécution contractuelle « dans la situation qui eût été la sienne si la défenderesse avait correctement rempli les obligations qui lui incombaient ». Mais aussi selon le principe mis en œuvre par la jurisprudence arbitrale internationale en vertu duquel l'indemnité compensatrice d'un préjudice doit être payée dans la monnaie où ce préjudice est subi. Deux sentences CCI reflètent ce principe. Il s'agit de la sentence rendue dans l'affaire n° 2103 en 1972 (*Clunet* 1974, p. 902) et de la sentence rendue dans l'affaire n° 2745/2762 en 1977 (*Clunet* 1978, p. 990). Dans la seconde l'arbitre fixe une indemnité en francs belges alors que la monnaie contractuelle était le dollar américain, au motif que le préjudice a été subi en Belgique : « *La conversion en francs belges s'impose plutôt parce que les deux sociétés créancières ... sont des sociétés belges. Elles tiennent leurs comptes en francs belges et tout le préjudice pécuniaire qu'elles subissent est, sauf circonstances particulières, un préjudice en francs belges* ». Le raisonnement suivi aurait pu s'appliquer à l'espèce ici rapportée.

Quant à la date de conversion retenue par la sentence — celle du jour où le préjudice a été subi — elle est la conséquence logique de la volonté des arbitres d'indemniser totalement le créancier de l'obligation inexécutée.

V. — Contrairement à ce qui s'était passé dans l'affaire CCI n° 5423 de 1987 (*Clunet* 1987, p. 1048) la partie défenderesse n'a pas soulevé l'incompétence de la Cour d'arbitrage de la CCI au motif que l'arbitrage n'était pas international. S'agissant d'un arbitrage à Anvers, entre deux parties belges, le droit belge étant applicable au fond et à la procédure, on aurait pu s'interroger légitimement sur le caractère international de l'arbitrage. Mais cette question ne se posait pas quant à la compétence de la CCI. En effet, l'article 1 du Règlement Intérieur de la Cour d'arbitrage de la CCI est libellé comme suit : « la Cour d'arbitrage peut accepter d'être saisie de différends n'entrant pas dans le champ des différends ayant un caractère international intervenant dans le domaine des affaires s'il existe une convention d'arbitrage lui attribuant compétence ». Ainsi, toute discussion sur le caractère international des différends devient inutile quand il s'agit de déterminer la compétence de la Cour d'arbitrage de la CCI.

Cette solution pratique est heureuse car les conceptions de l'arbitrage international varient d'un pays à l'autre, la Cour d'arbitrage ne pouvant en choisir une en particulier. Ainsi l'arbitrage ayant donné lieu à la sentence ici rapportée est indiscutablement un arbitrage international au sens du droit français en ce qu'il « met en cause des intérêts du commerce international », ainsi que l'exige l'article 1492 du Nouveau Code de Procédure Civile (sur l'interprétation de ce texte, *cf.* notamment Ph. Fouchard, « Introduction — spécificité de l'arbitrage international » : *Rev. arb.* 1981, 449, spéc. p. 462 s., et les références).

En effet, l'exportation de zinc de la Belgique vers le Pakistan, sans compter qu'une des parties faisait partie d'un groupe japonais, intéresse le commerce international.

Mais cette sentence rendue à Anvers ne jouit pas du statut des sentences « internationales » selon la loi belge du 27 mars 1985 sur l'arbitrage international. Cette loi par laquelle, ainsi qu'on l'a écrit « le juge belge devient purement et simplement incompétent pour annuler une sentence arbitrale internationale pour quelque raison que ce soit » (H. Van Houtte, « La loi belge du 27 mars 1985 sur l'arbitrage international » : *Rev. Arb.* 1986, p. 29) s'exprime en fait comme suit : « les tribunaux belges ne peuvent connaître d'une demande en annulation que lorsqu'au moins une partie au différend tranché par la sentence arbitrale est soit une personne physique ayant la nationalité belge ou une résidence en Belgique, soit une personne morale constituée en Belgique ou y ayant une succursale ou un siège quelconque d'opération ».

Cette différence d'approche n'oppose pas seulement la Belgique et la France. *Mutatis mutandis,* la récente loi fédérale suisse sur le droit international privé du 18 décembre 1987, n'aurait pas non plus considéré l'arbitrage en cause comme international, puisque son article 176 (1) exige pour cela que l'une des parties au moins n'ait pas, au moment de conclure la convention d'arbitrage, son domicile ou sa résidence habituelle en Suisse (*Cf.* Marc Blessing, « The New International Arbitration Law in Switzerland » : *Journal of International Arbitration,* 1988, Vol. 5 n° 2, p. 18). On constate ainsi qu'une affaire d'exportation maritime entre deux pays, donnant lieu au surplus à une saisie dans un pays tiers, ne donnerait pas lieu à un arbitrage considéré comme international dans deux pays qui ont récemment défini un régime spécial pour de telles procédures. Il serait facile, et sans doute exact, de dire que la conception du droit français est la plus proche des réalités économiques. Cependant, on ne peut que féliciter la CCI de s'être *de facto* placée en dehors de ces diversités d'approches nationales par une disposition appropriée de son règlement intérieur.

Y.D

I. — Amiable composition. — Portée des pouvoirs accordés au tribunal arbitral. — Faculté des arbitres d'écarter l'application du droit matériel. — Respect des dispositions d'ordre public. — Faculté de modifier le contrat (non). — Faculté d'écarter l'application de clauses non équitables. — Evolution de la jurisprudence française.

II. — Clause compromissoire. — Compétence du tribunal arbitral sur le dirigeant social signataire du contrat (non). — Notion de groupe de sociétés. — Formation du contrat.

III. — Résiliation fautive du contrat. — Dol ou fraude (non). — Usage par les arbitres des pouvoirs d'amiable composition. — Modération des effets dommageables de la clause de résiliation. — Evaluation du dommage. — Préjudice moral.

Sentence rendue dans l'affaire 4972 en 1989.

L'arbitrage fut introduit sur la base d'une clause compromissoire qui figurait dans un contrat de distribution exclusive passé entre d'une part X et Y (filiale de X) et d'autre part Z. Par ce contrat, Z accordait à X et à Y le droit exclusif de distribuer en France les produits de parfumerie qu'elle exploitait. Estimant que la résiliation du contrat par Z était fautive, X et Y déclenchent l'arbitrage contre elle ainsi que contre M. W (personne physique), dirigeant de Z et signataire du contrat litigieux. L'arbitrage s'est déroulé à Paris devant un tribunal formé par deux coarbitres français et un président de nationalité belge. Le tribunal arbitral était autorisé à statuer en amiable composition.

La première tâche des arbitres consistait donc à fixer la signification et la portée de leurs pouvoirs d'amiables compositeurs :

« *Qu'il soit d'abord permis au Tribunal Arbitral de rappeler qu'au regard du Règlement CCI comme du droit français, l'arbitre auquel sont confiés les pouvoirs d'amiable compositeur est dispensé de l'obligation d'observer le droit applicable au fond du litige, sous réserve des règles non susceptibles d'éviction telles les règles d'ordre public, et dispose également de certains pouvoirs à l'égard du contrat...*

*Il est exact que, comme le souligne (Z), l'article 13.5 du Règlement...
CCI dispose que :*

*"Dans tous les cas, l'arbitre tiendra compte des stipulations du contrat
et des usages du commerce".*

*Sur base de la jurisprudence des tribunaux arbitraux CCI quant à l'éten-
due des pouvoirs des amiables compositeurs à l'égard des clauses contractuelles, on constate que les amiables compositeurs CCI :*

*a) considèrent que ces pouvoirs ne les autorisent pas à réviser le contrat
(Clunet 1978, sentence 2694 ; Clunet 1974, sentence 1512 ; Clunet 1977,
n° 2708) par exemple à la suite de modifications de circonstances économiques en cours d'exécution du contrat (telles une hausse des prix imprévue
au jour de la signature du contrat) ou à en modifier les termes. A l'appui
de cette position est régulièrement invoqué l'adage* pacta sunt servanda *;*

*b) admettent néanmoins que l'article 13.5 précité ne fait nullement obsta-
cle à ce que :*

*"... l'arbitre siégeant en qualité d'amiable compositeur (refuse) de tenir
compte de droits légaux ou contractuels d'une partie quand la prétention
de s'en prévaloir équivaudrait à un abus de droit." (... Clunet 1980, 961...).*

*Dans une sentence ultérieure rendue dans la même affaire, les arbitres
ont à nouveau précisé leur position, et ce dans les termes suivants :*

*"In its first award, this arbitral tribunal already expressed its view on the
scope of its authority as amiable compositeur and intends to strictly adhere
to the principles so expressed. It is the duty of the ICC arbitrators to apply
the provisions of a contract even when empowered to act as amiable
compositeur but they may indeed disregard a party's legal or contractual
rights only when the enforcement of such rights amounts to an abuse
thereof." (... Yearbook, vol. XII, 1987).*

*Dans la note suivant la première sentence précitée... Derains précise
quant à lui que le cas de l'abus de droit n'est pas le seul dans lequel les
arbitres peuvent ainsi décider :*

*"on soulignera cependant que l'exercice d'un droit risque d'avoir des
conséquences inéquitables, que l'amiable compositeur pourra modérer,
sans qu'il y ait pour autant abus de ce droit. Tel sera le cas chaque fois
que ce droit sera exercé sans intention de nuire, dans un intérêt légitime,
et qu'il se heurte à un intérêt de même nature de l'autre partie."*

*Dans le même sens, Y. Derains précise, dans une note publiée sous la
sentence CCI n° 2694 (Clunet 1978, 985) :*

"*Que l'arbitre* amiable compositeur *ne soit pas en mesure de modifier un contrat, signifie-t-il que chacune des clauses de la convention des parties s'impose à lui et qu'il soit tenu de leur donner plein effet ? On concluera par la négative (...). Il semble, au contraire, que l'arbitre..., non tenu d'appliquer les dispositions supplétives de la loi, puisse se refuser à tenir compte de certaines clauses contractuelles qui ne sauraient s'imposer à lui avec plus de force que le droit qui confère au contrat son existence même.*"

Dans la note suivant la sentence n° 2119 (Clunet *1979, 977), il est encore souligné que :*

"*En réalité, l'expression* tenir compte des stipulations du contrat *ne crée pas une obligation générale de s'y soumettre et réserve l'éventualité de situations où ces stipulations devraient être écartées, que ce soit parce qu'elles heurtent des normes impératives applicables ou l'équité...*".

L'étendue des pouvoirs des amiables compositeurs a par ailleurs été... précisée, en droit français, dans trois arrêts de la Cour d'appel de Paris (15 mars 1984, 6 janvier 1984 et 12 mars 1985 publiés in Revue de l'Arbitrage 1985, p. 285-279-299).

Antérieurement à ces décisions, la question faisait l'objet d'une sérieuse controverse en droit français. S'il semblait y avoir une certaine unanimité sur le pouvoir modérateur de l'arbitre, il était contesté qu'il puisse écarter une clause contractuelle...

Il va de soi... que l'amiable compositeur, en exerçant son pouvoir modérateur, ne pourrait se rendre complice d'une fraude. De même le comportement dolosif de la partie qui souhaite bénéficier de ce pouvoir modérateur, excluerait que l'arbitre puisse en faire usage.

En conclusion de ce qui précède le Tribunal arbitral considère que s'il est tenu par les stipulations contractuelles encore a-t-il, en vertu des pouvoirs d'amiable composition qui lui ont été conférés, le pouvoir d'en modérer, c'est-à-dire de ne pas appliquer les dispositions contractuelles dans toute leur rigueur dès lors que pareille application heurterait l'équité... ».

C'est dans cet état d'esprit que le tribunal arbitral procède à l'examen de sa compétence, d'abord à l'égard de M. W et ensuite en ce qui concerne Z.

Invoquant la notion du groupe de sociétés et alléguant son rôle actif dans la négociation et dans l'exécution du contrat, les demanderesses affirment que leur véritable co-contractant était le groupe X et en particulier son principal animateur, M. W. A l'appui de leur thèse, les demanderesses produisent une décision de jurisprudence américaine reconnaissant aux sociétés du groupe X une réelle unité économique. Les arbitres font aussitôt apparaître la fragilité de la thèse :

« ... il paraît quelque peu audacieux d'appliquer en droit français et à une personne physique, une jurisprudence américaine visant des personnes morales... ».

Par ailleurs, les arbitres refusent d'accepter que le rôle joué par M. W dans la négociation et dans l'exécution du contrat ait pour effet de le rendre partie au contrat entre X, Y et Z. M. W est donc mis hors de cause :

« ... M.(W) n'est pas partie au contrat litigieux et... la clause compromissoire dont découle le présent arbitrage ne lui est pas opposable ».

Le deuxième volet de l'exception d'incompétence était, lui, plus complexe. Il concernait la défenderesse numéro 1 (Z) qui affirmait avoir acquis les actions de la demanderesse numéro 2 (Y), ce qui rend impossible son action en indemnisation. Cependant, l'analyse de l'opération ayant pour objet la cession d'actions montrait que, faute d'accord sur le prix, la vente n'avait pu être parfaite.

« (Y) est donc jusqu'à ce jour une société faisant partie d'un autre groupe que celui auquel appartient (Z, défenderesse numéro 1). »

L'existence dans le contrat d'une clause de résiliation automatique conduit les arbitres à examiner si les conditions de sa mise en œuvre par les défenderesses (Y et Z) ont été abusives. Cette clause contractuelle prévoyait certaines hypothèses entraînant la réalisation du contrat sans mise en demeure préalable. La lettre de résiliation des défenderesses reprochait aux demanderesses l'inexécution d'obligations découlant de cinq clauses du contrat de distribution exclusive, dont une seulement autorisait le recours à la clause de résiliation automatique. Toutes les autres violations alléguées devaient faire l'objet d'une mise en demeure préalable.

Mais, pour la violation autorisant la référence à la clause de résiliation automatique, les arbitres remarquent :

« Le revirement d'attitude de (Z, défenderesse numéro 1)... quant à l'application des règles prévues par le contrat paraît particulièrement brutal et inattendu : après avoir fait preuve de laxisme pendant près de trois ans, (Z) passe soudain à une intransigeance que rien ne pouvait laisser présager...

Vu l'absence de remarques ou de critiques quant à la commercialisation des produits... il eût été normal et plus conforme aux usages de la profession, de mettre (X et Y) en demeure de respecter les obligations contractuelles auxquelles il était estimé qu'elles faisaient défaut, avant de prendre des mesures plus drastiques. »

Ceci étant, le tribunal, investi des pouvoirs d'amiable composition, peut-il intervenir pour modérer les effets inéquitables de la clause de résiliation automatique ? La défenderesse s'y oppose aux motifs que la faute dolosive des demanderesses fait obstacle à l'usage des pouvoirs d'amiables compositeurs des arbitres. L'argument est rejeté par le tribunal :

« ... *(la défenderesse) ne rapporte nullement la preuve (d'un) comportement dolosif ou frauduleux des demanderesses... Le Tribunal arbitral considère par conséquent qu'aucun obstacle ne s'oppose à ce qu'il fasse usage de ses pouvoirs d'amiable compositeur.* »

Le tribunal peut donc procéder à la modération des effets inéquitables de la clause de résiliation automatique :

« ... *le Tribunal arbitral conclut... (que la défenderesse) ne lui paraît pas s'être conduite en conformité avec les usages de la profession qui s'opposent à tout usage brutal d'un droit.*

... le Tribunal Arbitral décide que les effets d'une application stricte de (la clause de résiliation automatique) sont, en équité, disproportionnés avec la fraude alléguée et qu'il conviendra d'atténuer les effets de la rupture prononcée sur cette base, en allouant ex aequo et bono *une indemnité en raison du préjudice subi...*

Statuant par conséquent en équité... le Tribunal Arbitral considère la rupture des relations contractuelles... abusive par son mode d'application immédiate...

L'exercice d'un droit aussi radical que celui de mettre fin à un contrat sans préavis, requiert que celui qui entend s'en prévaloir ait fait preuve d'exigence quant au respect des dispositions lui ouvrant ce droit tout au long de ses relations avec son cocontractant.

... le laxisme dont fait preuve (la défenderesse) au cours des trois années qui ont précédé la rupture... n'a pas permis (aux demanderesses) de prévoir la rupture qui a ainsi été prononcée... dans des circonstances qui heurtent les principes d'exécution de bonne foi des conventions et d'équité.

La décision... d'appliquer soudainement à la lettre les termes du contrat, sans tenir compte du fait qu'elle avait admis pendant des années le manquement dont elle se prévalait, ne peut par conséquent être considérée comme régulière.

... le Tribunal... estime que la lettre de résiliation... aurait dû consister en une mise en demeure de respecter les termes du contrat dans les délais fixés... ».

Modérant ainsi les effets dommageables de l'application pure et simple de la clause de résiliation automatique, les arbitres accordent aux demanderesses une indemnité pour rupture abusive du contrat par la défenderesse. Cette indemnité comprend une somme allouée à titre de préjudice moral subi par les demanderesses du fait de la rupture brutale du contrat.

OBSERVATIONS :

I. — Jusqu'où peut aller l'arbitre amiable compositeur ? Quelle est la portée des pouvoirs qui lui sont conférés par les parties ? Peut-il ou doit-il ignorer le droit ? Est-il obligé de tenir compte du contrat ? Loin de faire l'unanimité, les tentatives de réponse à ces questions n'ont fait qu'animer le débat scientifique sur le sujet (cf. par exemple E. Loquin, *L'amiable composition en droit comparé et international, Contribution à l'étude du non-droit dans l'arbitrage commercial,* Thèse publiée par l'Institut de Relations Internationales, Travaux du CREDIMI, vol. 7, Paris 1980, avec une riche bibliographie, et « Pouvoirs et devoirs » de l'amiable compositeur, à propos de trois arrêts de la Cour d'appel de Paris » : Rev. arb., 1985, 2 ; J.-D. Bredin, « L'amiable composition et le contrat : Rev. arb., 1984, 2). La jurisprudence arbitrale, quant à elle, révèle des hésitations dans son incursion en ce « non-droit », pour reprendre la suggestive terminologie de Loquin.

Toutefois, une nette différence se dégage sur l'étendue des pouvoirs de l'arbitre amiable compositeur face au droit et face au contrat. Autant on est prêt à lui reconnaître la faculté d'ignorer le droit au nom de l'équité, autant on s'oppose à son intervention pour modifier le contrat. Mais des nuances à cette affirmation s'imposent.

En effet, bien que la jurisprudence arbitrale soit pratiquement unanime sur la faculté de l'amiable compositeur d'ignorer le droit, encore faut-il qu'il respecte les dispositions d'ordre public (les arbitres en l'espèce en sont conscients ; cf. également : *J.D.I.* 1988, 1206, 1984, 922, 1984, 924 et 1984, 910). Il existe d'autre part certaines décisions arbitrales rendues en équité, mais très attachées au droit strict (*J.D.I.* 1987, 1027). N'est-il d'ailleurs pas encourageant d'assister à la confusion du droit et de l'équité ?

La jurisprudence arbitrale montre également que, dans certains cas, l'arbitre amiable compositeur peut « modérer » ou « tempérer » les dispositions contractuelles inéquitables (outre la présente espèce, cf. *J.D.I.* 1982, 971, 1982, 978 et 1980, 961). En revanche, l'interdiction à l'amiable compositeur de modifier ou d'adapter le contrat ne semble pas être contestée (cf. *JDI* 1984, 926, 1982, 971 et 1978, 985 et Bredin, *cit.,* p. 268). En l'espèce les arbitres reconnaissent ces limites.

S'estimant par conséquent investis du pouvoir de tempérer l'effet des dispositions contractuelles excessives ou inéquitables, les arbitres abordent l'incident de compétence ainsi que le fond. Nous constatons, néanmoins, que leur démarche est très proche de celle d'un arbitre statuant en droit. Autrement dit, les arbitres ne semblent véritablement pas s'aventurer dans l'énigmatique territoire du « non-droit » pour parvenir à la solution du litige.

II. — Sur la compétence, les arbitres décident que la clause compromissoire n'est pas opposable à M. W (défenderesse numéro 2), dirigeant de la société Z (défenderesse numéro 1), partie au contrat. En ce faisant, le tribunal arbitral confirme une tendance qu'il faut désormais observer avec intérêt ; faute de fraude, la signature du contrat par une personne physique au nom d'une société, ne rend pas la clause arbitrale opposable à cette personne. La notion de groupe de sociétés ne saurait par ailleurs perturber ce principe (les affaires qui retiennent cette notion concernent uniquement des personnes morales ; *JDI* 1988, 1207, 1983, 899 et 1978, 985).

Imposée par la nature consensuelle de l'arbitrage, conforme avec l'adage *res inter alios acta* et respectueuse des systèmes juridiques concernés, la solution retenue par les arbitres se passe d'une référence aux pouvoirs d'amiable composition. Il en va de même pour la décision du tribunal de retenir compétence à l'égard de Z (défenderesse numéro 1), au motif que la cession alléguée n'est pas devenue parfaite faute de détermination du prix des actions. Sur ce point, les arbitres font d'ailleurs référence expresse au droit français (« En droit français, il est constant que la vente n'est parfaite que s'il y a accord sur la chose et sur le prix »). Incontestablement imprégné de la démarche normalement suivie par les arbitres statuant en droit, le tribunal de l'espèce réserve ses facultés d'amiable composition pour trancher le fond.

III. — C'est à l'égard du fond que les arbitres déclarent expressément user de leurs pouvoirs de statuer en amiable composition. Les parties ayant consenti à l'incorporation dans le contrat d'une clause de résiliation automatique particulièrement sévère, il s'agit pour le collège arbitral de décider si, au vu des circonstances, ils peuvent écarter son application. En effet, la clause définit certaines hypothèses qui autorisent la résiliation automatique du contrat avec effet immédiat et sans mise en demeure préalable. Après trois ans de souplesse (laxisme disent les arbitres) dans l'exécution du contrat, la défenderesse met en œuvre la clause de résiliation automatique en invoquant cinq violations du contrat par les demanderesses jusqu'alors tolérées sans la moindre protestation. Uniquement une des violations alléguées autorisait le recours au mécanisme contractuel pour mettre un terme aux relations contractuelles entre les parties, et la défenderesse s'est abstenue de donner un préavis aux demanderesses.

Les arbitres sont donc confrontés au principe *pacta sunt servanda*. Ils reconnaissent d'abord que le recours à la clause de résiliation automatique par la défenderesse fut « brutal et inattendu », voire abusif. Sont-ils, dans ces conditions, autorisés à ignorer la clause contractuelle ? La réponse positive du tribunal est partiellement fondée sur les usages (« ... *il eût été... plus conforme avec les usages de la profession de mettre en demeure...* » ou encore « ... *la défenderesse ne s'est pas conduite en conformité avec les usages de la profession...* ») et, du bout des lèvres, les arbitres avancent la doctrine de l'abus de droit comme exception à la règle *pacta sunt servanda*.

Concernant les usages, leur application ne transforme point l'arbitre en amiable compositeur. Effectivement, l'article 13-5 du Règlement CCI invite les arbitres à en tenir compte quelle que soit la solution retenue pour le droit matériel applicable, et l'article 1496 du Nouveau Code de Procédure Civile français autorise les arbitres statuant en droit à s'y référer. « Les usages du commerce international sont des règles de droit... » (Bredin, *cit.,* p. 261).

Bonne foi, abus de droit et *pacta sunt servanda*. Voilà les clés de l'énigme. Les arbitres de cette espèce considèrent que l'exercice abusif et contraire à la bonne foi du droit à la résiliation automatique fait obstacle au respect strict de la règle *pacta sunt servanda*. D'autres tribunaux statuant en droit en ont fait autant sans dériver vers l'amiable composition (cette chronique a d'ailleurs contribué à mettre de telles solutions à la portée des arbitres internationaux ; *cf.* aussi la sentence *ad hoc* publiée dans le *Yearbook of Commercial Arbitration* 1982, 77 où des arbitres amiables compositeurs appliquent la *lex mercatoria*, et particulièrement le principe de l'abus de droit). Certes, les arbitres amiables compositeurs peuvent puiser dans la *lex mercatoria*, s'éloignant ainsi de l'amiable composition pour rejoindre la démarche de l'arbitre en droit. Toutefois, dans ce déplacement de l'amiable composition vers le droit, les arbitres se font accompagner de l'équité.

C'est probablement par prudence, ou craignant un contrôle judiciaire rigoureux (ou hostile à l'application de la *lex mercatoria*), que les arbitres justifient l'ignorance de la clause de résiliation automatique par référence à l'amiable composition. Il n'en demeure pas moins que leur démarche est très proche de celle d'un arbitre statuant en droit.

I. — Formation du contrat. — Commandes pour la fourniture de marchandises. — Acceptation des Conditions Générales d'Achat par le vendeur sous réserve de modifications. — Silence du vendeur. — Modification de l'offre. — Modification des Conditions Générales.

II. — Détermination de la loi applicable. — Choix des parties dans le contrat limité à des dispositions nationales administratives. — Système de droit incomplet. — Accord des parties pour l'application des principes et usages généraux et normaux du commerce international. — *Lex mercatoria*, complément de la loi du contrat. — Application du droit français à la détermination du taux d'intérêts. — *Lex fori.* — Obligation principale en francs français.

III. — Conformité des marchandises. — Inexécution partielle du vendeur de son obligation de livrer des marchandises conformes. — Retards dans la livraison. — Faute contractuelle du vendeur (non). — Annulation des commandes par l'acheteur justifiée (non). — Faute contractuelle de l'acheteur. — Preuve du dommage apportée par le vendeur (non).

Sentence rendue dans l'affaire 5904 en 1989.

Le litige opposant les parties découle d'une série de commandes passées par une société européenne auprès d'un fournisseur originaire d'un pays en voie de développement. A l'origine des relations commerciales entre les parties, l'acheteur européen avait adressé au vendeur des Conditions Générales d'Achat (CGA) contenant la clause suivante :

« *Ces conditions générales d'achat pourront être modifiées à la demande de (l'acheteur). Les modifications interviendront par voie d'avenant au présent contrat.* »

En réponse, le vendeur se déclarait :

« *... d'accord avec l'ensemble des conditions générales d'achat et des fiches d'instruction annexées.* »

Sous couvert d'une lettre de décembre 1985, le vendeur a renvoyé à l'acheteur le récépissé d'acceptation des CGA dûment signé. Toutefois, la lettre du vendeur précisait que l'accord était conditionné à une série de modifications aux CGA. Ces modifications portaient, *inter alia*, sur le traitement réservé au retard dans la livraison, sur la conformité des marchandises et l'application de certaines dispositions administratives du pays du vendeur. Faute de réaction de l'acheteur à la lettre du vendeur, les parties ont procédé à l'exécution du contrat sur la base des documents ainsi échangés.

Mais, compte tenu de l'affirmation de l'acheteur que le vendeur avait accepté les CGA sans réserves ni modifications, l'arbitre s'est penché sur le problème de la formation du contrat. Les CGA ont-elles été valablement modifiées par la lettre du vendeur de décembre 1985 ? L'arbitre donne une réponse positive à la question :

« *1. Bien que le libellé du récépissé d'accord ait bien l'intention d'éviter des modifications unilatérales par le fournisseur, il ne peut en aucun cas empêcher que les parties conviennent de commun accord de certaines modifications.*

2. Les modifications demandées par (le vendeur) ont apparemment été préalablement discutées avec (l'acheteur)... La lettre ne fait donc à toute évidence que refléter un accord oral antérieur.

3. Le dossier ne contient aucune trace de protestation de (l'acheteur) contre les modifications, ultérieure à la réception de la lettre (de) décembre 1985. Dans l'absence de protestation... il faut en conclure que (l'acheteur) a accepté les modifications apportées par (le vendeur). »

Parmi les modifications aux CGA proposées par le vendeur, figurait une mention de la loi applicable :

« *... en cas de litige, sa résolution juridique (doit) être conforme au droit... applicable aux sociétés dans la zone franche (du pays du vendeur).* »

En cours de procédure, aussi bien les parties que l'arbitre se sont prononcés pour une interprétation restrictive de cette référence au droit du vendeur :

« *... le droit désigné n'est pas, selon les parties, un système de droit complet, comprenant e.a. des règles de droit contractuel, mais est constitué* *uniquement d'une ou plusieurs lois réglant primordialement le régime fiscal et douanier des sociétés établies en zone franche. »*

L'application limitée de la loi du vendeur laissait donc entier le problème de la détermination du droit matériel applicable. Ici encore, l'accord des parties épargne à l'arbitre une démarche tendant à le déterminer :

« La clause en question ne constituant pas un choix du droit (du vendeur) dans sa totalité, il restait à l'Arbitre à déterminer le droit national applicable en complément du droit relatif aux sociétés en zone franche.

Les parties suggérèrent alors, en entente parfaite, que l'arbitre ne soit pas obligé de déterminer quel droit national est applicable, mais se laisse guider par les principes et usages normaux et généraux du commerce international...

Les parties ayant opté pour l'application des principes généraux et des usages normaux du commerce international, il faut quand même déterminer quel droit déterminera le taux d'intérêt, puisque la lex mercatoria ne contient évidemment pas de règles aussi détaillées que celles relatives aux taux d'intérêts.

Un argument en faveur de l'application du taux (du pays du vendeur) est que le créancier (éventuel) y a son domicile et souffre le dommage (dans ce pays).

Néanmoins, l'Arbitre considère que le taux français est plus adapté.

Il est logique que le droit du pays dans la monnaie duquel la créance est libellée s'applique pour déterminer le taux d'intérêt, qui est, en théorie, fonction de la situation de cette monnaie sur les marchés financiers. »

Quant au fond, et en particulier en ce qui concerne la conformité des marchandises, la sentence fait une distinction entre les vices découverts à la réception et les défauts constatés après :

« Pour ces derniers, (l'acheteur) se réserve le droit de réclamer même si le vice était apparent au moment de la livraison, dans les trois mois suivant la constatation du vice. Selon les CGA une telle réclamation doit être faite par lettre recommandée (au vendeur)...

En ce qui concerne les défauts constatés lors du contrôle systématique à la réception de la livraison... les CGA ne prévoient pas si, ou de quelle manière, le (vendeur) doit être informé du résultat de ce contrôle. De même, les CGA ne prévoient à ce sujet aucun droit de réponse du (vendeur), ni une procédure d'expertise contradictoire.

... il ne fait aucun doute que le vendeur ait été en défaut de remplir ses obligations contractuelles relatives au marquage des produits pour au moins une commande... En ce qui concerne les obligations de mensuration, teinture et composition des articles, (il) s'en déduit... une présomption de fait que (le vendeur) n'a pas toujours bien rempli ses obligations contractuelles relatives à la conformité des marchandises... »

Toutefois, faisant une analyse des mécanismes de réparation contractuels, l'arbitre décide que les défauts constatés n'étaient pas justificatifs de l'annulation des commandes en cours :

« *Pour marchandises non conformes, les CGA prévoient d'abord l'application d'une indemnité dans le cadre d'une procédure litiges... En outre, la répétition d'anomalies entraîne l'exclusion du fournisseur... Enfin, les CGA donnent (à l'acheteur) le choix entre trois remèdes :*

1. refus de la marchandise et retour aux frais du fournisseur ;

2. remise en état des marchandises par (l'acheteur) aux frais du fournisseur ;

3. résiliation du contrat aux torts du fournisseur et en renégociation sur la marchandise en question...

L'annulation des commandes en cours n'est pas mentionnée comme sanction possible. Elle ne serait d'ailleurs pas logique puisqu'elle ne remédierait pas aux défauts des marchandises livrées.

Par ailleurs, (l'acheteur) avait bel et bien opté pour la deuxième sanction...

Les défauts constatés... ne justifiaient donc pas l'annulation des commandes en cours. »

Pour la ponctualité dans la livraison des marchandises, la sentence souligne que, s'agissant d'un contrat FOB, la date à respecter est celle de la cargaison. Or, l'arbitre constate que, pour une part des commandes litigieuses, cette date ne figurait pas au dossier des parties. Pour les autres commandes, et notamment pour celles où l'acheteur n'a pas accordé une prolongation, l'arbitre se borne à vérifier s'il y a faute contractuelle du vendeur :

« *Les CGA insistent largement sur l'importance des délais de livraison... et ne prévoient ni le retard dû à une force majeure ou faute de (l'acheteur), ni l'extension conventionnelle des délais. Il est toutefois inconcevable que les fournisseurs souscrivant à ces CGA assument une obligation de garantie de délais de livraison, prenant ainsi sur eux toute responsabilité pour retard. Une telle interprétation stricte des CGA rendrait ces clauses léonines. Pour qu'il n'y ait donc pas d'abus de la part de (l'acheteur), concernant les sanctions prévues par les CGA, il faut que le retard soit attribuable au fournisseur (cf. M. Mustill, The Lex Mercatoria : The First Twenty-Five Years, Arbitration International, 1988, p. 111 : « The principle* pacta sunt servanda *is subject to the concept of* abus de droit, *and to a rule that unfair and unconscionable contracts and clauses should not be enforced* »).*

La cause du retard n'apparaît pas du dossier de (l'acheteur)...

Dans ces circonstances, il faut conclure que (le vendeur) n'a pas toujours respecté les délais contractuels, mais que le dossier ne permet pas de dire que ces retards ont constitué des défauts contractuels...

Ni la lettre (d'annulation de l'acheteur), ni un autre document du dossier n'indiquait que (l'acheteur) ait exercé ou voulu exercer son droit (aux remèdes contractuels). La lettre d'annulation des commandes ne disait nullement qu'elle annulait ces commandes parce que leur livraison était retardée. Elle n'a pas non plus été précédée d'une mise en demeure (du vendeur).

Enfin, il faut rappeler que l'annulation des commandes en cours n'était qu'une des quatre sanctions possibles. La lex mercatoria, *sur l'application de laquelle les parties se sont entendues, exige que les contrats soient exécutés de bonne foi. Ce principe exige que (l'acheteur) ait choisi la sanction la plus appropriée après avoir mis (le vendeur) en demeure...*

L'Arbitre conclut que les retards de livraison

... ne justifiaient pas l'annulation des commandes en cours... »

Mais, l'acheteur pouvait-il fonder l'annulation des commandes futures sur l'incapacité du vendeur d'honorer celles à venir ? Saisi de cette question, l'arbitre répond par la négative :

« *... (l'acheteur) a rompu les relations parce qu'il craignait le défaut* futur *(du vendeur) de remplir son obligation contractuelle de livrer des marchandises conformes.*

Ni les CGA, ni la lex mercatoria *ne donnent (à l'acheteur) un droit d'annuler des commandes pour défaut* futur *(du vendeur)...*

Ainsi, il n'y avait aucune justification pour l'annulation des commandes. »

Ceci étant, l'arbitre qualifie d'abusive l'annulation des commandes par l'acheteur. Naturellement, cette faute contractuelle ouvrait un droit à réparation pour le vendeur. Toutefois, faute de preuve du dommage subi, l'arbitre écarte l'essentiel de la demande du vendeur :

« *L'Arbitre est forcé de constater que (le vendeur)... reste en demeure de prouver (qu'il) a souffert une perte sur (les) marchandises...* » ;

ou encore :

« *... (le vendeur) n'a pas prouvé les dommages...* » Ceci conduit l'arbitre à n'admettre que très partiellement la demande du vendeur.

OBSERVATIONS :

I. — Confronté au problème classique de la formation du contrat dès lors que l'offre initiale d'un contractant fait l'objet de modifications émanant de son destinataire, l'arbitre devait se prononcer sur la portée qu'il convient de donner au silence de ce dernier. La solution adoptée en l'espèce retiendra sans doute l'attention des lecteurs de cette chronique : le silence vaut acceptation (« Dans l'absence de protestations... il faut en conclure que l'acheteur accepte les modifications apportées par le vendeur »). Le résultat final ne doit pas étonner, mais la démarche de l'arbitre mérite un examen plus attentif. En effet, s'exprimant en application des usages du commerce international (par accord des parties), l'arbitre donne au silence de l'acheteur une portée qui ne découle ni des droits potentiellement concernés ni des instruments internationaux qui ont codifié les usages en matière de vente internationale.

Si l'arbitre avait agi en application du droit français, il aurait dû convenir d'une solution inverse car la présomption d'accord en cas de silence n'est pas une règle retenue de manière générale. Selon une jurisprudence bien établie, le silence ne vaut acceptation que dans des circonstances limitées.

Mais, dégagé de l'obligation d'appliquer un droit national par accord des parties, l'arbitre aurait pu en revanche se référer à la Convention de Vienne de 1980 sur la vente internationale de marchandises. Véritable instrument codificateur des usages commerciaux en matière de vente internationale, cette Convention est d'une extrême utilité même lorsque les pays d'origine des parties en litige ne l'ont pas ratifiée. Bien entendu, il ne s'agit pas de son application à titre de loi nationale mais plutôt comme repère des usages du commerce international. Après tout, en l'espèce, l'arbitre n'était-il pas chargé par les parties de faire application des *principes et usages généraux et normaux du commerce international* ?

A l'image du droit français, le principe est posé par l'article 18 de la Convention de Vienne : « Le silence ou l'inaction à eux seuls ne peuvent valoir acceptation. » Autrement dit, l'acceptation de l'offre (ou de la contre-proposition) doit intervenir de façon expresse et dans un délai raisonnable. Pour sa part, le premier alinéa de l'article 19 dispose que la réponse à l'offre contenant des additions, des limitations ou autres modifications « est un rejet de l'offre et constitue une contre-offre ». Une exception au principe général de l'article 18 existe dans le deuxième alinéa de l'article 19 : si les modifications n'altèrent pas substantiellement l'offre, le silence de l'auteur de l'offre peut valoir acceptation. Finalement, sont substantielles les modifications portant sur le prix, son paiement, la qualité de la marchandise, les quantités à livrer, le lieu et le moment de la livraison, l'étendue de la responsabilité d'une partie et le règlement de différends (article 19 alinéa 3).

En l'espèce, les modifications proposées par le vendeur portaient sur des éléments substantiels de l'offre puisqu'elles cherchaient à atténuer le régime des CGA pour les retards de livraison et pour la responsabilité en cas de non conformité des marchandises. En outre, le vendeur proposait des modifications sur le mode de règlement des commandes. L'article 19.3 de la Convention de Vienne exige l'acceptation expresse de ces modifications substantielles par l'auteur de l'offre. En d'autres termes, l'application de la Convention de Vienne n'aurait pas permis de considérer que le silence de l'acheteur vaut acceptation.

En revanche, le comportement des parties après les modifications aux CGA proposées par le vendeur justifie aisément la conclusion de l'arbitre. La réception des marchandises et le paiement du prix par l'acheteur sont signe d'acquiescement s'ils interviennent dans le délai stipulé ou dans un délai raisonnable (*cf.* article 18 alinéa 3 de la Convention de Vienne). Ce fut le cas en l'espèce.

II. — On ne s'attardera pas sur la question du droit matériel applicable car la solution résulte entièrement de la volonté des parties. Elles ont d'une part limité le choix de la loi du vendeur aux seules dispositions administratives prévues pour les sociétés en zone franche et, de l'autre, elles autorisent directement l'arbitre à trancher en application des usages du commerce international. Notons cependant au passage que l'arbitre n'éprouve pas le besoin de puiser dans les dispositions administratives du droit du vendeur pour trouver la solution du litige. Quant à l'application des usages commerciaux, la solution est classique : faute d'autorisation directe des parties, l'arbitre aurait pu s'y référer en vertu de l'article 13-5 du Règlement de la CCI.

La nouveauté de la sentence résulte en fait dans l'accord des parties dispensant l'arbitre de rechercher le droit applicable au fond du litige. C'est en usant de cette faculté que l'arbitre peut se borner à identifier certains usages ou principes (à plusieurs reprises assimilés à la *lex mercatoria* ; voir M. Mustill, *cit.* p. 94 pour une précision terminologique) tels que la bonne foi, *pacta sunt servanda* ou l'abus de droit sur lesquels nous reviendrons. Cependant, l'arbitre reconnaît les limites de la *lex mercatoria* : « ... elle ne contient évidemment pas de règles aussi détaillées que celles relatives aux taux d'intérêts ». Dans ces conditions, quelle est la loi qui doit s'appliquer à la détermination du taux d'intérêts ? La question est elliptique et les conflits de lois qu'elle pose sont parfois complexes, car la solution finalement retenue doit être respectueuse de l'ordre public susceptible d'intervenir au moment de l'exécution de la sentence. Mais en l'espèce la démarche de l'arbitre est abrégée ; la dénomination des indemnités réclamées en francs français militent en faveur de l'application du taux légal applicable en France. Même si la conclusion de l'arbitre n'est pas en elle-même contestable, la sentence aurait pu être complétée par un examen, en termes de conflits de lois, de questions telles que le pouvoir de l'arbitre pour accorder des intérêts, la période pour laquelle ils courent et le taux applicable (*cf.* M. Hunter et V. Triebel, Awarding Interest in International Arbitration, Some Observations Based on the Comparative Study of the Laws of England and Germany, *Journal of International Arbitration,* mars 1989).

III. — La livraison de la marchandise est l'obligation principale du vendeur. L'intérêt principal de cette espèce est de révéler les manquements par le vendeur à son obligation de livrer des marchandises conformes dans les délais prévus, alors qu'il agit comme partie demanderesse à la procédure d'arbitrage. En effet, malgré l'inexécution de son obligation principale, le vendeur reproche à l'acheteur (partie défenderesse) l'annulation abusive des commandes. Cette situation paradoxale conduit l'arbitre à un examen minutieux des dispositions contractuelles et des éléments de fait susceptibles d'établir la responsabilité des parties. Tour à tour, l'arbitre analyse les questions de la conformité et des retards dans la livraison. Saluons au passage les efforts de l'arbitre pour rétablir l'équilibre contractuel parfois perturbé par l'incorporation de clauses léonines dans des conditions générales.

Pour ce qui est de la conformité des marchandises, l'arbitre puise dans les CGA en quête d'un mécanisme contractuel de communication au vendeur des défauts constatés par l'acheteur. Il ne trouvera qu'une solution partielle. L'acheteur est tenu de communiquer au vendeur, dans les trois mois de leur découverte, les vices apparus après la réception de la marchandise. En revanche, le contrat est muet en ce qui concerne les vices découverts à la réception de la marchandise. Ici encore, l'arbitre aurait pu s'inspirer de la Convention de Vienne dont les articles 38 et 39 fixent une succession de délais tendant à protéger le vendeur de réclamations tardives ou trop vagues de l'acheteur.

Mais l'aveu du vendeur qui reconnaît sa responsabilité pour le marquage des marchandises permet à l'arbitre d'établir une présomption de fait contre lui ; « ... *(le vendeur) n'a pas toujours bien rempli ses obligations contractuelles relatives à la conformité des marchandises...* ». Des différents moyens contractuels offerts pour remédier à cette situation, c'est la réparation (remise en état des marchandises aux frais du vendeur) que l'acheteur a choisi. Dans ces conditions l'annulation de commandes, sanction incompatible avec la remise en état des marchandises, n'est pas autorisée par le contrat. La solution est tout à fait compatible avec le régime de sanctions instauré par la Convention de Vienne, qui fait primer le maintien du contrat (*cf.* J.-P. Beraudo et Ph. Kahn, *Le nouveau droit de la vente internationale de marchandises, Convention de Vienne 11 avril 1980,* Marchés Internationaux, Chambre de Commerce et d'Industrie de Paris, août/septembre 1989, p. 97 ; « L'approche philosophique... consiste à privilégier la bonne foi, c'est-à-dire le maintien du contrat, son exécution matérielle, même si des équivalents monétaires peuvent compenser une inexécution totale ou partielle et s'ajouter ou se substituer à l'exécution en nature. »).

L'annulation des commandes par l'acheteur pour sanctionner les retards dans la livraison est également jugée abusive par l'arbitre. L'envoi par l'acheteur d'une lettre d'annulation non motivée et sans mise en demeure préalable ne peut être retenue comme étant conforme au principe de la bonne foi. Il faut d'ailleurs abonder dans le sens de l'arbitre lorsqu'il affirme, en interprétation des CGA, que le vendeur ne peut pas être tenu responsable pour les retards consécutifs à la faute de l'acheteur. Une clause contractuelle (purement potestative) qui fait dépendre les obligations d'une partie de la seule volonté de l'autre partie est susceptible de heurter l'ordre public de certains pays. Il faut en revanche se demander s'il n'est pas envisageable que des parties s'accordent pour que l'une d'entre elles prenne à sa charge certains événements de force majeure. Cette extension de responsabilité, généralement en contrepartie d'avantages financiers, serait-elle jugée abusive ?

La sentence de l'arbitre gagnerait à être nuancée sur ce point.

Finalement, le commentaire quant à la réparation contractuelle du vendeur ne peut qu'être bref. En effet, à plusieurs reprises dans la sentence, l'arbitre insiste sur la carence des dossiers des parties. Faute de preuve du préjudice subi, le vendeur ne peut rendre effectif le droit à réparation ouvert en sa faveur par la décision de l'arbitre.

I. — **Loi applicable.** — Application de la Convention de Vienne de 1980 (non). — Règles de conflit des pays concernés. — Application du droit yougoslave.

II. — **Vente internationale.** — Respect du prix convenu malgré l'augmentation des marchandises sur le marché. — Refus de livrer au prix convenu. — Faute contractuelle du vendeur. — Application du droit yougoslave. — Références à la Convention de Vienne de 1980 et à la Loi uniforme sur la vente internationale de La Haye.

Sentence rendue dans l'affaire 6281 en 1989.

L'affaire entre le vendeur yougoslave et l'acheteur égyptien a été tranché par un arbitre unique à Paris, lieu de l'arbitrage contractuel. Les parties avaient, en 1987, passé un contrat pour la vente FOB d'une certaine quantité d'acier au prix contractuel fixé. La première livraison eut lieu sans incident. Toutefois, le contrat accordait un délai à l'acheteur pour exercer une option d'achat d'une quantité supplémentaire d'acier aux mêmes prix et conditions prévus dans le contrat pour la première livraison. Se referant à cette disposition contractuelle, l'acheteur informa le vendeur de son intention d'exercer l'option. Au vu du refus du vendeur de respecter le prix convenu et à la suite de l'échec des négociations tendant à régler le différend, l'acheteur s'est adressé à un autre fournisseur sans pour autant renoncer à saisir l'instance arbitrale ultérieurement.

Devant l'arbitre, le vendeur a avancé trois arguments justificatifs de son refus. La première défense, tendant à établir que le contrat ne donnait qu'un *average effective price* fut abandonnée par le vendeur. En effet, la clarté de la disposition du contrat exigeant le respect de *the same price and conditions*, ne laissait planer aucun doute sur la portée de son obligation.

Le vendeur reprochait ensuite à l'acheteur l'inexécution de son obligation d'ouvrir une lettre de crédit rendant ainsi l'exercice de l'option inopposable. Cet argument fut aussitôt écarté par l'arbitre :

« ... *(le vendeur) n'a jamais accepté de livrer (l'acier) au prix convenu. Ceci étant, il serait irrationnel d'alléguer que la non-ouverture de la lettre de crédit est un obstacle à la validité de l'option ; après tout, (l'acheteur) aurait encouru des frais... en ouvrant une lettre de crédit, alors qu'il n'y avait pas de possibilité de livraison. (Le vendeur) ne saurait invoquer un acte de (l'acheteur) qu'il a lui-même causé.* »

Le vendeur invoque enfin le caractère déraisonnable d'une livraison au prix convenu alors que la hausse du prix mondial de l'acier venait s'ajouter à des frais de production importants. Sur ce point l'arbitre remarque à juste titre que :

« ... *les deux arguments ne sont ni économiquement interdépendants ni obligatoirement liés. Les coûts de production d'un entrepreneur sont déterminés par certains facteurs essentiellement locaux, alors que les prix mondiaux sont le résultat du jeu de l'offre et la demande.* »

Mais, pour trancher le fond, l'arbitre examine la doctrine du changement de circonstances à la lumière du droit matériel choisi.

« *A propos du caractère prétendu déraisonnable du prix convenu, compte tenu de la hausse des prix sur le marché mondial, il est primordial de déterminer les dispositions juridiques qui doivent s'appliquer à l'examen du contrat de vente et donc au nœud du problème. En tout état de cause, la Convention de Vienne des Nations Unies sur les contrats de vente internationale de marchandises, du 11 avril 1980, ne peut s'appliquer telle quelle. La convention est en vigueur en Egypte et en Yougoslavie, de même qu'en France, mais en vertu du § 2 de l'article 100, elle s'applique uniquement aux contrats de vente conclus après sa date d'entrée en vigueur, c'est-à-dire après le 1ᵉʳ janvier 1988. Le présent contrat de vente a été conclu le 20 août 1987.*

La question de la loi applicable doit donc être examinée sur la base des règles du droit international privé.

Selon le droit international privé égyptien, la loi qui s'applique est celle du pays où le contrat est signé, sauf convention contraire des parties, si elles ont leur principal établissement dans des Etats différents (article 19 du Code civil de 1949).

Selon le droit international privé yougoslave, la loi qui s'applique est celle du pays où le vendeur a son établissement principal au moment où il (ou l'autre partie) a reçu l'offre, s'il n'y a pas d'accord entre les parties sur la loi applicable (loi sur le droit international privé du 15 février 1982, Sluzbeni liste n° 43/1982).

La France est membre de la Convention sur la loi applicable aux contrats de vente internationale de marchandises, conclue à La Haye le 15 juin 1955. Le § 1 de l'article 3 de cette Convention stipule qu'à défaut de loi déclarée par les parties, le contrat est régi par la loi interne du pays où le vendeur a sa résidence habituelle au moment où il reçoit la commande (il importe peu que la « commande » fasse référence à l'offre en tant que telle ou à l'acceptation de l'offre ; en outre, aucune des exceptions de la Convention ne s'applique).

L'établissement principal et la résidence habituelle du vendeur au moment considéré étant en Yougoslavie et le contrat de vente ayant été conclu en Yougoslavie, toutes les règles applicables en matière de droit privé international font référence au droit matériel yougoslave. »

L'application du droit yougoslave, à plusieurs reprises confronté aux dispositions de la Convention de Vienne et à la Loi uniforme sur la vente internationale (La Haye), conduit l'arbitre à établir la responsabilité contractuelle du vendeur :

« Les paragraphes 1 et 2 de la loi yougoslave de 1978 sur les obligations stipulent (traduction libre) :

> *« 1) En cas de survenance après la conclusion du contrat de circonstances de nature à rendre difficile l'exécution de contrat par l'une des parties ou à empêcher que soit atteint l'objectif du contrat, et cela dans une mesure telle qu'il devient évident que le contrat cesse de correspondre à l'intention des parties et qu'il serait généralement considéré comme injuste de le maintenir en vigueur sous une forme inchangée, la partie dont l'exécution a été rendue difficile ou qui a été empêchée d'atteindre l'objectif du contrat par la modification des circonstances peut demander que le contrat soit résilié.*

> *« 2) La résiliation du contrat ne peut être demandée si la partie qui invoque la modification des circonstances aurait dû tenir compte de ces circonstances au moment de la conclusion du contrat ou aurait pu éviter ou surmonter ces circonstances ».*

La définition ci-dessus correspond à celle de la « frustration » en droit anglo-américain ou du « Wegfall der Geschäftsgrundlage » en droit allemand et autrichien. Les commentateurs yougoslaves (Blagojevic-Krulj ; Vizner) parlent de clause « rebus sic stantibus », essentiellement à cause du contexte historique de la loi yougoslave. Après tout, une « véritable » clause « rebus sic stantibus » ne maintiendrait (au sens positif) les relations juridiques qu'aussi longtemps qu'il n'y aurait aucun changement, indépendamment de toute prévisibilité ou applicabilité. Un tel concept ne figure ni dans la loi sur les obligations ni dans le droit commercial d'aucun pays (sauf, tout au plus, pour des obligations illimitées telles que les relations de location, mais essentiellement pour des obligations de soutien). Sinon, toute transaction commerciale serait exposée à l'incertitude ou serait même totalement impossible chaque fois que les conventions mutuelles ne seraient pas exécutées au moment même où le contrat est conclu.

En plus de l'article 133 de la loi sur les obligations, l'Usage n° 56 continue d'être en vigueur selon le droit yougoslave, qui inclut dans la liste des raisons entraînant une frustration des « événements économiques tels que des hausses ou des baisses de prix extrêmement soudaines et importantes ».

Par conséquent, il faut savoir si la hausse du prix de l'acier, admise par les deux parties... est une hausse de prix extrêmement soudaine et extrêmement importante (§ 1 de l'article 133 et Usage n° 56) ; et si c'est le cas, si le Défendeur aurait dû envisager cet événement au moment où le contrat a été conclu (§ 2 de l'article 133 ; en tout cas, l'événement ne pouvait être évité ou surmonté).

L'expérience montre que les prix du marché mondial de produits tels que l'acier fluctuent. Au moment où le contrat a été conclu, les prix de l'acier avaient commencé à augmenter légèrement — tendance qui s'est poursuivie entre la conclusion du contrat et l'exercice de l'option et est même devenue plus prononcée à la fin de 1988.

Selon Blagojevic-Krulj, dans les commentaires de la loi sur les obliga-tions, p. 351, le tribunal doit décider à partir de quel montant du préjudice l'exécution du contrat est encore ou n'est plus raisonnable, si l'une des parties subit un éventuel préjudice lorsqu'elle exécute ses obligations contractuelles sans modification du contrat. Quoi qu'il en soit, ce préjudice doit dépasser un risque commercial raisonnable. Dans le cas présent, l'aug-mentation des prix du marché mondial... est légèrement inférieure à 13,16 %. Devoir vendre un produit au prix convenu au lieu d'un prix supérieur de 13,16 % entre parfaitement dans la marge habituelle.

De plus, cette évolution était prévisible. Un vendeur raisonnable devait s'attendre à ce que les prix de l'acier puissent encore augmenter, peut-être même plus fortement que dans les faits. Savoir si le Défendeur s'est com-porté en vendeur raisonnable en accordant l'option « au même prix » pour une période relativement longue, dans ces circonstances, est une question qui n'entre pas dans le cadre de la mission de l'arbitre. Quoi qu'il en soit, même la loi yougoslave exclut qu'un vendeur puisse inciter un acheteur à signer un premier contrat contenant l'option « au même prix », tout en ayant pour arrière-pensée de pouvoir invoquer l'article 133 de la Loi sur les obligations si les prix devaient continuer à augmenter.

Blagojevic-Krulj conseillent également une approche stricte de l'évalua-tion de l'imprévisibilité. Ces auteurs vont même jusqu'à comparer l'article 133 aux dispositions du § 1 de l'article 74 de la Loi uniforme sur la vente internationale des objets mobiliers corporels (La Haye), qui reprend — presque littéralement — le § 1 de l'article 79 de la Convention de Vienne sur la vente. Les deux articles prévoient l'exonération en cas de circonstances que des personnes raisonnables placées dans une situation identique ne seraient pas tenues (ou susceptibles) de prendre en considération, ni d'éviter ou de surmonter. Par conséquent, les faits doivent être considérés comme proches d'un acte de force majeure...

L'arbitre estime donc qu'il n'y a pas lieu d'appliquer l'article 133. Il n'est pas non plus nécessaire de discuter en détail les paragraphes 3 à 5 de cet article, qui concernent la forme et le traitement d'une demande de résiliation ou de modification d'un contrat en vertu du § 1, ni l'article 134, qui stipule qu'une partie en difficulté doit en informer l'autre partie...

5. Le Défendeur maintient que l'achat par le Demandeur de... l'acier auprès d'un autre fournisseur ne peut être interprété comme un achat de remplacement, puisque le Défendeur n'a pas été informé à l'avance de l'intention précise d'achat du Demandeur...

Il est primordial de définir clairement l'interaction juridique entre les articles 262 et 525 de la loi yougoslave sur les obligations. L'article 262 accorde à toute partie contractante le droit de demander une indemnisation du préjudice qu'elle a subi en raison de la non-exécution, de l'exécution imparfaite ou du retard d'exécution des obligations de l'autre partie. L'article 525, qui concerne les achats de remplacement, ouvre un recours à la partie lésée, losqu'elle prouve le préjudice subi. Si l'on devait supposer que les dommages-intérêts ne sont pas dus en cas de non-respect de l'obligation de notification contenue dans l'article 525, aucune sanction ne pourrait être imposée en cas de non livraison de marchandises pour lesquelles il n'y a pas d'équivalent ni en cas de non livraison de marchandises lorsqu'il n'est plus possible de se procurer en temps utile leur équivalent par un achat de remplacement...

Il n'est pas non plus significatif que l'article 525 doive être interprété comme signifiant que la partie en défaut doit être informée à l'avance d'un achat de remplacement effectif. La demande d'indemnisation en raison de l'achat de remplacement est toutefois légèrement inférieure à la différence avec le prix sur le marché mondial au moment considéré, sur la base du fret le moins cher. En vertu de l'article 262 de la loi sur les obligations, le Demandeur ne peut réclamer plus que le montant du préjudice réel.

Il faut remarquer au passage que le résultat aurait été le même si l'on avait considéré les articles 74 à 77 de la Convention de Vienne sur la vente, qui compte actuellement 19 Etats membres et que l'on pourra bientôt qualifier de loi universelle, compte tenu du nombre important de ratifications et d'adhésions prévues dans un proche avenir.

Le résultat ci-dessus n'est absolument pas surprenant. Après tout, Blagojevic-Krulj précisent dans leurs Commentaires de la Loi sur les obligations, p. 1028, que l'article 525 de la loi correspond à l'article 85 de la loi uniforme (de la Haye) sur la vente internationale des objets mobiliers corporels. En commentant cette dernière, Tunc indique que l'acheteur doit au moins percevoir une indemnité résultant de la simple comparaison entre le prix convenu et le prix payé pour la marchandise achetée en remplacement. L'article 85 de la loi uniforme a été développé dans l'article 75 de la Convention de Vienne sur la vente, sans que le fond en soit modifié. Knapp, dans le Commentaire par Bianca-Bonell de la loi internationale en matière de vente, la Convention de Vienne de 1980 sur la vente, p. 551, confirme que si l'achat de remplacement n'est pas effectué de manière raisonnable ou dans un délai raisonnable, les dommages-intérêts devront être calculés comme si aucune transaction de substitution n'était intervenue, c'est-à-dire conformément aux autres dispositions relatives aux dommages-intérêts et notamment à l'article 74 (qui est la règle générale en matière d'évaluation des dommages-intérêts et remplit la même fonction que l'article 262 de la loi yougoslave sur les obligations). Dans certaines circonstances, des dommages-intérêts complémentaires peuvent être demandés en vertu de cet article 74, également (au-delà) des dommages-intérêts dus sur la base de l'achat de remplacement, conformément à l'article 75... ».

OBSERVATIONS :

I. — Outre son caractère très orthodoxe, la démarche adoptée par l'arbitre pour la détermination de la loi applicable est d'une grande netteté. Ainsi, a-t-il d'abord le réflexe de s'interroger sur l'application de la Convention de Vienne de 1980 relative à la vente internationale de marchandises, en vigueur dans les trois pays potentiellement concernés, à savoir, la France (lieu de l'arbitrage), l'Egypte (pays de la demanderesse) et la Yougoslavie (pays de la défenderesse). Dans un second temps cependant, il déclare ne pouvoir fonder sa décision sur ce texte lequel n'est applicable qu'aux contrats conclus postérieurement à sa date d'entrée en vigueur. Cette référence à la Convention de Vienne, caractéristique de la sentence, devrait, dans un proche avenir, inspirer d'autres arbitres du commerce international.

Faute d'application directe de ce traité, l'arbitre aborde le problème en termes de droit international privé. C'est ainsi qu'après examen des règles de conflit égyptienne (lieu de signature du contrat), française (lieu de résidence du vendeur) et yougoslave (lieu de l'établissement principal du vendeur), il retient le droit matériel yougoslave. En effet, toutes les règles de conflit conduisent à l'application de ce droit.

L'intérêt principal de la solution retenue réside dans le rapprochement opéré par l'arbitre entre les dispositions du droit yougoslave et celles de textes internationaux telles que la Loi uniforme de La Haye sur la vente internationale des objets mobiliers corporels ou la Convention de Vienne de 1980. Ainsi en est-il de la théorie de l'imprévisibilité ou du calcul de l'indemnité due à l'acheteur victime de l'inexécution.

II. — La vente internationale de matières, essentiellement premières, pose le problème de la fixation et du maintien du prix, particulièrement lorsque l'exécution s'étale dans le temps. En l'espèce, les parties ont renoncé à négocier une clause de réajustement du prix, préférant plutôt subordonner la livraison éventuelle à la condition de l'exercice par l'acheteur d'une option dont la validité était limitée dans le temps. Le vendeur, quant à lui, s'engageait à respecter le prix stipulé dans le contrat pour la première expédition d'acier. Ce mécanisme met l'acheteur à l'abri des augmentations de prix intervenues durant la période de validité de l'option. Les risques d'une hausse dans le prix mondial de l'acier sont par conséquent transférés au vendeur qui ne saurait les accepter avec l'arrière-pensée d'y échapper une fois que l'évolution du prix lui est défavorable. D'ailleurs, l'arbitre rappelle qu'il ne lui appartient pas de déterminer si la défenderesse s'est conduite comme un acheteur raisonnable en acceptant *the same price and conditions clause* pour un produit comme l'acier.

La défense du vendeur ne résiste pas à l'examen que l'arbitre lui fait subir en droit yougoslave. En effet, pour qu'il y ait *rebus sic stantibus*, l'article 133 de la Loi des obligations exige, d'une part, que l'augmentation du prix soit soudaine et importante et, d'autre part, qu'elle soit imprévisible. Or, en l'espèce, la hausse était à la fois progressive, raisonnable (13,6 %) et prévisible (« *Un vendeur raisonnable* » affirme l'arbitre « *devait s'attendre à ce que les prix de l'acier puissent encore augmenter...* »).

L'inexistence d'un changement brutal de circonstances au sens de la loi yougoslave engageait donc la responsabilité du vendeur. Et c'est en matière de calcul de la réparation à laquelle peut prétendre l'acheteur victime de l'inexécution que l'arbitre consacre à nouveau le rapprochement entre la loi yougoslave et la Convention de Vienne de 1980. Le principe posé par l'article 262 de la Loi des obligations (et par les lois nationales en général) correspond à celui de l'article 74 de la Convention de Vienne : les éléments constitutifs des dommages-intérêts sont la perte subie *(damnum emergens)* et le manque à gagner *(lucrum cessans)*. Mais à côté de ce régime général, l'article 525 de la loi yougoslave et 75 de la Convention de Vienne ouvrent en faveur de l'acheteur un droit de réparation spécifique. L'acheteur contraint de réaliser un achat de remplacement pourra récupérer la différence entre le prix contractuel non respecté par le vendeur et le prix de l'achat de remplacement. Nous approuvons la démarche de l'arbitre qui confronte la solution en droit yougoslave avec celle qui aurait résulté de l'application de la Convention de Vienne de 1980. En l'espèce, il y a coïncidence. N'est-ce pas un moyen de montrer les vertus d'unification de ce texte ?

I. — Clause compromissoire. — Arbitrage international. — Code de procédure civile égyptien, article 502 (3). — Nécessité de nommer l'arbitre dans la convention d'arbitrage (non). — Validité formelle de la convention d'arbitrage international.

II. — Contrat. — Conclusion par une succursale n'ayant pas la personnalité morale. — Principes généraux du droit des sociétés.

III. — Clause compromissoire. — Opposabilité de la clause au dirigeant social (non). — Usages du commerce international. — Bonne foi. — Recherche d'un fondement volontaire.

IV. — Résiliation. — Réparation du préjudice. — Devoir de minimiser les pertes.

V. — Garanties bancaires à première demande. — Compétence des arbitres pour statuer sur les relations entre la banque et le bénéficiaire (non). — Appel abusif de la garantie. — Compétence des arbitres (oui).

entence rendue dans l'affaire 5721 en 1990

Dans cette affaire, le Tribunal arbitral siégeant à Genève, était saisi d'une emande introduite par une société européenne à l'encontre de deux personnes norales X USA et X Egypte, ainsi que contre une personne physique M. Z, résident de X USA.

La demanderesse alléguait en effet que, désignée en qualité de sous-traitant ar le maître de l'ouvrage, elle avait en juin 1983 conclu avec X Egypte – qui s'était présentée comme filiale en cours de constitution en Egypte d'une société X USA représentée par son Président M. Z – deux contrats de sous-traitance our respectivement la fourniture de biens et la réalisation de divers travaux dans ne usine en construction située dans la banlieue du Caire. M. Z avait signé les eux contrats pour le compte de X Egypte.

Au termes des contrats, X Egypte, à qui incombait en qualité d'entrepreneur énéral un rôle de coordination technique et administrative, devait réaliser les ravaux de génie civil et le gros œuvre, et fournir à la demanderesse des installa-ions lui permettant d'exécuter ses propres obligations.

La demanderesse affirmait avoir rencontré de graves difficultés, X Egypte 'exécutant pas les obligations auxquelles elle s'était engagée. Cette situation urait alors conduit le maître de l'ouvrage à expulser X Egypte du site et à confier . la demanderesse la responsabilité directe du marché.

X Egypte ayant en particulier tenté d'appeler plusieurs garanties à première lemande relatives les unes à la restitution de l'acompte à la commande et les utres à la bonne fin des travaux qui lui avaient été fournies par la demanderesse, elle-ci demandait au Tribunal arbitral, entre autres, de constater la résiliation les contrats et de prononcer la caducité des lettres de garantie.

Les deux contrats précisent qu'ils sont expressément soumis au droit égyptien, es arbitres ayant les pouvoirs d'amiable compositeur.

Dans le cadre de la procédure arbitrale, l'ensemble des défenderesses avaient lésigné conjointement un arbitre. Ce n'est que par la suite – alors que X Egypte dmettait seule être liée par la clause compromissoire – que X USA et M. Z ont n particulier soulevé une exception d'incompétence au motif qu'ils ne sont pas oumis à la procédure d'arbitrage.

En tout premier lieu, le Tribunal arbitral siégeant à Genève a tenu à se prononcer sur la validité formelle de la clause compromissoire, un moyen tiré de 'invalidité de la clause par rapport à l'article 502 (3) du Code de procédure civile gyptien (CPCE) ayant été soulevé. Le Tribunal rejette ce moyen en ces termes :

L'article 502/3 CPCE dispose :

" Sous réserve de l'observation des dispositions de lois spéciales, il est requis de lésigner nommément les arbitres du Tribunal arbitral dans la clause contractuelle l'arbitrage, ou bien dans un accord séparé. "

L'une des défenderesses affirme que cette disposition du Code de procédure civile gyptien est applicable en l'espèce et que son inobservation entraîne la nullité de la lause d'arbitrage. On peut se demander si, même en droit interne, cette disposition onduit aux conséquences draconniennes énoncées. Le texte de la loi ne contient

401

en effet aucune disposition expresse relative à l'annulation en cas de violation de l'alinéa 3 ; cet article se contente de prévoir la nullité dans la seule hypothèse d'une violation du premier alinéa. Le Tribunal ne saurait en tout état de cause donner à cet article une portée internationale, étant donné les besoins du commerce international. Il est vrai que l'article 502/3 CPCE a donné lieu en Egypte à une importante jurisprudence et à des discussions doctrinales (voir en particulier Sigvard Jarvin, L'exécution des sentences arbitrales, Paris, 1989, notamment p. 32 s.).

Dans une décision du 26 avril 1982 (Mabrouk Trading Import and Export c. C. Arab Continental Navigation Co), la Cour suprême d'Egypte a établi qu'un arbitrage devant avoir lieu hors d'Egypte pourrait être valable et ne pas violer l'ordre public égyptien, même si les conditions de l'article 502/3 CPCE n'étaient pas réunies. Cette disposition n'est pas d'ordre public. Ce qui est contraire à la loi impérative égyptienne n'est pas nécessairement contraire à l'ordre public égyptien. Le Tribunal expose en particulier :

" Attendu que la clause arbitrale, établie dans le contrat de bail – objet de ce procès – stipule que tout litige qui découle de ce contrat sera référé à l'arbitrage à Londres.

Attendu que le législateur admet l'accord à procéder à l'arbitrage à l'étranger, et ne considère pas cela comme susceptible de porter atteinte à l'ordre public.

— Il s'ensuit que la validité et les effets consécutifs à la clause arbitrale sont soumis aux dispositions de la loi britannique, autrement dit, la loi du pays choisi comme lieu d'arbitrage, sous réserve que ces dispositions de la loi ne contredisent en rien les règles de l'ordre public en Egypte.

Attendu ce qui précède et que le jugement attaqué – après avoir dénié au requérant le droit d'invoquer la clause arbitrale – a prononcé et établi l'invalidité de cette clause, du fait qu'elle omet de mentionner nommément les arbitres choisis, comme requis par l'article 502/3 du Code de procédure, et contrevient donc à l'observation de cette loi, ayant failli à la subordination de cette clause à la loi britannique qui est la loi applicable.

Attendu qu'il est exclu d'écarter la loi britannique qui est ici applicable, sous prétexte qu'elle contrevient à l'article 502/3 du Code de procédure – en supposant même que ce soit le cas – parce que la seule condition pour écarter la loi britannique (en vertu de l'article 28 du Code civil) est qu'elle soit en contradiction avec les règles de l'ordre public en Egypte, c'est-à-dire contraire aux fondements d'ordre social, politique, économique et moral, sur lesquels repose l'Etat, mettant en cause l'intérêt supérieur de la nation, le fait qu'elle contredise un autre texte de la loi n'étant pas un motif valable pour en écarter l'application.

Attendu que l'article 502/3 du Code de procédure (stipulant que les noms des arbitres doivent nécessairement figurer dans la clause arbitrale ou dans un accord séparé) ne concerne en rien l'ordre public, comme démontré plus haut. "

Par la suite, et à plusieurs reprises, des parties égyptiennes ont contesté la validité des clauses d'arbitrage CCI. En particulier, plusieurs décisions ont été rendues dans lesquelles les parties égyptiennes ont plaidé, avec succès, que les entreprises publiques ne pouvaient pas donner leur accord à un arbitrage international... L'argumentation consistant à soutenir que la désignation des arbitres doit être faite impérativement par les parties elles-mêmes sous peine de nullité de la clause compromissoire est assurément contraire à l'esprit de l'arbitrage, d'autant plus lorsqu'elle est invoquée une fois le litige né et la procédure arbitrale entamée... Il semble d'ailleurs bien que la situation évolue dans un sens favorable à l'arbitrage international. »

Citant un extrait d'un jugement daté du 7 février 1987 du Tribunal de première instance de Giza (*Cf. JDI*, 1987, p. 1036) et mentionnant une décision du 18 février 1986 du Tribunal de première instance du Caire Sud, décisions qui toutes deux admettent la validité de la procédure arbitrale sans se référer d'office à l'article 502 (3) du CPCE, le Tribunal conclut :

« *Dans ces conditions, le Tribunal arbitral estime que l'exigence du droit égyptien interne exprimée à l'article 502/3 CPCE ne saurait être étendue au domaine de l'arbitrage international.* »

La validité formelle de la clause ayant été reconnue, il appartenait ensuite au Tribunal arbitral de se prononcer préalablement sur l'existence de X Egypte, seule défenderesse à admettre la compétence des arbitres. Celle-ci, au moment de la signature des contrats, s'était présentée comme filiale – en cours de constitution – de la société X USA.

« *La requête d'arbitrage est dirigée notamment contre les sociétés X USA et X Egypte. La réponse à la requête d'arbitrage indique séparément les entités égyptienne et américaine. M. Z affirme que les contrats en cause ont été passés par la " société " égyptienne et non par la société américaine...*

L'Acte de mission indique séparément le nom des deux entités, qui semblent juridiquement distinctes...

Les incertitudes qui ont existé dans l'esprit de la demanderesse, comme dans celui du Tribunal, ont été levées par le Mémoire en réponse déposé au nom de M. Z seulement.

Ce mémoire établit que la défenderesse appelée X Egypte n'est pas une entité juridique distincte d'X USA, mais une simple succursale de la société américaine (" a branch office "). Selon l'avis de M. Z, confirmé par les pièces du dossier (Replication memorandum, Annexes 1 et 2), X Egypte n'a eu aucune individualité juridique. Elle n'a jamais été qu'une succursale. C'est donc bien la société défenderesse n° 1, à savoir X USA, qui par l'intermédiaire de sa succursale égyptienne, a signé les contrats du 21 juin 1983. On relèvera d'ailleurs qu'à l'époque M. Z intervenait aussi bien en qualité de président du conseil de la société américaine que de représentant de la succursale égyptienne. La mention d'X Inc. sur le contrat ne peut être comprise que comme une référence à la société américaine dont l'adresse égyptienne était située en Egypte.

La nature même de X Egypte implique que seule la société X USA a pu signer le contrat. Soutenir que la société américaine n'est pas concernée par ce litige parce que le contrat n'a été signé que par la succursale égyptienne est contraire aux principes généraux du droit des sociétés, contraire même au bon sens : n'ayant pas d'existence propre, le " branch office " ne pouvait que représenter X USA.

Le Tribunal constatera donc que les conclusions qui sont prises à l'encontre d'X Egypte sont irrecevables et sans objet. Mais en même temps, le Tribunal admettra que l'activité de la succursale égyptienne est englobée dans celle de la société américaine. »

Ayant décidé d'englober les activités de la succursale X Egypte dans les activités de la société X USA (qui sera dorénavant identifiée dans les extraits de la sentence sous la lettre X) il restait encore au Tribunal arbitral à se prononcer sur l'éventuelle opposabilité de la clause d'arbitrage à M. Z qui était attrait à la procédure d'arbitrage ès qualité de Président de X :

« *La clause compromissoire qui établit la compétence du Tribunal arbitral est contenue dans les contrats du 21 juin 1983. La demanderesse entend étendre la portée de cette clause à M. Z, troisième défendeur. Elle veut, de ce fait, percer ou lever le voile social...*

Le Tribunal arbitral n'examinera pas cette délicate question à la lumière du seul droit applicable au fond du litige, le droit égyptien (voir l'arrêt Isover Saint-Gobain v. Dow Chemical France et autres, CA Paris 21 oct. 1983 : Rev. arb., 1984, 98). L'article 13, paragraphe 5 du Règlement d'arbitrage de la CCI invite le Tribunal à tenir compte des usages du commerce et des textes contractuels. Dans cette perspective, le Tribunal est en droit de se référer à la lex mercatoria. L'autonomie de la clause d'arbitrage, largement reconnue aujourd'hui, justifie cette référence à une règle non étatique déduite des seuls usages du commerce international. En particulier, il se justifie de dissocier le fond du contrat de la validité et la portée de la clause d'arbitrage. Ce sera donc en vertu de la notion générale de la bonne foi en affaires, et des usages du commerce international que le Tribunal arbitral se prononcera. Cela étant, il est intéressant de constater que les divers droits nationaux concernés par la présente cause conduisent à un résultat similaire. Il s'agit du droit américain, comme droit d'incorporation de la société X, du droit suisse, du lieu du siège du tribunal et du droit égyptien applicable au fond du litige.

Le problème posé par la levée du voile social n'est pas tout à fait récent, mais il a pris de l'importance notamment en raison du grand développement du droit des groupes de sociétés dès les années 1950.

Aux Etats-Unis, lieu d'incorporation de la défenderesse X et lieu de domicile de M. Z, le principe est, comme en droit continental, celui de la responsabilité de la société sur ses propres biens, à l'exclusion de celles de ses actionnaires (voir Rudolf Tschäni, Amerikanische Lehren für schweizerisches Konzernrecht ? in La Société anonyme suisse, 1980, p. 65 s.). En règle générale, ce principe n'est pas évincé par le seul fait que le capital d'une société est en main d'une autre et que les " officers " ou " directors " sont les mêmes pour la société mère et pour la société fille. Cependant, il est permis de s'éloigner de cette règle dans des circonstances particulières. C'est le cas lorsque la société fille est un " mere instrument " de la société mère, c'est-à-dire que l'une des parties est en réalité un simple représentant ou un simple instrument dans les mains de l'autre... La théorie de la levée du voile social... se justifie toutes les fois que le principe de la responsabilité limitée permet de conduire à des situations totalement injustes.

En droit suisse, lieu du siège du Tribunal d'arbitral, la doctrine et la jurisprudence se sont également prononcées sur la question de la levée du voile social (E. Homburger, Zum Durchgriff im schweizerischen Gesellschaftsrecht, Revue suisse de jurisprudence, 1951, p. 253 s.). La théorie du " Durchgriff " est fondée sur la prohibition de l'abus de droit. Dans cette optique, il faut toujours examiner concrètement si l'institution de la personne morale (et l'indépendance juridique qui s'y attache) est détournée de son but par les personnes qui en ont la maîtrise (ATF 112, II, 1, en matière immobilière par exemple). Il ne faut donc accepter l'exception de la levée du voile social qu'avec une prudente réserve. Il n'est fait abstraction de cette indépendance qu'exceptionnellement, lorsqu'elle est invoquée dolosivement, c'est-à-dire contrairement au principe de la bonne foi...

Le droit égyptien ne contredit pas ces règles générales. Il accorde lui aussi une importance décisive au principe de la bonne foi et sanctionne toute attitude abusive de droit (cf. les art. 5 et 148 CCE).

....

Il faut ajouter que l'essentiel de l'arbitrage est fondé sur le principe consensuel. De même, l'extension de la clause d'arbitrage doit avoir un fondement volontaire.

Certes, cette volonté peut être implicite seulement, sinon la discussion sur l'extension n'aurait aucun sens. Cette extension ne doit en revanche pas intervenir au titre de sanction du comportement d'un tiers. Une telle intervention doit être réservée aux tribunaux ordinaires devant lesquels une partie pourra toujours faire valoir l'argument tiré de la levée du voile social.

En résumé, l'appartenance de deux sociétés à un même groupe ou la domination d'un actionnaire ne sont jamais, à elles seules, des raisons suffisantes justifiant de plein droit la levée du voile social. Cependant, lorsqu'une société ou une personne individuelle apparaît comme étant le pivot des rapports contractuels intervenus dans une affaire particulière, il convient d'examiner avec soin si l'indépendance juridique des parties ne doit pas, exceptionnellement, être écartée au profit d'un jugement global. On acceptera une telle exception lorsque apparaît une confusion entretenue par le groupe ou l'actionnaire majoritaire. »

Ces principes une fois énoncés, le Tribunal arbitral procède alors à l'examen et à l'analyse des faits de la cause s'arrêtant sur chacune des présomptions pouvant apparaître sérieuses relatives tant au patrimoine qu'aux différentes adresses et au contrôle de X, qui tendraient à établir une confusion entre M. Z et la société X. De cette analyse, le Tribunal arbitral tire les conclusions suivantes :

« *Le Tribunal estime, après avoir mûrement considéré l'ensemble des éléments de preuve dont il dispose, qu'il ne doit pas étendre, en l'espèce, la clause arbitrale à M. Z. Cette conclusion se fonde sur les raisons suivantes.*

Une juridiction arbitrale doit être très circonspecte lorsqu'il s'agit d'étendre une clause à un dirigeant qui est formellement intervenu ès-qualité. L'extension suppose que la personne morale n'a été que l'instrument du commerce de la personne physique, de sorte que l'on puisse faire rejaillir sur celui-ci les contrats et engagements souscrits par celle-là. Or les présomptions énumérées ci-dessus ne permettent pas d'avoir une certitude totale à cet égard.

La demanderesse a admis, au cours de l'audience du 29-06-89, qu'au début des relations contractuelles elle a procédé à des vérifications, par son directeur commercial responsable des exportations, qui s'est rendu à New York, et constaté que la société X avait des bureaux et une activité effective.

Il n'est donc pas certain que la demanderesse ait eu l'intention de traiter avec M. Z à travers X, ni que M. Z ait eu l'intention d'être personnellement partie à la convention d'arbitrage. Si la demanderesse entend mettre en jeu la responsabilité de M. Z pour dol ou tout autre agissement, tel que, le cas échéant, le démantèlement ou l'appropriation de l'actif de X, il lui appartiendra de l'attraire devant les juridictions compétentes : l'extension de la clause d'arbitrage ne constitue pas la sanction d'une responsabilité, mais doit conserver, comme il a été dit, un fondement volontaire.

Le Tribunal estime donc que la clause arbitrale contenue dans les contrats du 21 juin 1983 ne s'applique pas à M. Z personnellement et que celui-ci doit être exclu de la procédure arbitrale, tous droits réservés pour la demanderesse à mieux agir devant les tribunaux ordinaires. »

S'étant déterminé sur sa compétence au regard de chacune des parties défenderesses telles qu'attraites à la procédure, le Tribunal arbitral en abordant le fond se prononce tout d'abord sur la résiliation des contrats conclus entre la demanderesse et X. Estimant que la dégradation de la situation invoquée par la demanderesse qui a conduit à la décision du maître de l'ouvrage, est due exclusivement à l'attitude fautive de X, le Tribunal aboutit à la conclusion que le contrat entre le maître de l'ouvrage et X est résilié, puis poursuit :

« *Quant au contrat X/demanderesse, il a été résilié, aux torts de X, conformément à l'article 157 CCE...*

Le contrat X/demanderesse a qualité de contrat accessoire par rapport au contrat principal conclu entre le maître de l'ouvrage et X. Le droit égyptien reconnaît une action directe aux sous-traitants. L'article 662 CCE statue que :

« *Les sous-traitants et les ouvriers qui travaillent pour le compte de l'entrepreneur à l'exécution de l'ouvrage ont une action directe contre le maître de l'ouvrage jusqu'à concurrence des sommes dont il est débiteur envers l'entrepreneur principal au moment où l'action est intentée. Cette action appartient également aux ouvriers des sous-traitants à l'égard tant de l'entrepreneur principal que du maître de l'ouvrage.*

Ils ont, en cas de saisie-arrêt pratiquée par l'un d'eux entre les mains du maître de l'ouvrage ou de l'entrepreneur principal, un privilège, au prorata de leurs droits respectifs, sur les sommes dues à l'entrepreneur principal ou au sous-traitant au moment de la saisie-arrêt. Ces sommes peuvent leur être payées directement.

Les droits des sous-traitants et ouvriers prévus par cet article, priment ceux de la personne à laquelle l'entrepreneur a cédé sa créance envers le maître de l'ouvrage. »

Il faut cependant observer que :

— *cette action directe est une garantie pour le sous-traitant et ne le prive pas du droit d'agir contre son cocontractant immédiat ;*

— *cette action directe est limitée à ce que le maître de l'ouvrage devrait à l'entrepreneur principal, ce qui ferait subir en l'espèce à la demanderesse tous les aléas des relations entre le maître de l'ouvrage et X. La demanderesse, dont le dommage de principe est reconnu en raison de l'inexécution fautive par son cocontractant direct de ses obligations, a donc une action contre X.*

La conclusion d'un protocole d'accord suivi de deux contrats entre le maître de l'ouvrage et la demanderesse ne change pas la situation sinon... au bénéfice de X. En effet, la reprise par le maître de l'ouvrage des grandes lignes des contrats X/demanderesse ont permis de diminuer le dommage qu'aurait subi la demanderesse si la poursuite de la réalisation d'ouvrage ne lui avait pas été confiée. Si donc un dommage existe pour la demanderesse, et qu'il n'a pas été supprimé par le nouveau contrat demanderesse/maître de l'ouvrage, X doit en assumer la réparation. »

Le Tribunal – usant de ses pouvoirs d'amiable compositeur – se prononce ensuite sur la détermination du dommage subi par la demanderesse avant d'aborder le véritable enjeu de cette procédure, à savoir la demande de constatation de la caducité de diverses lettres de garanties à première demande émises par une banque égyptienne en faveur de X et contre garanties par une banque européenne, lettres de garanties que X tentait d'appeler bien que le marché d'entreprise générale conclu avec le maître de l'ouvrage eût été résilié.

A cet égard, le Tribunal arbitral délimite le champ de sa compétence de la manière suivante :

« *Il n'est pas contesté que la relation établie entre le garant (la banque) et le bénéficiaire, entre le donneur (demanderesse) et la sous-garante (banque européenne), ne sont pas couvertes par la clause d'arbitrage des contrats de juin 1983. Le contrat de garanties est indépendant des contrats de juin 1983. L'arbitrage ne concerne donc que les relations entre la demanderesse et X.*

Le Tribunal serait donc incompétent pour donner des ordres à l'une ou l'autre banque. En revanche, il est compétent pour dire si le bénéficiaire des lettres de garantie, X, est en droit de se prévaloir des garanties par rapport à la demanderesse.

Il l'est également pour dire si les garanties sont valables dans le contexte des relations entre donneur d'ordre et bénéficiaire. Ces garanties ont leur fondement dans les contrats de juin 1983. Elles sont, pour les parties à l'arbitrage, liées à la validité, la portée et la résiliation du contrat de base.

Il est certain que dans la mesure où le contrat de base, soit ici les contrats du 21 juin 1983, font état de garanties bancaires, le Tribunal arbitral est en droit de se prononcer sur leur portée. Le caractère abstrait de la garantie ne signifie pas que la garantie n'a pas son origine dans le contrat de base et qu'elle ne lui est pas étroitement liée. C'est bien pour garantir une inexécution du contrat de base que la garantie a été exigée et donnée. Le Tribunal peut se prononcer sur le droit du bénéficiaire de faire valoir les garanties. Il est en droit de se prononcer sur le caractère illicite d'un appel en garantie (sur ce sujet voir notamment Jürgen Dohm, Bankgarantien und Schiedsgerichtsbarkeit, Bulletin de l'Association suisse de l'arbitrage, 1987, p. 92 s.).

En l'occurrence, il ne fait aucun doute qu'X a tenté d'appeler sans droit les lettres de garantie. Si l'on admet que le contrat de base est résilié (contrat de sous-traitance), la caducité des lettres de garantie en est la conséquence naturelle, puisqu'elles ont leur cause dans les contrats de sous-traitance. Il faut que le bénéficiaire ait une créance contre le donneur d'ordre. Or tel n'est pas le cas en l'espèce. En cherchant à encaisser les lettres de garantie, X a commis un acte contraire au droit. Si l'on devait admettre que X avait un droit formel et abstrait, elle en aurait alors abusé, rien ne justifiant l'appel des garanties. Aucun indice ne permet de supposer que la demanderesse ait été insolvable (garantie en restitution de l'acompte). Le contraire, en revanche, est pour le moins vraisemblable. Rien n'établit non plus que la demanderesse n'ait pas exécuté ses prestations contractuelles (performance bond). De surcroît, c'est aujourd'hui le maître de l'ouvrage seul qui aurait pu ou pourrait se plaindre d'une mauvaise exécution. Or le maître de l'ouvrage a délivré le 10 mars 1987, avec effet rétroactif au 31 décembre 1986, un certificat d'admission des travaux qui précise que la garantie prendra fin le 1er janvier 1988. Le risque couvert par les lettres de garantie a donc disparu pour le maître de l'ouvrage et, à l'époque, pour l'entrepreneur général X.

En conséquence, le Tribunal constate que les lettres de garantie mentionnées ci-dessus n'ont plus de cause. Leurs bénéficiaires n'ont plus aucun droit sur elles. En les faisant valoir, leurs bénéficiaires commettraient un acte illicite. En revanche, si le Tribunal ne prend directement aucune décision à l'égard des banques garantes ou contre-garantes, il relèvera qu'un paiement par elles, si elles ont connaissance des termes de la présente sentence, serait susceptible d'engager leur responsabilité. »

OBSERVATIONS. — I. — Une précédente chronique (*JDI* 1987, p. 1034) avait déjà attiré notre attention sur l'argumentation développée par certaines parties égyptiennes tendant à contester l'existence ou la validité de la convention d'arbitrage en se fondant sur l'article 502 (3) du Code de procédure civil égyptien (CPCE).

S'il avait pu toutefois être constaté qu'à la suite de nombreuses procédures, certaines juridictions égyptiennes s'étaient prononcées en établissant que l'article 502 (3) CPCE ne s'applique pas aux conventions d'arbitrage internationales et n'est pas d'ordre public, notre attention était attirée sur les doutes qui subsistent toujours au sujet de l'efficacité d'une convention d'arbitrage dans le contexte égyptien.

La présente sentence nous donne l'occasion non seulement de relever la vigueur avec laquelle les arbitres ont refusé de donner à l'article 502 (3) CPCE une portée internationale qui serait contraire à l'esprit de l'arbitrage et au principe reconnu de l'autonomie de la clause d'arbitrage mais aussi de faire état d'un arrêt récent de la Cour d'appel du Caire en date du 13 juin 1990.

Dans la sentence ici rapportée, le Tribunal arbitral indique d'emblée qu'il ne saurait donner à l'article 502 (3) CPCE « *une portée internationale étant donné les besoins du commerce international* ». Cette prise de position qui ne fait pas expressément référence au principe de l'autonomie de la clause compromissoire par rapport au contrat principal et par rapport à toute loi étatique, semble ériger en principe la validité de la convention d'arbitrage international à laquelle il conviendrait de conférer une efficacité propre lorsqu'elle est insérée dans un contrat international (voir sur ce principe, Paris, 20 avril 1988 : *Rev. arb.* 1988, p. 570).

Mais les arbitres ont pris soin, s'agissant de se prononcer sur la validité formelle de la clause d'arbitrage, d'asseoir leur décision en se référant à la jurisprudence étatique égyptienne évitant ainsi d'ériger la validité de la clause d'arbitrage international en principe absolu, tout en estimant que « *l'exigence du droit égyptien interne... ne saurait être étendue au domaine de l'arbitrage international* ».

Dans une affaire CCI 4746, il avait été interjeté appel d'un jugement rendu le 27 janvier 1987 par le Tribunal de première instance de Guizeh qui avait – quant à l'argument suivant lequel la clause d'arbitrage est frappée de nullité faute de nomination des arbitres – débouté les demanderesses au motif qu'une clause d'arbitrage prévoyait le règlement des litiges, et emportait renoncement de recourir aux tribunaux étatiques, que les arbitres soient ou non nommés dans la clause ou dans un accord séparé.

Par arrêt du 13 juin 1990, la Cour d'appel du Caire a confirmé le jugement en ces termes (traduction officieuse) :

« *Considérant que le moyen de défense des deux appelants, consistant à invoquer la compétence des tribunaux égyptiens à statuer sur le litige, n'est pas recevable eu égard au fait que les deux parties avaient convenu de recourir à l'arbitrage, écartant ainsi la compétence des tribunaux. D'autre part, dire que certains litiges ne sont pas soumis à l'arbitrage ou que la clause d'arbitrage ne peut s'appliquer à la disposition des droits, est également non recevable parce qu'il équivaut à la remise en cause des clauses du contrat de location dans son intégralité. L'absence de nomination des arbitres dans la clause d'arbitrage ne rend pas la clause nulle et non avenue.*

L'appel n'est donc pas fondé, sur le double plan des faits et du droit, il convient de le rejeter et de confirmer le jugement appelé. »

Alors que l'arrêt de la Cour de cassation égyptienne du 26 avril 1982, dans l'afffaire Mabrouk Trading Import Export c. The Arab Continental Navigation Co., à laquelle se réfèrent les arbitres dans la sentence rapportée, concernait une procédure d'arbitrage se déroulant hors d'Egypte, la décision de la Cour d'appel du Caire du 13 juin 1990, intervient quant à elle dans le cadre d'une procédure arbitrale se déroulant sur le territoire égyptien.

Cette dernière décision et surtout la promulgation attendue d'une nouvelle loi en Egypte sur l'arbitrage international dont le texte semblerait adopter en grande partie la loi modèle de la CNUDCI permettent aujourd'hui de se montrer plus optimiste en ce qui concerne l'avenir de l'arbitrage en Egypte.

II. — La société dont dépend une succursale qui n'a pas de personnalité morale est, suivant les principes généraux du droit des sociétés, tenue par les engagements souscrits par la succursale.

En relevant que le président de la société agissait aussi bien en qualité de représentant de la succursale, le Tribunal arbitral apparaît faire référence à la théorie des « *liens institutionnels* » ou encore de la « *réalité économique* » lui permettant de conclure que l'activité de la succursale est englobée dans celle de la société dont elle dépend. L'approche ainsi suivie par le Tribunal arbitral valide plus largement la convention d'arbitrage que s'il s'était attaché à la personnalité morale, signataire de la convention d'arbitrage.

Cette décision de bon sens est à rapprocher de la sentence 5065 rendue en 1986 (*JDI* 1987, p. 1039) où l'arbitre, saisi du « *problème classique d'une personne morale existante contractant pour le compte d'une société à créer* » conclut que « *selon les principes généraux du droit commercial international et les usages, et de la bonne foi... la personne morale existante est personnellement tenue* » (*ibid,* p. 1043).

III. — La démarche suivie par les arbitres dans la sentence ici rapportée est légèrement différente de celle adoptée dans l'affaire 4131 (*JDI* 1983, p. 899), mais aboutit au même résultat. Sans exclure a priori le droit applicable au fond (droit égyptien) le Tribunal arbitral se réfère à l'article 13 (5) du Règlement CCI qui précise que « *dans tous les cas, l'arbitre tiendra compte des stipulations du contrat et des usages du commerce* ». Pour justifier le recours à une règle matérielle non étatique qu'il dénomme *lex mercatoria*, le Tribunal fait appel au principe de l'autonomie de la clause d'arbitrage et en déduit devoir se prononcer en vertu de la notion générale de la bonne foi en affaires et des usages du commerce international. C'est sans doute pour veiller également à ce que la sentence soit susceptible de sanction légale que le Tribunal arbitral précise que les différents droits nationaux pouvant avoir vocation à s'appliquer en l'espèce, et qu'il examine, conduisent à un résultat similaire.

Cette approche des arbitres du commerce international pour déterminer les sources de droit devant être appliquées lorsqu'ils ont à trancher la question de leur compétence au regard d'un tiers non signataire du contrat apparaît justifié lorsque les parties n'ont pas expressément prévu de loi applicable non seulement à la validité, mais aussi à la portée et aux effets d'une clause compromissoire ou lorsqu'une règle impérative ne commande pas aux arbitres d'appliquer un droit déterminé.

Ce recours aux usages du commerce international, à la bonne foi en affaires, conduit les arbitres à rechercher dans l'examen et l'analyse des faits la commune volonté des parties, l'extension de la clause d'arbitrage qui doit rester l'exception, devant avoir un fondement volontaire.

On relèvera avec intérêt l'affirmation dans la présente sentence que l'extension de la clause compromissoire ne peut intervenir au titre de sanction du comportement du tiers, renvoyant au besoin la demanderesse à mieux se pourvoir devant les juridictions compétentes pour mettre en jeu la responsabilité du tiers pour dol ou tout autre agissement.

IV. — Le contrat de sous-traitance a qualité de contrat accessoire par rapport au contrat conclu entre l'entrepreneur et le maître de l'ouvrage.

En démontrant la dépendance qui existe entre le contrat principal et le contrat de sous-traitance et en relevant qu'après expulsion de l'entrepreneur du site, le maître de l'ouvrage a conclu directement avec le sous-traitant, les arbitres délimitent le champ de la réparation du préjudice consécutif à la résiliation en faisant appel au principe général de l'obligation faite au créancier de minimiser ses pertes.

Une précédente chronique (*JDI* 1988, p. 1216, observ. Yves Derains) a mentionné que cette obligation pour le créancier d'une obligation inexécutée de minimiser ses pertes est l'un des principes les mieux établis des usages de commerce international et de la *lex mercatoria*.

V. — A l'évidence, un Tribunal arbitral n'a de pouvoirs qu'à l'égard des parties à l'arbitrage et ne saurait prononcer aucune décision qui soit opposable à des banques non parties à la procédure.

La sentence relève à juste titre qu'une garantie bancaire – contrat de garantie conclu entre le garant et le bénéficiaire – est indépendant du contrat de base. Toutefois et parce que la garantie bancaire trouve son fondement dans le contrat de base, les arbitres restent compétents dans le contexte des relations entre le donneur d'ordre et le bénéficiaire : il en résulte que la garantie bancaire est liée à la validité, la portée et la résiliation du contrat de base.

Ayant admis la résiliation du contrat de sous-traitance, les arbitres constatent que les lettres de garanties n'ont plus de cause et prononcent en conséquence leur caducité.

I. Procédure arbitrale. — Règlement d'arbitrage de la CCI. — Article 8 (3). — Pouvoir de l'arbitre de statuer sur sa propre compétence.

II. Clause compromissoire. — Validité. — Droit applicable. — Droit du lieu de l'arbitrage.

III. Clause compromissoire. — Validité. — Droit français (art. 1443 NCPC). — Absence de signature. — Présomption de connaissance de la clause.

Sentence rendue dans l'affaire 5730 en 1988

Arguant du fait que M. Z. exerçait le commerce à titre personnel sous diverses dénominations voisines les unes des autres, la demanderesse a introduit une demande d'arbitrage à l'encontre de M. Z., de la société X SA et de l'entreprise X au motif que les défenderesses n'auraient pas réglé, en exécution d'un contrat de fourniture de lubrifiants pour navires en date du 2 novembre 1983, le montant de certaines factures.

Les faits étaient les suivants. A la suite d'un contentieux opposant les parties au titre de leurs relations commerciales antérieures, la demanderesse avait conclu le même jour, les deux documents contractuels suivants :

— d'une part, un procès-verbal ne comportant pas de clause compromissoire signé par M. Z. et un de ses employés (ci-après M. E.), relatif à l'échelonnement du règlement des fournitures impayées, établi sur papier à en-tête de la société X SA ; et,

— d'autre part, un contrat de fourniture établi sur un formulaire type normalement utilisé par la demanderesse, l'acheteur désigné étant l'entreprise X et mentionnant comme représentant M. Z. dont le nom fut néanmoins barré, son employé M. E. signant le contrat à sa place. Ce contrat qui contenait une clause d'arbitrage CCI avait pour objet de redéfinir les conditions dans lesquelles l'entreprise pourrait se procurer des lubrifiants marine dans les principaux ports du monde, nécessaires à 27 navires différents nommément désignés dont l'entreprise X n'est pas officiellement l'armateur.

Alors que M. Z. invoquait l'irrecevabilité de la demande dirigée à son encontre au motif qu'il n'était pas signataire du contrat de fourniture, la société X SA également non signataire, ne s'opposait pas à sa mise en cause indiquant qu'elle-même et l'entreprise X sont une seule et même personne, X étant le logo utilisé dans un but commercial. La demanderesse a néanmoins maintenu sa demande à l'encontre de l'entreprise X.

Comme la Cour internationale d'arbitrage l'y avait invité en faisant application des dispositions de l'article 8.3 de son Règlement lorsqu'elle a décidé de la mise en œuvre de la procédure, le Tribunal arbitral devait se prononcer sur sa compétence à l'égard de M. Z.

Avant d'examiner la question de l'opposabilité de la clause d'arbitrage à M. Z., les arbitres ont commencé à rechercher qui était le cocontractant de la demanderesse, les défenderesses soutenant que seule la société X SA pouvait être défenderesse.

De l'examen des contrats et de l'analyse du comportement des parties avant, pendant et après leur signature, les arbitres ont au contraire considéré que M. Z. était le véritable cocontratant en retenant notamment qu'en fait, l'entreprise X était une entreprise purement personnelle qui se confondait avec son propriétaire M. Z.

Le Tribunal arbitral relève à cet égard :

« *Pour résoudre cette première question, il n'y a pas lieu de dissocier les relations commerciales entre parties antérieures et postérieures au contrat du 2 novembre 1983, qui forment un tout. En effet, c'est à la fois pour régler l'arriéré et éviter des difficultés de paiement à l'avenir que les représentants de la demanderesse se sont rendus dans les bureaux des défendeurs, le 2 novembre 1983, et ont signé aussi bien le procès-verbal que le contrat... Il n'y a au surplus aucun indice que la demanderesse ait accepté à cette occasion de changer de cocontractant. En particulier, l'utilisation d'un papier à en-tête de la société X SA pour établir le procès-verbal de cet entretien n'a nullement été délibéré, mais opéré fortuitement ou à dessein par les défendeurs...*

Si donc l'on examine les antécédents de la convention de novembre 1983, on constate que les premiers contacts ont été pris en 1982 par les représentants de la demanderesse aussi bien avec M. E. qu'avec M. Z personnellement, et nullement avec la société X SA que le premier ne représentait pas. D'ailleurs, X SA n'apparaissait au régistre de la Lloyd ni comme propriétaire ni comme manager d'aucun des navires ravitaillés... Il s'agissait bien au contraire pour elle d'assurer le ravitaillement en lubrifiant de l'ensemble des navires du Groupe Z, et non de telle société particulière, navires dont la plupart sont d'ailleurs mentionnés dans l'Annexe au contrat du 2 novembre 1983.

Les défendeurs contestent en vain l'existence d'un tel Groupe, qui est notamment mentionné sur le papier à en-tête de la société X SA utilisé pour établir le procès-verbal du 2 novembre 1983 et sur la carte de visite de M. Z. Aux yeux des tiers, l'ensemble des sociétés dépendant du prénommé forment incontestablement un groupe de sociétés, soit propriétaires de navires, soit exploitants de lignes et d'agences maritimes, dont l'administration est assurée aux trois adresses mentionnées sur la carte de visite de M. Z dont au Pirée.

L'existence d'un tel groupe a d'ailleurs été reconnue dans la plupart des décisions judiciaires, tant grecques qu'étrangères, produites par la demanderesse. Le défendeur est d'autant plus mal venu de le contester qu'il a lui-même créé et entretenu l'apparence d'un tel groupe en utilisant des noms de navires et des raisons sociales proches les uns des autres au point de provoquer parfois même la confusion la plus complète, comme c'est notamment le cas pour les trois sociétés répondant à l'appellation X ainsi qu'en mêlant comme à plaisir la gestion et les comptes de ces diverses sociétés, ce qu'attestent notamment les modes de paiement utilisés en l'espèce...

A vrai dire, la demanderesse ne paraît guère s'être souciée d'identifier à l'époque ce groupe et l'expression X qui le qualifiait et figurait notamment sur ses factures. L'essentiel était pour elle de traiter soit avec M. Z personnellement soit avec une société faîtière dominant l'ensemble du groupe. Or, il s'est aujourd'hui avéré que cette désignation correspond à la raison commerciale individuelle, inscrite au Registre du Commerce de Jeddah, sous laquelle M. Z exerce personnellement ses activités maritimes en utilisant indifféremment en anglais les expressions X LINES ou LINE. Bien plus, M. Z lui-même et ses proches collaborateurs ont reconnu, à l'occasion d'un procès se déroulant devant la High Court of Justice, que les affaires traitées sous cette raison individuelle engageaient la responsabilité personnelle du premier, ce que confirment d'ailleurs les consultations de droit saoudien produites par la demanderesse...

Il est ainsi avéré qu'en traitant avec l'entreprise X et en établissant ses factures à ce nom, correspondant à la raison commerciale individuelle de M. Z, c'est bien avec celui-ci personnellement que la demanderesse traitait. Si M. Z n'entendait pas être lié personnellement par les affaires ainsi traitées et les factures ainsi établies au nom de sa raison individuelle, il lui appartenait de protester et d'indiquer clairement à son cocontractant quelle société en répondrait...

Si donc la demanderesse a traité jusqu'au 2 novembre 1983 avec M. Z personnellement, en sa qualité de commerçant individuel et de président du Groupe Z, le Tribunal considère qu'il n'en va pas différemment depuis lors. C'est d'ailleurs aux défendeurs qu'il appartiendrait d'établir un tel changement alors que la nature des affaires traitées et l'intitulé des factures établies au nom de l'entreprise X n'ont pas changé. On ne saurait en particulier considérer que l'utilisation du papier à en-tête de la société X SA, utilisé pour l'établissement du procès-verbal de la séance du 2 novembre 1983, implique une substitution de cocontractant... En outre, il n'est nullement mentionné dans ce procès-verbal que ce serait la société X SA qui serait débitrice des factures arriérées, ce qui aurait impliqué une reprise de dette nécessitant l'accord du créancier. Bien au contraire, l'article 3 de ce procès-verbal mentionne que l'engagement de payer émane de " X ", ce qui prouve que les défendeurs n'attachaient pas beaucoup d'importance aux désignations utilisées s'ils n'embrouillaient à dessein la situation. La quasi similitude de la raison individuelle de M. Z, utilisée jusqu'ici, et de la raison sociale figurant sur l'en-tête de ce procès-verbal expliquent d'ailleurs qu'on n'y ait pas prêté attention. Deuxièmement, la discussion relatée dans ce procès-verbal ne concernait en rien la SA, mais des factures arriérées établies au nom de X alias M. Z personnellement, et la saisie du navire appartenant à une société du Groupe, soit économiquement au défendeur mais nullement à la société X SA.

Ce procès-verbal s'insère donc dans les relations existantes et ne concerne en rien la société X SA. Certes, il a été signé par M. E pour X SA, mais précisément le représentant de la demanderesse ne s'en est pas accommodé et a exigé qu'il soit signé par M. Z, président du Groupe. Comme le précise le début du procès-verbal, c'est d'ailleurs avec M. Z, qualifié de " chairman ", par quoi il faut donc entendre président du Groupe et non de la société X SA, qu'a eu lieu la discussion... M. E qui n'avait d'ailleurs pas la qualité d'organe de la société défenderesse, n'a joué qu'un rôle d'exécutant lors de cette séance. C'est dire que même si, en établissant ce procès-verbal au nom de la société X SA, les défendeurs ont entendu substituer cette société à M. Z, personnellement engagé jusque-là, cette substitution n'a précisé-

ment pas été acceptée par la demanderesse qui a exigé de traiter, comme par le passé, avec M. Z.

On ne saurait davantage déduire du contrat signé immédiatement après (pièce 1) que la demanderesse ait accepté de changer de cocontractant et de traiter à l'avenir avec la société X SA. Tout d'abord, ce contrat a été établi expressément au nom de " l'entreprise X ", correspondant à l'intitulé des factures, et nullement au nom de la société X SA. D'autre part, comme le procès-verbal, il concerne aussi bien les factures arriérées, dues par M. Z personnellement, que les relations futures. Cela résulte en particulier de l'effet rétroactif au 1ᵉʳ janvier 1983 qui lui est attribué par l'article 3. Troisièmement, l'objet même du contrat, soit le ravitaillement des navires du Groupe Z, mentionnés dans l'Annexe I, confirme qu'il ne concerne pas la société X SA, propriétaire d'aucun de ces navires, mais le Groupe Z comme par le passé. Et, de fait, les relations ont continué comme par le passé : les livraisons ont été facturées à l'entreprise X et les télex adressés à X ou M. Z " chairman ".

Certes, alors qu'il était initialement prévu que ce contrat serait signé par M. Z, il l'a été seulement par M. E au nom de l'acheteur... M. E n'ayant ni la qualité d'organe de la société défenderesse ni même de pouvoir écrit pour agir en son nom, sa signature n'emporte nullement présomption qu'il aurait agi au nom de cette société. Il faut au contraire considérer que M. Z, seul interlocuteur de la demanderesse, a simplement laissé M. E signer à sa place et en sa présence ce contrat, les représentants de la demanderesse n'ayant pas exigé à nouveau la signature personnelle du premier sur ce document... »

Et de conclure :

« Aussi, sur la base de l'appréciation tant des pièces que de l'ensemble des témoignages, le Tribunal arbitral arrive-t-il à la conclusion que ni le procès-verbal ni le contrat du 2 novembre 1983 n'ont modifié la situation antérieure, savoir que la demanderesse a traité avec l'entreprise X, c'est-à-dire avec M. Z personnellement, agissant sous sa raison de commerce individuelle, et nullement avec la société X SA, société panaméenne qui n'était en rien concernée par ces relations commerciales...

Enfin, il résulte de ce qui précède que l'entreprise X, mise en cause comme troisième défenderesse, n'existe pas comme telle puisqu'il s'agit uniquement de la raison de commerce individuelle de M. Z, qui répond personnellement de l'activité exercée sous cette dénomination. »

Le tribunal arbitral s'est ensuite demandé si la clause arbitrale pourrait être opposée à M. Z, une discussion s'étant élevée sur la validité de la clause d'arbitrage. Le Tribunal arbitral procède d'abord à la détermination de la loi applicable à la convention d'arbitrage.

« Si les parties se sont entendues pour reconnaître que le contrat était, quant au fond, régi par le droit grec (art. 8 de l'Acte de mission) et si cet accord lie les arbitres conformément à l'article 13, alinéa 3 du règlement CCI, elles ont en revanche réservé expressément à l'article 7.1 dudit Acte de mission la détermination du droit applicable à la clause arbitrale contenue dans ce contrat du 2 novembre 1983. Il appartient donc au Tribunal arbitral de résoudre cette question. Pour cela, il ne saurait se contenter d'invoquer l'autonomie de la convention d'arbitrage par rapport au contrat pour en déduire qu'elle serait valable indépendamment de toute loi étatique, comme l'ont admis certains arrêts depuis celui rendu par la Cour de cassation le 4 juillet 1972 dans la cause Hecht (Clunet 1972, p. 843 avec note Oppetit ; cf. également CA Paris, 13 décembre 1975 : Rev. Arb. 1977, p. 147, note Fouchard ; Cass. 14 décembre 1983 : Rev. Arb. 1984, p. 483 ; cf. également les références données par Loquin, Clunet 1987, p. 947-948) et certaines sentences publiées (cf. notamment Rev. Arb. 1984, p. 137, confirmé par CA Paris, 21 octobre 1983 : Rev. Arb. 1984, p. 98). En effet, fidèle à la conception traditionnelle de

l'arbitrage même international, le présent Tribunal considère que la convention d'arbitrage, pour être efficace, doit tirer sa force de son rattachement à un ordre juridique, alors même que les parties seraient libres de désigner celui-ci. Il ne lui paraît pas davantage possible d'appliquer directement, comme un arrêt récent (CA Paris, 20 janvier 1987 : Rev. Arb. 1987, p. 482, note Kessedjian et Clunet 1987, p. 934, note Loquin, approuvé par l'une et critiqué par l'autre), l'article II de la Convention de New York à laquelle la France et la Grèce sont parties : comme l'observe Loquin (p. 961-963), cette règle conventionnelle s'adresse aux Etats contractants et non pas directement à l'arbitre international, qui ne statue pas au nom de l'un de ces Etats et doit rechercher librement quelle est, selon la volonté expresse ou présumée des parties, la règle la plus appropriée au litige. Il n'en demeure pas moins souhaitable de ne pas se départir sans raison sérieuse de la règle de forme autonome posée par l'article II de la Convention précitée afin que, d'une part, l'arbitre ne juge pas de sa compétence selon des critères contraires à ceux qui devraient être appliqués par le juge étatique selon cette disposition en vertu de l'article V, et non seulement VII, dans les pays parties à la Convention, ainsi que le le recommande Albert Jan van den Berg (Should an international arbitrator apply the New York Arbitration Convention of 1958 ? in : The Art of Arbitration, Deventer 1982, p. 39 s.).

De même le Tribunal arbitral ne saurait se contenter de constater qu'il s'agit en l'espèce d'un arbitrage international ayant son siège à Paris et, en conséquence, soumis aux articles 1492 s. NCPC, comme les parties l'ont reconnu à l'article 8, alinéa 2 de l'Acte de mission. En effet, ces articles ne déterminent pas la loi applicable à la validité de la convention d'arbitrage sous réserve de renvoi supplétif de l'article 1495 aux articles 1442 s. NCPC (cf. Jean Robert : L'arbitrage, 5ᵉ éd. 1983, p. 232, nᵒ 266 et p. 275-276, nᵒ 319 ; CA Paris, 20 janvier 1987, Clunet 1987, p. 937 et Rev. Arb. 1987, p. 484-485, qui confond toutefois la loi applicable au déroulement de la procédure et celle régissant la convention d'arbitrage, ainsi que le relève notamment Loquin dans sa note suivant cet arrêt, p. 953). On examinera donc les trois rattachements possibles, quitte à appliquer subsidiairement le renvoi de l'article 1495 s'ils ne conduisent à aucun résultat certain.

On pourrait tout d'abord être enclin à appliquer le droit grec à titre de loi du lieu de conclusion puisque le contrat a été passé en réalité au Pirée, contrairement à ce qu'il indique (cf. ch. 7 dernier al. ci-dessus). Alors même que ce rattachement est généralement reconnu en droit international privé français et même recommandé par certains auteurs en matière d'arbitrage international (cf. Robert, op. cit., p. 234-235, nᵒˢ 269 et 270), il n'a aucun caractère impératif et n'est pas consacré par le droit positif (cf. notamment les art. V de la Convention de New York et VI de la Convention de Genève) car le lieu de conclusion est le plus souvent accidentel dans le commerce international de telle sorte qu'on ne saurait présumer que les parties aient voulu soumettre à ce droit la validité de leur convention (cf. Loquin, Clunet 1987, p. 949-951 et les réf. citées ; Kessedjian, Rev. Arb. 1987, p. 491-493). Tel est précisément le cas en l'espèce où le projet de contrat, qui prévoyait sa conclusion à Paris, a été finalement conclu au Pirée simplement parce que les parties se sont rencontrées dans les bureaux de M. E et non dans ceux de la demanderesse. On ne saurait sérieusement faire dépendre le droit applicable de cette circonstance alors que la volonté clairement exprimée par les parties était de toute manière de se soumettre à un arbitrage de la CCI à Paris.

Deuxièmement, on pourrait songer à appliquer le droit grec à titre de loi de fond régissant le contrat selon la commune volonté des parties. Certes, l'autonomie de la convention d'arbitrage par rapport au contrat dans lequel elle est contenue, reconnue par la jurisprudence dès avant la nouvelle de 1981 (Cass. Gosset, 7 mai 1963 : Clunet 1964, p. 82, et Hecht, 4 juillet 1972 précité ; CA Paris, 13 décembre 1975 : Rev. Arb. 1977, p. 147, et 21 octobre 1983 : Rev. Arb. 1984, p. 98 ; Cass., 14 décembre 1983 = Rev. Arb. 1984, p. 483) et par la doctrine pratiquement una-

nime (cf. notamment Peter Sanders : L'autonomie de la clause compromissoire, in : Hommage à Frédéric Eisemann, Paris 1978, p. 31 s. sp. 38 ; Yves Derains, Yearbook Commercial Arbitration 1982, p. 6 ch. 4 ; Philippe Fouchard : L'arbitrage commercial international, p. 62 s., n° 105 s., spécialement n° 114 ; Loquin, op. cit., p. 951 ; Kessedjian, loc. cit., p. 490-491 et références), conduit à distinguer la loi applicable à la convention d'arbitrage de celle applicable au fond. Toutefois, comme l'observent notamment Fouchard (n° 115) et Loquin (loc. cit.) et l'admet un arrêt (CA Paris, 25 mars 1983 : Rev. Arb. 1984, p. 363, note Jean Robert), dans la majorité des cas, les parties entendent soumettre le contrat principal et la convention d'arbitrage qu'il contient à la même loi de telle sorte qu'il y aurait même présomption d'une loi unique lorsque les parties ont ainsi opté pour une loi de fond. Le Tribunal arbitral estime toutefois qu'en l'espèce une telle présomption ne saurait être retenue. En effet, rien n'indique que lors de la conclusion du contrat, les parties aient entendu le soumettre à la loi grecque. Celle-ci n'a été élue que dans l'Acte de mission, lequel réserve précisément la question du droit applicable à la convention d'arbitrage elle-même. On ne saurait donc en déduire un accord sur ce dernier point. Bien plus, la nature même des relations d'affaires entre les parties ne conduisait pas nécessairement à l'application du droit grec puisqu'il s'agissait, pour une société française, de ravitailler des navires dans le monde entier, navires qui n'étaient même pas nécessairement basés au Pirée et qui appartenaient à des sociétés non grecques ayant leur siège dans divers pays. Quant à M. Z, de nationalité saoudienne, il avait enregistré sa raison de commerce à Jeddah, vivait au Caire et administrait une partie au moins de ses affaires maritimes au Pirée. C'est dire que ce dernier rattachement n'apparaît nullement prépondérant.

En fin de compte, la seule disposition du contrat faisant allusion au règlement d'un litige éventuel entre parties est l'article 10 prévoyant un arbitrage selon les Règles de la CCI à Paris. Alors même que ce renvoi n'implique pas encore fixation du siège dans cette ville, mais laisse à la Cour d'arbitrage le soin de le fixer en application de l'article 12, la vraisemblance parlait en faveur d'un arbitrage à Paris, ce que la Cour n'a fait que confirmer en y fixant le siège. Le droit français est dès lors celui qui paraît avoir le mieux vocation à s'appliquer à la validité de cette convention d'arbitrage, cela au moins pour trois raisons.

Tout d'abord, en tant que loi du lieu de l'arbitrage, rattachement préconisé par une résolution fameuse de l'Institut de droit international (cf. Fouchard, p. 68, n° 114), consacré en l'absence de choix contraire des parties par l'article V, al. 1 lit. a de la Convention de New York, VI al. de lit. b et IX al. I lit. a de la Convention de Genève de 1961, admis encore par une partie importante de la doctrine et consacré par certains arrêts au moins à titre de critère subsidiaire pour déterminer la volonté implicite des parties (cf. notamment Fouchard, n° 123 ; P. Level, J. Cl. Droit international, Droit international judiciaire, fasc. 585, n°ˢ 67 et 68 ; Loquin, Clunet 1987, p. 951-952 et 954-955 ; Kessedjian, Rev. Arb. 1987, p. 492, citant plusieurs sentences en ce sens, bien qu'elle préconise plutôt à p. 493-494, comme l'arrêt Bomar commenté, l'application de la loi régissant la procédure à suivre, ce qui conduirait d'ailleurs au même résultat en l'espèce).

Deuxièmement, la loi française a vocation à s'appliquer au motif que la convention d'arbitrage a pour effet de priver en l'espèce la demanderesse du for de son domicile à Paris, dont elle bénéficierait sans cela en vertu de l'article 14 du Code civil pour agir contre M. E défendeur étranger non résident en France, pour une obligation contractée par lui en pays étranger envers cette société française. Il paraît dès lors logique que seule une clause d'arbitrage valable selon le droit français puisse priver la demanderesse du droit de s'adresser aux tribunaux français. Enfin, en l'absence même de ces critères et faute de toute indication de la volonté des parties quant au droit applicable à la convention d'arbitrage, le droit français devrait s'appliquer à titre supplétif en vertu du renvoi de l'article 1495 NCPC, ainsi que cela a été relevé plus haut. »

La question de l'opposabilité de la clause d'arbitrage à M. Z est ensuite examinée au regard du droit français déclaré applicable en l'espèce.

« En vertu de l'article 1443 NCPC, la clause compromissoire doit, à peine de nullité, être stipulée par écrit dans la convention principale ou dans un document auquel celle-ci se réfère. Or, en l'espèce, l'article 10 du contrat du 2 novembre 1983 passé par la demanderesse avec le défendeur Z, sous la raison de commerce individuelle de celui-ci respecte cette forme. En revanche, ce document n'est pas signé par M. Z mais en son nom par M. E. Toutefois, l'écrit contenant la clause compromissoire ne doit pas nécessairement, en vertu de l'article 1443, être signé (cf. notamment Philippe Fouchard : L'arbitrage international en France, Clunet 1982, p. 385, n° 19). Preuve en soit d'ailleurs que cette clause peut figurer dans un document annexe, conditions générales ou contrat type, auquel la convention signée se réfère ou être acceptée tacitement par le destinataire (cf notamment CA Paris, 25 mars 1983 : Rev. Arb. 1984, p. 363 s. note Jean Robert ; de Boisseson : Le droit français de l'arbitrage, p. 68 s. n°s 63-64 ; Loquin, Clunet 1987,p. 955-957 ; Jean Robert, op. cit., p. 67 s. n°s 83-84). Il importe dès lors peu que M. Z n'ait pas personnellement signé le contrat s'il est avéré que M. E avait pouvoir d'agir en son nom ou que le premier a valablement ratifié les engagements pris par le second.

Certes, la demanderesse soutient que le procès-verbal et le contrat du même jour constituaient une seule et même convention, de telle sorte qu'en signant le premier, M. Z souscrivait par là même au second. Il n'est pas contestable que par leur objet, ces deux documents constituaient en réalité un accord global concernant à la fois le règlement de l'arriéré et des relations futures...

Si cette unité de fond n'est pas sérieusement contestable, il n'en résulte pas encore qu'en signant le premier document, M. Z ait souscrit au second. En effet, le procès-verbal ne se réfère nullement au contrat signé immédiatement après, de telle sorte que l'on peut difficilement y voir une convention d'arbitrage par référence. Le Tribunal arbitral ne saurait en tout cas se contenter d'un tel rapprochement pour considérer que M. Z est lié par la clause arbitrale figurant à l'article 10 du contrat.

En revanche, ce procès-verbal n'est pas sans importance, pour apprécier les pouvoirs conférés à M. E. Alors même que la question n'a apparemment pas été jusqu'ici tranchée en matière d'arbitrage, on pourrait être enclin à soumettre le pouvoir de compromettre à la même forme en considérant que l'article 1443 NCPC a pour objet de protéger les parties contre une renonciation à la légère à la garantie des tribunaux étatiques (cf. Malaurie/Aynès, Cours de droit civil, Contrats spéciaux, 1985, n° 556, p. 238 ; D. Alexandre, Juris Classeur de Droit Civil, article 1964/1990 Code civil, Fasc. 2, n° 48). Dans ce cas, le pouvoir devrait revêtir la forme écrite et ne pourrait dès lors résulter que du procès-verbal signé par M. Z. En ratifiant par sa signature les engagements pris par M. E dans ce procès-verbal au sujet des relations passées, présentes et à venir avec la demanderesse, M. Z reconnaissait que M. E avait pouvoir de traiter cette affaire en son nom et, en particulier, de signer le contrat comportant la clause compromissoire qui avait d'ores et déjà été soumis par la demanderesse et dont la conclusion devait prendre place immédiatement après, en présence de M. Z. Il n'est toutefois pas nécessaire d'examiner plus avant si cela est suffisant pour constituer un pouvoir écrit de compromettre, cela pour trois raisons.

D'une part la forme écrite introduite en 1980 par l'article 1443 ne paraît pas avoir tellement une fonction de protection des parties que de sécurité du droit, en soumettant la volonté de compromettre à une preuve certaine qui coupe court ultérieurement à toute discussion (cf. notamment de Boisseson, op. cit., p. 65, n° 59 ; Jean Robert, op. cit., p. 67-68, n°s 82 et 83). On ne s'expliquerait d'ailleurs pas sans cela comment le législateur a pu admettre la convention d'arbitrage par simple référence à un document même non signé. Il ne serait dès lors pas indispensa-

ble que le pouvoir de compromettre soit donné par écrit (cf. Malaurie/Aynès, loc.
cit.*). De toute manière, même si M. Z n'avait pas valablement conféré pouvoir de
compromettre à M. E celui-ci bénéficiait à tout le moins de pouvoirs apparents. En
effet, M. Z a toléré que tout au long des relations avec la demanderesse, M. E se
comporte comme le mandataire autorisé de l'entreprise X, c'est-à-dire en réalité de
lui-même et de son groupe, qu'il signe le procès-verbal du 2 novembre 1983 et
même le contrat passé immédiatement après au nom de l'entreprise X. Bien plus,
M. Z avait parfaite connaissance de la clause arbitrale qui figurait dans le projet
qui lui avait été soumis au préalable, il n'a soulevé aucune objection à ce sujet et
a lui-même invité M. E à le signer en sa présence. Compte tenu de l'ensemble de
ces circonstances, la demanderesse était en droit de considérer que M. E avait le
pouvoir de signer et qu'il y était autorisé par M. Z lui-même, personnellement
présent...*

*Or, le mandat apparent peut s'étendre à tous les actes, même les plus graves,
donc à la souscription d'une clause compromissoire, d'autant plus qu'elle est usuelle
dans ce genre de contrat international. Enfin, même si M. E n'avait pas eu de
pouvoir suffisant pour compromettre au nom de M. Z celui-ci n'en aurait pas
moins confirmé ou ratifié cet engagement non seulement par sa présence lors de la
signature, mais en outre par la poursuite des relations d'affaires avec la demanderesse sur la base dudit contrat, de la correspondance et des télex échangés à ce
sujet sans que jamais les engagements pris aient été remis en question... Or, ces
engagements auraient été pris au nom de l'entreprise X, c'est-à-dire de M. Z lui-
même. Il ne saurait dès lors contester avoir par là même ratifié les engagements
pris en son nom et en sa présence par M. E dans le contrat du 2 novembre 1983.*

*Le Tribunal arbitral arrive dès lors à la conclusion que M. Z est lié par la clause
arbitrale contenue dans le contrat du 2 novembre 1983, signé en son nom, sur ses
instructions et en sa présence, par M. E, qui n'était que l'exécutant de la volonté
de M. Z et n'avait aucun autre titre à intervenir. A supposer qu'en se substituant
ainsi* in extremis *M. E lors de la signature de ce contrat, M. Z ait entendu par là
se soustraire personnellement à tout engagement pour pouvoir plaider ensuite les
arguments qu'il avance aujourd'hui, il faudrait considérer qu'un tel procédé astu-
cieux et même dolosif ne mérite pas d'être protégé par la loi. »*

Ayant de surcroît vérifié que l'on arrivait à la même solution selon le droit grec
invoqué par la demanderesse à supposer que ce droit soit applicable comme loi
du contrat, le Tribunal arbitral qui s'est déclaré compétent à l'égard de M. Z
ajoute qu'il l'est également à l'égard de X SA :

« *En effet, celle-ci l'a admis d'emblée dans ses diverses écritures, elle est entrée
en matière sur le fond sans aucune réserve et n'a pas contesté la compétence des
arbitres à son égard. Cela suffit non seulement en droit français (M.C. Rondeau-
Rivier, Juris Classeur de Procédure Civile, fascicule 1046, au n° 38, et Cour d'appel
de Paris, 15 mars 1979, Courtignon c. G.I.E. Gestion d'Assurances de la Construction, Rev. arb. 1979, 501.), mais également en droit grec, l'article 860 CPC Hell.
précisant que " si les parties à la convention comparaissent devant les arbitres et
participent sans réserve à la procédure arbitrale, le défaut d'écrit est couvert ". »*

Observations. — I. — La présente affaire et la sentence qui a été rendue
fournissent l'occasion d'examiner l'attitude qu'adopte la Cour internationale d'arbitrage lorsqu'elle statue, en application de l'article 8.3 de son Règlement, sur
l'existence d'une convention d'arbitrage *prima facie*, dans les affaires concernant
des groupes de sociétés ou des groupes animés par une personne physique.

Il résulte des dispositions combinées des articles 4.1 et 7 du Règlement, qu'une
partie qui entend décliner l'arbitrage de la CCI, doit le faire dans le délai de
30 jours qui lui est imparti pour faire parvenir sa réponse à la demande d'arbitrage.

L'absence d'objection dans la réponse à la demande d'arbitrage quant à l'existence ou la validité d'une convention d'arbitrage ne peut être interprétée que comme une acceptation de la compétence de la Cour pour organiser la procédure conformément à son Règlement, quitte à ce que le Tribunal arbitral se prononce lui-même sur sa compétence lorsque des exceptions sont ultérieurement soulevées.

Dans l'affaire 5721 (*cf. supra, p. 1020) la Cour avait accepté de mettre en œuvre la procédure telle qu'introduite par la demanderesse, alors même que deux des défenderesses n'étaient pas parties au contrat qui comportait la clause compromissoire, aucune exception de compétence n'ayant été soulevée à ce stade de la procédure, l'ensemble des défenderesses ayant par ailleurs désigné conjointement un arbitre.*

Une partie qui décline la compétence de la Cour entraîne l'examen par l'Institution de l'existence ou de l'absence prima facie d'une convention d'arbitrage liant les parties. C'est face à cette situation que la Cour s'est trouvée dans la présente affaire, M. Z ayant invoqué l'incompétence de la Cour. En l'espèce, la Cour a procédé à un examen des prétentions respectives des parties et a estimé que l'arbitrage pouvait se dérouler à l'encontre de M. Z dans les conditions visées par l'article 8.3 du Règlement, en retenant sans doute que celui-ci détenait 99,6 % de X SA et de chacune des sociétés propriétaires des navires approvisionnés par la demanderesse ou encore, en se référant au jugement du Tribunal de première instance d'Athènes qui avait autorisé la demanderesse à prendre une inscription d'hypothèque à titre conservatoire sur les biens immeubles de M. Z situés en Grèce.

Il est clair que si la Cour en l'espèce avait rendu une décision négative sur le fondement de l'article 8.3, celui que les arbitres ont retenu comme l'unique débiteur n'aurait pu être attrait à l'arbitrage en dépit de l'insertion d'une clause expresse d'arbitrage CCI, sans une procédure judiciaire préalable. Or, une telle solution aurait été « contraire aux tendances modernes de l'arbitrage : tous les progrès ont consisté en effet à faciliter la mise en œuvre de la clause arbitrale, laisser l'arbitre juge de sa compétence et maître de sa procédure, sous réserve d'un contrôle *a posteriori* de sa sentence » (selon les termes de P. Bellet, note sous Trib. gr. inst., Paris, ord. réf., 13 juill. 1988 : *Rev. Arb.* 1989, p. 99 ; *cf.* également Ph. Fouchard « Les institutions permanentes d'arbitrage devant le juge étatique » : *Rev. Arb.* 1987, p. 225 s.).

En fait, il apparaît que pour la Cour, une convention d'arbitrage *prima facie* existe dès lors que les prétentions de l'une des parties sont soutenues par quelque apparence et que leur admission éventuelle pourrait être de nature à justifier la compétence des arbitres.

La décision prise est de nature administrative, la Cour n'ayant en tant qu'organisatrice de la procédure, aucun pouvoir juridictionnel. Elle est en outre provisoire : c'est aux arbitres une fois saisis de se prononcer.

La nature administrative des décisions prises par la Cour trouve également une illustration en ce que l'Acte de mission dans cette affaire a été approuvé par la Cour, l'entreprise X ne l'ayant pas signé. Or s'il s'est révélé que cette entreprise attraite à la procédure n'était que le nom commercial de M. Z, il n'en demeure pas moins que la Cour a apprécié l'Acte de mission en fonction de données apparentes.

II. — L'un des intérêts de la présente sentence porte sur la recherche effectuée par les arbitres siégeant à Paris de la loi applicable à la clause compromissoire. Sa recherche est particulièrement intéressante car elle rappelle l'ensemble des rattachements possibles de la clause compromissoire.

Considérant que « *la convention d'arbitrage, pour être efficace, doit tirer sa force de son rattachement à un ordre juridique* », les arbitres refusent tour à tour d'invoquer l'autonomie de la convention d'arbitrage par rapport au contrat pour en déduire qu'elle serait valable indépendamment de toute loi étatique, d'appliquer l'article II de la Convention de New York qui s'adresse aux Etats contractants et non pas directement à l'arbitre international ; et enfin refusent de constater qu'il s'agit d'un arbitrage international se déroulant à Paris et soumis de par la volonté même des parties aux articles 1492 s. NCPC. Examinant dès lors les trois rattachements possibles en l'espèce, le Tribunal exclut la loi du lieu de conclusion du contrat de même que celle applicable au fond et retient finalement la loi du lieu de l'arbitrage. Ce faisant, la présente sentence se fait l'écho, comme dans l'affaire 4392 (*JDI* 1983, p. 907), de l'article 5 de la résolution de 1959 de l'Institut de droit international qui précise que « la validité de la clause compromissoire est régie par la loi du siège du Tribunal arbitral ». Cette conception de l'arbitrage international, qualifiée de procédurale ou encore juridictionnelle parce qu'elle assimile l'arbitre à un juge et confère une importance au siège arbitral, se heurte à certaines objections parmi lesquelles l'absence le plus souvent de rapport entre le lieu de l'arbitrage et le litige.

C'est pourquoi une précédente chronique (*JDI* 1986, p. 1102) se félicitait de l'émergence dans différents arbitrages de la CCI d'une présomption suivant laquelle la validité, la portée et les effets de la clause d'arbitrage sont régis par la volonté des parties et les usages du commerce international, sauf stipulation contraire des parties. Souhaitant qu'une telle présomption se renforce à l'avenir, il était toutefois fait mention de ce que son développement risque de se heurter au texte de l'article V (1)(a) de la Convention de New York de 1958. Suivant cette disposition, en l'absence d'indication des parties quant au droit auquel est soumise la convention d'arbitrage, un juge peut en effet refuser l'exécution d'une sentence reposant sur une convention d'arbitrage non valable en vertu de la loi du pays où la sentence a été rendue.

La présente sentence, permet de constater que la question de la détermination de la loi ou de la règle de droit applicable à la convention d'arbitrage est abordée de façon pragmatique par les arbitres. Ceux-ci, en effet, apparaissent veiller tout particulièrement à ce que la sentence soit susceptible de sanction légale. Ce faisant ils appliquent la loi du lieu de l'arbitrage ou d'autres normes, tout en indiquant qu'elles ne sont pas contraires à l'ordre public.

III. — La présente sentence dégage, par une analyse minutieuse des faits, les raisons qui conduisent à mettre en cause, en l'espèce, la responsabilité personnelle du dirigeant d'un groupe de sociétés. Ce n'est pas uniquement le comportement du dirigeant avant, pendant et après les négociations contractuelles qui est pris en compte, mais aussi le fait qu'il a créé et entretenu l'apparence d'un groupe « en utilisant des noms de navires et des raisons sociales proches les unes des autres... ainsi qu'en mêlant comme à plaisir la gestion et les comptes » de ses diverses sociétés. De par cette analyse, la sentence établit en particulier :

— la volonté de la demanderesse de traiter personnellement avec le dirigeant du groupe qualifié de « chairman » ;

— l'absence de volonté d'une des entités du groupe d'agir séparément ;

— la confusion résultant de la non-indépendance des entités constituant le groupe.

Par ailleurs, en vertu de la loi française déclarée applicable, c'est en raison de la « *parfaite connaissance de la clause arbitrale qui figurait dans le (contrat) qui lui avait été soumis au préalable* » que le dirigeant du groupe se voit étendre les effets de la clause compromissoire « *signée en son nom, sur ses instructions et en sa présence »* par son employé *« qui n'était que l'exécutant de sa volonté et n'avait aucun titre à intervenir ».*

Cette décision quant à sa motivation n'est pas sans rappeler la règle matérielle posée par la Cour d'appel de Paris dans deux arrêts rendus postérieurement à la présente sentence (*Rev. arb.* 1989, 691 note P.-Y. Tschanz) suivant laquelle :

« La clause d'arbitrage insérée dans un contrat international a une validité et une efficacité propres qui commandent d'en étendre les effets aux parties directement impliquées dans l'exécution du contrat, dès lors que leur situation et leurs activités font présumer qu'elles avaient connaissance de l'existence et de la portée de cette clause, stipulée conformément aux usages du commerce international. »

N'existerait-il donc aucune différence en la matière entre les usages du commerce international et la loi française applicable ? Il est intéressant de relever à cet égard, l'analogie du raisonnement suivi par les arbitres faisant application de la théorie des groupes. A la lecture des différentes sentences qui se sont prononcées sur la notion de groupe et ses conséquences (aff. 1434 : *JDI* 1975, p. 978 ; 2375 : *JDI* 1975, p. 973 ; 4131 : *JDI* 1983, p. 899), force est de constater que les arbitres ne se limitent pas à établir l'existence d'un groupe, mais recherchent également le rôle joué par l'un ou l'autre de ses membres non signataire. Comme le signale M. Ibrahim Fadlallah (*Clauses d'arbitrage et groupes de sociétés, Droit international privé* 1984-1985, éd. CNRS Paris 1987, p. 105 s.) *« c'est surtout la participation des diverses sociétés à l'opération objet de la convention qui est déterminante ».* C'est ainsi que la sentence rendue dans l'affaire 4504 (*JDI* 1986, p. 1118) a refusé d'étendre une clause compromissoire à un membre d'un groupe, après avoir constaté qu'il n'avait jamais manifesté une volonté d'exécuter et/ou de participer dans l'exécution du contrat avec la société mère. Il peut être aussi fait appel à cette notion lorsque les circonstances démontrent que la société partie à la convention d'arbitrage a été privée intentionnellement de toute substance.

I. — Clause compromissoire. — Autonomie. — Contrat. — Entrée en vigueur. — Effets sur la clause compromissoire.

II. — Litispendance. — Conflit de compétences judiciaires et arbitrales (non).

III. — Connexité. — Conflit de compétences judiciaires et arbitrales (non).

IV. — Lois de police. — *Lex contractus.* — Application d'office.

Sentence rendue dans l'affaire n° 6142 en 1990

Un arbitre unique siégeant à Paris, étant saisi d'un litige opposant une société française bailleresse de licence et demanderesse, à deux sociétés espagnoles, défenderesses. L'action de la demanderesse tendait entre autres à la constatation par l'arbitre de la résiliation d'un contrat de licence de fabrication et d'assistance technique et d'un contrat de licence de marque, conclus respectivement avec la première et la seconde défenderesse. Ces deux contrats, rédigés en deux versions, française et espagnole, de même qu'un contrat de base rédigé dans la seule langue espagnole, contenaient une clause compromissoire selon laquelle tous différends en découlant seraient tranchés à Paris selon le Règlement d'Arbitrage de la CCI. Le droit espagnol était applicable au fond.

La demanderesse fondait son action sur une disposition des versions françaises du contrat de licence de fabrication et d'assistance technique et du contrat de licence de marque prévoyant que leur résiliation anticipée pourrait intervenir au cas où le montant net des ventes servant de base de calcul de la redevance due par les sociétés espagnoles serait inférieur à un minimum annuel. Cette disposition n'apparaissait pas dans la version espagnole des contrats. Cependant, une lettre signée des sociétés espagnoles précisait que la version française prévaudrait en cas de divergences.

Antérieurement à l'introduction de la procédure arbitrale par la société française, la première défenderesse espagnole avait saisi une juridiction étatique de son pays pour, entre autres, faire constater l'inefficacité de la clause de minimum de vente figurant dans les versions françaises du contrat. Cette inefficacité résultait selon elle de ce que seule la version espagnole des contrats de licence, d'où la clause était omise, avait obtenu l'approbation du ministère espagnol de l'Industrie. Or, les accords des parties précisaient que cette approbation conditionnait leur entrée en vigueur. Cependant, la juridiction espagnole devait se déclarer incompétente en raison de la présence d'une clause compromissoire dans les accords litigieux, décision qui était frappée d'appel avant le prononcé de la présente sentence arbitrale.

Dans la procédure arbitrale, la première défenderesse avait repris son argumentation concernant l'inefficacité de la clause de minimum de vente et du droit de résiliation s'y attachant. Elle soutenait également que la clause compromissoire était sans effet, faute d'entrée en vigueur des contrats et opposait des exceptions de litispendance et de connexité découlant de la procédure en cours devant les juridictions étatiques espagnoles.

La deuxième défenderesse faisait défaut.

L'arbitre se prononça tout d'abord sur les effets de la clause compromissoire dans les termes ci-après :

« *Attendu que, comme le soutient à bon droit la demanderesse, il ressort du dossier que les contrats rédigés en espagnol ont effectivement été soumis au ministère de l'Industrie ;*

Que la première défenderessse elle-même plaidait ce fait dans les écritures qu'elle a soumises au Tribunal de première instance...

Que la clause compromissoire est donc entrée en vigueur puisqu'il ne peut être contesté que cette clause figure dans la version espagnole des contrats, laquelle a été soumise au ministère de l'Industrie, avec la conséquence que lesdits contrats, dans leur texte espagnol au moins, sont entrés en vigueur ;

Attendu que l'arbitre relève également que le contrat de base ne contient aucune disposition soumettant son entrée en vigueur à la condition préalable de sa présentation auprès du ministère de l'Industrie ;

Que, si la partie demanderesse ne demande certes pas la résolution dudit contrat, il n'en demeure pas moins que le litige opposant les parties se meut dans le cadre des droits et obligations qui y sont mis en œuvre, le contrat de licence de marque et le contrat de licence de fabrication et d'assistance technique en constituant d'ailleurs les annexes...

Que la clause compromissoire figurant au contrat de base était donc en tout cas entrée en vigueur dès la date de sa signature... »

L'arbitre aborda ensuite les exceptions de litispendance et de connexité :

« *Attendu que, dans ses premières conclusions, la première défenderesse demande le renvoi de la cause devant le Tribunal de première instance... pour raison de litispendance ou, à tout le moins, de connexité avec la demande qu'elle a elle-même introduite devant cette juridiction...*

Qu'elle souligne que cette demande est antérieure à la demande d'arbitrage... ;

Attendu, cependant, qu'il n'y a manifestement aucune litispendance entre les deux causes, les parties, si elles sont identiques, n'agissant pas en mêmes qualités ;

Que le Tribunal de première instance... est en effet saisi d'une demande dirigée par la première défenderesse au présent litige contre la demanderesse et la seconde défenderesse ;

Qu'en outre, il ne saurait y avoir de litispendance dès lors qu'une clause compromissoire est déclarée valable puisqu'elle a précisément pour objet d'écarter la compétence des juridictions ordinaires ;

Que le Tribunal de première instance... s'est, du reste, déclaré incompétent... en raison de la validité de la clause d'arbitrage figurant dans les contrats en litige ;

Que cette décision a, de plus, vidé la juridiction de l'instance devant laquelle la première défenderesse demandait le renvoi de sorte que cette demande est devenue sans objet ;

Attendu que si les deux causes sont, par contre, manifestement connexes, il n'en demeure pas moins que cette connexité n'autorise pas le renvoi, pour les mêmes motifs que ceux exposés aux trois alinéas qui précèdent ;

Qu'il en est d'autant plus ainsi que les deux litiges opposent les mêmes parties, sans intervention de tiers qui ne seraient pas liés par la clause compromissoire ;

Attendu, pour le surplus, qu'il n'entre pas dans les compétences de l'arbitre de faire la critique du jugement rendu par le Tribunal de première instance..., ni de se comporter en juridiction d'appel de cette décision, comme le demande la première défenderesse... »

Ayant ainsi constaté la recevabilité de la demande, l'arbitre la déclare néanmoins infondée :

« *Attendu que la demanderesse fonde son action sur l'article 6.03 (b) de la version française du contrat de licence de fabrication et d'assistance technique et l'article 8.03 (b) de la version française du contrat de licence de marque ;*

Qu'il est ici rappelé que ces clauses ne figurent pas dans les versions espagnoles des mêmes contrats ;

Que les défenderesses ont adressé une lettre à la demanderesse, reconnaissant la prévalence des versions françaises sur les versions espagnoles en cas de divergence entre elles ;

Attendu que la première défenderesse soutient que cette lettre est contraire à l'ordre public espagnol et qu'elle est, partant, frappée de nullité, les parties n'étant valablement liées, selon elles, que par les contrats rédigés en espagnol, étant les seuls qui ont été inscrits dans le registre du ministère de l'Industrie, en exécution de l'article 3 du décret 2343/1973 du 21 septembre 1973 réglementant les transferts de technologie (B.D.E. n° 236, 2 octobre 1973 rectifié dans le B.D.E. du 12 octobre 1973) ;

Attendu que, indépendamment même de l'exception ainsi invoquée par une partie, l'arbitre aurait d'ailleurs le devoir de soulever d'office la nullité de toute convention ou clause qui serait contraire à l'ordre public espagnol, au même titre qu'une juridiction ordinaire espagnole ;

Qu'en l'espèce, l'arbitre doit avoir égard à l'ordre public interne et non uniquement à l'ordre public international espagnol, les relations des parties étant soumises au droit espagnol ;

Qu'en cas de violation de l'ordre public, l'arbitre est donc tenu d'appliquer l'article 6 du Code civil espagnol qui consacre notamment la nullité des conventions contraires à l'ordre ou même à l'intérêt public ;

Attendu que les dispositions du décret 2343/1973 du 21 septembre 1973 touchent manifestement à l'intérêt public ;

Qu'une loi qui sauvegarde l'intérêt public est d'ordre public, à la différence de normes simplement impératives qui ne viseraient qu'à protéger des intérêts privés ;

Que le préambule du décret exprime clairement le souci du législateur de contrôler le choix et l'acquisition des technologies étrangères ainsi que les modalités des transferts ainsi opérés en vue de stimuler l'utilisation de ces technologies dans des conditions de rendement maximum pour l'économie nationale (" (...) supervisar la seleccion y adquisicion de tecnologia extranjera, asi como las modalidades segun las que esta adquisicion se produce y, asimismo, a fomentar una utilizacion de esta tecnologia en condiciones que procuren maximo rendimiento para la economia nacional. ") ;

Qu'il souligne également la nécessité d'une intervention publique régulatrice des aspects substantiels du transfert de technologies étrangères (" ... se estima la convenienza de una intervencion publica reguladora de los aspectos sustantivos de la transferencia de tecnologia extranjera. ") ;

Attendu que, dans l'esprit de la préoccupation exprimée au préambule, le législateur espagnol ne s'est pas contenté d'imposer une simple obligation d'inscription des contrats de transfert de technologie auprès du ministère de l'Industrie, mais investit celui-ci d'un véritable droit de regard sur le contenu de tels contrats ;

Que, plus spécifiquement, l'article 5 permet à l'administration de refuser l'inscription des contrats contenant des clauses restrictives qui font obstacle, portent préjudice au développement technologique du bénéficiaire du transfert ou le restreignent ;

Que l'administration peut également procéder à l'inscription avec annotations en formulant à cet égard toutes remarques utiles ;

Que, confirmant à cet égard les termes de l'article 5, dernier alinéa du décret susvisé, l'article 2.4 de l'Ordonnance du 5 décembre 1973 réglementant l'inscription des contrats de transfert de technologie, dispose que l'administration communique sa décision de refus d'inscription ou d'inscription avec annotations à l'intéressé afin qu'il apporte les modifications nécessaires au contrat initial, dans un délai de un mois ;

Attendu que, parmi les clauses contractuelles pouvant donner lieu à un refus d'inscription ou à une inscription avec annotation, figurent notamment :

— la fixation d'un niveau minimum d'activité ou la limitation de la liberté du licencié de décider des caractéristiques de sa production notamment quant à son niveau (art. 3, al. 2.6 de l'Ordonnance) ;

— l'imposition de la prédominance en matière d'interprétation d'une version en langue étrangère du contrat (art. 3, al. 2.15 de l'Ordonnance) ;

Que l'administration entend donc juger, dans chaque cas d'espèce, eu égard à ses spécificités, si de telles clauses justifient un refus d'inscription ou une inscription avec annotations ;

Qu'elle est tenue de s'enquérir de leur conformité avec l'intérêt public ;

Attendu que le refus du transfert de devises à l'étranger en exécution du contrat, tel que prévu par l'article 6 du Décret ne constitue pas l'unique sanction du défaut ou du refus d'inscription ;

Que l'article 5 de l'Ordonnance du 5 décembre 1973, dispose en effet que les contrats visés sont dénués de toute efficacité tant qu'ils ne sont pas inscrits au registre, avec ou sans annotation (" ... la eficacia de todo contrato, convenio o acuerdo documentado regulado en la presenta Orden, queda supeditada a su previa inscripcion, con o sin anotaciones en el Registro de Contratos de Transferencia de Tecnologia ") ;

Que cette inscription constitue, en d'autres termes, une condition suspensive de l'entrée en vigueur du contrat en cause ;

Que le législateur espagnol entend manifestement s'opposer, de la sorte, à l'exécution de contrats dont il n'aurait pu préalablement s'assurer de la conformité avec l'intérêt public ;...

Attendu que l'engagement souscrit par les deux défenderesses dans la lettre qu'elles ont adressée à la demanderesse le..., par laquelle elles invitaient celle-ci à contresigner les versions espagnoles des contrats de licence de marque et d'assistance technique à présenter aux autorités espagnoles aux fins d'inscription dans le registre, et acceptaient concomitamment de faire prévaloir les versions françaises si les versions espagnoles n'en reflétaient pas exactement le contenu, est donc frappé de nullité absolue en tant qu'il vise à donner plein et entier effet à des contrats qui divergeraient par leur contenu, de ceux qui seraient inscrits au registre du ministère de l'Industrie ;

Que le Tribunal arbitral ne peut donc avoir égard qu'aux versions espagnoles des contrats litigieux, telles qu'elles ont été présentées aux autorités espagnoles, de sorte qu'il ne peut prendre en considération les clauses de minimum de vente qui figurent dans les seules versions françaises ;

Qu'à défaut d'inscription dans le registre du ministère de l'Industrie, ces versions françaises sont en effet privées de toute efficacité, en vertu de l'article 5 de l'Ordonnance du 5 décembre 1973 ;

Attendu, à titre surabondant, qu'à supposer même que le Décret 2343/1973 du 21 septembre 1973 et son ordonnance d'application du 5 décembre 1973 ne soient pas d'ordre public et que, comme l'affirme la demanderesse, ces normes revêtent uniquement un caractère impératif, l'engagement contenu dans la lettre du... n'en serait pas moins nul de plein droit par application de l'article 6.3 du Code civil espagnol ;

Attendu, à titre encore plus surabondant, qu'à supposer même que cette nullité soit non pas absolue, mais simplement relative et qu'elle doive donc être invoquée par une partie qui y a un intérêt ou qu'il puisse y être renoncé, force serait de constater que la première défenderesse invoque précisément cette nullité ;

Attendu qu'il échet de souligner également que cette nullité, en tant qu'elle frappe l'engagement du..., s'ajoute à l'inefficacité des versions françaises des contrats de licence de marque et de licence de fabrication et d'assistance technique du... telle qu'elle est prévue par l'Ordonnance du 5 décembre 1973, la seconde sanction ne se substituant nullement à la première en application de l'article 6.3 du Code civil espagnol, dès lors qu'elles frappent des actes différents ;

Attendu que, au regard des motifs qui précèdent et sans qu'il y ait lieu d'examiner les autres moyens développés par les parties, la demande n'est pas fondée ;...

OBSERVATIONS. — I. — Dans la présente affaire, il n'était pas difficile à l'arbitre d'éluder le problème des effets de la non-entrée en vigueur d'un contrat sur la portée d'une clause compromissoire. En effet, il n'était pas contesté que les contrats de licence étaient entrés en vigueur dans leur version espagnole et l'efficacité du contrat cadre ne faisait pas problème. L'existence d'un accord d'arbitrage permettant à l'arbitre de se prononcer sur l'étendue des obligations des parties au contrat de licence était donc acquise.

Il reste que l'arbitre aurait pu se prononcer sur la demande de résolution qui lui était soumise, même si les contrats de licence n'avaient été signés qu'en leur version française et si, faute d'approbation par le ministère espagnol de l'Industrie, ils n'étaient jamais entrés en vigueur.

Une sentence rendue en 1983 dans l'affaire CCI n° 3987 (cf JDI 1984, p. 943, obs. Y. Derains ; Recueil des sentences arbitrales de la CCI par S. Jarvin et Y. Derains, p. 521), rappelle opportunément que lorsqu'un contrat conditionne son entrée en vigueur à l'obtention d'autorisations administratives, il n'en résulte pas que les parties n'aient aucune obligation contractuelle avant cette entrée en vigueur. Elles ont à tout le moins l'obligation de faire leur possible pour que les conditions d'entrée en vigueur du contrat se réalisent. Par conséquent, un litige qui porte sur l'effet obligatoire du contrat signé par les parties se situe nécessairement dans le champ d'application d'une clause prévoyant que tous les litiges découlant du contrat seront réglés par arbitrage.

De plus, l'autonomie de la convention d'arbitrage, règle aujourd'hui incontestée de l'arbitrage international (cf. inter alia la sentence rendue en 1986 dans l'affaire CCI n° 4381 : JDI 1986, p. 1103, obs. Y. Derains) s'oppose à ce qu'il suffise d'invoquer l'inefficacité du contrat pour en déduire l'inefficacité de cette convention. Si la convention d'arbitrage est matériellement reproduite dans le document qui définit les obligations économiques des parties – le contrat – il n'en est pas moins vrai qu'il s'agit de deux actes juridiques dont l'objet est différent : une opération économique d'un côté, la résolution des litiges susceptibles d'en découler de l'autre. C'est pourquoi la constatation de l'inexistence ou de la nullité du contrat n'entraîne pas l'inexistence ou la nullité de la convention d'arbitrage. Il se peut qu'une même cause affecte à la fois la validité du contrat et de la convention d'arbitrage – vice de consentement par exemple – mais dans ce cas les deux actes juridiques sont frappés de façon concomitante. C'est pourquoi on concluera, à fortiori, que l'absence d'une entrée en vigueur du contrat ne saurait entraîner une absence d'entrée en vigueur de la convention d'arbitrage, à moins bien entendu que contrat et convention aient été soumis à la même condition suspensive.

II et III. — Le rejet des exceptions de litispendance et de connexité au motif que l'existence d'une convention d'arbitrage s'oppose à la compétence des juridictions étatiques n'est pas nouvelle dans la jurisprudence des arbitres du commerce international. La solution était clairement posée dans une sentence rendue en 1988 dans l'affaire CCI n° 5103 (cf. JDI 1988, obs. G. Aguilar Alvarez) qui s'exprimait dans les termes suivants :

« La litispendance, à proprement parler, ne peut surgir qu'entre deux juridictions d'un même Etat ou de deux Etats différents, lorsque les règles de compétence de leur for les autorisent l'une et l'autre à connaître d'un même litige (sur l'admission récente de la litispendance internationale par la jurisprudence française qui la subordonne cependant à double compétence du juge français et du juge étranger, cf. Cass. civ, I, 26 nov. 1974 : Clunet 1975, 108, note A. Ponsard ; Rev. crit. dr. int. pr. 1975, 19, note D. Holleaux ; cf. A. Huet, J.Cl. dr. int., fasc. 581-D, n° 110 s.). Cette situation de compétence concurrente ne peut surgir entre une juridiction arbitrale et une juridiction étatique, pour la raison que leur compétence respective ne dépend que d'un seul facteur ; l'existence, la validité et l'étendue de la convention d'arbitrage. »

C'est qu'en présence d'une clause d'arbitrage, le problème de la vérification de la compétence d'une juridiction étatique ne se pose pas. La juridiction étatique ne peut être saisie du litige, comme l'a d'ailleurs en l'espèce confirmé la juridiction espagnole devant laquelle s'était présentée la première défenderesse. L'article II (3) de la Convention de New York de 1958 lui imposait de renvoyer les parties à l'arbitrage. Dans ces conditions l'exception de litispendance, de même que celle de connexité, ne peut trouver sa place.

IV. — Pour refuser de reconnaître la portée des clauses de minimum de ventes figurant dans les seules versions françaises des contrats, l'arbitre fait application de l'ordonnance espagnole du 5 décembre 1973 privant d'effet les contrats de transfert de technologie qui n'ont pas été inscrits dans les registres du ministère de l'Industrie. En effet, l'absence de ces clauses dans les versions espagnoles – seules à avoir été inscrites – fait qu'elles sont lettres mortes. Il est remarquable que l'arbitre ait pris le soin de souligner que si la première défenderesse ne s'était pas fondée sur ce texte espagnol, il aurait soulevé « d'office la nullité de toute convention ou clause qui serait contraire à l'ordre public espagnol, au même titre qu'une juridiction ordinaire espagnole ». Ceci appelle plusieurs observations.

Tout d'abord, on peut partager la conviction de l'arbitre qu'il avait le devoir de faire application du texte espagnol en cause, sans pour autant admettre qu'il agissait au même titre qu'une juridiction espagnole ordinaire. L'application par l'arbitre international des lois de police pose des problèmes différents de ceux que soulève l'application des lois de police par le juge (*cf.* sur ce point P. Mayer, « Mandatory rules of law in international arbitration », *in Arbitration International,* 1986, p. 274 s. ; Y. Derains, « L'ordre public et le droit applicable au fond du litige dans l'arbitrage international » : *Rev. Arb.* 1986, p. 375 s.).

En effet, le juge effectue naturellement une distinction entre lois de police du for et lois de police étrangères qui ne peut exister pour l'arbitre. Pour ce dernier toutes les lois qui prétendent appréhender le contrat ont a priori un titre égal à s'appliquer, à l'exception du droit choisi par les parties pour régir leur contrat, la *lex contractus.* Celle-ci s'impose à l'arbitre du fait de la volonté des parties, sans que l'arbitre ait à apprécier le choix qu'elles ont fait. Mais dans ce cas le devoir qu'a l'arbitre d'appliquer une loi déterminée est sans communauté de nature avec celui qu'a le juge d'appliquer la loi du for ou du moins le droit que cette loi désigne. Le devoir de l'arbitre se rattache à sa mission ; celui du juge à son office. Les premières destinataires du devoir de l'arbitre sont les parties ; le destinataire du devoir du juge est l'Etat au nom duquel il rend la justice. Cette différence a des conséquences pratiques. Le juge ne saurait se demander si les parties ont voulu écarter l'application d'une loi de police du for. L'arbitre, qui n'est pas le gardien de l'ordre public de l'Etat qui a édicté la loi de police dont l'application est demandée, ou qu'il envisage d'appliquer d'office, doit se poser la question qui se développe en deux branches : les parties ont-elles voulu écarter la loi de police ? (Si oui, le fait que celle-ci appartienne à la *lex contractus* qu'elles ont choisi est indifférent puisque leur choix se révèle avoir été un choix limité) ; la volonté des parties d'écarter la loi de police était-elle légitime ?.

Cette dernière question indique que si les parties sont bien les premières destinataires du devoir de l'arbitre, elles ne sont pas les seules. En effet, si l'arbitre n'a pas de devoirs vis-à-vis de l'Etat qui a édicté une loi susceptible d'appréhender le contrat, il en a vis-à-vis de la communauté du commerce international, la *Societas Mercatorum,* pour laquelle le développement de l'arbitrage international et sa coexistence pacifique avec les Etats et les ordres juridiques nationaux est indispensable. Or, cette coexistence serait compromise si l'arbitrage devenait un instrument de fraude aux intérêts légitimes des Etats et était perçu comme tel par ceux-ci. A moyen terme l'arbitrage ne pourrait survivre.

Par conséquent, s'il est exact qu'en l'espèce l'arbitre se devait d'appliquer la loi de police espagnole en cause, et éventuellement de l'appliquer d'office, ce n'est pas au même titre qu'une juridiction espagnole. Celle-ci aurait dû, dans tous les cas appliquer la loi de police en question, que les contrats de licence aient ou non été soumis au droit espagnol et que les parties aient ou non exprimé la volonté d'écarter cette loi de police. L'arbitre au contraire avait le devoir d'appliquer cette loi de police, soit parce que les parties s'y étaient expressément ou implicitement soumises, soit parce que l'ayant écartée (directement ou indirectement, en choisissant un autre droit que le droit espagnol pour régir leur contrat) elles portaient préjudice à un intérêt légitime d'un Etat, que l'arbitre doit faire respecter en raison de ses devoirs vis-à-vis de la *Societas Mercatorum*. La légitimité de l'intérêt de l'Etat à l'application de la loi de police semble pouvoir s'apprécier à la lumière de deux critères différents. Le premier, qui est le plus important, est le champ d'application que l'Etat donne à la loi de police. A cet égard, on peut estimer que les lois de police de l'Etat sur le territoire duquel le contrat est exécuté ont toujours un titre légitime à s'appliquer. Le second est le contenu de la loi de police, qui ne doit pas être incompatible avec l'ordre public international (*cf.* P. Lalive, « Ordre public transnational ou réellement international et arbitrage international » : *Rev. Arb.* 1986, p. 329 s.).

Dans l'espèce tranchée par la présente sentence, il ne semble pas que les parties aient voulu écarter l'application, même partielle, du décret espagnol réglementant les transferts de technologie. La lettre indiquant qu'en cas de contradiction entre les versions espagnoles et françaises des contrats, ces dernières auraient la prééminence, n'appelle pas nécessairement une telle interprétation. Au contraire, le fait qu'il ait été procédé à l'inscription des contrats au registre du ministère de l'Industrie révèle plutôt une volonté de se soumettre à ce décret. Cependant, au cas où cette volonté aurait réellement existé, l'arbitre aurait dû constater qu'elle était inopérante puisque contraire à une loi de police dont l'application correspondait à un intérêt légitime de l'Etat espagnol.

Le double critère du champ d'application et du contenu compatible avec l'ordre public transnational confirme en effet la légitimité de l'intérêt de l'Etat espagnol à l'application du décret réglementant les transferts de technologie. Par contre, on a quelque peine à suivre l'arbitre lorsqu'il précise, à titre surabondant, qu'à supposer que le Décret ne soit pas « d'ordre public », mais seulement de droit impératif, la lettre établissant la préeminence des versions françaises des contrats n'en seraient pas moins nulle. Si par « ordre public » l'arbitre vise la notion de loi de police – et cette acceptation ressort de l'ensemble de la sentence – et par droit impératif il évoque les normes auxquelles on ne peut déroger, on peut douter de la pertinence de l'observation. En effet, dans la mesure où en matière d'arbitrage international les parties sont libres de choisir le droit applicable, elles pouvaient en théorie soumettre leurs contrats à un autre droit que le droit espagnol. Dans cette hypothèse le décret, simple norme impérative, ne se serait pas appliqué. Toujours si le décret avait eu cette nature, on ne voit pas pourquoi les parties n'auraient pu faire un choix partiel du droit espagnol, excluant l'intervention du décret. Ce n'est en fait que parce que le décret n'est pas seulement de droit impératif mais une loi de police que l'arbitre doit l'appliquer, y compris contre la volonté des parties. Il est vrai que le caractère fluctuant de la terminologie suscite dans ce domaine bien des malentendus.

Rappelons enfin que si l'application de la loi de police espagnole avait été soulevée d'office, l'arbitre aurait dû soumettre le moyen aux observations des parties avant de l'invoquer. Mais le problème ne se posait pas en l'espèce.

Y. D.

I. — Paiement. — Taux d'intérêt. — Liberté de l'arbitre international.

II. — Dette. — Pays en voie de développement. — Rééchelonnement. — Usage du commerce international (non). — Commerce international (non). — Incidence sur contrat de droit privé.

Sentence rendue dans l'affaire CCI n° 6219 en 1990

Un arbitre unique, siégeant à Paris, était saisi d'un litige portant sur les conséquences des difficultés rencontrées par un Etat africain X pour rembourser un crédit fournisseur relatif à la vente de matériel de travaux publics par une société Y incorporée à Barhein. Le crédit était matérialisé par des billets à ordre libellés en Yens.

Ces difficultés apparurent avec la troisième échéance. Seul le billet à ordre représentant les intérêts de cette échéance fut honoré. Ni le billet à ordre portant sur le principal de cette échéance, ni aucun des billets à ordre des échéances suivantes ne devaient être payés.

Par un accord amiable Y et ses débiteurs de l'Etat X s'entendirent pour que les sommes dues à la date de l'accord portent intérêt au taux de 10,5 %, le paiement de ces intérêts devant intervenir, si possible, dans un délai d'un mois. Pour la période intérimaire comprise entre la date de l'accord amiable et de nouvelles négociations, X proposa que le taux d'intérêts soit le *prime rate* Japon à 6 mois, augmenté d'une marge de 1.7/8 % par an. Y s'engagea à examiner cette proposition.

Aucun nouveau paiement n'étant intervenu, Y en qualité de demanderesse a introduit une action en arbitrage contre ses débiteurs de l'Etat X, y compris l'Etat lui-même, en qualité de défenderesses. Devant l'arbitre les défenderesses ne contestaient pas leurs obligations de payer les sommes dues à Y. Elles invoquaient la situation financière difficile dans laquelle se trouvait la République de X et faisait valoir que ses créanciers étrangers, publics et privés, avaient consenti, respectivement dans le cadre du Club de Paris et du Club de Londres, des rééchelonnements de sa dette et que, tenue de traiter également tous ses créanciers, X avait conduit avec ceux qui n'étaient pas concernés par ces premiers arrangements, d'autres négociations au sein du « Club de Z » (capitale de X). Une telle négociation avait été engagée avec Y, comme en témoignait l'accord amiable, mais Y ne l'aurait pas poursuivie. Les défenderesses en conluaient que Y ne pouvait réclamer par voie d'arbitrage l'intégralité des sommes qui lui étaient dues sans que de réelles négociations, menées de bonne foi, et en accord avec les pratiques internationales reconnues, aient permis de rechercher les bases d'une solution à l'amiable.

L'arbitre commença par déterminer le montant des sommes impayées, et pour ce faire dut se prononcer sur le taux d'intérêt.

Il le fit dans les termes suivants :

« Le principal (c'est-à-dire le montant des billets à ordre impayés), sur la base duquel sont calculés les intérêts de retard, n'est pas contesté. Ne le sont pas davantage les dates à partir desquelles ont couru ces intérêts, et qui correspondent aux dates d'exigibilité des billets à ordre. Et comme enfin Y n'a jamais demandé que ces intérêts moratoires soient capitalisés et produisent eux-mêmes des intérêts avant la sentence, la seule question qui reste discutée est le taux qu'il convient de retenir.

Y fait valoir que si le taux contractuel était de 8,50 %, ce taux a été porté à 10,25 % par l'accord amiable... et que ce nouveau taux n'a jamais été contesté par les défenderesses jusqu'à l'audience...

428

Les défenderesses, à l'audience..., puis dans leur telex du... ont contesté cette argumentation. Elles se prévalent tout d'abord des termes du telex adressé le... par M. ..., directeur comptable de Y (Bahrein), d'où il résulterait que " le montant des intérêts a été obtenu par application d'un taux de 8,5 % pour chaque période d'intérêt ". Les défenderesses font également valoir que l'accord amiable limitait l'application du taux de 10,25 % au montant des billets à ordre impayés (a sa date) et que cet accord de portée limitée " ne saurait remplacer le taux contractuel de 8,5 % applicable à l'ensemble du prêt ".

« *L'arbitre estime que ni l'accord amiable, ni le comportement ultérieur des parties, ni le télex du... ne permettent de trancher complètement la question du taux d'intérêt moratoire applicable.*

En ce qui concerne l'accord amiable, il est vrai qu'il retient un taux d'intérêt moratoire de 10,25 % ; mais c'est seulement sur " le montant des billets à ordre en principal et intérêts échus et impayés a sa date ", c'est-à-dire sur une somme de 486.810.000 yens. Ces intérêts moratoires ont été calculés et fixés par le procès-verbal à 48.587.978 yens. Mais les parties déclaraient ensuite :

« *Concernant le taux d'intérêt à appliquer pendant la période intermédiaire allant du... jusqu'à la date de nouvelles négociations, X a proposé le prime rate Japon à six (6) mois, augmenté d'une marge de 1.7/8 % par an.*

Y prend l'engagement d'examiner cette proposition et répondre avant... »

Ainsi, il n'y a eu aucun accord, à la date de l'accord amiable, sur un taux définitif d'intérêts moratoires. Par la suite, Y n'a pas répondu à la proposition de X ; on ne saurait d'ailleurs lui en faire grief car l'inexécution complète, par les défenderesses, de leurs engagements et la cessation de tout versement de leur part rendait assez vaine toute discussion avec elles sur le taux des intérêts moratoires.

D'autre part, s'il est exact que toutes les réclamations postérieures de Y étaient calculées sur un taux de 10,25 %, et que ce taux n'a fait l'objet d'aucune contestation expresse avant l'audience..., on ne saurait assimiler ce silence prolongé à un consentement. En effet, invoquant les difficultés de la situation financière dans la République de X et leurs obligations vis-à-vis de la communauté financière internationale, les défenderesses ont constamment invité leur créancier à de nouvelles négociations, notamment dans le cadre de ce qu'elles appellent le « Club de Z ». Le but de celles-ci, comme de celles relatives aux autres composantes de la dette extérieure de X (Club de Paris, Club de Londres) est de « restructurer » cette dette dans ses différents aspects (montant, taux, délais). Quels que soient les mérites de la position de X, il suffit de retenir ici qu'elle était incompatible avec un accord quelconque des défenderesses sur le taux des intérêts moratoires consécutifs à leur défaillance.

Enfin, le télex de M. ... du... n'a pas davantage la portée que prétendent lui attribuer les défenderesses. Communiqué à l'arbitre sous la forme d'une simple copie redactylographiée, il se présente comme une " request for balance confirmation " au..., et se borne à reproduire la liste et le montant des 13 billets à ordre impayés (avec, en outre, une erreur de date, puisque chacune des échéances est retardée d'un an). Il aboutit au total de 827.457.500 yens. C'est celui du montant de tous les billets à ordre impayés ; il est incontesté, et a déjà été retenu ci-dessus au titre de la dette contractuelle. Le compte ainsi produit par Y ne comprend pas les éventuels intérêts de retard qui seraient dûs en raison du défaut de paiement, à leur échéance, de ces divers billets à ordre. Et ce sont ces intérêts moratoires qui sont réclamés dans le cadre de la procédure arbitrale et dont il convient de déterminer le taux.

Dans le cadre d'un arbitrage international, cette détermination n'est pas gouvernée par des règles rigoureuses et précises.

La tendance générale qui se dégage, en doctrine et dans la pratique arbitrale internationale, est de laisser à l'arbitre une grande liberté dans la fixation de ce taux

(V. notamment J. Gillis Wetter, " Interest for an element of damages in the arbitral process ", International Financial Law Review, dec. 1986, p. 20-25 ; S. Boyd, " Interest for the late payment of money ", Arbitration international, july 1985, p. 153 : Sentence had hoc Liamco c/ Libye, Genève, 12 juillet 1977, Revue de l'arbitrage, 1980.132, spéc. p. 187 et s. ; Sentence CIRDI AGIP c/ Gouvernement de la RP du Congo, 30 novembre 1979, Rev. crit. dr. int. pr., 1982.92, spéc. p. 104, Yearbook Commercial Arbitration, 1983.133, spéc. p. 142 ; Sentence CIRDI Benvenuti et Bonfante c/ Gouvernement de la RP du Congo, 8 août 1980, Yearbook Commercial Arbitration, 1983.144, spéc. p. 151 ; Sentence CCI 17 février 1984, n° 4237, Yearbook Commercial Arbitration, 1985.52, spéc. p. 59 ; Sentence du Tribunal irano-américain, McCollough & Company, Inc., 22 avril 1986, citée par T. G., Bulletin de l'Association suisse d'arbitrage, 1987.55, spéc. p. 57). Celui-ci n'est pas tenu de se référer au taux légal d'un système juridique national, qu'il s'agisse de celui de la loi contractuelle ou de celui du lieu de l'arbitrage.

En l'espèce, il convient d'ailleurs de constater que les parties n'ont soumis le contrat a aucune loi étatique déterminée, et que l'acte de mission ne précise pas davantage quel est le droit applicable au fond du litige. Bien plus, aucune partie ne sollicite, pour régler cette question, l'application d'un droit national déterminé, ni du taux légal en vigueur soit dans la République de X, soit dans le pays de Y.

Quant au taux légal français, s'il doit naturellement s'appliquer aux sommes qui seront allouées dans la sentence, à partir de celle-ci et jusqu'à leur paiement effectif, il n'a pas de titre particulier pour s'appliquer aux retards contractuels. Il n'est cependant pas inutile d'en rappeler l'évolution : fixé pendant longtemps à 9,50 % (loi du 11 juillet 1975), il est descendu à 7,82 % à partir du 15 juillet 1989 (loi du 29 juin 1989, article 12). Pour toute l'année 1990, il est de 9,36 % (décret du 4 janvier 1990).

Comme le relèvent de nombreuses sentences arbitrales, les intérêts moratoires sont alloués pour réparer le dommage résultant du fait que le créancier a été privé, pendant un certain délai, de l'usage et de la disposition de sommes qu'il aurait dû recevoir. Leur taux doit être raisonnable, et fixé en tenant compte de toutes circonstances pertinentes, et notamment de toute stipulation contractuelle significative..., de la nature des faits ayant engendré ce dommage... des taux en vigueur sur le marché de la monnaie concernée et du taux d'inflation de cette monnaie...

Dans la présente affaire, l'arbitre prend d'abord en considération le taux retenu dans le contrat, soit 8,5 %. Certes, ce taux était celui d'un crédit fournisseur d'une durée de 4 ans et demi, matérialisé par des billets à ordre à échéance déterminée... mais il était également stipulé " qu'à défaut de paiement à sa date d'une seule échéance..., le solde du montant contractuel majoré des intérêts accumulés ainsi que des frais et accessoires deviendra immédiatement et de plein droit exigible, si bon semble au vendeur ". Comme aucun autre taux d'intérêt n'était prévu, il est permis de déduire de cette clause qu'à tout le moins les parties n'avaient pas exclu l'éventualité de l'application du même taux de 8,5 % en cas de non-paiement des échéances. Certes, comme il a été dit plus haut, c'est un taux de 10,25 % qui a été ensuite convenu par accord amiable, mais il ne l'a été que jusqu'à la date de l'accord. Pour les retards ultérieurs, un autre taux devait être négocié, les défenderesses proposant le prime rate Japon à 6 mois majoré de 1.7/8 %.

Ce taux de 8,5 % ayant été accepté par les débitrices, l'origine et l'étendue des difficultés financières de l'Etat congolais sont telles que l'aggravation de sa dette en devises par l'augmentation des taux d'intérêt serait à la fois irréaliste et injustifiée...

Enfin, ce taux paraît d'autant plus raisonnable que, si les taux d'intérêts sur le yen se sont progressivement élevés de 1985 à ce jour, ils n'étaient encore que de 4 à 5 % en 1988 et une bonne partie de l'année 1989 (v. l'étude de l'OCDE : Tendances des marchés des capitaux, n° 44, octobre 1989, p. 99, 103). Aujourd'hui, quelle que soit leur durée, les prêts en euro-yens ne dépassent pas 8 %. Enfin, l'inflation au Japon, nulle en 1987 et 1988, est inférieure à 2 % en 1989, et reste de beaucoup la plus faible de tous les pays industrialisés : en d'autres termes, depuis la défaillance des défenderesses, à la fin de 1985, jusqu'à aujourd'hui, la dépréciation de la monnaie japonaise, en valeur absolue ou relative est – sinon insignifiante – du moins extrêmement modérée : un taux de 8,5 % la dépasse largement, et rémunère de manière raisonnable les capitaux dont la demanderesse a été privée pendant cette période. »

L'arbitre aborda ensuite le problème du rééchelonnement de la dette :

« *Les défenderesses ont à plusieurs reprises exposé que la situation financière de la République de X, depuis 1985, avait conduit celle-ci à chercher, par accord avec les institutions financières internationales et ses créanciers, à rééchelonner le paiement de ses dettes. Elles ont fait valoir qu'il s'agit là de pratiques bien établies au sein de la Communauté financière internationale, que le cadre de ces négociations est constitué par ce qu'il est convenu d'appeler les Clubs de Paris (créanciers publics) et de Londres (banques commerciales), et que les autres dettes (de X) font ou doivent faire l'objet de négociations parallèles au sein d'une instance locale, le " Club de Z ". Elles ajoutent qu'en demandant la restructuration de sa dette, la République de X se conforme aux obligations qui lui sont imposées par cette Communauté internationale.*

Dans leur mémoire en réponse, elles ont même prétendu que Y ne peut réclamer par voie d'arbitrage le règlement intégral de sa créance sans avoir recherché au préalable les bases d'un accord amiable, par de réelles négociations, menées de bonne foi.

Sans contester la gravité de la situation financière de X, Y, pour sa part, estime que ni celle-ci, ni les efforts menés çà et là pour rééchelonner sa dette publique ne peuvent lui être opposés. Pour elle, sa demande en arbitrage est à la fois recevable et bien fondée, et elle a un intérêt à obtenir, en tout état de cause, un titre exécutoire.

La gravité de l'endettement public externe et interne de l'Etat X a été exposée au cours des débats, de même que l'impossibilité dans laquelle il s'est trouvé, depuis plusieurs années, de procéder au moindre paiement significatif vis-à-vis de ses créanciers étrangers. Ont été également établies les circonstances dans lesquelles une négociation est intervenue avec les banques commerciales créancières de X, et aurait abouti à une restructuration des dettes (de X), dans le cadre du Club de Londres. Cependant, dans l'attente d'un accord de confirmation avec le Fonds monétaire international, cette restructuration n'est pas encore effective à la date de la présente sentence. Quant aux créanciers publics, il semble qu'un second " Club de Paris " soit envisagé.. ;

D'une part l'arbitre juge que Y n'a pas manqué à son obligation de rechercher de bonne foi un accord de rééchelonnement de sa créance (A) ; d'autre part, il estime que les pratiques de la communauté financière internationale en matière de rééchelonnement des dettes des pays en développement, quelles que soient leur importance et leur permanence, n'ont pas pour effet de priver la demanderesse de son droit de demander et d'obtenir dès maintenant une décision ayant autorité de la chose jugée, qui dira quelles sommes lui sont dues en suite de la défaillance de son cocontractant (B).

A) L'obligation de négocier de bonne foi

En présence de la quasi-cessation des paiements extérieurs de l'Etat X, Y était tenue de rechercher de bonne foi, avec sa débitrice publique, les voies et moyens d'un aménagement des échéances de sa créance.

Cette obligation résultait d'abord des termes du contrat, puisque l'article 19 de celui-ci stipulait que " tout désaccord entre les parties concernant l'interprétation du présent contrat et son exécution sera autant que possible réglé à l'amiable ", et que c'était seulement à défaut d'une telle solution que la contestation serait soumise à l'arbitrage.

Cette obligation découle en outre des principes généraux du droit du commerce international (V. notamment S. Jarvin, L'obligation de coopérer de bonne foi ; exemples d'application au plan de l'arbitrage international, L'apport de la jurisprudence arbitrale, les dossiers de l'Institut, CCI, publication n° 440/1, 1986, p. 157 ; L. J. Mustill, The New Lex mercatoria : the first twenty-five years, Arbitration international, april 1988, p. 86, spéc. p. 111 ; E. Loquin, La réalité des usages du commerce international, Revue internationale de droit économique, 1989.163, spéc. p. 175 et s.), qui imposent aux parties, lorsque l'exécution du contrat se heurte à de graves difficultés, de se concerter et de coopérer activement pour rechercher les moyens de les surmonter. La grave crise de l'endettement international, qui affecte, depuis le début des années 80, un certain nombre de pays en voie de développement, a engendré, chez leurs créanciers, quelles que soient leur qualité et la nature de leur créance, un tel comportement, et a donné lieu, avec des succès divers, à de nombreuses renégociations et à plusieurs accords de rééchelonnement de leurs dettes.

L'arbitre estime que Y a satisfait à cette obligation de négocier de bonne foi le rééchelonnement de sa créance. En effet, après les nombreuses réclamations présentées à partir du début de 1986, c'est seulement par une lettre du... 1987 que X faisait officiellement état des difficultés financières du pays et ajoutait :

" ... Il est préconisé un rééchelonnement de cette dette pour le Club de Z. Une convocation vous sera adressée le moment venu lorsque la tenue de ce Club aura été décidée par le Ministère des Finances et du Budget. "

C'est en réalité par une négociation de gré à gré entre les défenderesses et Y que l'accord (amiable) fut conclu. X n'effectua pas les paiements promis ; Y ne fit pas connaître son avis sur le taux des intérêts moratoires proposé pour les défaillances à venir, mais ne fut jamais convoqué au sein du " Club de Z " envisagé par les défenderesses.

Après une ultime réclamation en janvier 1988, Y engagea la procédure arbitrale en avril 1988... Tout au long de cette procédure, depuis la préparation de l'acte de mission et jusqu'à l'audience..., soit pendant deux ans, l'arbitre s'efforça de chercher les bases d'un éventuel accord de rééchelonnement. Les deux parties ont effectivement coopéré avec la plus grande bonne foi, dans la recherche d'une transaction. Malheureusement, les propositions qu'elles ont présentées, chacune de leur côté, étaient si éloignées qu'il a fallu prendre acte de l'échec de ces efforts...

B) L'incidence des pratiques de rééchelonnement de la communauté financière internationale.

... Les défenderesses ont constamment mis l'accent sur la nécessité, pour la République de X comme pour tous ses créanciers, de se plier aux procédures complexes de restructuration des dettes des pays qui, comme elle, se trouvaient dans l'impossibilité absolue d'honorer leurs engagements. La gravité de la crise financière frappant brusquement, à partir de 1982 (crise mexicaine) un grand nombre de pays en développement, à revenu faible ou même " intermédiaire ", du fait de la baisse des cours des matières premières, de la hausse du dollar et des taux d'intérêts (sur les causes, les manifestations et l'évolution de ce phénomène, v. : L'Endettement international-définition, couverture statistique et méthodologie, rapport d'un groupe de travail de la Banque mondiale, du FMI, de la BRI et de l'OCDE, Paris, 1988 ; Y. Gazzo, L'endettement dans le monde – de l'euphorie à l'inquiétude, La documentation française, notes et études documentaires, n° 4896, 1989), a en effet entraîné la mise en place, sous l'égide du FMI, de mécanismes de renégociation de

*leurs dettes auxquels sont appelés à participer, d'une part, les créanciers (ou garants)
publics, d'autre part, les banques commerciales.*

*Le Club de Paris est une instance assez empirique, réunissant à la Direction du
trésor du Ministère français des Finances les Etats créanciers ou garants auxquels
un débiteur souverain demande un réaménagement de ses dettes (P. Durant, Le
rééchelonnement des dettes à l'égard des Etats – Le Club de Paris : Revue de
jurisprudence commerciale, février 1985, p. 65 s. ; P. Beracha, Le Club de Paris,
in : H. Bourguinat et J. Mistral, La crise de l'endettement international, 1986,
CNRS, Paris, p. 181). Les banques commerciales créancières, de leur côté, généralement regroupées au sein d'un ou plusieurs syndicats internationaux ayant consenti
des crédits consortiaux, négocient avec leur débiteur des accords fort complexes de
rééchelonnement (sur ceux-ci, et ce que l'on appelait plus tardivement le Club de
Londres, v. D. Carreau, Le rééchelonnement de la dette extérieure des Etats :
Clunet, 1985.5 ; D. Carreau, Le rééchelonnement des dettes à l'égard des banques,
Revue de jurisprudence commerciale, février 1985, p. 77 et s. ; G. Peigney, Aspects
juridiques de la réorganisation des créances bancaires sur des emprunteurs étatiques,
Journal de droit des affaires internationales, 1985.339 ; L. Focsaneanu, endettement
extérieur, renégociation des dettes, contrôle du crédit transnational, Revue générale
de droit international public, 1985.299 ; C. Dufloux et M. Karlin, Le nouveau
contexte bancaire international de l'endettement des pays en développement, Banque, 1986, p. 491 et s., 588 et s. ; Ph. Fouchard, Financement et endettement
internationaux, aspects juridiques, Journées de la Société de législation comparée,
1986.635).*

*Les défenderesses, plus précisément, ont fait valoir que dans le cadre du Club
de Paris... la République de X... a pris l'engagement d'accorder à tous ses créanciers
un traitement uniforme. Cela lui interdirait de conclure avec Y un accord de
restructuration plus favorable à ce seul créancier, et obligerait ce dernier à se
soumettre à une sorte de " loi commune " du rééchelonnement.*

Cette argumentation n'emporte pas la conviction.

*Certes, la répétition de pratiques constantes, auxquelles participent activement ou
se plient à la fois les acteurs et les institutions de la communauté financière internationale, est de nature à faire apparaître de véritables usages en matière de relations
financières internationales. Il est cependant douteux que le procès-verbal de la
réunion du Club de Paris du... (seule pièce produite au titre de ces pratiques
internationales) constate ou consacre l'existence et la pleine force juridique d'un tel
usage, et surtout que celui-ci soit opposable en l'espèce à Y.*

*En effet, ce document se borne à mentionner que le Gouvernement de X " s'en-
gage à chercher à obtenir de ses créanciers extérieurs, y compris les banques et les
fournisseurs, un rééchelonnement ou un refinancement à des conditions semblables
à celles prévues par le présent procès-verbal pour les crédits d'échéance comparable,
et s'engage à n'établir aucune discrimination entre les différentes catégories de
créanciers ".*

*Or, les conditions de rééchelonnement convenues lors de cette réunion – et qui
devaient être mises en œuvre ensuite par des négociations bilatérales entre X et
chaque Etat créancier – n'ont pas été produites par les défenderesses. Celles-ci ne
démontrent pas qu'elles ont réellement cherché, avant ou au cours de la procédure
arbitrale, à en informer Y et à obtenir de ce fournisseur un rééchelonnement sur
des bases identiques. En l'absence d'une telle preuve, il est douteux que les accords
ou pratiques du Club de Paris soient opposables à Y.*

*En vérité, cette obligation d'un traitement égal ne pesait et ne pèse toujours que
sur la République de X. Il s'agit d'une obligation de nature contractuelle, qui doit
être considérée comme un fait dans les relations de celle-ci avec les tiers.*

Ces tiers, en l'occurrence Y, ne sont pas eux-mêmes tenus de se conformer à un accord international qui leur est étranger...

... La vérité est que les autorités publiques de X, face à une situation financière gravissime, et engagées dans de difficiles et constantes renégociations avec les institutions financières, les Etats créanciers et les banques étrangères, n'ont pu disposer des liquidités nécessaires à un règlement, même partiel, de leur dette à l'égard de Y. Elles ont cherché à gagner du temps, à obtenir des créanciers publics des refinancements – voire des abandons de créance – qui leur permettent, plus tard, de rencontrer plus utilement des créanciers privés étrangers comme Y. En l'état d'une véritable insolvabilité internationale, on ne saurait leur faire grief d'un tel comportement, d'autant qu'elles se sont refusé à proclamer un moratoire unilatéral et généralisé de leurs dettes.

Mais on ne saurait pas davantage reprocher à Y d'avoir engagé et poursuivi la présente instance arbitrale, pour obtenir une sentence qui dise ses droits et puisse donner lieu à un titre exécutoire. Aucune règle d'ordre public de X ne s'oppose à la condamnation des défenderesses à payer ce qu'elles doivent en vertu de relations internationales de droit privé. Bien plus, par leur contrat, elles ont expressément renoncé à toute immunité de juridiction et d'exécution à l'égard de leur fournisseur... Confronté aux difficultés nées de la situation financière et des éventuels engagements internationaux de la République de X il appartiendra à ce dernier, en toute connaissance de cause, de choisir les voies et moyens d'exécution de la présente sentence... »

OBSERVATIONS. — I. — Il est exact, comme le souligne la présente sentence que la pratique arbitrale reconnaît à l'arbitre une grande liberté dans la fixation des taux d'intérêts. L'examen de la jurisprudence des arbitres du commerce international révèle en effet plusieurs grandes tendances parmi les arbitres.

Tout d'abord, dans la majorité des cas, les arbitres appliquent le taux contractuel, lorsque les parties ont pris la précaution de le prévoir. Cette solution ne fait pas de difficulté lorsque la validité de ce taux ne peut être remise en cause, soit au regard du droit applicable au contrat, soit au regard du droit du pays du débiteur. Ainsi, le Code civil égyptien plafonnant d'intérêt légal à 7 %, par une disposition d'ordre public, l'arbitre pourra être amené à s'interroger sur l'efficacité d'une clause d'intérêts contractuels au taux de 10 % si le contrat est soumis au droit égyptien ou si le débiteur est égyptien. La réponse à la question semble passer par une analyse de la nature de la norme étatique limitant le taux d'intérêt.

S'il s'agit seulement d'une règle d'ordre public, par opposition à une loi de police, l'arbitre peut l'écarter. Cela est évident à l'égard d'une disposition du droit du pays du débiteur, puisque ce droit n'a pas, en soi, de titre à s'appliquer à la fixation du taux d'intérêt. Mais c'est également possible en ce qui concerne le droit applicable au contrat qu'il ait été ou non choisi par les parties. En effet, puisqu'en vertu de la liberté dont jouissent parties et arbitres en matière de choix ou de détermination du droit applicable, (*cf.* par exemple article 13 (3) du règlement d'arbitrage de la CCI, 33 (1) du Règlement d'arbitrage de la CNUDCI et la sentence CCI n° 1581 de 1974 : *JDI* 1974, p. 887, obs. Y. Derains) on peut exclure l'application de toute loi nationale en se référant aux principes généraux du droit ou à la lex mercatoria, restreindre le champ d'application du droit national en le combinant avec les principes généraux du droit, etc., on peut aussi, par un procédé de dépeçage, écarter du domaine du droit applicable au contrat à titre principal des normes qui sont incompatibles avec certaines clauses du contrat. Il suffit que la volonté des parties sur ce point soit claire. La fixation d'un taux d'intérêt non valide selon le droit applicable à titre principal semble exprimer une telle volonté, laquelle doit produire ses effets si elle n'est pas contraire à l'ordre public international (taux usuraire par exemple).

Il n'en va pas de même si le taux contractuel fixé par les parties se heurte à une loi de police. Dans ce cas son champ d'application ne dépend pas de la volonté des parties qui n'auraient pas eu la possibilité de l'éviter en soumettant leur contrat à un autre droit. L'arbitre doit alors prendre sa décision en évaluant la légitimité de l'intérêt de l'Etat qui a édicté la limitation du taux d'intérêt (sur ce point voir nos observations sous la sentence n° 6142, p. 1025).

En l'absence de taux contractuel de nombreuses sentences adoptent la solution classique qui consiste à déterminer le taux d'intérêt à partir du droit applicable au contrat (*cf.* H. Batiffol : *Rep. Dalloz dr. int. V°* Contrats et Conventions. n° 138 ; A. Toubiana, *Le domaine de la loi du contrat,* n° 142, p. 117). On peut citer en ce sens la sentence CCI n° 4237 de 1984 : *Yearbook Commercial Arbitration* n° X, p. 52 ; sentence CCI n° 5277 de 1987 : *Yearbook Commercial Arbitration* n° XIII, p. 80 ; sentence CCI n° 5649 de 1987 : *Yearbook Commercial Arbitration* n° XIV, p. 178 ; sentence CCI n° 5294 de 1988 : *Yearbook Commercial Arbitration* n° XIV, p. 137).

A cette tendance se rattache la sentence rendue dans l'affaire LIAMCO (*Rev. Arb.* 1980, p. 187) et celle rendue sous l'égide du CIRDI, dans l'affaire AGIP c/ République Populaire du Congo, en 1979 (*Yearbook Commercial Arbitration* n° VIII, p. 133).

D'autres arbitres s'en tiennent au taux d'intérêts légal du pays du créancier considérant que c'est dans ce pays que le préjudice subi doit être réparé (*cf.* sentence CCI n° 2375 de 1975 : *JDI* 1976, p. 973, obs. Y. Derains ; sentence CCI n° 5460 de 1987 : *Yearbook Commercial Arbitration,* n° XIV, p. 104).

Le souci d'un dédommagement plus exact que celui qui peut résulter de l'application des droits nationaux peut conduire l'arbitre à se référer aux taux réellement pratiqués par les banques. La sentence rendue dans l'affaire CCI n° 3572 en 1982 (*Yearbook Commercial Arbitration* n° XIV, p. 111) en fournit un exemple.

Bien entendu ce sont les arbitres qui ont reçu les pouvoirs d'amiables compositeurs qui se reconnaissent la plus grande liberté, se laissant guider essentiellement par des considérations d'équité. Ainsi, dans la sentence CCI n° 2879, rendue en 1977 (*JDI* 1978, p. 989, obs. Y. Derains) les arbitres décidèrent :

« *Considérant équitable que tous les intérêts prévus par cette sentence soient attribués dans la même mesure que les arbitres estiment raisonnable de fixer, à la charge de l'une et de l'autre partie, au taux de 10 % (dix pour cent) par an de sorte qu'on élimine ainsi le problème qui résulterait d'une différence de taux commerciaux et légaux en cours en France et en Yougoslavie ; »*

Les mêmes préoccupations se révèlent dans l'affaire CIRDI Benvenuti et Bonfante Srl c/ République Populaire du Congo (Sentence de 1980, *Yearbook Commercial Arbitration* n° VIII, p. 144), où le Tribunal Arbitral décide :

« *On account of the provisional agreement reached by and between the parties – - not confirmed by the Government – Claimant has claimed interest at the rate of 15 % annually on the total amount that would be awarded it. The Tribunal does not believe that it can accept this petition since the applicable law, that is to say, that of the Congo, provides for a legal rate of interest that is clearly lower. But the Tribunal notes that the Government, in its Defense Memorial, has proposed and interest rate of 10 % for its counterclaim. In view of its power to decide ex aequo et bono, the Tribunal deems it equitable to accept this rate for the compensation awarded to Claimant »*

Dans la présente affaire, l'arbitre estime visiblement que la diversité des solutions qui se rencontrent dans la jurisprudence des arbitres du commerce international exprime une liberté : celle de retenir le taux qui, tout en étant raisonnable, est à même de « réparer le dommage résultant du fait que le créancier a été privé, pendant un certain délai, de l'usage et de la disposition des sommes qu'il aurait dû recevoir ». Selon lui, ce taux n'a pas a être le taux légal d'un système juridique national. A cet égard, l'arbitre est aidé, ainsi qu'il le reconnaît, par le fait que les parties n'avait soumis leur contrat à aucune loi nationale. Cependant, l'application d'un droit étatique déterminé au contrat ne devrait pas entraver la liberté de l'arbitre puisqu'on a vu que certaines sentences décidaient de se référer au taux légal prévalant dans le pays du créancier plutôt qu'à celui fixé par le droit applicable au contrat. Il s'agit finalement pour l'arbitre de déterminer le domaine du droit applicable au contrat et il est libre de retenir une règle de conflit qui soumet le taux d'intérêt à une autre norme juridique que la lex contractus. Cette norme peut être puisée dans la lex mercatoria et ne pas désigner un taux précis, mais poser le principe d'une juste réparation.

On doutera enfin que la liberté de l'arbitre lui permette de ne pas appliquer le taux d'intérêt contractuellement choisi par les parties, même si, dans la présente sentence, l'arbitre le laisse entendre, en ne le retenant finalement qu'après avoir montré que son application constitue une réparation raisonnable.

II et III. — En ce qu'elle traite du délicat problème du rééchelonnement des dettes des pays du tiers monde, et de ses incidences sur l'arbitrage commercial international, la présente décision est d'un intérêt tout particulier. En effet, il ressort de la sentence que les défenderesses tiraient de la répétition des accords de rééchelonnement au plan international plusieurs arguments pour conclure au rejet de la demande de paiement dont elles étaient l'objet.

Le premier de ces arguments est classique. Il consiste à se fonder sur une disposition de la clause d'arbitrage prévoyant que tous les différends seraient, autant que possible, réglés à l'amiable et que ce n'est qu'en l'absence d'un tel règlement qu'ils seront soumis à l'arbitrage, pour prétendre que le litige dont est saisi l'arbitre n'est pas en état d'être arbitré. En l'espèce, les défenderesses considéraient que la demanderesse avait failli à une obligation de chercher une solution amiable au litige en ne participant pas à des négociations multilatérales sur le rééchelonnement de la dette de la République. L'arbitre écarte ce moyen en estimant que, dans les faits, la demanderesse avait, de bonne foi, cherché à aménager sa créance. Cependant, au-delà de cette constatation de fait, la sentence consacre l'existence d'une obligation de négocier de bonne foi, qui comporte celle d'aménager les échéances de la créance impayée.

Il ne fait pas de doute que la lex mercatoria contient une obligation de négocier de bonne foi. Les références que fournit la sentence à cet égard le montrent clairement (*cf.* également la sentence rendue dans l'affaire n° 5953 en 1989, *infra* p. 1056). On peut néanmoins se demander si cette obligation a la portée que lui donne la sentence. En effet, il n'est pas sûr que l'obligation de négocier de bonne foi, qui n'est qu'un aspect d'une obligation générale de coopération, implique celle de renoncer partiellement à l'exercice de droits incontestables et qu'à défaut d'une telle renonciation, même dans des limites raisonnables, une demande ne puisse être soumise à l'arbitrage. Les clauses d'arbitrage qui imposent une tentative de solution amiable avant l'introduction d'une procédure arbitrale obligent le demandeur à s'efforcer d'obtenir gain de cause par la voie de négociation et à négocier en ce sens de bonne foi. Elle ne l'oblige pas à abandonner une partie de ses droits, ce qui serait incompatible avec la force obligatoire des conventions, autre principe fondamental de la lex mercatoria (*cf.* sentence n° 5953 précitée). La sagesse doit parfois l'y inciter, et c'est le cas lorsque l'insolvabilité du débiteur diminue irrémédiablement la créance, mais on se situe ici hors du domaine juridique.

Le second argument développé par les défenderesses était que les accords de rééchelonnement passés dans le cadre du Club de Paris les engageaient à accorder à tous leurs créanciers un traitement uniforme. Cette position n'était pas tenable, et l'arbitre le relève fort justement. Il est vrai que les conventions de rééchelonnement contiennent souvent des clauses dites du « débiteur le plus favorisé » qui interdisent à l'Etat débiteur de traiter plus favorablement des dettes identiques non couvertes par la convention de rééchelonnement (cf I. Hautot, « Le surendettement des pays en voie de développement et la conversion des dettes » : *Revue du Droit des Affaires Internationales,* 1990, p. 253). Cependant, une telle obligation qui ne pèse que sur l'Etat qui la souscrit s'oppose à ce qu'il conclue un accord de rééchelonnement plus favorable pour des débiteurs tiers à la convention. Elles n'obligent pas ces tiers qui sont libres de se refuser à tout accord s'ils estiment que tel est leur intérêt. Comme le souligne l'arbitre, le rééchelonnement des dettes des pays du tiers monde, pour raisonnable qu'il soit, ne constitue pas un usage du commerce international qui s'impose à tous ses acteurs.

Y. D.

I. — Lex mercatoria. — Contenu. — Bonne foi. — *Pacta sunt servanda.*

II. — Lex mercatoria. — Contrat de fournitures. — Prix indéterminé. — Nullité du contrat (non).

III. — Lex mercatoria. — Contrat de fournitures. — Prix indéterminé — Nature de l'obligation de négocier.

IV. — Contrat de fournitures. — Fixation du prix. — Pouvoirs de l'arbitre.

Sentence rendue dans l'affaire n° 5953 en 1989

Un arbitre unique, siégeant à Paris, était saisi de difficultés d'exécution d'un contrat conclu entre une société espagnole X et une société américaine Y pour la livraison par la seconde à la première de charbon de qualité déterminée. Le prix devait être fixé de six mois en six mois par négociation entre les parties. Ceci fut fait pendant les trois premiers semestres, mais aucun accord ne put intervenir quant à la fixation du prix du quatrième semestre. Prétendant que X portait la responsabilité de cette situation, Y introduit une procédure d'arbitrage.

Appelé à se prononcer par une sentence partielle sur le droit applicable, l'arbitre décida que le litige serait « réglé selon les seuls usages du commerce international, autrement dénommés lex mercatoria » (cette sentence partielle, publiée à la *Rev. arb.,* 1990, 701, a fait l'objet d'un recours en annulation devant la Cour de Paris qui s'est soldé par un échec ; Paris 13 juill. 1989 : *JDI* 1990, 430, note Goldman ; *Rev. crit. dr. int. pr.,* 1990, 305, note B. Oppetit ; *Rev. arb.* 1990, 664, note P. Lagarde).

Statuant sur le fond du litige par la présente sentence, l'arbitre procéda tout d'abord à une analyse du contrat.

« Les griefs que les parties s'adressent relèvent de l'accusation, plus ou moins explicite selon le cas d'inexécution ou de mauvaise exécution par l'autre des obligations découlant du contrat.

Il n'est possible d'apprécier le bien ou le mal fondé de ces griefs que si les obligations découlant du contrat en cause sont, au préalable, clairement définies.

Mais les parties soutiennent aussi, soit sur la portée des obligations contractuelles, soit même sur leur existence ou validité, des thèses qu'il conviendra d'examiner.

A) Les obligations découlant du contrat

Comme on l'a vu, la caractéristique du contrat même s'il s'agit d'un type de convention qui n'est pas tout à fait inhabituel dans la pratique du commerce international des matières premières et notamment du charbon, est qu'il prévoit une fourniture sans que le prix en soit fixé.

Mais les spécifications du charbon à fournir sont précises ainsi que les quantités à fournir à l'intérieur d'une fourchette. Toutes les conditions importantes pour permettre les livraisons du charbon sont aussi précisées, sauf le prix.

Ce prix doit être déterminé au cours d'une période précédant chaque semestre, par négociation entre les parties. Cela résulte de la clause 12 du contrat qui prévoit, au cours de chacune des trois années, que pour le premier semestre, " les parties sont d'accord pour négocier le prix avant le 30 novembre de l'année précédente ", et que pour le second trimestre, " les parties sont d'accord pour négocier le prix avant le 31 mai de l'année calendaire ".

Du même coup, cela contribuait à donner à cette obligation de négocier, un caractère de simple formalité justifiée par les seules variations de prix dont les parties n'étaient pas maîtresses, mais qu'elles pouvaient constater sur le marché avant de se mettre d'accord. Autrement dit, si l'obligation de négocier ne constituait qu'une obligation de moyen, elle était en réalité très proche d'une obligation de résultat.

Il faut penser que cette position était raisonnable puique le contrat fut exécuté sans difficulté pendant la moitié de sa durée. Trois négociations aboutirent, confirmant le réalisme de la solution adoptée.

En présence d'un tel contrat, les parties, au cours de l'arbitrage, ont reconnu leur obligation de négocier, mais à partir de mai 1986, elles s'opposent sur la façon de la remplir.

B) Les thèses des parties

1. — Thèse de Y

La thèse de Y sur la portée des obligations contractuelles des parties est identique à l'analyse qui vient d'être faite. Cependant, au cours des négociations difficiles qui ont commencé en mai 1986 pour s'achever par une rupture en janvier 1987, elle a soutenu que leur désaccord sur le prix pourrait être résolu par voie d'arbitrage. Or, en droit, il est pour le moins douteux qu'un arbitre stricto sensu, même s'il jouit des pouvoirs d'amiable composition, puisse parfaire un accord important sur un élément aussi important que le prix.

D'autre part, au cas particulier, les parties, dans leurs négociations antérieures à la conclusion du contrat 320-120-84 avaient écarté la fixation du prix par arbitrage.

Enfin, pendant la période difficile, et même au cours de la procédure d'arbitrage, Y a essayé de soutenir que le contrat obligeait X, non seulement à négocier, mais aussi à acheter.

Cette thèse est exacte en ce qu'elle affirme, et fausse en ce qu'elle nie, à savoir que l'obligation d'achat était subordonnée à un accord sur le prix.

Cet engagement est donc une obligation contractuelle qui s'impose à chacune des parties. Leur obligation de négocier avant telle date de chaque semestre sur un seul point, à savoir le prix, n'est cependant pas une obligation d'aboutir.

Elle n'est assortie de précisions ni quant aux modalités de la négociation, ni même quant à la désignation de celle des parties qui doit en prendre l'initiative.

Mais il est intéressant de rappeler les circonstances qui ont précédé le contrat et les conditions dans lesquelles la clause de prix a été élaborée, pour en apprécier exactement la portée.

En effet, les parties avaient des relations suivies depuis près de deux ans quand elles décidèrent de signer un contrat de fourniture pour trois ans. Elles exprimaient ainsi la volonté certaine de se lier d'une certaine façon, pour une durée déterminée, mais à un prix non déterminé.

D'autre part, la négociation sur le mode de détermination du prix fut sérieuse et différentes méthodes furent envisagées, sur lesquelles elles ne purent se mettre d'accord, si bien qu'elles aboutirent à s'en remettre à des négociations partielles ultérieures.

Par ailleurs l'absence de prix déterminé s'explique par les variations relativement importantes que subit le prix du charbon sur le marché international, même s'il est difficile de parler de prix de marché au sens d'un cours de bourse ou d'une mercuriale. L'expérience avait montré, en outre, aux deux parties qu'il était prudent de ne pas se lier sur le prix trop longtemps à l'avance, en raison de ces variations. Mais elle leur montrait aussi, par leurs relations antérieures, qu'il était facile de se mettre d'accord pour des livraisons à court terme.

2. — Thèses de X

X de son côté soutient quatre thèses :

1) X soutient qu'à défaut d'accord sur le prix, le contrat n'avait pas d'objet et était donc nul, ainsi que le montreraient le droit espagnol et le droit français.

Cette thèse est contredite par le fait, admis par X que l'objet du contrat était la fourniture d'un certain type de charbon dans certaines quantités, sur trois ans et à un prix à négocier.

D'autre part, l'absence de prix préalablement convenu empêche, en général, la vente et son exécution, mais la thèse que le contrat de fourniture serait un contrat de vente ne peut être retenue et n'est d'ailleurs pas sérieusement soutenue, que ce soit par X ou par Y.

Indépendamment de la qualification comme contrat de vente, cette thèse ne pourrait sans doute être acceptée, que si le contrat était assorti d'une clause d'exclusivité mettant l'acheteur à la merci du fournisseur, qui pourrait alors lui imposer unilatéralement son prix.

Mais, le contrat n'est assorti d'aucune clause d'exclusivité.

Enfin, la loi de fond applicable au contrat et en fonction de laquelle l'arbitrage doit se dérouler, n'est ni la loi espagnole ni la loi française, ni celle d'aucun pays dont une jurisprudence similaire pourrait être invoquée (encoré qu'il ne soit pas assuré que cette jurisprudence soit applicable à un contrat international), puisque la sentence du 1er septembre 1988 a décidé que seuls devaient s'appliquer les principes généraux du droit et les usages du commerce international.

Or, aucun principe général de droit, ni aucun usage de commerce international ne peut être invoqué au soutien de la thèse de la nullité du contrat.

2) X soutient une thèse beaucoup plus radicale. Selon cette thèse, ab initio, la conception de X du contrat aurait été différente de celle de Y, de telle sorte que les parties n'ayant pas voulu la même chose, aucun contrat ne s'est jamais formé.

Outre que cette thèse est contredite par le comportement de X pour les trois premiers semestres, au cours desquels des avenants au contrat ont été signés chaque fois pour concrétiser, entre autres, les accords intervenus sur le prix, elle est erronnée en ce sens que X et Y ont toujours été d'accord au moins jusqu'à l'arbitrage et même ensuite, sur l'existence d'une obligation de négocier.

3) La thèse soutenue avec le plus de constance par X aussi bien au cours des négociations qu'au cours de la procédure d'arbitrage, est que l'obligation de négocier lui laissant une liberté absolue d'aboutir ou de ne pas aboutir, exactement comme dans une négociation qui n'aurait été précédée d'aucun engagement contractuel de négocier. Cette thèse ne peut être acceptée, car elle reviendrait à réduire le contrat à une simple obligation de consulter Y pour la mettre en concurrence avec d'autres " traders ", c'est à dire, en pratique, à le vider de son contenu.

4) Subsidiairement X a soutenu la caducité du contrat par la disparition de la source d'approvisionnement de... Mais cette thèse encore ne peut non plus être acceptée. Le contrat n'a jamais prévu une livraison d'origine..., mais seulement " Afrique du Sud ". Aucune raison extrinsèque n'est venue rendre le contrat caduc. »

Les caractéristiques du contrat étant ainsi déterminées, l'arbitre s'efforça de préciser les principes de la lex mercatoria qui y étaient applicables :

« Aucun usage particulier au commerce international du charbon n'a pu être mis à jour au cours des débats.

En particulier, l'usage de renégocier un prix convenu invoqué par X n'a fait l'objet d'aucune démonstration. Ce qui est vrai, c'est que dans l'exécution de contrats à long terme dont le prix est fixé, il est fréquent de prévoir une renégociation dans le cas où les conditions économiques viendraient à évoluer de telle sorte que l'équilibre du contrat initialement conclu par les parties se trouverait bouleversé. Mais, en l'absence d'une telle clause, il est au contraire à présumer que les parties, familières du commerce international, n'ont pas voulu de renégociation. Au cas particulier où les parties ont prévu un mécanisme de négociation pour chaque semestre afin de réduire au minimum le risque de variations trop importantes des prix, elles ont nécessairement exclu la possibilité d'une renégociation telles qu'on les trouve dans les clauses de " hardship ".

En effet, ce genre de clause est utilisé dans d'autres secteurs économiques que le commerce du charbon lorsqu'une longue période s'écoule ou doit s'écouler entre le moment où intervient l'accord sur le prix et celui où l'exécution de l'obligation de livrer une chose ou d'assurer une prestation de service. Or, rien de tel dans le présent contrat où la durée maximale s'écoulant entre ces deux moments était de sept mois.

Quant aux principes généraux du commerce international, leur liste ne se trouve dans aucun recueil. Leur application par la pratique les fait parfois assimiler à des usages du commerce international.

La doctrine s'est efforcée de les dégager par induction, à partir de la pratique et surtout à partir des sentences arbitrales connues (The Rt. Hon. Lord Justice Mustill, The new lex mercatoria : Twenty five years, in Liber Amicorum for the Rt. Hon. Lord Wilberforce, p. 149 s. ; Ole Lando, The lex mercatoria in International Commercial Arbitration, International and Comparative Law Quarterly, 1985, p. 747 sq ; B. Goldman, Frontières du droit et lex mercatoria, Arch. de philosophie du droit, 1964, p. 177 sq, et La lex mercatoria dans les contrats et l'arbitrage internationaux : réalité et perspectives, Clunet 1979, p. 475 s. ; et sur les usages du commerce international, Y. Derains : Le statut des usages du commerce international devant les juridictions arbitrales, Revue de l'arbitrage 1973, p. 122 s., et E. Loquin, La réalité des usages du commerce international, Revue internationale de droit économique, 1989/2, p. 161 s.).

Mais quelle que soit l'autorité de ceux qui ont tenté cet effort, il serait téméraire de les tenir tous pour établis de façon certaine avec l'autorité qui s'attacherait à un véritable droit coutumier.

En revanche certains principes relèvent de la morale naturelle, puisque aussi bien, si les affaires ne sont pas soumises à toutes les exigences de la morale, elles ne peuvent cependant échapper aux normes éthiques qui constituent le fondement de la vie en société, et ont alors une valeur de droit positif universellement reconnue, notamment dans le commerce international (Voir sentence du 28 août 1951 dans l'affaire de concession pétrolière Petroleum Development Ltd c/ Cheik d'Abu Dabi, citée par Ph. Fouchard, L'arbitrage commercial international, p. 428), mais aussi dans les relations internationales interétatiques (article 38 du statut de la Cour internationale de Justice).

Parmi ces principes, le plus général est sans doute celui de la bonne foi. Cette " exigence fondamentale de bonne foi... (se) trouve dans tous les systèmes de droit, qu'il s'agisse des droits nationaux ou du droit international " (Sentence AMCO du 25 septembre 1983 rendue dans le cadre du C.I.R.D.I. Revue de l'arbitrage, 1985, p. 268). Elle " est bien de l'essence de la lex mercatoria " (B. Goldman, La lex mercatoria dans les contrats et l'arbitrage internationaux : réalité et perspectives, Clunet 1973, p. 483).

La bonne foi qui est toujours présumée, doit présider à la négociation des contrats et à leur interprétation comme à leur exécution. La doctrine est unanime et les sentences publiées qui sont la source de droit privilégiée des arbitres le confirment, sans exception. On se contentera ici de citer, sur cette importance de la bonne foi, un passage de la sentence rendue dans le cas 3131 sous les auspices de la Cour d'Arbitrage de la C.C.I. le 26 octobre 1979 (Revue de l'Arbitrage, 1983, p. 530/1).

On peut y lire, à propos de la " lex mercatoria " :

« *L'un des principes qui inspirent cette dernière est celui de la bonne foi qui doit présider à la formation et à l'exécution des contrats. L'accent mis sur la bonne foi contractuelle est d'ailleurs l'une des tendances dominantes que révèle " la convergence des législations nationales en la matière... " Or, la bonne foi exprime non seulement un état psychologique, la connaissance ou l'ignorance d'un fait, mais aussi une " référence aux usages, à une règle morale de comportement... " ... Elle traduit alors une exigence de comportement qui peut être rapprochée du principe général de responsabilité. Conformément au principe de bonne foi qui inspire la " lex mercatoria " internationale, le Tribunal a recherché si, dans la présente espèce, la rupture du mandat était imputable au comportement de l'une des parties et si elle avait causé à l'autre un préjudice qui serait ainsi injustifié, et dont l'équité imposerait alors qu'il soit réparé.* »

Un autre principe d'un degré de généralité moindre, puisqu'il ne concerne que la seule exécution des contrats, est formulé par la maxime " Pacta sunt servanda ". Le respect de la parole donnée conduit à exécuter les engagements pris. Mais les modalités d'exécution ne sont pas indiquées. C'est le principe précédent qui apporte cette précision, si bien qu'on peut les réunir, en un seul, lorsqu'il s'agit de remplir une obligation, à savoir : " Pacta sunt servanda bona fide ".

C'est au regard de ces principes, au demeurant incontestés par les parties, qu'il convient d'examiner dans quelle mesure leurs griefs respectifs peuvent être fondés.

Mais on remarquera qu'au cas particulier ces deux principes vont se renforcer l'un l'autre.

En effet, si la bonne foi est toujours exigée dans les pourparlers et négociations préparatoires à un contrat, (faute de quoi la « culpa in contrahendo » peut être sanctionnée) elle doit l'être d'autant plus lorsque ces négociations sont consécutives à un contrat et résultent donc d'un engagement qui vise spécifiquement la négociation (Voir Jean Cedras, L'obligation de négocier, R.T.D.C. 1985, p. 265 s.). »

OBSERVATIONS. — I. — Dans sa sentence partielle, l'arbitre avait paru restreindre le contenu de la lex mercatoria « aux seuls usages du commerce international ». Sa sentence au fond montre qu'il n'en était rien, puisqu'il distingue les usages particuliers au commerce international de charbon des principes généraux du commerce international tout en relevant que l'application par la pratique « les fait parfois assimiler à des usages du commerce international ». Cette assimilation est sans aucun doute un abus terminologique dont la sentence rendue dans l'affaire n° 5721 (cf. *supra* p. 1020) constitue un nouvel exemple. On doit dissocier des usages du commerce, de portée sectorielle et dont l'arbitre doit toujours tenir compte d'après l'article 13 (5) du règlement d'arbitrage de la CCI des règles coutumières du commerce international dont l'origine se trouve dans la répétition d'un usage général (*cf* B. Goldman, note précitée, p. 437). Ces règles, de même que les principes généraux, n'interviennent que pour autant que les parties ou l'arbitre décident d'appliquer la lex mercatoria. Cependant, la lex mercatoria étant un ordre juridique en création, il n'est pas surprenant que la terminologie soit mal fixée. Ce n'est pas bien grave non plus, car les praticiens ont conscience de ce qu'ils visent lorsqu'ils écartent l'application d'un droit étatique pour s'en remettre à des normales anationales.

La prudence de l'arbitre dans le choix des règles de la lex mercatoria qu'il va appliquer peut sembler excessive. Les doutes qu'il émet quant à la réalité de certains principes qui ont été mis en lumière par la jurisprudence arbitrale et les commentateurs risquent d'étonner de la part d'un arbitre qui, dans une sentence partielle, a décidé de statuer sur la base de la seule lex mercatoria. Cette timidité affectée ne doit pas tromper. Elle n'a d'autre but que de renforcer la valeur du choix des principes retenus en l'espèce. Elle revient à dire que si l'on peut s'interroger sur le caractère de positivité de certaines règles dégagées par la jurisprudence arbitrale, une telle incertitude est exclue s'agissant de celles que l'arbitre va appliquer. Et, de fait, nul ne doute que le principe de la bonne foi et l'adage « pacta sunt servanda » fasse partie de la lex mercatoria.

Concernant la bonne foi, il serait fastidieux de faire l'inventaire des décisions arbitrales qui y voient un principe de la lex mercatoria (en dernier lieu voir les sentences rendues dans l'affaire n° 5721, *supra* p. 1020). On se référera utilement au « Dossier » de l'Institut du Droit et des Pratiques des Affaires Internationales de la CCI, « Apport de la jurisprudence arbitrale » et plus particulièrement à l'article de S. Jarvin, « L'obligation de coopérer de bonne foi », p. 157).

Pour ce qui est de l'adage *« pacta sunt servanda »,* on rappellera qu'une sentence rendue en 1971 dans l'affaire n° 1512 (*JDI* 1974, p. 905, obs. Y. Derains) n'a pas hésité à y voir un principe sacro-saint. La sécurité du commerce international exige qu'il ne soit pas remis en cause, sauf dans des circonstances exceptionnelles où, comme le relève B. Goldman, « la jurisprudence arbitrale ne refuse pas systématiquement de prendre en compte les exigences de la justice » (*cf.* B. Goldman « La lex mercatoria dans les contrats et l'arbitrage internationaux » : *JDI* 1979, p. 475). A cet égard, il n'était probablement pas utile que l'arbitre se réfère à « la morale naturelle », qui, si elle est le support de la bonne foi, ne trouve pas nécessairement son compte dans l'adage *« pacta sunt servanda ».* De plus, si ces principes de la lex mercatoria n'avaient qu'un fondement moral, on pourrait s'interroger sur leur juridicité, indispensable pour que l'arbitre ne puisse être soupçonné d'avoir tranché en amiable compositeur. Cependant, un tel soupçon n'aurait pas sa place ici, tant le caractère juridique des principes en cause – connus de la plupart des droits étatiques – n'est pas contestable.

II. — X soutenait qu'à défaut d'accord sur le prix le contrat n'avait pas d'objet et était nul, selon les solutions des droits espagnol et français. L'arbitre rejette cette conclusion en soulignant d'une part que le contrat n'était pas un contrat de vente mais un contrat de fournitures, à un prix à négocier, et d'autre part qu' « aucun principe général de droit ni aucun usage de commerce international ne peut être invoqué au soutien de la thèse de la nullité du contrat ».

Cette dernière approche a été critiquée au motif que le risque de trouver dans la lex mercatoria le fondement de la nullité du contrat n'était pas grand « dès lors que la lex mercatoria est généralement muette sur la validité du contrat » (*cf.* Paul Lagarde, note précitée, p. 670).

La critique est bien sévère et sans doute infondée. Il est exact que la lex mercatoria offre peu de solutions concernant « la validité du consentement ou la capacité des contractants » (en ce sens B. Goldman, « La lex mercatoria dans les contrats et l'arbitrage internationaux », *op. cit., loc. cit.* p. 478), encore que la jurisprudence arbitrale sur les groupes de sociétés montre qu'il ne faut pas exagérer la portée d'une telle réserve (*cf.* I. Fadlallah, « Clauses d'arbitrage et groupes de sociétés » : *Trav. Comité fr. dr. int. pr.* 1984-1985, p. 105 s.). Mais si la validité du contrat était en cause en l'espèce, ce n'est pas parce qu'était allégué un défaut de consentement ou de capacité. Il s'agissait de savoir si un prix déterminé constituait un élément fondamental du contrat dont le défaut aurait été une cause de nullité. Plus que de décider si un contrat dépourvu d'objet est néanmoins valable – problème de vice du consentement – l'arbitre devait définir cet objet en précisant le contenu des obligations des parties. Or, nul autre système juridique que la lex mercatoria, réceptacle d'accords contractuels nouveaux, pouvait permettre à l'arbitre d'apprécier la portée d'une convention conclue conformément à la pratique des contrats de fourniture de matière première. De plus, l'intervention d'une disposition d'ordre public national annulant le contrat eût été arbitraire. Les parties n'avaient soumis leur contrat à aucun droit national et, si elles l'avaient fait, elles n'auraient pas choisi un droit qui l'annulait. Autant on peut admettre qu'un arbitre assure le respect des lois de police correspondant à des intérêts légitimes des Etats et fasse prévaloir, dans des cas déterminés, ces lois sur la volonté des parties, autant il serait choquant d'annuler un contrat conclu en parfaite connaissance de cause au nom de l'ordre public d'un système juridique auxquelles les parties n'avaient aucune obligation de soumettre leur convention et auquel, dans les faits, elles ne l'ont pas soumises.

III. — L'arbitre déclare que si l'obligation de négocier ne constituait qu'une obligation de moyen, elle était proche d'une obligation de résultat. L'objet de l'obligation étant la négociation, les notions d'obligation de moyen et d'obligation de résultat ne sont pas facilement applicables, mais la formule a le mérite de souligner qu'un contrat de fournitures à prix indéterminé fait peser sur les négociateurs l'obligation de ne ménager aucun effort pour aboutir.

La jurisprudence arbitrale a souvent consacré l'obligation de négocier de bonne foi (*cf,* notamment les sentences n° 2478 de 1974 : *JDI* 1977, 942 ; n° 2291 de 1975 : *JDI* 1976, 989 ; n° 2508 de 1976 : *JDI* 1977, 939). Ce n'est qu'une application du principe de la bonne foi. Mais l'intensité de l'obligation générale de négocier de bonne foi est accentuée dans un contrat de fournitures qui fait de la négociation un mécanisme fondamental d'exécution du contrat. L'obligation de négocier trouve sa source dans le contrat lui-même et la lex mercatoria n'intervient que pour lui donner son plein effet.

IV. — La sentence rappelle qu'il est douteux qu'un arbitre, même amiable compositeur, puisse parfaire l'accord des parties en ce qui concerne le prix. C'est là une position traditionnelle, en droit français tout au moins, où l'on distingue la fonction juridictionnelle de l'arbitre de celle du mandataire des parties, à l'image du tiers qui peut être appelé à déterminer le prix de vente selon l'article 1592 du Code civil, et que ce texte n'appelle « arbitre » que comme synonyme de « volonté » (*cf.* C. Jarosson, note sous Paris, 17 mars 1989 : *Rev. arb.* 1990, p. 727, évoquant l'expression « libre-arbitre »). Il est vrai que cette distinction traditionnelle semble avoir été remise en cause, tout particulièrement lorsque l'arbitre est amiable compositeur (*cf.* E. Loquin, *L'amiable composition en droit comparé et international,* p. 295 ; *contra,* J. D. Bredin « L'amiable composition et le contrat » : *Rev. arb.* 1984, p. 267). De plus, la Cour de cassation a admis qu'un arbitre, même sans pouvoir d'amiable compositeur, pouvait fixer un loyer, pourvu que la volonté des parties en ce sens soit exprimée clairement (Cass. civ. II, 7 nov. 1974 : *Rev. arb.* 1975, p. 302, note E. Loquin ; *cf* aussi Paris 8 juin 1984 : *Rev. arb.* 1984, 516, note C. Jarosson ; Cass. civ. I, 9 oct. 1984, et 12 déc. 1984 : *Rev. arb.* 1986, 263, note P. Mayer). La situation reste assez confuse (plus généralement sur la question *cf.* C. Jarosson *La notion d'arbitrage,* n° 298 s.).

Comme l'a opportunément souligné B. Oppetit :

« Indiscutablement, les signes d'une évolution existent, en législation comme en jurisprudence. Mais l'effacement de la dualité de l'arbitrage juridictionnel et de l'arbitrage contractuel, pour pouvoir être tenu pour acquis en droit français, supposerait, compte tenu de la longue tradition historique et des interrogations pressantes des auteurs, des prises de position sans équivoque du droit positif et non pas seulement des recoupements ou des regroupements patiemment opérés par des commentateurs... » (*cf.* B. Oppetit, « Arbitrage juridictionnel et arbitrage contractuel » : *Rev. arb.* 1977, p. 315).

Y. D.

ICC Arbitral Awards

reprinted from *International Construction Law Review*

1986 - 1990

AWARD RENDERED IN CASE NO. 3790 IN 1983

I—Contract—Terms of the International Federation of Consulting Engineers (F.I.D.I.C.)—Role of the Engineer

II—Terms of the International Federation of Consulting Engineers (F.I.D.I.C.)—Article 67—Request for Arbitration—Communication with the Engineer—Method of Procedure

A dispute involving public works between a European contractor (plaintiff) and a Libyan employer (defendant), was submitted for arbitration at the I.C.C. The arbitration was held in Paris.

The contract which was subject to Libyan Law was drawn from the F.I.D.I.C. Conditions for Civil Engineering Works (2nd Edition). It stipulated in Clause 60 that payments should be made monthly on the basis of certificates submitted by the Contractor. Payment was to be made within 45 days following the delivery of completed documents to the engineer. The engineer had to approve the documents within 15 days of receiving them. An identical stipulation applied to payment of the final account. Nonetheless the employer had refused to make payment for a certain number of certificates approved by the engineer, claiming that the final balance included amounts which he had contested and which had been submitted to arbitration and, consequently, were not recognised.

The contract included a clause for settling disputes in accordance with Clause 67 of the F.I.D.I.C. terms (2nd edition) in the following terms:—

"Settlement of disputes—Arbitration.

If any dispute or difference of any kind whatsoever shall arise between the Employer or the Engineer and the Contractor in connection with or arising out of the Contract or the carrying out of the Works (whether during the progress of the works or after their completion and whether before or after the termination abandonment or breach of the Contract) it shall in the first place be referred to and settled by the Engineer who within a period of 90 days after being requested by either party to do so shall give written notice of his decision to the Employer and the Contractor. Save as hereinafter provided such decision in respect of every matter so referred shall be final and binding upon the Employer and the Contractor until the completion of the work and shall forthwith be given effect to by the Contractor who shall proceed with the Works with all due diligence whether he or the Employer requires arbitration as hereinafter provided or not. If the

445

Engineer has given written notice of his decision to the Employer and the Contractor and no claim to arbitration has been communicated to him by either the Employer or the Contractor within a period of 90 days from receipt of such notice the said decision shall remain final and binding upon the Employer and the Contractor. If the Engineer shall fail to give notice of his decision as aforesaid within a period of 90 days after being requested as aforesaid or if either the Employer or the Contractor be dissatisfied with any such decision, then and in any such case either the Employer or the Contractor may within 90 days (as the case may be) require that the matter or matters in dispute be referred to arbitration as hereinafter provided.

All disputes or differences in respect of which the decision of the Engineer has not become final and binding shall be finally settled under the Rules of Conciliation and Arbitration of the International Chamber of Commerce in Paris by one or more arbitrators appointed in accordance with the said Rules . . ."

1. The arbitrators had initially to decide whether or not the employer was obliged to make payment if the engineer had approved the certificates. Therefore they examined the legal aspects of the bond between the engineer and the employer in the following terms:

"The Tribunal considers that the contract entered into by both parties gives to the bond uniting the Engineer to the Employer two different legal characters depending on the clause applied. The Engineer is considered to be the Employer's agent:

   a) when he pays under clause 60;

   b) when, during the course of execution, he orders the renewal of all materials which he deems not to be in accordance with the Contract, by implementation of clause 39;

   c) when he orders to execute tests under clause 36(4);

   d) when he requires a return in detail of the supervision staff;

   e) when he orders the Contractor to stop works, under clause 40;

   f) when he gives the order to commence work;

   g) when he delivers a certificate after having satisfied himself that the works are provisionally executed;

   h) when he proceeds to variations under clauses 51 and 52;

   i) when he authorises payment for daywork under clause 52(4);

   j) when he checks and determines under clause 56 whether the value of the works complies with the Contract.

   k) when he issues the final completion certificate under clause 62.

There is an important difference however between the work executed by the Engineer in his capacity of the Employer's agent and his function when acting as an independent arbitrator under clause 67.

The Tribunal has noted the effect of article 699 of the Libyan Civil Code.

The Tribunal considers that the Engineer, with respect to the work which he carries out as the agent of the Employer, binds the latter and involves its financial responsibility with respect to such works.

When acting under clause 67, however;

   a) does not represent the Employer; and

   b) is independent and not bound by the Employer's orders.

Thus, the Engineer's decision under clause 67 can only bind the Employer if it does not object thereto, whereas the Engineer's orders and decisions as agent of the Employer do immediately bind the latter.

Clause 67 gives the Employer the possibility to object to the Engineer's certificate by presenting a claim to the Engineer, about which the latter is to render a decision within 90 days. Within 90 days, the Employer may object, before the Court of arbitration, to the Engineer's decisions relating to such certificates. In default of such objection, the Employer is finally bound by the decision."

Consequently, the arbitrators decided that the employer was bound by the approval of the engineer to the monthly and final certificates.

2. The second question to be settled was to decide whether the employer had acted in accordance with Clause 67 with regard to informing the engineer of the request for arbitration within the time given in that clause so as to avoid eight decisions of the engineer becoming final and binding on the employer.

The employer maintained that his request for arbitration submitted to the Court of Arbitration of the I.C.C. was sufficient proof of his rejection of the engineer's decision and that no additional communication with the engineer was necessary.

The Tribunal found that two different cases were possible under Clause 67.

"*First Case*:
The Engineer gives written notice of its decision to the Employer and the Contractor within 90 days after being requested to decide. In this case, should one of the parties be dissatisfied with the decision, or wish to object thereto, then a request for arbitration is to be made to the I.C.C. Court of Arbitration and such request should be communicated to the Engineer.

Second Case:
The Engineer does not give written notice of its decisions or does not take a decision within 90 days after being requested to decide. In such cases, the contract considers that the Engineer's negative behaviour constitutes a neglect of the claim presented by the Contractor or the Employer, which neglect entitled them to resort to Arbitration within a restricted period of time.

Only in the first case is the request for arbitration to be communicated to the Engineer, such communication is not a procedure of mere form but it is a fundamental procedure related to the Engineer's mission to establish the monthly payment certificates and particularly the final account.

Indeed, it is the Engineer who, under clause 60, adopts the final account which binds the Employer. Such final account varies, depending on whether the amounts fixed by the Engineer's decision are considered to be definitively due or not due subsequently to an objection thereto.

Unknowingly, the Engineer might order the payment to the Contractor of amounts of the final account, which amounts might be due or not due. It is to prevent such a serious risk that the Contract required that both parties communicate the request for arbitration to the Engineer.

In the case of the Engineer's not respecting the time-limits, the Engineer is considered by the contract as negligent and, in such case, the contract leaves the parties the choice to present a claim to arbitration either to the Court of Arbitration or to the Engineer as there is no need to help the latter to adopt the final account, which he is supposed to examine carefully, when he turns out to have failed to respect the proceedings by not taking the required decisions.

Moreover, a claim to arbitration without need for particular formalities is to be explicit and clear and clearly show the plaintiff's intention to submit the dispute to arbitration. On the contrary, the expression of a simple dissatisfaction is not enough to show clearly such intention and subsequently, the claim to arbitration expresses a dissatisfaction whereas a dissatisfaction does not express a claim to arbitration.

The expression of the dissatisfaction as to the decision is not enough in itself and it is to be accompanied by a claim to arbitration which is to be communicated to the Engineer himself as an objection to his explicit decision, as the mere dissatisfaction has no legal effect on the Engineer's decisions, only an explicit request for arbitration communicated to the Engineer within the 90 days period suspends the effect thereof.

The Tribunal rejects the Employer's contentions both grounds and finds that the Employer has not taken the necessary action under clause 67 of the relevant contract to prevent the eight decisions of the Engineer from being final and binding under that clause."

Consequently, the eight decisions of the engineer were held to be final and binding.

Observations

This case illustrates the double role of the engineer according to the F.I.D.I.C. terms: first, when he is acting as a representative of the employer; secondly, when he is responsible for settling disputes between the employer and the contractor.

The engineer's double role according to the F.I.D.I.C. terms requires a great amount of wisdom and experience as he is to act as both representative of the employer and "arbitrator." Article 2(1) of the 3rd edition of the F.I.D.I.C. terms describes the function of the engineer in the following manner: "to issue decisions, certificates and orders." In order for the various F.I.D.I.C. clauses to be applied successfully, it is necessary for both parties involved, the employer and the contractor, to have complete confidence in the engineer. Consequently, he should be both professionally qualified and impartial towards the parties in order to be able to make the necessary decisions for the work to run smoothly, without having to rely upon either the employer or the contractor. This may prove to be an extremely sensitive point given that the engineer is employed and remunerated by the employer. (*cf.* F.I.D.I.C. terms, article 1(1) (C).) The means by which the employer, a public corporation or a government agency, sometimes nominates a civil servant as engineer is not always to be recommended as there is the apparent risk that the engineer could show favouritism towards one party whereas he is obliged to act impartially.

The second question of procedure also deserves attention. The employer had maintained that his request, submitted to the I.C.C. Court of Arbitration, was sufficient evidence of his refusal to accept the engineer's decision, underlining the fact that the I.C.C. Court of Arbitration had not challenged the validity of the request for arbitration. In other words, should the I.C.C. Court of Arbitration verify if the formal procedures laid down in article 67 are respected by the parties before accepting their request for arbitration? In reply to this question, we must refer to articles 7 and 8 of the Rules of the I.C.C. Court of Arbitration. It is common practice for the Court to be limited to establishing the existence prima facie of a clause referring to I.C.C. arbitration so as to decide if the arbitration will take place or not.[1] In all cases, it is for the arbitrator to decide in his own jurisdiction to deal with the matter after having heard both parties' versions. Acceptance of a request for arbitration by the Court of Arbitration in no way pre-judges the arbitrator's jurisdiction, likewise if the Court of Arbitration raises no objection, it does not mean that the conditions set out in Clause 67 of F.I.D.I.C. have been fulfilled (see Article 8).

(For comments on the F.I.D.I.C. terms, *cf.* in addition to the standard comments of I. N. Duncan Wallace, Q.C., *The International Civil Engineering Contract*, Eric Petersen "Sale of industrial complexes and F.I.D.I.C. terms": D.P.C.I., International Trade Law and Practice (Droit et Pratique du Commerce International), 1978, p. 221.)

SIGVARD JARVIN

---

[1] Articles 7 and 8 of the I.C.C. Rules of Conciliation and Arbitration provide (*inter alia*) as follows:—

Article 7:
Absence of agreement to arbitrate.
Where there is no prima facie agreement between the parties to arbitrate or where there is an agreement but it does not specify the International Chamber of Commerce, and if the Defendant does not file an Answer within the period of 30 days provided by paragraph 1 of Article 4 or refuses arbitration by the International Chamber of Commerce, the Claimant shall be informed that the arbitration cannot proceed.

Article 8:
Effect of the agreement to arbitrate.
1. Where the parties have agreed to submit to arbitration by the International Chamber of Commerce, they shall be deemed thereby to have submitted *ipso facto* to the present Rules.
3. Should one of the parties raise one or more pleas concerning the existence or validity of the agreement to arbitrate, and should the Court be satisfied of the prima facie existence of such an agreement, the Court may, without prejudice to the admissibility or merits of the plea or pleas, decide that the arbitration shall proceed. In such a case any decision as to the arbitrator's jurisdiction shall be taken by the arbitrator himself.
4. Unless otherwise provided, the arbitrator shall not cease to have jurisdiction by reason of any claim that the contract is null and void or allegation that it is inexistent provided that he upholds the validity of the agreement to arbitrate. He shall continue to have jurisdiction, even though the contract itself may be inexistent or null and void, to determine the respective rights of the parties and to adjudicate upon their claims and pleas.
. . .

AWARD RENDERED IN CASE NO. 3902 IN 1984

I—Changes in Immigration Rules—Renewal of residence permits for foreign workers—Expulsion of contractors staff (Article 34(9) of the F.I.D.I.C. Terms)

II—State Sovereignty—Special risks according to Article 65 F.I.D.I.C. Terms—Public order.

A dispute involving public works between a European contractor (plaintiff) and an African State Agency, employer (defendant), was submitted for arbitration to the I.C.C. Court of Arbitration. The arbitration was held in Paris by three arbitrators (two named by and having the same nationality as each party and one British chairman). Under the contract, the contractor was to construct a factory for the manufacture of prefabricated-housing elements, buildings containing apartments erected from such elements, and a public utilities network, a drinking water system, rainwater and sewerage systems, electricity and telecommunications systems.

I—Circumstances of the case

Clause 34(9) of the Conditions of the contract stated: "The contractor shall have the right to bring into the Employer's country such number of expatriate staff and labour that the Contractor deems necessary for the execution of the works."

Sub-clauses (1) and (4) of clause 65 of the Conditions (which was in the same terms as the F.I.D.I.C. Conditions) obliged the employer to repay to the contractor any increase in costs of, or incidental to, the execution of the works which are the direct or indirect result of special risks, such as acts of war (whether war is declared or not) or a foreign invasion.

In early 1974, the contractor's personnel included more than 400 Tunisian and Egyptian workers representing 40% of the personnel.

In April 1974, the Director of the Immigration Bureau in the employer's country, advised the contractor that Ministry of the Interior approval would henceforth be required for the issue or renewal of residence permits for Egyptian and Tunisian nationals.

In May and July 1976, two government circulars were published to the effect that

(1) The employment of foreigners as "secretaries, 'medium-level' accountants, typists" was forbidden (the contractor noticed that this circular applied to the majority of its personnel).

(2) Renewal of the residence permits of all workers other than engineers,

draftsmen, quantity surveyors and "high-level" accountants would henceforth be subject to Ministry of Interior approval.

(3) Applications for renewal of the residence permits of all Egyptian and Tunisian workers had to be filed with the Ministry of the Interior at least three months before expiration of their current permits.

By letters in June, August and October 1976, the contractor protested against these measures, and in November 1976, it obtained an authorisation to retain those foreign employees who were already working on the site but could not hire new employees.

From October 1976 to July 1977, seven members of the contractor's staff were expelled on one week's notice, after an armed conflict between the employer's country and a neighbouring country.

Claim

The contractor stated that it was obliged to add three workers to its administrative staff to cope with the increased volume of work caused by the unforeseeable changes in immigration rules.

The contractor further contended that as a result of the expulsions, the number of employees in his payroll department was reduced and those remaining could not handle all the work. The contractor stated that it was thus obliged to computerise its payroll operations, and claimed for the increase in administrative staff (one person, one car and two interpreters during 24 months) and for the specialised computer (program, transport, cost of computerised monthly payrolls, site overhead 15% and general overhead 31%), an amount equivalent to more than U.S. $50,000.

Engineer's decision

The engineer concluded that these costs could have been foreseen by the contractor because expulsions are an ever-present political risk for non-indigenous personnel; that the contractor had bound itself to comply with local laws concerning expulsion of undesirable foreigners; and that no contractual provisions existed to allow the contractor's claim to be accepted so the engineer therefore rejected it.

The contractor's arguments

The fact that if bound itself to comply with the local laws did not oblige it to accept arbitrary and unexplained expulsions of its personnel. Clause 34(9) was expressly included to ensure that it could import and retain expatriate personnel.

Clauses 65(4) (special risks, which were defined in clause 65(1) as including war hostilities) was applicable and entitled the contractor to compensation for the increase in its costs of the work.

451

Employer's answer

The employer recalled that the right to deport aliens or to change immigration rules was a matter for the security and safety of the people of the employer's country. These measures clearly were part of "public policy", the definition of which is a typical attribute of the sovereignty of any state, upon its territory and upon all residents within its boundaries.

By expressly accepting to "observe all laws and orders in force in the Republic" (clause 71 of the General Conditions), the contractor was bound to respect the various circulars issued by the government of the employer's country.

Thus clause 34(9) of the Contract Conditions could be deemed to be a waiver of the sovereignty of the state. The employer could conceive how it could have been entrusted with such power—being an unchallenged and world wide recognised principle of public international law—which could only be vested in the official bodies of a state which have received such sovereignty. The employer as a state agency was a depository of such sovereignty and could not waive such sovereignty. It could only assist the contractor within the limit of his powers as provided in clause 73 of the Conditions.

The employer supported the engineer's decision saying that any reference to section 65 of the Conditions was totally irrelevant. Such clause defined what it calls "special risks" as: "destruction or damage to the works (. . .)." The employer's contended that none of the increase of costs detailed by the contractor were attributable to or consequent on or the result of or in any way whatsoever connected with the said special risks.

II—Award

The arbitrators made the following award:

On clause 34(9):

Clause 34(9) of the contract provides that "the Contractor shall have the right to bring into the Republic such number of expatriate staff and labour that the contractor deems necessary for the execution of the works".

The exercise of the right to expel and the exercise of the right to change immigration rules are not of the employer's capacity or authority, so that the employer's obligation is neither an obligation of means nor an obligation of outcome by which it would have bound itself but an obligation to stand bail.

The employer took upon itself the burden of the obligation to obtain from the competent authorities the authorisation for the contractor to "bring into the Republic such number of expatriate staff and labour that the Contractor deems necessary for the execution of the works".

The employer fulfilled its obligation as the contractor did succeed in obtaining from the relevant authorities to import the number of employees which he deemed necessary for the execution of the works.

As far as employee expulsion decisions or changes in immigration rules are concerned, these are administrative decisions and legislation which are not part of the employer's obligation as they are part of the state's sovereignty, which is a field of public order. Agreements and contractual obligations may not be extended to the field of public orders.

Therefore the Tribunal deems that, as far as the expulsion of personnel is concerned, the employer did not breach his obligations under clause 34(9).

On clause 65

Sub-clauses (1) and (4) of clause 65 oblige the employer to repay to the contractor any increase in costs of, or incidental to the execution of the works which are the direct or indirect result of special risks, such as acts of war (whether war is declared or not) or a foreign invasion.

The Tribunal held that this clause did not apply to those employees who originated from a country with which the employer's country had no hostilities. As far as the employees originating from countries with which there were hostilities, the Tribunal found there was no proof that the expulsion of the personnel was necessarily caused by war.

The Tribunal therefore rejected the claim.

III—Observations

(2)—Clause 34 of the F.I.D.I.C. conditions (1977 edition) (the "Red Book") contains 9 sub-clauses. The 9th sub-clause in the "Red Book" is not a clause with material content, but merely a reference to the possibility of setting out in Part II any other conditions affecting labour and wages.

Clause 34(9) as cited in the case at hand is therefore not a standard formulation from the Red Book, but a clause drafted for the particular contract, and its interpretation may therefore seem of limited interest for the users of F.I.D.I.C. Terms. However the clause and the case that the clause gave rise to is of utmost practical importance in today's construction environment, where foreign contractors perform work on distant sites, involving not only their own personnel brought overseas, but also third country nationals recruited in countries closer to the site.

The problem is one of risk sharing, at least at the tender stage when the parties have full freedom to allocate the hazards inherent in a large construction on either the owner or the contractor. Should the contractor or the employer carry the risks of changes in immigration laws and regulations? None of them seems more fit than the other to assess such risks in advance. One writer, Mr. Richard A. Eastman (*International Business Lawyer* July/August 1984, p. 293) holds that changes in laws or regulations is one of the risks which it is difficult to evaluate for purposes of pricing and that it is unwise to pass these risks to the contractor. Conscientious, skilled contractors may increase their prices substantially to account for them whereas careless contractors will disregard them. When the careless contractor, with the lowest bid, who got the contract, gets into difficulties, he will often succeed in passing the cost back on the owner after all.

It has been pointed out by Mr. McNeill Stokes at p.157 of *International Construction Contracts* (2nd edition, New York, 1980) that "the F.I.D.I.C. Conditions place the full burden of labour relations on the contractor where they should be".

The actual clause modified this principle only slightly by stipulating a duty for the employer to obtain immigration visas from the relevant authorities, leaving however all other burdens on the contractor. It is fair to think that employers do not generally undertake in addition to guarantee the risks of the host country changing its immigration laws during the performance of the contract, at least not in those (most frequent) cases when the employer has no influence on the competent body which takes the necessary measures.

One might therefore conclude that the clause as drafted, and its application in the actual case, both correspond to generally accepted terms of practice for the allocation of risks in respect of changes in regulations affecting labour and personnel in international construction contracts.

SIGVARD JARVIN

AWARD RENDERED IN CASE 4589 IN 1984

I—F.I.D.I.C. Terms—Article 67—compliance with the first step: to refer the dispute to the Engineer before arbitration.

II F.I.D.I.C. Terms—Article 67—Does the Engineer cease to have functions after the Contractor has terminated the contract? (No)

A. Circumstances of the case

In 1981 the Contractor, a European company, and the Employer, a Middle East company, signed a contract for the construction of a hotel in the Employer's country. During the execution of the construction several delays occurred in obtaining on time the imported furnitures and items required for the construction and the equipment, and the hotel was not completed in the contractual time agreed.

The Contractor contended that the delays were due to the Employer's failure to obtain all signatures and pay customs duties so as to allow timely customs clearance, causing the contractor considerable demurrage charges.

The contract contained a clause modelled on clause 67 (third edition) of the F.I.D.I.C. conditions. This paragraph read:

"*Settlements of Disputes*

'65'. If any dispute or difference of any kind whatsoever shall arise between the Empl and the Contractor or the Engineer and the Contractor in connection with, or arising out of the Contract, or the execution of the Works, whether during the progress of the Works or after their completion and whether before or after the termination, abandonment or breach of the Contract, it shall, in the first place, be referred to and settled by the Engineer who shall, within a period of ninety days after being requested by either party to do so, give written notice of his decision to the Employer and the Contractor. Subject to arbitration, as hereinafter provided, such decision in respect of every matter so referred shall be final and binding upon the Employer and the Contractor and shall forthwith be given effect to by the Employer and by the Contractor, who shall proceed with the execution of the Works with all due diligence whether he or the Employer requires arbitration, as hereinafter provided, or not. If the Engineer has given written notice of his decision to the Employer and the Contractor and no claim to arbitration has been communicated to him by either the Employer or the Contractor within a period of ninety days from receipt of such notice, the said decision shall remain final and binding upon the Employer and the Contractor. If the Engineer shall fail to give notice of his decision, as aforesaid, within a period of ninety days after being requested as aforesaid, or if either the Employer or the Contractor be dissatisfied with any such decision, then and in any such case either the Employer or the Contractor may within ninety days after receiving notice of such decision, or within ninety days after the expiration of the first-named period of ninety days, as the case may be, require that the matter or matters in dispute be referred to arbitration as hereinafter provided. All disputes or differences in respect of which the decision, if any, of the Engineer has not become final and binding as aforesaid shall be finally settled under the Rules of Conciliation and Arbitration of the International Chamber of Commerce (in Paris) by one or more arbitrators appointed under such Rules. The said Arbitrator/s shall have full power to open up, revise and review any decision, opinion, direction, certificate or valuation of the Engineer. Neither party shall be limited in the proceedings before such arbitrator/s as to the evidence or arguments put before the Engineer for the purpose of obtaining his said decision. No provisions shall disqualify him from being called as a witness and giving evidence before the arbitrator/s on any matter whatsoever relevant to the dispute or difference referred to the arbitrator/s as aforesaid. The reference to arbitration may proceed notwithstanding that the Works shall not then be or be alleged to be complete, provided always that the obligations of the Employer, the Engineer and the Contractor shall not be altered by reason of the arbitration being conducted during the progress of the Works. The Contractor shall not suspend the Works or any part thereof pending the Engineer's or the Arbitrator's decision on any question under the Contract."

By three letters in June, July and August 1982 the Contractor claimed extensions of time for completion of the works and additional payments. The Employer did not accept the claims and the Engineer gave an answer to this effect in a letter of July 1982.

In October 1982, the Contractor received a memorandum from the Engineer which the Contractor considered as a rejection of its claim and giving him the right to seek arbitration. Under the heading "General", this memorandum stipulated "It is assumed that all parties concerned are aware of the correspondence related to the following points . . ."

On 6 November 1982, the Engineer sent a letter to the parties in which he referred to his memorandum of October as being a decision under the arbitration clause.

In January 1983 the Contractor submitted a claim for arbitration to the ICC Court of Arbitration Secretariat in Paris.

The ICC Court of Arbitration appointed a sole arbitrator, M. M. Soumrani to decide the dispute. The place of arbitration was fixed at Paris (as indicated in the arbitration clause).

B. Claims

The contractor claimed damages for delay, extension of the time for completion, damages for keeping skilled labour idle, overhead costs, interests and costs of the proceedings. The Employer rejected the claims and presented a counter-claim.

Thereafter, on 16 May 1983, the Contractor terminated the Contract with effect from 30 May 1983. On that day he withdrew from the site. In August 1983 the Contractor submitted a revised and a supplementary claim, totalling amounts in excess of its original claim. These later claims, in his own opinion, superseded the original claims and took account of the consequences of the termination.

First issue—compliance with the arbitration clause

The Employer contested the right of the Contractor to go to arbitration on the ground that the Contractor had not referred the dispute to the Engineer before seeking arbitration, as provided in the arbitration clause. Since the Engineer had not been requested by either party to settle a dispute between them, the contractor should not be allowed to submit the claim to arbitration because in doing so he would avoid a first stage of reconciliation. The Employer asked the arbitrator to dismiss the claim for arbitration.

Second issue—the arbitrator's jurisdiction regarding the supplementary claim

The Employer's second defence was to contest the arbitrator's jurisdiction over the claims made after the termination of the contract. Following the termination of the contract by the contractor and his withdrawal from the site as from 30 May, the Engineer's functions were to be considered as having ceased. Therefore the arbitrator could deal only with matters referred to the Engineer before 30 May 1983.

C. Award

The arbitrator made the following award.

First issue

The Engineer's memorandum of October 1982 refers

"to the correspondence between the Contractor and the Employer. The reference made therein shows that a dispute had in fact arisen between the parties and was referred to the Engineer's consideration. In his letter dated, 6 November 1982, the Engineer made it clear that his memorandum of October 1982 was a decision as defined in clause 67 of the General Conditions of the Contract and therefore the Claimant was left without any other choice but to seek arbitration within the time limit set forth in clause 67."

Second issue

The contractor has argued that the arbitration clause provides for the case when the Engineer fails to give notice of his decision and that the present situation falls under that provision. What is at issue is to determine whether the Engineer, after the termination of the Contract and the withdrawal of the Contractor from the site, has lost his capacity to be addressed a claim by either of the parties. The arbitration concluded:

"Whereas the Contract states that any dispute that may arise between the parties 'whether during the progress of the works or after their completion and whether before or after the termination, abandonment or breach of the contract should in the first place, be referred to and settled by the Engineer'.
    Whereas the above wording shows that the Engineer cannot lose his capacity to act as Engineer by the mere fact of the termination of the Contract.
    Whereas the Engineer by refusing to consider the dispute between the parties after the termination of the Contract is to be considered as having failed to give notice of his decision.
    Whereas the claim for arbitration made under the above circumstances falls within the arbitrator's jurisdiction."

Finally the arbitrator decided that the claims were presented in accordance with the arbitration clause and that he had jurisdiction over the contractor's supplemental request.

D. Observations

On the first issue

It is not unusual in cases submitted to the ICC Court of Arbitration for a party to contest jurisdiction on the ground that the dispute has not first been referred to the Engineer for decision. As has been mentioned in comments on another case, (1984) 1 I.C.L.R. 375, the ICC Court of Arbitration does not verify whether the procedures of Clause 67 have been followed before accepting a case, but limits its control to verifying if there exists *prima facie* a clause referring to ICC arbitration. It is then for the arbitrator to decide on his jurisdiction having heard arguments from both parties, as was done in this case.

It has been stated (I. N. Duncan Wallace Q.C.: *The International Civil Engineering Contract* (London, 1974), p. 170, commenting on the 1973 version of the F.I.D.I.C. Conditions) that in English law at least the only and exclusive way of litigating a dispute between the parties to a Clause 67 contract is that, first, there must be a mandatory reference to the Engineer, and secondly, provided there has been the appropriate request within the relevant period, an arbitration under the rules of the ICC. The F.I.D.I.C. brochure "Notes on Documents for Civil Engineering Contracts", first published March 1977, reprinted 1979, does not contradict this opinion (p. 35). So unless the Engineer is seized with a claim by being asked to decide a dispute no arbitrator can be seized with it either. In other words the claim could never be arbitrated at all, nor could it, I presume, be referred to court where the arbitration clause operates as an exclusion of a court of law jurisdiction. The *ratio* for this might lie in the interest of both parties to a construction project in having a quick and concise procedure for the settlement of disputes. If claims were allowed to be taken up directly with arbitrators, avoiding the Engineer, who according to F.I.D.I.C. practice is generally the sole channel of communication between the Employer and the Contractor, the administration of the project would be more difficult and the risk of contradictory decisions by the Engineer and an arbitrator, the latter conceivably acting without the Engineer ever being notified, increases.

If the reference to the Engineer is thus a mandatory step, it is of vital importance to know how the reference to the Engineer may validly be made. The arbitrator in this case was satisfied that the Engineer was seized of the dispute because of the reference made by him in his October 1982 decision that the parties were aware of the correspondence etc. The requirement of the clause that the dispute shall "be referred to . . ." the Engineer was therefore met. Exactly in what terms can an Engineer be seized? Must a party actively approach the Engineer? The words "who shall, within a period of ninety days *after being requested by either party* to do so, give . . ." (emphasis added) seem to indicate, that this is the case, or may an Engineer choose to consider a decision to reject a claim as being both a negative decision on a request and a decision in his capacity as a quasi-arbitrator, simply by stipulating that his decision was one under Clause 67? It may be relevant that the contract does not start that *reference* if the dispute takes place at the same time as a decision is *requested:* there may be two steps.

A case where the arbitrator finds that a dispute has not been referred to the Engineer or where no decision was requested would be a welcome contribution to the jurisprudence on this point of Clause 67.

On the second issue

The Engineer is not a party to the construction contract. According to the F.I.D.I.C. Terms he is appointed by and reports to the Employer and is remunerated by him. The Engineer performs a number of duties delegated to him by the Employer. The F.I.D.I.C. "Notes on Documents for Civil Engineering Contracts" mention (p. 16) that "the Engineer's duty as regards supervision is towards the Employer" and that he owes no such duty to the Contractor.

The objection raised in this case, that the Engineer was to be considered as having ceased to have functions following the Contractor's termination of the contract, must be examined with the role and authority of the Engineer present in mind. Why shoud a termination of the construction contract make the Engineer *functus officio*? He is appointed by the Employer, with whom he has a contract to perform certain supervisory functions, and remains in that capacity until the contract between himself and Employer terminates. The contract relating to the project, the construction contract, may be repudiated by the Contractor without necessarily affecting the Engineer's authority to perform surviving duties and exercise remaining rights laid down in the F.I.D.I.C. conditions. As long as the appointment of the Engineer is notified to the Contractor, disputes must first be referred to him, and he must be prepared to examine new disputes after the termination of the construction contract until the Employer decides to replace him or otherwise. The Employer retains a control over the Engineer by appointing, replacing and withdrawing him, and the Employer—by withdrawing the Engineer—is in a position to modify the two-tier structure of Article 67. If namely the Contractor has been notified that the Engineer is no longer appointed, any dispute, it seems, may be referred directly to the ICC. Because the second link of the two-tier clause, to arbitrate possible disputes, there should be no doubt also in the case where no Engineer is appointed or has been withdrawn.

Finally an interesting question remains as to whether an Engineer can be held liable for not rendering a decision under Clause 67. He may be of the opinion, like a contractor who has terminated the construction contract, that it is a waste of time to decide the dispute at a time when the basic contract between the Contractor and the Employer is no longer operative, and the parties are heading towards a big conflict that arbitrators are best suited to decide. It is true that the parties are free to request arbitration under the ICC rules in the absence of an Engineer's decision within 90 days, but does the Engineer have a duty or free choice to make a Clause 67 decision and with what consequences for the parties who must wait 90 days to known whether or not he intends to do so?

SIGVARD JARVIN

AWARD RENDERED IN CASE NO 4416 IN 1985

F.I.D.I.C. Terms—Article 52 (5)—Article 67—the independent Engineer withdrawn and replaced by Owner's own staff; consequences on other terms of the contract—the "institutional" role of the Engineer.

A. Circumstances of the Case

In late 1975 a European Construction Company (Claimant), and an African State Corporation (Respondent), entered into a contract for the construction of certain public utilities. Clause 67 of the General Conditions of Contract (the F.I.D.I.C. Conditions) provided for arbitration under the I.C.C. Rules.

In March 1977 the contractual Engineer (an engineering firm from a European country) appointed by the Owner in accordance with the contract, was terminated by the Owner. No other engineering firm or person was appointed to succeed the engineering firm and the Owner notified the Contractor that the Owner's own supervisory staff "will handle this matter by itself".

The Contractor did not agree with this decision as, in its view, the Engineer's functions under the General Conditions of Contract (e.g. Clause 67 of the F.I.D.I.C. Conditions) could only be performed by an independent engineer as opposed to an employee of the Owner. Nevertheless, no independent engineer or engineering firm was appointed by the Owner.

The originally agreed time for completion, February 1982, was extended by the Owner on several occasions. The completion of the works therefore extended over a period of 49 months, whereas the contractual completion time was 24 months. Time extensions were granted by the Owner, upon the Contractor's request. In March 1980 the Claimant submitted the last certificate of completion. The request for arbitration was introduced in May 1982. No penalties were levied upon the Contractor. The contractor performed the work within the extended time period.

B. Claims

The extensions of time for completion brought about supplementary costs for which the Contractor (Claimant) sought relief.

The Owner/Respondent rejected the claims. The contract was, according to the view of the owner, to be considered as an administrative contract under the laws of the Owner's country. The Owner was therefore entitled, since public interest required such a measure, to appoint as Engineer a person and a team of experts of its own staff. In the Owner's view the claims for supplementary costs should have been introduced monthly to the engineer, after the dismissal of the engineering firm in compliance with Clause 52 (5) of the contract.

(NOTE: Clause 52 (5) of the F.I.D.I.C. Conditions reads:

> "The Contractor shall send to the Engineer's Representative once in every month an account giving particulars, as full and detailed as possible, of all claims for any additional payment to which the Contractor may consider himself entitled and of all extra or additional work ordered by the Engineer which he has executed during the preceding month.
>
> No final or interim claim for payment for any such work or expense will be considered which has not been included in such particulars. Provided always that the Engineer shall be entitled to authorise payment to be made for any such work or expense, notwithstanding the Contractor's failure to comply with this condition, if the Contractor has, at the earliest practicable opportunity, notified the Engineer in writing that he intends to make a claim for such work.")

Since the Contractor failed to do so the claims should be rejected for failure to comply with the contractual procedure for money claims.

C. Award

In their award the three arbitrators (three lawyers were nominated by each party and a chairman nominated by the I.C.C.) first set out that, although sanctity of contracts must be respected, the arbitrators must take into account the deviations from the contract which the parties themselves, explicitly or implicitly, had undertaken. The arbitrators did not limit their analysis to the wording of the contract alone, but took account of acts and deeds of the parties, giving rise to waivers of existing, and creating new, rights and obligations. A strict interpretation of the contract alone was thus excluded. The arbitrators went on to state.

> "A large portion of the contractual regulation has been inspired (often 'ad litteram') by the well-known F.I.D.I.C. International Standard Form Civil Engineering and Building Contract.
>
> It is equally well known that the F.I.D.I.C. Forms are built upon a number of key principles, among which one may cite, for their bearing upon our reasoning, the technical independence of the Contract Engineer, the due and reasonable appreciation of the effects, upon the parties' rights and obligations, of certain defined events occurring during the contractual performance, and, last but not least, the mechanism for settling disputes without affecting the completion of the works, within which mechanism the Engineer is entrusted with the function of an arbitrator, or better 'quasi-arbitrator', as the most attentive commentators would rather define it.
>
> In the present case, the dismissal of the Contract Engineer and the designation, in its stead, of members of Respondent's own Supervisory Staff appears to be no issue on which the Arbitrators are called to decide. This does not mean, however, that they are bound to ignore this circumstance, which *inter alia* is relied upon in Claimant's submissions.
>
> It is a plain fact that the parties have not complied with Clause 67 of the Contract, providing for a two-tier arbitration, whereby the submission of the dispute to the I.C.C. Court of Arbitration appears contingent upon the parties' expressed dissatisfaction with a prior decision of the Engineer, or else upon a failure of the same to decide the dispute submitted to it by the parties. Claimant's direct recourse to the I.C.C. Arbitration was not challenged by Respondent and the Arbitrators have no say on it. They have a say,

however, on a different proposition, pertinent to their finding, consisting of the following question: whether or not the absence of an independent Engineer may justify the parties' departure from a number of contractual (i.e. F.I.D.I.C.) rules, which are logically structured and hence to be interpreted and complied with) on the assumption that an independent Engineer is present and acting in compliance with the spirit and the letter of the whole body of the F.I.D.I.C. Rules. Specific reference is hereby made to the 'institutional role' of the Contract Engineer in the framework of the F.I.D.I.C. rules, with no implications whatsoever upon the technical competence and/or personal integrity of the natural persons which may have, individually, performed this task.

The Arbitrators are of the opinion that in the case at issue the absence of a Contract Engineer may have reasonably prevented Claimant, at the early stage of its claims, from seeking 'decisions' (in the F.I.D.I.C. Rules sense) from members of Respondent's own Supervisory Staff, who had no 'institutional capacity' to hand down any decisions carrying the legal implications inherent in the quality of an Engineer's decision under the F.I.D.I.C. Rules.

The Arbitrators are expressing no judgment on the reasons and/or legality of Respondent's choice to appoint members of its own Supervisory Staff as Contract Engineer. They are merely underlining the consequences of an act stemming from Respondent's own discretion and free volition, among which consequences account should be given of the '*ex parte*' frustration, by Respondent itself, of those contractual rules presupposing the active presence of the Contract Engineer. It follows from the above that Respondent, faced with Claimant's claims as put forward before the Arbitrators, cannot impute to Claimant the breach, on procedural grounds, of the same contractual provisions which Respondent itself frustrated by its own unilateral action. This answers, *inter alia*, in the Arbitrator's view, the Respondent's main argument whereby Claimant allegedly failed to comply with Article 52 (5) of the Contract. Irrespective of the question as to whether or not, in the case at issue, the works for which Claimant is claiming additional payments should be deemed 'extra' or 'additional' works within the meaning of Article 52, the Arbitrators believe that, especially in the absence of a Contract Engineer having the status as pointed out above, Article 52 (5) may not be construed in such a strict sense as to irreversibly bar Claimant's claim on the sole ground of non-compliance with the procedural rules provided for therein. All the more so, as the wording itself of said Article reveals that the rules in question are not mandatory in nature by stating:

> 'Provided always that the Engineer shall be entitled to authorise payment to be made for any such work notwithstanding the Contractor's failure to comply with this condition if the Contractor has at the earliest practicable opportunity notified the Engineer that he intends to make a claim for such work'.

It appears from the record that Claimant made no secret of its intent to make a claim for additional expense. It did so by turning directly to I.C.C. arbitration, a course of action which appears reasonable in view of the circumstances already commented upon, and which was not challenged by Respondent."

D. Observations

The role of the Engineer under the F.I.D.I.C. Conditions is much debated and is not easily defined. His authority to bind the Employer was touched upon in relation to an earlier case note in this review (refer Vol. 1, Part 4, July 1984, page 375). The wisdom and risk of appointing as Engineer a person who is not an independent engineer in the spirit of the F.I.D.I.C. Conditions, which was briefly mentioned in the cited case note, is explored in more detail in the case now reported.

If it is accepted that the professional advice of an engineer is necessary for the design of construction work, for the preparation of documents according to which the work is to be carried out and for the execution of the work, one may wonder why he must be an independent engineer. A person employed by the Owner could be just as qualified as an independent consulting engineer.

The problem is not one of the technical qualifications of the Engineer, but one of trust in a person having the far-reaching powers which the F.I.D.I.C. Conditions of Contract attribute to the Engineer. The F.I.D.I.C. Notes on Documents for Civil Engineering Contracts (first published in March 1977) describe the Engineer as the link between the Employer and the Contractor, based on the duties delegated to him by the Employer. The Notes state that the degree to which the Employer is prepared to leave to the Engineer decisions affecting the extent and cost of the Works will depend on the degree of confidence which the Employer has in the ability and professional integrity of the Engineer to act fairly and impartially (page 16). But the Engineer is and remains a person appointed and paid by the Owner and owes a duty of supervision towards the Owner and not the Contractor.

In this case the Owner, who lost confidence in the engineering firm, appointed a member of his own staff. By doing so, in my opinion, he contravened no letter of the F.I.D.I.C. Conditions, since the Owner has a right to appoint, remove and replace an engineer as he sees fit (F.I.D.I.C. Conditions Article 1 (c): "Engineer means the Engineer designated as such in Part II, *or other the Engineer appointed from time to time* by the Employer and notified in writing to the Contractor to act as Engineer for the purposes of the Contract in place of the Engineer so designated" (emphasis added). See also observations in Vol. 2, Part 3, April 1985, pages 302, 303). To appoint a member of his own staff is not in fact a breach of contract, since at least in U.K. practice from which F.I.D.I.C. Conditions originate an Engineer who is the Owner's employee is deemed to act impartially when acting as Engineer.

The arbitrators in this case expressed no judgment on the legality of Owner's choice to appoint members of its own staff as Engineer. The arbitrators seem to recognise that it was within the Owner's discretion to dismiss the Engineering firm. They do, however, attribute important consequences to the exercise of such discretion when they qualify the act as a "frustration" of contractual rules presupposing the active presence of the Contract Engineer. The arbitrators seem determined to restore the equilibrium which, by the authors of the F.I.D.I.C. Conditions, was supposed to exist through the presence of an *independent* engineer as Engineer; a practice which—as shown by this case and many others—has fallen into disuse as of late.

The decision in this case was confined to the application of Article 52(5). The reasons for the decision may pose questions regarding the extent to which a contractor may be relieved from having to comply with other clauses of the F.I.D.I.C. Conditions in a similar situation, where the removal by the Owner of an originally appointed independent Engineer may be considered a "frustration" of the spirit of the F.I.D.I.C. Conditions.

The F.I.D.I.C. Conditions (see F.I.D.I.C. cited "Notes" page 16) presuppose rightly that the Owner has confidence in the Engineer. The situation for an Owner who loses confidence in the Engineer and places confidence only in a person of his own staff may not be easy when he is to decide by whom to replace the original Engineer. Knowing that if the appointment will be deemed to breach the conditions, presupposing the presence of an independent Engineer, one or more of the clauses of the F.I.D.I.C. Conditions need not necessarily be strictly complied with by the Contractor.

SIGVARD JARVIN

I Saudi Arabia Royal Decree No. M/46—the scope of application on an international arbitration—Arbitrator's jurisdiction when contract stipulated I.C.C. arbitration.
II F.I.D.I.C. Conditions Article 67—Is a derogation to the conditions for the submitting of a dispute to arbitration permissible or is Art. 67 of a mandatory nature? —If derogation can be made, what form may such derogation take? (Parties' conduct or tacit agreement or express written agreement?)
III Applicable law on the merits in a case where the parties have made reference to some specific provisions only of the law of a particular country.

PARTIAL AWARD RENDERED IN 1986 IN CASE 4840

A. Circumstances of the case

In 1973 a Lebanese construction company (plaintiff) entered into two contracts with a company in Saudi Arabia (defendant) for the erection and completion of two office buildings in two Saudi Arabian cities. The time allowed for completion of the two contracts was 24 and 22 months respectively. The arbitration clause was of a type inspired by the F.I.D.I.C. Clause 67, second edition. It had the following wording:

Arbitration Clause (67 of the General Conditions):
"If any dispute or difference of any kind whatsoever shall arise between the Employer or the Consultant and the Contractor in connection with or arising out of the Contract or the carrying out of the Works (whether during the progress of the Works or after their completion and whether before or after the termination abandonment or breach of the Contract), it shall in the first place be referred to and settled by the Consultant who within a period of 90 days after being requested by either party to do so shall give written notice of his decision to the Employer and the Contractor. Save as hereinafter provided such decision in respect of every matter so referred shall be final and binding upon the Employer and the Contractor until the completion of the work and shall forthwith be given effect to by the Contractor who shall proceed with the Works with all due diligence whether he or the Employer requires arbitration as hereinafter provided or not. If the Consultant has given written notice of his decision to the Employer and the Contractor and no claim to arbitration has been communicated to him by either the Employer or the Contractor within a period of 90 days from receipt of such notice, the said decision shall remain final and binding upon the Employer and the Contractor. If the Consultant shall fail to give notice of his decision as aforesaid within a period of 90 days after being requested as aforesaid or if either the Employer or the Contractor be dissatisfied with any such decision, then and in any such case either the Employer or the Contractor may within 90 days after receiving notice of such decision or within 90 days after the expiration of the first named period of 90 days (as the case may be) require that the matter or matters in dispute be referred to arbitration as hereinafter provided. All disputes or differences in respect of which the decision (if any) of the Consultant has not become final and binding as aforesaid shall be finally settled under the Rules of Conciliation and Arbitration of the

International Chamber of Commerce by one or more arbitrators appointed in accordance with the said Rules.

The said arbitrator/s shall have a full power to open up review and revise any decision, opinion, direction, certificate or valuation of the Consultant and neither party shall be limited in the proceedings before such arbitrator/s to the evidence or arguments put before the Consultant for the purpose of obtaining his said decision. No decision given by the Consultant in accordance with foregoing provisions shall disqualify him from being called as a witness and giving evidence before the arbitrator/s on any matter whatsoever relevant to the dispute or difference referred to the arbitrator/s as aforesaid.

The arbitrator/s shall not enter on the reference until after the completion or alleged completion of the Works unless with the written consent of the Employer and the Contractor provided always:

1 that such reference may be opened before such completion or alleged completion in respect of the withholding by the Consultant of any certificate or the withholding of any portion of the retention money to which the Contractor claims in accordance with the conditions set out in Part II in the Clause numbered 60 to be entitled or in respect of the exercise of the Consultant's power to give a certificate under Clause 63(1) hereof or in respect of a dispute arising under Clause 71 hereof.

2 that the giving of a Certificate of Completion under Clause 43 hereof shall not be a condition precedent to the opening of any such reference."

B. Claims

The plaintiff claimed that he was confronted with a considerable increase in the construction costs and the occurrence of irresistible circumstances which could not have been reasonably foreseen and were completely beyond control. In the arbitration the construction company claimed compensation for damages incurred.

The defendant objected to the jurisdiction of the I.C.C., held that the reference to arbitration was time-barred and contended that the laws of Saudi Arabia were applicable on the merits. In developing the first point defendant suggested that the Royal Decree of the Kingdom No. M/46 dated 12/7/1403H clearly states that parties seeking arbitration are mandatorily required to file their dispute in Saudi Arabia before the competent authority, *viz.*, the Committee for Settlement of Commercial Disputes, and that any award given or decision taken by the arbitrators will be null and void and unenforceable.

C. Arbitrators and procedure

Three arbitrators were appointed, one of Lebanese nationality proposed by the plaintiff, one of Kuwaiti nationality proposed by the defendant. The I.C.C. appointed as chairman a Jordanese laywer.

Parties were represented by Lebanese and Saudi lawyers respectively.

The I.C.C. Court fixed the place of arbitration at Bahrain.

In the Terms of Reference it was decided that among the issues to be determined in a partial award were the jurisdiction of the arbitrators and the law applicable to the merits.

D. The award

(Where reference in the award is made to the "Consultant", this is to be understood as the "Engineer" according to the terminology of the F.I.D.I.C. Conditions (Author's note)).

On the question of the *application of the Saudi Royal Decree* the arbitrators held:

"Whereas the Defendant contests the Tribunal's jurisdiction on the basis that the above-mentioned Saudi Law—which was published and came into force before the filing of the Request for Arbitration by the Plaintiff—is a sovereign act which imperatively governs any agreement to arbitrate that is not in conformity therewith, especially that article 7 of the said Decree requires parties to disputes—whether their agreement to arbitrate was made before or after the dispute to comply with the rules spelled out in the Decree. According to the Decree, the Saudi Court having original jurisdiction over the dispute should approve the appointment of the arbitrators, and their Terms of Reference, and such Court has also liberty to uphold the award as being in conformity with the applicable laws in the Kingdom or to nullify same if not in conformity with such laws. The Defendant adds that, in our case the arbitration should have been held in Saudi Arabia, and that Bahrain was fixed fortuitously as a venue by the Court of Arbitration due to the fact that the arbitration clause did not fix the place thereof.

Whereas the Defendant submits that the principle of sovereignty commands—and despite any previous agreement to the contrary—the application of mandatory statutory provisions to any dispute whenever one or more of the parties is of Saudi nationality and the situs of the disputed transaction is in Saudi Arabia, and, therefore, by imperative application of the Decree M/46, the Parties seeking arbitration in the matter are required to file their disputes, pertaining to a project executed in Saudi Arabia, before the competent authority which is the Saudi Committee for Settlement of Commercial Disputes.

Whereas the Defendant adds that the dispute subject matter of this arbitration is of a domestic nature since the parties involved are Saudis or one or all of partners in the entities are of Saudi nationality and/or at least maintain their residence and/or carry on their business in Saudi Arabia, and, therefore, such dispute is out of the scope of the I.C.C.'s jurisdiction and should be settled by the Saudi Courts having jurisdiction.

Whereas the Tribunal after having examined the Contract, the arbitration clause making part thereof (cl. 67 of the General Conditions) and the Saudi Decree No. M/46, has reached the conclusion that it cannot accept the Defendant's point of view for the following reasons:

1 The dispute, subject matter of this arbitration, is an international dispute between a Lebanese company (Contractor) and a Saudi Employer for a project in Saudi Arabia.

2 It is true that the provisions of the Saudi Royal Decree M/46 are general and make no distinction between national disputes and disputes of international character. However, the provisions of the Decree, in spite of their generality, are limited to national arbitrations taking place in Saudi Arabia. Not only the Decree has no application to arbitrations that are held outside of Saudi Arabia, but also there is no provision in the Decree which forbids or precludes arbitration outside of the Saudi territory. In such case, the parties, knowingly, would renounce the advantages of a local Saudi arbitration under the Decree ending by an award enjoying the value of a 'Res Judicata' enforceable in Saudi Arabia, but the choice, under the Decree, remains open to the parties of the dispute between the two kinds of arbitration. This is the significance of the fact that the Decree does not forbid nor even makes any reference to arbitration outside the Kingdom.

It is up to the parties to weigh their interests when agreeing on an arbitration clause within or without the Kingdom.

3 Moreover, this construction of the Decree is in line with the fact that, as a general rule, and subject to some exceptions of a purely administrative nature, the agreement to arbitrate outside of the Kingdom is perfectly valid. The Saudi Law went even further, and the Kingdom adhered on 9–9–1979 to the I.C.S.I.D. Convention admitting thereby the enforceability of foreign awards in the Kingdom. Also, Saudi Arabia had already ratified on 5–4–1954 the Convention on the Enforcement of Foreign Judgements and Awards between the members of the Arab League.

4 The fact referred to by the Defendant that Bahrain as place of arbitration was fixed by the Court of arbitration and not by the parties is irrelevant. When the parties agreed in their Contract to settle their disputes through I.C.C. Arbitration without fixing the venue of the arbitration, they have accepted, in advance and since the signature of their Contract, to arbitrate in any place which the Court may fix under the Rules.

5 The Defendant's reference to article 7 of the Decree—as an imperative provision which automatically nullifies all inconsistent previous arbitration clauses between the parties—cannot be accepted by the Tribunal. Not only, as it is noted above, the whole Decree has no bearing on international arbitration clauses, but also nothing in article 7 of the Decree can be interpreted as giving to that provision a retroactive effect covering clauses validly agreed prior to 4–7–1983 date on which the Decree came into force.

Whereas, in view of all the above, it appears that the promulgation in Saudi Arabia of the Royal Decree M/46 prior to the filing of this arbitration is without effect to the jurisdiction of this Tribunal.

The Tribunal rules that the promulgation of the said Decree does not impair its jurisdiction over the dispute."

Thereafter, the arbitrators decided with respect of the allegation that the *claims were time-barred*:

"Whereas the Jurisdiction of this Tribunal is disputed by the Defendant on the basis that the Plaintiff's claims under the Contract were *either* not submitted to the Consultant for decision under Clause 67 of the General Conditions and therefore not ready for arbitration under the same Clause (requiring disputes to be referred to the Consultant for decision in the first place), *or* the above mentioned claims were submitted to the Consultant under Clause 67 and the Consultant either gave his decision or failed to give same but the Plaintiff has always failed to require, within the period of 90 days fixed by the Clause, the dispute to be referred to arbitration, and the claims are therefore, time-barred under the Contract and cannot be referred to arbitration, and consequently the Tribunal has no jurisdiction.

Whereas the Plaintiff denies the above allegation and maintains that he went on negotiating his claims with the Defendant in good faith and that it was quite clear that the Defendant had waived his right to invoke the provisions of Clause 67 and therefore, the Tribunal has full jurisdiction for all his claims.

Whereas the Tribunal has studied in detail all the documents submitted by the two parties and has noted the project's long span of time, the fact that the same claims were submitted or raised more than once on different occasions, and also that there is often no evidence of direct contact between the Plaintiff and the Consultant, and that some of the amounts claimed are dues for work executed and not for 'claims' in the proper sense of this word.

Whereas the Tribunal has in view of all the above factors, to examine one by one, but only as far as Clause 67 is concerned, the main categories of the amounts claimed by the Plaintiff.

1 *Claims for Phase I*

Whereas the facts, in this respect, are as follows:
— on 16–6–1976, the Consultant wrote to the Defendant (and not to the Plaintiff) stating that a minimum amount of S.R. 3,300,000 will be established as justifiable claims for reimbursable costs, extra works etc., out of which S.R. 1,367,276 were already certified and so leaving a balance of S.R. 1,932,724. The Consultant therefore recommended an advance payment on account of claims in round figures of S.R. 2,000,000.
— Negotiation followed, and on 24–4–1977, an agreement was reached by which the Plaintiff undertook to finish the works within 8 months and the amount of S.R. 1.5 million was granted to him as an interest free loan to be added to previous repayable loans (totalling S.R. 5.5 million), and the total amount (S.R. 7 million) was not to be reimbursed by the Plaintiff *until final settlement either amicably or through arbitration.* Claims of both parties were reserved.

Whereas from the above undisputed facts, the Tribunal concludes that the Consultant was not properly requested to give his decision under Clause 67 but the two parties preferred to settle the matter provisionally pending final amicable settlement or arbitration, while expediting the project's completion.

But whereas it is clear to the Tribunal—taking into consideration the dates, the amounts, the total loans becoming non-reimbursable until final settlement amicably or through arbitration, the reference to claims being reserved—that there had been a clear provisional settlement of the Phase I claims, and by virtue of that settlement it was accepted by the Defendant that in case of failure to reach an amicable settlement, the Plaintiff would have the way paved to file arbitration directly and without other formalities, especially that the Consultant had been already consulted and had given his assessment of these claims.

Whereas nothing in the Contract precludes the Parties from making any amendments to any of its provisions including the formalities laid down in Clause 67 and therefore these formalities can be validly waived, totally or partially, by subsequent agreement of the Parties.

Whereas such amendment can be made either expressly or implicitly provided such implicit amendment is clear and can be ascertained beyond doubt.

Whereas nothing in the Contract excludes implicit amendments. Moreover some of its provisions refer to such implicit agreement e.g. Clause (5) of the General Conditions recognizes the validity of whatever may be 'reasonably to be inferred from the Contract'.

Also according to Clause 51 a verbal variation order is deemed to be an order in writing by the Consultant if the confirmation thereof by the Contractor is not contradicted in writing by the Consultant.

Whereas nothing in the Trade Usages precludes implicit amendment by the Parties of their relationship.

Whereas the Saudi Law based on the principles of Islamic Law recognizes widely the Parties right to amend any aspect of their contractual relationship either in writing or verbally and either expressly or implicitly subject to the sole condition that they do not violate any imperative rule of law, and the formalities required in Clause 67 of the General Conditions cannot be considered as being a rule of public policy.

Whereas, in the light of the prevailing circumstances, the contracting practices, and the content and economy of the agreement reached by the Parties on 24–4–1977, the Tribunal is convinced that the waiver of the formalities laid down by Clause 67 of the General Conditions (as a condition precedent for arbitration in case no amicable settlement is reached,) is the sound and logical interpretation of the Parties will embodied in their written agreement dated 24–4–1977.

Whereas, in view of the above and in the presence of this tacit but clear agreement of both parties regarding Phase I claims, the Defendant should not be allowed to invoke in this arbitration the Tribunal's lack of jurisdiction based on the omission by the Plaintiff to request properly the Consultant's decision under Clause 67 on these claims."

Thereafter the arbitrators held as regards the Phase II claim:

"Plaintiff's Claim (Phase II):

Whereas, for this third category of claims, the Plaintiff recognizes in his submission dated 4–9–1985 (P:17) that he 'was not appealing to the function of the Consultant as provided for in article 67 but searched to find suitable arrangements with the Defendant on the way of the settlement of the dispute', and further alleges that negotiations with the Defendant were still engaged in February 1983 and that it was agreed with the top management of the Defendant that in case the claims are not settled within a reasonable time, the matter should be referred directly to arbitration, and that this agreement was acknowledged by the Defendant in his letter dated 7–2–1984 by which he declared his readiness to go to arbitration in Saudi Arabia and appointed his arbitrator.

Whereas the Defendant contends on his part that those claims were submitted to the Defendant and passed to the Consultant in early 1981, but the Consultant failed to give a decision thereon within 90 days, and the Plaintiff also failed to require that the matter be referred to arbitration as commanded by Clause 67, and that consequently, his claims are time-barred. The negotiations referred to by the Plaintiff took place but failed, and there was no agreement, express or tacit, that in case of failure the Plaintiff could initiate arbitration without observing the mandatory course of action laid down by Clause 67.

Whereas the Tribunal, after having examined all the documents submitted by the two parties, is convinced that the claims were not submitted to the Consultant for settlement in accordance with the terms of Clause 67, but were submitted to the Defendant who passed them to the Consultant for advice, and, therefore these claims cannot be considered time-barred as alleged by the Defendant.

Whereas the Plaintiff, on the other hand and unlike his position for his Phase I claims as aforementioned has failed to provide a conclusive evidence that the Defendant had accepted that the claims be submitted directly to arbitration.

Whereas the Defendant's letter dated 7–2–1984 cannot constitute such evidence, since it is subsequent to the filing of the I.C.C. arbitration by the Plaintiff and totally oriented to contest the I.C.C.'s jurisdiction to the benefit of a Saudi local arbitration.

Whereas it appears clearly to the Tribunal that the Plaintiff's claims for Phase II were referred to the I.C.C. arbitration directly without requesting the Consultant, acting as a quasi-arbitrator, to give his decision thereon in the first place as required by Clause 67 of the General Conditions.

And whereas such submission of claims 'in the first place' to the Consultant for settlement is *required* under Clause 67 and is a condition precedent to filing arbitration with the I.C.C., and that it appears, therefore, that the Plaintiff's claims for Phase II were prematurely and unduly referred to arbitration, and consequently this Tribunal does not have jurisdiction thereover.

The Tribunal rules that it does not have jurisdiction over these claims."

Thirdly the arbitrators had to decide the question of *applicable law*. They did so in the following terms:

"What is the applicable law to the merits of the case?

Whereas article 13 para 3 of the Rules for the I.C.C. Court of Arbitration stipulates that: 'The parties shall be free to determine the law to be applied by the Arbitrator to the dispute. In the absence of any indication by the parties as to applicable law, the Arbitrator shall apply the law designated as the proper law by the rule of conflict which he deems appropriate.'

Whereas the contracts under dispute do not refer to any National law to govern the said contracts.

Whereas the Defendant contends that Saudi Law is applicable over the dispute for the following reasons:

(a) The tacit choice by the parties of the Kingdom of Saudi Arabia evidenced by the reference made in the contracts (Part I, art. 16 and Part II, art. 10) to the rules of Saudi legal system.

(b) Art. 13 (3) of the I.C.C. Rules gives the arbitrators freedom to apply choice of law rules which have logical relationship and are appropriate for the particular dispute at hand.

(c) The most appropriate conflict of law rules lead to the choice of a system of law with which the contract is most closely connected.

(d) The criteria of 'objective localization' on the basis of objective connecting factors.

(e) The application of *Lex Mercatoria* is not a separate complete applicable system of law and is not a satisfactory solution.

Whereas the Plaintiff contends that the parties, willingly, did not refer to any specific law while adopting an international form (the Fidic form) for their contracts, and objects to the Defendants' request to apply Saudi Law to the merits of the case for the following reasons:

(a) The parties avoided the choice of their respective national laws as the applicable law to the contracts, by deleting the article of the Fidic form related to the law to which the contract is to be subject.

(b) The reference in two articles to specific Saudi laws (labour and boycott of Israel) exists in all international contracts and should be interpreted as a deliberate choice to restrict the application of Saudi law to these specific matters.

(c) The Defendant recognized implicitly that Saudi law does not apply by claiming interest which is strictly forbidden by Saudi law.

(d) The contracts provide for insurance in several articles which contravene the Sharia principles.

(e) The plaintiff could accept Saudi law as substantive law in as far as it is common to and in agreement with Lebanese law and the basic law of all nations and international commercial practice.

Whereas, in line with the provisions of art. 13 (3) of the I.C.C. Rules, the first duty of the Arbitral Tribunal is to determine whether an agreement, express or tacit, exists between the parties as to the law applicable to the substance of the dispute in which case the Tribunal should abide by the said agreement. In our case, there is obviously no such agreement.

Whereas, under article 13 para 3 of the Rules, the arbitrators should resort to the rules of conflict only in the absence of *any* indication by the parties as to the applicable law.

Whereas it is a fact that the parties have adopted the forms of conditions of contract prepared by the Federation Internationale des Ingenieurs—Conseils (Fidic) with some few exceptions and amendments.

Whereas the provision in the Fidic form related to the law of the country which is to apply to the Contract and according to which the contract is to be construed has been deleted while a reference to some specific Saudi laws was added.

Whereas the parties, one of which is non-Saudi avoided the reference to the Saudi law as being the law governing the Contract in spite of the fact that the place of negotiation, signature and performance are closely linked with Saudi Arabia.

Whereas the parties referred to the Saudi law only as far as the labour relationships and the boycott of Israel are concerned.

Whereas the Arbitral Tribunal believes that the above exception and amendments to the Fidic form agreed upon among the parties are a clear indication that they did not wish to subject their contracts '*in toto*' to the Saudi law.

Whereas, in view of the above, and due to the fact that the contracts under dispute are of an international nature, the Arbitral Tribunal believes that it should respond to the clear indication given by the parties at the date of signature of the contracts not to apply a national system to the said contracts '*in toto*'.

Therefore, in the light of the foregoing, *the Tribunal rules that it will give precedence in this dispute to the rules the parties have established for their relationship i.e. the terms of their contracts supplemented by the relevant trade usage applicable to the matter and, for issues directly related to the object of the contractual relationship that may arise in the course of this arbitration and which are not provided for in the contracts, the Tribunal would supplement by the Saudi law in the first place.*"

E. Comments

I. In his report on arbitration laws in Saudi Arabia in the *I.C.C.A. Yearbook, Commercial Arbitration,* (1984, p. 9), Dr. Albert Jan van den Berg states that one sometimes hears that reference to arbitration rules of a foreign arbitration institution is invalid. Mr. van den Berg goes on to say that this opinion needs to be qualified, and that the test is whether the contract concerns the Saudi Government or one of its agencies, "promoting the so-called Saudisation". Arbitration is prohibited with public Saudi bodies without the consent of the President of the Council of Ministers. In the private domain, between a Saudi and a non-Saudi, where the contract concerns a services agency agreement or a distributorship or commercial agency agreement it must be filed with the Ministry of Commerce, which does not accept arbitration abroad. The same applies to articles of a Saudi company. In these cases arbitration inside Saudi Arabia is permitted. But in all other cases there is no restriction to agree to arbitration abroad (*op. cit.*, page 10).

The award in this case confirms the opinion advanced in the *Yearbook*, holding that a dispute between a Saudi private party and a non-Saudi company may validly be submitted to arbitration by parties' agreement outside Saudi Arabia. There is no provision in the recently enacted Arbitration Regulation prohibiting a private Saudi party, outside the areas of agencies etc. (see above), from entering into arbitration agreements according to other rules than those laid down in the Arbitration Regulation issued by Royal Decree No. M/46, such as the Rules of the I.C.C. This unanimous award, rendered by three arbitrators from Arab Middle East countries, is a welcome contribution to the interpretation of the Saudi legislation. The full text of the Regulation is reprinted below (*see Annex*).

II. The question whether the strict conditions laid down in clause 67, regarding how and when a claim can be referred to arbitration, may be waived by parties' agreement is indeed an interesting one, since if it is possible it alters fundamentally the basic idea laid down in this clause 67, that disputes shall be referred (and settled) within a certain time-period..One of the purposes of clause 67 is said to be avoiding uncertainty as to whether there exists a dispute or not that shall be settled by the Engineer and possibly the arbitrator—and to avoid such uncertainty after the lapse of a fixed time period (the 90 days). Any waiver of the stipulated two-tier procedure, if permissible, risks upsetting this basic philosophy. If one accepts that parties will always be supreme and have the possibility of waiving the Article 67 conditions, the possibility of waiving the stipulated procedure may raise new difficulties. Extreme vigilance and care must be taken by the parties in the handling of such amendments in order to assure that the Engineer is kept informed of the parties' agreement to modify. Otherwise the Engineer's duty to manage the construction may be made more difficult and it may be difficult enough even if he *is* informed of the parties' amendment!

The Engineer is the Owner's agent and has not a contractual relationship with the Contractor, but the duty to inform him must probably be that of both the Owner *and* the Contractor in the interest of a smooth management of the works. The award in this case does not inform of what measures were taken, nor when, to keep the Engineer informed of the parties' negotiations and agreement (and I do not suggest this as a criticism of the award, since it is outside the scope of the arbitrator's mission).

Where waivers are accepted, and where not made in writing, the evidence that will be required to prove their existence will be—as in this case—decisive for the jurisdiction of the arbitrators. What rules of evidence shall be applied will be decided according to the contract and the law applicable on a case to case basis, but the drafters of the F.I.D.I.C. Conditions might wish to consider drawing parties' attention to the waiver possibility and to the establishment of guidelines in this respect, when they next revise the F.I.D.I.C. Conditions and notably its Clause 67.

III. The arbitrator's decision on the applicable law is in conformity with modern practices in I.C.C. arbitration cases. Arbitrators do not usually decide what shall be the law on the merits unless they have to (as is the case in Swiss Cantons where the Concordat applies). It is often only where the applicable law becomes a question of dispute that the arbitrators enter into a choice of law rules and deduce the applicable law on the merits from such rules of conflict. The terms of the contract and trade usages will often suffice for an arbitrator to settle a dispute, without the need of deciding what national law applies. This is not equivalent to applying *Lex Mercatoria*, an uncodified set of rules, by some said to have international recognition and expressing the general principles of international trade law, by others vividly contested. It is rather exploring the parties' intentions and applying their contract agreement and, where necessary, operating an interpretation on its terms. In the case at hand the arbitrators did not exclude the application of further laws, if necessary, since they decided to apply Saudi Law "in the first place".

SIGVARD JARVIN

ANNEX

ARBITRATION REGULATION OF SAUDI ARABIA*

Royal Decree M/46 of 25.04.1983G (1.07.1403 H)

Article 1
The parties may agree to arbitrate a specific existing dispute; a prior agreement to arbitrate may also be made in respect of any dispute resulting from the performance of a specific contract.

Article 2
Arbitration shall not be permitted in cases where a settlement (Arabic: *sulh*) is not allowed. An agreement to arbitrate (Arabic: *al-ittifaq ala al-tahkim*) may not be made except by those who have capacity to act.

Article 3
Government Agencies are not allowed to resort to arbitration for settlement of their disputes with third parties except after having obtained the consent of the President of the Council of Ministers. This ruling may be amended by resolution of the Council of Ministers.

Article 4
The arbitrator shall have expertise and be of good conduct and behaviour, and shall have full legal capacity. If there are several arbitrators, their number shall be uneven.

Article 5
The parties to the dispute shall file the arbitration instrument (Arabic: *wathiqat al-tahkim*) with the Authority originally competent to hear the dispute. The instrument shall be signed by the parties or their authorized attorneys, and by the arbitrators, and it must state the details of the dispute, the names of the arbitrators and their acceptance to hear the dispute. Copies of the documents relating to the dispute shall be attached.

Article 6
The Authority originally competent to hear the dispute shall record the applications for arbitration submitted to it, and take a decision approving the arbitration instrument (Arabic: *wathiqat al-tahkim*).

Article 7
If the parties have agreed to arbitrate before the occurrence of the dispute, or if the arbitration instrument relating to a specific existing dispute has been approved, then the subject matter of the dispute shall be heard only according to the provisions of this Regulation.

Article 8
The clerk of the Authority originally competent to hear the dispute shall be in charge of all the notifications and notices provided for in this Regulation.

Article 9
The arbitrators' decision shall be taken within the time-limit specified in the arbitration instrument (Arabic: *wathiqat al-tahkim*), unless it is agreed to extend it. If the parties have not fixed in the arbitration instrument a time-limit for the decision, the arbitrators shall take their decision within ninety days from the date on which the arbitration instrument was approved; otherwise any of the parties may, if he so desires, appeal to the Authority originally competent to hear the dispute which shall decide either hearing the subject matter or extending the time-limit for another period.

---

*Unofficial translation provided by the Law Offices of Van Doorne & Sjollema, Rotterdam, and published in *Yearbook Commercial Arbitration* (Volume IX—1984).

Article 10
If the parties have not appointed the arbitrators, or if either of them fails to appoint his arbitrator(s), or if one or more of the arbitrators refuses to assume his task or withdraws, or something prevents him from carrying out his tasks, or if he is dismissed, and there is no special agreement between the parties, the Authority originally competent to hear the dispute shall appoint the required arbitrators upon request of the party who is interested in expediting the arbitration, in the presence of the other party or in his absence after being summoned to a meeting to be held for this purpose. The Authority shall appoint as many arbitrators as are necessary to complete the total number of arbitrators agreed to by the parties; the decision taken in this respect shall be final.

Article 11
The arbitrator may not be removed except with the mutual consent of the parties, and the arbitrator so removed may claim compensation if he had already proceeded and if he had not been the cause of such removal. Furthermore, he cannot be removed except for reasons that occur or appear after the filing of the arbitration instrument (Arabic: *wathiqat al-tahkim*).

Article 12
The arbitrator may be challenged for the same reasons for which a judge may be challenged. The request for challenge shall be submitted to the Authority originally competent to hear the dispute within five days from the day on which the party was notified of the appointment of the arbitrator, or the day on which one of the reasons for challenge appeared or occurred. The decision on the request for challenge shall be taken in a meeting to be held for this purpose and attended by the parties and the arbitrator whose challenge is requested.

Article 13
The arbitration shall not terminate because of the death of one of the parties, but the time fixed for award shall be extended by thirty days unless the arbitrators decide on a further extension.

Article 14
If an arbitrator is appointed in place of the removed arbitrator or the one who has withdrawn, the date fixed for the award shall be extended by thirty days.

Article 15
The arbitrators, by the majority by which the award shall be made, may, through a justified decision, extend the periods fixed for the award on account of circumstances pertaining to the subject matter of the dispute.

Article 16
The decision of the arbitrators shall be taken by a majority vote and if they are authorized to reach a compromise solution (Arabic: *sulh*), their decision shall be by unanimity.

Article 17
The award document shall especially include the arbitration instrument (Arabic: *wathiqat al-tahkim*), a résumé of the depositions of the parties and their documents, reasons for the award and its text and date, and the signatures of the arbitrators. If one or more of them refuse to sign the award, such refusal shall be stated in the award document.

Article 18
All awards issued by the arbitrators, even if they are issued in relation to one of the procedures of investigation, shall be filed within five days with the Authority originally competent to hear the dispute and the parties shall be notified by copies of them. The parties may submit their objections against what is issued by the arbitrators to the Authority with whom the awards were filed, within fifteen days from the date on which they were notified of the arbitrators' awards; otherwise such awards shall be final.

Article 19
If the parties or one of them submitted an objection against the award of the arbitrators within

the period provided for in the preceding Article, the Authority originally competent to hear the dispute shall consider the dispute and shall either dismiss the objection and issue an order for execution of the award, or accept the objection and decide the case.

Article 20
The award of the arbitrators shall be due for execution, when it becomes final, by an order from the Authority originally competent to hear the dispute. This order shall be issued upon request of one of the concerned parties after confirming that there is nothing to prevent its execution legally.

Article 21
The award made by the arbitrators shall be considered, after issuance of the order of execution in accordance with the previous Article, as effective as a judgment made by the Authority which issued the order of execution.

Article 22
Fees of arbitrators shall be determined by agreement between the parties and unpaid sums of such fees shall be deposited with the Authority originally competent to hear the dispute within five days after approval of the arbitration instrument (Arabic: *wathiqat al-tahkim*), and shall be paid within a week from the date on which the order for execution of award is issued.

Article 23
If there is no agreement on the fees of arbitrators, and a dispute ensues, the matter shall be settled by the Authority originally competent to hear the dispute; which decision shall be final.

Article 24
The decisions required for the execution of this Regulation shall be issued by the President of the Council of Ministers, on the basis of a proposal made by the Minister of Justice after agreement with the Minister of Commerce and the President of the Board of Grievances.

Article 25
This Regulation shall be published in the Offical Gazette, and shall be effective thirty days after the date of its publication.

F.I.D.I.C.—conditions—time-bar under Article 67—must a request for arbitration be submitted to the I.C.C. Court of Arbitration within the 90 days period or is a notice to the Engineer sufficient, in order to prevent the Engineer's decision from becoming final and binding.

Introduction

In two awards rendered in the beginning of 1986 by arbitrators acting under the I.C.C. Rules of Arbitration, the issue determined was whether a party had taken the required measures under Clause 67 of the F.I.D.I.C. Conditions of Contract for works of Civil Engineering Construction to prevent the Engineer's decision from becoming final and binding. In one of the cases the issue arose with regard to the second edition of the F.I.D.I.C. Conditions and in the other with regard to the third edition. The arbitrators came to opposite conclusions in the two cases, in one considering that a request for arbitration must be filed with the I.C.C. Court of Arbitration within 90 days to prevent the Engineer's decision from becoming final and binding and to preserve the right to arbitration, in the other that a notification to the Engineer within 90 days requiring the dispute to be referred to arbitration is sufficient.

Case 4707

In this case a sole arbitrator sitting in Amman, Jordan, was to decide the issue under the Laws of the United Arab Emirates and with regard to the second edition of the F.I.D.I.C. Conditions.

In the award the arbitrator held:

"It is established that the Engineer sent his decision to the parties with courier on 2 March 1982. On 4 May 1982 the Respondent sent a letter rejecting the Engineer's Decision on the basis that it did not represent a fair settlement to the Claim. The Respondent was advised to take immediate action to notify the Claimant and the I.C.C. of his intention to refer the matter to Arbitration.

On 2 June 1982 the Respondent sent a telex to the Engineer confirming rejection of his decision and its wish to refer the dispute to Arbitration but took no steps to institute Arbitration proceedings before the I.C.C.

The Claimant had on 19 May 1982 informed the Respondent and the Engineer of their acceptance of the Engineer's Decision and when the Respondent contested the decision the Claimant submitted a request for Arbitration with the I.C.C.

The question is: Was the telex sent to the Engineer on 2 June 1982 sufficient to prevent the Engineer's Decision from becoming final and binding, or is it necessary in order to achieve this effect under Clause 67 of the Second Edition of F.I.D.I.C., that a formal request for arbitration be filed with the I.C.C. within 90 days from the date of the Engineer's decision?

In the hearing of 23 March 1985, held in Amman and attended by Counsel representing both parties, the Arbitrator, recognising that this is a controversial question which requires careful consideration, requested that the parties should submit further arguments and legal expert opinion.

The Arbitrator received written opinions from Mr I. N. Duncan Wallace Q.C., Mr Donald Keating Q.C., Mr Christopher Seppala, member of the New York Bar and *Conseil Juridique* in Paris, France, and Mr John Ward of Beale and Co, London.

After some keen deliberation and thorough examination of the issue in the light of the various arguments and opinions of the eminent experts presented by the parties, the Arbitrator concurs with and fully supports the following reasoning and analysis of Clause 67.

(a) Clause 67 requires strict observance by the parties of the 90 days period during which the Engineer should give his decision and the parties should take action to challenge such a decision if dissatisfied with it and wish to refer the matter to Arbitration. Failure to take the necessary measure within 90 days from receipt of the decision will result in the decision becoming final and binding. It is evident that the purpose of setting these fixed periods is to provide means for prompt settlement of Claims. The purpose of the Clause would be completely defeated if it should be interpreted in a sense leading to the delay or obstruction of settlement of disputes. The intention of the Clause is certainly to make arbitration always possible if the Engineer's Decision did not become final and binding. Otherwise, some matters may never be resolved and this could not be the intention of the Clause. To take the view that a mere telex to the Engineer without actually starting arbitration proceedings before the body designated in the contract renders the Engineer's decision ineffective would result in an absurd and unacceptable situation entirely incompatible with Clause 67 as we will neither have a binding decision nor will the matter be in Arbitration. The drafters of Clause 67 could not have contemplated such a situation.

Clause 67 requires 'Claim to Arbitration' to be communicated to the Engineer within a period of 90 days from receipt of the written notice of the Engineer's Decision. If such 'communication' is made within the said period, the Engineer's Decision will not become final and binding. In this case Arbitration should always be possible. To put it in Mr Seppala's words: 'Clause 67 cannot be read as envisaging a situation where the aggrieved party has taken such steps as might have been necessary to prevent the Engineer's Decision from becoming final and binding but had failed to take such steps as might have been necessary to enable it to arbitrate the matter'. Therefore, it is appropriate to construe the phrase, 'Claim to Arbitration' as assuming that such steps as may be necessary to commence arbitration should also be taken. These steps would be the filing of a request for arbitration with the Secretariat of the I.C.C. Court of Arbitration according to Article 3 of the I.C.C. Rules.

Mr Seppala lucidly presents the following convincing argument: 'It seems that the words "require that the matter or matters in dispute be referred to arbitration" can mean only one of two things. Either they mean that an arbitration must actually be commenced or that notice must be given to someone (the Employer, the Engineer or both) that arbitration is being required under Clause 67.

It seems that the second possibility gives rise to serious objections. If a party can "require" arbitration without actually commencing arbitration, what is the status of the matter after arbitration has been "required" but before it has commenced? The Decision on the matter would neither be final and binding nor in arbitration. Moreover, when would arbitration commence? There would be no time limit at all. This is not in harmony with a clause designed to promote the expeditious final settlement of disputes.'

As to how would arbitration be required, it is obvious that arbitration will not commence if the notice is sent to the Engineer only, as he has no competence to institute Arbitration proceedings nor is he under any obligation to pass the notice to the other party who would be very interested to know whether a Decision has become final and binding or subject to arbitration.

The term in the Clause is 'require' and not 'request' which implies that arbitration shall certainly take place. Therefore, since the Engineer cannot start Arbitration proceedings, how can a mere written notice to the Engineer or to the other party achieve this objective?

Clause 67 states: '. . . either the Employer or the Contractor may within a period of 90 days . . . etc. . . . require that the matter or matters in dispute be referred to arbitration as hereinafter provided'. It is provided in the next sentence of the Clause that arbitration should be according to the rules of the I.C.C., which require that a party wishing to have recourse to I.C.C. arbitration must submit a 'request for arbitration' to the I.C.C. The date the request is received by the Secretariat of the Court is deemed to be the date of commencement of proceedings. (Article 3.1). It is by the submission of a request for arbitration to the I.C.C. that the other party will be 'required' to arbitrate (actually compelled to arbitrate) and a certain means for the final settlement of the dispute shall be available.

To interpret 'require' as necessitating submission of a request for arbitration to the I.C.C. would be consistent with the purpose of Clause 67 which, as indicated above, is the expeditious and prompt settlement of claims. By such request a claim which has not been resolved by an Engineer's Decision shall necessarily be in arbitration and thus the purpose of Clause 67 shall be realized.

(b) A similar interpretation is expressed by Mr Donald Keating Q.C. as follows: 'The telex of 2/6/1982 rejects the decision and states that the owner had a wish to refer the dispute to arbitration. The question then becomes whether this telex is a "claim to arbitration" within the meaning of Clause 67. If the first sentence beginning with the words "if the engineer . . ." existed alone and without the second sentence and the sentences dealing with I.C.C. arbitration, it may be, I express no concluded view, that the telex could be considered a sufficient, "claim to arbitration". But it is elementary that in construing a contract one must read all its clauses together and give effect to them. Doing that, it is in my view, clear that it is not sufficient for one of the parties to express a desire in general terms to go to arbitration. It has to be the claim to the arbitration provided for by the terms of the contract. Further, such claim has to comply with the requirements of the second sentence beginning, "if the engineer . . .". It must require that the dispute be referred to arbitration "as hereinafter provided". What is provided is a requirement that the dispute be referred in such manner as to become finally settled under the Rules of Conciliation and Arbitration of the International Chamber of Commerce.

By construing the contract in this way the clause works in a clear and straightforward manner, whereas to construe the clause as providing for two different matters, a claim to arbitration which may be general and a requirement to refer a dispute in accordance with the I.C.C. Rules, immediately leads to great difficulties and absurdities. A clear plain meaning is to be preferred where the words permit to an unclear meaning giving rise to difficulties of operation of a Commercial Contract.

For the reasons set out above, I am of the opinion that the telex dated 2/6/82 did not prevent the Engineer's Decision from becoming final and binding upon the parties'.

On the basis of the above reasoning, the Arbitrator finds that a simple telex sent to the Engineer does not constitute the necessary measure under Clause 67 of F.I.D.I.C. and that a party wishing to prevent an Engineer's Decision from remaining final and binding should, within 90 days of receiving the Decision, file a request for Arbitration with the Secretariat of the I.C.C. Court of Arbitration and communicate a copy of that request to the Engineer. Consequently, since the Respondent in this case only expressed its dissatisfaction with the Engineer's Decision by its telex of 2 June 1982 but did not submit a request for arbitration to the I.C.C. and so could not have communicated a claim to arbitration within 90 days of having received notice of the decision as required under

Clause 67 of the Conditions of Contract, the Respondent continued to maintain a passive attitude and never at any time after the 90 days requested arbitration through the proper channels.

For the above reasons the Arbitrator finds that the Engineer's Decision on 26 February 1982 has become final and binding on the Parties in this arbitration case".

Case 5029

In the second case three arbitrators sitting in the Hague, the Netherlands, were to decide the time-bar issue under the laws of Egypt and with regard to the 3rd edition of the F.I.D.I.C. Conditions.

The arbitrators held in their award as to the facts:

"For each Claim, the Engineer issued a decision, rejecting Claimant's claim. For each Engineer's decision so given, the Claimant has communicated to the Engineer, within 90 days following the latter's decision that the Claimant required that the Claim be referred to arbitration. The Claims were actually filed in this arbitration after the expiration of the said 90 days' period. Claimant employed almost identical language in its letters to the Engineer, requiring the Claims to be referred to arbitration, reading: 'We hereby give you notice that we are dissatisfied with your decision and require that the dispute be referred to arbitration for resolution.' "

The defendant argued, *inter alia*, that:

"— The text of clause 67 is 'crystal clear'. According to article 150(1) of the Egyptian Civil Code, if the wording is clear, the text may not be deviated from in favour of the parties' intent.
— As Egyptian law is applicable to the Contract, it is not permitted to rely on foreign authorities, especially English case law and doctrine, as Claimant does."

The Claimant countered, *inter alia*, by contending that:

"Although the text of Clause 67 is clear, if it is considered ambiguous, article 150(2) of the Egyptian Civil Code allows to ascertain the common intention of the parties, taking into account the nature of the transaction as well as loyalty and confidence that should exist between the parties in accordance with commercial usage. Given the circumstances of the Contract, article 150(2) of the Egyptian Civil Code permits reliance upon English law."

The arbitrators decided in the following manner:

"Clause 67 of the Contract, which is identical to Clause 67 of the F.I.D.I.C. Conditions (3rd edition, 1977), provides for a two-tier system for the settlement of disputes between the parties.
. . .

The interpretation of Clause 67 is governed by Egyptian law, which is the law chosen by the parties in respect of the law governing the contract.

116. Defendant asserts that the text of Clause 67 is 'crystal clear', and that, hence, there is no room for an interpretation according to the second paragraph of article 150 of the Egyptian Civil Code. Claimant is also of the opinion that the text of Clause 67 is clear, although it reaches a conclusion on the basis of the same text which is entirely opposite to that of Defendant. Claimant, however, submits in the alternative an interpretation based on the second paragraph of article 150.

117. As it is observed by Mr D. N. Duncan Wallace in his article 'The Time Bar in F.I.D.I.C. Clause 67' [1981] I.C.L.R. 330 at p. 331: 'There are many infelicities and problems in the wording of this Clause'. As it will be seen below, the text of Clause 67 is

indeed not entirely clear. This fact is also demonstrated by the lengthy submissions of the parties on the issue and the differing conclusions reached by them on the basis of the same text. The Arbitral Tribunal, therefore, finds it justified to rely on the common intent of the parties in accordance with article 150(2) of the Egyptian Civil Code to the extent that the text of Clause 67 is unclear.

118. An important aspect for determining the parties' intent with respect to Clause 67 is the fact that the parties have relied on the F.I.D.I.C. Conditions to govern their contract. The parties' choice for these standard conditions is prompted by the desire to have conditions which are widely known and used in practice and hence to provide predictability in their contractual relations. The predictability can be maintained only if the manner in which they are generally interpreted and applied in the construction industry is taken into account. This is also in conformity with article 8(5) of the I.C.C. Rules which provides that in all cases the arbitral tribunal shall take account of the relevant trade usages.

119. What is clear in the text of Clause 67 is that if a party wishes to resort to arbitration in case he is dissatisfied with a decision of the Engineer, he must communicate a 'claim to arbitration' to the Engineer within the 90 days following the Engineer's decision. The text is less clear as to whether such notification to the Engineer is also required in case the Engineer has failed to give a decision. In the award in I.C.C. Case No. 3790 it was held that in such case no notification to the Engineer is necessary (see [1984] I.C.L.R. 372 at p. 374). Although the Arbitral Tribunal deems it at least advisable to send in any case a notification to the Engineer in this case too, it need not rule on this question because, as it appears from the factual circumstances stated above, the Claimant has indeed sent the notification to the Engineer for each of the Claims filed in this arbitration within the second 90 days.

120. The notifications sent by the Claimant to the Engineer are not mere reservations of right, as the Defendant asserts. In this respect, the Arbitral Tribunal adopts the test formulated in the aforementioned award in I.C.C. case no. 3790: '[A] claim to arbitration without need for particular formalities is to be explicit and clear and clearly show the plaintiff's intention to submit the dispute to arbitration'. As noted before, the letters written by the Claimant to the Engineer employ a standard language: 'We hereby give you notice that we are dissatisfied with your decision and require that the dispute be referred to arbitration for resolution'. This language, which is derived from Clause 67 itself, satisfies the above test. For the same reason Claimant must be deemed not to have accepted the Engineer's decisions as Defendant asserts.

121. The real question in the present case is whether, in addition to the notification to the Engineer, the Claimant should, as second step, also have filed a Request for Arbitration with the I.C.C. within the second 90 days. Defendant argues that Claimant, which has not taken the second step within the second 90 days, should have done so. Claimant argues that such second step is not required within the second 90 days under Clause 67.

122. Two sets of wording in successive sentences in Clause 67 appear to have a particular bearing on this question:

'If . . . no claim to arbitration has been communicated to him [i.e., the Engineer] . . . within a period of 90 days from receipt of such notice, the said decision [i.e. the Engineer's decision] shall remain final and binding.'

'[I]f either the Employer or the Contractor be dissatisfied with any such decision, then . . . either the Contractor or the Employer may within 90 days . . . require that the matter or matters in dispute be referred to arbitration as hereinafter provided.'

It is conspicuous that neither set of wording uses the technical term 'Request for Arbitration' as is used in article 3 of the I.C.C. Rules. Both sets of wording use the rather loose expressions of 'claim to arbitration' and 'require'. A time-bar for resorting to arbitration, as for litigation, is a very serious matter. A text therefore must make clear beyond any doubt under which conditions a time-bar becomes operative. Neither of the above quoted sets of wording achieves this result.

123. The question does not become clearer if one looks at the last sentence of Clause 67 which reads in relevant part: 'The reference to arbitration may proceed notwithstanding that the Works shall not . . . be complete'. Under customary English language, the words 'reference to arbitration' mean nothing more than 'arbitration'. The words 'may proceed' are ambiguous. They can mean: arbitration can be requested, or: arbitration, after having been requested, can continue. The last sentence of Clause 67 therefore does not clarify the words 'be referred' in the second set of wording quoted above.

124. The matter becomes clearer if one looks at the difference between the first (1957) and second (1969) edition of the F.I.D.I.C. Conditions on the one hand and the third (1977) edition on the other. As noted, Clause 67 is taken from the third edition. In all editions, the text of Clause 67 is almost identical, save for the last sentence. Under the first and second edition, arbitration could take place after completion of the works only. Under the third edition, the prohibition to arbitrate during the execution of the works was abolished as is reflected in the last sentence. The first and second edition have, as far as the Arbitral Tribunal is aware, never been interpreted as requiring the filing of a formal Request for Arbitration within the second 90 days (after which nothing would happen in the arbitration until after completion of the works). It was deemed sufficient to notify within the second 90 days that recourse to arbitration will be made in respect of an Engineer's decision. Since the relevant text has remained unchanged in the third edition, it must be interpreted in the same manner as in the first and second edition.

125. No argument can be derived from the fact that under the third edition arbitration can be held during the execution of the works. Defendant argues that for this reason Clause 67 needs to be re-interpreted. The change in the third edition merely means a relaxation of the system prevailing under the first and second edition according to which arbitration could take place only after completion of the works. This system was felt to be too cumbersome as it is not always desirable or necessary to wait with arbitration of disputes until after completion of the works. In the context of long term contracts, it can be burdensome for a party's financing resources to have to wait with the arbitration until completion. But the change does not mean that a dissatisfied party having a claim *must* now always file a Request for Arbitration within the second 90 days. A party may have good reasons not to do so. One of the reasons is to attempt an amicable settlement first, which can avoid costly and time consuming arbitration proceedings.

126. The Arbitral Tribunal need not consider the question as to whether a party should file a Request for Arbitration within a reasonable period of time after the lapse of the second 90 days. Even if such a condition were implied in Clause 67, Claimant's filing of the claims in arbitration was by all standards done within a reasonable period of time.

127. In conclusion, Clause 67 must be interpreted as requiring a party who is dissatisfied with a decision of the Engineer, in order not to lose his right to have the matter resolved by arbitration, solely to notify the Engineer, within 90 days after the Engineer has rendered his decision, that he requires the dispute be referred ' arbitration. Consequently, the Arbitral Tribunal rejects Defendant's jurisdictional defence and, accordingly, holds that it does not lack jurisdiction in this arbitration on account of this defence.''

Commentary

It is obviously unsatisfactory that such a vital question as how to present correctly a claim for arbitration under the terms of a standard and widely used set of general conditions gives rise to different interpretations. I shall not discuss the learned opinions and arguments presented in favour of one or the other solution; the readers of this *Review* have the benefit of the full quote from the awards on these points.

Fortunately F.I.D.I.C. is presently revising the third and latest edition of its "red book", and the two cases described in this case note will hopefully lead F.I.D.I.C. to improve the drafting of Clause 67 in the fourth edition. Let us hope that it will be done speedily so that the present state of uncertainty can be dispelled to the benefit of the parties of numerous international construction contracts.

Sigvard Jarvin

AWARD RENDERED IN CASE NO. 5625 IN 1987*

INTRODUCTION

The following case concerns a problem which arises with some frequency in international commercial arbitration, namely whether additional parties may be joined to an ongoing arbitration. The situation is one where a contract is entered into between two companies who sign an agreement, but where other companies, related to the companies party to the contract, are involved in the overall business transactions. The *Dow* v. *Saint-Gobain* case (*Journal du Droit International*, 1983, p. 899) is a well-known example in which four companies belonging to the same group of companies started an arbitration against a defendant company under a contract that only two of the claimant Dow companies had signed. The arbitrators found in that case that all four claimant companies had so actively participated in the formation, implementation and winding up of the contracts that they were all four parties to the arbitration agreement on which they relied. All four claimant companies were admitted as claimant parties in the arbitration.

In case 5625 below, the procedural situation is different. The arbitration is initiated by one claimant company belonging to a group of companies against one other company, belonging to another group of companies. It is only thereafter, when the arbitration has started, that the question arises whether it is possible to include the parent companies on both sides plus a third company, a sister company to the claimant, which company had signed the agreement in which the arbitration clause was contained.

The issue is therefore not— as it was in *Dow*—whether companies which have not signed an arbitration agreement can become party to an arbitration (one of the parties in case 5625 actually *was* party to the contract which contained the arbitration clause), but whether a party, whether it has signed an arbitration clause or not, may enter into an arbitration already started by another party.

The arbitrators decided that only those can become parties in an I.C.C. arbitration who name themselves as such in the request for arbitration or are identified as defendants in the claimants' request for arbitration. Arbitrators have no general discretion to add as parties to the arbitration persons or companies who were not identified as claimant or defendant in the request.

The interim award, rendered by three arbitrators of different nationalities, sitting in a Swiss city governed by the Concordat in a dispute between an

---

* Case note by Sigvard Jarvin

African claimant and a European defendant is reproduced in full, except for names and indications of nationalities where an indication thereof could lead to the identification of the parties.

THE AWARD

The undersigned, arbitrators in the above case, render the following interim award:

Considering:

I. As to the procedure

1. The arbitration is an arbitration under the Rules of Conciliation and Arbitration of the International Chamber of Commerce.

The undersigned have been nominated arbitrators in conformity with those rules and with the arbitration clause of the relevant agreement, being Article D4 of the agreement between claimant ("A"), company "B" and defendant "X" dated June 1973.

That Article lays down "arbitration in Berne in accordance with the Rules of Conciliation and Arbitration of the International Chamber of Commerce by three arbitrators, one appointed by X, one by A and/or B, and the third appointed by the two so chosen . . . .".

The undersigned arbitrator "W" has been nominated by A in its request for arbitration, the undersigned arbitrator "F" has been nominated by X in its answer to the request for arbitration and the undersigned arbitrator "S" has been appointed by W and F together, the appointment having been confirmed by the Court of Arbitration of the International Chamber of Commerce at its session of 19 August 1986.

2. The Terms of Reference, dated 29 December 1986, have been signed on behalf of A by its solicitor and on behalf of X by its president; the Terms have also been signed by the undersigned.

According to the Terms of Reference, the first issue to be decided is:

"Should the Arbitrators direct that Company 'B' be (made) a party to the arbitration and/or that 'C' Corporation and Company 'Y' should be (made) parties to the arbitration and do they have jurisdiction so to direct?"

During a session held in London on 20 December 1986, with the parties, the Tribunal has determined to decide on issue No. 1 as soon as possible after having received certain documents, and thus preliminary to any decision on other issues.

3. X has stated and explained its point of view in its answer to the request for arbitration of 30 July 1986.

A has stated and explained its point of view in its preparatory memorandum in response to the defendant's response dated 16 October 1986.

On 19 December 1986, in a session in London, the parties have argued their cause.

On 20 December 1986 the parties agreed to a decision by the arbitrators to proceed with the drafting of the Terms of Reference in which only the original claimant and the original defendant, as identified by A in its request for arbitration, would figure as parties, but in which the first item to be decided upon by the Tribunal would relate to this subject on which the Arbitral Tribunal, after the Terms of Reference would have come into effect, would give a preliminary ruling. It was agreed to by A and given to understand by the Tribunal that the signing by X of these Terms of Reference would in no way prejudice its position on this issue.

On 20 December counsel for defendant was given permission to hand over to the Tribunal a *"Note de Berthold Goldman sur l'applicabilité de la clause compromissoire à B et C (comme défenderesses) et à Y (comme demanderesse), du 15 décembre 1986"*, with the annotation that this document was not meant as a final text; and so he did.

The tribunal then decided that X would have until 12 January 1987 to submit the notes from which counsel for claimant had spoken and the case law and learned writers to which he referred, which submission would not go beyond the arguments which he and his co-counsels had pleaded, after which A would have until 9 February 1987 to reply, which reply neither should reflect other arguments than those advanced by counsel for claimant in 19 December session.

On 12 January 1987 counsel on behalf of X submitted a memorandum, together with a *mémoire* and photocopies of case law and a commentary by Professor Pierre Lalive in the *British Yearbook of International Law 1980*, pages 123–152 under the title "The First 'World Bank' Arbitration (*Holiday Inns* v. *Marocco*)—some Legal Problems", and some other documents.

On 6 February 1987 A submitted a memorandum in reply accompanied by a note of the submission of counsel and an opinion of Professor Eugene Bucher on certain aspects of Swiss Law.

II. The arguments of defendant X can be summarised as follows:

It states that it is artificial to limit the arbitration (*"l'instance arbitrale"*) to A (claimant) and X (defendant). It should be extended to company B on the one hand and to company Y and to C corporation on the other hand.

It should be extended to B because the latter is a party to the agreement which is at the basis of claimant's claim, and because it has an interest in the outcome of the arbitration.

It should be extended to Y and C corporation because these groups control defendant X and claimant A respectively and because as such they took this matter in hand in all stages (*"sont intervenues à tous les stades de cette affaire"*).

They have negotiated the agreement. Only at the last moment and for internal reasons each group has chosen companies belonging to their group to sign the agreement.

A "Memorandum of Agreement" referring specifically to the particular agreement on which claimant A bases its claim, has been signed the same day between company Y and C corporation. These companies have since the signing of the agreement remained in a permanent relationship and have got themselves involved in every phase of the re-negotiations and of the execution of the agreement.

In the execution of the agreement, X and its legal predecessors have found themselves to be in a permanent relationship with company D, a wholly owned subsidiary of C corporation, rather than with claimant A.

On these grounds defendant X in its answer to the request for arbitration demanded the Arbitral Tribunal to decide that company Y and the C corporation ought to be present in the arbitration (*"demande au Tribunal Arbitral de décider que X et C doivent être présentes à l'arbitrage"*).

In its answer to the request for arbitration defendant X furthermore states that company Y in 1972 started negotiations with a view of participating in the project, which concerned the exploitation of mineral deposits in Africa for which C had obtained a prospecting licence and for the exploitation of which it founded claimant A . . . The principal shareholder of that company was C corporation, but other nationalities got a minority interest.

After successful negotiations the C corporation had the agreement signed by (*"faisait signer le contrat par"*) claimant A and company B, two companies belonging to its group, and company Y had it signed by its wholly-owned subsidiary defendant X. This was in June 1973. On the same date the C corporation and company Y signed a Memorandum of Agreement which has been produced by defendant X with its answer to the request for arbitration. This Memorandum reads as follows:

"MEMORANDUM OF AGREEMENT

THE C CORPORATION and COMPANY Y having cognizance of the Agreement of even date between A/B (being subsidiaries of C on one hand, and X (being subsidiary of Y) the other hand, recognize that:
  (i) By X's loan to A, its stake in A, and its obligation to purchase 15,000 tons of A concentrates, X is contributing substantially to the development of A's mine and of its commercial outlets;
  (ii) It is the common interest of C and Y that the development of the mine, its exploitation, and the system of planned deliveries should take place in accordance with their desires;
  (iii) It is impracticable ·in such long-term Agreement to provide against every contingency which could arise during its life.
In the circumstances, Y and C have agreed to set out as follows, certain rules of fair behaviour between them in respect of the said Agreement.
1. If for one reason or another serious difficulties occur in the implementation of the Agreement C and Y will do everything reasonably possible to overcome such difficulties.

If, for example, the mining title of A or the right of the shareholders or of the lenders, or the rights of buyers of A's concentrates are threatened then C and Y will discuss between them the best way to approach the interested Authorities in an attempt to secure or cause to be secured in the best of the parties common interest that the mining operation and the delivery of the A products to the said buyer be maintained.

2. If by reason of *force majeur* A is unable to deliver the concentrates to X according to the Agreement, C shall use all reasonable efforts to cause supply X on essentially the same terms and conditions in the Agreement from other sources within the C Group.

3. C and Y further agree to use their voting powers in those subsidiaries concerned with the Agreement in favour of the performance of those subsidiaries obligations in the Agreement.

Signed on behalf of   Signed on behalf of
The "C" CORPORATION   COMPANY "Y"
LIMITED

Dated 18th June 1973"

Defendant X states that, in the spirit of the above mentioned Memorandum of Agreement it has agreed with the C corporation, on 21 February 1984, to adjust the price of certain quantities of concentrate.

Following an invitation of company Y, on the basis of the Memorandum of Agreement, to the C corporation of 16 October 1984, meetings between representatives of these parties have taken place to resolve fundamental difficulties which were encountered in the execution of the agreement. These have failed. Claimant A refused to adjust the price. This failure was the fault of claimant A and the C corporation which have not negotiated in good faith.

On this basis, defendant X has a right to demand the Arbitral Tribunal to pronounce the cancellation of the agreement and to condemn claimant A to pay damages, which defendant X will calculate later. ("... *est fondée à demander au tribunal Arbitral de prononcer la résolution au contrat, et de condamner A à des dommages et intérêts que X se réserve d'évaluer"*).

Furthermore, defendant X states that the Arbitral tribunal will have to draw all legal consequences of the non-performance by claimant A of its contractual obligations, which it will later on specify and calculate.

Finally, in its conclusion defendant X claims the Tribunal to

— *"dire à titre préalable, que company B, soit partie au présent arbitrage, de même que C corporation et company Y, notamment sur le fondement de la jurisprudence en matière d'opposabilité de la clause compromissoire à l'intérieur des groupes de sociétés;*

— *prononcer la résolution des relations contractuelles entre les parties, et condamner claimant A à des dommages et intérêts que defendant X se réserve d'évaluer;*

— *A titre subsidiaire, dire que les parties devront dans un laps de temps fixé par le Tribunal arbitral, déterminer une nouvelle méthode de fixation du prix. A défaut, se substituer aux parties pour procéder à cette détermination;*

— *Très subsidiairement, dire que l'exécution du contrat est devenue commercialement impossible pour defendant X, et qu'en conséquence, celle-ci doit être déliée de ses obligations, sur le fondement de la jurisprudence en matière de 'frustation';*

— *débouter claimant A de l'ensemble de ses demandes;*

— *dire que C corporation, company B et claimant A devront payer solidairement les frais d'arbitrage."*

Defendant X has sent its answer to the request for arbitration to the Court of Arbitration with a letter, dated 31 July 1986, in which it wrote, *inter alia,* *"Nous vous adressons ce mémoire en sept exemplaires, en raison de la demande de notre cliente pour que C corporation et company B fassent partie de l'arbitrage."*

By letter of 4 August 1986 the secretariat of the I.C.C. Court of Arbitration confirmed to counsel of defendant X the reception of the answer to the request for arbitration and of the counterclaim, and wrote furthermore:

> "We note from your letter that you wish company Y and C corporation to participate in this arbitration. We ask you to specify at your earliest convenience in what capacity you wish these corporations to participate, so that the Secretary can take appropriate actions in that respect."

Counsel of defendant X sent their answer to the President of C corporation with a letter of 18 August 1986, reading:

> ". . . *nous vous notifions officiellement le mémoire en réponse dans de mémoire . . . la société defendant X fait valoir auprés du tribunal arbitral que la convention d'arbitrage qui a été signée par X et A, est opposable à la société C corporation. De la même manière, la clause compromissoire est opposable à company Y, à laquelle la mémoire en réponse est officiellement notifié. En conséquence, nous avons l'honneur de sommer la société C corporation de participer à la procédure d'arbitrage."*

On the same date counsel of defendant X sent the answer to the President of company Y, with a letter reading:

> " . . . *nous vous prions de trouver ci-joint le mémoire en réponse. . . . Vous constaterez que dans ce mémoire, la société X soutient que la convention d'arbitrage est opposable a company Y et à la société C corporation . . . Nous suggérons que company Y appuie le point de vue de la société X et participe, à ces côtés, à l'arbitrage qui a engagé par la société A".*

A copy of the letter of that same date to the president of the C corporation was annexed.

By letter of 20 August 1986, the secretariat of the I.C.C. Court sent a copy of these two letters to claimant A.

In that letter the secretariat wrote, *inter alia,* ". . . as the undersigned discussed orally with counsel for both parties the inclusion of the fore-mentioned parties" (being C corporation and company Y) "in this arbitration will be a matter to be decided by the Arbitral Tribunal."

By letter of 28 August 1986 company Y has written to the Secretary General of the International Chamber of Commerce:

> *"Notre filiale, la société X nous a notifié en même temps qu'à la société C Corporation, le mémoire en réponse . . . . Il va de soi que nous partageons son point de vue quant à l'opposabilité de la convention d'arbitrage à notre compagnie et à C corporation. Nous sommes donc disposés à participer à la procédure d'arbitrage et nos intérêts étant communs avec ceux de X, nous désignons également comme conseils Maîtres . . . à qui vous voudrez bien adresser les documents et correspondances nous concernant. Nous vous précisions que nous ratifions les décisions prises à ce jour par la Cour d'arbitrage notamment en ce qui concerne la constitution du Tribunal arbitral . . . ".*

A copy of this letter was sent by the secretariat of the I.C.C. Court of Arbitration to the arbitrators, and counsel for parties, by letter of 1 September

1986, which reads: ". . . We believe that it is for the arbitral tribunal to decide whether company Y has, or can become part of the arbitration, and in the affirmative, in what capacity."

A copy of this letter was sent to company Y.

By letter of 29 August 1986 the secretary of the C corporation wrote to counsel for defendant X, *inter alia*.

> "You contend that the arbitration agreement made between is 'opposable à la société C corporation'. I am sure you will understand that we do not agree with your contention, and in the circumstances will not be taking any action. I therefore return the papers".

On a question by the tribunal, in the session of 19 December 1986, counsel for defendant answered that company Y was present, being represented by him and his co-counsels. On a question by the Tribunal whether anybody was present on behalf of company B responding on behalf of the C corporation, nobody replied in the affirmative.

In the oral pleadings on 19 December and in its brief of 12 January 1987, defendant X further developed its arguments. It maintained that company Y, company B and the C corporation are (*"sont"*) parties to the arbitration.

Company B because it signed the agreement, which is an indivisible whole, under which the dispute arises and because it is a party thereto, and the others because they are bound by the arbitration agreement signed by their subsidiaries. The claim, it was argued, is not a claim that third parties intervene, nor that additional parties join the original parties. Defendant X referred to Swiss, French and American case-law as to the binding force of an arbitration agreement within a group of companies, as to arbitration agreements *"per-relationem"*, and to the so-called *Holiday Inn* case (International Center for the Settlement of Investment Disputes (I.C.S.I.D.) ARB/72/1, see the above-mentioned publication by Professor Lalive). It also referred to the so-called *Dow Chemical* case (*Isover* v. *Dow Chemical*, arbitral award 23 September 1982, *Revue d'Arbitrage 1984*, pp. 137 *et seq.*) It résumés this award as follows:

> "*La sentence avait estimé que deux sociétés du groupe Dow Chemical dont la société mère, étaient en droit d'invoquer, comme demanderesses, une clause compromissoire qu'elles n'avaient pas elles-mêmes signées, mais qui figuraient dans un contrat signé par deux autres sociétés du groupe.*"

Defendant X also calls attention to the fact that in its answer it demands the cancellation of all contractual relations between the parties, which is to be understood not only as the cancellation of the agreement but also of the Memorandum of Agreement.

III. *The arguments of claimant A can be summarised as follows*

It disputes that company B has an interest in the outcome of the proceedings, the latter being only a party to that section of the agreement that relates to a transfer of shares in claimant A and not to the section dealing with the sale of concentrates. The only claim is made by claimant A. No claim is advanced by company B or the C corporation. In any event the latter is not a party to any arbitration agreement. No claim is made against any party other than defendant X.

The reference to arbitration cannot, and in any event should not, be widened to bring in other parties without the consent of all concerned, particularly the consent of those sought to be included.

Moreover it contends that if the defendant X wishes to raise any "claim against company B, they must do so by claiming arbitration against them under the arbitration clause in the agreement".

Claimant A denies that company Y and/or the C corporation are a party to any arbitration agreement with either itself or defendant X.

Both Article 29 of the Swiss International Arbitration Agreement [*sic*] and Article 7 of the Rules of the I.C.C. Court would preclude the joinder of these parties.

Claimant A admits that the C corporation negotiated the agreement on behalf of A, but that is no reason why it should be involved in the arbitration. The fact that company Y and the C corporation signed the Memorandum of Agreement on the same day as the agreement between company B, claimant A and defendant X was signed "is the clearest possible indication of the common intention that these companies were not to be parties to or bound by any part" of that latter agreement.

It is not denied that company Y and the C corporation both were involved in re-negotiating the agreement, but it is denied that the latter was directly involved in the execution of the agreement.

Claimant A furthermore refers to the Rules for the I.C.C. Court of Arbitration. In those rules, it says, one does not find explicitly a definition of the parties to an arbitration, but it results from various Articles, in particular Articles 3, 4 and 5, that parties are only the claimant and the defendant meant in the request for arbitration.

That company B has, or has not, an interest in the outcome of the procedure is irrelevant, since it is up to it to look after its own interests.

Claimant A does not read in the answer that any counterclaim is lodged against any other party than itself, but even if this were the case, this would be meaningless since a counterclaim can only be lodged against the claimant.

IV. *Considerations for the award*

1. The question to be decided is who are, or who are to be made, parties to the arbitration.

2. The question is not whether claimant A, company Y and C corporation are, or are not, bound by the agreement to arbitrate.

It is perfectly conceivable that a person is bound by one and the same agreement to arbitrate as are other persons but that does not prevent him from initiating an arbitration without joining as claimants those other persons nor does it oblige those other persons or any of them to join in an arbitration initiated by him. It is equally conceivable that a particular agreement entered into by other signatories is also binding on him, without his being a party in an arbitration initiated by those other signatories, against whoever they wish to identify as defendant.

The arbitration clause (D.4) in fact clearly recognises the right of claimant A to bring arbitration proceedings without company B.

3. The question whether a person is or is not bound by an agreement to arbitrate, and the debate whether and under what circumstances companies belonging to one group are bound by an agreement to arbitrate which has been signed by other companies belonging to that same group, can only arise in a situation where they identify themselves as claimants, or are being identified by a claimant as defendants, in a request for arbitration.

4. The rules for the I.C.C. Court of Arbitration leave no doubt as to who is, or are, to be identified as a claimant/claimants: it is that person that submits, on the basis of Article 3, a request for arbitration. In this particular case the request for arbitration has been submitted by claimant A, and by it only.

Neither do the rules leave any doubt as to who is, or are, the defendant/defendants: it is that person which is being identified as such in the request. In this particular case the request for arbitration identifies the defendant as defendant X, and it only.

5. Article 5 of the Rules reads:

> "1. If the Defendant wishes to make a counterclaim, he shall file the same with the Secretariat. It shall be open to the Claimant to file a Reply with the Secretariat within 10 days from the date when the counter claim was communicated to him."

From this it follows that a counter-claim is a claim by the defendant—that is, the person identified as such by the claimant in its request for arbitration—against the Claimant—that is, the person that has submitted the request and identified himself as being the claimant.

That follows not only from the text of Article 5, but is moreover in conformity with the meaning of the word counter-claim and the way that mechanism is understood in many national legislations.

6. Both the fact that company B is a signatory to the agreement on which claimant A bases its claim and the fact that it would have an interest in the outcome of the arbitral proceedings are irrelevant to the question whether it is, or should be made, a party to the arbitration. It is up to the interested person involved to determine whether it wishes to be a claimant in a procedure through the mechanisms thereto prescribed, i.e., in this case through the mechanism of Article 3 of the Rules.

7. The debate whether company Y and the C corporation are bound, as far as the Memorandum of Agreement is concerned, by the agreement to arbitrate in the agreement between claimant A, company B, and defendant X cannot be argued, as a procedural point, given the proceedings as they have been framed by claimant A; it can only arise when and after defendant X and/or company Y would have submitted, on the basis of Article 3 of the

Rules, a request for arbitration identifying C corporation, whether or not together with claimant A and/or company B as defendants. This was the case in *Dow Chemical* and in *Holiday Inns;* this is not the case here.

8. There is one way only in which one can become a party in an arbitral procedure under the I.C.C. rules: that is by way of Article 3, by a request in which one constitutes oneself a claimant or is being identified by such a claimant as a defendant.

9. The present arbitration proceedings are entirely regular from a procedural point of view. They are brought by a claimant—A—under an arbitration clause which applies to it against a respondent—X—which is bound by the arbitration clause in respect of a subject matter which (as *is not* contested) is covered by the arbitration clause.

The arbitrators have been nominated in accordance with the same clause. They are competent to and (under the I.C.C. rules) are bound to proceed with the arbitration so constituted on the basis of the parties' contentions as to substance.

10. The above paragraphs leave aside the problem of intervention of parties or of joinder, because defendant X has explicitly stated in the second paragraph on page 10 of its brief of 12 January 1987: "*Cette demande*" (i.e., "*que les sociétés company B, company Y et C corporation, soient parties à la procédure d'arbitrage*") "*ne constitue pas une demande d'intervention de sociétés tierces, ou ne consiste pas à demander que des 'parties additionnelles' viennent, en quelque sorte par surcroît, s'adjoindre aux parties initiales defendant X et claimant A*".

11. Under the I.C.C. rules, the arbitrators once they have been nominated, have no discretion to add as parties to the arbitration claimant(s) or defendant(s) who were not identified as such in the request for arbitration. Thus it follows that, in the present case, articles 8(3) and 16 of the Rules can be of no assistance to defendant X.

12. A different situation might have arisen if company Y and defendant X had attempted to file a request for arbitration naming claimant A, company B and the C corporation as defendants. Then the question might have to be faced whether A can be a defendant and whether Y and C corporation are or are not bound to the agreement to arbitrate to which they are not signatories. But that is not the case.

13. The above conclusions appear to be in accord with the provisions of the Swiss Concordat.

14. Any question of substance as to whether claimant A can claim under the contract of June 1973 without the presence of company B as a co-claimant (and the Tribunal is not sure if any such question is raised) or as to whether the claim of claimant A is affected by the Memorandum of Agreement of the same date, cannot be considered at the present stage, but is open to be argued at the hearing on the merits.

15. In consequence of the decision of the Tribunal no change is necessary in the terms of reference, which accordingly, remain effective.

Therefore and on these grounds,
the undersigned,
have decided and decide,
on the issue No. 1 of the terms of reference:

Company B, the C corporation and company Y are not parties to this arbitration, nor can they be (made) parties thereto.
So awarded at this   day of March 1987, at Berne, Switzerland.

Signed by Arbitrators.

Multiparty arbitration—Arbitration clause in main contract based on F.I.D.I.C. Clause 67—Arbitration clause in subcontract based on Federation of Civil Engineering Contractors (U.K.)—Interpretation of multiparty arbitration clause—Is it a condition to enjoin the subcontractor in the dispute between the owner and the main contractor that this dispute has developed beyond the stage of difference of opinion and reached the stage of an arbitration proceeding? (Yes).

Partial award in I.C.C. case No. 5333, rendered in 1986.

INTRODUCTION

The award in this case sheds light on the difficulties that may arise in interpreting the undertakings of the parties regarding the settlement of disputes in a complex construction project. Where several parties are bound by separate but linked contracts, the settlement of disputes between two of the many parties may involve the rights of a third party involved in the same project. A mechanism for the settlement of disputes related to more than two parties and related to more than one contract is sometimes desirable in order to avoid contradictory findings, in order to shorten proceedings since witnesses may only appear once before one and the same tribunal of arbitrators and in order to reduce the total costs of the settlement of the dispute as compared to having two or more separate arbitrations. However, there are disadvantages related to the so-called multiparty disputes; principally as regards aspects of confidentiality: information exposed during the arbitration becomes available to more than the other party, e.g., a subcontractor may be informed of prices, costs and margins in the contract between the owner and the main contractor, etc.

In Case 5333 three arbitrators, all of British nationality, sitting in London, had to decide as a first point whether they had jurisdiction to hear and determine the claims made by the claimant, a British company, against two defendants, one British and one Egyptian construction company.

THE AWARD

"1. Introduction

1.1. In this Arbitration the Terms of Reference dated 6th March 1986 stated that one of the issues to be determined was:

'Whether the Arbitrators have jurisdiction to hear and determine any and if so which of the claims made by the Claimants.'

1.2. By Order No. 1 dated .... 1986 we ordered that an Interim Award should be made as to that issue and that there should be a hearing of that issue on .... 1986.

1.3. In accordance with Order No. 1 the hearings were held on those days and were supplemented by written submissions from the parties. Accordingly we now make this Award on that issue. As will appear the issue is not one which strictly falls within Articles 8.3 and 8.4 of the Rules of Conciliation and Arbitration of the International Chamber of Commerce but even if it did we would, by virtue of those Articles, have power to determine that issue.

2. The contractual background

2.1. The Claimants (subcontractors) are a United Kingdom company which entered into two sub-contracts. The first, dated 15th December 1981, was made between the subcontractors and the First Defendants, (the main contractors), another U.K. company. It has been termed the 'offshore' contract since under its provisions the subcontractors were to supply materials to a Mediterranean port and to provide certain offshore technical services, both for the purposes of a main contract which the main contractors had made with 'X' acting on behalf of 'X Investment Company'. The main contract was for the construction of the 'X Building'.

2.2. The second sub-contract was dated 28th January 1982 and was made between the subcontractors and the Second Defendants, an Egyptian company to which the main contractors had assigned the construction, completion and maintenance of the building of the X tower (excluding goods and services provided offshore).

2.3. For the purpose of the issue which we have to determine it was common ground between the parties that there were no material differences between the terms of the sub-contracts. As a matter of convenience we shall in general therefore make reference only to the terms of the first 'offshore' sub-contract and we shall also refer to the other contracting party to the second sub-contract as the main contractor. Both sub-contracts were expressed to be governed by English law.

2.4. The main contract contained many provisions which were the same or substantially the same as those to be found in the F.I.D.I.C. Conditions for Civil Engineering Works, 3rd Edition. Clause 67(1) of the General Conditions of the main contract provided as follows:

'If any dispute or difference of any kind whatsoever shall arise between the Employer and the Contractor, the Architect and the Contractor or the Quantity Surveyor and the Contractor in connection with or arising out of the Contract, or the execution of the Works, whether during the progress of the Works or after their completion and whether before or after termination, abandonment or breach of the Contract, it shall in the first place be referred to and settled by the architect, who shall within a period of ninety days after being requested by either party to do so, give written notice of his decision to the Employer or the Quantity Surveyor and the Contractor. Subject to arbitration, as hereinafter provided, such decision in respect of every matter so referred shall be final and binding upon the Employer or the Quantity Surveyor and the Contractor, who shall proceed with the execution of the Works with all due diligence whether he or the Employer or the Quantity Surveyor requires arbitration as hereinafter provided or not. If the Architect has given written notice of his decision to the Employer or the Quantity Surveyor and the Contractor and no claim to arbitration has been communicated to him by the Employer, the Quantity Surveyor or the Contractor within a period of ninety days from receipt of such notice, the said decision shall remain final and binding upon the Employer or the Quantity Surveyor and the Contractor. If the Architect shall fail to give notice of his decision as aforesaid, within a period of ninety days after being requested as aforesaid, or if the Employer or the Quantity Surveyor or the Contractor be dissatisfied with any such decision, then and in any such case the Employer or the Quantity Surveyor or the Contractor may within ninety days after receiving notice of such decision or within ninety days after expiration of the first-named period of ninety days, as the case may be, require that the matter or matters in dispute be referred to arbitration as hereinafter provided. All disputes or differences in respect of which the decision, if any, of the Architect has not become final and binding as aforesaid shall be finally settled under the Rules of Conciliation and Arbitration of the International Chamber of Commerce by one or more arbitrators appointed under such Rules of which the language shall be English and the venue shall be Paris. The said arbitrator/s shall have full power to open up, revise and review any decision, opinion, direction, certificate of the Architect or valuation of the Quantity Surveyor. Neither party shall be limited in the proceedings, before such arbitrator/s, to the evidence or arguments put before the Architect for the purpose of obtaining his said decision. No decision given by the Architect in accordance with the foregoing provisions shall disqualify him from being called as a witness and giving evidence before the arbitrator/s on any matter whatsoever relevant to the dispute or difference referred to the arbitrator/s as aforesaid. The reference to arbitration may proceed notwithstanding that the Works shall not then be or be alleged to be complete, provided always that the obligations of the Employer, the Architect, the Quantity Surveyor and the Contractor shall not be altered by reason of the arbitration being conducted during the progress of the Works.'

2.5. Similarly the sub-contract conditions were in many instances substantially the same as or comparable to provisions to be found in a form of sub-contract originally published in the United Kingdom by the Federation of Civil Engineering Contractors suitable for use within the United Kingdom in conjunction with the I.C.E. Conditions of Contract (a main contract form) but now widely used in conjunction with the F.I.D.I.C. Conditions which, as is well-known, closely follow the I.C.E. Conditions, 4th Edition.

2.6. Clause 18 of the first sub-contract reads as follows:

'(1) If any dispute arises between the Contractor and the Sub-Contractor in connection with this Sub-Contract it shall subject to the provisions of this Clause be referred to arbitration and final decision of a person agreed between the parties or failing such agreements shall be finally settled under the Rules of Conciliation and Arbitration of the International Chamber of Commerce by one or more arbitrators appointed in accordance with the said Rules of which the language shall be English and the venue London.

(2) If any dispute arises in connection with the Main Contract and the Contractor is of the opinion that such dispute touches or concerns the Sub-Contract Works then provided that an arbitrator(s) has not already been agreed or appointed in pursuance of the preceding sub-clause the Contractor may by notice in writing to the Sub-Contractor require that any dispute under this Sub-Contract shall be referred to the arbitrator(s) to which the dispute under the Main Contract is referred and if any such arbitrator(s) (hereinafter called the 'joint arbitrator(s)') be willing so to act such dispute under this Sub-Contract shall be so referred. In such event the joint arbitrator(s) may subject to the consent of the Employer give such directions for the determination of the two said disputes either concurrently or consecutively as he may think just and convenient and provided that the Sub-Contractor is allowed to act as a party to the dispute between the Employer and the Contractor the joint arbitrator(s) may in determining the dispute under this Sub-Contract take account of all material facts proved before him in the dispute under the Main Contract.

(3) If at any time before an arbitrator(s) has been agreed or appointed in pursuance of sub-clause (1) of this Clause any dispute arising in connection with the Main Contract is made the subject of proceedings in any court between the Employer and the Contractor and the Contractor is of the opinion that such dispute touches or concerns the Sub-Contract Works he may by notice in writing to the Sub-Contractor abrogate the provisions of sub-clause (1) of this Clause and thereafter no dispute under this

Sub-Contract shall be referable to arbitration without further submission by the Contractor and Sub-Contractor.'

The comparable clause in the second sub-contract was Clause 20. We were also referred to other clauses of the Sub-Contract Conditions including (references in the case of the first sub-contract) 2, 3, 5, 7, 10, 14 and 22. It is not necessary to reproduce either these clauses or the comparable clauses in the second sub-contract for the purposes of determining this issue.

2.7. The law governing each sub-contract was English law.

3. The facts

3.1. The parties agreed that all the facts relevant to our decision on the issue were to be found in or to be derived from certain documents presented to us, principally a bundle of correspondence together with another larger bundle of 'Claim Submissions'. No witnesses were called to give evidence.

3.2. The following are the principal facts which we consider to be directly relevant to the issue.

3.2.1. On 28th August 1984 the main contractors wrote to the Architect appointed under the main contract setting out 36 Heads of Claim in respect of which a detailed Statement of Claim was to be submitted. The main contractors were then seeking an extension of time as well as certain additional payments. The list of Heads of Claim included a claim from the subcontractors and the subcontractors were subsequently informed of the fact that such a claim had been made in respect of their work.

3.2.2. The Architect on 29th August 1984 granted an extension of time of 56 days. On 16th October 1984 the Architect stated that such an extension of time was not to be considered as an 'interim award'. That extension of time was subsequently approved by X Investment Company, as envisaged by Clause 93 of the main contract conditions.

3.2.3. A detailed Statement of Claim was submitted in two parts on 30th October and 30th November 1984. It included claims from the subcontractors. On 1st November 1984 the Architect acknowledged receipt of the first of such claims but stated that the method of presentation left much to be desired and needed clarification.

3.2.4. On 7th December 1984 the main contractors wrote to the subcontractors informing them that a claim from them had been incorporated in full in the claim submitted to the Architect on 30th October 1984. Thereafter discussions took place between the main contractors and the subcontractors and on 8th January 1985 the subcontractors wrote to the main contractors in respect of both sub-contracts recording that they had been informed by the main contractors that the Architect had been requested to make a decision under Clause 67(1) of the Conditions of Contract and asking for a copy of the relevant request. On 17th January 1985 the main contractors replied denying that there had been any reference to a request being made under Clause 67 of the main contract and stating that the main contractors were thinking about making such a reference but had postponed doing so.

3.2.5. On 21st January 1985 the main contractors wrote to the subcontractors informing them that if certain discussions with the Employer did not lead to a settlement then formal notice of the dispute in accordance with Clause 67 would be served in February or at the latest early March 1985. This letter was acknowledged by the subcontractors on 25th January 1985.

3.2.6. On 1st March 1985 the main contractors wrote to the Architect referring to the claims which had been submitted on 30th October and 30th November 1984 and also to claims by the subcontractors which had been adopted by the main contractors and submitted at other dates to the Architect, and went on to say:

'The validity of these claims has not been accepted by the Employer and accordingly disputes have arisen between the Employer and the Contractor. In accordance with Clause 67 of the Conditions of Contract we request your formal Decision in respect of a proper extension of time and a valuation of loss, expense and additional costs incurred by us.'

3.2.7. On 6th March 1985 the main contractors also wrote to the subcontractors stating that they regarded themselves as being in dispute with the Employer under the main contract and that they were of the opinion that that dispute touched or concerned the sub-contract works. The letter went on to say:

'We have received claims from you which we have transmitted to the Employer in the usual manner without admission on our part that we are in any way liable to yourselves. If and to the extent that you regard yourselves as being in dispute with us in connection with these claims, we hereby give notice in writing in accordance with Clause 18(2) of your sub-contract that we require any dispute under this sub-contract shall be referred to the arbitrator(s) to which the disputes under the main contract or the Assignment are referred. We hereby reserve our rights under Clause 18(3) of the sub-contract.'

A similar letter was sent in relation to the second (onshore) sub-contract.

3.2.8. On 7th March 1985 the Architect replied to maincontractor's letter of 1st March stating simply: 'The matter is still undergoing review'.

3.2.9. On 25th March 1985 solicitors acting for the subcontractors wrote to the main contractors and to the Egyptian Company letters requiring disputes to be referred to arbitration pursuant to Clause 18(1), alternatively Clause 20(1) of the relevant sub-contracts.

3.2.10. On 3rd April 1985 the Architect wrote again to the main contractors in relation to their letter of 1st March 1985 stating, on that occasion, that:

'We are not aware of any dispute having arisen between you and the Employer and no dispute has been referred to us as is required by Clause 67. Reference to Clause 67 is inapplicable to the determination of a normal claim by the Architect. The claim documents are receiving attention. Our analysis has been hampered by the way in which the documents were presented and the need to research the subject-matter, most of which is several years out of date.'

3.2.11. On 4th April 1985 solicitors acting for both Defendants replied to the letters from the solicitors acting for the subcontractors invoking Clause 18(2) alternatively Clause 20(2) of the sub-contract conditions. On 25th April 1985 the same solicitors wrote a longer and fuller letter again invoking the relevant provisions of the sub-contract requiring the disputes to be referred to the arbitrators under the main contract.

3.2.12. On 25th April 1985 the Architect also wrote to the main contractors re-iterating that there was no dispute to be referred for decision under Clause 67 since there had only been the presentation of a normal claim which did not fall within that category.

3.2.13. On 8th May 1985 the main contractors answered the Architect's letter of 25th April 1985, referring to their letter of 1st March 1985 and stating:

'In the event that a decision under Clause 67 which is acceptable to us has not been received from you by 30th May 1985 then we shall give notice of our intention to proceed to arbitration and act accordingly. We therefore await your decision in accordance with Clause 67.'

The Architect replied to that letter on 10th May 1985 again stating that the letter of 1st March 1985 was not a notice and did not specify any dispute and that it only related to a claim which would not be a ground for any action under Clause 67.

3.2.14. The Architect gave no decision as requested by the main contractors by 30th May 1985. On 6th June 1985 the solicitors acting for the subcontractors purported to make a request for arbitration under the I.C.C. Rules of Conciliation and Arbitration. On 18th June 1985 the main contractors replied to that letter objecting to it as a request falling within the Rules and arguing that the subcontractors were not entitled to arbitration pursuant to Clause 18(1) of the sub-contract conditions and that there was no dispute between the subcontractors and either of the main contractors.

3.2.15. On 21st June 1985 the Architect wrote to the main contractors giving the results of their consideration of the main contractors claims.

3.2.16. On 23rd August 1985 the main contractors replied to the Architect's letter of 21st June 1985 recording that it was not regarded by the Architect as a Clause 67 decision and stressing that they were not at all happy with the determination and were presently reviewing its contents. The letter went on to say:

'Given that we are concurrently concluding a further interim claim for discussion with you, we are of the opinion that it would be counter-productive to us all at this stage to take the step of filing proceedings and are prepared to concede that the Clause 67 machinery ought to be set in motion once we have considered your letter of 21st June 1985 and its contents in detail. You should, however, regard this as Notice that we intend to refer our claims to arbitration in due course if a resolution is not forthcoming.'

3.2.17. Nearly 6 months later, on 7th February 1986, the main contractors wrote to the Architect referring to the Architect's letter of 21st June 1985 and stating:

'It is now clear that disputes have arisen between the Contractor and the Employer, Architect and Quantity Surveyor in connection with the contract. The matters in dispute are summarised in Appendix II to this letter and those disputes are hereby referred to you for settlement in accordance with Clause 67 of the Conditions of Contract. We hereby request that you give written notice of your Decision thereon in accordance with Clause 67.'

3.3. The requests for arbitrations (numbers 1 and 2) had been received by the I.C.C. on 2nd September 1985. The answer and counterclaim were received by the I.C.C. on 3rd December 1985. In the answer and counterclaim the Defendants raised the issue as to whether or not the arbitrators had jurisdiction to determine the claims the subject of the request for arbitration. Paragraph 11 of the answer and counterclaim, inter alia, argued that a written notice requiring that the dispute should be referred to arbitration under the main contract was given in answer to the subcontractors' letters in 1985; that there was in fact a main contract dispute in existence because the Defendants had submitted extensive claims to the Architect which the Architect had either rejected or not accepted and that that matter would need to be resolved by main contract arbitration; and that in the alternative to those contentions:

'The Contractor now gives the required written notice under Clauses 18(2) (offshore) and 20(2) (onshore) that a dispute or disputes have arisen in connection with the main contract which in his (the Contractor's) opinion touch or concern the sub-contract works and no sub-contract Arbitrators or Arbitrator having been agreed or appointed the Contractor now requires that subcontractor's claims should be referred to the Arbitrators or Arbitrator to which the dispute or disputes under the Main Contract is or are referred.'

3.5. In so far as it is a question of fact and if or in so far as it was not agreed between the parties we find for the purposes of this issue only that the claims made by the Defendants by March 1985 touched or concerned the sub-contract works. We make no findings as to the extent to which the Claimants' claims are disputed between the Claimants and the Defendants and we assume for the purposes of this issue that a bona fide dispute exists as to each of them.

4. The arguments

4.1. We do not consider it necessary to set out all the arguments presented to us on behalf of the parties.

4.2. In essence the Defendants who had raised the issue as to our jurisdiction contended that either:
(a) By their letter of 6th March 1985; alternatively
(b) By their letter of 18th June 1985; alternatively
(c) By their Answer in Counterclaim; alternatively
(d) By their written submissions for the hearing;

they had effectively invoked Clause 18(2) of the relevant sub-contract conditions since there was on every such occasion a 'dispute in connection with the main contract' falling within Clause 18(2) of the sub-contract conditions. It was part of their case that the word 'dispute' in the first line of Clause 18(2) of the sub-contract conditions was to be read widely and that such a dispute might arise under the main contract at any time after a claim had been submitted particularly if it was clear that the claim was not to be accepted. Furthermore it was submitted that it was not necessary that there should be a reference to the Architect for decision under Clause 67 or a decision or failure to decide or that the arbitral tribunal should have been formed before a valid notice could be given under the sub-contract conditions requiring the sub-contract dispute to be referred to the main contract arbitral tribunal.

4.3. For the Claimants it was argued that for the purposes both of Clause 18(2) of the sub-contract conditions and of Clause 67 of the main contract it was not enough that a claim should have been submitted and not accepted; there had for the purposes of the main contract to be a dispute in existence which had been referred to the Architect for decision and either decided or failed to have been decided and that there had been notice of dissatisfaction with it; not every dispute that was decided or not decided would necessarily be referred to arbitration and a notice under the sub-contract could not validly refer to a dispute which was not a real dispute under the main contract. Accordingly a 'dispute' for the purpose of the first line of Clause 18(2) of the sub-contract had to be a dispute which had either been referred to arbitration or was capable of being referred to arbitration at the time when the sub-contract notice was given. On the facts there was no such dispute at any of the dates contended for by the Defendants.

5. Conclusions

5.1. The recitals to the sub-contract and Clause 3(1) of the sub-contract conditions make it clear that the sub-contractor is to be treated as having read the conditions of the main contract which was itself identified in the Schedule to the sub-contract. The word 'dispute' in the first line of Clause 18(2) of the sub-contract conditions should therefore be given a meaning consistent with the meaning in the main contract.

5.2. The purpose of Clause 18(2) of the sub-contract conditions is quite clear: the Contractor is given a unilateral right to require certain disputes between himself and the sub-contractor to be referred to the decision of the arbitral tribunal appointed under the main contract. Provided that the machinery of Clause 18(2) is operated properly the sub-contractor has agreed to submit those disputes to that tribunal. However this is a departure and derogation from the ordinary rights of the sub-contractor which are contained in Clause 18(1). We have accordingly approached the interpretation of Clause 18(2) bearing in mind the observations of Harman L.J. in *Monmouthshire C.C.* v. *Costelloe & Kemple Ltd.* (1965) 5 B.L.R. 83 at page 91:

> 'This is a process by which the defendants can be deprived of their general rights at law and therefore one must construe it with some strictness as having a forfeiting effect. It is not a penal clause, but it must be construed against the person putting it forward who is, after all, trying to shut out the ordinary citizen's rights to go to the courts to have his grievances ventilated. Therefore, I think that it will require very clear words . . . to shut the defendants out of their rights.'

The judge was there referring to the position of a contractor under a clause very similar to the clause in the main contract conditions.

5.3. Under the main contract there are the following stages before an arbitral tribunal can properly be seized of a dispute:

(1) A dispute or difference must have arisen: in our view the observations of Lord Denning M.R. in the *Monmouthshire C.C.* case (1965) 5 B.L.R. 83 at page 89 are apposite:

> 'It is accepted that, in order that a dispute or difference can arise on this contract, there must in the first place be a claim by the contractor. Until that claim is rejected, you cannot say that there is a dispute or difference. There must be both a claim and a rejection of it in order to constitute a dispute or difference.'

(2) The dispute or difference must be referred to the Architect for decision under Clause 67: clearly this will ordinarily mean something which conveys to the Architect the fact that the issue has progressed beyond the mere submission of a claim and requires something other than consideration or further consideration of the claim simply for the purposes for example of determining whether or not a certificate should be issued or some other similar step taken; the point at issue arising from the previous exchanges must be capable of being identified for the purposes of obtaining a decision on it.

(3) Such a point at issue being the dispute or difference must then have been decided by the Architect or there must have been a failure to decide within the prescribed period of 90 days.

(4) Dissatisfaction must then have been expressed in accordance with Clause 67 within a further 90 day period after the decision or failure to decide, by requiring that the matter or matters in dispute should be referred to arbitration as provided by Clause 67, namely under the requirements of the Rules of Conciliation and Arbitration of the International Chamber of Commerce.

It is clear therefore that an arbitral tribunal constituted as envisaged by Clause 67 will not be seized of a dispute or difference for its determination until after all four stages have been completed. The machinery of Clause 67 is however plainly intended to give an opportunity (perhaps the last) to have the dispute resolved primarily by the Architect's decision or by amicable agreement following the Architect's decision. Not every dispute that comes into existence will, even if it is referred to the Architect for decision, therefore necessarily be referred to arbitration, and come before an arbitral tribunal.

5.4. We therefore consider that the word 'dispute' in the first line of Clause 18(2) of the sub-contract conditions must be read as referring not to a dispute which is in existence or which has been referred to the Architect for decision but one in respect of which dissatisfaction has been expressed and which has been required to be referred to arbitration. Otherwise the normal method of resolving disputes under the contract by means of Clause 18(1) could easily be blocked by a contractor by reference to a supposed dispute or a dispute in respect of which there was no need or intention to seek arbitration.

5.5. It therefore follows in our view that it is not competent for a contractor to give notice under Clause 18(2) of the sub-contract conditions unless the dispute is one which is thus capable of being referred to arbitration under the main contract. In other words stages (1) to (4) described above must have been completed before the Contractor may invoke Clause 18(2) in relation to a dispute which in his opinion touches or concerns the sub-contract works. (We were not asked to decide why the sub-contract refers to 'the sub-contract works' rather than 'the sub-contract'.) (In addition of course the conditions set out in the proviso in Clause 18(2) must not have occurred i.e. an arbitrator or arbitrators must not have been agreed or appointed as provided by Clause 18(1). Agreement or appointment of an arbitrator or arbitrators would preclude the operation of Clause 18(2) even if Stages (1) to (4) had been completed.)

5.6. This conclusion is not only consistent with but supported by the remainder of Clause 18(2) which provides for certain conditions to be satisfied before the sub-contract dispute can effectively come before the arbitral tribunal under the main contract. Clause 18(2) envisages that the dispute notified 'shall be referred to the arbitrators to which the dispute under the main contract is referred': the words 'is referred' must mean 'is *presently* referred' or in effect 'has been referred', rather than 'is to be referred' for otherwise there is no certainty as to the next stage. That stage is that the tribunal has to express a willingness to act. It is in our view incompatible with the scheme of this clause that there should be an indeterminate period of uncertainty before a tribunal is constituted so as to find out whether it is willing to act. This predicament would be easily resolved if the clause presupposes, as we hold that it does, that the arbitral tribunal is either already in existence or is in the process of being formed so that either at or at least very shortly after the time of the Contractor's notice the arbitral tribunal will be in existence and in a position to state whether or not it is willing to act. Before the tribunal can give its consent, it must obviously be aware both of the dispute under the main contract and the dispute under the sub-contract, the Contractor's opinion that the former touches or concerns the sub-contract works and all other considerations relevant to the giving of consent.

5.7. In our view the scheme of Clause 18(2) is based on the assumption that an arbitral tribunal has already been constituted or is in the process of being constituted to decide the dispute under the main contract. Reading Clause 18 as a whole the word 'dispute' must for these reasons therefore mean a dispute which is not only capable of being referred to arbitration but which is being referred to arbitration.

5.8. We now apply these principles to the facts before us. In our judgment no dispute or difference under the main contract had been referred or was in the course of being referred to arbitration at the time when any of the notices relied on by the Contractor under Clause 18(2) of the sub-contract conditions was given.

5.8.1. *6th March 1985:* We are not convinced that at this date there was a dispute between the main contractors and any other party capable of being referred to the Architect for decision under Clause 67. The Architect certainly regarded the matters referred to him as being claims which had not yet been considered, still less rejected by him; the main contractors did no more than refute that contention and did not support their position by referring to the prior history of the submission of the claim so as to show that a dispute had truly crystallised (as they subsequently were able to do on 7th February 1986). Even if there was a dispute or difference in existence on 6th March 1985 it had not been decided by the Architect at that date and accordingly the dispute had not passed through the stages which we have described above as necessary for the existence of a dispute for the purpose of Clause 18(2). Furthermore, as appears below, consideration of these questions became academic as a result of the main contractors' subsequent action.

5.8.2. *18th June 1985:* By this date the Architect had not given a decision as requested by the main contractors but the main contractors had not expressed any dissatisfaction with such a failure or required the supposed disputes to be referred to arbitration. The subcontractors had commenced an arbitration on 6th June 1985 but in our view there was still no 'dispute' for the purposes of Clause 18(2) of the sub-contract conditions since none of the stages described above had been completed.

5.8.3. *Answer and Counterclaim (December 1985):* By this date the main contractors had in their letter of 23rd August 1985 decided that they would not proceed to file proceedings for the purposes of furthering their dissatisfaction with the Architect's failure to decide the dispute referred on 1st March 1985, alternatively with the 'decision' given by him on 21st June 1985. In our judgment by their letter of 23rd August 1985 the main contractors effectively withdrew the request for a decision which they believed that they had made to the Architect on 1st March 1985 and announced their intention that they would not file proceedings (i.e., by submitting a Request for Arbitration to the I.C.C. Court of Arbitration as required by Clause 67 of the main contract conditions). Even if the latter is not to be read in this manner, by the date of the Answer and Counterclaim there was for the purposes of determining the issue before us, either no dispute or no dispute capable of being referred to arbitration for the reasons that we have given, namely that the requisite stages for the formulation of a dispute referable to arbitration under Clause 18(2) had not been met. It is not necessary for us to reach a conclusion as to whether by this date or subsequently the main contractors' rights under Clause 18(2) of the sub-contract conditions were still available, having regard to the progress made in appointing arbitrators in the arbitration initiated by the subcontractors under Clause 18(1).

5.8.4. *The hearing:* the main contractors argued that by their written submissions prior to and at the hearing they could still give the relevant notice. On the assumption that this could be done (as to which we have considerable doubts) we are unable to accept the main contractors' submissions that the requirements of Clause 18(2) had by then been satisfied. On 7th February 1986 the main contractors purported to refer to the Architect certain disputes but the extracts from the documents presented to us were uninformative and did not identify what were the matters which by then were said to be in dispute and which might in the main contractors' opinion touch or concern the sub-contract works. It appears that the Architect did not decide that dispute and that apparently on or about 19th May 1986 the main contractors had filed a Request for Arbitration with the Court of Arbitration of the I.C.C. in purported compliance with the requirements of Clause 67 of the main contract conditions. We were however given insufficient information as to the nature of the main contractors' dissatisfaction which led to the reference to arbitration for us to be able to form an opinion as to whether or not there was a bona fide dispute referable to arbitration between the main contractors and the Employer or the Architect (or indeed the Quantity Surveyor) for the purposes of the main contract conditions. We were therefore not satisfied that the necessary stages described above had been completed.

5.8.5. For these reasons we have decided that the Defendants' objections fail and that the preliminary issue must be answered in favour of the Claimants.

6. Costs

6.1. Subsequent to the hearing the parties delivered written submissions as to costs, those for the Claimants being submitted on 29th May 1986 and those for the Defendants by a letter dated 3rd June 1986. The Claimants submitted that the costs should follow the event of the Arbitrators' decision on jurisdiction. The Defendants submitted that if the Arbitrators' were to decide that they had no jurisdiction to deal with the claims then the Defendants should be awarded their costs but that if the Arbitrators' decided that the tribunal had been properly constituted under the terms of the sub-contracts then the question of costs should be reserved or that costs should be awarded to the Claimants 'contingently upon the Claimants establishing some appreciable liability in respect of some (at least) of the claims being advanced'.

6.2. In our judgment the costs should 'follow the event' as contended by the Claimants. We have decided that the Defendants' objections to our jurisdiction are and were not well-founded and that accordingly no issue as to our jurisdiction should have arisen nor should any hearings have taken place nor was it necessary for this award to be made. We therefore make our award to reflect these factors.

7. Accordingly, for the reasons set out above, we AWARD AND ADJUDGE

1. That we, the Arbitrators in this arbitration No. 5333/GAA between the above-named Claimants and Defendants, have jurisdiction to hear and determine all the claims so far made by the Claimants in this arbitration.

2. That the Defendants pay the Claimants' legal costs of and occasioned by the hearing of this issue, to be agreed by the parties or to be fixed by the Arbitrators in the final award.

3. That the proportion of the costs of the arbitration referable to the hearing of the preliminary issue, such costs being those defined by Article 20.2. of the I.C.C. Rules of Conciliation and Arbitration (but excluding 'the normal legal costs incurred by the parties') shall be borne by the Defendants, such proportion to be determined in our final award in accordance with Article 20.1 of the I.C.C. Rules of Conciliation and Arbitration.

DATED at London this ... day of ... 1986."

COMMENTS

1. Both the subcontract and maincontract were in standard form—the main contract was a modified F.I.D.I.C. 3rd Edition. The subcontract was one which is very frequently used in combination with the F.I.D.I.C. form and the subcontract arbitration clause was virtually identical to that used in United Kingdom domestic subcontracts. The subcontract form owes its origin to a

standard form published by the Federation of Civil Engineering Contractors in that country.

2. In the case referred to above the parties had decided to tackle the multiparty disputes problem by providing for such an eventuality in the subcontract. The clause is one according to which the decision to proceed in a multiparty arbitration lies with the contractor, and only with him. Where the contractor decides to exercise his choice and requires that the disputes with the subcontractor be submitted to the arbitrators appointed for the settlement of the main contract dispute, then the subcontractor is obliged to follow. On the other hand, we are not informed whether the owner is contractually bound to follow by virtue of a separate contract between him and the contractor or otherwise. Clause 67 in the main contract does not provide for the possibility of the owner participating in the dispute between the contractor and the subcontractor nor for the subcontractor joining the arbitration between owner and the main contractor.

3. The question never arose in the case and we may suppose that the owner might have been willing to let the subcontract dispute into "his" arbitration since he sits with two important trump cards in his hand:

(a) The owner will have had an opportunity to appoint one arbitrator, which arbitrator remains on the panel to hear the subcontract dispute. The subcontractor, on the other hand, will not be able to appoint an arbitrator, nor will he have any influence on the choice of any of the three arbitrators, which may be a serious drawback. Since all arbitrators appointed under the Rules of the I.C.C. are required to be independent of the party appointing them, the owner should theoretically not have a particular advantage from appointing one of the arbitrators. Other factors than independence of the arbitrator may, however, play to the subcontractor's disadvantage. Suppose the subcontractor were not English or not English-speaking. The subcontractor and his foreign lawyer might feel at a disadvantage to explain their case in such circumstances, particularly where the law applicable was English.

(b) The owner may influence the conduct of the arbitration, since he, according to Article 18(2), must give his consent to the directions that are to be given by the joint arbitrators. The owner may thereby—it seems—avoid concurrent proceedings and for legitimate reasons, protect his business secrets from the ears of the subcontractor.

The way the clause is written, it does not give equal rights to all parties involved.

4. The multiparty arbitration clause in the subcontract, Article 18(2), offers to the contractor the same advantage as it offers to the owner under the main contract, i.e., the right to appoint an arbitrator. Here again, the subcontractor has no influence on the choice of any of the arbitrators who are going to decide a dispute in which the situation in many instances is one

where the subcontractor is attacked by the contractor and the owner (although the situation is different in case 5333 where the subcontractor is claimant).

5. It is crucial to the operation of the subcontract clause (both in commercial and legal terms) that arbitrators should have been appointed under the main contract and seised of the main contract dispute. The reader's attention is drawn to those parts of the award which show that:

(a) there must first be a dispute under the main contract;
(b) the dispute must have been referred to the engineer for decision;
(c) dissatisfaction must have been expressed with that decision under clause 67 and the ensuing dispute duly referred to arbitration;

before the main contractor could properly operate his option under the subcontract arbitration clause.

It therefore makes sense to impose restrictions on the reference of a subcontract dispute to a main contract arbitration if all three above steps have first to be followed since otherwise odd results might occur, e.g.:

(a) What was a "promising" dispute between the contractor and the engineer/employer might prove to have no connection with the subcontract dispute;
(b) The engineer might render a decision which removed the potential dispute between contractor and subcontractor from the ambit of any future arbitration;
(c) One or the other of the parties dissatisfied with the engineer's decision might not refer the part relevant to the subcontract dispute to arbitration under the main contract.

6. For the reasons given by the arbitrators, i.e., the possibility of a contractor blocking a subcontractor from the Article 18(1) procedure by reference to a supposed dispute or a future arbitration with the owner and for the reasons given above relating to the appointment of an arbitrator, one can easily agree with the findings of the arbitrators. The clause in the subcontract should be construed in a way as to protect the interests of the subcontractor; so as to enable him to submit a dispute with the contractor to an arbitration panel over the constitution of which he has had some influence. But this interpretation puts the contractor under some pressure. In practice, the contractor will have to make up his mind very quickly after a subcontractor has required a dispute between the two of them to be decided by arbitration if the contractor is of the opinion that the dispute is one that touches or concerns the main contract. Where it would be advantageous to have it settled in a joint arbitration with the owner (which is a legitimate wish of the contractor), the contractor must take quick action to bring the two disputes together. It is worth noting that in this situation the arbitration panel can be established rather quickly under Article 18(1) since a dispute does not have to be processed by an engineer as a first step; it is a question of two or three months

in present I.C.C. practice. Once established, the subcontractor can block the situation under Article 18(2), and the contractor will not, as a right, be able to refer the dispute to a joint arbitration. Even if the contractor sets in motion the mechanism provided for under clause 67 of F.I.D.I.C. as soon as he is informed about the subcontractor's request for arbitration, it is most unlikely that a contractor could submit a request for arbitration to the I.C.C. before the arbitrators are appointed according to Article 18(2).

7. The award indirectly touches the much discussed question of whether a request for arbitration under clause 67 must be submitted to the I.C.C. in Paris within 90 days in order to be validly made, or whether an expression of dissatisfaction within 90 days is sufficient, leaving it open when, at the latest, the request must ultimately be submitted to the I.C.C. The award seems to assume that in order for the multiparty scheme to be able to operate efficiently the request under F.I.D.I.C. clause 67 must be submitted to the I.C.C. within the 90 days. If this were not the case, the contractor could prevent the subcontractor from requesting arbitration according to Article 18(1) by giving notice under Article 18(2) to the subcontractor requiring any dispute under the subcontract to be referred to the arbitrators under the main contract long before such arbitrators have been appointed and even long before the contractor has requested arbitration at the I.C.C. One must, therefore, agree with the arbitrators in point 5.7 of the award where they hold that Article 18(2) of the subcontract assumes that an arbitral tribunal has already been constituted or is in the process of being constituted. A contrary decision would have afforded too great a measure of discretion to the contractor as to when he wanted a dispute to be decided and put the subcontractor in a situation where he had no influence over the time when his dispute with the contractor would be decided. He already has no influence over the choice of an arbitrator as we have seen above where Article 18(2) applies.

Sigvard Jarvin

I—F.I.D.I.C. Conditions—Clause 67—Period for submitting a Request for Arbitration.
II—Procedure—Injunction by a state court to stop the arbitration proceedings—the form required for an injunction—the effect of an injunction on arbitrators sitting in another jurisdiction.
Partial award rendered in 1986 in Case No. 4862. *

A dispute arose on a Public Works Contract between a joint venture of three European firms (all of different nationalities) and a state organisation of the Yemen Arab Republic (Y.A.R.). The European Contractor who had undertaken the construction of a road claimed in his Request for Arbitration the recovery of additional costs. The contract was for a fixed price and was governed by the F.I.D.I.C. Conditions, Second Edition. The Engineer was a firm of consulting engineers who had in August 1978 taken a decision in accordance with Article 67 of the F.I.D.I.C. Conditions and had approved part of the Contractor's claim for additional costs but had rejected the greater part of the claim. Before making this decision on the claim the Engineer had issued a Final Acceptance Certificate in April 1978 in respect of which payment had been made in July 1978.

By a letter of October 1978 the Contractor informed the Engineer that he did not accept the decision and formally notified him in accordance with Article 67 that the disputes and differences had to be submitted to arbitration. The Contractor added that he still hoped that an amicable solution could be found and that in consequence he did not intend to take any steps towards commencing the arbitration.

In June 1981 the Contractor wrote to the Secretariat of the I.C.C. Court of Arbitration in order to inform it that he had a dispute with the Employer, that the dispute had not been resolved and that he was in the course of preparing his request in due and proper form and that he was going to submit it unless an amicable solution could be found.

On 21 December 1983 the Secretariat of the I.C.C. Court of Arbitration received a complete request for arbitration accompanied by an advance on

---

* This is primarily a translation of the note which first appeared in *Journal du Droit International* (Clunet), 1987, 4th part, p. 1018, and is reproduced by permission of the editor, Professor Berthold Goldman, and publishers. However, it also includes a part of the award not previously published, relating to the limitation issue.

account of costs of $450 (following the request of June 1981 and a formal payment of $50 at that time).

In May 1984 the Employer delivered an Answer limited to the defence that the Request for Arbitration was time-barred according to the law of the Y.A.R. The Defendant also pleaded that it had commenced on 13 May 1984 proceedings against the Contractor before a Commercial Court in Yemen in which it had asked, amongst other things, that the court should declare that the Request for Arbitration made to the I.C.C. was in conflict with the laws of Yemen because of prescription.

The Court of Arbitration of the I.C.C. decided that there was *prima facie* an arbitration agreement and set the arbitration in motion. A panel of three arbitrators (a Lebanese President with co-arbitrators from the Federal Republic of Germany and from the United Kingdom) was appointed and the place of arbitration was fixed by the I.C.C. in Paris.

The three arbitrators and the Claimant took part in meetings in order to draw up the Terms of Reference but the Defendant refused to take part relying upon an order of the Commercial Court at Sana'a and said that to have taken part would be in violation of that order.

The Terms of Reference were signed by the arbitrators and the Claimant and approved by the I.C.C. Court of Arbitration in March 1986 (under Article 13.2 of the I.C.C. Rules of Arbitration).

Subsequently the arbitrators dealt with certain of the issues in the Terms of Reference in the following terms (the award was written in English):

Concerning the time limit to preserve the right to go to arbitration in accordance with Clause 67 of the F.I.D.I.C. Conditions:
1. The Defendant alleged that there was no jurisdiction to proceed with the arbitration under Clause 67 because the Claimant had not made its Request for Arbitration within 90 days of the Engineer's decision, i.e., it was not sufficient for the Claimant only to give formal notice to the Engineer within 90 days "requiring" the matters to be referred to arbitration. This question was answered in the following terms:

"Whereas the Claimant did fulfil all the requirements of Clause 67 pertinent to this case, viz.: (1) he did inform the Engineer on 24 May of his non-acceptance of the Engineer's assessment of his claims—thereby defining the 'dispute', (2) he did request the Engineer on 24 May 1978 for a decision under Clause 67 on the amount of such claims, and (3) he did notify the Engineer on 19 October 1978 (66 days after the Engineer issued on 14 August 1978 his decision under Clause 67, i.e., well within the 90-day period allowed for notifying such dissent) that he required the matter in dispute to be referred to arbitration.

Whereas nothing in Clause 67 may be construed as obliging a dissenting party to actually file with the I.C.C. Court of Arbitration a formal Request for Arbitration (as required by the I.C.C. rules) within the 90-day period following receipt of the Engineer's decision, the words 'require that the matter or matters in dispute be referred to arbitration' clearly meaning that the dissenting party wishes to put on record that he opts to avail himself of the opportunity offered him by the Clause to have the dispute settled by arbitration under the auspices of the I.C.C. rather than be bound permanently by the Engineer's decision which he rejects,

Whereas the quoted sentence actually purports to express the dissenting party's serious intention to apply for arbitration and is therefore to be construed as a notification by him that he will at a certain time file a formal Request for Arbitration, and serves meanwhile the important purpose of avoiding that the Engineer's decision becomes permanently final and binding,

Whereas, should the opposite be true, i.e., should the text of the Clause be interpreted to mean that an actual Request for Arbitration has to be filed within 90 days of receipt by the dissenting party of the Engineer's decision, one could imagine that in many cases there would be several formal Requests for Arbitration filed, all related to the same Contract, which would then have to be resolved according to different calendars overlapping one another, with possibly different arbitrators appointed in the different cases, the whole at great cost and misery to all concerned, a situation which could not have been intended either by the authors of the text of Clause 67 or even by the parties at the time of signing the Contract,

Whereas a leading specialist in such questions, I. N. Duncan Wallace, Q.C., in a well-documented article on just this matter, in the July 1985 issue of *The International Construction Law Review*, has also concluded that the only action required to prevent the Engineer's decision from becoming permanently binding was for the dissenting party to express within the time limit specified in the Clause his requirement 'that the matter or matters in dispute be referred to arbitration', the formal Request for Arbitration itself being filed at a later date,

Whereas the contention of the Respondent—that the Claimant has contravened the requirements of Clause 67 by making his request for reference to arbitration conditional upon his failure to reaching a solution by negotiation—has no legal ground, the Claimant having consistently and constantly stated that in case of failure in such negotiation he would be left with no other choice that to file a Request for Arbitration,

The Tribunal unanimously rules that the Claimant has correctly adhered to the requirements of Clause 67 of the Contract and therefore the fact that his Request for Arbitration was not filed within 90 days from his receipt of the Engineer's decision does not invalidate the arbitration."

2. The following questions were raised:
   What is the law of limitation, if any, which applies to this arbitration?
   If section 43 of the Yemeni Law relating to Legal Evidence and the Duties of a Judge and Arbitration applies to this arbitration:
   (a) Does the 5-year limitation period apply to arbitration as opposed to bringing a case in a Yemeni Court?
   (b) Is the Claimant seeking the determination as to an "amount already due under the Contract"?

These questions were answered as follows:

"Whereas Clause 76 of the Contract provides that 'the Contract shall be governed by and construed according to the laws for the time being in force in the Yemen Arab Republic',

Whereas the laws referred to are the Substantive Laws and not the Rules of Procedure, the latter being those of the I.C.C.,

Whereas Y.A.R. Law No. 90/1976 quoted by the Respondent as applicable to this dispute is a Law of Procedure and not a Substantive Law, and in any event a Law which—according to the unanimous finding of this Tribunal—is obviously intended and designed for local proceedings in the Y.A.R.,

Whereas, in any case, Article 43 of the said Y.A.R. Law deals with debts that have become due, not with those that have still to be determined, which is the substance of this arbitration,

Whereas, also, the said Article 43 stipulates that in order to bar proceedings in court, a period of five years should have elapsed from the date the amount has become due without a demand having been made,

Whereas the Claimant has, several times since he notified the Engineer and the Employer of his rejection of the Engineer's decision and his intention to start arbitration proceedings if no satisfactory solution could be negotiated, kept following up his claims. In particular (1) by his letter of 15 June 1979 to the Respondent, (2) by his letter of 30 June 1981 to the Prime Minister of the Y.A.R. Government who, in the Respondent's own words 'passed on the letter to the Minister of Public Works' (see item 7, page 18 of the Defendant's Preliminary Objections), (3) by the repeated efforts over the years since 1981 by the Embassy of [a European country] to bring the dispute to the attention of the Y.A.R. Government and in particular of the Ministry of Public Works (as certified by the Embassy's Chargé d'Affaires a.i.) and (4) by other representations properly documented in the Claimant's submission, e.g., to the Central Planning Organisation and the I.D.A.,

Whereas the Respondent's contention—that despite the above follow-ups he made it clear at various dates to his Government that the Engineer's decision was final and binding and that no negotiation was possible—cannot alter the Claimant's right to resort to arbitration, this being the course of action contractually agreed by the parties to resolve disputes. Indeed it rather shows that the Claimant did make demands subsequent to his notification of 14 August 1978 requiring the matter in dispute to be referred to arbitration,

Whereas, in view of the above findings, the Tribunal finds it unnecessary to deal with the different contentions of the parties regarding the meaning and effect of Article 43 of Y.A.R. Law No. 90/1976 though had it been necessary, the Tribunal would have held:
(a) that the article does not apply to a situation such as this where the unliquidated claim of the Claimant has not matured i.e., the debt has not 'become due' in the words of the article, and
(b) even if it had 'become due', the Claimant would benefit from the exception that he had made a number of demands subsequent to the Engineer's decision, which would at least have the effect of prolonging the 5-year limitation period, and
(c) that the opening words of Article 43 and the position of the article in a particular section of the law and in the context of other articles suggest that it applies to cases commenced in Court and not to arbitration.

Whereas the Y.A.R. Law No. 10/1979 provides in Articles 32 and 33 that the applicable law of procedure shall be either that of the country where the case is initiated or the law of the forum, thus incorporating the general rules of private international law on the subject,

Whereas, therefore, the rules of procedure which apply to this arbitration are the I.C.C. Rules supplemented, when required, by rules settled by this Tribunal,

Whereas although the said Rules (Article 3) do not impose a time limit for submitting a formal Request for Arbitration, it is accepted that there must be some time limit for the filing of such a formal Request after a notice has been served,

Whereas the Claimant's delay in filing a formal Request for Arbitration is not so inordinate as to lead to the inevitable conclusion that the Claimant had slept upon his rights and acquiesced in the position taken by the Engineer. This is evidenced by the repeated demands made by the Claimant and herein alluded to.

Whereas the Tribunal's approach on this issue of delay and time-bar is consistent with the view taken in the English decision of the House of Lords in *Bremer Vulkan Schiffbau und Maschinenfabrik* v. *South India Shipping Corporation Ltd.* [1981] A.C. 909, recently followed and applied in *Allied Marine Transport Ltd.* v. *Vale Do Rio Doce Navegacao S.A.* [1985] 1 W.L.R. 925.

Whereas the Claimant's acceptance of payment of the amounts approved by the Engineer without protest, demur or reservation cannot in the circumstances of this dispute be construed to mean that he waived his right to the claims he had previously submitted, such a waiver having to be the subject of an unequivocally explicit document. The Claimant's position with respect to such claims was quite clear to the Respondent before said payment.

The Tribunal rules unanimously that:
(1) The Claimant is not barred from pursuing his claims in arbitration on account of the lapse of time between his rejection of the Engineer's decision and the formal filing of his Request for Arbitration.
(2) The Claimant's acceptance of payment without protest, reservation or demur of whatever amounts the Engineer certified in his decision does not bar the claims from being pursued in arbitration."

3. This required the arbitrators to decide the effect of the proceedings pending in the Commercial Court of the Y.A.R. on the present arbitration. As to this the Tribunal's decision was as follows:

"Whereas the parties to this dispute have clearly agreed in Clause 67 of the Contract that disputes or differences of any kind have at first to be referred to the Engineer and thereafter to I.C.C. arbitration,

Whereas the Respondent has not disputed the validity of Clause 67,

Whereas the Respondent's case introduced in the Y.A.R. First Commercial Court was commenced on 13 May 1984, i.e., nearly five months after the Request for Arbitration was filed by the Claimant and one day before the Respondent filed with the I.C.C. his Preliminary Objections,

Whereas the letter No. 515 dated 24 October 1984 which the President of the First Commercial Court of Sana'a addressed to the "Chairman and Members of the Chamber of International Arbitration in Paris", cannot be construed as an injunction notified to the I.C.C. Court of Arbitration to freeze arbitration proceedings and similarly not an injunction to the Arbitral Tribunal when notified by the Respondent to it on 26 June 1986,

Whereas the subsequent letters Nos. 61 and 63 addressed on 13 February 1985 by the same President of the First Commercial Court of Sana'a to the Claimant and the Respondent respectively are also not injunctions notified to the I.C.C. Court of

Arbitration and similarly not injunctions to the Tribunal when notified to it by the Respondent on 10 February 1986,

Whereas in any event the said letters are not orders of a Yemeni Court but letters addressed by the President of the Court requesting the parties to refrain from proceeding with the arbitration pending the decision of the Y.A.R. Court,

Whereas an interim decision was made by the First Commercial Court on 9 February 1985 in the said case, which decision was not communicated to the Arbitral Tribunal by the Respondent but came to its attention in the documents supplied by the Claimant on 30 July 1986,

Whereas that decision has nothing to do with this arbitration but is simply refuting two preliminary objections made by the Claimant herein (Defendant in the Y.A.R. Court) as to the Y.A.R. Court's jurisdiction,

Whereas in any event those orders are under appeal to a higher Court in Y.A.R.,

Whereas there is nothing in the case instituted in the Y.A.R. Court that could possibly affect the jurisdiction of this Tribunal,

Whereas this Tribunal does not accept that it is in contempt of any order or ruling made by the Y.A.R. Court,

The Tribunal unanimously rules that:
1. The proceedings pending in the Y.A.R. court have no effect on the present arbitration.
2. The Y.A.R. Court has made no formal orders which have the effect of postponing or stopping the proceedings of this arbitration.
3. The letters emanating from the President of the First Commercial Court of Sana'a are not injunctions addressed to this Tribunal nor to the I.C.C. Court and consequently have no bearing on this arbitration.
4. This Tribunal does not consider that it is in contempt of any order or ruling made by the Y.A.R. Court.
5. This Tribunal considers that it has jurisdiction to hear and resolve this arbitration.
6. All other questions including costs will be dealt with later.

Observations

I. Clause 67 of the F.I.D.I.C. Conditions creates a stage for settlement of disputes prior to proceedings. The Engineer is required to make his decision in a period of 90 days from the dispute having been referred to him. From the time of that decision—or from the time of the expiry of a period of 90 days if the Engineer has not made a decision—the two parties, the Contractor or the Employer, have a further period of 90 days to request that the dispute or disputes between them should be submitted to arbitration. The arbitral tribunal explicitly designated by the clause is the Court of Arbitration of the I.C.C.

In default the decision of the Engineer is treated as final and binding on both parties (except in the case of fraud or irregularity). A request for arbitration which was presented outside the period would not be permissible in so far as the object would be to review the Engineer's decision.

A failure by a party to observe the period of 90 days is, as one can see, full of consequences. It is therefore important to know the exact conditions which must be fulfilled by a party before it can be thought to have decided that the decision should be submitted to arbitration. Is it necessary that during the period of 90 days a Request for Arbitration must be submitted to the I.C.C. Court of Arbitration in Paris or is it sufficient that the party should simply notify the Engineer of its intention of going to arbitration?

In the latter case the Request for Arbitration would be submitted to the I.C.C. at a later date. This question has arisen on several occasions in I.C.C. arbitrations in recent years. Arbitrators have given conflicting interpretations.

First, in Case No. 3790 (see *Clunet*, 1983, p. 910) three arbitrators—in *obiter dictum*—interpreted the clause in favour of the necessity of delivering the Request to the I.C.C. within the 90-day period (see pp. 911–2).

In Case No. 4707 decided in 1986 a sole arbitrator (a Jordanian) sitting in Amman and applying the law of the United Arab Emirates in relation to the second edition of the F.I.D.I.C. Conditions decided that a Request for Arbitration must be presented to the I.C.C. within the period of 90 days in order to avoid the decision of the Engineer becoming final and binding.

In a third case, No. 5029, also decided in 1986, three arbitrators of different nationalities sitting at The Hague and applying Egyptian law in relation to the third edition of the F.I.D.I.C. Conditions arrived at a decision which was diametrically opposed to the other decisions. They decided that a simple notification to the Engineer of an intention to go to arbitration was sufficient to prevent the decision of the Engineer becoming final and binding. (These two last cases were published in *The International Construction Law Review* (1986) 3 I.C.L.R. 470 *et seq.*)

We now have Case No. 4862 on the interpretation of the 2nd Edition of the F.I.D.I.C. Conditions which has been described above.

Finally, in an award published in 1987—in Case No. 5634 (not published) three arbitrators (of Irish and British nationalities) sitting in Paris and applying English law on a clause drawn from the third edition of the F.I.D.I.C. Conditions decided that it was not necessary to submit a Request to the I.C.C. but simply to notify the decision to the Engineer within 90 days.

The arguments advanced for and against the necessity of submitting a Request for Arbitration to the I.C.C. within the 90-day period may be summarised as follows:

Arguments for:
The determination of the fixed period of 90 days has the object of giving means for the prompt settlement of claims. The object of the clause would be completely destroyed if it had to be interpreted in a sense which would lead to delay or to impede the settlement of disputes. The intention of the clause is surely to make arbitration possible so long as the decision of the Engineer has not become final and binding. Otherwise some cases would never be resolved and that cannot be the intention of the clause.

It would result in the adoption of the opposite view that the despatch of a simple telex to the Engineer, without truly commencing an arbitration proceeding before the body designated in the contract, would have the effect of making the decision of the Engineer null and without effect—a situation which is absurd and unacceptable and entirely incompatible with Clause 67 because there would be no binding decision and neither would the case be the object of an arbitration. The authors of Clause 67 would not have envisaged such a situation.

If one of the parties can "require" an arbitration without really commencing it, what is the situation in a case after the arbitration has been "required" but before it has been commenced? The Engineer's decision on the dispute would not be definitive and binding nor submitted to arbitration. Furthermore when would the arbitration commence? There would be no limit at all to the period. It is not in accordance with a clause whose object is to promote the prompt and final settlement of disputes and differences.

The word used in Clause 67 is "to require" and not "to request": this implies that the arbitration will certainly take place. Accordingly, seeing that the Engineer cannot commence the arbitration proceedings how can that objective be obtained by the simple notification to the Engineer or to the other party?

Clause 67 envisages that "the Employer or the Contractor may within a period of 90 days require that the dispute or disputes or differences may be submitted to arbitration according to the methods hereinafter provided". It is envisaged from the following part of the clause that the arbitration will be commenced in accordance with the Rules of Arbitration of the I.C.C. which themselves require the party desiring recourse to arbitration to submit a "Request for Arbitration" to the I.C.C. The date of receipt of the Request by the Secretariat is deemed to be the date of the commencement of the proceedings (see Article 3.1 of the Rules of Arbitration).

It is by virtue of the Request for Arbitration addressed to the I.C.C. that the other party will be "required" to arbitrate (in fact obliged to arbitrate) and that there will be a certain means of settling the dispute finally.

To interpret "require" as necessitating a Request for Arbitration to be addressed to the I.C.C. would be compatible with Clause 67—that is the speedy and prompt settlement of requests.

Arguments against:
In the course of a long period of construction under the terms of a civil engineering contract where the parties become at arm's length, the Engineer's decisions relating to several different matters in dispute can be taken up and contested—for example, those regarding quantities, variations and their valuation, claims arising out of physical conditions, extensions of time, late information, problems of ownership or rights of ways or problems with sub-contractors. If it were necessary to address a formal Request to the I.C.C. to avoid binding decisions, it would be necessary to commence several quite different arbitrations at different times to conform to the fairly strict time

limits set out in the regulations, leading to a multiplication of formal Requests and Answers and (in the case of the 2nd Edition) an embargo on the instruction of the case until the works are completed.

The clear commercial wish of parties contemplating arbitration in a construction contract is to defer the final decision until the results of all the various claims and counterclaims are known, which they will be towards the end of the contract at the time of the final certificate or maintenance certificate at the stage when the negotiations on the final claim usually take place. It is at this stage that the parties will want to review the situation, before deciding finally whether to incur considerable expense and the other disadvantages and risks of undertaking a far-reaching arbitration. The contrary view would insist on frequent formal requests, the payment of several preliminary advances perhaps quite considerable in amount, different time limits for the production of different replies/responses and the possibility, which is not entirely academic, that different arbitrators will be appointed according to the types of dispute which emerge one by one.

We think that the difficulties envisaged by the solution which asks for a Request for Arbitration to be presented to the I.C.C. within a 90-day period are somewhat exaggerated. It is true that since 1 July 1986 each Request for Arbitration to the I.C.C. costs $2,000 payable by the Claimant instead of $500 payable between both parties. Repeated Requests for Arbitration can weigh more heavily on the Claimant's cash flow than one single request made at the end of the contract. However, the more important consideration, in our opinion, is the interests of clarity at all times between the Employer and the Contractor concerning which decisions of the Engineer are to be contested or accepted as binding.

Even where several Requests for Arbitration are submitted to the I.C.C. within a shorter or longer period the parties could appoint the same arbitrators, who could with the parties' consent co-ordinate these Requests in a single proceedings. Provided that the first Request for Arbitration has not reached the stage of the Terms of Reference when the later Requests are presented, the Court of Arbitration can exercise its right to join cases (see Article 18 of the internal regulations of the Court). Attempts to settle can still be made by the parties independently of the fact that one or more Requests for Arbitration have been made. The parties can jointly extend the periods originally provided in the Rules for rendering the award if they wish the first Request for Arbitration to be dealt with at the same time as later ones.

The answer which requires only a simple notification of intention to go to arbitration can weigh very heavily on a party which risks living with uncertainty for years and years, in the worst cases, before knowing definitely whether its opposite number, having made such a notification, is going to decide for or against arbitration procedure. Neither the F.I.D.I.C. Conditions nor any arbitrators in arbitration cases have prescribed the period within which a Request for Arbitration must be presented following a notification of intention made within the 90 days. The question may be asked whether the limit should follow the limitation period which of course varies according to the law applicable. It is not always possible to know in advance which law applies to a dispute arising from an international contract, as the chronicles of I.C.C. awards published since 1974 show.

In September 1987 F.I.D.I.C. produced a fourth edition of its Conditions, including a new Clause 67 which resolves the question raised here. This new edition will be very welcome to practitioners of international construction.

Experience shows, however, that previous editions continue to be used in many contracts long after the date they have been replaced by a new edition. Hence the point in reporting here arbitral decisions on the 2nd and 3rd F.I.D.I.C. Conditions. It is hoped that the case law reported here will alert parties and encourage them either to take the necessary precautions when drafting their contract if it incorporates the 2nd and 3rd editions of the F.I.D.I.C. Conditions or to act quickly when a dispute arises based on the Engineer's decision.

II. For several years instances have become more frequent in I.C.C. arbitrations where a State tribunal issues orders to suspend or stop an arbitration while it is proceeding. In most cases it is a court of the place of residence of one of the parties which, at the request of the party to the arbitration, orders the other party and/or the arbitrators, and/or even the I.C.C. Court of Arbitration to interrupt its hearings while waiting for a decision to be made by the court. Unfortunately, but undeniably, we have to see here a proof of the "proceduralisation" of modern international commercial arbitration.

Such demands arise out of the existence and validity of the arbitration agreement being called into question. When the validity of the arbitration agreement is contested before an arbitral tribunal, it is generally accepted that such a tribunal is competent to examine such a claim and to pronounce judgment on the validity of the agreement and decide whether it is competent or not. It is also accepted, or at least understood, under the law of several States that a party to an arbitration agreement is able to apply to the courts to obtain a declaratory judgment that the arbitration agreement is null and non-existent.

However, if a question as to the validity of the arbitration agreement is raised by the defendant before the Arbitral Tribunal, is it consonant with the spirit of international arbitration at the same time to commence an action before a court of law which raises the same problem?

A party who hopes that the arbitrators will refrain from studying the question and will not pronounce on their competence at the same time as the judges give judgment can easily put a spoke in the wheels of arbitral procedure by launching a court case. Are arbitrators who wait for a legal decision, and who abstain from exercising their right to consider the matter until there is a legal decision, really acting in the general interest of the rapid resolution of international commercial disputes?

If it is accepted that it is consonant with the spirit of international arbitration for a party who has signed an arbitration agreement to contest its validity or existence before a court of law (and I doubt this), then the question arises whether it is equally "good manners" for a party to ask a State judiciary to order the suppression of an arbitration while awaiting judgment.

The New York Convention, in Clause II.3, raises the possibility of a party applying to a court of law about a problem which is already subject to an arbitration agreement, but it goes no further and does not foresee the possibility of injunctions for the time during which the court of law examines the exception of lapse from the arbitration agreement.

If the party is happy just to apply to the law court without applying for an injunction, there is a risk that both tribunals, judicial and arbitral, will arrive at different conclusions, one declaring the agreement to be null and the other that it is competent to deal with the dispute.

It is conceivable that the arbitral tribunal may choose not to wait for the judgment of the law court, even though some people think that it should (see Nordenson in *60 years on—a look at the future,* I.C.C. Publishing Ltd., Paris, 1984, p. 317). If the arbitral tribunal does not accept the decision of the law court which has declared the agreement null, and it is possible to have doubts about the tribunal's obligation to do this when it sits in another country to that of the court, the party risks later complications. His attitude is more easily understood when he asks for an injunction to prevent two tribunals considering the same problem at the same time.

What attitude should arbitrators take faced with an injunction coming from a foreign jurisdiction? Are they bound by all injunctions, and what is the I.C.C.'s position in this respect?

The attitude of the Court of Arbitration varies according to the cases. It examines carefully the extent to which an injunction has a restraining effect on the arbitrators, or one of them or on one or other of the parties, before making recommendations. The final decision is naturally that of the arbitrators, the court does not have restraining powers to force an arbitral tribunal to continue a case where there is an injunction emanating from a jurisdiction on which it depends. The case in question is an example of the methods used by arbitrators. The dispositive part of the award suggests—*a contrario*—that if an injunction in good and due form had been taken by the Tribunal at Sana'a and presented to the arbitrators, they would have bowed to such a decision.

The I.C.C. Court of Arbitration refuses in principle to accept that injunctions are issued against it or the I.C.C. itself. Every time it has happened, the Court of Arbitration has systematically drawn the attention of the foreign court to the manner in which I.C.C. arbitration functions, explaining the role of the court, (which is of an administrative nature) and that of the Arbitrators (which is of a judicial nature). In the opinion of the Court of Arbitration it makes no sense to issue an injunction to the institution of the I.C.C. itself whose task is only to organise an arbitration but not to settle the differences between parties.

Sigvard Jarvin

*I Contract—Building contract—revision of original fixed price—abandonment of site—
     Libyan law and* lex mercatoria—*obligation to co-operate in good faith.*
II Lex mercatoria—Imprévision—*obligation of creditor to take all possible steps
                             to reduce his loss.*

Award made in case 4761 in 1987 *

A partial award was made earlier by the arbitral tribunal in Paris in this dispute between Italian and Libyan parties.[1]

The claimant was a consortium—a legal entity in Italian law formed by two Italian companies—created for the purpose of doing civil engineering work in Libya. The respondent was a company formed with Libyan share capital, to carry out building and civil engineering works in Libya. In 1978 the respondent was appointed to carry out certain building works for a Libyan employer and on 22 October 1978 it subcontracted to the claimant some of the main contract works such as foundations, electrical installations, heating, plumbing, etc.

The parties had stipulated a fixed price in the contract, which provided that the price for the work "would be set for the whole duration of the contract and would not be subject to any revision".

The contract was expressly made subject to Libyan law. The period for completion was 24 months. Payment on account was to be made against the issue of an advance payment guarantee and a performance guarantee.

From the beginning of the works there were considerable delays on site such as:
— delay in issuing import permits by the Libyan customs administration for the necessary materials and tools to carry out the work;
— delay in issuing entry visas for foreign workers by the Libyan administrative authorities;
— irregularities in the plans;
— the necessity to demolish some buildings;
— bad weather;

* This note is based on Mr. Jarvin's note of the case which first appeared in *Le Journal du Droit International* (*Clunet*), and the Editors-in-Chief and publishers of this *Review* are therefore most grateful to Professor Berthold Goldman, the editor, and to the publishers of *Clunet* for permission to use it.
[1] Reported in *Clunet*, 1986, p. 1137.

— difficulties in supplying basic materials such as sand and cement.

In consideration of these difficulties the respondent asked the employer to defer completion for eight months. In the same letter the respondent also asked the employer to approve an increase of 30% of the contract price on the grounds that the price of wood, cement and sand had risen greatly since the contract was agreed. By 1 May 1980 only about 10% of the total value of the works had been completed, which shows clearly the difficulties experienced on site.

The parties met representatives of the employer several times, particularly in October 1980, to try to find a solution which would resolve the difficulties relating to completion of the works. These meetings finally produced a variation to the sub-contract dated 28 October 1980 which provided basically as follows:

— The works were to be handed over on 15 June 1982, i.e. 21 months from 15 October 1980;
— The respondent accepted the principle of a revision of the contract price subject to approval by the employer;
— The respondent accepted that it would procure financial facilities for the claimant to enable it to continue the works.

By a separate agreement on the same day the respondent undertook to give an "official reply" within a period not exceeding two months, to the question of a possible raising of the contract price—which had been admitted in principle, although subject to certain reservations in the variation of 28 October 1980.

After the variation had been concluded in October 1980 the works continued. The variation did not resolve all the problems arising on site and in 1981 the claimant insisted that it was necessary to revise the price. The respondent applied to the employer for the contract price to be increased by 45%. The claimant continued to carry out the works in spite of the absence of any "official reply" as to the possible raising of the price of the works, promised by the respondent in the separate agreement signed on the same day as the variation of 28 October 1980.

In December 1981 the parties agreed a protocol which set out, among other things, that the determination of the increase of the contract price would be effected and paid by 31 December 1982 at the latest. This protocol led in January 1982 to a further variation to the contract. Right up to July 1982 the number of people employed by the claimant on site was somewhat higher than the number agreed in the variation of January 1982. On the other hand, the respondent neither quantified nor paid any amount to the claimants under the heading of price revision; in fact the employer had never accepted any revision of the contract price.

In spite of the facts that the price increase was not fixed and other agreed conditions were not met, the claimant still carried on its activities on site because the respondent stated that this default was due solely to bureaucratic delays.

In July 1982, taking advantage of a holiday period, the claimant evacuated all its personnel from the site, considering that it was no longer obliged to carry out its obligations, since the respondent was delaying carrying out its own obligations to which it had agreed in the variation of January 1982. This decision was not preceded by any formal notice, as the claimant was afraid that, if previous written notice had been given, the respondent would take reprisals against the workers employed on the site. (These fears were realised subsequently, as two people who remained were forced to stay in Libya for 10 and 18 months respectively.) The claimant had completed a little less than 20% of the works when it left the site.

A certificate of payment had been signed not only by the parties' representatives but also by the Employer. All the payments provided by the certificate had been made unconditionally.

After the break in relations in July 1982 the parties met on several occasions in December to try to resolve the situation.

It was then that the respondent invoked the two guarantees given in the context of the contract of 22 October 1978. The banks made the payments which were debited to the claimant's account.

After some attempts at settling the dispute, the respondent wrote to the claimant in July 1983, stating that it repudiated the sub-contract on the grounds of the claimant's actions.

After this the claimant submitted a request for arbitration to the I.C.C. seeking a declaration that the contract was null and void by virtue of the respondent's serious wrong, restitution of any money paid under bank guarantees and an award in respect of all loss suffered. The parties were agreed on the amount due to the respondent from the claimant, consisting of the cost of materials and goods bought by the respondent for the claimant's account, financial advances and projected expenses.

In the partial award made with the parties' consent in 1984, the arbitral tribunal held that the applicable law[2] was in principle Libyan law but that the arbitrators might apply a *lex mercatoria* where Libyan law had not been proved or if it had lacunae or was incomplete.

In this final award, under the heading "law and discussion", the Arbitrators declared that they would apply Libyan laws in the first place, and in the second place *lex mercatoria* and general principles of law. The following is an extract from the award.

> "Each party brought the contract of 22 October 1978 to an end by a free declaration, by invoking a series of contractual violations by the other, justifying the anticipatory repudiation of the contract and payment of damages and interest in respect of loss suffered."

Having established that the parties had agreed variations to the contract after the initial difficulties arising on site, so that there was no need to examine

---

[2] See *Clunet*, 1986, p. 1137.

to what extent certain losses were attributable to the claimant, the arbitrators continued:

"There now remains the matter of the sudden withdrawal from the site on June/July 1982: this action would certainly constitute a motive for repudiating the sub-contract on the grounds of the claimant unless provoked by the behaviour of the respondent, which leads the Arbitral Tribunal to examine the actions relied on by the claimant against the respondent.

The claimant maintains that it had the right to leave the site in June/July 1982 and to repudiate the contract of 22 October 1978 on account of the actions of the respondent by relying on the following matters against its opponent:

— the respondent's failures to carry out the obligation undertaken by the agreements of 28 October 1980, 11 December 1981 and 14 January 1982 to settle the raising of the price of the work and to pay the amount due under this heading.

It is not contested that the respondent did not settle nor pay any sum in respect of any rise in price stipulated in the contract.

In its defence, the respondent alleges on the one hand that this revision of the contract price was conditional on the employer's approval, which was never given, and on the other hand that Libyan law does not allow for the principle of a revision of a fixed price so that any agreement which it might have made for such purpose would have no effect at law.

So far as the first argument was concerned, the arbitral tribunal holds that although it was true that the variation of 28 October 1980 made the respondent's agreement to the principle of price revision subject to the employer's approval, this commitment was undertaken without any reserve of condition in the later agreements.

Moreover, the variation of 14 January 1982 specifies that the principle of price revision 'has already been accepted for a long time by the employer'.

Since the principal contract concluded between the employer and the respondent must be considered separately from the legal relationship between the defendant and the claimant, and that in agreements of 11 December 1981 and 14 January 1982 the respondent undertook unconditionally to determine an increase in the contract price which it agreed to pay within a fixed time, any position which the employer might take as to the principle of revision of the contract price is irrelevant to the solution of the present case.

There remains the second argument drawn from Libyan law: with regard to this the arbitral tribunal acknowledges that while it is true that Article 657, ch. 1 of the Libyan Civil Code does exclude in principle any revision of contract price where it is fixed, subsection 4 of this chapter gives the judge the power to raise the price or to repudiate the contract where the economic basis of the agreement is upset owing to exceptional and unforeseen events arising after the contract was agreed.

This being so, Libyan law, in the same way as other national laws such as German or Swiss law or even the *lex mercatoria* (*cf.* I.C.C. award 1512, *Clunet* 1974, 905; I.C.C. award 2291, *Clunet* 1976, 999) gives effect to the theory of the unforeseen (*imprévision*) which arises from the principle that the rule *"pacta sunt servanda"* is superseded by the higher principle of good faith.

Within this perspective, the arbitral tribunal points out also that Libyan law, just like Swiss and German law, not only stipulates that parties must fulfil their obligations in conformity with the rules of good faith (*cf.* Art. 148, ch. 1 of Libyan Civil Code) but also forbids any abuse of the law (*cf.* Art 5 of Libyan Civil Code).

Art. 657, ch. 4 of the Libyan Civil Code is merely one application of these two principles—albeit interdependent—because it is quite clearly contrary to the principle of good faith, and consequently an abuse, to insist on obligations imposed by the contract on the debtor, if the circumstances existing after it is concluded are so changed that the economic basis of the contract is upset.

Decree/Law dated 6 May 1980 promulgated by the people's committee of the Arab

Libyan Popular and Socialist Jamahirya which the respondent invoked also in support of its argument does not alter the preceding considerations at all. Certainly, Article 104 of the Decree excludes any raising of a fixed price; however, Article 114 tempers this rule by providing for a corrective rule identical in every way to that contained in Art. 657, ch. 4 of the Libyan Civil Code.

Consequently, and contrary to the respondent's submission, Libyan law does not forbid adaptation or revision of a fixed price, where extraordinary and unforeseen circumstances arise; further, in such circumstances, it authorises the judge expressly to raise the price fixed in the contract or repudiate the agreement, and in this is not to be distinguished from other judicial systems such as Swiss and German law, which recognise expressly the theory of the unforeseen.

The result is that an agreement such as the variation of 14 January 1982 which, in Art. 7, makes one party liable to revise the contract price within a specified time and pay the amount of any rise is neither unlawful nor illegal and therefore can be fully effective at law.

The respondent has maintained also, as an auxiliary argument, that such an agreement could not bind it, because even if the parties had accepted the principle of a rise in price, they had not agreed the amount which, when the variation was concluded, was neither settled nor able to be settled.

The respondent seemed to deduce from this that the agreement between the parties was imperfect, because it did not address an essential element of agreement, that is, the amount of the rise. To this the claimant retorted that agreement as to *quantum* resulted implicitly from the letter addressed by the defendant to the employer on 4 June 1981, a copy of which had been sent to the claimant, in which a rise of 45% of the contract price was claimed from the employer.

It is not necessary to decide whether this letter constitutes an implicit agreement between the parties to a rise in price, as it is obvious, looking at the papers produced in the current case, in particular the report on increases in the costs of materials, works, transport and other services, that it was possible to determine the rise in price objectively on the basis of existing statistics and thus was not susceptible to an arbitrary and artificial determination by one of the parties, which could have made the agreement illegal or at least ineffectual.

In other words, supposing that the respondent had proceeded to determine the rise in contract price as it should have done and that the claimant had not accepted it, the case could have been brought before an arbitral tribunal which would have fixed the price rise following objective data arising from statistics and other methods of economic analysis.

In truth the respondent in alleging that the agreement only refers to the principle of a rise is mistaken as to the nature of its undertaking. In fact, Article 7 of the variation of 14 January 1982 obliges it to proceed to the determination of a rise in the contract price within a certain time limit, thus an obligation to perform, that is to say, negotiate or more exactly, co-operate in good faith during the performance of the contract. (*Cf.* Morin, *Le devoir de co-opération dans les contrats internationaux D.P.C.I.*, 1980, pp. 1 *et seq.*; S. Jarvin, 'The Duty of Co-operation in Good Faith in International Commercial Arbitration,' contribution on arbitral case law—Paris Conference, 7 and 8 April 1986.)

By refusing to undertake any step towards determining *quantum* of the rise in contract price the respondent has violated this duty and therefore has become liable.

The arbitral tribunal decides therefore that the claimant's second claim is well founded.

The arbitral tribunal has now to set the amount of damages and compensatory interest to be allowed to the claimant and it will proceed to do this by reference to the principles set out in articles 224 *et seq.* of the Libyan Civil Code, among which must first be quoted that one which provides that the extent of compensation must be determined according to the circumstances and the seriousness of the debtor's fault (art. 224, ch. 1 of Libyan Civil Code) so in this case it is obvious that the respondent was somewhat imprudent in binding itself when it was not in a position to carry out its promises. However, this being said, there was no question of trying to cause loss to the claimant but only an attempt, cost what it may, to collaborate in the hope of completing the two buildings. The fact that, in the course of the building works, the respondent had agreed important advances with the claimant without any contractual obligation, provides the best possible proof of this attitude and if it is to be penalised it should not be too severely done.

The arbitral tribunal recalls also the provision of Libyan law which requires the creditor to take any measures within his power to reduce the extent of his loss (art. 224, ch. 2, Libyan Civil Code: in so far as reference is made to *lex mercatoria*: see awards I.C.C. 2103 and 2142, *Clunet*, 1974; 902, 2478, *Clunet*, 1975; 925, 2291, *Clunet* 1976; 989, 2520, *Clunet*, 1976; 992, 3344, *Clunet* 1982; 978 which apply the same rule)."

Observations

I and II

The award reported here is particularly worthy of note because it is the parties—and not just the arbitrators as is often the case—who chose to apply the *lex mercatoria*.

Lex mercatoria, according to the interim award, should only be applied where Libyan law is contrary to "international public policy" or "the principles of good faith". Further, *lex mercatoria* would be applied where Libyan law had not been proved or was incomplete.

It must be accepted that *lex mercatoria* plays only a small part in this case since the arbitrators arrived at their conclusions on the essence of the case after detailed analysis of Libyan Law; on the one hand, that Libyan law does give effect to the theory of the unforeseen, and on the other hand that it forces the creditor to take all the measures in his power to reduce the extent of his loss. It was not a case where Libyan law was not proved or was incomplete. The only obstacle to its application would be if it were contrary to international public policy or the principles of good faith. By referring to identical solutions in German and Swiss law the arbitrators can be seen to have dismissed a possible conflict of Libyan law with international public policy. At least for the theory of the unforeseen it is said to comply with the principles of good faith.

What of the *lex mercatoria?* Does it add some extra elements which are not to be found in Libyan law?

If there are references to the *lex mercatoria* in the award—which in our opinion would not be essential once Libyan law was proved—is it to emphasise international public policy? If it happened that Libyan law did not comply with the *lex mercatoria*, would it give way to *lex mercatoria*, given that the latter represents international public policy? This would give *lex mercatoria* a priority over Libyan law, which in our opinion would be dangerous. First, because the parties agreed that Libyan law should be applied in the first place. Secondly, because *lex mercatoria* should remain an expression of international commercial practice but should not be raised to a higher status unless the parties expressly wish it.

The hierarchy should not be turned upside down. Even if the English Court of Appeal recognised recently that *lex mercatoria* is not contrary to public policy[3] it still must not be seen as identical with the notion of public policy itself.

Sigvard Jarvin

---

[3] *Bulletin of the Swiss Arbitration Association*, No. 2, 1987, pp. 165 et seq. *Deutsche Schachtbau-und-Tiefbohrgesellschaft mbh* v. *The R'as Al Khaimah National Oil Company* [1987] 2 Lloyd's Rep. 257.

Performance Guarantee—its nature: subordinate security or independent guarantee— intervention by an expert as a condition for calling the guarantee—Refusal of bank to pay.

Award made in Case 5639 in 1987 *

By a contract in September 1982 a European company (the contractor) contracted with an employer from an African country to build a port complex for fishing and ship maintenance for sums amounting to several hundred million francs.

In the contract the contractor undertook to obtain a performance guarantee from a European bank for the benefit of the employer for a sum equal to 20% of the contract price.

In November 1984 a bank issued a guarantee in favour of the employer to secure the successful completion of the works, services and equipment supplied by the contractor. The bank declared that if would stand as joint surety for the contractual obligations of the contractor to the amount of a sum representing 20% of the contract and stated:

> "We shall pay the whole or part of the sum indicated above (and renounce expressly any benefit of discussion and division) on receipt of your written demand accompanied by a report drawn up by an expert from the International Centre of Expertise of the I.C.C."

In addition it was understood that the amount of the guarantee would diminish as the works progressed.

Finally, the bank concluded by submitting the guarantee to the uniform rules for contractual guarantees and accepting that any disputes relating to its interpretation or execution would be referred to the Court of Arbitration of the I.C.C.

Upon completion of the works in 1984 a dispute arose between the employer and the contractor which resulted in a request for arbitration being made on 10 September 1985 with the object of establishing whether the parties had

*   Mr.
Jarvin's note of the case first appeared in *Le Journal du Droit International (Clunet)* and the Editors-in-Chief and publishers of this *Review* are therefore most grateful to Professor Berthold Goldman, the editor, and to the publishers of *Clunet* for permission to use it.

fulfilled their obligations. These proceedings were still taking place when the arbitrators made their award in this case.

The employer for its part made a request on 10 October 1985 to the International Centre of Technical Expertise of the I.C.C. for the nomination of an expert under the terms of the bank guarantee issued in its favour.

By a decision of 12 November 1985 the President of the Centre, having recalled that an expert was only empowered to make findings of fact, nominated Mr. G., a Swiss national, assisted by two consulting engineers. The centre advised the bank of this nomination on 27 November 1985 and the expert informed the contractor at the same time.

The expert began his task, went to the sites, visited several other installations in the presence of managers of the contractor, questioned representatives of both parties and finally submitted his report in April 1986.

In his conclusion, the expert valued the amounts required for completion of all the works to be tens of millions of francs. Further he broke down these amounts into three categories.

By a letter of 21 April 1986 the employer required the bank to pay these sums fixed by the expert by virtue of the above-mentioned agreement.

In a letter of 2 May 1986 the bank replied that it did not question its liability but that it was astonished to receive this demand when arbitration proceedings were already in progress to establish the parties' obligations. Further, the bank felt obliged to make reservations as to the conditions under which the expert's report had been made, adding that there were difficulties of interpretation making it impossible to carry out the guarantee and that the bank had decided to have recourse to arbitration.

An arbitral tribunal consisting of three arbitrators was constituted. The place of arbitration was Paris. According to its request dated 22 May 1986 the bank asked the arbitrators to decide:

"(1) Whether the report compiled by Mr. G. sent to it by the employer on 21 April 1986 was the type of report envisaged by the guarantee.
(a) Whether in fact it should not have been advised previously of the request for the nomination of this expert.
(b) Whether the contractor should not have been party to the setting in train of the expertise procedure.
(c) Whether, therefore, Mr. G.'s report fixing the amount of the sums which he estimates to be necessary for the satisfactory completion of the complex by the employer is capable of being challenged by the contractor on the one hand and by the bank on the other, allowing it to carry out its obligations of November 1984.
(2) Whether, consequently, Mr. G.'s report should be interpreted as being the one envisaged by the letter of guarantee.
(3) Whether, therefore, the bank should pay the amounts claimed by the employer, in spite of the fact that the contractor was contesting the invocation of the guarantee.
(4) By way of subsidiary request, whether it should not suspend any payment while awaiting the result of the dispute existing between the employer and the contractor currently submitted to the Arbitration Court of the I.C.C."

By a submission in July 1986 the employer asked the tribunal to decide:

"1. That the bank's liability only arose on the production of an expert's report made by an expert from the International Centre for Technical Expertise of the I.C.C.
2. That Mr. G.'s report fulfils these requirements, the only ones set out in the letter of guarantee.
3. That the conclusions which the expert reached, taking into account the reversible and irreversible inconsistencies which he had established by examination were the elements necessary but sufficient to enable the employer to bring the guarantee into operation.
4. That the bank's liability was independent of the contractor's.
5. That consequently, the refusal proferred to the employer was improper and dilatory.
6. That the expertise envisaged by the letter of guarantee and brought into play by the employer was quite separate from any other arbitral procedure and/or expertise."

Furthermore it presented grounds for a counterclaim.

"The bad faith and manifestly dilatory behaviour of the bank by instituting arbitration procedure with the sole objective of gaining time and avoiding its obligations should be certified by the arbitrators."

Terms of Reference were drawn up and signed by the parties, specifying that the issue submitted to the arbitration was the interpretation and consequences of the letter of guarantee of November 1984.

Extract from the award

"The bank maintains:
1. If the guarantee which it made has to be considered a surety, its outcome should depend on that of the principal dispute between the employer and contractor which is not yet resolved.
2. If this guarantee is a documentary guarantee subject to the production of an expert's report, the report was obtained in fraudulent conditions thus preventing the employer from relying on it.
3. That the report results in such difficulties of interpretation that it is impossible to carry out the guarantee.
4. That it is not liable to pay the sums claimed, that there is cause to delay payment in any event and in the absence of any fault on its part it is not liable for any damages.

The employer for its part maintains that the disputed report was properly obtained, that it meets the requirements laid down in the letter of guarantee, that the guarantee should be brought into effect to the extent of the sums reserved by the expert, that the guarantee is autonomous and quite distinct from any other procedure; consequently the bank's refusal to pay immediately is unsound. The employer asks by way of counterclaim:
1. Payment of the amount of the reserves estimated by the expert together with interest for the delay from 21 April 1986.
2. Reimbursement of the expert's costs, and costs and fees arising from the current dispute.
3. Payment of 1,500,000 francs to compensate it for economic and material loss suffered."

Reasons given by the arbitral tribunal

A. As to the claim

1. On the issue as to whether the arbitrators are dealing with a subordinate surety or an independent guarantee.

The letter of guarantee is couched in very equivocal terms. On the one hand the bank uses such expressions as "banker's security as to completion", "joint security", "renunciation of benefit of discussion and division", which are characteristic of a surety.

However, on the other hand, the bank undertakes to pay: "on receipt of your written request, accompanied by a report drawn up by an expert." Certainly the bank emphasises three other traits which in its view characterise it as a surety.

In the first place, in fact, according to the bank, if it promised to pay "all or part" of a sum indicated in its letter, that was because this payment would be dependent on the settlement of the principal debt which would become due.

Secondly, it recalled that the guarantee was to be reduced progressively as the work advanced.

Thirdly, the bank said that the insertion of an arbitration clause in respect of any difficulty of interpretation or execution would show that the guarantee was not to be brought into operation automatically.

However, these three points in no way characterise a surety rather than an independent guarantee. As to the first point, the obligation to pay all or part arises simply from the fact that the sum due to the employer might be less than the amount of the guarantee.

As to the second point, the fact that the guarantee was reduced as the works progressed is entirely separate from the issue of whether the guarantee is independent or collateral.

Finally, as to the third point, the insertion of an arbitration clause in order to deal with any difficulties of interpretation or execution does not imply that the guarantee was not independent. On the contrary, if its application had depended on the outcome of the arbitration between the employer and the contractor, there was no need at all to provide for a second arbitration. In truth the reduction of the guarantee as the works progressed was enough to raise difficulties making it necessary to have recourse to arbitration.

Thus there remains the contrast between the phrases "guarantee as to completion", "joint guarantee" and the obligation to pay "on demand".

The arbitral tribunal, forced to make a choice between these contradictory terms, and regretting that a bank could allow such contradictions to exist, considers that in the present case it is faced with a banking guarantee of the documentary type—that is to say independent of the principal liability and subject only to the production of a document.

Further, the bank, when it refused to pay on 2 May 1986, never contended that its liability was subject to the result of a dispute arising between the employer and the contractor, but merely alleged that it was "impossible" to carry out its guarantee. Otherwise, it would be impossible to understand why the employer was obliged to produce a report, if the bank had only been bound to honour the guarantee after the dispute between the employer and contractor had been resolved.

In itself the existence of a report was to prevent an improper call (as the contractor had said in a letter to a subcontractor in November 1984) without being as rigorous for the employer as "strict" proof of loss as the bank proposed originally.

This intermediate solution was, however, more advantageous for the bank and thus for the contractor, than tying up a certain sum in the bank's hands under the form of a stand-by letter of credit.

In fact the ambiguity in the terms used arises from the fact that it was a compromise solution between

— the indemnity (*caution*) *stricto sensu* proposed by the bank in its letter in October 1984 which it is not contested was excluded.

— and the guarantee on demand pure and simple sought by the employer, which was also excluded.

However, the bank continued to use the term "*caution*" in its general meaning of guarantee *lato sensu* and not in its specific legal meaning. It is, therefore, ill founded to claim that the letter of 9 November 1984 is an indemnity (*caution*).

Having held that the bank did indeed agree to give the employer a documentary guarantee, the arbitral tribunal decides that Mr. G.'s report is the condition (set by the bank itself) which brings it into operation.

2. On the issue of whether the expert's report was obtained in fraudulent or irregular circumstances.

This question asked by the bank is only of interest in so far as it implies of necessity the answer which has just been given to the preceding issue, that is that we are concerned with a documentary guarantee.

The report which had to be produced was in no way intended to facilitate or accelerate the outcome of the dispute- between the employer and the contractor—it was intended, as the builder wrote, to prevent any improper use of the guarantee by the employer, by submitting the amount of the sums claimed by the employer from the contractor to the control of a competent and neutral technical expert to bring the guarantee into operation.

This report does not have any legal authority, either with reference to the arbitrators or parties, in the arbitral procedure commenced against the contractor. The contractor did not need to be heard before the report was drawn up since the report has no binding effect on him.

The expert was nominated in accordance with the terms of the letter of guarantee and with the regulations relating to technical expertise to which the letter referred.

Moreover, not only the bank but also the builder were informed of the nomination, the expert met them and listened to them, he had meetings with them and visited the site.

There is no irregularity, even less, fraud, here in the sense understood in case law on bank guarantees. Consequently, the report cannot be set aside.

3. On the issue whether the difficulties of interpretation of the report make it impossible for the guarantee to operate.

This is the essential argument relied on by the bank in refusing to pay. Subsequently, the bank stated that the expert would have made inaccurate findings, that he would have come to an erroneous appreciation of the contract terms and would have made hypothetical conclusions.

On this point also, it is necessary to have regard to what has just been said about the nature of the guarantee; the production of a report from an expert nominated according to the prescribed conditions must in principle suffice, on condition, naturally, that the conclusions of this expert do not contradict the employer's allegations. Certainly, if the expert had concluded that there was no point in any claim, the employer would not have been able to succeed in his request.

Far from that, after detailed research the expert succeeded in calculating precisely the amount of the employer's claims and it is this sum which the employer took up in his request.

In the absence of any obvious or glaring errors on the part of the expert, it is not possible to exercise any control of fact or law on his work. He did not indulge in hypotheses, but he was keen to classify his calculations and valuations in three different categories as though to add, as a matter of duty, that his valuations could be modified if circumstances were to change. These estimates are not in doubt.

Similarly, there is no point in seeing whether the amount of the guarantee could have diminished as the works progressed, because the bank did not make any request on this subject, nor did it present any specific facts which might confirm these allegations. Therefore there is no contradiction, doubt, nor any difficulty which would make execution of the guarantee impossible. No stay of proceedings relating to the execution of the principal contract will be ordered.

B.   On the counterclaim

It follows from this that the employer is right to insist on the execution of the promised guarantee. Further, the bank is obliged to make reparation for the employer's loss resulting directly from its refusal to pay.

On this point the employer is entitled to claim in addition to the amounts fixed by the expert:

1. Interest on these sums for the period from 21 April 1986 when formal notice was addressed to the bank by registered letter, such interest to be calculated according to French law, namely at the rate of 9.5% per annum.
2. Compensation for moral and material loss suffered by the employer therefrom independently of the delay in the execution of the guarantee.

The arbitral tribunal values this—all causes and loss included—subject to what will be said on the costs of the expert—in the sum of 1,300,000 French francs. The employer is not entitled, however, to claim reimbursement of such costs of the expert for which it was liable in any case.

As to the costs of the arbitration (administrative costs of the I.C.C. and arbitrators' fees) properly so called, the tribunal considers the equitable division to be that three-quarters should be paid by the bank and one-quarter by the employer.

Comments

Public works contracts as well as turnkey installations often stipulate that a third person should provide guarantees or securities in favour of the employer as to "completion" of the contractor's undertakings. A recurrent problem is to find a contractual means to protect the contractor from improper dealings on the part of the employer allowing the guarantee to be invoked without having to prove any faults in the builder's execution of the works. Tribunals in different countries have granted little protection to contractors in cases of guarantees being invoked in bad faith, where the contractor has accepted, when the contract was signed, the right of the beneficiary to invoke the guarantee at once and without having to prove any fault on the contractor's part and still less without having to produce an arbitral award or judgment from a judicial tribunal in favour of the employer.

This case indicates the use that can be made of the services of the Centre of Technical Expertise of the I.C.C. in this respect. Other instances have already occurred where the services of the Centre of Technical Expertise (whether or not there has also been agreement for submission to I.C.C. Arbitration), have been used by parties in order to obtain an expert's advice as a necessary condition to invoke a guarantee or bond.

Even if the opinion of a third party has no binding effect on the contractor in his relationship with the employer, the very fact that an expert is to express his opinion on the state of the works discourages an employer from making an ill-founded claim. If the expert does not find any fault in the installation executed by the contractor, it would be contrary to good faith on the employer's part to invoke the guarantee. On the other hand, if the expert holds that there are defects, an invocation of the guarantee could, a priori, not be treated as improper; everything will then depend on the circumstances of the case in question.

It is surprising, moreover, that the guarantee in this case did not even lay down as a condition for invoking it, that according to the expert's opinion, defects in the execution of the work were attributable to the contractor. A simple statement of non-compliance of actual completion and the contract specifications may suffice.

The intervention of an expert, nominated by an organisation which has no interest in the case, can therefore be useful in calming the contractual parties and preventing improper appeals by the employer. But it is also necessary that whoever gives the guarantee, whether a bank or another, should execute its obligations in good faith in accordance with the conditions stipulated in the guarantee which it has given.

Sigvard Jarvin

Arbitration clause—determination of the law applicable as to form, validity and power to arbitrate. Necessity for a written authority signed for and on behalf of the company party to the contract (yes).

Arbitration clause—formation of contract. Existence of an arbitration agreement before the contract was completed (no)—pre-contractual reference in the general conditions by one party.

Award made in case 5832 in 1988. *

Having secured a contract for works to be carried out in a middle eastern country, an Austrian company (the Defendant) received an offer to carry out part of the works from a Liechtenstein firm (the Claimant). After negotiations over several months the Defendant sent the Claimant an "Order Letter" in September 1982 setting out the contractual conditions for the operation and inviting it to indicate its acceptance or, where necessary, to indicate any modifications desired. The Order Letter was signed by two duly authorised directors of the Austrian company and referred to general conditions containing an I.C.C. arbitration clause for the settlement of disputes. Shortly afterwards, (three weeks) the Claimant signalled its acceptance subject to certain modifications but leaving the arbitration clause intact. Finally, in January 1983 the parties had concluded an agreement set out in an Order and Minutes signed by two employees of the Austrian company as well as by a representative from the Claimant company. Making a preliminary award on jurisdiction, the arbitral tribunal (sitting in Zürich) had to examine the Austrian Defendant's defence based on the lack of authority of the signatories to the contract of January 1983, thus rendering the arbitration clause inoperative so far as it was concerned. Prior to deciding this issue, the arbitrators had to determine the law applicable to the arbitration clause.

---

* Mr. Alvarez' note of the case first appeared in *Le Journal du Droit International (Clunet)* and the Editors-in-Chief and publishers of this *Review* are therefore most grateful to Professor Berthold Goldman, the editor, and to the publishers of *Clunet* for permission to reproduce a translation of it.

OBSERVATIONS

Both Swiss jurisprudence and case law as quoted by the arbitrators allow the *lex fori* to be applied to assess the validity of the arbitration clause. This solution can be questioned where the parties themselves have not selected the place of arbitration, despite its being equally recognised by the 1958 New York Convention (article V 1.a) and by the 1961 Geneva Convention (articles VI 2.b and IX.1. a).

However, other criteria could have been considered by the arbitrators. Although recognised by some jurists (in France *cf*. Robert, "L'Arbitrage droit interne, droit international privé", p. 234, n. 269) the law of the country where the contract was completed would only be applied where there were indications that the parties fully intended to submit their agreement to that law. The actual place where the contract is finalised is often fortuitous and any tendency to make it more significant might lead to the introduction of an artificial connection. In the instant case, this rule, referred to as an "alternative solution" is purely and simply put aside by the arbitral tribunal.

In the absence of a choice of law clause, the arbitrators did not have to research whether the substantive law chosen by the parties should be applied to the arbitration agreement. Naturally, an agreement between the parties as to the substantive law would allow the arbitrators to presume that, in spite of the principle of severability of the arbitration clause, both the contract and the arbitration agreement are subject to the same law (for a different solution, *cf*. awards made in case 4504: *Clunet* 1986, 1118, observ. S. Jarvin).

We should note in passing that Article 178 of the new Swiss Federal Law on Private International Law puts an end to the debate as to which law applies to the validity of an arbitration clause. Accordingly, the arbitration agreement will be valid "as regards its substance . . . if it conforms either to the law chosen by the parties, or to the law governing the subject-matter of the dispute, in particular the law governing the main contract, or if it conforms to Swiss law" (Article 178.2, Swiss P.I.L.). Thus Swiss law has accepted the principle of the autonomy of the parties' will and the fall back character of the *lex fori*.

In the present matter the arbitrators decided that the form and validity of the arbitration clause should be considered under Zürich law (*lex fori*). That being so, the tribunal took care to point out that the same did not apply to the issue of an agent's power to sign an arbitration agreement on behalf of a company. This decision should be considered according to the law of the principal (existence of the power) or by applying the law of the place of the deed (extent of the power).

Imposed by the Swiss rules of private international law, this rule led the arbitrators to apply Austrian law both to the existence and extent of the power. Caution is, however, necessary, as the separation of these two aspects may lead to the application of state laws which produce quite different results.

In this case the solution resulting from the application of Austrian law is severe (in favour of such severity, *cf.* R. David, "L'arbitrage dans le commerce international", *Economica* 1982, pp. 270–271). In the absence of a written authorisation to its signatories, the 1983 contract was not binding on the Austrian company. But having recourse to the *théorie de l'apparence* validity, would it not have been possible to find a real agreement justifying the legitimate hope of seeing the dispute resolved by way of arbitration?

Restricted by the position which they took on this crucial issue, the arbitrators examined the period of the formation of the contract in order to decide whether an agreement to have recourse to arbitration existed prior to 1983.

In the pre-contractual dealings between the parties there was already an offer in September 1982 signed by duly authorised managers of the Austrian company incorporating an I.C.C. arbitration clause by reference. However, the arbitrators refused to recognise a final arbitration agreement here in spite of a reply from the Claimant communicating its acceptance of the offer subject to certain modifications which did not bear upon the principle of I.C.C. Arbitration to resolve disputes. Did these modifications address the essential elements of the contract? The award contains an affirmative response: "According to the corresponding statements of both parties the still open dispositions of the contract must be considered as *essentialia negotii* . . .".

Accordingly, the arbitrators considered that the reply to the offer (*i.e.*, "acceptance of the order is subject to modification") really constituted a "rejection of the Order Letter". This interpretation renders the pre-contractual exchanges ineffective ("with the rejection of the order . . . the entire offer of the defendant became invalid, including the arbitration agreement") whereas the reality of international trade seems to favour an examination of the totality of the relations between the parties (*cf.* Y. Derains' commentary on Award 5065 made in 1985, *Clunet* 1987, 1039, and especially B. Haniotiau, M. Demideleer and N. Gerryn "Vers la Conclusion du Contrat: Les éléments caractéristiques de la Convention et les Pouvoirs des Négociateurs" in *Le Contrat en Formation*, Brussels 1987, as well as Kahn's observations on the importance of pre-contract exchanges in "L'Interpretation des Contrats Internationaux", *Clunet* 1981, p. 5). Moreover it can be seen that this restrictive approach has also been adopted in considering good faith, examined from the point of view of a national law (Austrian law) and limited to the problem defined by the arbitrators as "abusive reliance on a defect in the form of the power of attorney".

This leads the arbitrators to a declaration that they had no jurisdiction. In so doing they state that the formal severity of Austrian law excluded any reference to the principle of good faith.

Recourse to the general and a-national principle of good faith by reason of the parties' lack of choice of the substantive law and of giving precontractual exchanges the importance which they merit would certainly have produced a different result (*cf.* E. Loquin, "L'application de règles anationales dans l'arbitrage commercial international" in *L'apport de la jurisprudence arbitrale, Les Dossiers de l'Institut du Droit et des Pratiques des Affaires Internationales*, Paris 1986, pp. 98 and 99: "The needs of international trade give rise ... to the creation of a-national rules which, taking account of the hazards and costs of international commercial operations, impose co-operation in good faith upon the parties whose scope exceeds that normally required by national law in internal operations"; and the award given in case 4381 in 1986, *Clunet* 1986, 1102).

AWARD

In case 5832

1.(a) The Claimant is a company limited by shares organised under the laws of the Principality of Liechtenstein with its registered office in Vaduz (FL). According to the extract of the Register of Commerce its object is the "participation on its own account or for third parties in other companies, financings and execution of fiduciary transactions" and it can perform all businesses which are appropriate to promote the development of the company and the achievement of the company's objects. The Defendant is a company limited by shares organised under the laws of Austria with its registered office in Vienna. According to the extract of the Register of Commerce its object is "Supplementation and preparation of steel, iron and other materials", the sale of "relevant" products, as well as the planning, development etc. of any kind of plants. Both parties are experienced in the procurement and/or installation of industrial plants in the countries of the Middle East.

(b) In accordance with the corresponding presentation of the facts by the parties the Claimant made an offer to the Defendant in connection with the erection of the construction-sections Nos. 7 and 8 of a power station on 1 March, 1982 (Exhibit to the claim, Contract Document, No. 15).

(c) After several months of negotiations between the parties the Defendant finally sent an "Order letter" to the Claimant on 20 September 1982. At the same time the Claimant was asked to disclose possible wishes for the alterations of the offered conditions or to approve the offer by counter-signing it with the signature and stamp of the company. In addition to the detailed establishment of the mutual contractual obligations the Order letter contained a reference to the "General Conditions for the execution of erection work of a power station, Edition February 1982" (hereinafter referred to as "General Conditions"). The Order letter was signed on behalf of the Defendant by Messrs. Dr. J. S. and Dr. P. S. who, according to the corresponding statements of the parties, were authorised to sign jointly by two on behalf of the Defendant. The General Conditions which were declared as an integral part of the Order letter contained an arbitration clause with the following wording:

"24.   *Valid and Applicable Law, Venue/Jurisdiction, Arbitration*
24.1.   All disputes and disagreements arising from, or connected with this contract,

which cannot be settled amicably by the parties to the contract, shall—at the complainant's choice—either be adjudicated by the regular court of jurisdiction at the defendant's location of headquarters, or, disbarring legal action or litigation, by arbitration.

24.2 Arbitration proceedings shall be in accordance with the Rules of Conciliation and Arbitration of the International Chamber of Commerce.

24.3 Place of venue for the Court of Arbitration shall be Zürich, Switzerland. The decision/verdict of the Court shall be announced in Zürich, too.

24.4 The Court of Arbitration shall base its decision on the original wording of the order and—inasmuch as no settlement of the issue can be adduced from this wording—on the *"Schweizerisches Obligationenrecht"* (Swiss Bond and Debenture Law).

24.5 The decision/verdict handed down by the Court of Arbitration shall be deemed final and irrevocable. The parties to this contract shall consider themselves bound to carry out and fulfil the verdict of the Court of Arbitration unconditionally and without delay.

24.6 An appeal to a Court of Arbitration or filing suit with a regular court of law shall not release the parties to this contract from implementing and carrying out their other contractual obligations, which are not subject of the dispute or disagreement leading to litigation or arbitrations."

(d) On 11 October, 1982 the Claimant declared towards the Defendant its agreement to the Order letter subject to the points mentioned in the attached letter: "Our acceptance of the order is subject to modifications as mentioned in the attached schedule No. 1A." (Order Confirmation, Exhibit to the claim, Contract Document No. 3.)

According to the statements of both parties, the contract between the parties was not concluded (yet) on the basis of these declarations, because essential dispositions of the contract (*"essentialia negotii"*) were still left open.

(e) During the mutual negotiations in late autumn 1982, the parties finally agreed upon the remaining open dispositions of the contract. The final agreement and therewith the conclusion of the contract took place "on" or "at the earliest on" 13 January, 1983 on the occasion of a meeting in Linz. Mr. P. representing the Claimant and [eight people] representing the Defendant attended this meeting. The final sentence of the minutes of the said meeting (Exhibit to the claim, Contract Document No. 1) reads as follows: "The above clarification finalises order of Defendant and its confirmation of Claimant."

Mr. P. signed these minutes as well as the Confirmation Order of 11 October, 1982 on behalf of the Claimant. Mr L. of the department "Montage" and Mr. P. of the purchasing department signed on behalf of the Defendant. The Defendant alleged in its Statement of Defence that the two persons signing the minutes on behalf of the Defendant were not authorised to do so. The Claimant does not contradict this allegation.

(f) The points of litigation of the present arbitration proceedings are set out in the following (Terms of Reference) of 21 August, 1987, lit. F; ICC-Rules Art. 13 para. lit. 1 d):

(i) Does the Arbitral Tribunal have jurisdiction to decide this matter?

(ii) Is Claimant entitled to a payment of DM14,705,695.00 by the Defendant?

(iii) Is Claimant entitled to interest payments at the rate of 10% p.a. on the amount of DM14,705,695.00, as from 1 January, 1987 until full payment of the principal amount?

(iv) Is Defendant entitled to (counter-) claims (to be substantiated)?

(v) Costs of the arbitration proceedings according to Art. 20 of the I.C.C. Rules, including recourse of one party against the other for amounts advanced to the I.C.C. Court.

2.(a) The arbitration proceedings are determined by the Rules of the Court of Arbitration of the International Chamber of Commerce, ("I.C.C. Rules"), the Swiss Intercantonal Arbitration Convention of 27 March, 1969 ("Convention") and—to the extent not otherwise agreed by the parties or decided by the arbitrators—by the Code of Civil Procedure of the Canton of Zürich ("ZPO"). For the issue of jurisdiction the Arbitrators are free to deviate from the procedure rules hereinabove and to apply the applicable procedural conflict of law rules.

(b) The Statement of Claim submitted by the Claimant on 16 December, 1986 to the Secretariat I.C.C. Court of Arbitration was considered as complaint in accordance with §§103, 106 and 126 ZPO. The statements submitted by the Defendant to the Court of Arbitration of the International Chamber of Commerce were considered as an *objection* to the *jurisdiction* of the Arbitral Tribunal in accordance with §111 ZPO and Art. 8 Convention.

In accordance with the Terms of Reference the Arbitral Tribunal shall limit the proceedings at first to the question of its jurisdiction. The Claimant was invited by the order of the Chairman to submit its response to Defendant's objection to the jurisdiction of the Arbitral Tribunal in writing. In compliance with this order the Claimant submitted its response and requested:

> "1. The Defendant's objection to the jurisdiction of the Arbitral Tribunal is to be dismissed and the arbitration claim of the Claimant shall be decided on substantive grounds;
> 2. the decision on the jurisdiction of the Arbitral Tribunal shall be postponed until a final decision in the matter itself is reached;
> with costs and attorney's fees."

On the occasion of the oral hearing held in Zürich, both parties maintained their original point of view.

(c) The Defendant substantiated its *objection to the jurisdiction* of the Arbitral Tribunal as follows: that there was no legally binding arbitration clause; that the arbitration clause on which the Claimant bases its claim was not signed in a legally binding way by either the Claimant or the Defendant; that this question has to be decided in accordance with the law of the country which governs the relationship between the principal and its authorised agent; that in accordance with §577 para. 3 of the Austrian Law on Civil Procedure ("AZPO") an arbitration agreement has to be in writing or in form of a telegram or telex; that the object of this formality is not only to clarify and simplify the manner of proof, but also to protect the parties against a precipitated conclusion of an agreement; that if a contracting party is

represented by someone else than its legal representative, the formal requirement referring to the agreement which has to be in writing in accordance
with Austrian law is equally applicable to the relationship between the
principal and the authorised agent; that according to the extract of the
Register of Commerce the Defendant may be represented in a legally binding
way by either two executive members authorised to sign jointly by two or by
an executive member together with a holder of procuration; that the contract
between the parties referring to the construction works on the power station
"was concluded on January 13, 1983"; that the persons who signed the
minutes of the meeting of 13 January, 1983 were not the legal representatives
of the Defendant and that they were not authorised in writing to sign the
arbitration agreement, either; that on the basis of these reasons the arbitration
agreement was not concluded in accordance with Austrian law; that according
to the laws of Liechtenstein a legally binding arbitration agreement has to
be in writing and publicly certified and that the same refers to a power of
attorney; that Mr. P. who signed the Minutes of 13 January, 1983, on behalf
of the Claimant was neither a director of the Claimant nor a holder of
procuration and that a power of attorney in writing cannot be presented;
that, therefore, the arbitration agreement is not valid under the laws of
Liechtenstein, either; that on the basis of these grounds an arbitral award in
this matter is not enforceable in Austria; furthermore, that the arbitral
agreement did not become effective by the release of the Order Confirmation,
either; that up to the conclusion of the contract on 13 January, 1983 the
Defendant was free to conclude the contract with a competitor of the Claimant
and that it had entered into such negotiations; and that the allegation of the
invalidity of the arbitration clause is no *venire contra factum proprium*, either.

(d) The Claimant replied as follows: that Mr. P. had been duly authorised
with a general power of attorney to sign an arbitration agreement on behalf
of the Claimant; that the Order letter of 20 September, 1987 had been signed
on behalf of the Defendant by Messrs. Drs. S. and S. who were authorised to
sign; that the General Conditions which incorporated the said arbitration
clause formed an integral part of the Order letter; that the order of the
Defendant had been accepted by the Claimant with the Order Confirmation
subject to certain conditions which questioned the conclusion of the contract
as a whole but not the valid acceptance of the arbitration clause; that the
issue of the conclusion and the contents of the arbitration agreement has to
be determined in accordance with the *lex fori*; that the form of the arbitration
agreement has to be in accordance with the laws of the Canton of Zürich
and Switzerland; that alternatively, an arbitration agreement can also be
valid, if the formal requirements in force at the place where it was concluded
(Austria or Liechtenstein) are fulfilled; that the arbitration clause had been
accepted without reservation in the Order Confirmation of 11 October, 1982;
furthermore, that the undisputed parts of the contract which also formed a
part of the binding offer of the Defendant of 20 September, 1982 had been
accepted on 13 January, 1983; that this acceptance included the arbitration

agreement to which reference was made; that the formal requirement that the arbitration clause had to be in writing in accordance with the law of the Canton of Zürich had been fulfilled; that further formal requirements did not exist; that both the parties who signed on behalf of the Defendant as well as Mr. P. who signed on behalf of the Claimant had been duly authorised; that besides that the Defendant's allegations of the invalidity of its own General Conditions represent a *venire contra factum proprium* which is against the principle of good faith; that the Defendant is not allowed to refer to the non-existence of a valid power of attorney for Mr. P. who acted on behalf of the Claimant, as only the Claimant can do so; and that an arbitral award handed down on the basis of the said arbitration clause is enforceable in accordance with the applicable treaties in Liechtenstein as well as in Austria.

3.(a) In accordance with the Swiss doctrine and case law, an *arbitration agreement* is not a contract of the substantive law, but of the procedural law (Rüede/Hadenfeldt, *Schweizerisches Schiedsgerichtsrecht*, Zürich 1980, p. 38; Sträuli/Messmer/Wiget, *Kommentar zu §238 ZPO, N. 6;* Guldener, *Schweizerisches Zivilprozessrecht*, 3. edition, Zürich 1979, p. 601; Jolidon, *Commentaire du Concordat Suisse sur l'arbitrage*, Bern 1984, p. 135; Federal Court decisions 103 II 75, 101 II 170, 96 I 338, 85 II 151; *Schweizerische Juristenzeitung* 71, 1975, p. 337). The issue as to which law is applicable with respect to the arbitration agreement is to be decided in accordance with the principles of the Swiss international procedural law which is applicable in the present case. According to the unanimous Swiss doctrine the *validity* of an arbitration agreement is to be decided in accordance with the *lex fori* which is the law of the Canton of Zürich as the law at the seat of the Arbitral Tribunal (Sträuli/Messmer/Wiget, §238 N. 6; Guldener, *Das interkantonale und internationale Zivilprozessrecht der Schweiz*, Zürich 1951, p. 111; Federal Court decisions 101 II 170, 96 I 340, 85 II 151; *Schweizerische Juristenzeitung* 71, 1975, p. 337; *Blätter für Zürcherische Rechtsprechung* 48 (1949) Nr. 78). As far as procedural rules are missing, the rules of the private law are applicable by analogy (Federal Court decision 96 I 340).

(b) In general, the *form* of an arbitration agreement has to be in accordance with the law at the seat of the Arbitral Tribunal. However, in an international case the form may also be in accordance with the law at the place of the conclusion of the agreement according to the principle of *locus regit formam actus* (Sträuli/Messmer/Wiget, §238 N. 10; Guldener IZR, p. 111; Federal Court decision 57 I 303).

According to the main doctrine and case law (Guldener, IZR, p. 111; Federal Court decision 57 I 303) the above-mentioned connecting rule is an alternative solution. According to the law applicable at the seat of the Arbitral Tribunal (which according to the undisputed statements of the Defendant—Statement of Claim pp. 6, 11—is in conformity with the applicable law at the place where the contract was concluded) an arbitration agreement has to be in writing. It is not relevant whether the ZPO of the Canton of Zürich (§238 para. 1) in effect at the time of the possible conclusion of the contract or the convention which is now binding also in the Canton of Zürich (Art. 6 para. 1) is applicable.

(c) Another issue is whether the arbitration agreement was signed by *authorised* persons and in particular, which law governs the authority *for executive organs, employees or representatives* of the company. According to the Swiss international private and procedural law the latter issue is not generally subject to the *lex fori*. Different laws may be applicable depending on whether a representative is acting under a power of attorney for an executive organ or under an ordinary power of attorney and in the latter case whether the relevant issue concerns the existence or the scope of the said power of attorney *(Schweizerische Juristenzeitung* 71, 1975, p. 337). If the representative acted under a power of attorney for an executive organ, the existence and scope of this power of attorney is to be decided in accordance with the personal statute of the respective legal entity (Federal Court decision 95 II 448, *Schweizerische Juristenzeitung* 71, 1975, p. 337; Schönenberger/Jäggi, *Zürcher Kommentar, Allg. Einleitung*, N.145; Jolidon, *op. cit.*, Art. 4 N. 34 c). If the representative did not act in his capacity as an executive organ, but as an authorised agent of the litigant party, the issues referring to existence and scope of the power of attorney have to be separated. The existence of the power of attorney, i.e., the question whether the arbitration agreement had been concluded by a person who was authorised to act on behalf of the principal, has to be decided in accordance with the law of the registered office or domicile of the represented person (Federal Court decision 76 I 338; *Schweizerische Juristenzeitung* 71, 1975, p. 337; Rüede/Hadenfeldt, *op. cit.*, p. 48). The question as to the scope of a power of attorney has to be decided in accordance with the law of the place where the representative concluded the arbitration agreement with the third party, i.e., at the so-called "place of effect" (Rüede/Hadenfeldt, *op. cit.*, p. 49; *Blätter für Zürcherische Rechtsprechung* 48, 1949, No. 78; *Schweizerische Juristenzeitung* 71, 1975, pp. 338, 354; Schönenberger/Jäggi, *Einleitung*, N. 159 ff.; Vischer/von Planta, *Internationales Privatrecht*, 2. edition, Basel und Frankfurt a.M. 1982, p. 191). According to Jolidon *(op. cit.*, Art. 4 c) the issue whether the applicable law governing a power of attorney is the personal statute of the represented person or the statute of effect has not been decided in a final way by the Swiss doctrine and practice (yet). However, Jolidan also tends to agree that the statute governing the power of attorney should be the statute of effect. One part of the doctrine believes that the form of a power of attorney has to be in compliance with the statute of effect (Vischer/von Planta, *op. cit.*, p. 192). Other authors argue that the *lex causae* (of the authorisation) should be the relevant statute, i.e., the personal statute of the represented person (Schönenberger/Jäggi, *Einleitung*, N. 158), but even the latter authors agree to the alternative application of the statute of effect.

(d) The *Defendant* has its registered office in Vienna. Its representative(s) made use of the possibly existing power of attorney in Linz. Therefore, the personal statute and the effect statute of the Defendant are identical, and in either case Austrian law is applicable.

(e) With respect to the *Claimant* the law of Liechtenstein would be applicable as the personal statute (registered office of the company is in Vaduz) and the statute of effect would be either the law of Liechtenstein or Austrian law. The issue which law is applicable in respect of the Claimant need, however, not be decided because, as will be shown below (paras. 4.–6.), the form of a power of attorney, if any, on behalf of the Defendant was not in accordance with the Austrian law. In so far, the decision as to whether the Arbitral Tribunal has jurisdiction or not depends merely on the issue whether the persons who acted on behalf of the Defendant had the authority to do so.

4.(a) The Austrian Code of Civil Procedure regulates the arbitration proceedings in §§577 ff. The provision referring to the form of an arbitration agreement in §577 para. 3 AZPO reads as follows: "The arbitration contract must be in writing or it must be contained in a telegram or telex exchanged between the parties."

(b) According to the undisputed allegation of the Defendant, which is supported by the opinion of Prof. Dr. Wolfgang Jelinek, the formal requirement that (according to Austrian law) an arbitration agreement has to be in writing is extended to the relationship between the principal and the authorised agent, if one contracting party is represented by a person other than its legal representative. The doctrine and case law mentioned in the opinion of Jelinek is clear and unequivocal: The arbitration clause must be covered entirely by the signatures given on behalf of both parties. Should the arbitration agreement not be signed by the party itself, but by an authorised agent, the authorisation to conclude such an arbitration agreement forms a part of the arbitration agreement itself and completes it in such a way that the arbitration agreement cannot be acknowledged as a valid agreement without such a power of attorney. "Therefore, in case a party is represented by an agent, the latter's power of attorney which refers to the conclusion of the arbitration agreement has to be in writing, too, and it has to be submitted to the Arbitral Tribunal," (OHG 3,2,1915, Spruch 250, cited in the opinion of Jelinek, p. 9). As mentioned in the opinion of Jelinek and not disputed by the defendant in a substantiated form this precedent has become the basis of a consistent Austrian case law (opinion of Jelinek, p. 10). Exhibit 5 to the Statement of Defense, a recent decision of the Oberlandesgericht Graz (OLG Graz 20.2.1985, 4 R 28/85, in the Austrian *Juristenzeitung* 40, 1985, No. 130), shows that this practice is still to be considered as relevant.

(c) A tacit or express oral granting of a power of attorney for the agent or the subsequent acceptance of his declarations is not sufficient because it would make void the object of the formal requirements (opinion of Jelinek, p. 13). Neither the proof of a so-called "*Anscheinsvollmacht*" (appearance of a power of attorney) nor of a subsequent approval of the arbitration agreement by the Defendant can—according to Austrian law—lead to a different result. This would also be the case, if the substantive provisions of the contract would have been informally approved (OHG 16.1.1924, ZBI 1924 No. 92, cited in the opinion of Jelinek, p. 13). In recapitulation of the above it can be said that according to the substantive Austrian law which is the relevant law for the Defendant the authorisation to represent another person has to be *in writing* as long as no respective entry has been made in the Register of Commerce.

(d) Both parties agree that the persons who signed the Order letter of 20 September, 1982 on behalf of the Defendant had the authorisation to sign and were allowed to conclude an arbitration agreement on behalf of the Defendant. However, this was not the case for Messrs. L. and P. who signed the minutes of the meeting of 13 January, 1983 on behalf of the Defendant, which fact has not been disputed by the Claimant. A valid submission to the arbitration clause included in its General Conditions by the Defendant may have taken place only, if the Order letter of 20 September, 1982 in connection with the Order Confirmation of the Claimant of 11 October, 1982 formed a binding agreement, but not if this agreement was concluded on 13 January, 1983. The reason *why* the document of 13 January, 1983 was signed by the two unauthorised persons is irrelevant. Due to the fact that a tacit granting of an authorisation is not valid under Austrian law and that a written power of attorney had not been issued, a legally binding effect of the signing of the 13 January, 1983 document cannot be concluded from the conduct of the Defendant.

5.(a) The issue, how the three relevant written declarations of 20 September, 11 October, 1982 and 13 January, 1983 have to be qualified with respect to the conclusion of an arbitration agreement, has to be decided in accordance with the Swiss procedural law and—as mentioned above (4.(d))—if procedural provisions are missing, the Swiss substantive private law has to be applied by analogy.

(b) An essential condition for the binding effect of the arbitration clause in dispute is that the Order letter of 20 September, 1982 in connection with the Order Confirmation—with respect to the arbitration clause—had a contractually binding effect, because—as mentioned above (4.(d))—only the Order letter had been signed by duly authorised persons on behalf of the Defendant (executive organs or holders of procuration). The Order letter of 20 September, 1982 is, therefore, the only relevant declaration for the Defendant in this respect.

(c) The Order letter of September, 1982 may only contain a valid arbitration clause, if

— it could be regarded together with the Order Confirmation as an independent arbitration agreement which, by itself, i.e., independently of the other—substantive—parts of the contract, could have been agreed and was agreed upon, or

— one assumes that a conditional agreement had been concluded—together with the Order Confirmation—which would have been perfected with the fulfilment of the condition, i.e., the conclusion of the main contract on 13 January, 1983; or finally

— the offer—to conclude an arbitration—agreement contained in the Order letter had stayed valid while the contractual discussions were continuing and had been accepted by the counter-party on (or "at the earliest" on) 13 January, 1983.

(aa) According to the ruling doctrine and case law it is quite possible that an arbitration agreement may have an *independent significance* and that it may have an independent destiny as compared to the substantive provisions of the contract (Sträuli/Messmer, §238 N. 9; Jolidon, *op. cit.*, pp. 137 ff.; Craig/Park/Paulsson, *International Chamber of Commerce Arbitration*, New York 1985, Part II §5.04; Rüede/Hadenfeldt, *op. cit.*, p. 75; Federal Court decisions 71 II 116, 59 I 179). It may happen that an arbitration agreement remains valid, even if the validity of the—substantive—main contract which includes the arbitration clause is disputed, for example, because of the absence of a mutual consent (Federal Court decisions 88 I 105, 71 II 116, 65 I 22; Rüede/Hadenfeldt, *op. cit.*, pp. 75 f.; Sträuli/Messmer, §238 N. 9; Jolidon, *op. cit.* pp. 138 f.; Craig/Park/Paulsson, *op: cit.*, §5.04).

In the present case the situation is, however, different. There is no separation of the substantive provisions of the contract from the arbitration agreement. When the question arises whether the arbitration clause has a legally independent destiny from the main contract, the intentions of the parties have to be regarded as decisive. Neither the allegations of the parties nor the documents submitted to the Arbitral Tribunal allow the conclusion that the parties had the intention to conclude an independent agreement on the arbitral judgment of the mutual relationship by the exchange of the Order letter and Order Confirmation and, therefore, *before* they had agreed on the substantive contents of the contract.

(bb) A further possibility which has to be examined is, if the parties agreed upon the conclusion of an arbitration agreement on 20 September, 1982 and 11 October, 1982 subject to the *condition*, that the main contract would be concluded in the future. If this was the case the parties would have agreed upon certain parts of the contract such as the arbitration clause, subject to the condition of a future agreement on the contract as a whole.

Contrary to this assumption the majority of the Arbitral Tribunal holds that generally a comprehensive contract is concluded at the end of contractual negotiations. Only as an exception it may be assumed that individual questions are settled in advance under the condition of a subsequent conclusion of the full contract. For example, if a frame contract which is supposed to be binding for future individual contracts is concluded, or if sureties (guarantees) are agreed upon in view of the future conclusion of the main contract and in respect of the obligations to be secured. In the present case, such an intention of the parties cannot be deduced from either what the parties have alleged or from the documents submitted, and there have not been any allegation by the parties of the like.

(cc) A last possibility is that the offer of the Defendant contained in the Order letter of 20 September, 1982 had *remained valid and open* during the whole period of the subsequent negotiations between the parties and that the order had finally been accepted in a binding way on 13 January, 1983, as far as the arbitration clause is concerned.

According to Art. 1 of the Swiss Code of Obligations ("CO") it is essential for the conclusion of a contract that the parties have communicated to each other their corresponding mutual intentions. For this purpose it is necessary that they have agreed at least upon all objectively and subjectively important contractual dispositions (von Tuhr/Peter, *Allg. Teil des Schweiz. Obligationen-rechts*, Vol. I, 3. Edition, Zürich 1979, p. 183; Gauch/Schluep, *Schweizerisches Obligationenrecht*, Allg. Teil, 4. Edition, Zürich 1987, No. 307 ff.; Schönenberger/Jäggi, N. 84 to Art. 1 CO, N. 2 F. to Art. 2 CO; Federal Court decision 54 II 305). Only if the parties have agreed on all essential contractual dispositions, can a contract be considered as concluded. If the parties have agreed on all essential points, it is to be assumed that a reservation as to the secondary dispositions does not impede the binding effect of the contract (Art. 2 para. 1 CO).

At the conclusion of a contract the declarations of the intentions of the parties are mutually exchanged. The offer of one party to another party which is not present is valid until the offeror can expect an acceptance of it (if no specific period of time had been agreed upon by the parties in accordance with Art. 5 para. 1 CO), if his offer gets to the other party in time and if the acceptance has been duly sent back in time. If this period of time lapses unused the offer is no longer valid unless an intention to the contrary of the offeror can be assumed (von Tuhr/Peter, *op. cit.*, p. 185; Gauch/Schluep, *op. cit.*, No. 365; Bucher, Schweiz. *Obligationsrecht*, Allg. Teil, Zürich 1979, p. 108). The acceptance must be in accordance with the offer, in order that a mutual and corresponding declaration of the intentions, which is essential for the conclusion of the contract, can be achieved. If the declaration of acceptance deviates from the offer, the acceptance is not regarded as an acceptance in the sense of Art. 3 ff. CO, but constitutes, in turn, a new offer (Schönenberger/Jäggi, N. 48 to Art. 3 CO; Gauch/Schuep, *op. cit.* No. 379).

The Order letter of the Defendant of 20 September, 1982 was followed by the Order Confirmation (probably within time limit for such an acceptance according to Art. 5 CO). The Claimant declared in this Order Confirmation that it agreed with most of the dispositions of the offer, but it also clearly and unequivocally declared that this "acceptance" could only be considered as such, if an agreement in respect of the still open dispositions of the contract could be reached. According to the corresponding statements of both parties (Statement of Claim p. 37, Statement of Defence p. 4) the still open dispositions of the contract must be considered as *essentialia negotii*, so that Art. 2 Code of Obligations cannot be applied. One can agree with the parties that at least those open dispositions which referred to the prepayment, the conditions for the falling due of the penalty for delays and the dispositions with respect to the insurance questions were absolutely *essential parts of the contract*. This interpretation is in accordance with the wording of the declaration of the Claimant: "acceptance of the order is subject to modifications" (see

Statement of Claim, Exhibit 3). This leads to the conclusion that it cannot be said that the offer of 20 September, 1982 was basically accepted unchanged on 13 January, 1983 by the Claimant. The Order Confirmation of 11 October, 1982 of the Claimant constituted a *rejection* of the Order letter and—in accordance with the above-mentioned doctrine—a new (counter)-offer to the Defendant. The original offer was, therefore, not—as the law requires—forthwith accepted, but a modified counter-offer was returned which could have been accepted by the Defendant. According to the majority of the Arbitral Tribunal the fact that the—on the occasion of the (alleged) conclusion of the contract—minutes of 13 January, 1983 made reference to the earlier offer and counter-offer of the Claimant does not change the conclusion reached by the Court of Arbitration. With the rejection of the Order letter of 20 September, 1982 the entire offer of the Defendant became invalid, including the arbitration agreement. That the parties did not consider themselves bound any longer is shown by the fact that the counter-offer of the Defendant was not accepted, either, and that the parties continued their contractual negotiations until 13 January, 1983.

In recapitulation of the above it can be said that the main contract between the parties was concluded only on—or "at the earliest on" (which is of no importance)—13 January, 1983 and independently of the offer of 20 September, 1982. As the arbitration clause had no independent destiny, it could have become effective only at that time, too. The possibility that the offer (for the conclusion of an arbitration agreement) contained in the Order letter remained valid during the subsequent contractual negotiations before being finally accepted by the counter-party on 13 January, 1983 must be denied under the present circumstances.

(d) Therefore, it must be concluded that the Defendant did not enter into an *arbitration agreement* in a legally binding way.

6.(a) Finally it has to be examined whether this result is to be considered as against the principle of good faith as the Claimant also argues.

In order to answer this question it first has to be examined whether Swiss or Austrian law is applicable. The issue to be decided is if it is an abusive reliance on a defect in the form of the power of attorney and not if there is an abusive reliance on defects in the arbitration clause as such. *The statute governing the power of attorney* is, therefore, relevant to decide whether a possible offence against the principle of good faith by the Defendant has taken place, i.e., it is Austrian law which applies (Vischer/von Planta, *op. cit.* p. 191; Schönenberger/Jäggi, *Einleitung*, N. 156 ff.).

(b) The opinion of Jelinek shows that a reference to the principle of good faith is excluded under the present circumstances. The reason for this rejection is that the severe formality provisions which are instituted for the purpose of securing a clear and simple manner of proof as well as to protect the parties against the waiver of the procedural guarantees exclude any possible allegation of an offence against the principle of good faith under Austrian law. "The defence referring to the principle of good faith is excluded when the mandatory rule of §577 (3) AZPO is applicable." (OHG, of 11.9.1957; OHG, of 5.6.1935). This description of the legal situation under Austrian law has not been disputed in a substantial way by the Claimant and, at present, there is no reason why it should not be considered as being correct.

(c) Even if Swiss law would be applicable, the arbitration clause could not be qualified as validated by reference to the principle of good faith: according to the predominant Swiss doctrine and case law the allegation of a defect in form may be abusive under certain circumstances, for example if the parties—knowing that there was a defect in form—fulfilled the contract in a legally binding way. Such a situation is, however, not given here. There is no reason to believe that the Claimant did not raise the issue of the invalidity of the arbitration clause immediately when it so realised. A *venire contra factum propium* cannot be detected in the conduct of the Defendant. Under the given circumstances it cannot be accepted that there was a "reasonable trust" (Egger, *Zürcher Kommentar* to Art. 2 of the Swiss Civil Code, N. 36) of the Claimant in the existence of the arbitration clause. Any other case of abuse of rights cannot be detected, either. If a party refers to the protection which is granted to it by a formality rule, there may often be a hardship for the counter-party, a hardship, however, which has been taken into account by the legislatures. Other reasons—such as that the Defendant might have knowingly had the contract signed by non-authorised persons—are not given.

7. On the basis of this result it is no longer necessary to examine the lack of authority to represent on the side of the Claimant as well as the questions referring to the enforcement of the arbitral award.

8. On the basis of these conclusions the Claimant is to be ordered to pay the costs for the arbitration proceedings as well as to pay to the Defendant a—reduced—compensation for attorney's fees.

Accordingly the Arbitral Tribunal renders its Awards as follows:

1. The claim is dismissed for lack of jurisdiction of the Arbitrators.

. . .

3. The Claimant is ordered to pay the costs.

Table of Cross-Referenced Cases

Table de correspondance des références

Case/ Affaire	Award rendered in/ Sentence rendue en:	Reference: (JDI: "Journal du Droit International") ("Yearbook Commercial Arbitration") (I.C.L.R.: "International Construction Law Review")	Obs.:	Collection of ICC Awards/ Recueil: (Volume/page)	
n° 369	1932:	JDI 1974, 902,	YD	I	204
n° 519	1932:	JDI 1974, 892,	YD	I	193
n° 536	1933:	JDI 1974, 901,	YD	I	203
n° 953	1956:	Yearbook Comm. Arb'n III (1978) 214		I	17
n° 1110	1963:	JDI 1984, 921,	YD	I	498
n° 1250	1964:	Yearbook Comm. Arb'n V (1980) 168		I	30
n° 1350	1968:	JDI 1975, 931,	YD	I	239
n° 1397	1966:	JDI 1974, 879,	YD	I	179
n° 1422	1966:	JDI 1974, 884,	YD	I	185
n° 1434	1975:	JDI 1976, 978,	YD	I	263
n° 1455	1967:	Yearbook Comm. Arb'n III (1978) 215		I	18
n° 1507	1970:	JDI 1974, 913,	YD	I	215
n° 1512	1967:	Yearbook Comm. Arb'n V (1980) 170		I	33
	1970:	Yearbook Comm. Arb'n V (1980) 174		I	37
	1971:	Yearbook Comm. Arb'n I (1976) 128		I	3
		JDI 1974, 905,	YD	I	207
n° 1526	1968:	JDI 1974, 915,	YD	I	218
n° 1581	1971:	JDI 1974, 887,	YD	I	188
n° 1598	1971:	Yearbook Comm. Arb'n III (1978) 216		I	19
n° 1641	1969:	JDI 1974, 888,	YD	I	189
n° 1675	1969:	JDI 1974, 895,	YD	I	197
n° 1677	1975:	Yearbook Comm. Arb'n III (1978) 217		I	20
n° 1689	1970:	JDI 1974, 886,	YD	I	186
n° 1703	1971:	JDI 1974, 894,	RT	I	195
		Yearbook Comm. Arb'n I (1976) 130		I	6
n° 1704	1977:	JDI 1978, 977,	YD	I	312
n° 1717	1972:	JDI 1974, 890,	YD	I	191
n° 1759	1972:	JDI 1974, 886,	YD	I	186
n° 1776	1970:	JDI 1974, 886,	YD	I	186
n° 1782	1973:	JDI 1975, 923,	YD	I	230
n° 1784	1975:	Yearbook Comm. Arb'n II (1977) 150		I	10
n° 1803	1972:	Yearbook Comm. Arb'n V (1980) 177		I	40
n° 1837	1971:	JDI 1979, 988,	YD	I	346
n° 1840	1972:	Yearbook Comm. Arb'n IV (1979) 209		I	27

Case/ Affaire	Award rendered in/ Sentence rendue en:	Reference: (JDI: "Journal du Droit International") ("Yearbook Commercial Arbitration") (I.C.L.R.: "International Construction Law Review")	Obs.:	Collection of ICC Awards/ Recueil: (Volume/page)	
n°1850	1972:	JDI 1974, 910,	YD	I	213
n°1939	1971:	JDI 1974, 919,	YD	I	222
n°1990	1972:	JDI 1974, 897,	YD	I	199
		Yearbook Comm. Arb'n III (1978) 217		I	20
n°2068	1973:	JDI 1974, 892,	YD	I	193
n°2073	1972:	JDI 1975, 932,	YD	I	240
n°2074	1973:	JDI 1975, 924,	YD	I	232
n°2090	1976:	Yearbook Comm. Arb'n VI (1981) 131		I	56
n°2096	1972:	JDI 1974, 886,	YD	I	186
n°2103	1972:	JDI 1974, 902,	YD	I	204
		Yearbook Comm. Arb'n III (1978) 218		I	21
n°2114	1972:	Yearbook Comm. Arb'n V (1980) 186		I	49
n°2119	1978:	JDI 1979, 997,	YD	I	355
n°2129	1972:	Yearbook Comm. Arb'n III (1978) 219		I	23
n°2136	1974:	JDI 1982, 993,	YD	I	456
n°2138	1974:	JDI 1975, 934,	YD	I	242
n°2139	1974:	JDI 1975, 929,	YD	I	237
		Yearbook Comm. Arb'n III (1978) 220		I	23
n°2142	1974:	JDI 1974, 892,	RT	I	194
		Yearbook Comm. Arb'n I (1976) 132		I	7
n°2216	1974:	JDI 1975, 917,	YD	I	224
n°2249	1973:	JDI 1975, 924,	YD	I	231
n°2272	1975:	Yearbook Comm. Arb'n II (1977) 151		I	11
n°2291	1975:	JDI 1976, 989,	YD	I	274
n°2321	1974:	JDI 1975, 938,	YD	I	246
		Yearbook Comm. Arb'n I (1976) 133		I	8
n°2347	1979:	JDI 1980, 961,	YD	I	376
n°2374	1972:	JDI 1978, 997,	YD	I	333
n°2375	1975:	JDI 1976, 973,	YD	I	257
n°2376	1976:	JDI 1977, 949,	YD	I	303
n°2391	1976:	JDI 1977, 949,	YD	I	302
n°2404	1975:	JDI 1976, 995,	YD	I	280
n°2438	1975:	JDI 1976, 969,	YD	I	253
n°2443	1975:	JDI 1976, 991,	YD	I	276

Case/ Affaire	Award rendered in/ Sentence rendue en:	Reference: (JDI: "Journal du Droit International") ("Yearbook Commercial Arbitration") (I.C.L.R.: "International Construction Law Review")	Obs.:	Collection of ICC Awards/ Recueil: (Volume/page)	
n°2444	1976:	JDI 1977, 932,	YD	I	285
n°2462	1974:	JDI 1975, 925,	YD	I	232
n°2476	1976:	JDI 1977, 936,	YD	I	289
n°2478	1974:	JDI 1975, 925,	YD	I	233
		Yearbook Comm. Arb'n III (1978) 222		I	25
n°2502	1977:	JDI 1978, 989,	YD	I	325
n°2508	1976:	JDI 1977, 939,	YD	I	292
n°2520	1975:	JDI 1976, 992,	YD	I	278
n°2521	1975:	JDI 1976, 997,	YD	I	282
n°2540	1976:	JDI 1977, 943,	YD	I	296
n°2546	1976:	JDI 1977, 945,	YD	I	299
n°2558	1976:	JDI 1977, 952,	YD	I	306
n°2559	1976:	JDI 1977, 949,	YD	I	302
n°2583	1976:	JDI 1977, 950,	YD	I	304
n°2585	1977:	JDI 1978, 998,	YD	I	334
n°2602	1976:	JDI 1977, 949,	YD	I	303
n°2605	1977:	JDI 1978, 989,	YD	I	325
n°2626	1977:	JDI 1978, 981,	YD	I	316
n°2637	1975:	Yearbook Comm. Arb'n II (1977) 153		I	13
n°2654	1976:	JDI 1977, 949,	YD	I	303
n°2673	1976:	JDI 1977, 947,	YD	I	301
n°2680	1977:	JDI 1978, 997,	YD	I	334
n°2689	1977:	JDI 1978, 998,	YD	I	335
n°2694	1977:	JDI 1978, 985,	YD	I	320
n°2699	1976:	JDI 1977, 945,	YD	I	299
n°2708	1976:	JDI 1977, 943,	YD	I	297
n°2730	1982:	JDI 1984, 914,	YD	I	490
n°2734	1972:	JDI 1978, 997,	YD	I	333
n°2735	1976:	JDI 1977, 947,	YD	I	301
n°2745	1977:	JDI 1978, 990,	YD	I	326
n°2762	1977:	JDI 1978, 990,	YD	I	326
n°2763	1980:	Yearbook Comm. Arb'n X (1985) 43		I	157
n°2795	1977:	Yearbook Comm. Arb'n IV (1979) 210		I	28
n°2801	1976:	JDI 1977, 949,	YD	I	303

Case/	Award rendered in/	Reference: (JDI: "Journal du Droit International")	Obs.:	Collection of ICC Awards/
Affaire	Sentence rendue en:	("Yearbook Commercial Arbitration") (I.C.L.R.: "International Construction Law Review")		Recueil: (Volume/page)

n°2811	1978:	JDI 1979, 984,	YD	I 341
n°2879	1978:	JDI 1979, 989,	YD	I 346
n°2886	1977:	JDI 1978, 996,	YD	I 332
n°2930	1982:	Yearbook Comm. Arb'n IX (1984) 105		I 118
n°2977	1978:	Yearbook Comm. Arb'n VI (1981) 133		I 58
n°2978	1978:	Yearbook Comm. Arb'n VI (1981) 133		I 58
n°3031	1977:	JDI 1978, 999,	YD	I 335
n°3033	1978:	Yearbook Comm. Arb'n VI (1981) 133		I 58
n°3043	1978:	JDI 1979, 1000,	YD	I 358
n°3055	1980:	JDI 1981, 937,	YD	I 422
n°3086	1977:	JDI 1978, 996,	YD	I 332
n°3093	1979:	JDI 1980, 951,	YD	I 365
n°3099	1979:	Yearbook Comm. Arb'n VII (1982) 87		I 67
n°3100	1979:	JDI 1980, 951,	YD	I 365
		Yearbook Comm. Arb'n VII (1982) 87		I 67
n°3130	1980:	JDI 1981, 932,	YD	I 417
n°3131	1979:	JDI 1981, 922,	YD	I 407
		Yearbook Comm. Arb'n IX (1984) 109		I 122
n°3202	1978:	JDI 1979, 1003,	YD	I 362
n°3226	1979:	JDI 1980, 959,	YD	I 374
n°3235	1980:	JDI 1981, 925,	YD	I 410
n°3243	1981:	JDI 1982, 968,	YD	I 429
n°3267	1979:	JDI 1980, 962,	YD	I 376
		Yearbook Comm. Arb'n VII (1982) 96		I 76
	1984:	Yearbook Comm. Arb'n XII (1987) 87		II 43
n°3281	1981:	JDI 1982, 990,	YD	I 453
n°3292	1980:	JDI 1981, 924,	YD	I 409
n°3316	1979:	JDI 1980, 970,	YD	I 385
		Yearbook Comm. Arb'n VII (1982) 106		I 87
n°3327	1981:	JDI 1982, 971,	YD	I 433
n°3344	1981:	JDI 1982, 978,	YD	I 440
n°3380	1980:	JDI 1981, 928,	YD	I 413
		Yearbook Comm. Arb'n VII (1982) 116		I 96
n°3383	1979:	JDI 1980, 978,	YD	I 394

Case/	Award rendered in/	Reference: (JDI: "Journal du Droit International")	Obs.:	Collection of ICC Awards/
Affaire	Sentence rendue en:	("Yearbook Commercial Arbitration") (I.C.L.R.: "International Construction Law Review")		Recueil: (Volume/page)

		Yearbook Comm. Arb'n VII (1982) 119		I 100
n°3460	1980:	JDI 1981, 939,	YD	I 425
n°3472	1982:	JDI 1983, 895,	YD	I 461
n°3493	1983:	Yearbook Comm. Arb'n IX (1984) 111		I 124
n°3515	1980:	JDI 1981, 938,	YD	I 424
n°3540	1980:	JDI 1981, 915,	YD	I 399
		Yearbook Comm. Arb'n VII (1982) 124		I 105
n°3572	1982:	Yearbook Comm. Arb'n XIV (1989) 110		II 154
n°3742	1983:	JDI 1984, 910,	YD	I 486
n°3779	1981:	Yearbook Comm. Arb'n IX (1984) 124		I 138
n°3790	1983:	JDI 1983, 910,	SJ	I 476
		Yearbook Comm. Arb'n IX (1984) 119		II 3
		(1983) 1 I.C.L.R. 372	SJ	II 445
n°3820	1981:	Yearbook Comm. Arb'n VII (1982) 134		I 115
n°3879	1984:	Yearbook Comm. Arb'n XI (1986) 127		II 11
n°3880	1983:	JDI 1983, 897,	YD/SJ	I 462
		Yearbook Comm. Arb'n X (1985) 44		I 159
n°3881	1984:	JDI 1986, 1096,	SJ	II 257
n°3894	1981:	JDI 1982, 987,	YD	I 449
n°3896	1982:	JDI 1983, 914,	SJ	I 481
		Yearbook Comm. Arb'n X (1985) 47		I 161
n°3902	1984:	(1984) 2 I.C.L.R. 49	SJ	II 450
n°3913	1981:	JDI 1984, 92O,	YD	I 497
n°3916	1982:	JDI 1984, 930,	SJ	I 507
n°3938	1982:	JDI 1984, 926,	SJ	I 503
n°3987	1983:	JDI 1984, 943,	YD	I 521
n°4023	1984:	JDI 1984, 950,	SJ	I 528
n°4126	1984:	JDI 1984, 934,	SJ	I 511
n°4131	1982:	JDI 1983, 899,	YD	I 465
		Yearbook Comm. Arb'n IX (1984) 131		I 146
n°4132	1983:	JDI 1983, 891,	YD	I 456
		Yearbook Comm. Arb'n X (1985) 49		I 164
n°4145	1983:	Yearbook Comm. Arb'n XII (1987) 97		II 53
	1984:	JDI 1985, 985,	YD	I 559

Case/ Affaire	Award rendered in/ Sentence rendue en:	Reference: (JDI: "Journal du Droit International") ("Yearbook Commercial Arbitration") (I.C.L.R.: "International Construction Law Review")	Obs.:	Collection of ICC Awards/ Recueil: (Volume/page)	
		Yearbook Comm. Arb'n XII (1987) 97		II	53
	1986:	Yearbook Comm. Arb'n XII (1987) 97		II	53
n°4156	1983:	JDI 1984, 937,	SJ	I	515
n°4187	1982:	JDI 1983, 895,	YD	I	460
n°4237	1984:	Yearbook Comm. Arb'n X (1985) 52		I	167
n°4265	1984:	JDI 1984, 922,	YD	I	499
n°4338	1984:	JDI 1985, 982,	YD	I	555
n°4367	1984:	Yearbook Comm. Arb'n XI (1986) 134		II	18
n°4381	1986:	JDI 1986, 1103,	YD	II	264
n°4392	1983:	JDI 1983, 9O7,	YD	I	473
n°44O2	1983:	Yearbook Comm. Arb'n IX (1984) 138		I	153
n°4415	1984:	JDI 1984, 952,	SJ	I	530
n°4416	1985:	JDI 1985, 969,	SJ	I	542
		(1986) 3 I.C.L.R. 67	SJ	II	460
n°4434	1983:	JDI 1983, 893,	YD	I	458
n°4467	1984:	JDI 1984, 924,	X	I	501
n°4472	1984:	JDI 1984, 946,	SJ	I	525
n°4491	1984:	JDI 1985, 966,	SJ	I	539
n°4504	1985:	JDI 1986, 1118,	SJ	II	279
	1986:	JDI 1986, 1118,	SJ	II	279
n°4555	1985:	JDI 1985, 964,	SJ	I	536
		Yearbook Comm. Arb'n XI (1986) 140		II	4
n°4567	1984:	Yearbook Comm. Arb'n XI (1986) 143		II	27
	1985:	Yearbook Comm. Arb'n XI (1986) 143		II	27
n°4589	1984:	Yearbook Comm. Arb'n XI (1986) 148		II	32
		(1985) 2 I.C.L.R. 298	SJ	II	454
n°4604	1984:	JDI 1985, 973,	YD	I	546
n°4650	1985:	Yearbook Comm. Arb'n XII (1987) 111		II	67
n°4667	1984:	JDI 1987, 1047,	YD	II	338
	1985:	JDI 1986, 1136,	YD	II	297
n°4695	1984:	Yearbook Comm. Arb'n XI (1986) 149		II	33
n°4707	1986:	(1986) 3 I.C.L.R. 470	SJ	II	477
n°4761	1984:	JDI 1986, 1137,	SJ	II	298
	1987:	JDI 1987, 1012,	SJ	II	302

Case/ Affaire	Award rendered in/ Sentence rendue en:	Reference: (JDI: "Journal du Droit International") ("Yearbook Commercial Arbitration") (I.C.L.R.: "International Construction Law Review")	Obs.:	Collection of ICC Awards/ Recueil: (Volume/page)	
		(1989) 6 I.C.L.R. 330	SJ	II	519
n°4840	1986:	(1986) 3 I.C.L.R. 277	SJ	II	465
n°4862	1986:	JDI 1987, 1018,	SJ	II	309
		(1989) 6 I.C.L.R. 44	SJ	II	508
n°4972	1989:	JDI 1989, 1101,	GAA	II	380
n°4975	1988:	Yearbook Comm. Arb'n XIV (1989) 122		II	165
n°4996	1985:	JDI 1986, 1132,	YD	II	293
n°4998	1985:	JDI 1986, 1139,	SJ	II	300
n°5029	1986:	Yearbook Comm. Arb'n XII (1987) 113		II	69
		(1986) 3 I.C.L.R. 473	SJ	II	480
n°5065	1986:	JDI 1987, 1039,	YD	II	330
n°5073	1986:	Yearbook Comm. Arb'n XIII (1988) 53		II	85
n°5080	1985:	Yearbook Comm. Arb'n XII (1987) 124		II	80
n°5103	1988:	JDI 1988, 1207,	GAA	II	361
n°5117	1986:	JDI 1986, 1113,	YD	II	274
n°5118	1986:	JDI 1987, 1027,	SJ	II	318
n°5195	1986:	Yearbook Comm. Arb'n XIII (1988) 69		II	101
n°5269	1986:	JDI 1987, 1029,	SJ	II	320
n°5277	1987:	Yearbook Comm. Arb'n XIII (1988) 80		II	112
n°5294	1988:	Yearbook Comm. Arb'n XIV (1989) 137		II	180
n°5333	1986:	(1987) 4 I.C.L.R. 321	SJ	II	495
n°5418	1987:	Yearbook Comm. Arb'n XIII (1988) 91		II	123
n°5423	1987:	JDI 1987, 1048,	SJ	II	339
n°5428	1988:	Yearbook Comm. Arb'n XIV (1989) 146		II	189
n°5460	1987:	Yearbook Comm. Arb'n XIII (1988) 104		II	136
n°5477	1988:	JDI 1988, 1204,	GAA	II	358
n°5485	1987:	Yearbook Comm. Arb'n XIV (1989) 156		II	199
n°5505	1987:	Yearbook Comm. Arb'n XIII (1988) 110		II	142
n°5625	1987:	(1987) 4 I.C.L.R. 239	SJ	II	484
n°5639	1987:	JDI 1987, 1054,	SJ	II	345
		(1989) 6 I.C.L.R. 417	SJ	II	526
n°5649	1987:	Yearbook Comm. Arb'n XIV (1989) 174		II	217
n°5713	1989:	Yearbook Comm. Arb'n XV (1990) 70		II	223
n°5721	1990:	JDI 1990, 1020,	X	II	400

557

Case/	Award rendered in/	Reference: (JDI: "Journal du Droit International")	Obs.:	Collection of ICC Awards/	
Affaire	Sentence rendue en:	("Yearbook Commercial Arbitration") (I.C.L.R.: "International Construction Law Review")		Recueil: (Volume/page)	
n°5730	1988:	JDI 1990, 1029,	X	II	410
n°5779	1988:	JDI 1988, 1206,	GAA	II	360
n°5832	1988:	JDI 1988, 1198,	GAA	II	352
		(1990) 7 I.C.L.R. 421	GAA	II	533
n°5904	1989:	JDI 1989, 1107,	GAA	II	387
n°5910	1988:	JDI 1988, 1216,	YD	II	371
n°5953	1989:	JDI 1990, 1056,	YD	II	437
n°5989	1989:	Yearbook Comm. Arb'n XV (1990) 74		II	227
n°6076	1989:	Yearbook Comm. Arb'n XV (1990) 83		II	236
n°6142	1990:	JDI 1990, 1039,	YD	II	420
n°6219	1990:	JDI 1990, 1047,	YD	II	427
n°6281	1989:	JDI 1989, 1114,	GAA	II	394
		Yearbook Comm. Arb'n XV (1990) 96		II	249

GAA: Guillermo Aguilar Alvarez
RT: Robert Thompson
SJ: Sigvard Jarvin
YD: Yves Derains

Statistics

Statistiques

Statistics / Statistiques

Number of requests for arbitration (per year)/
Nombre de demandes d'arbitrage (par an):

1977	1978	1979	1980	1981	1982	1983	1984	1985	1986	1987	1988	1989	1990
205	235	285	250	262	267	291	296	339	334	285	304	309	365

Arbitrators, nationalities/
Arbitres, nationalités représentées:

1980	1981	1982	1983	1984	1985	1986	1987	1988	1989	1990
34	25	38	38	38	49	46	44	44	41	49

Number of Arbitrators in ICC Cases/
Nombre d'arbitres dans les affaires CCI:

(Pourcentages)	1980	1981	1982	1983	1984	1985	1986	1987	1988	1989	1990
Three Arbitrators/ Trois arbitres:	-	55	47	58	64	57	58	62	62,1	62,3	58,3
Sole Arbitrator/ Arbitre unique:	-	45	53	42	36	43	42	38	37,9	37,7	41,7

Seats of arbitration (number of countries)/
Siège de l'arbitrage (nombre de pays):

1980	1981	1982	1983	1984	1985	1986	1987	1988	1989	1990
21	31	20	23	29	31	29	24	31	32	29

Place of Arbitration/
Lieu de l'arbitrage

(Pourcentages)	1980	1981	1982	1983	1984	1985	1986	1987	1988	1989	1990
Place fixed by the Court/ Lieu fixé par la Cour:	46,8	47,6	37,4	33,3	18,5	32,1	19,5	22,1	20,6	14	13,8
Place confirmed by the Court/ Lieu confirmé par la Cour:	53,2	52,4	62,6	66,7	81,5	67,9	80,5	77,9	79,4	86	86,2

Statistics/statistiques

Origin of the Parties/
Origine des parties:

(Pourcentages)	1980	1981	1982	1983	1984	1985	1986	1987	1988	1989	1990
Western Europe/ Europe occidentale:	60	63,5	62	57,2	56,9	52,5	54,9	56,5	57,1	56,2	59,8
Central & Eastern Europe/ Europe centrale et orientale:	8	2,4	5,8	3,8	4,1	2,6	3,5	3,7	4,2	2,2	2,3
Middle East/ Moyen Orient:	10	6,6	5,8	8	7,4	5,9	7,4	4	5,1	5,1	4,3
North Africa/ Afrique du Nord:	5	4,8	3,9	5,1	6,6	5,6	6,2	6,2	4,3	4,4	3
Africa/ Afrique:	2	4,4	2,5	3,1	3	4,2	3,2	4	5,5	5,5	2,2
North America/ Amérique du Nord:	10	7	9,1	12,5	10,5	15,3	15	13,5	13,1	12,9	14,9
Latin America & Caribbean/ Amérique Latine et Caraïbes:	2	3,7	5,8	3,4	4,9	4,2	3,5	3,8	4,1	4,4	2,3
Asia & Oceania/ Asie et Océanie:	3	7,6	5,2	6,9	6,6	9,7	6,3	8,4	6,6	9,3	11,2

Parties (number of Nationalities/
nombre de nationalités représentées):

1980	1981	1982	1983	1984	1985	1986	1987	1988	1989	1990
61	75	60	80	70	81	89	77	86	90	94

Number of Cases involving more than Two Parties/
Nombre d'affaires impliquant plus de deux parties:

(Pourcentages)	1980	1981	1982	1983	1984	1985	1986	1987	1988	1989	1990
	-	-	-	18	24	20	22	19	22,6	38	21

Repartition by Economic Sectors/
Répartition par secteur économique:

(Pourcentages)	1980	1981	1982	1983	1984	1985	1986	1987	1988	1989	1990
Foreign Trade: Commerce extérieur:	-	-	37,3	31,5	33,3	33	35	31,8	26	26	27,1
Licences/Transfer of Technology/ High Technology/Patent: Licences/transfert de technologie/ technique de pointe/brevets:	-	-	8,6	10	7,8	13	11	13,3	17	18	16,4

562

			1980	1981	1982	1983	1984	1985	1986	1987	1988	1989	1990
Joint Ventures & Industrial Cooperation: Joint ventures et coopération industrielle:	-	-	12,7	11,9	14,1	5	8	4,7	2,4	5,4	6,5		
Agency & Distribution: Agence et distribution:	-	-	6	5,1	8,3	7	7	14	10,7	13	17,1		
Construction:	-	-	17,1	25,3	28,7	28	24	18,5	26,4	21	18,9		
Finance & Banking: Finances et banque:	-	-	7,&	0,9	4,2	1	4	6	5,2	6	5,8		
Others*: Autres*:	-	-	11,2	15,3	3,6	13	11	11,6	12,3	10,6	8,2		

Amounts in dispute/
Montants en litige:

(Pourcentages)	1980	1981	1982	1983	1984	1985	1986	1987	1988	1989	1990
Less than/ Moins de $50 000:	-	9,2	8,2	10,5	8,6	12,8	6,1	3,8	5,8	5	4
From -- to/ De $50 000 à $200 000:	-	22	22	20	19,5	14,8	11,2	13,9	15,1	14,5	12,5
From -- to/ De $200 000 à 1 million:	-	29,5	32,1	30	26,2	24,4	23,8	24,4	20,6	25,5	30
From -- to/ De $1 million à 10 millions:	-	31,3	24,4	31	25,7	28	31,4	33	39,9	34,1	30
More than/ Plus de 10 millions:	-	8	13,3	8,5	13,8	13,6	9,8	8,4	7,4	12,7	11,3
Unspecified amount/ Montant non spécifié:	-	-	-	-	6,2	6,4	17,7	16,5	11,2	8,2	12,2

(* Maritime Transportation, Employment, etc.)
Transport maritime, emploi, etc.)

Key word indexes

Index des mots-clés

Key-word index, English

567

Key-word in English	_Corresponding notion in French_
Changed circumstances	Changement de circonstances
Claim	Demande
Company	Société
Competence of arbitrator	Compétence de l'arbitre
Competence-competence	Compétence-compétence
Competition	Concurrence
Concordat on Arbitration	Concordat Suisse sur l'Arbitrage
Concurrent Court proceedings	Connexité, litispendance
Conflict of law rules	Conflit de lois
Construction contract	Contrat de construction
Contract	Contrat
Costs of Arbitration	Frais de l'Arbitrage
Damages	Dommages-intérêts, préjudice
Delay	Retard
Delivery	Livraison
Depreciation	Dévalorisation
Devaluation	Dévaluation
Dissolution of party during arbitration	Faillite d'une partie à l'arbitrage, liquidation
Distributorship contract	Contrat de distribution, de représentation
Engineer	FIDIC
Equity	Amiable composition
Error _in contrahendo_	_Culpa in contrahendo_
Estoppel	_Venire contra factum proprium (Nemo auditur turpitudinem suam allegans)_
European Economic Community	Traité de la CEE
Ex aequo et bono	_Ex aequo et bono_
Exceptio non adimpleti contractus	_Exceptio non adimpleti contractus_
Exchange losses	Risque de change
Expatriate staff	Personnel
Expert	Expert technique
Fait du Prince	Fait du Prince
FIDIC	FIDIC
First demand guarantee	Garantie bancaire
Force majeure	Force majeure, 'Frustration'
Foreign exhange regulations	Contrôle des changes

Key-word in English	Corresponding notion in French
Frustration	*Force majeure*, 'Frustration'
General conditions (of sale)	Conditions générales (de ventes)
General principles of Law	Principes généraux du Droit
General principles of International Law	Principes de portée internationale
Geneva Convention	Convention européenne de Genève
Good faith	Bonne foi; obligation de coopérer, d'informer, de négocier
Group of companies	Groupe de sociétés
Guarantee	Garantie
Hague Convention	Convention de La Haye
Hostilities	Hostilités, conflit armé
ICC rules	Règlement de la CCI
–article 8.3	*–Prima facie*
ICSID Convention	Convention de Washington
Immunity	Immunité
Indexation clause	Clause d'indexation
Injuction	Injonction
Interest	Intérêt
Interim measures	Mesures provisoires/conservatoires
International Commerce	Commerce international
International trade	Usages du commerce
usages	international
Interpretation of	Interprétation de
Joint venture	Consortium, contrat d'association
Jurisdiction	Compétence, (juridiction)
Letter of credit	Crédit documentaire
Lex fori	*Lex fori*
Lex loci solutionis	*Lex loci solutionis*
Lex Mercatoria	*Lex Mercatoria*
Liability	Responsabilité
Licence (contrat)	Licence (contrat de)
Limitation	Limitation

Key-word in English	Corresponding notion in French
Liquidated damages	'Liqudated damages', pénalités contractuelles
Lis pendens	Litspendance, connexité
Loss of profit	Perte, préjudice
Merchantability	Conformité des marchandises
Mitigation of damages	Obligation de minimiser les pertes
Multiparty arbitration	Arbitrage multipartite
Nationalization	Nationalisation
New York Arbitration Convention (1958)	Convention de New York (1958)
Notice	Réclamation
Nullity of contract	Nullité de contrat
Oil	Pétrole
Ordre public	Ordre public
Pacta sunt servanda	*Pacta sunt servanda*
Parallel Court proceedings	Connexité/litispendance
Partial award	Sentence partielle
Party	Partie
Performance Bond	Garantie de bonne fin
Personnel	Personnel
Place of arbitration	Lieu de l'arbitrage
Price	Prix, révision de prix
Proof	Preuve, *Actori incumbit probatio*
Proper law of the contract	'Proper law of the contract'
Public policy	Ordre public
Rebus sic stantibus	*Rebus sic stantibus*
Renvoi	Renvoi
Res judicata	Autorité de la chose jugée
Sales/purchase contract	Contrat d'achat/vente

570

Key-word in English	*Corresponding notion in French*
Scrutiny of the draft award by the ICC Court of Arbitration	Règlement CCI (article 21)
Set-off	Compensation
Settlement	Transaction
Sovereign immunity	Immunité
Stabilization clause	Clause de stabilisation
State	Etat
Stay of arbitral proceeding	Sursis à statuer
Subcontract	Soustraitance
Technical expertise	Expert technique
Termination	Résiliation, annulation
Terms of reference	Acte de mission
Time limit	Prescription
Tort	Responsabilité délictuelle
Trade usages	Usages de commerce
Treaty of Rome	Traité de la CEE
ULIS	Loi uniforme sur la vente internationale
Uniform Customs and Practices for Documentary Credits	Règles et usances uniformes relatives aux crédits documentaires
Vienne Sales Convention	Convention de Vienne
Voie directe	'Voie directe'
Waiver	Renonciation
War	Conflit armé, hostilités
Warranty	Garantie, Conformité des marchandises

571

Index des mots-clés

Mot-clé (Français)	*Notion ou rubrique correspondante (Anglais)*
Change	Exchange losses / Foreign Exchange Regulations
Changement des circonstances	Changed circunstances / *Rebus sic stantibus*
Chose jugée	*Res judicata*
Clause d'arbitrage	Arbitral clause / Arbitration agreement
Clause compromissoire	Arbitral clause / Arbitration agreement
Clause d'indexation	Indexation clause
Clause résolutoire	Termination of contract
Clause de révision de prix	Price
Commerce international	International commerce
Commission de la CEE	European Economic Community
Compensation	Set-off
Compétence de l'arbitre	Competence of arbitrator / Jurisdiction/
Compétence-compétence	Competence-competence
Concession de distribution exclusive	Distributorship contract
Concordat suisse sur l'arbitrage	Concordat on Arbitration, Swiss
Concurrence	Antitrust Law / Competition
Conditions générales	General conditions
Conflit de loi	Conflict of law rules
Conflit armé	War, Hostilities
Conformité des marchandises	Merchantability / Warranty
Connexité (exception de --)	Concurrent.../ Parallel Court proceedings / *Lis pendens*
Consortium	Joint venture
Contrat	Contract
Contrat d'adhésion	Adhesion contract
Contrat d'agence commerciale	Agency contract
Contrat d'association	Joint venture
Contrat de construction	Construction contract
Contrat de distribution	Distributorship contract
Contrat de fourniture de longue durée	Delivery
Contrat de licence	Licence contract
Contrat de représentation	Agency contract, Distributorship
Contrat de sous-traitance	Sub-contract
Contrat de travaux publics	Construction contract
Contrat de vente	Sales/purchase contract
Contravention essentielle au contrat	Breach of contract
Contrôle des changes	Foreign exchange regulations
Convention européenne de Genève	Geneva Convention of 1961
Convention de la Haye	Hague Convention

Mot-clé (Français)	*Notion ou rubrique correspondante (Anglais)*
Convention de New York	New York Arbitration Convention
Convention de Vienne	Vienna Sales Convention
Convention de Washington, CIRDI	ICSID Convention
Corruption	Bribery
Crédit documentaire	Letter of credit
Culpa in contrahendo	*Error in contrahendo*
Délai	Time-limit
Délai de dénonciation des vices cachés	Notice
Délai de réclamation	Notice
Demande nouvelle	Amendment of claim
Dévalorisation	Depreciation
Dévaluation	Devaluation
Devoir de limiter le préjudice	Mitigation of damages
Dommages-intérêts	Damages
Droit applicable	Applicable law
– à la convention d'arbitrage	– to validity of arbitration agreement
– au fond	– to substance
– à la procédure	– to procedure
Etat	State
Etat souverain	State
Evaluation du préjudice	Calculation of damages
Ex aequo et bono	*Ex aequo et bono*
Exceptio non adimpleti contractus	*Exceptio non adimpleti contractus*
Expert technique	Expert / Technical expertise
Faillite d'une partie à l'arbitrage	Dissolution of party during arbitration
Fait du prince	Fait du prince
FIDIC	FIDIC / Engineer
Force majeure	*Force majeure*, Frustration
Frais de l'arbitrage	Costs of arbitration
Frustration	Frustration
Garantie bancaire	Bank guarantee / First demand guarantee
Garantie de bonne fin	Performance bond
Garantie contractuelle	Guarantee

575

Mot-clé (Français)	Notion ou rubrique correspondante (Anglais)
Garantie de performance/d'exécution	Performance bond
Groupe de sociétés	Group of companies
Hostilités	Hostilities / War
Immunité de juridiction	Immunity
Indexation	Indexation
Injonction	Injunction
Intérêts	Interest
Interprétation de la clause compromissoire	Interpretation of arbitration clause
Lex fori	*Lex fori*
Lex loci solutionis	*Lex loci solutionis*
Lex mercatoria	*Lex mercatoria*
Licence	Licence
Lieu de l'arbitrage	Place of arbitration
Liquidated damages	Liquidated damages
Limitation de responsabilité	Limitation / Liability
Litispendance	Parallel Court proceeding / *Lis pendens*
Liquidation	Dissolution
Livraison	Delivery
Loi applicable	Applicable law
Loi uniforme sur la vente internationale	ULIS
Mesures provisoires/conservatoires	Interim measures
Modifications des circonstances	Changed circumstances
Monnaie étrangère	(Foreign) Currency
Multipartite	Multiparty
Nationalisation	Nationalization
Nemo auditur turpitudinem suam allegans	Estoppel
Nomination d'arbitre	Appointment of arbitrator
Normes anationales	Anational rules
Nullité du contrat	Nullity of contract

576

Mot-clé (Français)	Notion ou rubrique correspondante (Anglais)
Obligation de coopérer/d'informer/de négocier	Goodfaith
Obligation de minimiser les pertes	Mitigation of damages
Ordre public	Ordre Public / Public policy
Ordre public international	Ordre public / Public policy
Pacta sunt servanda	*Pacta sunt servanda*
Partie	Party
Pénalité contractuelle	Liquidated damages
Personnel	Personnel / Expatriate Staff
Perte	Damages / Loss of profit
Pétrole	Oil
Préjudice	Damages / Calculation of damages
Prescription	Time limit
Preuve	Proof
Prima facie	ICC Rules (article 8.3)
Principes généraux du droit	General principles of law
Principes de portée internationale	General principles of international law
Prix	Price
Procédure arbitrale	Procedure
Proper law of the contract	Proper law of the contract
Rebus sic stantibus	*Rebus sic stantibus*
Réclamation	Notice
Règlement CCI	ICC Rules
Règlement d'Expertise Technique	Expert
Règles et usances uniformes (CCI) relatives aux crédits documentaires	Uniform customs and practices for documentary credits
Renvoi	Renvoi
Résiliation (d'un contrat)	Termination of contract / Rescission
Résiliation unilatérale	Termination of contract / Rescission
Responsabilité	Liability
Responsabilité délictuelle	Tort / Liability
Retard	Delay
Révision de prix	Revision of price / Price
Risque de change	Exchange losses

Mot-clé (Français)	Notion ou rubrique correspondante (Anglais)
Sentence	Award
Sentence partielle	Partial award
Société	Company
Soustraitance	Subcontract
Stabilisation	Stabilization clause
Succession	Succession
Traité de la CEE	European Economic Community
Transaction	Settlement
Travaux publics	Construction contract
Usages du commerce	Trade usages
Usages du commerce international	International trade usages
Venire contra factum proprium	Estoppel
Vente	Sales, purchase contract
Violation du contrat	Breach of contract
Visa	Visa
Voie directe	Voie directe